Academic Integrity in the Age of Artificial Intelligence

Saadia Mahmud
Australian Institute of Business, Australia

A volume in the Advances in Educational Marketing, Administration, and Leadership (AEMAL) Book Series

IGI Global
PUBLISHER of TIMELY KNOWLEDGE

Published in the United States of America by
IGI Global
Information Science Reference (an imprint of IGI Global)
701 E. Chocolate Avenue
Hershey PA, USA 17033
Tel: 717-533-8845
Fax: 717-533-8661
E-mail: cust@igi-global.com
Web site: http://www.igi-global.com

Library of Congress Cataloging-in-Publication Data

Names: Mahmud, Saadia, 1968- editor.
Title: Academic integrity in the age of artificial intelligence / Edited by Saadia Mahmud.
Description: Hershey, PA : Information Science Reference, [2024] | Includes bibliographical references and index. | Summary: "This book seeks to understand the higher education landscape with the advent of generative AI. More importantly, it seeks to promote a culture of academic integrity in the face of unprecedented pressure to breach academic integrity by members of the academic community"-- Provided by publisher.

Identifiers: LCCN 2023049176 (print) | LCCN 2023049177 (ebook) | ISBN 9798369302408 (hardcover) | ISBN 9798369302415 (paperback) | ISBN 9798369302422 (ebook)
Subjects: LCSH: Artificial intelligence--Educational applications. | Education, Higher--Moral and ethical aspects.
Classification: LCC LB1028.43 .A27 2024 (print) | LCC LB1028.43 (ebook) | DDC 371.9--dc23/eng/20231103
LC record available at https://lccn.loc.gov/2023049176
LC ebook record available at https://lccn.loc.gov/2023049177

This book is published in the IGI Global book series Advances in Educational Marketing, Administration, and Leadership (AEMAL) (ISSN: 2326-9022; eISSN: 2326-9030)

British Cataloguing in Publication Data
A Cataloguing in Publication record for this book is available from the British Library.

Advances in Educational Marketing, Administration, and Leadership (AEMAL) Book Series

Siran Mukerji
IGNOU, India
Purnendu Tripathi
IGNOU, India

ISSN:2326-9022
EISSN:2326-9030

Mission

With more educational institutions entering into public, higher, and professional education, the educational environment has grown increasingly competitive. With this increase in competitiveness has come the need for a greater focus on leadership within the institutions, on administrative handling of educational matters, and on the marketing of the services offered.

The **Advances in Educational Marketing, Administration, & Leadership (AEMAL) Book Series** strives to provide publications that address all these areas and present trending, current research to assist professionals, administrators, and others involved in the education sector in making their decisions.

Coverage

- Governance in P-12 and Higher Education
- Faculty Administration and Management
- Advertising and Promotion of Academic Programs and Institutions
- Enrollment Management
- Academic Administration
- Technologies and Educational Marketing
- Educational Marketing Campaigns
- Educational Management
- Direct marketing of educational programs
- Educational Leadership

IGI Global is currently accepting manuscripts for publication within this series. To submit a proposal for a volume in this series, please contact our Acquisition Editors at Acquisitions@igi-global.com or visit: http://www.igi-global.com/publish/.

The Advances in Educational Marketing, Administration, and Leadership (AEMAL) Book Series (ISSN 2326-9022) is published by IGI Global, 701 E. Chocolate Avenue, Hershey, PA 17033-1240, USA, www.igi-global.com. This series is composed of titles available for purchase individually; each title is edited to be contextually exclusive from any other title within the series. For pricing and ordering information please visit http://www.igi-global.com/book-series/advances-educational-marketing-administration-leadership/73677. Postmaster: Send all address changes to above address.

Titles in this Series

For a list of additional titles in this series, please visit:
http://www.igi-global.com/book-series/advances-educational-marketing-administration-leadership/73677

Promoting Crisis Management and Creative Problem-Solving Skills in Educational Leadership
Afzal Sayed Munna (University of Sunderland in London, UK) Uzoechi Nwagbara (University of Sunderland in London, UK) and Yahaya Alhassan (University of Sunderland in London, UK)
Information Science Reference • copyright 2024 • 321pp • H/C (ISBN: 9781668483329) • US $215.00 (our price)

Strategic Opportunities for Bridging the University-Employer Divide
William E. Donald (University of Southampton, UK & Ronin Institute, USA)
Information Science Reference • copyright 2024 • 329pp • H/C (ISBN: 9781668498279) • US $225.00 (our price)

Enrollment and Retention Strategies for 21st Century Higher Education
Rayshawn L. Eastman (Mount St. Joseph University, USA)
Information Science Reference • copyright 2024 • 300pp • H/C (ISBN: 9781668474778) • US $215.00 (our price)

Interrogating Race and Racism in Postsecondary Language Classrooms
Xiangying Huo (University of Toronto, Canada) and Clayton Smith (University of Windsor, Canada)
Information Science Reference • copyright 2024 • 370pp • H/C (ISBN: 9781668490297) • US $215.00 (our price)

Supporting Students' Intellectual Freedom in Schools The Right to Read
Danielle E. Sachdeva (University of North Georgia, USA) Samantha L. Hull (Old Dominion University, USA) Sue C. Kimmel (Old Dominion University, USA) and Westry A. Whitaker (University of North Georgia, USA)
Information Science Reference • copyright 2024 • 303pp • H/C (ISBN: 9781668496558) • US $230.00 (our price)

Challenging Bias and Promoting Transformative Education in Public Schooling Through Critical Literacy
Lyndsey Aubin Benharris (Fitchburg State University, USA) and Katharine Covino (Fitchburg State University, USA)
Information Science Reference • copyright 2024 • 300pp • H/C (ISBN: 9781668496701) • US $230.00 (our price)

Promoting Quality Hybrid Learning Through Leadership and Educational Management
Edgar Oliver Cardoso Espinosa (Instituto Politécnico Nacional, Mexico)
Information Science Reference • copyright 2024 • 264pp • H/C (ISBN: 9798369300947) • US $220.00 (our price)

Handbook of Research on Critical Issues and Global Trends in International Education
Megel R. Barker (TASIS England, UK) Robyn Conrad Hansen (Northern Arizona University, USA) and Liam Hammer (International School of Lusaka, Zambia)
Information Science Reference • copyright 2024 • 744pp • H/C (ISBN: 9781668487952) • US $270.00 (our price)

IGI Global
PUBLISHER of TIMELY KNOWLEDGE

701 East Chocolate Avenue, Hershey, PA 17033, USA
Tel: 717-533-8845 x100 • Fax: 717-533-8661
E-Mail: cust@igi-global.com • www.igi-global.com

Table of Contents

Detailed Table of Contents

Artificial intelligence offers the opportunity to revolutionise work and it is now ubiquitous globally. In higher education the use of generative artificial intelligence has raised concerns about the integrity of assessment and research. The current study analyses the academic integrity policy and practice at leading universities globally to assess the early response to the use of artificial intelligence. A sample of twenty universities (N=20) from four different countries—USA, UK, Australia, and Canada—were selected. Data was collected and analysed in May-June 2023. Fostering of academic integrity at the higher education institutions was assessed using the core elements of exemplary policy and framework for enacting exemplary academic integrity policy. A minority (45%) of the universities mentioned the use of artificial intelligence in their academic integrity policy. Higher education institutions globally need to update academic and research integrity policy and practice to facilitate the ethical use of artificial intelligence.

The rise of GenAI in HE has brought both opportunities and challenges, including threats such as plagiarism, data fabrication, and misrepresentation of original works. This chapter scrutinises the publicly available websites of 130 universities across Great Britain and evaluates documents pertinent to 67 of them to the interplay between academic integrity and AI. The integration of GenAI into higher education has significantly impacted how British universities provide guidance and support for staff and students. In England, 59.3% of universities possess GenAI guidance and have integrated it into their academic misconduct policy. However, only 18.6% have announced a statement concerning GenAI. British universities display a more even distribution of stances towards GenAI, with most exuding a positive stance. British universities are increasingly focusing on academic integrity and implementing GenAI tools to foster AI literacy among students and faculty.

Academic integrity is considered under threat in the age of artificial intelligence owing to new technologies. The sector has questioned exemplary responses in institutional academic integrity policy and proposed changes to what is exemplary. This chapter examines three issues seen in proposed academic integrity policy changes. The first issue is whether to ban or accept the use of generative artificial intelligence (GenAI) tools. The second issue is whether the proposed changes are sufficient to cover what is needed in academic integrity policy. The third issue is what other changes are needed to support academic integrity throughout a student's interactions with an institution. The chapter concludes with a proposal of how the work of the exemplary academic integrity project should not be added to but modernized to address questions raised in the age of artificial intelligence.

There are many generative AI (GenAI) tools available, and their rapid advancement has caused concerns relating to academic integrity. This chapter will consider concerns relating to academic integrity in the age of AI, including plagiarism and cheating. Awareness and education will be discussed as strategies for upholding academic integrity, as will proactive measures such as assessment design, and the need for institutional policies concerning the use of AI in education. The chapter concludes by stating that students should be taught to use generative AI ethically, responsibly and transparently and highlights how the integration of AI can foster creativity and enhance students' learning experiences.

This chapter presents a roadmap for teacher educators to equip their graduates with the ability to recognize and mitigate the limitations and risks of using ChatGPT in educational settings. With the rise of artificial intelligence (AI), the incorporation of AI-powered technologies like ChatGPT has the potential to enhance student learning. However, it also raises concerns about psychosocial harm for both students and educators. By sharing the burden of responsibility and fostering a safe working environment, teacher educators can prepare future teachers to leverage ChatGPT safely, harness its benefits, and navigate the complex landscape of a phenomena introduced in this chapter as 'technorisk' while promoting positive educational outcomes.

This chapter explores the impact of generative AI technologies on academic integrity in higher education, within the context of a business capstone course in a Canadian polytechnic. Using a case study and leveraging the Double Diamond framework for innovation, the chapter illustrates how generative AI tools can support known pedagogical supports for academic integrity: (1) Building relational trust between instructors and students; (2) student agency; (3) assessment mastery; and (4) choice in grading and assessment. The chapter concludes with recommendations for continuing to integrate generative AI technologies into practice.

Recent advances in artificial intelligence (AI) and generative artificial intelligence (GenAI) are beginning and will continue to have a profound impact on industry and higher education (HE). This chapter presents an overview of the relationship between AI, industry, and HE with a focus on higher education institutions (HEI) and students who are beginning to navigate the implications of AI. Following a review of global HE institution's approaches and responses to GenAI, the current impact of AI on student's education journeys and their preparedness for an AI ready world is explored through a review of the opportunities and challenges AI presents, resulting in a thematic framework for HE institution considerations for traversing this new terrain.

This study addresses the limitations of traditional assessment practices and proposes a conceptual model to reframe assessments for authenticity in the context of generative artificial intelligence (AI). Traditional assessment practices often fail to capture diverse knowledge and can be exploited by students' misuse of generative AI tools for unfair academic advantages, which underscores the need for robust assessment mechanisms. This study explores how authentic assessments can be integrated with generative AI tools to mitigate academic dishonesty and enhance the learning experience. Building on existing AI approaches in higher education, this study develops a model integrating generative AI in authentic assessments. This model can serve as a framework for incorporating authenticity in assessment practices while leveraging the capabilities of generative AI. An example illustrating the conceptual model, along with several reimagined authentic assessment types, and mitigation strategies for reframing authentic assessment design, are provided.

While generative AI is often discussed in terms of challenging notions of academic integrity, it is increasingly looked at as a potential tool to break down barriers in post-secondary education. In particular, this chapter considers how generative artificial intelligence technologies could be leveraged to provide multiple means of engagement, representation and expression (CAST, n.d.). In other words, how can

that has been created for the student, typically contract cheating or use of generative AI, then it is less straightforward. The first challenge is detecting a potential breach of integrity. The second challenge is for the marker to have both the time and the will to report it. Next, the marker needs to know what evidence is needed and how to report it. There are many reasons why a marker may decide not to raise allegations. Addressing doubts and concerns like these can make a huge difference to how many cases of conduct are reported and investigated. This chapter suggests what actions can be taken within institutions to ensure that fairness and integrity prevail.

This chapter explores how generative artificial intelligence, which poses a threat to academic integrity, can also be used to address some of the root causes of breaches in academic integrity. The root causes discussed are primarily derived from the largest self-reported academic integrity survey conducted across Australia's leading universities. Some of these root causes that the chapter will address include dissatisfaction with the teaching and learning environment, challenges related to English as an additional language, and the perception of easy access to cheating opportunities. By embracing generative artificial intelligence and incorporating it into the classroom, educators are afforded the opportunity to discuss its acceptable use in assessments and to bring attention to the academic integrity policies and procedures of the institution.

The arrival of 'free to access' generative AI platforms in late 2022 has irrevocably changed the educational landscape. Of concern to many is how to uphold academic integrity in assessments ensuring students are able to demonstrate their learning in this new environment where a 'machine' can research and write for you. In this chapter, the authors present a process which is designed to uncover the true nature of the 'work' expected to be performed by students during assessment, which then allows GenAI tools to be knowingly used by students as just another research tool. While it is still early days, changing our understanding that what should be assessed is 'the work' expected of students rather than the 'output' suggests that all is not lost when it comes to academic integrity.

In recent decades, technology has advanced exponentially, ushering in the widespread integration of artificial intelligence (AI) to daily life. AI is now omnipresent, from smart home devices to autonomous vehicles, and it has gained significant traction across various industries. In higher education, educators must adapt to this cultural shift by revising curriculum, learning environments, and teaching methods. AI has the potential to revolutionize higher education but raises concerns about academic integrity. This chapter explores AI's impact on global society, discusses AI-related academic integrity issues, proposes

Preface

Some moments in history are pivotal. The advance of artificial intelligence is one such moment, a time of transformative change. With the phenomenal take-up of generative artificial intelligence (AI) applications, the world has seen rapid and turbulent change. The wide-ranging impact of generative AI is reverberating across industries as diverse as higher education, medicine, and the arts. The ability for AI to produce text and images creatively based on user prompts has opened the door to vast possibilities that promise greater productivity and reduced processing time. However, it is a double-edged sword with risks such as falsification of information, infringement of copyright and in the case of higher education, a breach of academic integrity. There has been increasing concern in the press and social media about the risks of generative AI such as ChatGPT and other applications. The response to this phenomenon has been mixed in the higher education sector with some institutions banning the use of the technology while others seeking to use it in an educative capacity. Regardless of the stance taken by individuals and institutions, generative AI is here to stay, and the proverbial genie cannot be put back into the bottle.

This book seeks to understand the higher education landscape with the advent of generative AI. More importantly, it seeks to promote a culture of academic integrity in the face of unprecedented pressure to breach academic integrity by members of the academic community. The foundations of higher education are being shaken with many questioning the merits of pursuing degrees. The structure of assessment is under review, and academic integrity policy and practice are effectively out of date. For tackling a multi-faceted issue, the need of the hour is to consider the implications from a variety of angles and stakeholder perspectives. Multiple stakeholders include academics, higher education policy makers, higher education institutions, regulatory bodies, students, researchers, technology solution providers that deal with detection of a breach in academic integrity, legislators, government, and society at large.

The journey for this book started two decades ago with my first research project on detecting plagiarism by Australian researchers using the text-matching software Turnitin. The need for academics to uphold academic integrity standards was contentious and my colleague Dr Tracey Bretag and I wrote a paper on 'self-plagiarism' which remains a source of debate. Over the subsequent years, I worked on academic integrity research in higher education policy and practice. A pivotal moment was managing the *Academic Integrity Standards Project* (2010-2012) which collected the largest data set on student's understanding of academic integrity and institutional academic integrity policy. Over fifteen thousand students responded to the survey and the student voice was resounding in the appeal to be taught about how to uphold academic integrity. Our paper 'Teach us how to do it properly' echoes the students' call for help. Analysing the data for the Contract *Cheating and Assessment Design Project* (2016-2017) highlighted the reasons why students cheat and 'opportunities to cheat' was a leading reason. Some argue that generative AI provides students with an easy and accessible opportunity to cheat. With the advent of the age of artificial intelligence, we need to build on our understanding of academic integrity in this new reality. The issue is multi-faceted, and this publication seeks to further our understanding and propose ways to address the issue.

This book is borne out of a need to make a positive change with integrity. My research over the past two decades in academic integrity and research integrity has underscored the challenges faced in upholding standards in higher education. The challenge posed by the advent of generative AI is unprecedented. In deciding how to make a meaningful contribution to higher education, industry, and society at large, I was influenced by my own doctoral research. My PhD proposed open and honest communication and trust between agents of a complex adaptive system as the way to build adaptive capability. Using the complexity theory lens for the current scenario, I view higher education as a complex adaptive system. The need of the hour is for us to collaborate as agents with high levels of autonomy to find ways to forge ahead. The contributors to this publication each bring their expertise and perspective on the issue of academic integrity in the age of artificial intelligence. Their unique contributions are greatly appreciated. My role has been to bring together this collective understanding to be a catalyst for positive change.

In Chapter 1 “Fostering academic integrity in the age of artificial intelligence,” Saadia Mahmud from the Australian Institute of Business reports on a study that uses the lens of exemplary academic integrity policy and practice to assess the responsiveness of twenty leading universities across the USA, UK, Australia, and Canada to the use of generative AI tools. In this comprehensive analysis conducted in May-June 2023, Mahmud identifies a minority (45%) of universities acknowledging the use of artificial intelligence in their academic integrity policies and with varied stances. The chapter emphasizes the urgent need for higher education institutions worldwide to update their academic and research integrity policies to align with the ethical use of artificial intelligence.

In Chapter 2 “British battle for authenticity: Defending academic integrity in the age of AI,” Edyta Kostanek, Roopa Nagaraju and Anna Michalska from various UK institutions present a meticulous examination of 130 British universities, shedding light on the integration of generative AI (GenAI) into higher education. The chapter reveals that while a significant portion of universities (59.3%) in England provide GenAI guidance and integrate it into their Academic Misconduct Policy, only a fraction (18.6%) explicitly address GenAI in their official statements. The varied stances of British universities towards GenAI underscore the importance of academic integrity and the implementation of AI tools to foster literacy among students and faculty.

In Chapter 3 “Revising Australian academic integrity policy for the age of artificial intelligence,” David Morgan from the Polytechnic Institute in Australia explores the evolving landscape of academic integrity in Australia in the face of artificial intelligence. The chapter scrutinizes proposed changes to academic integrity policy, addressing key issues such as whether to ban or accept the use of generative artificial intelligence tools. Morgan advocates for the modernization of existing frameworks, emphasizing the need to adapt to the challenges posed by the age of artificial intelligence while maintaining the exemplary standards set by the Exemplary Academic Integrity Project.

In Chapter 4 ‘Embracing AI in the classroom whilst being mindful of academic integrity’, Lynsey Meakin from the University of Derby, UK expands on potential solutions to using generative artificial intelligence tools in an academic setting. The chapter explores strategies for upholding academic integrity, including awareness, education, and proactive measures like thoughtful assessment design. Meakin emphasizes the importance of teaching students to use generative AI ethically and responsibly, highlighting the potential for AI integration to foster creativity and enhance the overall learning experience.

In Chapter 5 "Redefining classroom readiness: how initial teacher training can mitigate risks and capitalize on the potential of GenAI," Janine Arantes from Victoria University, Australia questions what classroom readiness means for graduate teachers in their ability to capitalise on the potential of emerging technologies such as artificial intelligence while mitigating the risks. She provides a roadmap for teacher educators to be trained to enhance student learning while using artificial intelligence tools appropriately. She argues for academic integrity concerns about artificial intelligence to be addressed early in a teacher's training to facilitate the use of these tools in a non-punitive manner.

In Chapter 6 "(A)I'm a believer, but (A)I'm also responsible," Blake Kanewischer and Sonja Johnston from the Southern Alberta Institute of Technology in Canada present a case study of a capstone course in a business degree in which generative AI tools are used innovatively to foster creativity. The chapter leverages the Double Diamond framework for innovation to explore ways in which AI technologies can uphold academic integrity principles such as building trust, supporting student agency, and enhancing assessment practices.

In Chapter 7 "Exploring the profound impact of AI on higher education and students: Shaping tomorrow's workforce," Amy Emanuel and David Stone from Christian Heritage College in Australia present an overview of the relationship between AI, industry, and higher education. As students undertake studies to prepare for their careers, higher education needs to consider how to address the opportunities and challenges presented by AI. Examining the existing policy and practice of higher education institutions and the imperatives of industry, the authors propose a framework for higher education institutions to start a proactive approach towards the use of AI.

In Chapter 8 "Reframing assessments: designing authentic assessments in the age of generative AI," Peter Matheis and Jubin John from Navitas in Australia address the limitations of traditional assessment practices and propose a conceptual model to reframe assessments for authenticity in the context of generative artificial intelligence (AI).

In Chapter 9 "AI as an accessibility Tool: Using generative AI to support Universal Design for Learning Approach," Brenda McDermott from the University of Calgary, Canada, argues for the debate on the use of generative AI to consider individuals with disabilities. She proposes a shift to the Universal Design for Learning approach to promote social justice in higher education. Assessments need to be set up to focus more on the process as opposed to the product of learning.

In Chapter 10 "The inherent uncertainties of AI-text detection and the implications for courses and assessment: An overview," Robin Crockett and Rob Howe from the University of Northampton in the UK discuss the implications of generative AI 'chatbot' technologies and the challenges associated with AI-text detection. The chapter emphasizes the inherent uncertainties and inaccuracies in AI-text detection and explores how institutions must navigate the growing use of AI while addressing the unreliability of detection technologies review the systematic AI-text detection methods.

In Chapter 11 "AI detection's high false positive rates and the psychological and material impacts on students," Whitney Gegg-Harrison and Claire M. Quaterman present a chapter highlighting the inherent challenges of AI detection and its impact on students. The authors bring together their expertise in computational linguistics, cognitive science, and data science, to examine a corpus of texts and show that the rate of false positives is much higher than reported. They highlight the emotional and mental harm to students of being falsely flagged as having submitted work written by AI. The authors argue for the ethical considerations surrounding the use of AI detection tools in academia.

In Chapter 12 "Detecting is just the start, deciding whether to take action and generating evidence is harder," Irene Glendinning from Coventry University, addresses the challenges institutions face in detecting and addressing breaches of academic integrity, particularly in cases involving generative AI. The chapter highlights the complexities of investigating and reporting breaches, emphasizing the importance of institutional actions to ensure fairness and integrity prevail.

In Chapter 13 "Harnessing the power of generative artificial intelligence to promote academic integrity," Nadia Koren and Brent Anders from TAFE NSW in Australia draw on research on why students commit a breach of academic integrity to propose ethical ways AI tools can be used to minimise the instances of such breaches. The chapter provides practical advice on how AI tools can be used to mitigate language barriers and improve understanding of complex topics. The insights are valuable for a range of stakeholders including students, teaching staff and university management to foster a culture of academic integrity.

In Chapter 14 "Empowering students from assumptions to knowledge, making integrity everyone's business," Lynn Gribble and Janice Wardrop from UNSW in Australia present a process designed to uphold academic integrity in assessments in the era of "free to access" generative AI platforms. The chapter proposes a shift in understanding assessment to focus on the expected work of students rather than the output, allowing generative AI tools to be used knowingly as research aids without compromising academic integrity.

In Chapter 15 "New innovations in higher education's academic integrity and classroom strategies," Maya Jaber from the University of Wisconsin-Platteville explores the transformative impact of AI on higher education, emphasizing the need for educators to adapt to the cultural shift. The chapter discusses AI-related academic integrity issues and offers practical strategies for nurturing students' evolving thinking processes in the age of artificial intelligence.

This edited volume explores the intersection of academic integrity and artificial intelligence from several dimensions. Evidence-based recommendations on updating academic integrity policy and practice are complemented by a deeper understanding of the issues in the detection and handling of a breach involving generative AI use. Innovation and creativity in assessment design and practical classroom strategies are proposed to foster ethical use. The discourse is extended with a debate for social justice and a proposed framework for higher education institutions to take a proactive approach towards the use of AI.

As the editor, I express my appreciation to the contributors who have generously shared their time, insights, research, and expertise, in the joint effort to promote academic integrity in a time of transformative change. We hope this volume serves as a valuable resource for academics, policymakers, practitioners, and all those invested in upholding the integrity and quality of higher education in the age of artificial intelligence.

Saadia Mahmud
Australian Institute of Business, Australia

Chapter 1
Fostering Academic Integrity in the Age of Artificial Intelligence

Saadia Mahmud
https://orcid.org/0000-0001-5133-9416
Australian Institute of Business, Australia

ABSTRACT

Artificial intelligence offers the opportunity to revolutionise work and it is now ubiquitous globally. In higher education the use of generative artificial intelligence has raised concerns about the integrity of assessment and research. The current study analyses the academic integrity policy and practice at leading universities globally to assess the early response to the use of artificial intelligence. A sample of twenty universities (N=20) from four different countries—USA, UK, Australia, and Canada—were selected. Data was collected and analysed in May-June 2023. Fostering of academic integrity at the higher education institutions was assessed using the core elements of exemplary policy and framework for enacting exemplary academic integrity policy. A minority (45%) of the universities mentioned the use of artificial intelligence in their academic integrity policy. Higher education institutions globally need to update academic and research integrity policy and practice to facilitate the ethical use of artificial intelligence.

INTRODUCTION

The dishonest behaviour of students in higher education has been documented by researchers throughout the decades (Bowers, 1964; Bretag et al., 2019; McCabe et al., 2012; McCabe & Trevino, 1993). In the past decade, the discourse has shifted from a punitive focus on misconduct to an educative focus on academic integrity (Mahmud & Ali, 2023). A widely accepted definition of academic integrity is "a commitment to six fundamental values: honesty, trust, fairness, respect, responsibility, and courage" (ICAI, 2021). At the core of ethical behaviour in academia lies the ability to make ethical choices guided by these values. The advent of artificial intelligence and in particular generative artificial intelligence tools has raised concerns about a potential rise in unethical conduct by students.

Content generated by artificial intelligence is easily accessible, highly capable, and problematic to detect thus it can provide students an opportunity to cheat and effectively circumvent the systems

DOI: 10.4018/979-8-3693-0240-8.ch001

in place to safeguard academic integrity (Abd-Elaal et al., 2019; Cotton et al., 2023; Sweeney, 2023). Generative artificial intelligence applications can generate content based on analysis of large datasets using algorithms from natural language processing, neural networks, and deep learning. The launch of ChatGPT in November 2022 – a generative artificial intelligence that uses Large Language Models (LLM) is a watershed moment. Attracting a million subscribers in just five days (Baidoo-Anu & Owusu Ansah, 2023) and one hundred million in three months (Lo, 2023). The mass adoption of this technology is a double-edged sword. Universities need to be proactive in their response to the use of artificial intelligence tools as Cotton et al. (2023) argue:

ChatAPIs and GPT-3 can be used to facilitate cheating, and it can be difficult to distinguish between human and machine-generated writing. Universities must carefully consider the potential risks and rewards of using these tools and take steps to ensure that they are used ethically and responsibly. This may involve developing policies and procedures for their use, providing training and support for students and faculty, and using a variety of methods to detect and prevent academic dishonesty.

Fostering a culture of academic integrity in higher education institutions has been advocated to promote ethical conduct (Bertram-Gallant, 2011; Bretag et al., 2011). Academic integrity policy and practice as a cornerstone in such a culture, offers a powerful lens to analyse the response of higher education institutions to promote ethical choices in the use of artificial intelligence tools. This discussion is an ongoing dialogue with the landscape constantly changing as new artificial intelligence tools are developed and existing ones learn and adapt their responses over time. This chapter is an early glimpse at the effort to foster academic integrity in the age of artificial intelligence and highlights the need for concerted action and further research in this area.

ARTIFICIAL INTELLIGENCE AND ACADEMIC INTEGRITY

Though the term 'age of artificial intelligence' is being used in the current context, the conceptualisation of artificial intelligence as machines simulating human intelligence is not new. Almost seven decades ago, the Dartmouth Artificial Intelligence conference in 1955 proposed that "every aspect of learning or any other feature of intelligence can in principle be so precisely described that a machine can be made to simulate it" (McCarthy et al., 2006). Artificial intelligence (AI) has been defined as "systems that display intelligent behaviour by analysing their environment and taking actions – with some degree of autonomy – to achieve specific goals" (Sheikh et al., 2023). In a learning and teaching context, artificial intelligence (AI) is conceptualised as "computing systems that are able to engage in human-like processes such as learning, adapting, synthesizing, self-correction and use of data for complex processing tasks" (Popenici & Kerr, 2017).

The ubiquitous use of artificial intelligence globally offers the opportunity to revolutionise work in a variety of fields including business, finance, and healthcare (Davenport, 2018; Gruetzemacher & Whittlestone, 2022; Krakowski et al., 2023). The use of artificial intelligence is anticipated to improve learning outcomes, student engagement, and the efficiency and effectiveness of education (Adiguzel et al., 2023; Alam, 2022; Holmes et al., 2023; Thurzo et al., 2023). The casualisation of the teaching staff at many higher education providers (Andrews et al., 2016) may see further reliance on artificial intelligence tools for academic work such as tutoring and marking assessments (Baidoo-Anu & Owusu Ansah, 2023; Crompton & Burke, 2023). Though offering opportunities, artificial intelligence also poses significant risks such as a lack of transparency, privacy and bias (Varsha, 2023). A contributor to bias in machine learning models is that they learn from data input into the system which may encode and further amplify the bias (Illia et al., 2023). The European Union has taken the lead in the regulation of artificial intelligence to mitigate risks (Justo-Hanani, 2022; Satariano, 2023), with other nations now working towards the enactment of safeguards. A recent study revealed a mixed response by universities and public opinion about the use of artificial intelligence with strong concerns about academic integrity (Sullivan et al., 2023).

Considerable research on academic integrity in higher education has focused on plagiarism as a major form of academic misconduct (Carroll & Development, 2002; Devlin, 2006; Glendinning, 2014; Howard, 2007) with more contemporary threats coming from social media (Cole et al., 2019) essay mills and contract cheating (Bretag et al., 2019). Plagiarism or "the representation of a source's words or ideas as one's own" (Howard, 1995) and contract cheating or "outsourcing of student work to third parties" (Lancaster & Clarke, 2016) share the core issue of whether the work is the student's work. A core concern is that a rise in unethical conduct such as plagiarism and contract cheating using artificial intelligence will occur undermining the credibility of the assessment (Alkhaqani, 2023; Picciano, 2019). Therefore, higher education institutions may risk being sidelined as providers of credentials recognised by the industry. The possible breach of academic integrity is not limited to students as learners. The potential for unethical conduct by academics is a real risk (Lund et al., 2023; Pickler, 2023). In research, trust in an academic's endeavour is critical to the pursuit of new knowledge. Submissions of papers listing ChatGPT as an author have already occurred and the detection of AI-written content is problematic (Anderson et al., 2023). However, AI-generated content does not always meet the requirements of authorship and publishing guidelines have needed to be updated to make this explicit (Flanagin et al., 2023).

To assess the response by universities to the ethical use of artificial intelligence tools, this study used the lens of academic integrity policy and practice. A culture of academic integrity at higher education institutions can be fostered by an exemplary academic integrity policy (Bretag et al., 2011). The core elements of an exemplary academic integrity policy access, approach, responsibility, detail, and support are part of a robust model that has been used to analyse academic integrity policies in several countries (Möller, 2023; Stoesz & Eaton, 2022). An exemplary policy is easy to access, has an educative approach, includes the responsibility of all stakeholders, extensive detail and support (Bretag et al., 2011). The six components of the framework that can enact exemplary policy into practice are academic integrity education, student engagement, academic integrity champions, robust decision-making systems, record keeping for evaluation, and regular review of policy and process (Bretag & Mahmud, 2016).

The main research question of this study was 'How have higher education providers addressed the use of artificial intelligence tools in their academic integrity policy and practice?'. An educative approach to upholding academic integrity sees the provision of support such as training (Foltýnek & Glendinning, 2015; McCabe et al., 2001). Therefore, the secondary research question was 'Is academic integrity education about the use of artificial intelligence tools accessible to staff and students?'.

RESEARCH METHODOLOGY

Secondary data collected included a review of current literature and media on the subject to inform the study. Website content analysis has been used as a research tool in previous studies (Hasim et al., 2018; Nejati et al., 2011; Zhang, 2005). The current study analysed qualitative data on the publicly available websites of universities to analyse academic integrity policy and practice concerning the use of artificial

Table 1. List of universities by country

Country	University	Country Ranking	THE World Ranking
USA	Harvard University	1	2
	Stanford University	2	3
	Massachusetts University of Technology	3	5
	California University of Technology	4	6
	Princeton University	5	7
UK	University of Oxford	1	1
	University of Cambridge	2	3
	Imperial College of London	3	10
	University College of London	4	22
	University of Edinburgh	5	29
Australia	University of Melbourne	1	34
	Monash University	2	44
	University of Queensland	3	53
	The University of Sydney	4	54
	Australian National University	5	62
Canada	University of Toronto	1	18
	University of British Columbia	2	40
	McGill University	3	46
	McMasters University	4	85
	University of Montreal	5	111
Source: https://www.timeshighereducation.com/world-university-rankings/2023/world-ranking			

intelligence tools. Using purposeful sampling (Palinkas et al., 2015) to provide a global perspective of leading universities, the most highly ranked five universities were selected from four different countries – the USA, the UK, Australia, and Canada. The ranking was obtained using the Times Higher Education University World Rankings in May 2023 (https://www.timeshighereducation.com/world-university-rankings/2023/world-ranking) as a leading measure of institutional reputation (Safón, 2019; Zhang et al., 2021). A total of twenty universities were selected (N=20) as listed in Table 1 below. Data was collected and analysed in May-June 2023. The calendar year for study varies between the four countries in this study. The universities in this study had at least one teaching term/semester since the launch of generative artificial tools such as ChatGPT. Table 1 (below) lists all the universities in the current study according to their location and ranking in their own country and the world.

For each university, secondary data was collected using the publicly accessible website of the university to analyse the academic integrity policy and procedure. The search words 'academic integrity policy' and 'academic misconduct policy' were used. For the universities with an academic integrity policy that mentioned the use of artificial intelligence tools, the academic integrity policy was further analysed for the five core elements of *access*, *approach*, *responsibility*, *detail*, and *support* based on the methodology of Bretag et al. (2011). The following items were analysed for each academic integrity policy:

1. Title of policy
2. Title of supporting document
3. The effective date of the policy
4. Scope of the policy – whether it applied to students and staff
5. Access – ease of finding policy on the university website
6. Approach – educative, punitive, mixed
7. Responsibility – university, staff, students
8. Detail – description of a range of breaches with levels of severity, process for identification, reporting and recordkeeping, outcomes, and process for appeals.
9. Support - training for students and professional development for staff
10. Mention of artificial intelligence tools

Previous research indicates that exemplary academic integrity policy and practice provide stakeholders – including staff and students *support* through access to academic integrity information (Bretag et al., 2011). The availability of integrity information on university websites is useful for comparative analysis (Zhang et al., 2021). To analyse easily accessible academic integrity information each university website was queried using the search words 'academic integrity and artificial intelligence' and 'academic misconduct and artificial intelligence'. The first ten hits for each search were analysed and coded by the researcher. Content analysis was used to analyse each link regarding academic integrity education with support consisting of resources, training, and procedures specifically addressing academic integrity/academic misconduct relating to the use of artificial intelligence tools. The proportion of support targeted at staff and students was calculated as a percentage of the twenty hits based on the coding. In terms of the online search, the first ten results were displayed on a single web page. This offers a practical and efficient way to analyse the most relevant content generated by the search algorithm that would be viewed by most users. Market research on Google search results suggests that most (92%) of users only click on the results of the first page (Insights, 2013). The overall assessment of each university included triangulation of the data with the analysis of the relevant academic integrity policy and procedure. The universities were deidentified in the reporting of results.

FINDINGS

Academic Integrity Policy and Practice

The use of artificial intelligence tools was included in a minority of academic integrity policies reviewed in the current study. As Table 2 (below) shows, nine out of the twenty universities (9/20 or 45%) had a policy for academic integrity/academic misconduct that specifically mentioned artificial intelligence tools. The proportion of policies that mentioned artificial intelligence tools was consistent for universities in almost all four countries. The UK had a slightly higher proportion (3/5 or 60%) of universities that specifically mentioned artificial intelligence tools.

The nine policies which mentioned artificial intelligence tools were analysed against the five core elements of exemplary academic integrity policy. *Access* based on ease of locating a policy was found to be easy for less than half of the policies (4/9 or 44%). The *approach* of the policies was mainly educative (6/9 or 66%) with the remainder being punitive (3/9 or 33%). The title of the policies included the

Table 2. Mention of artificial intelligence tools in the academic integrity policy

Country	Universities No.	Documents No.	AI mention No	University
US	5	9	2	D and E
UK	5	8	3	H, I and J
Australia	5	11	2	L and N
Canada	5	7	2	Q and T
Total	20	35	9	

terms academic integrity (3/9 or 33%), plagiarism (2/9 or 22%), academic misconduct (2/9 or 22%) and others such as code (2/9 or 22%). In terms of *responsibility*, most policies included students, staff, and the university (5/9 or 55%) with the remainder being students (3/9 or 33%), students and staff (1/9 or 11%). In terms of *detail*, most policies had limited detail (6/9 or 66%). Policies were coded as limited detail where information was not provided such as the levels of the breach, process for identification of the breach, consideration of contextual factors, and outcomes. *Support* was mentioned in a minority of policies (3/9 or 33%). The policies are now discussed further below.

A total of nine documents were analysed regarding academic integrity/academic misconduct policy and procedure at US universities. The use of artificial intelligence tools was specifically mentioned in two US universities (2/5 or 40%) in their academic integrity policy (University D and University E). In the context of academic integrity regulations, the use of artificial intelligence tools was dealt with under plagiarism (University E) and as an unpermitted aid if there was no specific permission from an instructor (University D). A total of eight policy and procedure documents for UK universities were analysed that referred to academic misconduct. Three universities (3/5 or 60%) specifically mentioned the use of artificial intelligence tools in their academic integrity policy. In all three universities, the use of artificial intelligence tools was dealt with under plagiarism (University H, University I and University J). A total of eleven academic integrity policy and procedure documents were analysed for the five Australian universities. Among the Australian universities, the use of artificial intelligence tools was specifically mentioned in two (2/5 or 40%) academic integrity policies (University L and University N). The unethical use of artificial intelligence was dealt with as plagiarism (University N) and under unauthorised use for content generation and contract cheating (University L). In two of the universities that did not mention artificial intelligence in their academic integrity policy, statements were included on the university website to guide students and staff about the use of such tools (University M and University O). In both universities unethical use of artificial intelligence tools was dealt with under plagiarism. A total of seven documents with related links were analysed about academic integrity/academic misconduct policy and procedures at Canadian universities. Two Canadian universities (2/5 or 40%) specifically mentioned the use of artificial intelligence in academic integrity policy and dealt with it under 'unauthorised aid' if not permitted by an instructor. (University Q and University T).

Some US universities in this study appear to be cautious about the use of artificial intelligence tools with resigned acceptance of the use of these tools by students. One US university referred to the resistance of artificial intelligence tools as 'futile' given they are ubiquitous and that students will use them even if they are banned. There was recognition of the need to restructure learning objectives to focus on each step of the process rather than the finished product (University C). Another US university acknowledged that artificial intelligence tools can foster student learning however it cautioned that such tools can be used to bypass learning objectives (University D). A third US university website included a blog article to encourage educators to adopt artificial intelligence tools rather than resist them. In the approach staff may take the possibilities include ignoring the technology, banning it, outflanking it, or leaning into it (University E).

In two universities in the UK (University I and University J), the use of artificial intelligence tools was prohibited. One university considered content produced by ChatGPT as not representing original work by a student and submission of such work as a form of academic misconduct dealt with under the university's disciplinary procedure. However, there was recognition that over-regulation of AI tools may widen the gap making the institutional position irrelevant (University I). At the other university, the use of artificial intelligence in assessments required specific prior authorisation or a reasonable adjustment for a student's disability. Students were cautioned that the unauthorised use of AI tools in exams and other assessed work is a serious disciplinary offence (University J). At a Canadian university, students were discouraged from using such tools based on the factual errors, low level of sophistication and citation errors in the content generated (University T).

Individual instructors were free to set their course policies about the use of generative artificial intelligence tools at some US universities in this study. The centre for teaching and learning was a common academic integrity champion across the US universities. Overall, in the US universities, limited guidance for students was found about the ethical use of artificial intelligence. The use or consultation with generative AI was construed as assistance from another person unless permitted by the instructor for the course. Substantial use of generative AI for an exam or assignment was prohibited. Disclosure of the use of generative AI through an acknowledgement was required (University D). The use of AI technologies was mentioned in academic integrity guidance reminding students that while the new technologies 'might be tempting to use for writing and other assignments' under the academic integrity policy they were forbidden to represent work as their own that they had not written or created (University E). At two US universities (University A and University B), artificial intelligence was not mentioned in the academic integrity regulations, however, teaching resources were provided for instructors regarding the use of artificial intelligence.

In all the UK universities in the sample, some guidance was provided about the use of artificial intelligence with academic integrity. There was guidance available on the use of AI tools in research and the statement on research integrity included a reference to the use of artificial intelligence tools (University J). In one university, clear guidance for staff and students about the use of AI tools was evident with links to the academic misconduct policy that addressed the use of AI tools. This university also advocated for an educative approach to the use of AI-generated content in its educational programmes (University H). Though not specifically dealing with AI tools in its academic integrity policy, one university included a statement supporting the use of AI tools ethically and transparently rather than prohibiting their use stating they are 'transformative' and 'disruptive' (University G).

In a majority (4/5 or 80%) of Australian universities, guidance was provided encouraging the ethical use of AI tools. Examples of the guidance provided to students included a reminder to appropriately acknowledge and cite AI-generated material in their assessment, a library guide for students to reference the use of AI tools and a link to the academic integrity policy (University O). The guidance to staff included a resource on adapting assessments to mitigate the risk of cheating and plagiarism posed using ChatGPT, and external resource links (University O). At another Australian university, the guidance for staff was more explicit with webinars and templates for student conversations and a commitment was expressed to provide students and staff resources to guide their use of generative artificial intelligence tools (University N). In one Australian university, no clear guidance was evident about the use of artificial intelligence tools (University K). The use of technology to detect AI written content in assessments was disclosed as being used in two (2/5 or 40%) Australian universities (University M and University O).

In most Canadian universities (3/5 or 60%) the use of generative artificial intelligence tools was not considered academic misconduct automatically by the university as the decision about the permitted use is made at a course level by the instructor. A minority of Canadian universities (2/5 or 40%) had clear guidance for staff and students about the use of AI tools. One of these universities echoed the caution and resigned acceptance of US universities stating a ban on AI tools was unlikely to reduce its use to subvert academic honesty. The decision not to use AI detection technology was explained as testing for accuracy is in an early stage (University S).

Academic Integrity Education About AI for Staff and Students

The relative proportion of academic integrity education targeted at each stakeholder varied across the universities in each of the countries (see Tables 3-6). Out of the twenty universities, two in the US (University C and University D) and two in Canada (University S and University T) could be identified as having a high level of staff support. This was defined as fifty per cent (50%) or more of the search results being coded as academic integrity education for staff. Most Australian universities had a higher level of support for students as compared to universities in the three other countries. The proportion of search results coded as academic integrity education for students was twenty-five per cent (25%) or more for most (4/5) Australian universities compared to a minority of universities in the other countries (0/5) US, (2/5) UK, and (1/5) Canada.

In each of the four countries, most universities had some information available for staff and students on the use of artificial intelligence tools. However, a low level of *support* for staff and students was found in most universities (13/20).

Table 3. Support for staff and students about AI use at US universities

Category	A	B	C	D	E
Support for staff	20	10	55	75	45
Support for students	5	0	10	10	10
Miscellaneous	75	90	35	15	45
Total %	100	100	100	100	100

Table 4. Support for staff and students about AI use at UK universities

Category	F	G	H	I	J
Support for staff	5	10	15	10	20
Support for students	5	35	10	30	10
Miscellaneous	90	55	75	60	70
Total %	100	100	100	100	100

Table 5. Support for staff and students about AI use at Australian universities

Category	K	L	M	N	O
Support for staff	5	10	25	35	10
Support for students	5	40	25	35	50
Miscellaneous	90	50	50	30	40
Total %	100	100	100	100	100

Table 6. Support for staff and students about AI use at Canadian Universities

Category	P	Q	R	S	T
Support for staff	5	10	10	55	50
Support for students	5	20	0	15	30
Miscellaneous	90	70	90	30	20
Total %	100	100	100	100	100

LIMITATIONS

The current study has a few limitations. The sample of twenty universities is small and may not be representative of the universities in each country. The sample selection rationale was that global leading universities would be at the forefront of addressing academic integrity challenges due to the use of artificial intelligence tools. The universities are all from English-speaking countries and are not representative of other universities globally where English is not the language of instruction. In consideration of drawing useful insights, the four countries selected in the sample have led the research, policy, and practice in academic integrity over the past two decades. The subjective judgement of the researcher has been used in coding the policies against the five core elements of exemplary policy. The findings from this study may not be generalisable. Relevant content may not be publicly available on some university websites; therefore, the findings at the time of investigation are limited to the information that was found in the search conducted. Data was collected in May-June 2023 and provides a glimpse of the early response to the introduction of generative artificial intelligence tools. There have been rapid developments in the higher education sector and the policy response to the use of artificial intelligence tools may have changed. The accessible academic integrity education measured was based on university website search results.

DISCUSSION AND IMPLICATIONS

The use of generative artificial intelligence tools has raised concerns about academic integrity such as the risk of a potential rise in unethical conduct by students and academics. This study examined the response of higher education providers to address these concerns using the lens of exemplary academic integrity policy and practice. The sample included twenty leading universities across four countries, providing a global perspective on the issue. The study found that most universities have yet to explicitly address the issue of the use of artificial intelligence tools in their academic integrity policies. This finding is concerning as research suggests strong academic integrity policies can promote a culture of academic integrity and reduce academic misconduct.

The study found that only a minority of universities (9/20 or 45%) mention the use of artificial intelligence tools in their academic integrity policies, indicating a global gap in policy response. In the US, Australia, and Canada the proportion was even lower (2/5 or 40%), while the UK had a higher proportion (3/5 or 60%). Only one university in the UK had a statement on research integrity that included a reference to the use of artificial intelligence tools. These findings highlight the need for higher education providers to update their academic integrity and research integrity policies to address the use of artificial intelligence tools.

Further analysis of the nine policies against the core elements of exemplary academic integrity policy provides insights into areas of strength and weakness. A positive finding is that most policies had an educative *approach* (6/9 or 66%) and stated the *responsibility* of all stakeholders (5/9 or 55%). The existing base of such policies can be built upon to address the ethical use of artificial intelligence tools. In an educative *approach*, the policy focus would be on guiding students in the responsible use of artificial intelligence applications. An educative *approach* was reflected in the positive commitment found in one university policy that specifically mentioned its responsibility to provide resources to staff and students to guide their understanding and use of artificial intelligence tools (University N). *Access* is essential to build awareness of academic integrity policy and it is a concern that it needs to be improved for most policies (5/9 or 55%). A lack of *detail* and *support* in most policies (6/9 or 66%) is a major concern as this can lead to a lack of shared understanding, consistency, and transparency in the enforcement of policy. Therefore, a review of academic integrity policies should include *detail* such as identification of a breach, levels of a breach, and consideration of contextual factors and outcomes. Furthermore, the policy should include *support* for staff and students such as training and provision of academic integrity information to foster ethical conduct. Training is also needed to *support* staff in the investigation of academic misconduct cases.

Universities differ in their academic integrity policy concerning the use of artificial intelligence tools. The approach varied from a ban on the use, to restricted use with permission, to an educative approach. It is anticipated that with time, universities will re-evaluate their policy response. Evidence of a shift to a more educative approach is the new principles announced by the twenty-four universities of the UK-based Russell Group to support the ethical use of generative artificial intelligence tools (Group, 2023). Workers in the age of artificial intelligence need AI literacy skills that enable them to collaborate effectively with AI tools (Lodge et al., 2023). With the rapid uptake of artificial intelligence tools by industry, the higher education sector needs to keep pace with technological change. Resistance to change such as a ban on the use of artificial intelligence tools or a punitive approach may limit higher education providers in equipping students with skills to realise the transformative potential of artificial intelligence (Adiguzel et al., 2023).

The unethical use of artificial intelligence tools is currently being dealt with primarily as a 'student issue' as the focus is on their use by students in the completion of assessments. An exemplary approach to fostering academic integrity needs to address ethical conduct by all members of the academic community including students and academics. Therefore, it can be argued that updated academic integrity and research integrity policies should have a scope that explicitly addresses the use of artificial intelligence tools by students and academics. Furthermore, the *responsibility* for ethical use of artificial intelligence tools lies with all stakeholders including the university, staff, and students.

A common theme in academic integrity policies in this study was to deal with academic misconduct arising from the use of artificial intelligence tools under 'plagiarism' (5/9 or 55%). Past research has highlighted that a lack of understanding about plagiarism can contribute to the breach of academic integrity by students (Bretag & Mahmud, 2014; Bretag et al., 2014). In the context of the use of artificial intelligence tools, issues may be compounded about the lack of understanding regarding appropriate acknowledgement or citation of content generated by AI. The author concurs with Perkins (2023) who argues:

it is not the student use of any AI tools that defines whether plagiarism or a breach of academic integrity has occurred, but whether any use is made clear by the student. Deciding whether any particular use of LLMs by students can be defined as academic misconduct is determined by the academic integrity policies of any given HEI, which must be updated to consider how these tools will be used in future educational environments.

An exemplary academic integrity policy needs to include sufficient *detail* of what constitutes a breach of policy. Consideration will be needed for the discipline-specific use of artificial intelligence tools when setting the parameters of permitted use.

Creating a shared understanding of academic integrity entails *support* for students and staff through guidance about the ethical use of artificial intelligence tools (Rudolph et al., 2023). Cases or scenarios that differentiate between ethical and unethical use of artificial intelligence tools can be part of clear guidance, so students understand what constitutes academic misconduct. To aid students in making informed decisions, training should also include the limitations of generative AI models such as the provision of false information, incorrect or out-of-date information and bias (Mijwil et al., 2023). Easily accessible academic integrity education for students on the use of artificial intelligence tools was low in most universities in the study (13/20 or 65%), though relatively speaking Australian universities provided students with higher access. An Australian university with a high level of support for students provided clear guidance to students on the institutional position on the use of AI tools, a list of permitted AI tools, a link to academic integrity policy, and a guide to appropriately acknowledge and cite AI-generated material in their assessment (University O). Going forward, an important consideration in the provision of guidance and support about the use of AI tools is the variance across different disciplines such as computer science, healthcare, social sciences, and the arts (Kelly et al., 2023). Tailored support will be needed as the ways students use AI tools will vary across disciplines. Further research is needed about the use of AI tools and the academic integrity challenges faced by students in different disciplines to inform the support provided.

A minority of universities (4/20 or 20%) in this study, provided staff with a high level of easily accessible *academic integrity information* about the use of artificial intelligence tools. Interestingly, two of these universities based in the US and Canada, refer to the use of artificial intelligence tools in their academic integrity policies (University D and T). This could be an indicator of the proactive approach taken at each of these institutions to provide support to instructors. In most US and Canadian universities in this study, instructors make the key decision at the course level whether the artificial intelligence tools are permitted or an unauthorised aid. Instructors in other countries also need to consider what constitutes ethical use of such tools in the courses they teach. While this study did not assess the confidence and competence of staff in the use of artificial intelligence tools, adjusting to new technology may cause stress for users. Therefore, *support* professional development activities that include sharing best practices in assessment and evaluation can assist staff in addressing the challenges of using artificial intelligence tools (Khan et al., 2021). By taking a comprehensive approach to AI literacy, such as its inclusion in learning and teaching policy, universities can empower educators to use artificial intelligence tools in a way that enhances their teaching and research practice. This promotes a learning environment that incorporates technological innovation while balancing ethical responsibility.

This study found that in some proactive universities, *support* through clear guidance has been provided to educators about the use of artificial intelligence tools including materials to use in courses, conversations with students and assessment redesign. Artificial intelligence creates new challenges for educators with existing performance evaluation approaches being limited in their ability to assess student learning outcomes (Chaudhry et al., 2023; Sparrow, 2022) and ensure academic integrity (Ventayen, 2023). Eaton et al. (2023) argue for educators' responsibility to take an ethical approach to the use of artificial intelligence tools in teaching, learning and assessment to ensure student success. The new reality is a world with humans plus AI and higher education needs to keep pace with how to assess student learning in this space (Dawson, 2020). The ongoing need is for assessment to be redesigned to relate it to 'workplaces that are immersed in the digital' (Bearman et al., 2023). Changes to assessment to address the risks posed by artificial intelligence is an emerging area. Focusing on assessments such as critical appraisal where humans have greater thinking capabilities than machines such as personal epistemology and evaluative judgement is one approach (Bearman & Luckin, 2020). A few measures proposed to address the risks and promote academic integrity include personal viva and oral examinations and in-person assessments, however, such measures may not suit large online courses (Kortemeyer, 2023). Therefore there is a need to re-evaluate guidelines for online examinations given artificial intelligence (Dawson et al., 2023). Ongoing research on assessment, learning, and teaching is needed as artificial intelligence technology improves (Lodge et al., 2023). Educators and researchers need to explore how advances in AI technology can be used to improve teaching practice and enhance student learning outcomes while safeguarding academic integrity.

There is an ongoing challenge in establishing *robust decision-making systems* for a breach of academic integrity relating to the use of artificial intelligence tools. Plagiarism detection systems are typically a key building block of plagiarism policies (Foltýnek et al., 2019). However, the ability of plagiarism-detection software to deter plagiarism has been questioned (Anson & Kruse, 2023; Youmans, 2011). The ability of detection software to establish academic misconduct in the use of artificial intelligence tools is limited even further with concerns about the accuracy and effectiveness of technologies to detect AI-written content (Khalil & Er, 2023). Hybrid human-ai writing cannot be detected using conventional similarity-checking software and there is an incidence of false positives in tools detecting AI content (Brainard, 2023). Therefore, it is not surprising that only two Australian universities in this study were found using technological tools to detect AI-written content in assessment submissions. While some UK universities (2/5 or 40%) were found to have banned the use of AI tools, advice from the Quality Assurance Agency (QAA) and JISC in the UK discourages the banning of AI tools and highlights the inability to conclusively detect their use and adequately investigate the number of false positive cases (currently 1%). The current scenario where the detection of AI written content is problematic may already be causing students considerable stress. There are media reports of students falsely accused of submitting AI-written work. International students who tend to be overrepresented in academic integrity breach data, are particularly vulnerable to being picked up by AI detection tools (Zhao & Brookes, 2023). The adverse impact on students of a false accusation of misconduct and the difficulties in investigation raise practical issues in the implementation of AI-detection tools. Further research is needed to examine the accuracy and effectiveness of AI detection tools as technological advances occur in AI tools. Moving forward the need for multi-modal detection is anticipated with text, audio and images generated by AI being embedded in content.

Multi-stakeholders uphold academic integrity in higher education ranging from the individual 'micro' level to the 'mega' community level (Eaton, 2021). In this study, most Australian universities had clear statements for staff and students on the use of AI tools. This finding may be attributed to previous work in the development of exemplary academic integrity policy (Bretag et al., 2011) and the structure of the Australian higher education sector where the approach has been to facilitate the ethical use of AI within a strong regulatory framework. The regulator TEQSA has published advice for higher education providers and students on the use of AI (TEQSA, 2023a). At an industry level, the Australasian Academic Integrity Network (AAIN) Generative AI Working Group is acting as an *academic integrity champion*. AAIN has released guidelines to support existing and new guidance for students, teaching staff, professional staff, university administrators and decision-makers. These guidelines align with the Higher Education Standards Framework (Threshold Standards) 2021 which requires providers to ensure the quality of teaching, learning, research, and research training, concerning content and skills developed, assessment and determination of learning outcomes, and the mitigation of foreseeable risks to academic and research integrity. Providers have been advised to 'document their decisions and monitor their progress in addressing generative AI' (Munoz et al., 2023). The sector is still playing 'catch-up' with the rapid technological change with all Australian universities needing to submit credible action plans to TEQSA by June 2024 about how they are addressing the risks posed by generative artificial intelligence (TEQSA, 2023b).

Like the approach in Australia with AAIN guidelines, the European Network for Academic Integrity (ENAI) has prepared guidelines for the ethical use of AI in education (Foltynek et al., 2023) that include student education on the need to complete their own assessments and the ethical content production skills, teacher training on the ethical use of AI in developing learning outcomes, assessments, and activities. ENAI has called for national and institutional policies to be updated to include AI. Clear definitions and policies are needed to distinguish unauthorised content generation and inappropriate use of AI from appropriate use of services and tools by students and staff. *Academic integrity champions* are also needed at an institutional level as evident at a Canadian university that has set up a task force to enhance teaching and learning using artificial intelligence and handle challenges, and at a US university where the learning and teaching department acknowledged that many queries are being received from instructors about the use of artificial intelligence tools.

As AI is increasingly embedded in frequently used software, the need to maintain academic integrity while using these tools will be more challenging. Most universities in this study dealt with academic misconduct using artificial intelligence tools under 'plagiarism'. The focus of the policy response is on appropriate acknowledgement of content which is possible where content is distinct and identifiable. However, in the future, this may not be the case as AI tools become more integrated into frequently used software, and the current approach may no longer be applicable. As Eaton (2021, p.213) contends "defining plagiarism will become even more impossible as technology becomes more intertwined with our lives". The current practice of dealing with the use of artificial intelligence as 'unauthorised assistance', 'plagiarism', or 'contract cheating' will not suffice. It is anticipated that redefining academic misconduct will be necessary as new forms of academic misconduct arise from the use of AI tools. This highlights the importance of regularly *reviewing policies and processes* (Bretag & Mahmud, 2016). The knock-on effect of the changes in the use of artificial intelligence tools will require updates to the academic integrity education provided to staff and students.

This study has examined academic integrity concerns about the use of artificial intelligence tools. The response of universities to address these concerns has been limited and the sector is playing catch up with the impact of the technological advancements. Academic integrity as an institutional issue (Whitley Jr & Keith-Spiegel, 2001) warrants that higher education providers must respond proactively and promptly to the challenges posed by the use of artificial intelligence tools.

CONCLUSION

The systematic evaluation of the higher education policy and practice response to artificial intelligence underlines the gap in academic integrity policy and practice where only a minority of policies refer to the use of AI tools. The policy response by higher education providers needs to go beyond an update to include details on the permitted use of artificial intelligence tools and the provision of comprehensive academic integrity education for staff and students. Future research is needed to understand the impact of AI tools on academic integrity with its varied use across disciplines by students and academics. The ethical guidelines for AI use in education need to balance its benefits with the potential risks. Clear guidelines are needed for institutions, academics and students that are adaptable to AI technologies that are constantly evolving.

Given the limitations of the detection of AI content, an educative approach is advocated centred on ethical values. In the longer term, higher education providers need to change how a student is assessed. Research is needed to design assessments that are less susceptible to academic misconduct using AI tools. With the increasing integration of AI tools in frequently used software, it is anticipated that academic misconduct will be reconceptualised. The responsiveness of higher education institutions, regulators, and industry practitioners to the use of artificial intelligence will determine the outcome for society at large. If they do not adequately consider the effective and ethical use of AI tools, higher education institutions may risk being sidelined as providers of credentials recognised by the industry. All stakeholders must come together to foster a culture of academic integrity at this critical time to realise the potential of artificial intelligence while mitigating the risks.

REFERENCES

Adiguzel, T., Kaya, M. H., & Cansu, F. K. (2023). Revolutionizing education with AI: Exploring the transformative potential of ChatGPT. *Contemporary Educational Technology*, *15*(3), ep429.

Alam, A. (2022). Employing adaptive learning and intelligent tutoring robots for virtual classrooms and smart campuses: Reforming education in the age of artificial intelligence. In *Advanced Computing and Intelligent Technologies Proceedings of ICACIT*. Springer.

Alkhaqani, A. L. (2023). ChatGPT and Nursing Education: Challenges and Opportunities. *Al-Rafidain Journal of Medical Sciences (ISSN 2789-3219)*, *4*, 50-51.

Anderson, N., Belavy, D. L., Perle, S. M., Hendricks, S., Hespanhol, L., Verhagen, E., & Memon, A. R. (2023). AI did not write this manuscript, or did it? Can we trick the AI text detector into generated texts? The potential future of ChatGPT and AI in Sports & Exercise Medicine manuscript generation. *BMJ Open Sport & Exercise Medicine*, *9*(1), e001568. doi:10.1136/bmjsem-2023-001568 PMID:36816423

Andrews, S., Bare, L., Bentley, P., Goedegebuure, L., Pugsley, C., & Rance, B. (2016). *Contingent academic employment in Australian universities*. LH Martin Institute.

Anson, C. M., & Kruse, O. (2023). Plagiarism Detection and Intertextuality Software. In O. Kruse, C. Rapp, C. M. Anson, K. Benetos, E. Cotos, A. Devitt, & A. Shibani (Eds.), *Digital Writing Technologies in Higher Education: Theory, Research, and Practice* (pp. 231–243). Springer International Publishing. doi:10.1007/978-3-031-36033-6_15

Baidoo-AnuD.Owusu AnsahL. (2023). Education in the era of generative artificial intelligence (AI): Understanding the potential benefits of ChatGPT in promoting teaching and learning. SSRN 4337484. doi:10.2139/ssrn.4337484

Bearman, M., & Luckin, R. (2020). Preparing university assessment for a world with AI: Tasks for human intelligence. *Re-imagining university assessment in a digital world*, 49-63.

Bearman, M., Nieminen, J. H., & Ajjawi, R. (2023). Designing assessment in a digital world: An organising framework. *Assessment & Evaluation in Higher Education*, *48*(3), 291–304. doi:10.1080/02602938.2022.2069674

Bertram-Gallant, T. (Ed.). (2011). *Creating the ethical academy: A systems approach to understanding misconduct and empowering change*. Routledge. doi:10.4324/9780203840481

Bowers, W. J. (1964). *Student dishonesty and its control in college*. Bureau of Applied Social Research, Columbia University.

Brainard, J. (2023). Journals take up arms against AI-written text. *Science*, *379*(6634), 740–741. doi:10.1126/science.adh2762 PMID:36821673

Bretag, T., Harper, R., Burton, M., Ellis, C., Newton, P., Rozenberg, P., Saddiqui, S., & van Haeringen, K. (2019). Contract cheating: A survey of Australian university students. *Studies in Higher Education*, *44*(11), 1837–1856. doi:10.1080/03075079.2018.1462788

Bretag, T., & Mahmud, S. (2014). *Embedding and extending exemplary academic integrity policy and support frameworks across the higher education sector*. A. Government. https://ltr.edu.au/resources/SP12_2327_Bretag_Report_2014.pdf

Bretag, T., & Mahmud, S. (2016). A conceptual framework for implementing exemplary academic integrity policy in Australian higher education. Handbook of academic integrity, 463-480.

Bretag, T., Mahmud, S., Wallace, M., Walker, R., James, C., Green, M., East, J., McGowan, U., & Patridge, L. (2011). Core elements of exemplary academic integrity policy in Australian higher education. *International Journal for Educational Integrity*, *7*(2). doi:10.21913/IJEI.v7i2.759

Bretag, T., Mahmud, S., Wallace, M., Walker, R., McGowan, U., East, J., Green, M., Partridge, L., & James, C. (2014). 'Teach us how to do it properly!' An Australian academic integrity student survey. *Studies in Higher Education*, *39*(7), 1150–1169. doi:10.1080/03075079.2013.777406

Carroll, J., & Development, O. C. f. S. (2002). *A handbook for deterring plagiarism in higher education*. Oxford Centre for Staff and Learning Development Oxford.

Chaudhry, I. S., Sarwary, S. A. M., El Refae, G. A., & Chabchoub, H. (2023). Time to Revisit Existing Student's Performance Evaluation Approach in Higher Education Sector in a New Era of ChatGPT—A Case Study. *Cogent Education*, *10*(1), 2210461. doi:10.1080/2331186X.2023.2210461

Cole, M. T., Shelley, D. J., & Swartz, L. B. (2019). *Re launching a new vision in education and e-learning: Fostering a culture of academic integrity in e-learning. In Smart Education and e-Learning*. Springer.

Cotton, D. R., Cotton, P. A., & Shipway, J. R. (2023). Chatting and cheating: Ensuring academic integrity in the era of ChatGPT. *Innovations in Education and Teaching International*, 1–12. doi:10.1080/14703297.2023.2190148

Crompton, H., & Burke, D. (2023). Artificial intelligence in higher education: The state of the field. *International Journal of Educational Technology in Higher Education*, *20*(1), 1–22. doi:10.1186/s41239-023-00392-8

Davenport, T. H. (2018). *The AI advantage: How to put the artificial intelligence revolution to work*. MIT Press. doi:10.7551/mitpress/11781.001.0001

Dawson, P. (2020). *Defending assessment security in a digital world: preventing e-cheating and supporting academic integrity in higher education*. Routledge. doi:10.4324/9780429324178

Dawson, P., Nicola-Richmond, K., & Partridge, H. (2023). Beyond open book versus closed book: A taxonomy of restrictions in online examinations. *Assessment & Evaluation in Higher Education*, 1–13. doi:10.1080/02602938.2023.2209298

Devlin, M. (2006). Policy, preparation, and prevention: Proactive minimization of student plagiarism. *Journal of Higher Education Policy and Management*, *28*(1), 45–58. doi:10.1080/13600800500283791

Eaton, S. E. (2021). *Plagiarism in higher education: Tackling tough topics in academic integrity*. ABC-CLIO. doi:10.5040/9798400697142

Flanagin, A., Bibbins-Domingo, K., Berkwits, M., & Christiansen, S. L. (2023). Nonhuman "authors" and implications for the integrity of scientific publication and medical knowledge. *Journal of the American Medical Association*, *329*(8), 637–639. doi:10.1001/jama.2023.1344 PMID:36719674

Foltynek, T., Bjelobaba, S., Glendinning, I., Khan, Z. R., Santos, R., Pavletic, P., & Kravjar, J. (2023). ENAI Recommendations on the ethical use of Artificial Intelligence in Education. *International Journal for Educational Integrity*, *19*(1), 12. doi:10.1007/s40979-023-00133-4

Foltýnek, T., & Glendinning, I. (2015). Impact of Policies for Plagiarism in Higher Education Across Europe: Results of the Project. *Acta Universitatis Agriculturae et Silviculturae Mendelianae Brunensis*, *63*(1), 207–216. doi:10.11118/actaun201563010207

Foltýnek, T., Meuschke, N., & Gipp, B. (2019). Academic plagiarism detection: A systematic literature review. *ACM Computing Surveys*, *52*(6), 1–42. doi:10.1145/3345317

Glendinning, I. (2014). Responses to student plagiarism in higher education across Europe. *International Journal for Educational Integrity*, *10*(1). doi:10.21913/IJEI.v10i1.930

Group, R. (2023). *New principles on use of AI in education*. Russell Group. https://russellgroup.ac.uk/news/new-principles-on-use-of-ai-in-education/

Gruetzemacher, R., & Whittlestone, J. (2022). The transformative potential of artificial intelligence. *Futures*, *135*, 102884. doi:10.1016/j.futures.2021.102884

Holmes, W., Bialik, M., & Fadel, C. (2023). Artificial intelligence in education. Globethics Publications.

Howard, R. M. (1995). Plagiarisms, authorships, and the academic death penalty. *College English*, *57*(7), 788–806. doi:10.2307/378403

Howard, R. M. (2007). Understanding "internet plagiarism". *Computers and Composition*, *24*(1), 3–15. doi:10.1016/j.compcom.2006.12.005

ICAI. (2021). *The Fundamental Values of Academic Integrity* (3 ed.). International Center for Academic Integrity. https://academicintegrity.org/images/pdfs/20019_ICAI-Fundamental-Values_R12.pdf

Illia, L., Colleoni, E., & Zyglidopoulos, S. (2023). Ethical implications of text generation in the age of artificial intelligence. *Business Ethics, the Environment & Responsibility*, *32*(1), 201–210. doi:10.1111/beer.12479

Insights, C. (2013). The value of Google result positioning. Westborough: Chitika Inc, 0-10.

Justo-Hanani, R. (2022). The politics of Artificial Intelligence regulation and governance reform in the European Union. *Policy Sciences*, *55*(1), 137–159. doi:10.1007/s11077-022-09452-8

Kelly, A., Sullivan, M., & Strampel, K. (2023). Generative artificial intelligence: University student awareness, experience, and confidence in use across disciplines. *Journal of University Teaching & Learning Practice*, *20*(6). doi:10.53761/1.20.6.12

Khalil, M., & Er, E. (2023). Will ChatGPT get you caught? Rethinking of plagiarism detection. *arXiv preprint arXiv:2302.04335*. doi:10.1007/978-3-031-34411-4_32

Khan, Z. R., Sivasubramaniam, S., Anand, P., & Hysaj, A. (2021).. . *International Journal for Educational Integrity*, *17*, 1–27. doi:10.1007/s40979-020-00063-5

Kortemeyer, G. (2023). Could an artificial-intelligence agent pass an introductory physics course? *Physical Review. Physics Education Research*, *19*(1), 010132. doi:10.1103/PhysRevPhysEducRes.19.010132

Krakowski, S., Luger, J., & Raisch, S. (2023). Artificial intelligence and the changing sources of competitive advantage. *Strategic Management Journal*, *44*(6), 1425–1452. doi:10.1002/smj.3387

Lancaster, T., & Clarke, R. (2016). Contract cheating: The outsourcing of assessed student work. Handbook of academic integrity, 1, 639-654.

Lo, C. K. (2023). What is the impact of ChatGPT on education? A rapid review of the literature. *Education Sciences*, *13*(4), 410. doi:10.3390/educsci13040410

Lodge, J. M., Thompson, K., & Corrin, L. (2023). Mapping out a research agenda for generative artificial intelligence in tertiary education. *Australasian Journal of Educational Technology*, *39*(1), 1–8. doi:10.14742/ajet.8695

Lund, B. D., Wang, T., Mannuru, N. R., Nie, B., Shimray, S., & Wang, Z. (2023). ChatGPT and a new academic reality: Artificial Intelligence-written research papers and the ethics of the large language models in scholarly publishing. *Journal of the Association for Information Science and Technology*, *74*(5), 570–581. doi:10.1002/asi.24750

Mahmud, S., & Ali, I. (2023). Evolution of research on honesty and dishonesty in academic work: A bibliometric analysis of two decades. *Ethics & Behavior*, *33*(1), 55–69. doi:10.1080/10508422.2021.2015598

McCabe, D. L., Butterfield, K. D., & Trevino, L. K. (2012). *Cheating in college: Why students do it and what educators can do about it*. JHU Press. doi:10.1353/book.18818

McCabe, D. L., & Trevino, L. K. (1993). Academic dishonesty: Honor codes and other contextual influences. *The Journal of Higher Education*, *64*(5), 522–538. doi:10.1080/00221546.1993.11778446

McCabe, D. L., Trevino, L. K., & Butterfield, K. D. (2001). Cheating in Academic Institutions: A Decade of Research. *Ethics & Behavior*, *11*(3), 219–232. doi:10.1207/S15327019EB1103_2

McCarthy, J., Minsky, M. L., Rochester, N., & Shannon, C. E. (2006). A proposal for the dartmouth summer research project on artificial intelligence, august 31, 1955. *AI Magazine*, *27*(4), 12–12.

Mijwil, M. M., Hiran, K. K., Doshi, R., Dadhich, M., Al-Mistarehi, A.-H., & Bala, I. (2023). ChatGPT and the future of academic integrity in the artificial intelligence era: A new frontier. *Al-Salam Journal for Engineering and Technology*, *2*(2), 116–127. doi:10.55145/ajest.2023.02.02.015

Möller, A. (2023). An analysis of university academic integrity policies in New Zealand. *Journal of Further and Higher Education*, *47*(3), 338–350. doi:10.1080/0309877X.2022.2130195

Munoz, A., Wilson, A., Pereira Nunes, B., Del Medico, C., Slade, C., Bennett, D., Tyler, D., Seymour, E., Hepplewhite, G., & Randell-Moon, H. (2023). *AAIN Generative Artificial Intelligence Guidelines*.

Nejati, M., Shafaei, A., Salamzadeh, Y., & Daraei, M. (2011). Corporate social responsibility and universities: A study of top 10 world universities' websites. *African Journal of Business Management*, *5*(2), 440–447.

Palinkas, L. A., Horwitz, S. M., Green, C. A., Wisdom, J. P., Duan, N., & Hoagwood, K. (2015). Purposeful sampling for qualitative data collection and analysis in mixed method implementation research. *Administration and Policy in Mental Health*, *42*(5), 533–544. doi:10.1007/s10488-013-0528-y PMID:24193818

Perkins, M. (2023). Academic Integrity considerations of AI Large Language Models in the post-pandemic era: ChatGPT and beyond. *Journal of University Teaching & Learning Practice, 20*(2), 07.

Picciano, A. G. (2019). Artificial Intelligence and the Academy's Loss of Purpose. *Online Learning : the Official Journal of the Online Learning Consortium*, *23*(3), 270–284. doi:10.24059/olj.v23i3.2023

Pickler, R. H. (2023). Artificial "Intelligence" and Scientific Integrity, *72*(3), 165-166.

Popenici, S. A., & Kerr, S. (2017). Exploring the impact of artificial intelligence on teaching and learning in higher education. *Research and Practice in Technology Enhanced Learning*, *12*(1), 1–13. doi:10.1186/s41039-017-0062-8 PMID:30595727

Rudolph, J., Tan, S., & Tan, S. (2023). ChatGPT: Bullshit spewer or the end of traditional assessments in higher education? *Journal of Applied Learning and Teaching*, *6*(1).

Safón, V. (2019). Inter-ranking reputational effects: An analysis of the Academic Ranking of World Universities (ARWU) and the Times Higher Education World University Rankings (THE) reputational relationship. *Scientometrics*, *121*(2), 897–915. doi:10.1007/s11192-019-03214-9

Satariano, A. (2023). Europeans Take a Major Step Toward Regulating A.I. *New York Times*. https://www.nytimes.com/2023/06/14/technology/europe-ai-regulation.html

Sheikh, H., Prins, C., & Schrijvers, E. (2023). Artificial Intelligence: Definition and Background. In Mission AI: The New System Technology (pp. 15-41). Springer.

Sparrow, J. (2022). The machines are learning: How artificial intelligence is already affecting journalism education. *Australian Journalism Review*, *44*(2), 163–169. doi:10.1386/ajr_00101_7

Stoesz, B. M., & Eaton, S. E. (2022). Academic integrity policies of publicly funded universities in western Canada. *Educational Policy*, *36*(6), 1529–1548. doi:10.1177/0895904820983032

Sullivan, M., Kelly, A., & McLaughlan, P. (2023). ChatGPT in higher education: Considerations for academic integrity and student learning. *Journal of Applied Learning & Teaching*, *6*(1), 1–10.

Sweeney, S. (2023). Who wrote this? Essay mills and assessment–Considerations regarding contract cheating and AI in higher education. *International Journal of Management Education*, *21*(2), 100818. doi:10.1016/j.ijme.2023.100818

TEQSA. (2023a). *Artificial Intelligence*. TEQSA. https://www.teqsa.gov.au/guides-resources/higher-education-good-practice-hub/artificial-intelligence

TEQSA. (2023b). *Protecting sector integrity: Assessment reform and AI*. TESQA. https://www.teqsa.gov.au/about-us/news-and-events/latest-news/protecting-sector-integrity-assessment-reform-and-ai

Thurzo, A., Strunga, M., Urban, R., Surovková, J., & Afrashtehfar, K. I. (2023). Impact of artificial intelligence on dental education: A review and guide for curriculum update. *Education Sciences*, *13*(2), 150. doi:10.3390/educsci13020150

Varsha, P. (2023). How can we manage biases in artificial intelligence systems–A systematic literature review. *International Journal of Information Management Data Insights*, *3*(1), 100165.

VentayenR. J. M. (2023). OpenAI ChatGPT generated results: Similarity index of artificial intelligence-based contents. *Advances in Intelligent Systems and Computing*.

Whitley, B. E. Jr, & Keith-Spiegel, P. (2001). *Academic dishonesty: An educator's guide.* Psychology Press. doi:10.4324/9781410604279

Youmans, R. J. (2011). Does the adoption of plagiarism-detection software in higher education reduce plagiarism? *Studies in Higher Education, 36*(7), 749–761. doi:10.1080/03075079.2010.523457

Zhang, J. (2005). *Content analysis of web sites from 2000 to 2004: a thematic meta-analysis.* Texas A&M University.

Zhang, Y., Lin, H., Zhang, X., & Ye, Q. (2021). The next steps in academic integrity—Education, awareness, norms, duty and law. *Forensic Sciences Research, 6*(4), 341–346. doi:10.1080/20961790.2021.1970887 PMID:35111353

Zhao, I., & Brookes, S. (2023). International students and researchers concerned tools to detect AI-generated text may be inaccurate. *ABC News.* https://www.abc.net.au/news/2023-06-02/international-students-say-ai-detectors-are-inaccurate/1023948944

Chapter 2
The British Battle for Authenticity:
Defending Academic Integrity in the Age of AI

Edyta Kostanek
https://orcid.org/0000-0002-2854-2587
University College London, UK

Roopa Aruvanahalli Nagaraju
Oxford Brookes University, UK

Anna Michalska
University of Warwick, UK

ABSTRACT

The rise of GenAI in HE has brought both opportunities and challenges, including threats such as plagiarism, data fabrication, and misrepresentation of original works. This chapter scrutinises the publicly available websites of 130 universities across Great Britain and evaluates documents pertinent to 67 of them to the interplay between academic integrity and AI. The integration of GenAI into higher education has significantly impacted how British universities provide guidance and support for staff and students. In England, 59.3% of universities possess GenAI guidance and have integrated it into their academic misconduct policy. However, only 18.6% have announced a statement concerning GenAI. British universities display a more even distribution of stances towards GenAI, with most exuding a positive stance. British universities are increasingly focusing on academic integrity and implementing GenAI tools to foster AI literacy among students and faculty.

DOI: 10.4018/979-8-3693-0240-8.ch002

INTRODUCTION

Higher education is undergoing transformative shifts, primarily influenced by global paradigms such as globalisation, privatisation, and the meteoric rise of communication technologies and social media platforms (Tierney & Almeida, 2017). The advent and proliferation of communication technology have ushered in an era where higher education is more accessible, fostering greater global collaboration and unprecedented innovation in teaching methodologies and research. Nevertheless, these positive strides are offset by the looming spectre of compromised academic integrity, which stands as the cornerstone of scholarly and educational pursuits (Manly et al., 2015).

Within the academic realm, integrity is not merely a term but a guiding principle (Padillah, 2023). It underscores the commitment to time-honoured values such as honesty, fairness, trust, respect, and responsibility, evident across a spectrum of activities including but not limited to research, teaching, learning, and assessment (Sefcik et al., 2019). While ushering in myriad advantages, the digital age also presents pervasive threats to this principle. We see this in the proliferation of digital malpractices like plagiarism, data fabrication, and the misrepresentation of original works. Disturbingly, the Internet has given rise to platforms offering students off-the-shelf or customised academic work.

Furthermore, emerging technologies that generate authentic-seeming content – text, imagery, or video – can confound even the most astute human evaluators. ChatGPT, a state-of-the-art generative artificial intelligence (GenAI) system, epitomises this challenge. Its potential for crafting sophisticated, nuanced, and subject-specific content has catalysed debates and concerns regarding its possible misuse within academic spheres. Other essay bots, text generators, and grammar checkers are available, such as Quillbot, ChatGPT, Perplexity.ai, Chimp Rewriter, Grammarly, etc. There are also artefact generators such as Github Co-pilot, DALL.E 2, Melobites.com, Midjourney, Stable Diffusion, etc. GenAI is also being built into search engines to improve results from natural language prompts (e.g., Bing) and computational knowledge engines used to perform calculations, analyse data sets, and provide insights into complex problems, such as Wolfram.

Macfarlane et al. (2014) astutely observed that while strides have been made in academic integrity, a knowledge gap persists, especially concerning identifying and implementing the most effective, sustainable, and adaptable strategies. This chapter aims to bridge this gap, focusing mainly on the transformative responses of British universities to emerging tools such as ChatGPT and comparable artificial intelligence (AI) innovations. Our goal is to provide an analysis of the current situation in Great Britain, taking into consideration important aspects such as the effect that AI has on academic integrity, the rethinking of assessment methods, the safeguarding of academic integrity through laws and practises, and the instruction of staff and students on how to make responsible use of AI. By doing so, we intend to contribute to the understanding of AI's scope, benefits, and challenges in the context of higher education teaching, learning, and assessment, as well as to provide an institutional perspective on how AI could be exploited in the context of the higher education industry.

AI AND ITS IMPACT ON EDUCATION

Artificial Intelligence (AI), posited within contemporary computer science literature, seeks to simulate facets of human cognitive function within computational frameworks (Di Vaio et al., 2020). An emergent sub-discipline within the AI domain is GenAI. This paradigm, predicated on algorithmic intelligence, is characterised by its ability to engender novel content or data structures predicated upon extant informational parameters. Such a dimension of AI elucidates transformative potentialities for pedagogical practices, scholarly research, and academic assessments, offering methodologies that conflate efficacy with efficiency (Zawacki-Richter et al., 2019). GenAI can amplify assessment modalities' validity, reliability, and alacrity while enhancing the granularity and pertinence of feedback mechanisms (Zawacki-Richter et al., 2019). For the learner, this culminates in a pedagogical milieu enriched by bespoke feedback, content modulated to cater to individualised learning trajectories, and simulations possessing a high degree of immersion (Mohd et al., 2020). For educators, GenAI emerges as an auxiliary, facilitating the creation of robust instructional materials, diverse learning activities, and multifaceted pedagogical scenarios (Latif et al., 2023).

In the rapidly evolving domain of AI, profound implications arise, especially when juxtaposed with the hallowed tenets of higher education and its intrinsic pedagogical frameworks. One symbolic manifestation of this confluence is ChatGPT, which can articulate natural language constructs across a vast spectrum of topics underpinned by existing data or information paradigms. Beyond its technological finesse, ChatGPT's multifaceted applicability resonates profoundly with a range of educational objectives, be it the generation of tailored learning resources, the provision of bespoke feedback mechanisms, or the nuanced formulation of evaluative matrices. However, this suite of capabilities also casts a shadow of potential misuse, particularly within the HE context. The seductive allure of ChatGPT and its AI contemporaries extends a dual-edged sword: while they hold the promise of revolutionising education, they also harbour the potential for academic deceit. The threat is not confined to students substituting their intellectual endeavours with algorithmic outputs; it cascades further into the dangerous realm of jeopardising the inviolable principles of academic integrity. By leveraging GenAI in an academically inauthentic manner, students could produce textual or visual artefacts devoid of original thought and engagement.

Given this intricate mosaic of potential and pitfall, the custodians of education — the institutions themselves — must rationally re-evaluate their guiding pedagogical philosophies and assessment frameworks. It becomes incumbent upon them to harmonise their educational strategies with a zeitgeist wherein AI platforms are no longer novel but normative. This entails an endeavour that reaches deeper than mere policy reformulations. At its core, it calls for nurturing an enlightened student and faculty cohort, individuals steeped in the ethical ramifications of GenAI engagement. This involves the conceptualisation and diligent implementation of robust frameworks that not only deter the misuse of AI but are also equipped with the insight to detect such transgressions.

AI AND ITS IMPACT ON ACADEMIC INTEGRITY

One of the main issues that ChatGPT and other GenAI systems may bring for higher education assessment is the threat to academic integrity. At the core of higher educational pursuits lies the quintessential doctrine of academic integrity. Turner and Beemsterboer's (2003, p. 1122) articulation of academic integrity as emblematic of "honesty in all academic endeavours" anchors the integrity debate. This is not merely an abstract construct; it fundamentally influences the perceived credibility, reliability, and authenticity of educational and research outcomes (Macfarlane et al. 2014). Some authors believe that integrity is essential to enhance every part of human life (Zadauer, 1992).

Over the past decade, a noteworthy evolution in the academic world has shifted from a punitive stance on violations of academic integrity to an educative, preventive approach. Rather than being an intricate labyrinth of rules to navigate, academic integrity has metamorphosed into an ethos, an intrinsic part of the academic culture to be collectively embraced (Bretag et al., 2016). Nevertheless, the global academic community grapples with breaches of this virtue, as evidenced by studies like those by Mirshekary and Lawrence (2009) and Ison (2012). The battle against plagiarism, as highlighted by McKillup and McKillup (2007) and Löfström and Kupila (2013), exemplifies the struggle against one of the most insidious manifestations of academic deceit.

Empirical research underscores the imperativeness of crafting robust policy blueprints that embrace holistic paradigms to navigate the intricate maze of academic integrity (Boehm et al., 2009). As Morris et al. (2018) elucidate, policies are the guiding star that illuminate the development and execution of academic integrity precepts within institutional precincts. These policies are anchored in transparent definitions, principles, and ethical constructs, providing a roadmap for students and faculty (Bretag et al., 2016). Adherence to these principles becomes a non-negotiable tenet of academic life. Pedagogical interventions, like academic integrity courses posited by Whitley and Keith-Spiegel (2001), have proven to be efficacious in bolstering academic integrity competence, underscoring the need for proactive rather than reactive measures to preserve the academic realm's sanctity.

Furthermore, institutions should consider augmenting traditional pedagogies with educational interventions tailored to the digital age to navigate this complex terrain. As Whitley and Keith-Spiegel (2001) posited, courses centred around academic integrity can foster awareness, promote understanding, and cultivate a sense of ethical responsibility. In this constantly evolving academic landscape, proactive measures are not merely desirable but imperative, ensuring that the cherished edifice of academic integrity stands robust and unyielding.

METHODOLOGY

Sample

In our research, spanning June to September 2023, we scrutinised the publicly available websites of 130 universities across Great Britain (GB) to identify and evaluate documents pertinent to the interplay between academic integrity and AI. Our primary objective was to locate official documents such as institutional declarations on academic integrity, policies addressing academic misconduct, and pedagogical guidelines for faculty and students. Navigating the plethora of documents available across the various British universities presented a complex task. Several factors contributed to this complexity. Many institutions had multiple iterations of pertinent documents, and in some cases, these documents were undergoing revisions concurrently with our data collection period. Of the 130 GB universities, we successfully retrieved relevant documents from 67: 59 from England, seven from Scotland, and one from Wales (see Table 1).

It is imperative to highlight that our analysis exclusively encompasses publicly accessible documents as of 15 September 2023. We did not access any proprietary or internal documents, which implies that while some universities may have crafted guidelines concerning AI utilisation, such documents might not have been publicly disclosed during our research window. Additionally, for the scope of this study,

Table 1. Characteristics of the reviewed sample of institutions

Characteristic	*n*	%
Country		
England	59	88.06
Scotland	7	10.45
Wales	1	1.49
Grouping		
Unassigned	23	34.33
The Russell Group	18	26.87
University Alliance	10	14.93
MillionPlus Group	10	14.93
GuildHE	3	4.48
The Cathedrals Group	3	4.48
Size		
under 10,000 students	8	11.94
10,001-20,000 students	34	50.75
20,001-30,000 students	15	22.39
30,001-40,000 students	6	8.96
above 40,001 students	4	5.97

Note. N = 67

academic misconduct policies were only deemed relevant if they explicitly alluded to the role or influence of AI.

Analysis Approach

We employed a dual approach for our comprehensive data analysis, integrating thematic and quantitative manifest content analyses. This combined method enabled us to delve into the intricacies of our documents, gaining insights from multiple perspectives. Thematic analysis, a qualitative technique, was instrumental in deciphering emergent themes, discerning underlying patterns, and identifying dominant narratives within our data. We drew inspiration from Braun and Clarke's (2006) six-step framework and used NVivo14 to achieve a consistent coding process. NVivo proved invaluable in our research, aiding in streamlined coding, visually representing our data, and facilitating intricate data mapping. On the other hand, the quantitative manifest content analysis supplemented this by quantifying the prevalence of these themes. By assessing theme prevalence, we were able to establish empirical evidence of the significance and prominence of themes across the documents we analysed.

The British HE Context

Higher education in Great Britain (i.e., England, Scotland, and Wales) is renowned globally, with many universities in the region having historical significance and world-class reputations. British universities consistently rank highly in global university rankings. The constellation of universities in Great Britain, currently exceeding 130, remains fluid due to periodic institutional amalgamations, the conferment of university statuses, and other metamorphic processes. There are over 130 universities across Great Britain. England houses over 100 of these, Scotland has 19, and Wales holds 8. However, these numbers can change due to mergers or when new universities are created. Also, exact numbers might vary depending on the specific inclusion criteria (like the inclusion of small, specialised postgraduate institutions or institutions that have a university title but do not have degree-awarding powers).

Several university groupings exist within Great Britain. Encompassing 24 premier public research-intensive institutions, the Russell Group[1] is emblematic of its stringent research proclivity, academic distinction, and elevated admission requisites. The University Alliance[2] comprises predominantly technical and vocational institutions renowned for their industry and public sector affiliations. Notable members are Coventry University, University of Hertfordshire, Liverpool John Moores University, and Manchester Metropolitan University, among others. MillionPlus[3] represents modern universities that offer diverse courses and strongly focus on innovation, industry engagement, and accessibility. Notable members include the University of Bedfordshire, London Metropolitan University, Middlesex University, and the University of Wolverhampton. GuildHE[4] represents some of Britain's smaller and specialised institutions, including several art schools, agricultural institutions, and more. Notable examples include the Royal Agricultural University, Ravensbourne University London, and Rose Bruford College of Theatre & Performance. Finally, the Cathedrals Group[5] consists of 17 universities and college institutions that are faith-based. Notable Examples include Canterbury Christ Church University, University of Chester, Liverpool Hope University, and York St John University, among others.

RESULTS AND DISCUSSION

The landscape of British higher education has long been contending with multifaceted challenges, even before the onset of the COVID-19 pandemic. A particularly vexing concern during this period was the burgeoning prevalence of contract cheating. This malpractice involves third-party entities undertaking academic tasks on behalf of students, who subsequently present these outputs as their original work. Universities with substantial cohorts of international students found themselves particularly vulnerable to such misconduct. Various factors, ranging from the aspiration for immaculate academic submissions to challenges in linguistic proficiency in English, have driven students to engage with proofreading services. While seemingly innocuous, these services occasionally modify student work to an extent that violates institutional guidelines on proofreading.

The emergence of the COVID-19 pandemic magnified existing challenges and introduced a fresh slew of complications. Universities across the globe were compelled to swiftly recalibrate their modus operandi in response to the new normal. The almost overnight transition to online teaching and reconsidering traditional assessment paradigms became exigent. While logistically convenient, the initial tactical shift to online examinations – obviating the need for expansive physical venues – became numerous institutions' de facto assessment strategy. However, this evolution was not without pitfalls. The virtual examination ecosystem became rife with issues of unauthenticated content appropriation from online sources and tacit collaborations among examinees.

The global unveiling of ChatGPT in December 2022 further exacerbated the academia's apprehensions. Preliminary experiments by educators found that posing typical assessment questions to this programme

Table 2. Inclusion of AI aspects in university documents

Characteristic	University has GenAI guidance in place			The university released a statement on GenAI.			The university included GenAI in the Academic Misconduct Policy.	
	n	%		n	%		n	%
Country								
England	35	59.3		11	18.6		35	59.3
Scotland	4	57.1		2	28.6		2	28.6
Wales	1	100.0		0	0.0		1	100.0
Grouping								
Unassigned	13	56.5		6	26.1		12	52.2
The Russell Group	12	66.7		1	5.6		9	50.0
University Alliance	6	60.0		2	20.0		7	70.0
MillionPlus Group	6	60.0		2	20.0		7	70.0
GuildHE	2	66.7		1	33.3		2	66.7
The Cathedrals Group	1	33.3		1	33.3		1	33.3
Size								
under 10,000 students	2	25.0		2	25.0		5	62.5
10,001-20,000 students	21	61.8		10	29.4		18	52.9
20,001-30,000 students	11	73.3		0	0.0		10	66.7
30,001-40,000 students	4	66.7		1	16.7		3	50.0
above 40,001 students	2	50.0		0	0.0		2	50.0
Total instances	40	59.7[1]		13	19.4[1]		38	56.7[1]
Note. [1] *N = 67*								

yielded answers of commendable quality, often warranting pass grades. The reflexive institutional response was to revert to traditional, in-person examination modalities as a bulwark against the potential misuse of advanced AI, especially the GenAI subset, famed for human-like response generation.

Given the student access to Chat GPT, the response of the Universities is varied. Some Higher Education Institutions in GB, such as Oxford and Cambridge, decided to ban ChatGPT in assessment immediately. However, many others believed such a solution was too drastic and would only worsen the problem (ITVnews, 2023). However, this move was criticised, likened to historical aversions against innovations like calculators and search engines. This period of introspection led several universities to discern the potential pedagogical merits of A, its capacity to bolster teaching, learning, and evaluation processes, promote autonomous learning, ensure equity, and bridge achievement differentials among diverse learner demographics. Some universities have responded positively and tried to educate the students and encourage them to use Chat GPT constructively, ethically, and responsibly (e.g., University College London, University of Warwick, etc.)

Table 2 indicates how British universities responded to this evolving area is of significant interest. Notably, 59.3% of universities in England possess GenAI guidance and have integrated it into their Academic Misconduct Policy (e.g., Brunel University London, City University London, University College London, University of Westminster). However, 18.6% have announced a statement concerning GenAI (e.g., SOAS University of London, Lancaster University, University of Brighton). Universities in Scotland display a notable engagement, with 57.1% having GenAI guidance (e.g., Heriot-Watt University, University of Glasgow). Equally, 28.6% have disseminated and integrated statements into their misconduct policies (e.g., Abertay University, Edinburgh Napier University). The Swansea University in Wales (100%) has established GenAI guidance and integrated it into its policy framework, albeit without a public statement.

56.5% of Unassigned universities offer guidance (e.g., the University of Dundee, Swansea University), 26.1% have made public statements (e.g., University of Surrey), and 52.2% have accounted for it in their misconduct policies (e.g., Royal Holloway, University of London). 66.7% of Russell Group have issued guidance. London School of Economics and Political Science has only released a statement. At the same time, 50% of Russell Group institutions acknowledge GenAI in their misconduct guidelines (e.g., University of Exeter, University of Manchester). University Alliance and MillionPlus Group exhibit similar trends, with 60% formulating guidance (e.g., University of Portsmouth), 20% broadcasting statements (e.g., University of Greenwich), and a substantial 70% embedding it within misconduct policies (e.g., University of Salford, Birmingham City University). Within GuildHE, two-thirds have provided guidance and adjusted their misconduct policies, whereas Leeds Arts University issued a public statement. A consistent 33.3% of The Cathedrals Group within this collective have undertaken each action.

Universities with less than 10,000 students have seen 25% issue guidance and statements, but a robust 62.5% have integrated GenAI in misconduct policies (e.g., University of Cumbria, Harper Adams University). Those with student bodies ranging from 10,001 to 20,000 show 61.8% with guidance, 29.4% releasing statements (e.g., Solent University, Glasgow Caledonian University), and 52.9% revising their misconduct policies. For institutions hosting between 20,001 and 30,000 students, 73.3% have formulated guidance (e.g., University of Bristol, University of Liverpool), yet none have issued statements. However, 66.7% have adapted their misconduct policies. Institutions sized 30,001 to 40,000 reflect 66.7% with guidance, 16.7% releasing statements, and 50% amending misconduct policies. Large institutions with over 40,001 students depict 50% with guidance and corresponding policy changes but lack public statements.

59.7% of all reviewed universities have created GenAI guidance, 19.4% have issued statements, and 56.7% have adapted their Academic Misconduct Policies. Many universities have acknowledged GenAI's significance, primarily through guidance and policy amendments. However, fewer feel the compulsion to release public statements. Variations across groupings and sizes may illuminate differing priorities, resources, or perceptions of GenAI's relevance within their academic spheres.

Student and Staff Guidance

The diffusion of GenAI into academic and administrative echelons necessitates a thorough comprehension of how educational institutions facilitate awareness and education regarding this paradigm.

Canterbury Christ Church University (2023), in their staff guidance, states that they aim to "encourage academic staff to co-create with students and look for opportunities to build learning communities, (...) upskilling ourselves, revisiting current working and teaching practices and considering new ways of learning, teaching and assessing, using AI as a part of our toolkit."

Oxford Brookes University (2023) offers specific guidance for students introducing the CAUTION approach when using AI tools that urges students to "Check [their] prompts. (…) / Approach any information the AI tool produces cautiously (…). / Understand that Large Language Models (…) won't do the thinking (…). / Take the time to verify any claims made and check the reliability of any sources. / Identify any use of AI tools (…) Always declare (…) use of AI tools and explain how you used them. / Observe the principles of Good Academic Practice at all times. /Never submit chunks of text produced by AI as your work (…)".

Table 3 shows that in the English higher education landscape, 25.4% of institutions have proactively offered guidance concerning GenAI to their staff (e.g., Canterbury Christ Church University, Imperial College London, University College London, University of Reading), paralleled by 30.5% directing such guidance towards their student body (e.g., City University of London, Manchester Metropolitan University). Scotland's universities, intriguingly, demonstrate a divergent trend: only Edinburgh Napier University extended guidance to staff, but an augmented 42.9% have done so for students (e.g., Heriot-

Table 3. Guidance was issued to university staff and students

Characteristic		The university provided guidance on GenAI to its staff.			Student University provided guidance on GenAI to its students.	
		n	%		n	%
Country						
England		15	25.4		18	30.5
Scotland		1	14.3		3	42.9
Wales		0	0.0		1	100.0
Grouping						
Unassigned		4	17.4		8	34.8
The Russell Group		6	33.3		7	38.9
University Alliance		2	20.0		4	40.0
MillionPlus Group		4	40.0		2	20.0
GuildHE		0	0.0		1	33.3
The Cathedrals Group		0	0.0		0	0.0
Size						
under 10,000 students		0	0.0		0	0.0
10,001-20,000 students		8	23.5		12	35.3
20,001-30,000 students		5	33.3		4	26.7
30,001-40,000 students		2	33.3		4	66.7
above 40,001 students		1	25.0		2	50.0
Total instances		16	23.9[1]		22	32.8[1]

Note. [1] N = 67

Watt University, University of Glasgow). Wales presents a particularly distinct case, where its institutions have yet to cater to the staff in this domain, but Swansea University offers guidance to its students.

Unassigned universities evince a distribution of 17.4% for staff and a moderately higher 34.8% for students. Institutions within The Russell Group, reputed for their research-driven ethos, manifest a more robust engagement: 33.3% have dispensed guidance to their staff, and 38.9% to their student populace. The University Alliance showcases 20.0% of its institutions promulgating guidance to staff, contrasted with a higher 40.0% targeting students. The MillionPlus Group displays a reversal in this trend, with 40.0% catering to staff and 20.0% to students. Interestingly, universities within the GuildHE domain have eschewed staff-oriented guidance, with their engagement solely directed towards students at 33.3%. The Cathedrals Group, on the other hand, remains reticent, with neither staff nor students receiving any specific GenAI guidance.

Small-scale universities harbouring fewer than 10,000 students have refrained from disseminating any GenAI guidance. Those accommodating between 10,001 to 20,000 students depict 23.5% furnishing guidance to staff and 35.3% to students. The middle-tier universities, with populations ranging from 20,001 to 30,000, exhibit a 33.3% rate for staff and a slightly decreased 26.7% for students. Larger institutions hosting 30,001 and 40,000 students convey guidance to 33.3% of staff but show an intensified commitment towards students, evidenced by a 66.7% rate. The most expansive institutions, with student bodies surpassing 40,001, showcase a balanced approach with only University College London guiding staff and a doubled 50.0% guiding students (the University of Glasgow and University College London).

Surveying the academic panorama, it is discernible that 23.9% of universities have extended GenAI guidance to their staff, with a marginally enhanced 32.8% directing such guidance towards their students. This aggregated insight underscores the prevailing inclination of universities to prioritise student-oriented GenAI guidance over their staff counterpart.

Universities' Stance

As we navigate the evolving landscape of GenAI in higher education, comprehending institutional stances is pivotal. Table 4 presents information on British universities and their stances towards AI. Within the English academic realm, 45.8%, to be precise, exude a positive stance (e.g., Buckingham New University, University of Bournemouth, University of the West of England, etc.). A smaller contingent, 11.9%, remains neutral (e.g., University of Chester, University of Lincoln, etc.), while a minute fraction, 3.4%, seem to harbour a negative perception (the University of Oxford and the University of Westminster). Scottish universities display a more even distribution: 28.6% are positive, with both neutral and negative stances at 14.3%. Contrarily, Welsh institutions remain enigmatic, with no available data on any stance.

Among the unassigned institutions, positivity prevails at 43.5%, followed by neutrality at 13% and negativity at 4.3%. The eminent Russell Group showcases a conspicuous positivity, mirrored in 50% of its institutions, with neutral and negative stances cited in 5.6%. The University Alliance exudes 30% positivity, 10% neutrality, and a conspicuous absence of negativity. The MillionPlus Group presents a more diverse palette: 20% positive, 20% neutral, and 10% negative. The GuildHE, much like its Welsh counterparts, offers no discernible data. Meanwhile, The Cathedrals Group balances positivity and neutrality at 33.3%, with negativity absent.

Institutions harbouring fewer than 10,000 students predominantly lean positive at 14.7%, with no data on neutral or negative stances. Those accommodating 10,001 to 20,000 students manifest a resounding positivity at 93.3%, complemented by 40% neutrality and 13.3% negativity. Institutions within the 20,001

Table 4. University stance towards AI

Approach	Positive stance		Neutral stance		Negative stance		No particular stance[1]	
	n	%	n	%	n	%	n	%
Country								
England	27	45.8	7	11.9	2	3.4	23	39.0
Scotland	2	28.6	1	14.3	1	14.3	3	42.9
Wales	0	0.0	0	0.0	0	0.0	1	100.0
Grouping								
Unassigned	10	43.5	3	13.0	1	4.3	9	39.1
The Russell Group	9	50.0	1	5.6	1	5.6	7	38.9
University Alliance	3	30.0	1	10.0	0	0.0	6	60.0
MillionPlus Group	2	20.0	2	20.0	1	10.0	5	50.0
GuildHE	0	0.0	0	0.0	0	0.0	3	100.0
The Cathedrals Group	1	33.3	1	33.3	0	0.0	1	33.3
Size								
under 10,000 students	5	62.5	0	0.0	0	0.0	3	37.5
10,001-20,000 students	14	41.2	6	17.6	2	5.9	12	35.3
20,001-30,000 students	4	26.7	1	6.7	1	6.7	9	60.0
30,001-40,000 students	3	50.0	1	16.7	0	0.0	2	33.3
above 40,001 students	3	75.0	0	0.0	0	0.0	1	25.0
Total instances	29	43.3	8	11.9	3	4.5	27	40.3

Note. N = 67.

[1]*Some universities in our sample issued concise statements or include information on AI in Academic Misconduct policies however without explaining their specific approach further.*

to 30,000 student brackets display a 50% positivity, 12.5% neutrality, and an equivalent 12.5% negativity. Those hosting between 30,001 and 40,000 students predominantly lean positive at 50%, complemented by 16.7% neutrality and an absence of negativity. The most expansive institutions, those with student bodies surpassing 40,001, radiate a 75% positivity, with no insights into neutral or negative stances.

When assessed in aggregation, the stances crystallise as follows: 43.3% positive, 11.9% neutral, and 4.5% negative. This overarching perspective underscores the prevailing optimism across British universities towards GenAI, albeit nuanced by size and grouping.

The rise of tools like ChatGPT, while met with scepticism in certain quarters, has inadvertently engendered crucial pedagogical debates concerning the adequacy of prevailing assessment methods. This development precipitated an essential discourse around the concept of authentic assessment. Indeed, it sheds light on the palpable limitations of online examinations. Initially introduced as an interim modality during the tumultuous COVID era, these examinations inadvertently evolved into the predominant assessment paradigm within the expansive ambit of mass education. The advent of GenAI tools provided an opportune juncture to reconsider the fundamental objectives of education, especially in the context of equipping students for a rapidly metamorphosing global landscape.

Ultimately, the British higher education sector discerned three potential trajectories in assessment design vis-à-vis AI: i. Design AI 'into' the assessment - Integrate AI into the assessment framework; ii.

Design AI ‘out of’ the assessment, deliberately exclude AI from the evaluative process; iii. Do neither and accept its use by students. Adopt a neutral stance, implicitly allowing student reliance on AI.

Some British universities, recognising the potential advantages of integrating modern technologies, have begun incorporating AI and tools like ChatGPT into their pedagogical strategies (‘Design in’). A salient example of this incorporation entails prompting students to utilise AI to generate preliminary ideas or drafts, which are then elaborated upon or refined in subsequent phases of academic engagement.

For instance, Birkbeck, University of London acknowledges explicitly that there are legitimate uses for AI, especially in the preparatory stages of assessments and “recognises that AI-powered tools can support and assist the learning and development process in constructive ways” (Birkbeck, University of London, 2023). Similarly, Canterbury Christ Church University states they “recognise the potential of GenAI to support learning, teaching, research and working practices. However, we know the tools’ limitations and the ethical complexity of their widespread use within the University. Therefore, our approach to the adoption and use of these tools is educative rather than punitive.” (Canterbury Christ Church University, 2023). University of Birmingham (2023) suggests that “marking criteria and rubrics should be updated for all assessments and assignments (…) should reflect how the use of GenAI is being assessed (…) [and] proportionately reward successful demonstration of the higher-order thinking skills of Bloom’s Taxonomy which GenAI currently finds difficult to replicate.”

However, the ‘Designing in” has engendered a concomitant debate surrounding the equitable accessibility of such technological tools, especially in scenarios where proprietary charges might be levied on users. Should the deployment of these tools become a mandatory component of academic assessments, the financial onus would shift to universities to ensure universal access for their student populace.

‘Designing out’ typically implies outright prohibiting a particular tool or method. Nevertheless, even within this context, it is paramount to differentiate between the broad spectrum of AI tools available. For instance, even though it is a rudimentary form of AI, spellcheckers are ubiquitously utilised and have garnered widespread acceptance in academic circles.

To maintain the integrity of assessment, some British universities also have shown greater interest in returning to the in-person exams. However, educators think this is not the answer as this method does not accurately assess the students’ learning. Instead, there is a greater emphasis on oral presentations and vivas to assess students’ grasp of the subject and their learning. However, these methods are resource-intensive, and many experts think it is vital to use a hybrid assessment method to ensure it is inclusive, as there is reasonable pressure on the staff to carry out the assessment.

Adopting a more neutral stance would entail permitting ChatGPT and analogous GenAI tools but with stipulations. Ensuring that any deployment of such technologies within academic submissions is meticulously articulated and duly cited is vital. However, this opens another intricate dimension of the discourse.

Though seemingly straightforward, citing the use of GenAI tools becomes fraught with complexities when delving into the intricacies of intellectual ownership and responsibility. Unlike traditional citations attributing human authors, referencing AI-generated content transcends the conventional paradigm since these tools do not possess human-like agency or responsibility. This evolving dynamic raises intricate questions about the aptness of citations, especially when the originality of the idea is AI-derived.

Types of Misconduct

Numerous academics opine that the emergence of ChatGPT mirrors the perennial struggle against academic misconduct. It is perceived as merely an evolved manifestation of students' proclivity to seek expedient routes, sidestepping the rigours of genuine learning (Times Higher Education, 2023).

Prominent universities are increasingly advocating for cultivating a robust ethos of academic integrity. In a landmark move in June 2023, the Russell Group universities unveiled a quintet of guiding principles for deploying GenAI tools in academia. These principles encompass a spectrum of objectives, from fostering AI literacy among students and faculty to ensuring academic rigour remains inviolate. A collaborative spirit, wherein best practices are synergistically shared, is envisaged as GenAI's educational applications evolve.

The nexus of higher education, GenAI, and the pertinent regulations is rapidly evolving. To fathom this intricate relationship, it is essential to understand how university policies across Great Britain address different types of misconduct associated with GenAI usage. We have noticed varying levels of terms used to describe academic misconduct instances. For instance, Birkbeck, University of London (2023) understands submitting work for assessment that has been generated by a chatbot or AI tool as an academic offence and states that "the words and ideas generated by the chatbot or AI tool would make use of other, human authors' ideas without referencing them, which is plagiarism." Others like London Metropolitan University (2023) refer either to "Plagiarism, where AI tools are used to generate output and ideas that are presented or submitted as if they were the student's own work, without proper citation or references", or a much stricter Contract Cheating "where a complete assignment is created using GenAI and represented as a student's own work (…) [regarded] in the same way as commissioning an 'Essay Mill' or other third party to complete your work."

As Table 5 shows, in the English context, 'plagiarism' conspicuously stands out as the predominant misconduct type, cited in 16.9% of university policies. This is trailed by 'contract cheating' at 13.6%. On the contrary, 'AI misuse', 'falsification', and 'lack of authorship' are marginally acknowledged, each appearing in 1.7% of policies. Scottish universities manifest an emphatic focus on plagiarism, highlighted in 57.1% of their policies, and contract cheating follows at 28.6%. Swansea University referred solely to 'academic misconduct'.

Unassigned universities predominantly address 'plagiarism' and 'academic misconduct', cited in 26.1% and 30.4% of policies. Institutions within The Russell Group exhibit an accentuated focus on 'contract cheating', referenced in 22.2% of their guidelines. University Alliance offers an equanimous approach, referencing 'academic misconduct' and 'contract cheating' in 30% of policies. The MillionPlus Group, conversely, singles out 'academic misconduct', highlighted in 30% of their regulations. GuildHE emphasises 'plagiarism' and 'cheating', appearing in 33.3% of their policies. The Cathedrals Group splits its attention between 'academic misconduct' and 'plagiarism', each cited in 33.3% of guidelines.

Smaller institutions with fewer than 10,000 students primarily address 'academic misconduct', evidenced by an 8.8% reference rate. Institutions accommodating 10,001 to 20,000 students evince a strong inclination towards 'academic misconduct' and 'plagiarism', as mentioned in 60% and 53.3% of policies. The trend of highlighting 'academic misconduct'' persists for institutions sized 20,001 to 30,000, with a mention rate of 62.5%. Interestingly, universities catering to 30,001 to 40,000 students pivot their attention towards 'contract cheating', referenced in 50% of their policies. The largest institutions, with a student populace surpassing 40,001, revert the focus to 'plagiarism', referenced in 50% of their guidelines.

Table 5. Types of academic misconduct related to AI use

Characteristic	Academic Misconduct		Plagiarism		Contract Cheating		Cheating		Cheating (*while on exams*)		AI misuse		Falsification		Lack of authorship		Malpractice	
	n	%	n	%	n	%	n	%	n	%	n	%	n	%	n	%	n	%
Country																		
England	15	5.0	10	16.9	8	13.6	3	5.1	3	5.1	1	1.7	1	1.7	1	1.7	2	3.4
Scotland	1	14.3	4	57.1	2	28.6	1	14.3	0	0.0	0	0.0	0	0.0	0	0.0	0	0.0
Wales	1	100.0	0	0.0	0	0.0	0	0.0	0	0.0	0	0.0	0	0.0	0	0.0	0	0.0
Grouping																		
Unassigned	7	30.4	6	26.1	2	8.7	1	4.3	1	4.3	0	0.0	1	4.3	0	0.0	1	4.3
The Russell Group	3	16.7	3	16.7	4	22.2	1	5.6	1	5.6	0	0.0	0	0.0	0	0.0	1	5.6
University Alliance	3	30.0	1	10.0	3	30.0	0	0.0	0	0.0	1	10.0	0	0.0	1	10.0	0	0.0
Million+ Group	3	30.0	2	20.0	1	100	1	10.0	1	10.0	0	0.0	0	0.0	0	0.0	0	0.0
GuildHE	0	0.0	1	33.3	0	0.0	1	33.3	0	0.0	0	0.0	0	0.0	0	0.0	0	0.0
The Cathedrals Group	1	33.3	1	33.3	0	0.0	0	0.0	0	0.0	0	0.0	0	0.0	0	0.0	0	0.0
Size																		
under 10,000 students	3	8.8	1	2.9	0	0.0	1	2.9		0.0	0	0.0	0	0.0	0	0.0	0	0.0
10,001-20,000 students	9	60.0	8	53.3	3	20.0	2	13.3	0	0.0	0	0.0	1	6.7	0	0.0	1	6.7
20,001-30,000 students	5	62.5	1	12.5	3	37.5	1	12.5	2	25.0	1	12.5	0	0.0	1	12.5	0	0.0
30,001-40,000 students	0	0.0	2	33.3	3	50.0	0	0.0	1	16.7	0	0.0	0	0.0	0	0.0	0	0.0
above 40,001 students	0	0.0	2	50.0	1	25.0	0	0.0	0	0.0	0	0.0	0	0.0	0	0.0	1	25.0
Total instances	17	25.4[1]	14	20.9[1]	10	14.9[1]	4	6.0[1]	3	4.5[1]	1	1.5[1]	1	1.5[1]	1	1.5[1]	2	3.0[1]

Note. [1] N = 67

When holistically evaluating all instances, the 'academic misconduct' label emerges as the most recurrent theme at 25.4% (e.g., University of Cumbria, University of Gloucestershire, Newcastle University), succeeded by 'plagiarism' (e.g., York St John University, the Birkbeck University of London, University of Derby, Goldsmiths University of London) at 20.9% and 'contract cheating' (e.g., Sheffield Hallam University, University of Exeter, University of Southampton) at 14.9%. Contrastingly, 'AI misuse' (Birmingham City University), 'falsification' (City University London), and 'lack of authorship' (University of Salford) languish at the periphery, each acknowledged in a single university policy.

From the data, we can infer that while GenAI might be a new technological consideration, traditional labels like plagiarism and academic misconduct still dominate the discussions in university policies across Great Britain. 'AI misuse', while relevant, is less frequently addressed in these policies, suggesting that many institutions may not yet have adapted their guidelines to the evolving technological landscape or may not see it as a significant threat.

Authorisations and Declarations

As GenAI becomes increasingly influential in the academic world, understanding the regulatory measures established by universities becomes paramount. For instance, Oxford Brookes University (2023) requires that "Brookes students are required to use the form in Moodle to declare which AI tools you have used and how you have used them (….) [and] must then paste [the completed declaration] into an appendix at the end of your assignment." Other British universities require students to obtain authorisation before using GenAI for their assessments.

Table 6 shows how various British universities, differentiated by country, grouping, and size, have responded to GenAI, specifically requiring authorisation and necessitating students to include an explicit declaration when employing GenAI. In England, a relatively modest 23.7% of universities mandate authorisation for utilising GenAI (e.g., University of Birmingham, University of Westminster, University of Kent, City University of London, etc.), and 13.6% demand an explicit declaration from students (e.g., the University of Cumbria, University of Brighton). Scotland sees a more proactive stance, with 57.1% of universities necessitating authorisation (e.g., Glasgow Caledonian University, University of Edinburgh) and the University of Dundee insisting on an explicit declaration. Interestingly, universities in Wales have refrained from imposing either of these stipulations.

Among the unassigned universities, 30.4% stipulate authorisation, and 13.0% demand a declaration. In the prestigious Russell Group, 27.8% require authorisation, contrasted with a mere 5.6% calling for a declaration. The University Alliance displays a unified approach, with 30.0% of its member institutions mandating authorisation and declaration. Similarly, the MillionPlus Group sees 30.0% of its members imposing an authorisation requirement, with a slightly lesser 10.0% seeking a declaration. In contrast, neither the GuildHE nor The Cathedrals Group have chosen to impose authorisation. However, The Cathedrals Group is unique, with 33.3% of its universities demanding an explicit declaration.

For universities with student populations under 10,000, authorisation and declaration are expected by 12.5%. Those hosting between 10,001 to 20,000 students see 29.4% imposing an authorisation requirement and 17.6% necessitating a declaration. Institutions with a student body between 20,001 and 30,000 show a modest 13.3% advocating for authorisation and a mere 6.7% for declaration. Remarkably, universities accommodating 30,001 to 40,000 students display a heightened regulatory stance, with half (50.0%) imposing authorisation and 16.7% seeking a declaration. The most sizable institutions, with student populations exceeding 40,001, exhibit a 50.0% authorisation requirement but surprisingly abstain from the declaration stipulation.

Considering the broader landscape, 26.9% of instances demand authorisation for deploying GenAI, and 13.4% insist on an explicit declaration. One could discern various interpretations from this data, but a salient observation is the consistent precedence of the authorisation requirement over the declaration stipulation across different delineations. Notably, universities with larger student populations tend to exhibit heightened regulatory inclinations. This may stem from heightened concerns surrounding misuse on a grander scale.

Table 6. University requiring authorisation of AI use and declaration of AI use

Characteristic	The university requires authorisation to use GenAI.		The university requires students to include an explicit declaration on using GenAI.	
	n	%	n	%
Country				
England	14	23.7	8	13.6
Scotland	4	57.1	1	14.3
Wales	0	0.0	0	0.0
Grouping				
Unassigned	7	30.4	3	13.0
The Russell Group	5	27.8	1	5.6
University Alliance	3	30.0	3	30.0
MillionPlus Group	3	30.0	1	10.0
GuildHE	0	0.0	0	0.0
The Cathedrals Group	0	0.0	1	33.3
Size				
under 10,000 students	1	12.5	1	12.5
10,001-20,000 students	10	29.4	6	17.6
20,001-30,000 students	2	13.3	1	6.7
30,001-40,000 students	3	50.0	1	16.7
above 40,001 students	2	50.0	0	0.0
Total instances	18	26.9[1]	9	13.4[1]

Note. [1] N = 67

Detection

Numerous entities have posited claims of devising impeccable AI tools, ostensibly capable of discerning the use of other AI tools in student submissions. Turnitin used extensively in Higher education to detect plagiarism, has launched a new tool to detect language written with AI (Drozdowski, 2023). Regrettably, extant research casts a shadow on these assertions, and early studies have shown these tools are easily circumvented by changing just a few words in a paragraph. Preliminary findings also indicate a propensity for these so-called 'AI detectors' to generate false positives, an outcome that carries potentially detrimental ramifications for students' academic journeys and psychological well-being.

The British universities are also split in their opinion about such tools' accuracy and reliability. Some universities like Birkbeck or the University of East Anglia decided to opt into Turnitin's AI writing detection tool and stated that they "reserve the right to include this as evidence in any proceedings against [students] should an allegation of an assessment offence be made" (Birkbeck, University of London 2023). Many Universities have rejected the adoption of the AI detection tool as they feel Turnitin needs to provide detailed information about the working process of the tool, as well as the accuracy of the measurements. The Universities have set up working groups to assess the challenges posed by AI text-generating technology and try to get to grips with the fast-evolving situation. Other universities, such as Canterbury Christ Church University, believe that "controlling the use of AI with surveillance and detection software is not feasible" (2023) and believe that "altering our teaching and assessment practices is a more pedagogically sound alternative to relying on detection and punitive arrangements to manage the arrival of open access AI writing tools" (2023).

CONCLUSION

The discourse surrounding the integration of AI into the landscape of higher education has intensified considerably in recent times. A survey of contemporary literature reveals dichotomous viewpoints. While a subset of academic papers underscores AI's prospective advantages in augmenting student engagement and cognitive immersion, a contrasting body of work highlights potential quandaries, particularly concerning evaluations and the adjudication of grades. Institutions of higher learning in the United Kingdom are in a phase of contemplative exploration, gauging the optimal means of assimilating AI within their pedagogic paradigms.

As the frontier of AI continues its expansion, it becomes imperative for educational entities to exhibit both adaptability and foresight. Their strategies ought to champion the augmentation of student preparedness in navigating the intricacies of a progressively digitised global landscape while simultaneously fortifying the bedrock principles of academic honesty. Indeed, sophisticated AI derivatives, like GenAI platforms, introduce an intricate web of ethical dilemmas by potentially equipping learners with the means to generate or procure multimedia content that either lacks originality or appropriate attribution. However, juxtaposed against these challenges, AI also embodies a catalyst for pedagogical evolution, potentially revolutionising aspects like student-centric engagement, formative feedback mechanisms, collaborative learning environments, and fostering a milieu of innovation. To strike an equilibrium, institutions must cultivate a holistic strategy that harmoniously amalgamates educational prerogatives, technological acumen, and revamped evaluative frameworks. By engendering a climate that prioritises ethical discernment and collective knowledge-building, learners will be better equipped to thrive in an AI-centric era.

Limitations

Like many in the academic realm, our study has its limitations. These limitations and the resultant suggestions for future inquiries are delineated as follows. Our dataset encapsulates a subset of 67 universities from 130 British institutions. This partial representation inherently curtails comprehensive sector-wide insights. The geographical distribution of these universities—59 from England, seven from Scotland, and one from Wales—might also introduce regional biases. A more exhaustive survey encompassing the entire spectrum of British universities could proffer a holistic perspective.

Multiple versions of pertinent documents were extant across institutions. Concurrent revisions to these documents during our data acquisition phase could skew interpretations. Chronicling the evolutionary trajectories of these guidelines might have furnished insights into the dynamism of policy adaptations. Longitudinal studies could be instrumental in tracing the metamorphosis of institutional policies over time. Our investigative purview was confined to documents within the public domain as of 15 September 2023. Proprietary or internal communiqués remained beyond our reach. This limitation presupposes that some universities, while potentially formulating AI guidelines, might not have made such doctrines publicly accessible within our study's timeframe. Moreover, only documents directly referencing AI's influence or role in academic malfeasance were deemed pertinent. Collaborative ventures with universities to access internal documents or employ surveys could provide additional layers of understanding.

The compartmentalisation of data into discernible themes carries the inherent risk of distilling intricate ideas into oversimplified constructs. This could attenuate the data representation's nuance, depth, and granularity. Methodological augmentations, such as incorporating narrative or phenomenological analysis, can offer complementary insights. The recurrence of a theme may signal its importance. However, frequency alone is an inadequate arbiter of significance. The onus on recurrent themes might inadvertently eclipse those less prevalent but with intrinsic importance. Future studies could develop metrics that weight themes by frequency and contextual impact or relevance.

Finally, content and thematic analyses are only sometimes generalizable in quantitative studies. Our scrutiny is circumscribed to the British milieu, replete with its unique idiosyncrasies. Strategies discerned may lack direct applicability to extraneous contexts. An examination of further education or vocational establishments was absent from our analysis, a domain ripe for future inquiry given potential shared challenges and solutions.

In conclusion, while our study endeavours to offer pivotal insights, scholars and policymakers must interpret the findings within the context of its inherent limitations and consider the avenues of future research elucidated herein.

REFERENCES

Birkbeck, University of London (2023). *Appendix 1: AI (AI) and academic integrity*. BBK. https://www.bbk.ac.uk/downloads/registry/student-policies-2022-23/ai-and-academic-integrity-appendix.pdf

Boehm, P. J., Justice, M., & Weeks, S. (2009). Promoting academic integrity in higher education. *The Community College Enterprise*, *15*(1), 45–61.

Braun, V., & Clarke, V. (2006). Using Thematic Analysis in Psychology. *Qualitative Research in Psychology*, *3*(2), 77–101. doi:10.1191/1478088706qp063oa

Bretag, T. (Ed.). (2016). *Handbook of academic integrity*. Springer Singapore. doi:10.1007/978-981-287-098-8

Canterbury Christ Church University. (2023). *Generative AI (AI): Guidance for Staff*. Canterbury Christ Church University. https://www.canterbury.ac.uk/learning-and-teaching-enhancement/resources-for-academics/Docs/Generative-Artificial-Intelligence-AI-Guidance-for-Staff.pdf

Di Vaio, A., Palladino, R., Hassan, R., & Escobar, O. (2020). AI and business models in the sustainable development goals perspective: A systematic literature review. *Journal of Business Research*, *121*, 283–314. doi:10.1016/j.jbusres.2020.08.019

Drozdowski, M. J. (2023, April 23). *Testing Turnitin's New AI Detector: How Accurate I sit?* Best Colleges. https://www.bestcolleges.com/news/analysis/testing-turnitin-new-ai-detector/

Duin, A. H., & Pedersen, I. (2021). *Writing futures: Collaborative, algorithmic, autonomous*. Springer. doi:10.1007/978-3-030-70928-0

Huggins-Manley, A. C., Booth, B. M., & D'Mello, S. K. (2022). Toward Argument-Based Fairness with an Application to AI-Enhanced Educational Assessments. *Journal of Educational Measurement*, *59*(3), 362–388. doi:10.1111/jedm.12334

International Center for Academic Integrity. (2014). *The fundamental values of academic integrity*. Second Edition. https://academicintegrity.org/wp- content/uploads/2017/12/Fundamental-Values-2014.pdf

Ison, D. C. (2015). The influence of the Internet on plagiarism among doctoral dissertations: An empirical study. *Journal of Academic Ethics*, *13*(2), 151–166. doi:10.1007/s10805-015-9233-7

ITVnews. (2023, 28 February). Oxford and Cambridge ban ChatGPT over plagiarism fears, but other universities choose to embrace AI bot. *ITVNews*. https://inews.co.uk/news/oxford-cambridge-ban-chatgpt-plagiarism-universities-2178391

Latif, E., Mai, G., Nyaaba, M., Wu, X., Liu, N., Lu, G., Li, S., Liu, T., & Zhai, X. (2023). Artificial general intelligence (AGI) for education. *arXiv preprint arXiv:2304.12479.*

Löfström, E., & Kupila, P. (2013). The instructional challenges of student plagiarism. *Journal of Academic Ethics*, *11*(3), 231–242. doi:10.1007/s10805-013-9181-z

London Metropolitan University. (2023). *Guidance on the use of AI.* London Metropolitan University. https://student.londonmet.ac.uk/your-studies/student-administration/guidance-on-the-use-of-artificial-intelligence/

Macfarlane, B., Zhang, J., & Pun, A. (2014). Academic integrity: A review of the literature. *Studies in Higher Education*, *39*(2), 339–358. doi:10.1080/03075079.2012.709495

Manly, T. S., Leonard, L. N., & Riemenschneider, C. K. (2015). Academic integrity in the information age: Virtues of respect and responsibility. *Journal of Business Ethics*, *127*(3), 579–590. doi:10.1007/s10551-014-2060-8

McKillup, S., & McKillup, R. (2007). An assessment strategy that pre-empts plagiarism. *International Journal for Educational Integrity*, *3*(2). doi:10.21913/IJEI.v3i2.163

Mirshekary, S., & Lawrence, A. D. (2009). Academic and business ethical misconduct and cultural values: A cross national comparison. *Journal of Academic Ethics*, *7*(3), 141–157. doi:10.1007/s10805-009-9093-0

Mohd, C. K. N. C. K., Shahbodin, F., Mohd, S., Nor, A. M., Mohamad, S. N., & Saaya, Z. (2020). Educational technologies in a personalised learning environment (PLE): An overview. *World Transactions on Engineering and Technology Education*, *18*(4), 485–490.

Morris, E. J. (2018). Academic integrity matters: Five considerations for addressing contract cheating. *International Journal for Educational Integrity*, *14*(1), 15. doi:10.1007/s40979-018-0038-5

Oxford Brookes University. (2023). *AI*. Oxford Brookes University. https://www.brookes.ac.uk/students/academic-development/online-resources/artificial-intelligence

Padillah, R. (2023). Ghostwriting: A reflection of academic dishonesty in the AI era. *Journal of Public Health*. doi:10.1093/pubmed/fdad169

Sefcik, L., Striepe, M., & Yorke, J. (2019). Mapping the landscape of academic integrity education programs: What approaches are effective? *Assessment & Evaluation in Higher Education*.

Tierney, W. G., & Almeida, D. J. (2017). Academic responsibility: Toward a cultural politics of integrity. *Discourse (Abingdon)*, *38*(1), 97–108. doi:10.1080/01596306.2015.1104855

Times Higher Education. (2023, 13 March). Keep calm and carry on: ChatGPT doesn't change a thing for academic integrity. *Times Higher Education*. https://www.timeshighereducation.com/campus/keep-calm-and-carry-chatgpt-doesnt-change-thing-academic-integrity

Turner, S. P., & Beemsterboer, P. L. (2003). Enhancing academic integrity: Formulating effective honor codes. *Journal of Dental Education*, *67*(10), 1122–1129. doi:10.1002/j.0022-0337.2003.67.10.tb03705.x PMID:14587677

University of Birmingham. (2023). *Generative AI and its Role Within Teaching, Learning and Assessment*. University of Birmingham. https://www.birmingham.ac.uk/university/hefi/gai/index.aspx

Whitley, B. E. Jr, & Keith-Spiegel, P. (2001). Academic integrity as an institutional issue. *Ethics & Behavior*, *11*(3), 325–342. doi:10.1207/S15327019EB1103_9

Zauderer, D. G. (1992, October). Integrity: An essential executive quality. *Business forum*, *17*(4), 12.

Zawacki-Richter, O., Marín, V. I., Bond, M., & Gouverneur, F. (2019). Systematic review of research on AI applications in higher education–where are the educators? *International Journal of Educational Technology in Higher Education*, *16*(1), 1–27. doi:10.1186/s41239-019-0171-0

ENDNOTES

1. https://russellgroup.ac.uk/
2. https://www.unialliance.ac.uk/
3. https://www.millionplus.ac.uk/
4. https://guildhe.ac.uk/
5. https://cathedralsgroup.ac.uk/

Chapter 3
Revising Australian Academic Integrity Policy for the Age of Artificial Intelligence

David Morgan
https://orcid.org/0000-0001-9597-1800
Polytechnic Institute Australia, Australia

ABSTRACT

Academic integrity is considered under threat in the age of artificial intelligence owing to new technologies. The sector has questioned exemplary responses in institutional academic integrity policy and proposed changes to what is exemplary. This chapter examines three issues seen in proposed academic integrity policy changes. The first issue is whether to ban or accept the use of generative artificial intelligence (GenAI) tools. The second issue is whether the proposed changes are sufficient to cover what is needed in academic integrity policy. The third issue is what other changes are needed to support academic integrity throughout a student's interactions with an institution. The chapter concludes with a proposal of how the work of the exemplary academic integrity project should not be added to but modernized to address questions raised in the age of artificial intelligence.

INTRODUCTION

In the present age of artificial intelligence, many questions have arisen about the proliferation of new tools available to students and their impact on academic integrity. While institutional decision-makers are questioning what skills students and staff need to be equipped with, what is the ethical use of generative artificial intelligence (GenAI) and what changes should be made to assessments considering these deliberations, there has been little consideration as to the larger framework in which these decisions are made. For Australian Higher Education institutions this larger framework is shaped by government legislation, regulator advice, institutional regulations, policies, and procedures. This paper explores the need to revise academic integrity policy to address, at an institutional policy level, the impact of these new tools.

DOI: 10.4018/979-8-3693-0240-8.ch003

Recent work reviewing Higher Education academic integrity policies in the Australian context has stressed the need for reviews of policy (Morgan, 2023) and proposed restructuring policy to respond to and be centred on the affordances of e-cheating (Tertiary Education Quality and Standards Agency, 2023, based on Dawson, 2021). Earlier work in the Australian context, by Bretag and others, created a website that allows the generation of an institution's academic integrity policy using a template based on exemplary work in the sector, a requirement to be educative and the need for a clear process when misconduct is suspected (Bretag & Mahmud, 2013; Bretag et al., 2011; Bretag et al., 2011; EAIP, 2013; Exemplary Academic Integrity Project, n.d.-b). All these earlier works were written before GenAI became familiar to the public.

Internationally, Perkins and Roe (2023) proposed an addition to the Exemplary Academic Integrity principles with a recommendation of a new category on "Technological Explicitness" to specify which technologies are permitted. Glendinning (2023), from the UK, raised the issue of what type of artificial intelligence institutions are concerned about impacting academic integrity because not all have the same impact on demonstrating learning. The Australasian Academic Integrity Network (AAIN) (2023) published material on changes made in academic integrity policies with the increased availability of GenAI. These issues indicate that there is a consistent question trying to be answered, "What is useful for academic integrity policy in the age of artificial intelligence?" In that light, this chapter argues there is a need to revise academic integrity policies in Australia because artificial intelligence is no longer an emerging threat, but a present reality. The question this chapter addresses is in what ways should this revision occur. The issues and solutions proposed here are relevant not only to the academic integrity policies of institutions in Australia but internationally as well.

This chapter explores three lines of argument for the revision of policy. First, it considers the role of policy in the academic integrity and academic misconduct processes of higher education institutions. This argument considers whether permitting or banning the use of GenAI in policy is a useful stance and shows where there are changes in policies in the Australian context supporting both.

Second, this chapter explores the necessity that any changes to policy must support more than just digital contexts. This is a consequence of focusing on the problem of artificial intelligence and its writing occurring in digital environments and not on the larger context of why this is a problem in the first place. The perception that viva voces, oral examinations of students' submissions, and invigilated examinations are a "gold standard" to prevent interference from GenAI will be shown to not be realistic. The actions and consequences to those who would undertake to breach the integrity of these forms of assessment must be included in any rewritten policy. This means interrogating the four affordances that Dawson (2021) proposed to see if they help structure academic integrity policy.

Third, this chapter considers that academic integrity policy is part of a web of policies that needs revising in an age of artificial intelligence. It shows that what is needed in policy to support academic integrity is other policies, such as misconduct regulations and assessment policies supporting requirements to ensure academic integrity. This chapter will show a need to address both e-cheating and other forms of cheating and that for consistency the negative behaviors enabled by digital environments need to be incorporated into policies. This chapter explains that rewriting an academic integrity policy successfully requires it not to be an isolated updated document, but to know it relies on supporting material in assessment policies and misconduct regulations as well. This extends the work of the exemplary academic integrity project to specify requirements elsewhere in other policies.

Finally, given that a need for revision to policy is demonstrated, the material of the Exemplary Academic Integrity Project (EAIP) (n.d.-a) is reexamined to see where updates are required. Bretag's work was written at a time when academic integrity policies were perceived as punitive and not educational. One could argue that Bretag's writing and research projects such as the EAIP on academic integrity changed academic integrity in Australia to include the responsibilities of educational institutions toward students, but what was exemplary a decade ago may now need an update. What is being educated about, what the decision-making processes are, and who brings accusations of breaches of academic integrity to the notice of institutions are all in flux, changed, or under review. Given the aforementioned points, the chapter finishes with an outline of what exemplary academic policy may look like in the age of artificial intelligence. The aim is to show that exemplary academic integrity policy in the 2020s remains similar to, yet also different from the policies of the 2000s and the 2010s.

THE ROLE OF POLICY IN ACADEMIC INTEGRITY AND MISCONDUCT PROCESSES

The role of academic integrity policies in Australian institutions has been described in multiple ways that have varied over time. The Tertiary Education Quality and Standards Agency (TEQSA) commissioned Good Practice Note by Bretag (2017) describing the published research on academic integrity states:

By and large, the emphasis has been on developing and promoting clear academic integrity policy and processes for undergraduate students, coupled with appropriate support services and resources. Various research projects and investigations demonstrated that all Australian universities had appropriate policies in place (Grigg, 2009), and generally speaking, there had been a shift in emphasis from a punitive to educative approach in relation to academic integrity.

Sutherland-Smith (2010) put forward a similar argument regarding the standing of academic integrity policy, often based on plagiarism at the time: The language of plagiarism policies from 18 institutions used "legal discourse in framing plagiarism, particularly the language of criminal law" (Sutherland-Smith, 2010, p. 7). The nature of these policies meant that:

Plagiarism management processes are generally passed by the Academic Board or Academic Council of each university and therefore have university-wide standing and apply to all staff and students across the particular institution. Hence, plagiarism is not something that is able to be defined or administered differently across the institution, and there is an expectation in the discourse of the regulations that there is consistency in managing plagiarism across faculties, schools and departments (Sutherland-Smith (2010, p. 7).

Whether these policies are followed the same way by everyone across an institution is not discussed.

Examples of other views include Anohina-Naumeca et al.'s (2018) statement that "the publication of university policies linked to some extent with academic integrity is an important means of substantiating university social responsibility" (p. 2), or this view by Miron et al. (2021): "Policy and procedure is one important aspect of a systemic approach that helps ensure clarity for all members of the learning community to address contract cheating" (p. 64). The Impact of Plagiarism in Higher Education Across Europe (IPPHEAE) project surveyed institutions to establish how policies, procedures and processes

Table 1. Position regarding GenAI in policy examples

Institution	Material
Australian Catholic University (ACU)	You should seek clarification from the lecturer-in-charge (LIC) of your unit to see if it is permissible to use AI in your assessments. According to the university's 2023 Student Academic Integrity and Misconduct Policy, "unauthorised or undisclosed use of artificial intelligence" is a form of academic misconduct. (8.1.c).
Central Queensland University (CQU)	Section 3.19: Contract cheating may also include the use of machine generated text or artificial intelligence (AI) software that can generate text, or paraphrase, rewrite, edit, and improve textual content (also known as washing or text spinning) (2023).
Federation University Australia	In the "Definitions" section of the Academic Integrity Procedure, the definition for Academic misconduct lists the "unauthorised use of artificial intelligence to create part thereof or all assessable content" as a breach of academic integrity in its own right, separate from plagiarism and contract cheating, although it lists unauthorised use of Gen-AI as an example of contract cheating.
La Trobe University (LTU)	Clause 6c: While students are encouraged to seek assistance from academic staff and other university supports as needed, all work submitted by a student for assessment purposes, or a group of students for group assessment purposes, must be their independent and original work. The ideas and work of others, including any that may arise from the use of any artificial content production tools, must be acknowledged appropriately and in accordance with relevant conventions.

were "preventing, detecting and penalising cases of student plagiarism" (Foltýnek & Glendinning, 2015, p. 208).

The themes that emerge concerning the role of academic integrity policy is that these policies are to ensure clarity and consistency in educating, preventing, detecting and managing academic misconduct when it is suspected or detected. This view shows an evolution away from a plagiarism-only approach but does not provide sufficient detail. Elsewhere, Morgan (2023) argued that policy must be concrete enough to guide the staff that must execute such policy when misconduct occurs and be able to provide direction to students as to what academic misconduct is.

Given that the role of policy is to provide clarity and consistency, the question arises about what is given to students and staff regarding academic integrity in an age of artificial intelligence. The two approaches toward GenAI tools have been to ban the use of this technology by students or to allow it under some constraints such as the publication of citations.

The Australasian Academic Integrity Network (AAIN) has produced material on 39 institutions and their positions regarding GenAI (2023). A series of examples from that list are included in Table 1.

The institution where the author is employed, Polytechnic Institute Australia (PIA), has taken the approach that other academic misconduct includes "unauthorised use of generative artificial intelligence that is contrary to guidelines published by the Institute and in relevant Institute documentation (e.g., Unit Outline)" (PIA, 2023, p. 2).

These policies show a range of clear positions, from outright bans such as CQU defining the use of GenAI as contract cheating; a number of institutions saying it is permitted where the lecturer or documentation has said so (PIA, ACU, Federation) to the permitted when cited stance of LTU. This lack of consistency in the sector would make it more difficult to know what the correct behavior is when transferring from one institution to another.

Furthermore, the literature published so far does not include sensible guidance regarding what measures are useful to educate in the ethical use of artificial intelligence, what actions to take to prevent

Table 2. Glendinning's (2023) types of artificial intelligence

Type	Description	Production	Software Products
1	Conversion and translation tools	Speech <-> Text, Predictive text	Google Translate, Dragon
2	Spelling checkers, paraphrasers, grammar checkers	Improved writing	Grammarly, Quill Bot, Microsoft Office
3	Essay bots, text generators	Essays	ChatGPT, Quill Bot
4	Artifact generators	Programming code, graphics, artwork, maths, music	GitHub, co-pilot, DALL-E 2

the abuse of artificial intelligence use, and what ways to detect its use when not allowed. For instance, 29 of the 39 examples provided in the AAIN list mention support for students, and only four of these examples mention the ethical use of artificial intelligence. The preventive strategies are often limited to student-initiated conversations about whether the use of artificial intelligence tools is permitted. Policy statements requiring students to initiate conversations seems to be a return to a non-educative approach in institutions. The lack of a reference to detection may be due to wording in policies such as La Trobe University's 2022 Student Academic Misconduct Policy:

The University uses various methods to identify academic misconduct, including: a. work submitted by students for assessment may be checked using text, code, or other comparative software, or manually reviewed using web search engines, checking of student sources, comparison with other assignments, and consultation with colleagues (C, [18]).

The wording in this policy allows for tools of detection to be used. The other reason may be the difficulties, theoretical and practical, in the accurate detection of text being produced by generative artificial intelligence (Elkhatat et al., 2023), and thus, silence is chosen as a more modest option.

One other aspect connected to the role of policy is the use of the term artificial intelligence. Artificial intelligence is an overarching term describing little; what it is can be harder to define. One description of artificial intelligence, used by computer scientist Ross Quinlan when the author was his student, was that artificial intelligence is the "use of weak methods" (personal communication, 1985). These weak methods are "programs based upon general standards which do not consider knowledge specific to any certain employment or field strong techniques" (N., 2013). The use of a generative pre-trained transformer (GPT) is the use of a non-specific generator of text that is able to produce not only text but also computer programs and mathematical proofs. There are other tools now producing images (DALL-E 2) and still others to support the production of music (see Ditto Music, 2023). These descriptions of how the output is produced are not so useful as the implications of the affordances named by Dawson (2021) or the categories presented by Glendinning (2023).

The affordances will be discussed in the next section, so only Glendinning's categories will be addressed here. According to Glendinning (2023), the use of artificial intelligence can be divided into four types, as shown in Table 2.

These different types of artificial intelligence have various impacts on determining whether a student has met the learning outcomes of an assessment. Converting material from one language to another, although often being poor grammatically, does not take away from what a student has understood. The translated material may not have the clarity desired, but it is their understanding. Text generators and artifact generators are tools that make it very difficult to determine what is the student's work and what is generated by algorithms. These are the types of artificial intelligence that are causing panic in the higher education sector (Glendinning, 2023), and yet, a blanket ban on artificial intelligence in academic integrity policy would catch all types.

An academic integrity policy that includes such a generic ban on artificial intelligence, as found previously in some policies (Morgan, 2023), would have a number of effects on students. For example, international students using phones with autocorrect to submit assignments may be in breach of such an academic integrity policy. Students who use the spelling and grammar tools built into software such as Microsoft Office would also be caught by poorly worded policies banning artificial intelligence. At the same time, students in the context of a class learning a language that is foreign to them would not be able to show their own work using translation tools. Without recognizing that there needs to be a nuanced approach to the different types of artificial intelligence, combined with the context for the assessment, poorly written policy will hinder supporting academic integrity and generate unnecessary and wrongful academic misconduct cases.

The aforementioned statements do not mean, however, that a policy should include nothing about GenAI. Essential in this analysis is the fact that the use of GenAI threatens assessment validity because it stops the assessor from being able to determine what is the student's own work. Effectively without assessment security, there is no assessment validity. Dawson (2021) described assessment security's main purpose as "ensuring that cheating does not stop assessment from doing what it is meant to do … Assessment's summative purpose involves certifying and credentialing that students have achieved particular learning outcomes" (p. 128). Assessment validity is commonly described as assessing what is meant to be assessed or measuring what is supposed to be measured. Without sufficient security, there is no way to know that the student completing the assessment is the one who has completed the work. Even a measure of a grade such as a high distinction means nothing if the student is not the one who has earned it by their own work. Where there is not sufficient security to determine the validity of a response being from the student, means of verification that this is the student's response are needed. Thus, in academic integrity policy, GenAI must be considered in a nuanced manner to ensure assessment validity.

This section has shown that academic integrity policy has been revised for an age of artificial intelligence, but the response has not been consistent across the sector or nuanced enough to ensure or maintain assessment validity. Both the task being undertaken, and the type of artificial intelligence being used to demonstrate meeting a learning outcome need consideration when rewriting academic integrity policy. Yet, as the next section will show, not all assessment occurs in digital environments, and thus, the focus of academic integrity policy cannot neglect the nondigital environment.

POLICY REVISIONS TO SUPPORT DIGITAL AND NONDIGITAL ENVIRONMENTS

A solution to prevent changing an academic integrity policy for each new as yet unknown threat has been proposed to incorporate the affordances of e-cheating (Tertiary Education Quality and Standards Agency, 2023, based on Dawson, 2021). The author has not found these affordances embedded in an academic integrity policy at this time. This section discusses the limits to this proposal by considering what e-cheating is, the taxonomy of affordances, and the need that any changes to academic integrity policy must support both digital and nondigital environments.

A consequence of focusing on the problem of artificial intelligence, particularly GenAI, being able to produce written texts can easily ignore that this occurs only in digital environments. This approach neglects the larger context of why this is a problem in the first place. Given a take-home or un-invigilated assessment, the assessment conditions do not ensure that assessment security is maintained. The issue is not artificial intelligence per se, but rather, the same opportunities that allowed contract cheating to thrive during the COVID-19 pandemic—namely, a lack of assessment security. If an academic integrity policy is to be rewritten, then it must also cover where students can attempt to circumvent assessment security in nondigital environments using digital and nondigital means. Lancaster (2020b) discussed the use of devices to compromise the assessment of invigilated examinations, and deMontigny (2022) proposed the use of trained invigilators to circumvent breaches during in-person invigilated examinations. Similarly, viva voces could be compromised with either a human or an artificial intelligence ultimately at the other end of an unseen communications channel. These cross over all four of Dawson's (2021) e-cheating affordances, but none can occur in a purely digital environment because they additionally rely on nondigital means. This perception that viva voces and invigilated examinations are a "gold standard" to prevent interference using generative artificial intelligence is no longer realistic. The actions by, and consequences to, those who would undertake to breach the integrity of assessment, using e-cheating or nondigital means must still be included in any rewritten policy.

Young (2022) stated that the concept of "affordances" originated in the work of Gibson (1979); in another published work, Young et al., stated that "Gibson defined affordances as the *action possibilities* resulting from the relationship between user and environment" (2019, p. 694). This definition takes in the concerns already mentioned recognising the environment users find themselves in will affect the actions that can be taken. Dawson (2021) proposed an affordance-based taxonomy of approaches to e-cheating (pp. 8–17) and then examined attempts or known methods to prevent these to some degree or another. However, the focus here is on the affordances Dawson proposed plus the environment to which they apply. These are summarized in Table 3.

The summary in Table 3 shows several issues that can be summarized as follows: First, traditional forms of academic misconduct, such as cheating in an exam, plagiarism, and collusion, are not explicit in Dawson's taxonomy. Second, cognitive offloading to a tool is only expected in digital environments. Third, thwarting anti-cheating approaches as a form of disrupting the assessment process is considered to occur only in the digital environment. Fourth, the use of GenAI is considered cognitive offloading to a tool because the use of Open AI GPT2 is explicitly discussed as a bespoke essay writing tool (Dawson, 2021, p. 13). The implications of these issues for academic integrity policy will now be discussed.

To revise academic integrity policy in an age of artificial intelligence and ignore traditional forms of misconduct would lead to policies that do not address issues still facing current assessments. The role of programmatic assessment, and the need to update assessments, will be considered in the next section, but many current assessments will need to remain to assess lower-level threshold concepts or underpinning knowledge. If these assessments are not invigilated, and current practice shows they are not, then the risks of plagiarism and collusion remain as well as forms of e-cheating. If students deliberately do not show where they have obtained their ideas, one question that would have to remain is where did this answer originate from? These forms of misconduct seem to sit under Dawson's (2021) taxonomy of "providing access to unauthorised information" (p. 9). Similarly cheating in an exam may be using an information smuggling device such as unauthorized notes, notes kept in the exam room's bathrooms, or the signalling for which deMontigny (2022) trained invigilators to look. This cheating seems to remain in the same taxonomy of "providing access to unauthorised information," (Dawson, 2021, p.

Table 3. Summary of Dawson's taxonomy of affordances with the relevant environment added

Affordance Example	Environment(s)
Affordance: Providing access to unauthorized information	
Subcategory: Breaching information restrictions	
Information smuggling devices	Nondigital, digital
Circumventing online examination limitations by using virtual machines	Digital
Text input hardware	Digital
Subcategory: Accessing questions, solutions, answers, and exemplars	
Brain dumps of exam questions	Nondigital, digital
Essay banks and assignment trading sites	Nondigital, digital
Affordance: Cognitive offloading to a tool	
Essay spinning, auto-paraphrase, and back-translation tools	Digital
Translation tools	Digital
Computer algebra solvers	Digital
Bespoke essay writing tools	Digital
Affordance: Outsourcing work to a person	
Contract cheating	Digital
Online course-taking	Digital
Remote coaches	Nondigital, digital
Expert input	Digital
Affordance: Disrupting the assessment process	
Subcategory: Thwarting anti-cheating approaches	
Bypassing text-matching software	Digital
Defeating remote proctoring software	Digital
Bypassing website blocking with a VPN	Digital
Pulling the plug	Digital
Subcategory: Causing problems for students and teachers	
Denial-of-service attacks	Digital
Fire alarm or bomb threat (mentioned as an analogy for the digital)	Nondigital

Based on Dawson (2021, pp. 9–17).

9) but possibly a different subcategory. The use of impersonation—that is, sending a different person, possibly with fraudulent identity documents, into the exam—is also known to occur. This is not a form of disruption, but it destroys the validity of answers to the examination for the impersonated student, even if the answers are all correct. Although this may be a form of "providing access to unauthorised information," it seems to need a category of its own because it is closer to "defeating remote proctoring software," but there is no software involved.

An academic integrity policy that limits cognitive offloading to a tool to occur only in a digital environment may be reasonable because any access to such a tool when not permitted is "providing access to unauthorised information." This implies in the taxonomy a potential overlap that must be decided in a policy or procedure to make clear which affordance should take precedence when misconduct is suspected. This would mean when there is evidence of cognitive offloading, such as the term "as an AI language model" appearing in written submissions, as found by Gao (2023), the context of where this occurred, examination or otherwise, may decide which affordance is being used.

Thwarting anti-cheating approaches as a form of disrupting the assessment process only occurring in the digital environment seems to be consistent because the anti-cheating approaches are only for digital assessment. However, this would be the equivalent of defeating invigilation in a face-to-face exam. There are two issues here — attempting to defeat invigilation is one; being detected doing it, is the other. There are known ways that students have tried to defeat invigilation, including bringing unauthorized material into examination rooms and using in-the-ear devices (Lancaster, 2020a). These fall under other affordances. The use of an impersonator, as already mentioned, is the closest to thwarting an anti-cheating, by falsifying the identity check to prevent a form of cheating. This form of misconduct is known to occur as well as invigilators catching it (Carter, 2022). This will be raised again later as a form of fraud that policies must address.

Finally, Dawson (2021) considers the use of GenAI as a cognitive offloading tool. This raises the issue of whether cognitive offloading is a form of misconduct, and thus, the discussion returns to the same issues as discussed regarding Glendinning's view of artificial intelligence. A ban on the use of GenAI in policy would mean that if an industry was using such a tool, the graduates would not have all the skills needed to be part of that industry. This is again the issue of context needing to be considered added to which is the question of the wider environment the students will find themselves in. Banning GenAI may be good for assessment validity, but potentially damaging for graduate employability; there needs to be a way to ensure both are being achieved. Such a way would require changes to more than just an academic integrity policy permitting GenAI in some situations but to the web of policies in which the academic integrity policy is found.

This section has shown that Dawson's (2021) work does not consider the traditional forms of academic misconduct sufficiently to solely rely on the affordances for the writing of academic integrity policy. What has been argued is that changes to policy can use these concepts for both digital and nondigital environments, but there need to be categories added to support the nondigital environments and other policies changed to maximize assessment validity.

POLICY REVISIONS IN A WEB OF POLICIES

The previous section raised the idea that the maintenance of assessment validity requires responses to several issues. Of particular concern is how to deal with the fraud of impersonation when it occurs in any assessment context, whether it is cognitive offloading to a person or as described by the Australian Federal Police as identity theft (2022). At the same time, there is a trend to recognize that new or revised processes of assessment are needed to maintain assessment validity in an age of artificial intelligence (Chen, 2023). Requiring such changes is both cultural and often outside of the scope of an academic integrity policy. Such changes could be expected as part of an assessment policy revision. Bearman and Luckin (2020) argued that there are two aspects of knowledge or learning needed to ensure that students are assessed on what computers will not do in the future: one aspect is meta-knowing; the other aspect is self-efficacy and evaluative judgment. This meta-knowing is the building of personal epistemology such that students understand their own beliefs about knowledge and how knowing occurs. Ensuring that assessment is scaffolded to support these two aspects requires training and support for academic staff, as well as changes to an institution's assessment policy.

One other proposed change has been a move to programmatic assessment, which Dawson describes as a "continuous, connected and planned programme" (2021, p. 137) of assessment, rather than a series of "one-off, disconnected and haphazard tasks" (2021, p. 137) which is common in current course designs. If programmatic assessment is introduced, changes would need to be made to the assessment policy. Then, if an approach of programmatic assessment is taken at an institutional level, rather than just at a course or school level, courses would need a different design process, meaning any course design policy or course approval policy would require changes.

The previous section raised the issue that e-cheating occurs in digital environments, and some forms of cheating occur in nondigital environments. These two environments are brought together in an academic integrity policy, but where else do they need to be brought together? Is it appropriate for cyberbullying to be listed as unacceptable behavior in a use of computer resources policy, but not listed in the institution's code of conduct or general misconduct rules? These issues of fraud, programmatic assessment, course design, and general misconduct show that academic integrity is not an isolated policy, but one in a web of policies to maximize assessment validity and ensure that there are consequences for breaching the community standards of academic integrity and expected behavior to ensure a safe learning environment.

The idea that impersonation of someone in an assessment setting is a form of identity crime may be novel. The Australian Federal Police (2022) describes identity theft as a type of identity crime that has "theft or assumption of a pre-existing identity (or significant part thereof), with or without consent and whether, in the case of an individual, the person is living or deceased" (para. 2). The impersonation of a student in an assessment setting would be the assumption of a pre-existing identity with consent. Such impersonation, as stated already, has implications for assessment validity because the measurement of the assessment is not against what the actual student can demonstrate. If such impersonation were detected, would the academic integrity policy or other institutional policies or regulations require this to be divulged to law enforcement? This is legally a type of fraud and is known to occur elsewhere in the student life cycle (Eaton et al., 2023), particularly at admissions, meeting visa requirements, or as the author once witnessed documentation of, when seeking employment through providing forged credentials. Such fraud in the author's state is a criminal offense with penalties ranging from 5 to 10 years for the maximum sentence (State Government of Victoria, pp. 233-238). Institutions that use legal language for academic integrity policy also need to connect such policy to the legal system or have such concerns raised elsewhere in the web of policies.

Dawson (2021) suggested a method of ensuring assessment security is programmatic assessment security (p. 137). The implications of such an approach have not yet been seen in Australian policy because no institutions have implemented a whole-of-institution adoption of programmatic assessment, and programmatic assessment has often been focused on health sciences education (Baartman et al., 2023). Because programmatic assessment "decision-making is based on aggregating information from the data points" (Baartman et al, 2022, p. 3), these data points themselves need to be valid. Focusing assessment security on specific assessment tasks where there is security may not generate enough data points to make decisions. Furthermore, with nested awards such as a diploma as the first year of a bachelor's level award within the Australian Qualification Framework (2013) and the possibility of an associate degree as the first two years of the same bachelor's award, there are multiple points where decision-making to allow progress must be explicit. Most assessment policies do not allow for this because they tie assessment to a unit of study. Furthermore, this process would also affect the granting of credit when there are not units of study assessed as currently happens. This would disrupt movement between providers in a system designed for flexibility that from earlier reforms wanted "credit transfer and articulation … between higher education and other education and training providers" (Baldwin, 1991, 1.19). Programmatic assessment will make credit transfer harder except at the boundary points, such as the completion of a diploma in a bachelor's level award. For programmatic assessment to be implemented, an institutional policy would need to address how assessment is conducted to be valid, how to collect enough data points to aggregate and make decisions, and how to assess credit transfers. Sector-wide acceptance of such practices would also need to occur.

If the policy changes mentioned already are enacted, this has an impact on course design. Units of study may disappear as points of assessment and the process of assessment may be turned on its head. Students may be told what to study through some mechanism, such as a mentor or program guide. Data points would be collected along the way to be aggregated to make decisions regarding who passes or fails to go on to the next level. This requires mentors or tutors to work with individual students. The staffing required in a course would be different from the current unit-based staffing. The points of assessment would need to be clear to an academic board or an accrediting body. This would look very different to the course design requirements of the moment as expressed in the Higher Education Threshold Standards (2021) where everything is packaged as units (or equivalent) that are specified (Standard 3.1.1 c) and assessed (Standard 1.4.4) with results given back to students in official documents as weighted and graded (Standard 1.5.7 a-d). An institution's course design policy would need to give direction regarding the institutional expectation of programmatic assessment and would not be the same as current policy.

The incorporation of e-cheating into an academic integrity policy should not be an isolated change of bringing the digital environment into the policy. General misconduct policies that are often centered on acts against property or persons through physical means ensure that a safer learning environment is maintained. The equivalent of this for digital environments is the Use of Computer Resources Policy or equivalent in which the consequence of a breach may be prevention from using the institution's computing resources. This policy ignores the issues of cyberbullying, students sending unwanted sexts through personal phones, or other ways that technology can be used to harass students. These forms of harassment are not directly connected to the institution's computer or network provision. It is possible, for example, that a distributed denial-of-service attack could be launched at an individual student's internet service provider and no institutional technology used. These forms of misconduct need to be considered if consequences for e-cheating are being meted out so that the consequences of general misconduct should be paralleled in response to e-assault or e-harassment. This type of policy would also start to consider the role of e-cheating in admission and credit transfer policies where documents obtained through e-cheating are treated the same as fraudulent physical documents.

This section has shown that ensuring assessment validity and dealing with both the digital and nondigital worlds consistently in an age of artificial intelligence requires further changes to policy than just the academic integrity policy. What these changes become when focused on exemplary academic integrity can now be discussed.

CONSIDERATION OF EXEMPLARY ACADEMIC INTEGRITY POLICY

The Exemplary Academic Integrity Project (EAIP) created an electronic toolkit (n.d.-b) to generate academic integrity policies for providers. The second web page of the toolkit (Exemplary Academic Integrity Project, n.d.-a) requests responses to a series of prompts that are:

1. Policy scope
2. Policy purpose
3. Definition of academic integrity
4. Roles and responsibilities
5. Promoting academic integrity
    - 5.1. Promoting a culture of academic integrity
    - 5.2. Ensuring academic integrity in assessment
6. Academic integrity breaches
    - 6.1. Specify what constitutes an academic integrity breach at your institution
    - 6.2. Classification of academic integrity breaches
    - 6.3. Academic integrity breach outcomes
    - 6.4. Academic integrity breach decision-makers
7. Academic integrity decisions
    - 7.1. Academic integrity decision-making process
    - 7.2. Identification of potential academic integrity breach
    - 7.3. Notification of breach to an appropriate authority
    - 7.4. Referral of breach to academic integrity decision-maker
    - 7.5. Preliminary assessment by decision-maker
    - 7.6. Communication of students' rights in the decision-making process
    - 7.7. Student's response to allegation of academic integrity breach
    - 7.8. Consideration of relevant matters in determining outcome
    - 7.9. Communicating the decision
8. Recordkeeping
9. Appealing the decision

Recently, Perkins and Roe (2023) suggested that a new category of "technological explicitness" be added to the Exemplary Academic Integrity model. They stated that this new category "emphasizes that academic integrity policies should explicitly define and explain the acceptable and unacceptable uses of emerging technologies in academic work" (Perkins & Roe, 2023, p. 15). However, this seems to already be covered by prompt 6.1 where the definition of a breach would minimally need to define what is unacceptable use of emerging technologies.

In the age of artificial intelligence, the findings of the EAIP need to remain unchanged; however, ways of responding to those findings need to be updated. It is argued that several toolkit prompts need revisions to be made as proposed in Table 4.

These changes presuppose that the level of assessment security is sufficiently robust to not need to verify that a submitted response to an assessment is a student's or group's own work. Where there is not total assessment security this means there may also be a need for more changes related to the toolkit prompts as proposed in Table 5.

Table 4. Proposed revisions to the EAIP content

Prompt	Proposed Change
Policy scope	Incorporate aspects of admissions and credit transfer affected by e-cheating and fraudulent documents.
Ensuring academic integrity in assessment	Incorporate staff training to ensure assessment is appropriate in an age of artificial intelligence using meta-knowing, self-efficacy, and evaluative judgment.
Specify what constitutes an academic integrity breach at your institution	Include the acceptable and unacceptable use of emerging technologies. Define e-cheating through the affordances. Specify the priority of the breaches for a single incident to ensure a student is not accused of multiple, potentially contradictory, breaches. Academic staff to be required to make explicit the use of tools rather than the student being the one who must initiate actions.
Academic integrity breach decision-makers	Include who decides regarding fraudulent documents at admission or credit transfer.
Identification of potential academic integrity breach	Include who reports when there are concerns of fraudulent documents at admission or credit transfer.
Communication of students' rights in the decision-making process	Incorporate how applicants can or cannot respond to concerns of fraudulent documents.

Table 5. Proposed revisions to the EAIP content where there is insufficient assessment security

Prompt	Proposed Inclusion
Ensuring academic integrity in assessment	Design a way to verify that work is a student's own work when there is a question of validity
Appealing the decision	Ensure the designed verification process can be appealed as necessary to ensure procedural fairness and natural justice

This shows that there is not a need to change the categories of exemplary academic integrity, but rather, to revise the responses within them to address e-cheating, artificial intelligence, and the wider aspects of academic integrity in an academic integrity policy.

CONCLUSION

In an age of artificial intelligence, it seems easy to argue that exemplary academic integrity needs to modernize. What has been argued in this chapter is that the findings of previous work in exemplary academic integrity remain with no additional categories added. These historic findings, however, need revising to include more modern answers to the questions raised historically. Institutions are wrestling with the incorporation of artificial intelligence into their assessment practices and academic integrity policies, but it can have the unintended consequence of banning tools used which may have broader consequences. Responses to artificial intelligence in an academic integrity policy require nuance and need to be contextualized. The affordances proposed by Dawson (2021) are not sufficient to structure academic integrity policy, but neither is academic integrity policy in isolation sufficient to ensure and maintain academic integrity in an age of artificial intelligence.

Dawson's work does not consider the traditional nondigital forms of academic misconduct sufficiently to solely rely on the affordances for the writing of an academic integrity policy. The incorporation of misconduct that has digital components must also be handled in the suite of regulations, rules, and policies that an institution maintains. Finally, in an age of artificial intelligence an institution's academic integrity policy, to remain exemplary, needs to be updated in a way that incorporates e-cheating, artificial intelligence, and the impact of either of these elements on other aspects of the student's journey. Where there is not sufficient assessment security, incorporating verification processes to ensure assessment validity is required.

REFERENCES

Anohina-Naumeca, A., Tauginienė, L., & Odineca, T. (2018). Academic integrity policies of Baltic state-financed universities in online public spaces. *International Journal for Educational Integrity*, *14*(1), 8. doi:10.1007/s40979-018-0031-z

Australasian Academic Integrity Network. (2023). *Summary of institutional responses to the use of generative artificial intelligence.* AAIN. https://wordpress-ms.deakin.edu.au/academicintegrity/wp-content/uploads/sites/290/2023/06/AAIN-Institutional-Responses-to-the-use-of-Generative-Artificial-Intelligence-V1.1.pdf

Australian Catholic University. (2023, July 25). *Artificial intelligence (AI) tools.* ACU. https://libguides.acu.edu.au/referencing/artificial-intelligence-tools

Australian Federal Police. (2022). *Identity crime.* AFP. https://www.afp.gov.au/what-we-do/crime-types/fraud/identity-crime

Australian Government Department of Education. (2021). *Higher education standards framework (threshold standards) 2021*. Legislation. https://www.legislation.gov.au/Details/F2022C00105

Australian Government Tertiary Education Quality and Standards Agency. (TEQSA). (2023). *TEQSA module 3 — Policies and procedures.* TEQSA. https://learning.teqsa.gov.au/mod/scorm/player.php?a=3&currentorg=TEQSA_Module_3_-_Policies_and_procedures_ORG&scoid=12

Australian Qualifications Framework Council. (2013). *Australian qualifications framework second edition January 2013*. AFQ. https://www.aqf.edu.au/framework/australian-qualifications-framework

Baartman, L., Baukema, H., & Prins, F. (2023). Exploring students' feedback seeking behavior in the context of programmatic assessment. *Assessment & Evaluation in Higher Education*, *48*(5), 598–612. doi:10.1080/02602938.2022.2100875

Baartman, L., van Schilt-Mol, T., & van der Vleuten, C. (2022). Programmatic assessment design choices in nine programs in higher education. *Frontiers in Education*, *7*, 931980. doi:10.3389/feduc.2022.931980

Bearman, M., & Luckin, R. (2020). Preparing university assessment for a world with AI: Tasks for human intelligence. In M. Bearman, P. Dawson, R. Ajjawi, J. Tai, & D. Boud (Eds.), *Re-imagining university assessment in a digital world* (pp. 49–63). Springer. doi:10.1007/978-3-030-41956-1_5

Bretag, T. (2017). *Good practice note: Addressing contract cheating to safeguard academic integrity*. Australian Government Tertiary Education Quality and Standards Agency (TEQSA). https://www.teqsa.gov.au/sites/default/files/good-practice-note-addressing-contract-cheating.pdf?v=1507082628

Bretag, T., & Mahmud, S. (2013). *Academic integrity standards: Aligning policy and practice in Australian universities*. Australian Government Office for Learning and Teaching. https://ltr.edu.au/resources/PP10_1783_Bretag_report_2013.pdf

Bretag, T., Mahmud, S., East, J., Green, M., James, C., McGowan, U., Partridge, L., Walker, R. G., & Wallace, M. (2011). Academic integrity standards: A preliminary analysis of the academic integrity policies at Australian Universities. In *Proceedings of AuQF 2011 Demonstrating Quality* (pp. 48–53). AuQF. https://ro.uow.edu.au/asdpapers/323/

Bretag, T., Mahmud, S., Wallace, M. C., Walker, R. G., James, C., Green, M., East, J., McGowan, U., & Partridge, L. (2011). Core elements of exemplary academic integrity policy in Australian higher education. *International Journal for Educational Integrity*, *7*(2), 3–12. doi:10.21913/IJEI.v7i2.759

Carter, S. (2022). *Academic integrity and testing: Digging deeper into impersonation*. International Center for Academic Integrity. https://academicintegrity.org/resources/blog/99-2022/may-2022/370-academic-integrity-and-testing-digging-deeper-into-impersonation

Central Queensland University. (2023). *Student academic integrity policy and procedure*. CQU. https://delivery-cqucontenthub.stylelabs.cloud/api/public/content/student-academic-integrity-policy-and-procedure.pdf

Chen, J. (2023). Four directions for assessment redesign in the age of generative AI. *The Times Higher Education*. https://www.timeshighereducation.com/campus/four-directions-assessment-redesign-age-generative-ai

Dawson, P. (2021). *Defending assessment security in a digital world: Preventing e-cheating and supporting academic integrity in higher education*. Routledge.

deMontigny, D. (2022). Managing academic integrity in Canadian engineering schools. In S. E. Eaton & J. Christensen Hughes (Eds.), *Academic integrity in Canada: Ethics and integrity in educational contexts* (pp. 291–306). Springer International Publishing. doi:10.1007/978-3-030-83255-1_15

Ditto Music. (2023 v). AI for music production: 10 tools to produce like a pro. *Unsigned Advice*. Retrieved July 30, 2023, from https://dittomusic.com/en/blog/ai-for-music-production-tools-for-musicians/

Eaton, S. E., Carmichael, J. J., & Pethrick, H. (Eds.). (2023). *Fake degrees and fraudulent credentials in higher education*. Springer Cham., doi:10.1007/978-3-031-21796-8

Elkhatat, A. M., Elsaid, K., & Almeer, S. (2023). Evaluating the efficacy of AI content detection tools in differentiating between human and AI-generated text. *International Journal for Educational Integrity*, *19*(1), 17. doi:10.1007/s40979-023-00140-5

Exemplary Academic Integrity Project. (n.d.-a). *Academic integrity policy toolkit*. APP. https://app.secure.griffith.edu.au/policy-form/index.php?pageno=2

Exemplary Academic Integrity Project. (n.d.-b). *Academic integrity policy toolkit*. Griffith. https://app.secure.griffith.edu.au/policy-form/

Foltýnek, T., & Glendinning, I. (2015). Impact of policies for plagiarism in higher education across Europe: Results of the project. *Acta Universitatis Agriculturae et Silviculturae Mendelianae Brunensis*, *62*(1), 207–216. doi:10.11118/actaun201563010207

Gao, A. K. (2023). *Go to Google Scholar and look up 'As an AI language model" -"ChatGPT"'* [Tweet]. Twitter [X]. https://twitter.com/itsandrewgao/status/1689634145717379074

Gibson, J. J. (1979). *The ecological approach to visual perception*. Houghton, Mifflin and Company.

Glendinning, I. (2023). *Academic integrity: Responding to advances in artificial intelligence* [Video presentation]. Aga Khan University. https://www.youtube.com/watch?app=desktop&v=JGxtHxXH79I

La Trobe University. (2022). *Student academic misconduct policy*. La Trobe University. https://policies.latrobe.edu.au/document/view.php?id=221

Lancaster, T. (2020a). *Academic integrity 2020 – Keynote presentation slides* [Blog]. https://thomaslancaster.co.uk/blog/academic-integrity-2020-keynote-presentation-slides/

Lancaster, T. (2020b). *Contract cheating in the context of Covid-19: Five key ideas to consider* [Slideshare presentation]. https://www.slideshare.net/ThomasLancaster/contract-cheating-in-the-context-of-covid19-five-key-ideas-to-consider

Miron, J., McKenzie, A., Eaton, S. E., Stoesz, B., Thacker, E., Devereaux, L., Persaud, N., Steeves, M., & Rowbotham, K. (2021). Academic integrity policy analysis of publicly-funded universities in Ontario, Canada: A focus on contract cheating. *Canadian Journal of Educational Administration and Policy*, *197*(197), 62–75. https://files.eric.ed.gov/fulltext/EJ1316334.pdf. doi:10.7202/1083333ar

Morgan, D. (2023). An autoethnography and analysis of Australian academic integrity policies amidst emerging threats. In U. G. Singh, C. S. Nair, & R. Watson (Eds.), *Academic integrity and quality assurance in the new digital higher education environment* (pp. 1–21). Elsevier. https://www.sciencedirect.com/book/9780323954235/academic-quality-and-integrity-in-the-new-higher-education-digital-environment

N., S. M. S. (2013, April 29). *Weak methods*. Psychology Dictionary. https://psychologydictionary.org/weak-methods/

Perkins, M., & Roe, J. (2023). Decoding academic integrity policies: A corpus linguistics investigation of AI and other technological threats. *Higher Education Policy*. Advance online publication. doi:10.1057/s41307-023-00323-2

Polytechnic Institute Australia. (2023). *Academic integrity and misconduct policy*. PIA. https://docs.pia.edu.au/wp-content/uploads/Academic-Integrity-and-Misconduct-Policy.pdf

Sutherland-Smith, W. (2010). Retribution, deterrence and reform: The dilemmas of plagiarism management in universities. *Journal of Higher Education Policy and Management*, *32*(1), 5–16. doi:10.1080/13600800903440519

University of South Australia. (2013). *The exemplary academic integrity project*. https://www.unisa.edu.au/EAIP

Victorian Legislation. (2023). *Crimes act 1958*. https://www.legislation.vic.gov.au/in-force/acts/crimes-act-1958/299

Young, F. (2022, 28 February). Affordances of innovative learning environments. In *Scholarly Community Encyclopedia online*. https://encyclopedia.pub/entry/19677

Young, F., Cleveland, B., & Imms, W. (2019). The affordances of innovative learning environments for deep learning: Educators' and architects' perceptions. *Australian Educational Researcher*, *47*(4), 693–720. doi:10.1007/s13384-019-00354-y

Chapter 4
Embracing Generative AI in the Classroom Whilst Being Mindful of Academic Integrity

Lynsey A. Meakin
https://orcid.org/0000-0002-2236-8602
University of Derby, UK

ABSTRACT

There are many generative AI (GenAI) tools available, and their rapid advancement has caused concerns relating to academic integrity. This chapter will consider concerns relating to academic integrity in the age of AI, including plagiarism and cheating. Awareness and education will be discussed as strategies for upholding academic integrity, as will proactive measures such as assessment design, and the need for institutional policies concerning the use of AI in education. The chapter concludes by stating that students should be taught to use generative AI ethically, responsibly and transparently and highlights how the integration of AI can foster creativity and enhance students' learning experiences.

INTRODUCTION

"AI is a tool that we should use to enhance and augment our own abilities."

(Fitzpatrick et al, 2023:22)

This chapter will explore concerns relating to academic integrity when it comes to the use of generative artificial intelligence (GenAI) in education and will propose practical strategies in the classroom to tackle these concerns. Rather than simply analysing or manipulating existing data, generative AI, as its name suggests, is designed to generate new content and this ability to generate an original response, in various languages, to user prompts in a conversational way has meant that GenAI, such as ChatGPT, has caused controversy (Kumar et al, 2022; van Dis et al, 2023). Many educators responded by banning GenAI or calling for software capable of detecting text created by GenAI to be made immediately

DOI: 10.4018/979-8-3693-0240-8.ch004

available. This response can be explained because of the concern about the impact that GenAI and its use in content production could have on academic integrity (Eke, 2023; Sullivan et al, 2023). Academic integrity is defined by the European Network for Academic Integrity (ENAI) as "Compliance with ethical and professional principles, standards, practices and consistent system of values, that serves as guidance for making decisions and taking actions in education, research and scholarship" (ENAI, 2022: online). In practice this relates to the expectation that teachers, students, researchers, and all members of the academic community act with honesty, trust, fairness, respect and responsibility. Breaching academic integrity is also known as 'academic misconduct' or 'academic dishonesty'.

Generative AI systems are designed to generate content or output (such as text, images, audio, simulations, video and codes) from the data they are trained on (Eke, 2023). AI tools provide multiple modes of representation, engagement, and communication (Delisio & Butaki, 2019) and there are a wide range of tools on offer that use GenAI, including chat bots like ChatGPT and Google Bard, AI that generate text responses; there are also image generative AI tools like DALL-E, VIZCOM and OpenArt; and video generative Ai like Fliki, Hour One and Rephrase.ai. The rapid advancement of GenAI is very real, and its capabilities are astounding including its potential to empower students and enhance their educational experiences and resources (Dai et al, 2023). It therefore makes sense to educate students into the effective, efficient and transparent use of ChatGPT and other generative AI.

McMurtrie (2022) argues that GenAI tools like ChatGPT will become part of everyday writing in some shape or form, in the same way that calculators and computers have become part of math and science. Similarly, Sharples (2022) suggests engaging students and instructors in shaping and harnessing these AI tools to support learning rather than stopping the students from using it. If this is the case, then academic integrity is regarded as a teaching and learning imperative (Bertram Gallant, 2008, 2017) and the role of educators includes facilitating student understanding of how to use GenAI ethically and transparently. This can be achieved through classroom activities and assessment design, which will in turn enhance the employability potential of these students.

This chapter suggests that generative AI should be embraced in the classroom and supports this argument by defining academic integrity and identifying academic integrity concerns in the age of AI. Strategies for addressing these concerns and upholding academic integrity in educational settings are proposed, including the adoption of a model of academic integrity institutionalization and an approach to teaching and learning that situates integrity practices within the goal of improving student learning, as well as reassessing assessment design and purpose so that students are taught to use GenAI effectively and transparently, and so enhance their employability.

ACADEMIC INTEGRITY CONCERNS IN THE AGE OF AI

The principles of academic integrity are embraced by educators, administrators and students because they are aware of the need for an ethical environment for the goals of teaching, learning, and research to be successfully accomplished. Educational institutions, however, have a propensity for addressing academic integrity by identifying and outlawing behaviours that are contrary to the principles of integrity rather than demonstrating their commitment to these principles in positive and pragmatic terms (ICAI, 2021:4). The fundamental values of honesty, trust, fairness, respect, responsibility, and courage serve to inform and improve behaviour and ethical decision-making, and so they can effectively create academic communities with academic integrity as a foundation. It has long been accepted that educational institutions contribute to the overall and holistic development of citizens of the world rather than just focusing on subject knowledge acquisition (Kibler, 1993). This being the case, a more holistic institutional approach should be adopted whereby academic integrity is regarded as an institutional issue that recognises the need for a shared responsibility between the student, staff and institution, supported by external quality agencies (Macdonald & Carroll, 2006).

Artificial Intelligence had been defined as "computing systems that are able to engage in human-like processes such as learning, adapting, synthesizing, self-correction and use of data for complex processing tasks" (Popenici & Kerr, 2017, p. 2). Generative Artificial Intelligence (GenAI), or algorithmic text-generating software, are writing technologies that are capable of creating or generating original text either ex nihilo or from user prompts (Dans, 2019). The general concern around GenAI is that students will start outsourcing their writing to GenAI, and some early responses to university level essay questions suggest that educators should be worried about the future of essays as a form of assessment (Stokel-Walker, 2022). Eaton, Mindzak & Morrison (2021) claim that students across all disciplines will utilise text-generators and continue to push the boundaries of academic integrity when there is a reduced likelihood of detection. This highlights the need for practical guidance on teaching academic integrity to students (Eaton & Kumar, 2023).

Plagiarism and AI

Plagiarism, the act of presenting someone else's work, ideas, or intellectual property as one's own without proper attribution, has been a long-standing concern in academia. The availability of AI-powered content generation tools has raised concerns about the potential for facilitating plagiarism and about the impact GenAI will have on academic integrity (Foltynek et al, 2023).

Technological change has made it easier to plagiarise, for example the internet provides access to a vast amount of information that can be easily copied and pasted without proper citation or acknowledgement (Amzalag et al 2021). Until recently it also allowed for plagiarism to be detected, for example online tools and services that can scan and compare texts for similarities and identify potential sources of plagiarism, such as Turnitin. The advent of GenAI, however, makes plagiarism harder to detect, as some AI tools can produce texts that are very similar to human-written ones, and may not be easily distinguished by conventional plagiarism detection methods. This has a two-fold consequence: firstly, to educate students and researchers about the ethical and academic standards for writing and research; secondly to adopt an institutional theory, a model of academic integrity institutionalization (Bertram Gallant and Drinan, 2008; Drinan and Bertram Gallant, 2008), whereby academic integrity is a multi-stakeholder, multi-faceted concept that applies to everyone in an educational institution (Bretag et al, 2013) and responsibility for academic honesty is removed exclusively from students and is shared by staff and the entire educational organization. Bertram Gallant (2020) argues that educational institutions must address cheating and plagiarism as a systemic rather than individual conduct challenge in order to leverage institutional integrity for the betterment of education.

AI has the capability to generate human-like text that can mimic the style, tone, and structure of academic writing. This raises concerns about students using AI to create essays, research papers, or assignments that appear original but are, in fact, generated by AI. Traditional plagiarism detection tools may struggle to identify AI-generated text because rather than relying on copying and pasting from existing sources, GenAI generates a brand-new response every time a prompt request is entered. AI-generated content can also be a mix of original ideas and phrases, making it harder to detect through conventional means. Students can also collapse writing detector accuracy by making small changes in text output or by prompting GenAI to rewrite the content in the same way that a human would write (Bauschard, 2023). There are tools available to predict the likelihood that a text originates from machines or humans, but such detection methods can likely be circumvented by evolved AI technologies and clever prompts (van Dis et al, 2023). LLM-output detection tools have also been shown to provide false positives, identifying academic work as having been generated by LLM or GenAI (Gegg-Harrison, 2023).

In order to avoid a futile race between text generators and text generator detection tools, educators and educational institutions should foster a culture of integrity and ethical responsibility that discourages plagiarism and promotes genuine learning (Dai et al, 2023). Educational institutions should utilise a strategy on academic integrity that focuses primarily on education and on developing and reinforcing student's appreciation of the value of academic integrity, before considering discipline (Bertram Gallant and Drinan, 2008). This proactive approach will enhance student awareness and likelihood to adhere to the values and principles of academic integrity rather than facing the potential consequences of breaching these (Whitley and Keith-Spiegel, 2001). McCabe and Makowski (2001) claim that such an approach, involving students, will "encourage students to accept greater responsibility for their behaviour . . . [and result in] lowered levels of self-reported cheating." (2001:337).

Students should clearly attribute the AI's contribution in their work when they use AI tools to generate content. This includes specifying the AI model used, the dataset, and any parameters or modifications applied. Students should be taught how to cite AI-generated content appropriately to maintain transparency and give credit where it is due.

Cheating and AI

Cheating, particularly during exams and assessments, is a significant concern for academic integrity. Research indicates that a large percentage of higher education students will cheat during tests and exams if they do not expect to be caught and state that the reason for engaging in practising academic misconduct is a natural outcome of the competitive society we live in (Caldas et al 2023). Common breaches of academic integrity and values include plagiarism, collusion, contract cheating, dishonesty, cheating, data fabrication, and ghost authorship (Pavletić & Hammerbauer, 2022). The advent of GenAI has introduced new and sophisticated ways for students to cheat, posing increased challenges for educators and institutions.

A longer-term implication on academic integrity is an over-reliance on AI for idea generation and actual writing, which can deter students from engaging deeply with the topic or content and exercising their own thinking and problem-solving abilities. Students could get used to looking for quick answers from GenAI systems instead of working through challenges, which will eventually lead to the erosion of creativity and originality (Dai et al, 2023).

STRATEGIES FOR UPHOLDING ACADEMIC INTEGRITY

Awareness and Education

Students may not always be aware of the ethical concerns surrounding the use of AI in academic work. Educators need to make students aware of these issues and the importance of maintaining academic integrity, to understand why it is important to produce original work, give credit to sources, and follow ethical guidelines in academic pursuits. Educators should teach students how to use AI tools responsibly, ensuring that AI is a supplementary tool to enhance their learning rather than a shortcut to academic success. Students need to be educated that while AI can assist in research and idea generation, it should not replace critical thinking, analysis, and creativity.

To reduce the likelihood of students plagiarising using GenAI, it is important that they are educated on what plagiarism is and why it is wrong. This could involve providing information on plagiarism in programme and course materials, discussing plagiarism in class, and highlighting the consequences of plagiarism. It could also be a requirement that students complete a written declaration stating that their work is their own and that they have not used any AI language models to generate it or have acknowledged its use if they have. This can help to deter students from using GenAI without acknowledging it and serve to hold them accountable for their actions (Cotton et al, 2023). Clear guidelines for the use of GenAI should be set and communicated to students. This could include guidelines on when and how GenAI can be used, as well as the proper citation and attribution of AI-generated text (Cotton et al, 2023).

Proactive Measures

Proactive measures are designed to prevent academic misconduct from occurring in the first place and are essential for maintaining academic integrity in educational institutions. Assessment is an integral part of education, serving as a means of evaluating student learning and progress (Cotton et al, 2023). The impact of GenAI and other text generators on assessment could be significant (Kumar, Eaton, Mindzak & Morrison, 2023), but herein lies an opportunity for educators to fundamentally change assessment methods and introduce innovative assessments, strengthening the design of assessment to improve academic integrity and actively discourage students' from cheating (Slade et al.,2016).

Assignment Design

Assignments and assessments should be constructed in such a way that they are challenging to complete using AI tools or by copying from external sources (Rudolph et al, 2023). Assignments with easily searchable answers should be avoided and questions should be rotated, or question banks should be used to discourage sharing of answers among students. Assignments could require analysis of texts that are too long to fit in a GenAI prompt or require writing about events that are recent and so not in the training data for the text generator (Mills, 2023).

Students could be asked to write about a highly specific and niche topic on which GenAI may find it difficult to find relevant information. In addition, students could be tasked with including personal experiences or perspectives in their writing, as it is difficult for AI systems to replicate this (Nowik, 2022). GenAI can be embraced in the writing of assignments but when they are designed so that students write about topics that genuinely interest them, in which their voices come through, and their opinions are valued (McMurtrie, 2022), GenAI cannot replicate this and so it can be used as a writing assistant rather than as a tool to write the assignment for the student.

Authentic Assessments

Authentic assessment is a form of evaluation of student learning by having students apply what they learned to real-life scenarios, thereby assessing deeper understanding and abilities. This provides students with the opportunity to demonstrate learning of the material by transferring classroom knowledge to situations that resemble the outside world. Examples of authentic assessments include:

- Carrying out interviews or journaling about the use of fractions in one day.
- Engage in group discussions, presentations, or other interactive activities that involve application of knowledge and skills.
- Student debates (individual or group).
- Ask students to create an app that solves a need.
- Ask students to design a tool to resolve a problem (for example a solution for plastic pollution).

Further opportunities for using authentic assessments arise when educators provide the "real-world" scenario, for example, educators could create a sick patient report and have students design a plan of care; or develop a fake company and ask students to design a marketing plan with a set goal. These assessments are designed to evaluate if students can put their knowledge to use to solve real-world problems, which is an essential skill for success in the workforce. Authentic assessments and effective teaching about academic integrity provide students with skills that can advance their employability (Sotiriadou et al 2020).

Emphasise Critical Thinking

Assignments that require critical thinking, problem-solving, and analysis rather than regurgitation of facts and projects that demand students to apply their knowledge in unique ways are less susceptible to cheating and are less likely to be generated by AI. Assignments should be created that foster students' creative and critical thinking abilities (Rudolph et al, 2023); for example, assessments could be created that require students to deliver presentations or performances.

Project-Based Learning

Project-based learning, group projects, and presentations should be promoted as they encourage collaborative learning and discourage individual cheating. Tasks can be assigned within projects that require each team member to contribute their unique skills and expertise.

In-Class Assessments

Conduct in-class assessments, both written and oral, to reduce opportunities for AI-assisted cheating. Such in-class assessments could include analysis that draws on class discussions (Mills, 2023). These in-class assessments are formative – assessment for learning – and so also allow educators to monitor student progress and measure a student's real-time understanding of the material.

Oral Assessments

If students are able to speak intelligently on the topic and defend their position or arguments, then they have demonstrated learning regardless of whether AI has been used or not (Kumar et al, 2023). As such, oral assessments could be a key way of assessing learning and allowing students the opportunity to demonstrate their knowledge, application and further learning of the topic being assessed.

Adaptive Testing

Adaptive testing techniques should be used where questions are tailored to a student's performance. This makes it difficult for students to share answers since each test may be unique.

Timed Exams

Implementing timed exams to limit the time available for students to consult external sources or use AI-generated content. Ensure that the time allocated is reasonable for the scope of the assessment.

Open-Book Exams With a Twist

If using open-book exams, include questions that require higher-order thinking or apply concepts in novel ways. This makes it less advantageous for students to rely solely on reference materials.

Assignment Variability

Assignments and assessments should be regularly updated to make it challenging for students to reuse old solutions or readily find available answers online and past papers should not be used in their entirety for mock exam purposes.

Peer Review and Evaluation

Students can be involved in peer evaluations and 'teach-back' (Sharples, 2022), which is a communication confirmation method whereby students demonstrate their understanding in speech. The incorporation of peer review and evaluation processes for assignments and projects can help identify discrepancies in group work and encourage students to hold each other accountable.

By implementing these proactive measures, educational institutions can create an environment where academic integrity is the norm and infringements on academic integrity are reduced (Bretag et al 2019). These measures not only deter academic misconduct but also promote learning experiences that emphasise critical thinking, problem-solving, and ethical conduct, preparing students for success in their future careers.

Institutional Policies

In an effort to mitigate the potential risks to academic integrity posed by GenAI, in addition to raising awareness, educating students about ethical and transparent use of GenAI, and the use of proactive measures, educational institutions must ensure that they have clear policies and guidance to guide the adoption of GenAI in Programmes of study. These policies should provide a framework specifying the acceptable and unacceptable uses of AI tools as well as the protocols for reporting AI usage in a transparent and accountable manner.

The reality is that Microsoft intends to integrate ChatGPT's technology into its suite of Microsoft products, including Bing search engine, Word, PowerPoint, Excel and Publisher (Metz & Weise, 2023). When this happens, GenAI will be mainstream, and students may not even be aware of their use of GenAI or the impact of GenAI on their work. This highlights the importance of educational institutions updating their academic integrity policies to address AI-generated plagiarism explicitly. These policies should clarify what constitutes AI-generated plagiarism and the consequences for such actions. Penalties and consequences for students who engage in AI-generated plagiarism must be clearly defined. These consequences should be in line with existing academic integrity policies and reflect the seriousness of the offense.

Academic integrity as an educational institutional issue includes students, faculty members, administrators and librarians (Whitley and Keith-Spiegel, 2001). This institutional approach could include asking students to explain the nature and extent of institutional cheating; giving student leaders support and guidance; assisting student leaders to educate their peers; giving a voice to interested students and staff in setting policy; keeping faculty members and senior administrators informed; developing fair, prompt and efficient due process procedures; and allowing students a significant part in resolving contested cases (McCabe and Pavela, 2000).

Students must be familiarised with the specific academic integrity policies of the institution and provided with a clear understanding of what constitutes academic misconduct and the penalties for violating these policies. Current definitions of misconduct, such as contract cheating and plagiarism, may not explicitly include the type of misconduct that GenAI could result in and so Foltynek et al (2023:2) propose an umbrella definition for all types of unauthorised content generation, including contract cheating and inappropriate use of AI:

"Unauthorised content generation (UCG) is the production of academic work, in

whole or part, for academic credit, progression, or award, whether or not a payment

or other favour is involved, using unapproved or undeclared human or technological assistance."

Educational institutional policies should define default rules on when and how the students, teachers, researchers and other educational stakeholders are allowed to use different kinds of AI tools. There should be space for specific rules at course level and the policy and the rules should be clearly communicated to all stakeholders. Users should also be guided on how to correctly and transparently acknowledge the use of AI tools in an assignment, dissertation, thesis, paper, article, book chapter, computer programme, graphic, artwork and other types of artefact (Foltynek et al, 2023). Dumin (2023) points out that a good policy should take into account the diverse ways educators may employ or restrict the use of AI in the educational setting while also accommodating their decision-making. Crucially, given the rapid advancement of AI, institutional policies should strike a balance by allowing for technological advances, changes and adaptations while providing sufficient guidance to ensure both educators and students feel at ease with the information provided.

Students should be provided with resources, guidelines, and handbooks on academic integrity and offered practical advice on how to avoid unintentional plagiarism, cite sources correctly, and use AI responsibly in academic work. Educators should actively promote and model ethical behaviour, they can share personal experiences and challenges related to academic integrity, making the topic more relatable to students. Clear channels of communication must be established for students to seek guidance or report concerns related to academic integrity, ensuring that students feel comfortable reporting violations.

An institutional approach to academic integrity can promote a philosophy of integrity for teaching, learning, and student support, as well as provide an approach for managing academic misconduct with a process that is accessible, consistent, and equitable (Morris, 2023). Institutional policies should include definitions of academic dishonesty, examples of behaviours that comprise violations, a description of the process followed when alleged violations occur, and a description of the sanctions usually imposed (Kibler, 1993). Most importantly, academic integrity policies should not be regarded as written in stone, but rather should be reviewed and updated on a regular basis (Eaton et al., 2021).

Embracing GenAI into the classroom must come with conditions, including appropriate acknowledgment of its use and recognition of its limitations, but this adoption of GenAI brings enormous opportunities to enhance student learning (Sullivan et al, 2023). Students should be guided on the benefits and limitations of AI tools in order to learn and use AI ethically and uphold academic integrity. With increasing automatization of modern societies, students will likely use AI tools in their professional life and so should be given opportunities to learn these skills during their education (Foltynek et al, 2023).

TEACHING STUDENTS TO USE GENERATIVE AI EFFECTIVELY AND TRANSPARENTLY

Students today are often digital natives who have grown up with technology, computers, and the Internet and who think, learn and understand the world differently from people who are not as familiar with digital technologies (Thomas, 2011). These digital natives are comfortable with and fluent in the use of technology, often using technology more effortlessly and intuitively than their teachers (Rudolph, 2023). Regardless of this pre-existing digital capability, education still has a role in ensuring that students are digitally literate and master AI tools (Zhai, 2022) and enhance their employability as a result. Selwyn (2009) argues that educators have a role to play in supporting young people in the digital age.

AI literacy refers to the application of a range of skills and knowledge to understand, use, and critically evaluate AI technologies and their impact on society (Ng et al., 2021; Su et al., 2022). GenAI can be used as a real-world AI application to empower teachers and students to develop their digital skills and AI literacy, including understanding the ethical, legal, and social implications of AI, and the ability to communicate effectively about AI issues and ideas (Su et al., 2023). Glendinning (2023) proposes that the subject of integrity could be gradually introduced throughout pre-university education, culminating in successful transition to tertiary education or working life and Eaton and Kumar (2023) have compiled a book of comprehensive lesson plans at elementary, secondary, and higher education levels that focus on instilling skills and values related to academic integrity.

There is a lack of clarity in differentiating students' seeking to cheat from those trying to find assistance (Dawson, 2020; Vaccino-Salvadore and Hall Buck,), which further highlights the need for educators to ensure that students are fully informed and digitally literate.

Bertram Gallant (2017) proposes an approach to teaching and learning whereby educators situate integrity practices within the goal of improving student learning, transferring the focus from how educators can stop students from cheating to how they can ensure students are learning (Bertram Gallant, 2008). Sefcik, Striepe & Yorke (2020) argue that academic integrity should draw on an educational approach for skill development that incorporates learner feedback into the process with a greater emphasis on underpinning values. In an effort to reduce the likelihood of infringements on academic integrity, this approach can be applied by "fostering a learning-oriented environment, improving instruction, enhancing institutional support for teaching and learning, and reducing institutional constraints to teaching and learning" (Bertram Gallant, 2008, p. 89).

This learning approach with a positive orientation to academic integrity could focus on building students' skills and competencies, rather than focusing on consequences for committing academic misconduct (Eaton & Kumar, 2023). Fostering a learning-oriented environment focused on mastery rather than being performance oriented encourages students to want to develop their meta-cognitive skills, enabling students to set goals, select strategies to enhance their learning experiences, and use self-assessment or self-questioning to monitor their own learning. Bertram Gallant (2017) argues that Mastery orientations can be developed by using meaningful assessments, providing students choice and control over grading, and fostering deeper approaches to active learning by allowing multiple attempts at an assessment or scaffolding assessments to lead to a final culminating demonstration of mastery.

Ethical Use of AI

To fully embrace GenAI in the classroom and remain mindful of academic integrity, educators should create an environment in which students are invested in their learning (McMurtrie, 2022). Students should take ownership and share responsibility for their learning. Students should be made aware that participating in classwork and assessments are forms of thinking and progressing and that a critically important form of learning is being missed if they try to delegate their work and writing to GenAI (Rudolph, 2023).

Although the detection of cheaters remains a challenge for educators, if GenAI is embraced in the classroom and students are not only allowed, but are actively encouraged, to utilise GenAI and its many benefits, strategies could be adopted to account for this. Perkins et al (2023) have developed an AI Assessment Scale (AIAS) which allows for the integration of GenAI tools into educational assessment by detailing different levels of AI usage in assessments based on the learning outcomes. This usage ranges from AI not being used at any point during the assessment, through three levels of increased AI use, to full AI use whereby AI may be used throughout the assessment to support the student's work.

Transparency in Attribution

All persons, sources, and tools that influence the ideas or generate the content of work submitted should be properly acknowledged, therefore, when GenAI is used, it should be recognised. Making students aware that they need to cite uses of AI tools and giving them the tools for doing may be sufficient motivation to comply with academic integrity policies (Kumar et al, 2023). The acknowledgement may be done in different ways, according to the context, the institutional policies, or other requirements. Ordinarily, the input or prompt given to the GenAI should be specified, when possible. It is important to note that GenAI cannot be listed as a co-author in a publication or piece of work because it cannot take responsibility for the content and findings reported (Foltynek et al, 2023). The student is always accountable for the content, whether or not it was generated by AI.

If students do not have the opportunity to learn about the ethical use of AI and the correct way to acknowledge its use, they will be more susceptible to engaging in inappropriate use of AI, which may constitute academic misconduct (Foltynek et al, 2023). Embracing GenAI in the classroom means that students should be encouraged to use GenAI as a resource, as a set of tools to improve writing skills and generate new ideas, rather than simply copying and pasting text (Rudolph, 2023).

Following the approach of academic integrity being integrated into teaching and learning, Kibler (1993) identifies ways that academic institutions can promote this within the context of student development, including "recognizing the importance of clearly written policies, offering opportunities for discussion and dialogue, establishing equitable adjudication procedures, acknowledging the role of sanctions, and recognizing the importance of instructional settings" (1993:264-265). Developing student awareness of the values and principles of academic integrity can reduce student academic misconduct, especially when students are involved in designing and enforcing campuswide academic integrity policies, and in educating other students about the importance of academic integrity, encouraging students to take responsibility for their own behaviour (McCabe and Pavela, 2000).

Pitt, Dullaghan & Sutherland-Smith (2021) conducted a qualitative study with higher education students accused of contract cheating and found that students found the experience the most challenging of their life that resulted in hypervigilance around future assignment submission but also encouraged them to stay on track and guide other students to practice academic integrity. The researchers recommend that staff ensure that formal university contract cheating processes are primarily a learning experience, from which students can emerge and progress to complete their studies, again emphasising the importance of teaching students the importance of academic integrity and regarding this as a learning experience. White (2000) developed an academic integrity board game and trialled it with hundreds of her own students, demonstrating a move away from regarding academic integrity as a moral issue that invokes strong emotions and instead implementing an interactive games-based approach to academic integrity that encourage students to engage more deeply with academic integrity.

If students are fully aware of the importance of academic integrity, they are less likely to violate the expectations and if they are offered a choice in how they learn and how they are assessed, this too could reduce academic misconduct in general (Kumar et al, 2023; Perkins, Gezgin & Roe, 2020).

Critical Evaluation of AI-Generated Output

Incorrect, Inaccurate or Mis-Information

GenAI, including ChatGPT and other Large Language Models (LLMs) generate text that is convincing, but that can also be wrong, with the consequence that their use can distort scientific facts and spread misinformation (van Dis et al, 2023). The responses generated by GenAI may not always be accurate or factually correct because GenAI, like ChatGPT, will have 'hallucinations' where information, answers or references are made up when it does not know how to reply. AI hallucinations occur when the AI generates content that cannot be grounded in any of its training data or the source content provided (Fitzpatrick et al., 2023).

Inaccuracies could also be the result of a failure to filter relevant information or being unable to distinguish between credible and less-credible sources. Such errors could, therefore, be due to an absence of the relevant information or data in the LLMs training set, a failure to extract the relevant information or simply the reality that LLMs are unable to distinguish between credible and less-credible sources (van Dis et al, 2023). This makes clear the need for students to critically evaluate the output they receive from GenAI.

Biased, Prejudiced, or Stereotypical

Prejudices and stereotypes that were present in the set of text data used to build the GenAI could be replicated in its generated responses. AI models are trained on datasets that reflect historical and societal prejudices, and so have the potential to perpetuate those biases in their predictions (Eke 2023; Fitzpatrick et al, 2023). Issues like availability, selection and confirmation biases, can be reproduced and so there is a distinct need for students to fact-check and verify the results generated by AI (Alvero, 2023).

No Understanding of the Context

Generative AI will process and generate natural language, but it has no understanding of the content of the queries, the context of the prompts, or of the physical world (Alvero, 2023). Following the algorithm that has programmed the GenAI, it will take the set of words provided in the prompt or query, access its vast set of training data, and determine what the most likely word is to come next, and then after that. GenAI does not understand the query and will not source relevant documents or appropriate sources of information. Thus, although the responses seem authentic and authoritative, GenAI cannot fully understand the context and meaning of the text and cannot self-evaluate its outputs (Grobe, 2023). The fact that GenAI is not able to assess the value or accuracy of the information it provides further highlights the need for students to be critical of the GAI-generated responses and content (Dobrin, 2023).

Fact-Checking and Cross-Referencing Information

GenAI responds to prompts in a confident, and seemingly knowing manner, regardless of whether the provided information is accurate or not. Fitzpatrick et al (2023) point out that while GenAI can process data very quickly, it does not have the ability to think critically or creatively to arrive at new insights. Students need to be made aware that the system is simply a smart predictive text that does not understand the context of the prompts and can unpredictably misrepresent or invent information (Meyer et al, 2023). Students should view the responses and text generated by AI with a degree of scepticism, and should confirm all information, fact-checking and cross-referencing information from multiple sources to ensure informed decision-making (Fitzpatrick et al, 2023).

GenAI in its current iteration does have a number of limitations, and many of these are made clear to users, for example, ChatGPT-3.5 clearly states at the bottom of the home page: "Free Research Preview. ChatGPT may produce inaccurate information about people, places, or facts. ChatGPT August 3 Version". These limitations should not hinder the use of GenAI or prevent it being embraced into the classroom, rather it presents the opportunity to guide students about these limitations. Students should be informed about the importance of using GenAI ethically and about being transparent in its use and attributing the contributions of GenAI. Students should be encouraged to think critically about the AI-generated content they incorporate into their work, they should be able to explain, defend, and expand upon the

AI-generated portions, demonstrating their understanding of the material. This will allow GenAI to be incorporated into student work and actively encourage critical engagement in the content.

STRATEGIES TO FOSTER CREATIVITY THROUGH INTEGRATION OF AI

The interface of GenAI, like ChatGPT, is a simple dialog format, with a text input area for users and a text output area from the GenAI, which results in the conversation always being initiated by the user, and the direction of the conversation is primarily controlled by the user. This user interface ensures that GenAI remains user-driven and as such is empowering to students who are not passively receiving notifications or tasks pushed through predefined commands but who are responsible for deciding on the topic, path, and process of the conversation (Dai et al, 2023). This reliance on student inputs for successful conversation echoes the principle of student-centred learning which identifies students as the owners of their learning, taking a leading role in planning, organising, and personalising their learning process (Lee & Hannafin, 2016). This need for user-controlled conversation also requires that students have a set of competencies to carry out and manage an inquiry and so inputs. These skills can be further enhanced because students can challenge and clarify information by asking GenAI to respond to follow-up questions, encouraging integration with existing knowledge and promoting a deeper understanding of multiple meanings and concepts (Rospigliosi, 2023).

The use of generative AI can enhance student creativity in several ways:

Idea Generation

GenAI has enormous sets of training data and a massive knowledge base, and so can be used to generate ideas, provide suggestions, and assist in brainstorming on given topics or prompts (Dai et al, 2023). This enables students to explore different perspectives, identify potential solutions, and think about various possibilities. Fitzpatrick et al (2023) state that we could use GenAI to generate initial ideas or even contrary ideas, but caution "we shouldn't rely on it to do our thinking for us" (2023:34) and this point must be emphasised to students.

Creative Content Generation

Opportunities for students at all levels include using GenAI as a source of creative inspiration, it can provide quick direct answers to specific questions, and as a content generator to draft, format, summarise, and/or edit academic work. GenAI can help students to write essays by suggesting topics, providing ideas, outlining structures, and improving their academic writing (Su and Yang, 2023).

Simulation and Experimentation

A major benefit of GenAI is that it allows students to learn through hands-on experiential learning experimentation and experience (Rudolph et al, 2023). GenAI can be used to create interactive learning tools, increasing student engagement, and facilitating group activities (Meyer et al, 2023), by presenting students with complex problems and scenarios that require critical thinking, problem-solving, and decision-making.

Interactive GenAI-powered content can captivate students by simulating real-world scenarios, virtual laboratories, and dynamic visualisations, making learning more engaging and enhancing understanding. This experiential learning emphasises learning by doing and allows students to engage with real-world contexts. Simulations generated by GenAI can also facilitate "what if" scenarios that encourage students to explore hypothetical situations and observe the outcomes, which encourages students to consider various possibilities, encouraging critical thinking and complex decision-making. Simulation and experimentation experiences offered by GenAI can help students learn and develop skills in realistic scenarios that might otherwise be difficult to access, for example participating in a surgery in an operating theatre (Fitzpatrick et al, 2023). Coverstone (2023) argues that critical thinking skills need to be practiced and that the practice should reflect the actuality of real-life. The use of GenAI to create simulations, case studies and experiential learning situations allows for students to practice critical thinking skills in a variety of different real-world contexts and scenarios.

Collaborative Creativity

By employing effective and suitable teaching methods, GenAI can be harnessed to promote collaboration and teamwork among participants. For instance, it can be employed to form student groups, enabling them to collaborate on various projects and assignments (Cotton et al, 2023). GenAI can generate different scenarios for students to work together to solve problems and achieve goals, fostering a sense of community and allowing students to learn from one another and support one another (Rudolph et al, 2023).

Whether working on an individual or a group project, students can communicate and consult with others and GenAI can facilitate this.

Personalised Learning Experiences

GenAI has the advantage of context awareness because the conversational tool can reference recent texts and contexts provided by users when generating responses. This capacity allows GenAI to gain a contextual understanding of student input and better identify the needs, goals, and areas of difficulty for individual students, so personalised learning support can be offered to students in a coherent and sensitive way, offering real-time assistance (Dai et al, 2023). This personalised learning experience can be further harnessed by GenAI generating questions that are tailored to each student's level of proficiency and that challenge them to demonstrate their knowledge and skills (Cotton et al, 2023). GenAI can provide students with targeted instruction customised to their individual needs. For example, if students need assistance with a math problem, they can receive detailed instructions on how to solve the issue (Su & Yang, 2023).

GenAI has the ability to translate across and between languages, making educational content available to students in languages other than their native tongue. This makes it possible for students to access a wider range of sources and expand their knowledge further than what is available in their primary language (Fitzpatrick et al, 2023). When used for language translation GenAI can serve as a conversation partner to language-learners whereby students practice their speaking and listening skills in a safe and non-judgmental environment. Furthermore, GenAI can receive and output text in multiple languages, providing translations of reading passages or re-writing classic text to accommodate specific learner needs, such as learning difficulties, and is beneficial for non-native speakers studying in English (Hosseini et al, 2023).

GenAI also has the benefit of offering instant feedback, enhancing its potential as a learning aid. GenAI will process the student input and provide immediate responses to and guidance on the inquiries and prompts inserted. The advantages of this instant feedback include enabling students to learn and make progress at their own pace and on their own schedules; allowing students to clarify any confusion and resolve misconceptions in real time; and the application of new understandings to subsequent tasks and topics. Dai et al (2023) argue that this immediate feedback is likely to enhance student learning engagement and increase the efficiency of education.

Embracing GenAI in the classroom further allows for the principles of student-centred learning to be embraced because GenAI facilitates students to "generate learning opportunities and reconstruct knowledge dynamically in an open-ended learning environment" (Lee & Hannafin 2016:708). This enables students to accept increased autonomy and responsibility for their own learning, they can use GenAI to build on their existing background knowledge and experiences.

CONCLUSION

In an age where technology accelerates the pace of change, academic integrity remains the bedrock of education, ensuring that the pursuit of knowledge remains a noble and ethical endeavour. As we move forward, let us continue to adapt, innovate, and uphold these principles, fostering an educational ecosystem where AI enhances learning without compromising the integrity of our educational mission.

This chapter advises against a policing approach that focuses on discovering academic misconduct, such as detecting the use of ChatGPT and other AI tools and instead favours an approach that builds trusting relationships with students in a student-centric pedagogy, advocating for a curriculum that embraces GenAI and the creation of assessments for and as learning rather than solely assessments of learning.

Educators have the responsibility of developing the skills that students need to thrive in the modern world, including the ability to question, be curious, think critically, converse with others in dialogue and be able to apply their knowledge in real-world situations. These skills will help students to solve complex problems and to think creatively, preparing them for future careers. This will ensure that students can become responsible digital citizens prepared for a future where AI is ubiquitous (Fitzpatrick et al, 2023).

It remains true that Gen AI could undermine academic integrity in the way it is used; but GenAI is equally capable of revolutionising academia. Students must be taught the importance of fact-checking, of validating the GenAI information received against other sources and formats, and the criticality of thoroughly checking every reference provided by GenAI generated text. Generative AI should be embraced enthusiastically in the classroom and students encouraged to use it as a tool to facilitate personalised learning and allow the development of creative thinking and critical evaluative skills. Students should also be educated to use GenAI ethically, transparently and with good intentions to maintain academic integrity.

REFERENCES

Alvero, R. (2023). ChatGPT: Rumors of human providers' demise have been greatly exaggerated. *Fertility and Sterility, 119*(6), 930–931. doi:10.1016/j.fertnstert.2023.03.010 PMID:36921837

Amzalag, M., Shapira, N., & Dolev, N. (2021). Two Sides of the Coin: Lack of Academic Integrity in Exams During the Corona Pandemic, Students' and Lecturers' Perceptions. *Journal of Academic Ethics, 20*(2), 243–263. https://doi-org.ezproxy.derby.ac.uk/10.1007/s10805-021-09413-5. doi:10.1007/s10805-021-09413-5 PMID:33846681

Bauschard S, Rao A, Shah P, and Shryock C (2023) *Chat(GPT): Navigating the Impact of Generative AI Technologies on Educational Theory and Practice: Educators Discuss ChatGPT and other Artificial Intelligence Tools.* Independently published.

Bertram Gallant, T. (2017). Academic Integrity as a Teaching & Learning Issue: From Theory to Practice. *Theory into Practice, 56*(2), 88–94. doi:10.1080/00405841.2017.1308173

Bertram Gallant, T. (2020). Leveraging the teachable moment: What, if anything, can students learn from cheating? In T. Bretag (Ed.), *A Research Agenda for Academic Integrity* (pp. 55–68). Edward Elgar Publishing Ltd. doi:10.4337/9781789903775.00011

Bertram Gallant, T. & Drinan, P. (2008) Toward a Model of Academic Integrity Institutionalization: Informing Practice in Postsecondary Education. *Canadian journal of higher education (1975) 38* (2), 25-43.

Bretag, T., Harper, R., Burton, M., Ellis, C., Newton, P., Rozenberg, P., Saddiqui, S., & van Haeringen, K. (2019). Contract cheating: A survey of Australian university students. *Studies in Higher Education, 44*(11), 1837–1856. doi:10.1080/03075079.2018.1462788

Caldas, I. M., Pereira, M. L., Azevedo, R., & Madureira-Carvalho, Á. (2022). Self-Report of Academic Misconduct Practices Among University Students in Portugal. In S. Bjelobaba, T. Foltýnek, I. Glendinning, V. Krásničan, & D. H. Dlabolová (Eds.), *Academic Integrity: Broadening Practices, Technologies, and the Role of Students. Ethics and Integrity in Educational Contexts* (Vol. 4). Springer. https://doi-org.ezproxy.derby.ac.uk/10.1007/978-3-031-16976-2_13

Cotton, D., Cotton, P., & Shipway, J. R. (2023) Chatting and Cheating: Ensuring academic integrity in the era of ChatGPT. *Innovations in education and teaching international.* https://www-tandfonline-com.ezproxy.derby.ac.uk/doi/full/10.1080/14703297.2023.2190148

Coverstone, A. (2023) Generative AI and Teaching Students to Think Critically. In Bauschard S, Rao A, Shah P and Shryock C (Eds.) (2023) Chat(GPT): Navigating the Impact of Generative AI on Education theory and Practice. Great Britain: Pedagogy Ventures.

Dai, Y., Liu, A., & Lim, C. P. (2023) Reconceptualizing ChatGPT and generative AI as a student-driven innovation in higher education. *Procedi 33rd CIRP*, 119. https://www.sciencedirect.com/science/article/pii/S2212827123004407

Dans, E. (2019, February 6). Meet Bertie, Heliograf and Cyborg, the new journalists on the block. *Forbes*. https://www.forbes.com/sites/enriquedans/2019/02/06/meet-bertie-heliograf-and-cyborg-the-new-journalists-on-the-block/?sh=669bf965138d

Delisio, L. A., & Butaky, C. A. (2019). UDL and assistive technology. In W. W. Murawski & K. L. Scott (Eds.), *What really works With Universal Design for Learning* (pp. 157–172). Corwin.

Drinan, P. M., & Bertram Gallant, T. (2008). Plagiarism and Academic Integrity Systems. *Journal of Library Administration*, *47*(3-4), 3–4, 125–140. doi:10.1080/01930820802186472

Dumin, L. (2023) Developing Acceptable Use Policies for the College Classroom. In Bauschard S, Rao A, Shah P and Shryock C (Eds.) (2023) Chat(GPT): Navigating the Impact of Generative AI on Education theory and Practice. Great Britain: Pedagogy Ventures.

Eaton, S. E. (2021). *Plagiarism in higher education: Tackling tough topics in academic integrity*. Libraries Unlimited. doi:10.5040/9798400697142

EatonS. E.KumarR. (Eds.). 2023 Academic Integrity Lessons: Practical Ideas for Teaching, Learning, and Assessment. University of Calgary. Calgary, Canada. https://dx.doi.org/ doi:10.11575.PRISM/42226

Eaton, S. E., Mindzak, M., & Morrison, R. (2021). *The impact of text-generating technologies on academic integrity: AI & AI*. Paper presented at the Canadian Association for the Study of Educational Administration (CASEA), University of Alberta. http://hdl.handle.net/1880/113569

Eke, D. O. (2023). ChatGPT and the rise of generative AI: Threat to academic integrity? *Journal of Responsible Technology*, *13*, 1–4. https://www.sciencedirect.com/science/article/pii/S2666659623000033. doi:10.1016/j.jrt.2023.100060

European Network for Academic Integrity (ENAI). (2023) *Glossary: Academic Integrity*. ENAI. https://www.academicintegrity.eu/wp/

Fitzpatrick, D., Fox, A., & Weinstein, B. (2023). *The AI Classroom: The Ultimate Guide to Artificial Intelligence in Education*. TeacherGoals Publishing.

Foltynek, T., Bjelobaba, S., Glendinning, I., Khan, Z. R., Santos, R., Pavletic, P., & Kravjar, J. (2023). ENAI recommendations on the ethical use of Artificial Intelligence in Education. *International Journal for Educational Integrity*, *19*(12), 1–4. https://edintegrity.biomedcentral.com/articles/10.1007/s40979-023-00133-4. doi:10.1007/s40979-023-00133-4

Gegg-Harrison, W. (2023) Against the use of GPTZero and other LLM-output Detection Tool. In Bauschard S, Rao A, Shah P and Shryock C (Eds.) (2023) Chat(GPT): Navigating the Impact of Generative AI on Education theory and Practice. Great Britain: Pedagogy Ventures.

Glendinning, I. (2023). Educational Integrity in Schools: A Framework for Young Learners. In S. E. Eaton & Z. R. Khan (Eds.), *Ethics and Integrity in Teacher Education. Ethics and Integrity in Educational Contexts* (Vol. 3). Springer. doi:10.1007/978-3-031-16922-9_11

Grobe, C. (2023). Why I'm Not Scared of ChatGPT. [+ https://www.chronicle.com/article/why-im-not-scared-of-chatgpt]. *The Chronicle of Higher Education*, *69*(11), 32.

Hosseini, M., Rasmussen, L. M., & Resnik, D. B. (2023) Using AI to write scholarly publications. *Accountability in Research*. Taylor and Francis. https://www.tandfonline.com/doi/full/10.1080/08989621.2023.2168535

Kibler, W. L. (1993). Academic Dishonesty: A Student Development Dilemma. *NASPA Journal*, *30*(4), 252–267. doi:10.1080/00220973.1993.11072323

Kumar, R., Eaton, S. E., Mindzak, M., & Morrison, R. (2023). Academic Integrity and Artificial Intelligence: An Overview. In S. E. Eaton (Ed.), *Handbook of Academic Integrity*. Springer. doi:10.1007/978-3-031-39989-3_153

Lee, E., & Hannafin, M. J. (2016) A design framework for enhancing engagement in student-centered learning: own it, learn it, and share it. *Educational technology research and development*. [Online] *64*(4), 707–734. https://link.springer.com/article/10.1007/s11423-015-9422-5

Macdonald, R., & Carroll, J. (2006). Plagiarism—A complex issue requiring a holistic institutional approach. *Assessment & Evaluation in Higher Education*, *31*(2), 233–245. doi:10.1080/02602930500262536

McCabe, D., & Pavela, G. (2000). Some Good News About Academic Integrity, Change. *Change*, *32*(5), 32–38. doi:10.1080/00091380009605738

McCabe, D. L., & Makowski, A. L. (2001). Resolving Allegations of Academic Dishonesty: Is There a Role for Students to Play? *About Campus: Enriching the Student Learning Experience*, *6*(1), 17–21. doi:10.1177/108648220100600104

McMurtrie, B. (2022, December). AI and the future of undergraduate writing. [Online] [Available at: https://www.chronicle.com/article/ai-and-the-future-of-undergraduate-writing]. *The Chronicle of Higher Education, 13*.

McMurtrie, B. (2023) Teaching: Will ChatGPT change the way you teach? *The Chronicle of Higher Education*. https://www.chronicle.com/newsletter/teaching/2023-01-05

Metz, C., & Weise, K. (2023). Microsoft bets big on the creator of ChatGPT in race to dominate A.I. *The New York Times*. https://www.nytimes.com/2023/01/12/technology/microsoft-openai-chatgpt.html

Mills, A. (2023). AI Text Generators: Sources to Stimulate Discussion Among Teachers. Google Docs. https://docs.google.com/document/d/1V1drRG1XlWTBrEwgGqd-cCySUB12JrcoamB5i16-Ezw/edit#heading=h.sot8caygc8jr

Morris, E. J. (2023). Integrating Academic Integrity: An Educational Approach. In S. E. Eaton (Ed.), *Handbook of Academic Integrity*. Springer. doi:10.1007/978-981-287-079-7_96-1

NeumannM.RauschenbergerM.SchönE.-M. (2023) "We Need To Talk About ChatGPT": The Future of AI and Higher Education. 2023:4. doi:10.1109/SEENG59157.2023.00010

Ng, D. T. K., Leung, J. K. L., Chu, S. K. W., & Qiao, M. S. (2021). Conceptualizing AI literacy: An exploratory review. *Computers and Education: Artificial Intelligence*, *2*, 100041. doi:10.1016/j.caeai.2021.100041

Nowik, C. (2022, December 17). The robots are coming! The robots are coming! Nah, the robots are here. *Substack*. https://christinenowik.substack.com/p/the-robots-are-coming-the-robots#detail

Pavletić, P., & Hammerbauer, M. (2022). The Role of Students in the Preservation of Academic Integrity. In S. Bjelobaba, T. Foltýnek, I. Glendinning, V. Krásničan, & D. H. Dlabolová (Eds.), *Academic Integrity: Broadening Practices, Technologies, and the Role of Students. Ethics and Integrity in Educational Contexts* (Vol. 4). Springer. https://doi-org.ezproxy.derby.ac.uk/10.1007/978-3-031-16976-2_18

Perkins, M., Gezgin, U. B., & Roe, J. (2020). Reducing plagiarism through academic misconduct education. *International Journal for Educational Integrity*, *16*(1), 3. doi:10.1007/s40979-020-00052-8

Pitt, P., Dullaghan, K., & Sutherland-Smith, W. (2021). Mess, stress and trauma': Students' experiences of formal contract cheating processes. *Assessment & Evaluation in Higher Education*, *46*(4), 659–672. doi:10.1080/02602938.2020.1787332

Popenici, S. A., & Kerr, S. (2017). Exploring the impact of artificial intelligence on teaching and learning in higher education. *Research and Practice in Technology Enhanced Learning*, *12*(1), 1–13. doi:10.1186/s41039-017-0062-8 PMID:30595727

Rospigliosi, P. (2023). Artificial intelligence in teaching and learning: What questions should we ask of ChatGPT? *Interactive Learning Environments*, *31*(1), 1–3. https://www.tandfonline.com/doi/full/10.1080/10494820.2023.2180191. doi:10.1080/10494820.2023.2180191

Rudolph, J., Tan, S., & Tan, S. (2023). ChatGPT: Bullshit spewer or the end of traditional assessments in higher education? *Journal of Applied Learning and Teaching*, *6*(1), 342–363. https://journals.sfu.ca/jalt/index.php/jalt/article/view/689

Sefcik, L., Striepe, M., & Yorke, J. (2020). Mapping the landscape of academic integrity education programs: What approaches are effective? *Assessment & Evaluation in Higher Education*, *45*(1), 30–43. doi:10.1080/02602938.2019.1604942

Selwyn, N. (2009). The digital native - myth and reality. [Online]. *Aslib Proceedings*, *61*(4), 364–379. doi:10.1108/00012530910973776

Sharples, M. (2022). Automated essay writing: An AIED opinion. *International Journal of Artificial Intelligence in Education*, *32*(4), 1119–1126. https://link.springer.com/article/10.1007/s40593-022-00300-7. doi:10.1007/s40593-022-00300-7

Slade, C., Rowland, S., & McGrath, D. (2016). *Student dishonesty in assessment: Issues paper for UQ assessment sub-committee. Institute for Teaching and Learning Innovation*. The University of Queensland. uq.edu.au

Sotiriadou, P., Logan, D., Daly, A., & Guest, R. (2020). The role of authentic assessment to preserve academic integrity and promote skill development and employability. *Studies in Higher Education*, *45*(11), 2132–2148. doi:10.1080/03075079.2019.1582015

Stokel-Walker C (2022) AI bot ChatGPT writes smart essays — Should professors worry? *Nature*. doi:10.1038/d41586-022-04397-7

Su, J., Ng, D. T. K., & Chu, S. K. W. (2023). Artificial intelligence (AI) literacy in early childhood education: The challenges and opportunities. *Computers and Education: Artificial Intelligence*, *4*, 100124. doi:10.1016/j.caeai.2023.100124

Su, J., & Yang, W. (2023) Unlocking the Power of ChatGPT: A Framework for Applying Generative AI in Education. *ECNU review of education, 6*(3), 355–366. https://journals.sagepub.com/doi/full/10.1177/20965311231168423

Su, J., Zhong, Y., & Ng, D. T. K. (2022). A meta-review of literature on educational approaches for teaching AI at the K-12 levels in the Asia-Pacific region. *Computers and Education: Artificial Intelligence, 3*, 100065. doi:10.1016/j.caeai.2022.100065

Sullivan, M., Kelly, A., & McLaughlan, P. (2023). ChatGPT in higher education: Considerations for academic integrity and student learning. *Journal of Applied Learning and Teaching, 6*(1), 31–40. https://journals.sfu.ca/jalt/index.php/jalt/article/view/731

The International Centre for Academic Integrity (ICAI). (1999). Fundamental values project. Academic Intregity. http://www.academicintegrity.org/icai/resources-2.php

Thomas, M. (Ed.). (2011). *Deconstructing digital natives: young people, technology and the new literacies* [Online]. Routledge. https://ebookcentral.proquest.com/lib/derby/reader.action?docID=684081 doi:10.4324/9780203818848

Vaccino-Salvadore, S., & Hall Buck, R. (2021). Moving from plagiarism police to integrity coaches: Assisting novice students in understanding the relationship between research and ownership. *International Journal for Educational Integrity, 17*(20), 1–18. doi:10.1007/s40979-021-00085-7

van Dis, E A M., Bollen, J., Zuidema, W., van Rooij, R., & Bockting, C. L. (2023) ChatGPT: five priorities for research. *Nature, 614*(7947), 224–226. https://www.nature.com/articles/d41586-023-00288-7.pdf

White, A. (2020). Interactive approaches to learning about academic integrity: The role of fun and games. In T. Bretag (Ed.), *A Research Agenda for Academic Integrity* (pp. 86–99). Edward Elgar Publishing Ltd. doi:10.4337/9781789903775.00013

Whitley, B. E. Jr, & Keith-Spiegel, P. (2001). Academic Integrity as an Institutional Issue. *Ethics & Behavior, 11*(3), 325–342. doi:10.1207/S15327019EB1103_9

ZhaiX. (2022) ChatGPT User Experience: Implications for Education. SSRN. https://ssrn.com/abstract=4312418 doi:10.2139/ssrn.4312418

Chapter 5
Redefining Classroom Readiness:
How Initial Teacher Training Can Mitigate Risks and Capitalize on the Potential of GenAI

Janine Aldous Arantes
https://orcid.org/0000-0002-0301-5780
Victoria University, Australia

ABSTRACT

This chapter presents a roadmap for teacher educators to equip their graduates with the ability to recognize and mitigate the limitations and risks of using ChatGPT in educational settings. With the rise of artificial intelligence (AI), the incorporation of AI-powered technologies like ChatGPT has the potential to enhance student learning. However, it also raises concerns about psychosocial harm for both students and educators. By sharing the burden of responsibility and fostering a safe working environment, teacher educators can prepare future teachers to leverage ChatGPT safely, harness its benefits, and navigate the complex landscape of a phenomena introduced in this chapter as 'technorisk' while promoting positive educational outcomes.

INTRODUCTION

As technology continues to advance, the landscape of education is evolving, presenting both opportunities and challenges for future educators. Among the emerging technologies, Generative Artificial Intelligence (GenAI) tools, such as ChatGPT, have garnered attention for their potential to revolutionize the teaching and learning process (Adiguzel et al., 2023). ChatGPT, developed by OpenAI, has had a significant global impact by enhancing language understanding and generation across diverse applications, including content creation, code generation, education, customer support, and fostering innovation in the field of natural language processing. According to Shewale (November 8, 2023) ChatGPT has a user base of

DOI: 10.4018/979-8-3693-0240-8.ch005

over 100 million weekly active users, with more than 2 million developers utilizing the platform and over 92% of Fortune 500 companies incorporating ChatGPT. The user demographic is comprised of 59.67% males and 40.33% females, and the model is anticipated to generate $200 million in revenue by the end of 2023. OpenAI expends $700,000 daily to operate ChatGPT, which has accumulated over 10 billion all-time page visits, receiving an average of over 1 billion page visits each month. Over 88% of ChatGPT's traffic comes directly, with 4.22% originating from social media platforms. Notably, seven nations, including China and Russia, lack access to ChatGPT and 53% of readers fail to recognize content generated by ChatGPT as AI-written. This brings about unique risks in the context of Education. The integration of GenAI in education comes with concerns, particularly related to academic integrity and assessment (Cotton et al., 2023). Secondly, concerns about "consumer well-being, bias, misinformation, lack of context, privacy concerns, ethical considerations and security" (Paul et al., 2023, 1) are increasingly being regulated. With teachers a prosumer of ChatGPT, this chapter adopts a novel approach to understanding the impacts and implications of GenAI in education, by considering how GenAI may be associated with psychosocial hazards.

Moving beyond pedagogy, assessment and practice, this chapter considers teachers' workplace rights in the context of Australian classrooms. Working through a lens of Australia's Safework "Model Work Health and Safety Regulations" (Safework, 2023), psychosocial hazards are described as a hazard that arises from, or relates to, in part, workplace interactions or behaviours that may cause psychological harm, whether or not it may also cause physical harm. With teacher burnout at all-time highs, this lens is significant, as it encourages us to consider to what extent GenAI may present as a psychosocial risk to teachers' working conditions. Examining how teachers navigate assessment and academic integrity within the context of how these processes are "managed, organized, and supported" and the guidance provided in terms of "information, training, instruction, and supervision" (Safework, 2023, 62), potential psychosocial hazards such as job demands, limited job control, inadequate support, and a lack of role clarity (Safework, 2022) are discussed. I offer a means of prompting discourse around such matters, and do not claim any form of legal advice or direction to legal matters. With this in mind, the purpose of this chapter is to reposition teachers' workplace rights within the discourse around GenAI.

SETTING THE SCENE: TECHNORISK AND THE BURDEN OF THE UNKNOWN

For many years, technology has been seen as an innovation that could *save* education and teachers (Milan, 2020). Education institutions and educators, in general, have often been portrayed as lacking in some way; and technology has been promoted as 'better' (Morozov, 2013). Often referred to as *techno-solutionism*, this perception that technology can solve the problems education faces, has been amplified in recent times by the claims of AI evangelists, sparking critique and debate about claims that robots will eventually replace teachers (Hrastinski et al., 2019). Notably, those who challenge this rhetoric have long been dismissed as merely virtue signalling, as this debate has become both profitable and sensationalized in media (Mockler, 2022). Taking a rights-based approach, I aim to encourage more thorough discussions about the hazards associated with AI's deficiencies, using ChatGPT within initial teacher training programs as an example. I introduce the term *technorisk*, to refer to the hazards that arise from the use, adoption, and reliance on technology. Technorisk encompasses a wide range of risks associated with the use of digital technologies, software, hardware, and data to encourage debate beyond how we are engaging with AI. There is a true and real risk that without greater teacher training in addressing the psychosocial harm of navigating the academic integrity issues tied to AI, while we wait for legislation to mandate AI's deficiencies are rectified, educators negotiating assessment and academic integrity will burnout, adding to the global teacher shortage. What follows is a case writing exercise, to illustrate how psychosocial harm might emerge for graduate teachers due to the presence of AI such as ChatGPT.

THE BURDEN OF THE UNKNOWN

Mr. Thompson, a graduate educator fresh out of university, reflected on the introduction of GenAI with Mr Anderson, a highly experienced leader in the school. It had promised innovation and efficiency. But its implications on academic integrity loomed large. As Mr Thompson marked student's assignments, he noticed that the line between AI-generated content had become blurred with who and why students were or were not submitting authentic work. Mr Anderson was quick to point out, that the majority of students do not maliciously cheat. The sense of equity and access, pillars of a fair education system, faced disruption as a result of GenAI. He explained, "While some students will seamlessly engaged in the digital landscape, leveraging GenAI to enhance their work, others will seemingly struggled to adapt. But it isn't that simple." After talking with Mt Anderson, Mr Thompson realised that although he had provided the class with the same digital literacy skills, some faced digital poverty. Some could afford the newer versions of AIs and were sailing through the digital landscape, and others were sitting at the back of McDonald's using the free Wi-Fi in a paddle boat. The digital divide had widened with GenAI, encompassing financial constraints, and limited infrastructure, exacerbating social and economic inequalities. Mr Anderson understood, that ChatGPT had begun casting shadows over the principle of equal opportunities for all learners, muddying the waters of academic integrity with notions of why students used GenAI at all.

Once Mr. Thompson understood the growing disparity among his students, he started to identify that assessment with GenAI, was significantly more complex and entangled that simply identifying authentic work. Alongside the growing question of 'But, did they actually write it?' was an ill ease with making accusations. Mr Anderson, drew on research that, pointed out, that such accusations are more commonly targeted towards culturally and linguistically diverse students, who were being falsely identified for plagiarism by 'AI detection tools'. Secondly, as Mr Anderson led the student appeals process, he explained students and staff were increasingly expressing feelings of stress, and anxiety of either being falsely accused or falsely accusing a student. He was increasingly providing mental health supports for his staff and students – a role he took on, above and beyond his full time work. He explain that Mr Thompson, had his full support, and that while juggling the demands of being a new teacher, if he felt that he was in a constant state of anxiety, where he seemed to be spending more time teaching to the tech and troubleshooting its deficiencies, than teaching with the students – he was not alone. The psychosocial toll on Mr. Thompson and Mr Anderson, was palpable.

The constant questioning of the authenticity of student work created an atmosphere of mistrust. The constant need to stay abreast of the technology was draining. As they faced the responsibility of addressing plagiarism issues stemming from GenAI-generated content and navigating the onslaught of marketing claims, they found themselves in a constant state of unease. The once-clear path of assessing academic progress had become a labyrinth, with guidelines and support to navigate the challenges posed by these deficient tools in a constant state of development. Mr Anderson found himself taking on more and more to support students, and staff. While Mr Thompson found himself feeling overwhelmed, knowing the support from colleagues was there, but the burden of not knowing if this was going to last, was depressing. The human connection, a cornerstone of education, that drew both teachers to education, waned as deficient and defunct technologies claiming to increase efficiencies, inserted intangible forms of bias, and consent, privacy and IP issues into education.

As their students became data points and they became conduits for tools to enter the classroom, they lost the human connection and became prosumers of data. The technological push towards self-regulated learners, rather than active participants in a collaborative learning environment with complex learning needs and differences, was further monetized and exploited. This made them both reflect on the initial promises of efficiency and advancement. Both decided that the benefits of ChatGPT, were hugely outweighed by the ethical and psychosocial concerns GenAI introduced. On reflection, Mr Thompson thought about the workload and cognitive load of navigating academic integrity, equity, and access as a new teacher vs a job that pays the same, without the same hazards. My Anderson, supporting new staff, demanded a reconsideration of the role of GenAI in shaping the future of education. But it became clear that the evolution of technology was funded by tech behemoths that profit from dehumanization and was not going to stop without a balance of innovation and regulation through legislation. Mr Anderson's demands were smothered with more claims of efficiencies and innovations, and Mr Thompson, left the profession. Mr Anderson was only a year from retirement, and decided that he didn't want to be part of education anymore either.

The story underscores the urgent need for clarity, support, and guidelines to ensure integrity and equity in education, or risk teachers like Mr. Anderson joining the myriads of teachers leaving the workforce at scale. The pivotal role of initial teacher training programs in providing graduate teachers with the knowledge and skills to navigate the intricacies of GenAI, uphold academic integrity, and create a supportive learning environment for students while safeguarding their psychosocial well-being is significant. A novel way of imagining 'classroom readinesses could potentially provide an innovative approach to address these challenges.

By reimagining classroom readiness and embracing a comprehensive approach to GenAI integration, pre service teacher education can effectively harness the benefits of AI while upholding academic integrity principles. What follows is a brief background into the teacher shortage and classroom readiness in the context of the Australian Education system, followed by how ITE providers are burdened with the responsibility of fixing the teacher shortage and then a roadmap to move us away from Techno solutionism and towards assessing Technorisk as a means of, in part addressing the teacher shortage.

CRISIS IN THE CLASSROOM: THE TEACHER DROUGHT

The shortage of qualified teachers is a growing concern worldwide. In 2022, UNESCO (2022, 5) stated that "[a]n increase in the supply of qualified teachers is urgently needed to achieve universal primary and secondary education." Darling-Hammon & Podolsky (2019) suggest that this has been a growing issue since at least the 1930s. Policy measures across continents have sought to tackle challenges related to attracting, recruiting, and retaining teachers. In the context of the Australian education system, strategies such as offering financial incentives, creating accelerated career development paths or leadership opportunities, and establishing formal recruitment programs that aim to address specific areas of demand by bypassing conventional qualification routes have occurred (Heffernan et al., 2022). The global shortage of teachers, stems from various causes. Causes including demographic changes, low teacher retention rates, and unequal distribution of teachers (See et al., 2022). The teacher shortage is complex social, economic, and political issue. Addressing the worldwide shortage of qualified teachers requires a multi-faceted approach which in recent years has sought novel ways to positively impact education.

Classroom readiness, in this context, refers to the ability of teachers to possess the necessary skills, knowledge, and adaptability to meet the diverse needs of students in an ever-changing educational landscape (Ma & Cavanagh, 2018). As the number of qualified teachers decreases, there is an increased need for new educators who can step into the classroom and effectively engage with the demands of the role, including the technologies that are part of the changing landscape of the classroom from day one. Often touted as innovative and responding to the imperative for improving instructional practices (Edwards & Cheok, 2018), technology has significantly influenced global education. Automation of administrative tasks has been a key aspect, claiming to alleviate teachers' workloads and enhance teacher-student interactions. While technological interventions have brought positive changes and innovative solutions, they also introduce risks and challenges for teachers, contributing to the multifaceted reasons behind the teacher shortage. Further, Edtech has often benefited from a narrative around teachers' having inherent deficits (Mockler, 2022). That is, technology cannot provide a solution to educations' problems, if there are no problems that need a solution. This negative perception of teachers allows the increased sales and marketing of technologies to 'save' education (García & Guerra, 2004), whilst potentially exacerbating teacher shortages as individuals may be discouraged from pursuing a career in teaching due to the prevailing negative narratives and attitudes surrounding the profession. With tools such as Generative Artificial Intelligence now intensifying challenges with assessment and academic integrity (Cotton et al., 2023), and further feeding into the increase challenges of being a teacher, it is thought that by incorporating practical training and hands-on experiences to equip aspiring teachers with the necessary skills to negotiate emerging technologies from a rights based approach that more people will be attracted to, and be retained in the profession. Notably, this does not in any way place the burden of responsibility on schools and teachers – platforms who profit the most, must design their tools with safety as a priority. This potential solution to the problem of teacher shortages, assumes training is needed, while regulation is developed and implemented.

Where much of research into Artificial Intelligence in Education and the notion of being Classroom Ready, focuses on pedagogy and practice, there is a need to focus on Teachers Rights at work, as a means of addressing the teacher shortage. Teachers, like all other occupations, have workplace rights that safeguard their well-being, working conditions, and job security. These rights include fair employment practices, a safe and healthy work environment, freedom of association, academic freedom, and contractual rights ensuring fair compensation and benefits (Arantes, 2022). These workplace rights contribute to fostering a supportive environment that empowers teachers to focus on providing quality education to their students, in a context that supports their rights to a safe workplace – arguably decreasing teacher burnout and addressing the teacher shortage in part. What follows is consideration of how the teacher shortage is being addressed in the context of the Australian Education System.

EMBRACING THE ERA OF GENAI: SHARING THE BURDEN OF RESPONSIBILITY IN TEACHER EDUCATION

How have we been addressing the teacher shortage? In Australia, a Teacher Education Expert Panel was established in response to concerns raised at the Teacher Workforce Shortage Roundtable and the Quality Initial Teacher Education Review (TEMAG 2014). The panel aimed to provide advice on four reform areas to improve initial teacher education in Australia. The panel sought feedback and discussion to achieve the goal of delivering confident, effective, classroom-ready graduates and improve the quality of practical experience in teaching, attract mid-career entrants, and link performance with funding of ITE programs. On 6th July 2023, the final report was published, containing 14 recommendations aimed at enhancing teacher training and equipping educators for the classroom. The recommendations are categorized as follows: the first three focus on fortifying Initial Teacher Education (ITE) programs to produce confident and effective beginning teachers. The next four emphasize creating a stronger connection between performance and funding of initial teacher education. The subsequent four concentrate on enhancing practical teaching experience. Lastly, the remaining three recommendations are dedicated to improving postgraduate initial teacher education programs to cater to mid-career entrants. The Panel acknowledged "that more could be done nationally to support beginning teachers as they enter the teaching profession" (Scott et al., 2023, 72) and that

"…teachers are operating in an environment that is more difficult than at any other time.

Schools are at the forefront of managing the impacts of constant changes shaping our

society, such as mobile technology, social media, [and] artificial intelligence... There

are greater expectations placed on teachers than ever before." (Scott et al., 2023, 6).

There is a systemic issue far beyond Initial Teacher Education Programs that needs to be addressed to come close to tackling the teacher shortage problems faced on a global scale. The 'greater expectations placed on teachers than ever before' cannot simply be fixed by placing the burden of change onto initial teacher educators and the teachers themselves. With this stated, the chapter focuses on what could occur to support beginning teachers as they enter the teaching profession, to become 'classroom ready', by focussing on their right to a psychosocially safe workplace in an era of Generative Artificial Intelligence.

Generative AI tools, including ChatGPT, introduce significant academic integrity challenges that require careful consideration and proactive measures. One of the primary concerns in education, is the potential for plagiarism (Cotton et al., 2023). The ability of AI models to generate text that closely resembles human-written content can make it difficult to distinguish between original work and AI-generated material. This raises questions about the authenticity and authorship of academic papers, essays, or other assignments (including written text, visual or audio production). Further, generative AI tools are associated with the manipulation of information and the dissemination of misinformation, and can be vulnerable to biases present in training data (Perrotta et al., 2022). If students rely solely on AI-generated content without critically evaluating its accuracy and reliability, it can undermine the integrity of their assessments, decrease critical thinking, increase addictive tendencies and the unauthorized assistance and outsourcing of academic tasks. There are multiple, complex ethical implications of using generative AI tools in assessments that require a re-examination on what it means to be 'classroom' ready during the age of AI.

The integration of GenAI technologies in assessment practices has given rise to new forms of psychosocial risks for educators. Risks are yet to be fully considered, researched and documented, but may include heightened work demands, increased pressure to identify GenAI work, and feelings of insecurity among staff regarding fair assessment. Where much of the current research focuses on pedagogy and practice, concerns around the psychosocial impact to teachers around assessing work with fairness, free from bias when suspecting GenAI has been used, and the erosion of trust if questioning students in the assessment process is noticeably lacking. This constant exposure to AI-driven assessments and the lack of definitive means to identify AI generated work, may be leading to increased stress levels, reduced self-esteem, and anxiety among staff, impacting their overall psychosocial well-being. A process, that Australian workplaces are mandated to assess and mitigate risk of harm.

As such, this we need to consider how these two approaches – technology and teacher training may relate to the teacher shortage through the notion of being 'classroom ready' when faced with increased forms of psychosocial harm due to academic integrity issues with GenAI. What follows, is a provision of provocations around what it means to be a 'classroom ready' graduate teacher, by prompting consideration of the developing nexus between integrity policy, psychosocial health, policy and practice in Australian higher education initial teacher education providers. The following Roadmap, aims to prompt discussion around what it means to be a 'class-room ready' educator with GenAI tools abound, and calls for the concept of being classroom ready to be reconsidered due to the risks associated with academic integrity, assessment and staff wellbeing. As an initial teacher educator, recognizing the importance of holistic and diverse approaches to problem-solving, the roadmap does not claim to solve the issues present here. Rather it has been written to explore the integration of ChatGPT within ITE courses to highlight the significance of preparing future educators to consider various perspectives, how to increase psychosocial safety and utilize technological advancements to address multifaceted issues in educational assessment and academic integrity.

A ROADMAP TO BE 'CLASSROOM READY' TO WORK WITH CHATGPT SAFELY IN THE CLASSROOM

A novel way of considering the teacher shortage, through the lens of being classroom ready, is via a roadmap to work with AI in education safely in the classroom. The disruption of GenAI, discussed here through the tool ChatGPT, can be likened to driving a car without a roadmap or navigation system. More akin to driving without a safety belt. Without clear guidance, a safe environment and a predetermined route, there is a risk of getting lost, taking inefficient or incorrect paths, or encountering unexpected obstacles along the way that lead to unintended consequences without appropriate safety to protect us. Just as a roadmap provides a structured plan for reaching a destination efficiently, a well-defined roadmap for deploying and utilizing ChatGPT helps ensure responsible and effective use. But, how can we increase psychosocial safety when GenAI is part of education? This roadmap to psychosocial safety has to include considerations such as ethical guidelines, data privacy, bias mitigation, transparency, and human oversight. Without such a roadmap, the unguided use of ChatGPT in education may result in issues such as generating misleading or inaccurate information, propagating biases, or producing inappropriate or harmful content. Just as a roadmap and seat belts assist in navigating and reaching the desired destination safely and efficiently, a well-constructed roadmap for ChatGPT in Initial Teacher Education Programs can guide its deployment, minimize risks, and maximize its potential benefits. One option is to mandate that educational institutions implement comprehensive training for teachers, emphasizing emotional well-being and effective communication. But this places, the burden of responsibility on an already strained workforce. Fostering open communication channels, providing mental health resources, and integrating psychosocial topics into the curriculum, will not address the defunct and deficiencies technologies that insert bias and privacy and consent issues into the classroom. It may help to navigate the path, by establishing boundaries, safeguards, and responsible practices to ensure that ChatGPT's capabilities are harnessed in ways that align with ethical standards, educational expectations, and societal well-being, but it does not ensure a seatbelt in protecting the driver.

What follows is the first iteration of a roadmap for teacher educators to better prepare their graduates to recognize the limitations and risks of ChatGPT while still using it to enhance student learning as part of a safe working environment. By providing a roadmap for teacher educators that considers GenAI as a risk to be negotiated through the lens of psychosocial harm, Higher Education providers can embed ways we may train the next generation of teachers about the academic integrity concerns associated with the use of ChatGPT, in a non-punitive manner. Through discussion of pedagogical change and educative processes such as Mastery Learning (Bloom, 1968) and Formative Assessment (Lane et al. 2019), what follows, is a means to promote the idea of how we may develop a culture of academic integrity and equip ITEs and PSTs with the knowledge and skills they need to effectively integrate ChatGPT in their teaching practices while mitigating the risks associated with its use.

Starting the Car: Shift From Techno Solutionism to Technorisk to Navigate the Hazards of AI in Education

While ChatGPT and similar generative AI tools have the potential to enhance teaching and learning experiences, they also introduce challenges that can impact teachers' psychosocial well-being, particularly in relation to academic integrity and assessment. The challenges associated with academic integrity in the context of ChatGPT can place additional stress and burden on teachers, with K-12 teachers required to ensure academic honesty and address instances of plagiarism involving AI-generated content. This requires teachers to invest more time and effort in verifying the authenticity and originality of student work. This increased workload can lead to heightened pressure, particularly when considering the large volume of assignments and assessments to be evaluated; and the huge diversity in learners within each classroom. The need to continuously adapt and update assessment strategies to detect AI-generated content can further contribute to the psychosocial strain experienced by teachers. Moreover, the reliance on ChatGPT and similar tools for assessment purposes poses risks to the validity and reliability of evaluations. Second, the potential for biases in AI-generated content can also raise concerns about equity and objectivity in the evaluation process, exposing teachers to these uncertainties and challenges as they, like their academic tutors, try to negotiate how to best engage with these tools. Undoubtedly, the process of being classroom ready, when working with teachers' anxiety and stress levels increased, as they navigate the complexities of ensuring fair and valid assessments in the presence of AI-generated content, highlights a need for a new roadmap that positions digital technologies such as ChatGPT as a risk to psychosocial health.

Putting it Into Gear: The Notion of Classroom Readiness Needs to Change

The psychosocial impact on teachers, is complex and multifaceted. Whether stemming from a need for continuous professional development and adaptation to technological advancements, through to the rapid pace at which AI technologies evolve, this constant learning and adaptation process places pressure on Initial Teacher Educators (ITE) to look for new ways that don't demand that they keep up with technological advancements. One such approach, is to mitigate these psychosocial risks, by providing teachers with comprehensive support systems around their psychosocial health. This includes professional development programs that address the ethical considerations and challenges associated with AI tools, promoting a culture of collaboration and peer support, and providing resources and guidelines to navigate issues of academic integrity and assessment. Open communication channels and opportunities for dialogue can also facilitate the sharing of experiences and strategies among teachers where the technology is no longer innovative – but assessed as a risk, may foster a sense of collective problem-solving and reduce the potential isolation that teachers may feel when facing these challenges. By recognizing the potential psychosocial impact and providing the necessary support mechanisms, educational institutions can help teachers navigate the complexities associated with academic integrity and assessment in the context of generative AI tools like ChatGPT, ensuring their well-being and promoting a positive teaching environment.

As a language model, ChatGPT has the potential to significantly impact the notion of classroom readiness. Traditionally, classroom readiness has been defined as the ability of a student to engage in and benefit from classroom instruction, based on their mastery of foundational academic skills (Ma & Cavanagh, 2018). However, with the emergence of advanced technologies like ChatGPT, the notion of classroom readiness needs to change. One way in which ChatGPT can contribute to this change is by providing pre service teachers with a more personalized and adaptive teaching and learning experience (Kasneci et al, 2023). Another way in which ChatGPT can contribute to this change is by facilitating a shift towards more project-based and collaborative learning and teaching (Cooper, 2023). However, ChatGPT also challenges the traditional notion of classroom readiness and questions how to best train PSTs to evaluate and assess student work (Cotton et al. 2023), and how to ensure that students are developing the skills and knowledge that they need to succeed in the modern world that includes Artificially intelligent (AI) tools such as ChatGPT.

To achieve this goal, ITE programs need to be evidence-based and grounded in best practices that have a high impact on student learning. Specifically, graduate teachers need to be equipped with a strong understanding of how students learn, what classroom practices work best, how to manage classrooms effectively, and how to be culturally responsive to diverse learners – as well as how to negotiate the risks and benefits of emergent technologies in terms of both their own and the students' psychosocial health. Pre service teachers need to know how to mitigate risks such as the falsification of information and infringement of copyright, and ITE providers need to emphasize the importance of teachers recognizing these risks and ensuring that work produced using ChatGPT is authentic and upholds academic integrity – and how to best manage the situation when unsure. This requires a re-evaluation of what it means to be 'classroom ready'. Pre-service teacher training programs arguably need to integrate instruction on rights based considerations of AI tools, and how to assess the authenticity and academic integrity of work produced with the use of AI tools.

According to Australia's Quality Initial Teacher Education (QITE) Review conducted in 2022, a significant number of beginning teachers face challenges in essential areas of teaching, such as reading, cultural responsiveness, supporting diverse learners, classroom management, and family/carer engagement. The review also emphasized the need to strengthen the focus on evidence-based teaching strategies to better prepare Initial Teacher Education (ITE) students to highlight that this review is lacking in content around teachers' rights at work; a pressing issue when working with AI in education. To address this issue, I invite you to consider how accredited ITE programs may ensure that all graduate teachers are equipped with sufficient evidence-based practices, to enable them to enact their workplace rights when employed in an AI informed classroom. Just like a roadmap provides streets to drive down, and seatbelt provide the protections, what follows are suggestions for how to increase psychosocial safety in Initial Teacher Education Programs when GenAI is a mundane edtech tool in the classroom.

Let's go Driving – With Our Seatbelts On

Topic One: The Misuse of AI Tools

Without sufficient training, pre-service teachers may not understand how to use AI tools appropriately, nor how to teach and assess with GenAI tools. This should not however sit as a further expense to be covered by ITE intuitions through micro credentials, as new content may not be added due to accreditation issues. AI is profiting from education. AI providers within the context of education, should provide funding to ITE intuitions to develop local and tailored programs for their individual cohort of pre service teachers. This should be in consultation with non for profit organisations, to address issues such as overreliance on AI-generated content by students (ie new forms of addiction) or the use AI tools to automate tasks that should be done manually (sponsor time to develop policy and guidelines). Without doing so, we may see inaccurate or unreliable results that undermine the credibility of the educational process. Which in turn raises various ethical dilemmas, such as privacy concerns and issues related to bias and discrimination. Without training, first year out pre-service teachers may not be able to recognize or address these dilemmas, which could result in unintended consequences for students and themselves.

Topic Two: Your Rights at Work, During an Era of AI

The potential misuse of AI tools, such as ChatGPT, can have psychosocial implications for both teachers and students. The psychosocial harm can manifest in several ways. Firstly, teachers may experience increased stress and self-doubt when relying heavily on AI-generated content without fully understanding its limitations or how to integrate it effectively into their teaching practices. Furthermore, the ethical dilemmas associated with AI tools can contribute to teachers' psychosocial strain. Privacy concerns arise when AI tools collect and analyse student data, potentially compromising students' personal information. Issues related to bias and discrimination also come into play, as AI models can inadvertently perpetuate existing biases present in the training data. Teachers may feel a sense of ethical responsibility and pressure to address these dilemmas but may lack the knowledge and training to effectively do so. This can lead to feelings of moral distress, as teachers grapple with the implications of using AI tools without fully understanding their potential consequences. To mitigate the psychosocial harm associated with the misuse of AI tools, comprehensive training and professional development programs are crucial. Providing teachers with the knowledge and skills to understand the limitations and ethical considerations of AI tools can help alleviate their anxieties and empower them to make informed decisions about their usage. Additionally, creating supportive environments that encourage open dialogue, collaboration, and continuous learning can foster a sense of psychological safety for teachers, allowing them to navigate the complexities of AI tools with confidence and minimize the potential psychosocial impact on themselves and their students.

Topic Three: Student Belonging, Trust, and Their Right to Voice

Where unintended consequences emerge, a lack of trust follows. If GenAI tools are used inappropriately or if ethical considerations are not taken into account, it could erode the trust that students and parents have in the educational system. This could lead to a decrease in student engagement and a decline in academic performance; and if associated with protected attribute assessment issues. Using GenAI tools inappropriately could result in issues such as plagiarism and the unfair treatment of assessment in K-12 settings. This may contribute to feelings of frustration, disillusionment, and decreased self-esteem among students; which in turn increases the risk of psychosocial harm for teachers. This can result in feelings of injustice, inequality, and a sense that their efforts are not being fairly evaluated. Such experiences can negatively impact students' and teachers' self-perception, motivation, and overall psychosocial well-being. It is crucial to integrate instruction on ethical considerations and provide training on assessing the authenticity and academic integrity of work produced with the use of GenAI tools in pre-service teacher training programs. By doing so, the psychosocial harm to students and teachers can be minimized, and the credibility and trustworthiness of the educational process can be maintained.

PUTTING ON THE BRAKES: MITIGATING RISKS

To mitigate risks associated with emerging technologies like GenAI, ITE programs must incorporate training on psychosocial harms and rights based considerations related to AI tools, such as ChatGPT. This training should be included as part of any reform, as it currently lacks consideration of risk to teachers' psychosocial wellbeing. Teachers need to understand the limitations and risks of using such tools while enhancing student learning, and this roadmap based on academic integrity in the context of ChatGPT may offer the opportunity to strengthen ITE programs and produce confident, effective, and classroom-ready graduates who can manage the risks associated with ChatGPT while leveraging its potential. This roadmap emphasizes that psychosocial risk is to be view alongside key teaching practices for upholding academic integrity and ensuring a safe working environment for teachers. Being a rights-based approach, by considering teachers' well-being and addressing potential psychosocial hazards associated with AI tool usage we promote critical thinking skills, provide practical training, whilst also emphasising pedagogical strategies, fostering collaboration, and engaging in continuous professional development, ITE programs can effectively mitigate the risks of using GenAI tools. Ongoing evaluation and adaptation will ensure the roadmap remains responsive to evolving needs and supports teachers in navigating academic integrity issues and psychosocial well-being. Redefining classroom readiness to include awareness of rights based considerations, academic integrity, and psychosocial health will prepare teachers to effectively use ChatGPT and similar AI tools responsibly. Redefining classroom readiness, requires us to then mitigate 'technorisk'.

Technorisk

The notion of Technorisk is not new. Hughes (1997) has discussed Technorisk in regards to technology-related loss, such as computer viruses and Sliter (2004) has discussed Technorisk in terms of fraud and digital privacy concerns. More recently, Stephen and Jummai (2022) have discussed socio-technorisk in relation to Information ownership and privacy control, and Singh, Goel and Baral (2022) have considered the legal right of the data subject to access, use, and collection of data. What has occurred over the years is a shift away from the risk of technology being corrupt, and towards the rights humans have given the presence of technology.

Technorisk does the same shift in gear. Here Technorisk refers to the potential risks and challenges that arise from the use and integration of emerging technologies, particularly in various professional and educational settings. It involves identifying and addressing the negative impacts, limitations, and rights based considerations associated with adopting and implementing technological and digital tools. As technology continues to advance, there are concerns about how certain technologies can bring unintended consequences or unforeseen risks, both in terms of social implications and individual well-being and the notion of Technorisk, repositions technology away from being a 'solution' and towards being a 'risk'. By actively addressing Technorisk, individuals and organizations can strike a balance between harnessing the advantages of technology and safeguarding against potential harm. This includes integrating rights based considerations, adhering to data protection and privacy regulations, promoting digital literacy, and continuously evaluating the effects of technology on various stakeholders. Effectively managing Technorisk contributes to building a more sustainable and secure technological landscape that benefits society while mitigating potential downsides. The following steps can be incorporated into this roadmap to capitalise on the benefits of GenAI, whilst also teaching about Technorisk

1. Integration of rights based considerations: ITE programs to embed discussions on privacy, bias, data security, and the responsible use of AI-generated content.
2. Promoting critical thinking: educational systems to shift away from technology being a solely seen as a solution, and to increasingly assess it as a risk.
3. Providing practical training: ITE programs to include hands-on experiences, simulations, and real-world case studies that allow them to navigate ethical dilemmas and make informed decisions when using these tools in their classrooms.
4. Emphasizing pedagogical strategies: ITE tutors to guide student discussions, promoting critical engagement with ai-generated content, and encouraging assessment design as a graduate teach that thinks critically about the limitations and implications of such tools.
5. Collaboration and continuous professional development: policy makers and governance systems must recognise that there will be a need for ongoing training and support and as such provide funding for it.
6. Comprehensive risk assessment: partnering with institutions that enable the ongoing examination of potential stressors, workload demands, and rights based considerations associated with using AI tools beyond the employer – employee context are required.
7. Supportive policies and guidelines: an examination of current educational policies to emphasize the importance of maintaining a healthy work-life balance, provide guidance on workload management, and establish protocols for addressing any psychosocial issues that may arise as per new legislation is required.

8. Protected collaborative support systems: creating communities of practice where teachers can openly and without punishment, discuss the challenges and share strategies for managing psychosocial risks associated with ai tool usage must be established on a global scale.
9. Ongoing evaluation and adaptation: consider establishing feedback mechanisms and regular assessments to identify areas for improvement and ensure that the roadmap remains responsive to evolving needs on a local scale is needed.

By incorporating a rights-based approach that acknowledges teachers' rights to a safe workplace, ITE programs can address the psychosocial risks associated with technology integration. This ensures that teachers' well-being is protected, promoting a positive and sustainable teaching environment that maximizes the benefits of GenAI tools while minimizing potential harm to teachers' psychosocial health.

CONCLUSION

In conclusion, the integration of ChatGPT and similar AI tools in initial teacher education programs has the potential to revolutionize the concept of classroom readiness, based around the complex and intertwined notions of psychosocial harm and technorisk. While these tools offer exciting opportunities for personalized and adaptive learning experiences, they also pose challenges that must be addressed to ensure ethical usage and maintain the integrity of the educational process. To navigate these challenges, it is imperative for ITE programs to be grounded in evidence-based practices that emphasize best practices in AI integration. Pre-service teachers must be equipped with the knowledge and skills necessary to critically assess the authenticity and academic integrity of work produced with AI tools like ChatGPT. By providing comprehensive training and support, ITE programs can empower pre-service teachers to navigate the ethical considerations associated with AI tools effectively. Failure to address these challenges can have detrimental consequences. Pre-service teachers who are ill-prepared may unintentionally cause harm to students, compromising their learning experiences and overall well-being. Additionally, the credibility of the educational process may be undermined, eroding trust in the system and hindering student engagement and performance.

By recognizing and proactively addressing these challenges and risks, teacher educators can play a pivotal role in preparing confident, effective, and classroom-ready graduates. Through a combination of evidence-based practices, ongoing professional development, and a focus on ethical considerations, ITE programs can empower teachers to leverage the potential of ChatGPT while effectively mitigating its risks. Ultimately, by embracing the integration of AI tools like ChatGPT in initial teacher education, educators can shape a future where technology enhances teaching and learning without compromising academic integrity or students' well-being. By prioritizing rigorous training, ethical guidelines, and ongoing support, we can harness the transformative power of AI tools while ensuring that teachers are equipped to navigate the evolving educational landscape with confidence, competence, and a commitment to the highest standards of academic integrity.

REFERENCES

Adiguzel, T., Kaya, M. H., & Cansu, F. K. (2023). Revolutionizing education with AI: Exploring the transformative potential of ChatGPT. *Contemporary Educational Technology*, *15*(3), ep429. doi:10.30935/cedtech/13152

Arantes, J. A. (2022). Personalization in Australian K-12 classrooms: How might digital teaching and learning tools produce intangible consequences for teachers' workplace conditions? *Australian Educational Researcher*, 1–18. doi:10.1007/s13384-022-00530-7 PMID:35505893

Bloom, B. S. (1968). Learning for Mastery. Instruction and Curriculum. *Evaluation Comment, 1*(2).

Cooper, G. (2023). Examining Science Education in ChatGPT: An Exploratory Study of Generative Artificial Intelligence. *Journal of Science Education and Technology*, *32*(3), 1–9. doi:10.1007/s10956-023-10039-y

Cotton, D. R., Cotton, P. A., & Shipway, J. R. (2023). Chatting and cheating: Ensuring academic integrity in the era of ChatGPT. *Innovations in Education and Teaching International*, 1–12. doi:10.1080/14703297.2023.2190148

Darling-Hammond, L., & Podolsky, A. (2019). Breaking the cycle of teacher shortages: What kind of policies can make a difference? *Education Policy Analysis Archives*, *27*, 34–34. doi:10.14507/epaa.27.4633

Edwards, B. I., & Cheok, A. D. (2018). Why not robot teachers: Artificial intelligence for addressing teacher shortage. *Applied Artificial Intelligence*, *32*(4), 345–360. doi:10.1080/08839514.2018.1464286

García, S. B., & Guerra, P. L. (2004). Deconstructing Deficit Thinking: Working with Educators to Create More Equitable Learning Environments. *Education and Urban Society*, *36*(2), 150–168. doi:10.1177/0013124503261322

Heffernan, A., Bright, D., Kim, M., Longmuir, F., & Magyar, B. (2022). 'I cannot sustain the workload and the emotional toll': Reasons behind Australian teachers' intentions to leave the profession. *Australian Journal of Education*, *66*(2), 196–209. doi:10.1177/00049441221086654

Hrastinski, S., Olofsson, A. D., Arkenback, C., Ekström, S., Ericsson, E., Fransson, G., Jaldemark, J., Ryberg, T., Öberg, L.-M., Fuentes, A., Gustafsson, U., Humble, N., Mozelius, P., Sundgren, M., & Utterberg, M. (2019). Critical Imaginaries and Reflections on Artificial Intelligence and Robots in Postdigital K-12 Education. *Postdigital Science and Education*, *1*(2), 427–445. doi:10.1007/s42438-019-00046-x

Hughes, M. L. (1997). Technorisk: Who's responsible? *Risk Management*, *44*(11), 20–24.

Love, T. S., & Love, Z. J. (2023). The teacher recruitment crisis: Examining influential recruitment factors from a United States technology and engineering teacher preparation program. *International Journal of Technology and Design Education*, *33*(1), 105–121. doi:10.1007/s10798-022-09727-4

Ma, K., & Cavanagh, M. S. (2018). Classroom ready?: Pre-service teachers' self-efficacy for their first professional experience placement. *The Australian Journal of Teacher Education*, *43*(7), 134–151. doi:10.14221/ajte.2018v43n7.8

Milan, S. (2020). Techno-solutionism and the standard human in the making of the COVID-19 pandemic. *Big Data & Society*, *7*(2), 2053951720966781. doi:10.1177/2053951720966781

Mockler, N. (2022). *Constructing Teacher Identities: How the Print Media Define and Represent Teachers and Their Work*. Bloomsbury Publishing., doi:10.5040/9781350132917

Morozov, E. (2013). *To save everything, click here: The folly of technological solutionism*. Public Affairs.

Perrotta, C., Selwyn, N., & Ewin, C. (2022). Artificial intelligence and the affective labour of understanding: The intimate moderation of a language model. *New Media & Society, 14614448221075296*. doi:10.1177/14614448221075296

See, B. H., Gorard, S., Morris, R., & Ventista, O. (2022). Rethinking the complex determinants of teacher shortages. The Palgrave Handbook of Teacher Education Research, 1-28. doi:10.1007/978-3-030-59533-3_2-1

Singh, T., Goel, R., & Baral, S. K. (2022). A Study on Big Data Privacy in Cross-Industrial Challenges and Legal Implications. In *Cross-Industry Applications of Cyber Security Frameworks* (pp. 112–123). IGI Global. doi:10.4018/978-1-6684-3448-2.ch006

Sliter, J. (2004). "Techno risk"-technology and intelligence data need to be pushed. *Journal of Financial Crime*, *11*(4), 322–324. doi:10.1108/13590790410809266

Stephen, G. L., & Jummai, N. M. (2022). Information Ownership and Privacy Control in Information Society. [IJSRM]. *International Journal of Scientific Research and Management*, *10*(06), 25–33. doi:10.18535/ijsrm/v10i6.lis01

TEMAG. (2014). *Action Now: Classroom Ready Teachers – Report of the Teacher Education Ministerial Advisory Group (TEMAG)*. Australian Government Department of Education.

UNESCO. (2022). *Transforming teaching from within – Current trends in the status and development of teachers*. United Nations Educational, Scientific and Cultural Organization. https://unesdoc.unesco.org/ark:/48223/pf0000383002.

Chapter 6
(A)I'm a Believer, but (A) I'm Also Responsible

Blake Kanewischer
https://orcid.org/0000-0002-9978-548X
Southern Alberta Institute of Technology, Canada

Sonja L. Johnston
Southern Alberta Institute of Technology, Canada

ABSTRACT

This chapter explores the impact of generative AI technologies on academic integrity in higher education, within the context of a business capstone course in a Canadian polytechnic. Using a case study and leveraging the Double Diamond framework for innovation, the chapter illustrates how generative AI tools can support known pedagogical supports for academic integrity: (1) Building relational trust between instructors and students; (2) student agency; (3) assessment mastery; and (4) choice in grading and assessment. The chapter concludes with recommendations for continuing to integrate generative AI technologies into practice.

INTRODUCTION

Academic integrity is foundational to post-secondary education, and addresses "[c]ompliance with ethical and professional principles, standards, practices, and [a] consistent system of values, that serves as guidance for making decisions and taking actions in education, research, and scholarship" (European Network for Academic Integrity (ENAI), 2022). This definition is intentionally broader than assessing or "catching" violations, such as plagiarism, cheating, or misrepresenting contributions in team assignments. Because this definition bridges academia into practice, it is well-suited to capstone courses in undergraduate programs.

In alignment with the context set out by Hauhart and Grahe, this capstone, "as the culminating experience for students' undergraduate careers, … is intended to tie together previous courses in theory, method,

DOI: 10.4018/979-8-3693-0240-8.ch006

and substantive knowledge within most disciplines" (2015, p. x). This requires a degree of fluidity on the part of students and the instructor, as the integration is most critical to the culminating experience.

Faculty at a Canadian polytechnic implemented an integrative capstone course in its undergraduate business program, with the intent of exposing students to ambiguous situations without a clear "correct" answer (Hauhart & Grahe, 2015), while working with live project clients and working through client interaction and customer validation opportunities. The capstone course made use of several high-impact strategies (Kuh, 2008), which will be elaborated in the next section, to support students in delivering good work products for their clients.

In a capstone course, including the case study presented here, greater emphasis is placed on working with skills, tools and technologies that are used in the workplace (Hauhart & Grahe, 2015). Thus, business students may be reactivating dormant knowledge of finance and accounting, marketing, or business law. They may be using tools such as Canva to map out customer personas, Excel to build *pro forma* financial statements, or analyzing government demographic data. In short, there are a plethora of tools and techniques that students are expected to have available, both individually and collectively within a team environment. Students begin to navigate the transition to their future professional identities here, taking on the ethics of professional practice in using the tools available, creating an opportunity to integrate generative artificial intelligence (AI) tools into a capstone environment in a natural manner.

There is a tension between the concept of academic integrity espoused here and the approach taken institutionally in the course that is the subject of this case study. From an institutional perspective, at a minimum, students are expected to comply with the institution's procedure on Student Academic Conduct, which outlines approximately 25 ways violations of the policy may occur (Southern Alberta Institute of Technology [SAIT], 2022). Formally, students are responsible for ensuring they know and comply with these policies and procedures, as well as related ones. Similarly, faculty are expected to enforce and monitor compliance with these policies and procedures. However, this removes focus from substantive engagement with students' work on behalf of capstone project clients. Thus, rather than supporting students in navigating academic integrity in a professional context, faculty are required to respond to suspected violations of this procedure. This negatively affects the quality of recommendations to project clients and students' learning because, instead of developing critical thinking and ethical reasoning skills, students are pressured to conform to a rigid set of rules that may not reflect the realities and complexities of their chosen fields. Therefore, we propose a more holistic approach to academic integrity in this context.

As previously mentioned, generative AI tools are a natural fit with the client-centred design of this capstone course, since they are likely to be used in a professional context, and the principles of academic integrity associated with their usage are emergent. These tools open a new frontier for students, faculty, and capstone project clients to consider in their learning and work.

This chapter will address common academic integrity violations and explore how the case study course may have worked to mitigate these causes in an environment that predated the widespread adoption of generative AI tools. Considering the rapid expansion of generative AI tools, this chapter will outline how subsequent offerings of the capstone course are intended to incorporate these tools to further enhance students' confidence and self-efficacy. Simultaneously, students' iteration velocity is expected to improve, resulting in improved outcomes for students, their instructors, as well as their clients. In the next section, an overview of the antecedents of academic integrity violations will be provided, along with mitigation strategies.

ACADEMIC INTEGRITY

As noted, the operational definition of academic integrity in this chapter extends beyond avoidance of academically dishonest behaviours (ENAI, 2022). However, common definitions of academic dishonesty focus on several specific behaviours: (1) failing to cite material; (2) adding superfluous citations to work; (3) unauthorized actions (e.g., copying or unauthorized disclosure) on examinations; (4) unauthorized collaboration on work; or (5) submitting work completed by others (McCabe et al., 2012). Research suggests that business students, in particular, recognize a conflict between the need for ethical behaviour in business and their actions as students (Lawson, 2004). Despite this, business students still report that they engage in academic dishonesty (Lawson, 2004), and at higher rates than their colleagues outside business schools (McCabe et al., 2012).

Simply put, students often take a utilitarian approach to academic integrity violations, reasoning that the practical benefits (i.e., passing) of academic dishonesty, outweigh the perceived consequences of these acts (Lawson, 2004). Factors that have been shown to influence academic dishonesty include gender, age, GPA, and participation in outside groups, such as sports or extracurricular activities (McCabe et al., 2012). These are generally less correlated with academic dishonesty than the institutional context within which students find themselves, including acceptance of dishonesty by peers and the severity of sanctions applied for dishonesty (McCabe & Treviño, 1997). Most importantly, faculty have the ability to influence levels of academic integrity in their classrooms by explicitly naming and discussing these issues, along with delineating the boundaries of academic integrity in their specific course context (McCabe et al., 2012). They note that an "aspirational" culture can be created by faculty, but do not fully discuss all components of that culture (McCabe et al., 2012).

One component that should be included in creating a normative culture of academic integrity is the design and structure of assessments. However, McCabe et al. pay minimal attention to this facet, merely noting that assessments that do not provide perceived value are more likely to have "shortcuts" taken (2012, p. 49). The nature of a capstone course, coming, as it does, later in a degree program, lends itself to authentic assessments, which should "reflect the tasks seen in real professions and workplaces, … [solving problems that] are complex and sustained, requiring intensive effort" (Herrington & Herrington, 2006, p. 2). Some evidence suggests that authentic assessments may improve academic integrity, because they promote student engagement (Mercer & Vogt, 2022; Miles & Foggett, 2019). Contextually, when there is relational trust between students and instructors and student agency, students are more likely to engage in behaviours that reinforce academic integrity (Minarcik & Bridges, 2015). This leads naturally into the question of academic integrity in capstone courses, since they provide fertile ground for strong relational trust and student agency.

There does not appear to be significant research evaluating academic integrity in capstone courses specifically, though a number of situational and pedagogical factors can frame students' experiences in these courses. From a situational perspective, the learning experiences within a capstone course occur against a backdrop of students preparing to graduate and transition into the workplace, which is an additional source of stress for students (Hettich, 2010). Between ambiguity, new types of interactions, and impending graduation and transition to the workplace, students may feel overwhelmed (Kanewischer et al., 2023). This stress sometimes leads students to make choices that do not conform to the norms of academic integrity (Tindall et al., 2021). These factors are exacerbated by assessment design, including high-stakes assessments (Tindall et al., 2021), which are often endemic to capstone-type courses.

From a pedagogical perspective, student agency and relational trust in the classroom mitigate the risk of academic integrity violations (Minarcik & Bridges, 2015). Additionally, mastery-oriented learning, choice in grading, iterative attempts of assessments, and problem-based learning also reduce the likelihood of academic integrity violations (Bertram Gallant, 2017). These pedagogical foundations lend themselves to a capstone course, which will be explored in the next section.

COURSE CONTEXT

The business capstone course serves as the culminating course in a 40-course, undergraduate Bachelor of Business Administration (BBA) degree sequence. Students complete this double-credit course, usually in the final 15-week semester of study, and it is scheduled in sections of 40 students with one instructor assigned per section. Six distinct majors are represented, each with their own professional norms and standards: accounting, supply chain management, human resource management, marketing, financial services, and management (SAIT, 2023).

Students work in a project-based environment with a team of approximately five students that are tasked with agency to determine the path of interest for their experience. The course allows student teams to partner with one of three types of clients: (1) instructor-sourced clients with a business challenge; (2) student-sourced clients, vetted by the instructor, with a business challenge; or (3) developing an entrepreneurial venture and working to develop a minimum viable product, complete with customer empathy and ideation. This permits students authentic learning opportunities to expand their work experience or to deep dive into the exploration, development, and validation of start-up ventures.

Due to the program's structure, students are often funneled into their major courses from the second year, meaning there are relatively few opportunities to work with colleagues from different disciplinary backgrounds. This compounds existing sources of stress for capstone students, generating situational challenges for many students: (1) the heterogeneity of their team; (2) the need to integrate concepts from prior coursework; and (3) the ambiguity of the capstone project, due to working with live project clients and customers, forcing students to transcend their disciplinary background. All three of these factors influence the anxiety and stress students face, which may increase susceptibility to academic integrity violations (Fu & Tremayne, 2022). The authors took advantage of a research opportunity to pilot a restructured version of the course, with the intent of improving client results as the primary outcome. As a secondary outcome, pedagogical and structural elements were redesigned to better support academic integrity.

As a foundational element, faculty worked to support students in managing their stress and situational challenges, by acting as mentors in this workplace-integrated learning course (Johnston & Glancey, 2022). Additional material was introduced on teamwork and conflict management, building effective client relationships, and agile project management techniques. Collectively, these were designed to help students work with teammates who brought different disciplinary perspectives to the course, model working with clients in a discovery-oriented manner, and provide techniques to manage ambiguous and evolving projects. This gives students tools to support self-efficacy and mitigate some of the stress that can lead to making poor academic choices. From there, we could lay the groundwork for pedagogical changes that supported academic integrity.

Several pedagogical factors were identified as supporting student learning and academic integrity: (1) fostering strong instructor-student relationships; (2) nurturing agency for students; (3) developing mastery-oriented approaches to assessments; and (4) providing choice in grading and assessment. To strengthen the instructor-student relationship, the demonstrated technique of instructor-as-coach was used (Bolton, 1999). The role of instructor-coach is foundational: as the name implies, the instructor assumes a dual role. While retaining the subject matter expertise of an instructor, they also assume the mindset of a coach, "building student self-confidence for the task, raising the team performance level, and building more self-sufficiency by the end of the learning period" (Bolton, 1999, p. 244). Ultimately, the goal is to provide students with the ability to believe in themselves and their abilities.

To support task ownership, students were provided agency to choose the task or project they wanted to work on, and were taught the Lean Canvas framework espoused by Maurya (2022). This framework explicitly encourages testing assumptions and working through iterations of problems and solutions, meaning that students can focus on improving the quality of their work over time, reducing the pressure to deliver a "perfect" deliverable. The design framework used to support the Lean Canvas is the similarly-iterative Double Diamond methodology, which helps students discover potential customer problems, define them, develop potential solutions to those problems, and deliver those solutions to the customer (Design Council, 2023b). Finally, students were provided choice in grading and assessment using ungrading, referring to a philosophy where grades as a control and feedback mechanism are replaced by students themselves providing their assessment of their own work (Kohn, 2020), giving students the ability to build confidence and self-efficacy (Spurlock, 2023). Of course, none of this is possible without instructor-coaches and supporting students in managing their stress and situational challenges.

During the pilot delivery of the course (during the January 2023 term), there was expanding awareness and usage of generative artificial intelligence (AI) tools, such as ChatGPT and Midjourney, so the faculty did not have an opportunity to integrate these tools into the course delivery – but intend to do so in subsequent course offerings, which is the intent of this chapter.

Lean Canvas Framework

The Lean Canvas framework is comprised of nine boxes, conventionally laid out on a letter-sized page in landscape orientation, as shown in Figure 1.

The Lean Canvas construction begins by identifying customer segments and specifying who early adopters are, and then specifying what the customers' problems are, along with their existing solutions. The unique value proposition encapsulates what makes your business solution compelling, and often uses a high-level concept (i.e., X for Y) as a pitch. The solution is fleshed out, followed by identifying how customers are reached. A high-level revenue plan and cost structure ensure the viability of the endeavour, while key metrics demonstrate the operational effectiveness of the business. Finally, the unfair advantage represents what makes the service offering distinctive, such as the company's brand or expertise. Maurya (2022) argues that the Lean Canvas should be completed quickly, updating with the results of assumption testing. In a student context, this frenetic pace is somewhat adapted to account for their competing priorities that may include (but are not limited to) other courses, employment, and commitments, but the model is (deceptively) simple enough for students to grasp at a glance – without realizing that they are integrating work across their entire knowledge base.

Figure 1. Lean canvas with fill order
(Maurya, 2019)

Double Diamond Model

The Double Diamond model is also an innovation model, which is increasingly paired with Lean Startup methodologies, including the Lean Canvas model. The two are complementary, but have different foci (Marion et al., 2021). The Double Diamond "is a visual representation of the design and innovation process. It's a simple way to describe the steps taken in any design and innovation project, irrespective of methods and tools used" (Design Council, 2023). This model is illustrated in Figure 2.

The Double Diamond by the Design Council is licensed under a CC BY 4.0 license.

The leftmost diamond comprises the processes of ideation and customer empathy, or discovery and definition. By understanding the challenges customers face, the problem is clarified; a problem is rarely what a potential customer articulates at first. Having an open mind, while difficult, is a necessity in this process. From there, the definition phase works to redefine the customer's problem. As a simple example, if we were looking to improve public transportation in a city, we could survey transit users and non-transit users, supplementing this with data on travel times and bottlenecks. Then, using that information, we might discover that there isn't enough service at off-peak hours such as nights or weekends, the buses aren't particularly clean, and schedule adherence is problematic.

Figure 2. Double diamond model
(Design Council, 2023b)

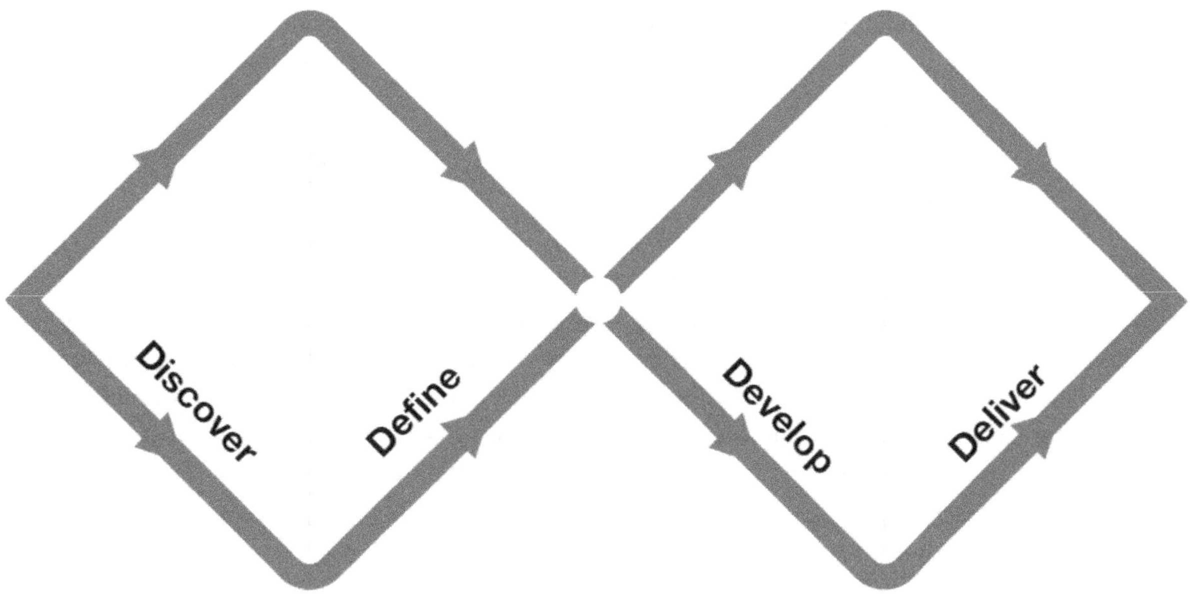

The rightmost diamond works to refine the problem definition and propose solutions, or in the Design Council vernacular, the develop and deliver phases. Here, we might propose trialing off-peak service, adding trash receptacles by bus doors, and offering real-time tracking for buses. These solutions are developed via brainstorming, exploring other jurisdictions, and working with (potential) customers directly. In the delivery phase, these can be tested on a small scale and data can be gathered to test their effectiveness. This iterative approach may reveal that trash receptacles alone are not sufficient to keep the buses clean, or that real-time tracking may not be an adequate replacement for reducing headway between buses.

Designing a Course to Incorporate the Double Diamond Model

In the pilot iteration of the course, students faced challenges in mastering two core processes: customer empathy and ideation. Upholding the principles of academic integrity, which demand compliance with ethical and professional standards, is crucial in this learning context. Since the instructor-coach is not present in meetings with students and their clients, it becomes imperative for students to independently apply these values in their interactions and decision-making, which helps ensure that students' learning and the subsequent outputs from these processes are genuinely reflective of their understanding and ethical practice. Faculty, relying on discussions with student teams and their process outputs, must foster an environment that encourages these standards of integrity, despite the challenges in directly overseeing the students' learning journey.

In the context of customer empathy, students often prematurely narrowed their focus, either by not critically analyzing the broader context or hastily diagnosing a problem without fully understanding its nuances. For example, when a team of students faced an extraordinarily complex destination tourism scenario involving intricate financing transactions, their failure to recognize the complexity of financing as a pivotal challenge led to underwhelming client interactions. This highlights a missed opportunity for applying the principles of academic integrity by thoroughly investigating all aspects of the problem. Additionally, students' reluctance to engage with potential customers outside their personal networks indicates a gap in applying ethical and professional standards in market analysis and prototype validation. These challenges underscore the need for more effective coaching and tool support to help students adhere to the principles of academic integrity in their learning process.

One of the challenges that teams face in ideation is crafting a broad and diverse array of solutions to identified problems. Demonstrating academic integrity during this process is crucial, and can be done by identifying potential solutions, showing how they build on prior work, respecting the principles of originality and acknowledgment of sources. In collaboration with instructor-coaches, teams are encouraged to shift their perspectives on the problems, fostering the generation of a wider range of ideas and thus enhancing their self-efficacy. For instance, a team that wants to improve recycling adherence on campus should consider the existing recycling infrastructure and can also extend their thinking to a full lifecycle approach, under the guidance of their instructor-coach. With an expanded perspective, they can consider incentivizing reusable mug usage, implementing crockery and utensils in food service outlets, or using attendants to sort waste in cafeterias.

Another challenge teams face is being able to empathize with the perspective of an intended customer. For example, the destination tourism team took a "Field of Dreams" (if you build it, they will come) approach to their solution, focusing on a singular solution, without considering the diverse preferences of multiple customer groups. This approach did not bring a comprehensive understanding of the customer base, but working with an instructor-coach, students can learn to use data effectively to understand customer personas, integrating this information with publicly available data, such as Statistics Canada, and survey data. This approach not only enhances their understanding and self-efficacy but also reinforces their skills in academic integrity by ensuring their analysis and innovations are grounded and complete. These challenges and the opportunities they present for enhanced coaching models underscore the importance of integrating academic integrity into the learning process, ensuring that students develop solutions that are not only innovative but also ethically and professionally responsible.

From an academic integrity perspective, several different challenges are illustrated in these processes: (1) students need to develop the ability to independently apply their ethical values; (2) premature focus and inadequate analysis; (3) insufficient customer empathy; (4) not acknowledging prior work; and (5) not leveraging appropriate information sources. Instructor-coaches can work with students to develop these skills, and support students in iteratively developing their ideas, which allows the students to recognize that their initial ideas can always be improved. In the next section, the role of iteration in both innovation models and academic integrity is explored.

THE ROLE OF ITERATION

Iteration, as noted previously, supports both innovation and academic integrity; it is explicit in the Double Diamond model (Design Council, 2023b), and is a pedagogical intervention that supports academic integrity (Bertram Gallant, 2017). In the Double Diamond model, iteration allows for continuous refinement and improvement of solutions, fostering a deeper understanding and more creative outcomes. This process involves repeated cycles of discovery, definition, development, and delivery, ensuring that the final product is both innovative and user-centred. Similarly, in the context of academic integrity, iteration plays a crucial role. It encourages students to engage in a continuous learning process, where they can develop their ideas and understandings over time. This approach reduces the temptation to engage in academic shortcuts, promoting a more genuine and thorough exploration of subjects. Iteration, therefore, not only enhances the quality of academic work but also instills a culture of honesty and ethical practice, which can extend beyond academic context into the workplace.

Two significant challenges to implementing iterative approaches in an academic context include students' meta-cognitive skills (i.e., their ability to critically evaluate their work) and faculty time and energy. Since part of the goal of a capstone course is to replicate work situations without definitive answers, helping students build their meta-cognition skills is a key task of the instructor-coach (Bolton, 1999). The instructor-coach plays a vital role in guiding students to reflect on their learning processes, encouraging them to question, evaluate, and adjust their strategies for better outcomes. However, this level of personalized guidance demands substantial time and energy from faculty, who must balance this intensive coaching with their other academic responsibilities. Potential solutions include peer feedback, but this is challenging, given the disparate contexts within which student teams are operating, as well as the confidentiality inherent in working with live project clients. Sharing feedback with multiple groups at once might help, but this also limits the transferability of feedback.

The goal of iterative work in both an innovation context and an academic context is to improve iteration velocity, as the more ideas students have, the more likely it is that one or more, or some combination thereof, will be better than others. This acceleration in generating and refining ideas not only enhances the quality of solutions but also fosters a culture of continuous improvement and innovation. In the Double Diamond model, rapid iteration enables teams to quickly test hypotheses, learn from mistakes, and evolve their ideas in response to real-world feedback. Academically, this process cultivates critical thinking and problem-solving skills, as students learn to rapidly adapt and refine their thoughts based on new information and insights. Furthermore, increased iteration velocity encourages resilience and adaptability, qualities essential for success in both academic and professional spheres. Ultimately, by prioritizing the speed and efficiency of iterative work, students can develop a more agile and proactive approach to learning and problem-solving, preparing them for the complexities and dynamics they will face in the workplace. Generative AI tools can be used to increase iteration velocity, to which we now turn.

A ROLE FOR GENERATIVE AI

With the release of ChatGPT on November 30, 2022, generative AI chatbots became more generally available to the public (Hines, 2023). Microsoft's Bing was released on February 22, 2023, and competing products from Anthropic (Claude) and Google (Bard) were released in March 2023 (Hines, 2023). These tools can develop contextually-appropriate responses to a diverse array of prompts, showcasing their adaptability and depth of understanding. This makes them particularly valuable in Design Thinking frameworks, especially in educational settings like capstone courses. In such contexts, these tools can facilitate brainstorming sessions, offering diverse perspectives and prompting creative thinking. They can also assist in the iterative process of the Double Diamond model by providing rapid feedback and suggestions, enabling students to refine their ideas and approaches more efficiently. Moreover, their capacity to simulate various stakeholder viewpoints can be instrumental in developing empathy – a core aspect of applying the Double Diamond model. By integrating these AI tools into capstone projects, educators can enhance the learning experience, providing students with a unique opportunity to interact with cutting-edge technology while also nurturing their problem-solving and critical thinking skills. Although, as with any new tool, there are new skills needed to use them efficiently and effectively.

New Skills Required to Use Generative AI

Prior to using generative AI tools to augment student and faculty experiences in future iterations of the capstone course, we need a basic understanding of the emergent skills required to effectively use these tools. Three primary skills required to use these tools effectively include: (1) prompt engineering, which is the set of principles and practices regarding the design and structure of prompts made to generative AI tools; (2) an awareness of the ethical considerations associated with using the tools, including understanding the sources of data for the tools, as well as the considerations associated with securing the data and information used to prompt the tool; and (3) an awareness of the strengths and limitations of the available tools. Different tools have different underlying models, which influence their abilities to respond to certain types of prompts.

Prompt engineering is defined as "the practice of designing and refining specific text prompts to guide transformer-based language models … in generating desired outputs." (Takyar, 2023). The goal of prompt engineering is to allow generative AI tools to progressively iterate towards a desired outcome, which is particularly salient for more complex problems requiring a chain of reasoning (Takyar, 2023). For generative AI chatbots, or Large Language Models (LLMs), providing the LLM with information about the role or persona to be adopted when considering the input, the context and constraints associated with the problem to be solved, and a description of the desired output supports improved usability of outputs (Takyar, 2023). Table 1 demonstrates one possible framework for prompting a generative AI chatbot.

Until recently, generative AI tools have not made a significant impact, because data is their fuel, and there was not enough data available to train the tools. Text-based tools such as ChatGPT, Bing, and Bard rely upon having large quantities of human-generated text to draw upon when constructing their models. These texts have been sourced (or "scraped") from a variety of sources, including websites like X (formerly Twitter), Reddit, Stack Overflow and others ("Digging For Digits," 2023). Image generation tools such as DALL-E and Midjourney similarly rely upon a corpus of designs and artwork, such as material found on websites like Shutterstock and others ("Digging For Digits," 2023). As many students have discovered, the mere presence of information on the internet does not abrogate creators' intellectual property rights, save under appropriate licensing (e.g., Creative Commons licenses or public-domain

Table 1. Generative AI chatbot prompt framework (extends Takyar, 2023)

Prompt Component	Rationale
Role	By defining the role the chatbot is asked to adopt, this helps the chatbot "understand" its context and knowledge base. Various roles might be used, depending on what is to be done. For example, it may be appropriate to have Tim Brown, a Design Thinking pioneer, critique aspects of a design. Or, it may be helpful to understand a specific customer segment when evaluating a proposed solution to a problem.
Request	Explaining the request helps the chatbot determine what it is to do, whether it is to critique, evaluate, engage in a role play, brainstorm, refine, or create. Requests should be stated positively, rather than negatively.
Request Context	What constraints are placed on the request? Consider cost, materials, legislation, integration with existing products or services, etc.
Output	How should the chatbot output its work? Consider the format – an interactive dialogue, a table, bullet points, etc.

licenses). As a result, there are serious and unresolved questions regarding the provenance of material used to train generative AI models, as well as the exploitation of humans who review and classify inputs and outputs to these systems (Williams et al., 2022).

As an additional consideration, generative AI tools, by their very nature, use the information provided to them in prompts to augment their transformer models. This means, effectively, that no information provided as input into a generative AI tool should be considered secure, since these inputs augment subsequent versions of the model ("Digging For Digits," 2023). At minimum, great care needs to be taken to consider the commercial sensitivity or privacy implications of data fed into these models, which is different from using non-generative AI computing applications, such as cloud computing office productivity tools. Of course, from an academic integrity perspective, disclosing material uses of these tools should also be discussed (Committee on Publication Ethics, 2023).

There are many publicly-available generative AI models, including commercially-supported ones and open-source models, such as LLaMA, LLaMA 2, Alpaca, and Falcon (Sahota, 2023). Depending on how the models are implemented, there are strengths and limitations endemic to each model. As a simple example, ChatGPT's training data ends sometime in 2021, whereas Bing has access to the internet, and can combine this information with its training model to return results that might otherwise be outside the scope of its training data (Alston, 2023). Google's Bard model, in certain configurations, can draw upon material in Gmail and Google Docs (Pinsky, 2023), which enables greater contextual sensitivity in its responses. Visual generative AI models include DALL-E 2, Midjourney, and Stable Diffusion, with varying degrees of ease of use and customization; each has its preferred use cases (Guinness, 2023).

One of the most fundamental concepts of generative AI models is that they are just that, generative. Thus, because they have evolving models, and have randomness built in, their output cannot be replicated directly (Mollick & Mollick, 2023). Transparency can be achieved by documenting the generative AI prompts and describing or summarizing the outputs, as demonstrated in some of the early papers in this field (e.g., McGee, 2023; Mollick & Mollick, 2023). Generative AI users must learn to document their workflow and document it in a consistent manner; an emergent practice is to do so in a manner akin to a systematic literature review protocol (Tranfield et al., 2003). With this baseline understanding of the new skills required for effective use of generative AI tools, we can proceed to integrating AI tools into the capstone course workflow, by way of a case study.

A team of students in the capstone course tackled the challenge of improving coffee cup recycling adherence on campus. They chose this opportunity based on their own experiences of struggling to identify which components of a takeout coffee, with cup, lid, and cardboard sleeve, were recyclable in which bins. The campus has several different purveyors of coffee, and three- or four-bin recycling stations were located strategically throughout the campus. Three-bin recycling stations had bins for refundable beverage containers, paper, plastics, and other recyclable materials, and garbage. Four-bin stations added an organics bin. Each bin was labeled with pictographic signage both above the bin and on the bin proper. The campus has approximately 15,000 students enrolled, with an additional 2,000 faculty and staff. Occupancy peaks from approximately 7:00 AM to 3:00 PM weekdays, and there are fewer occupants during the evenings and weekends. Additionally, members of the public taking continuing education programming tend to use the campus outside peak occupancy hours. We will now demonstrate the potential to apply generative AI tools across the Double Diamond innovation process of discovery, definition, development, and delivery.

Using Generative AI to Accelerate Discovery

In the case study scenario, the students identified that recycling adherence of coffee cups (and their constituent components) was lower than they felt appropriate. This problem was identified from personal experience and observations of various locations on campus. The problem is quite specific in its formulation and may needlessly bind students to a potential solution. In the discovery phase of the Double Diamond framework for innovation, we seek to understand the problem, by observing and speaking to those affected by the potential problem (Design Council, 2023a).

To further validate whether this problem is worthy of tackling, additional observations would be appropriate—examining "successful" recyclers and "unsuccessful" ones, and perhaps having conversations with members of each group to better understand the incentives, motivations, and barriers associated with task completion. Several questions emerge from this problem formulation: (1) Are disposable coffee cups the most important contaminant in recycling bins? (2) What are the characteristics of a disposable coffee cup that make it difficult to recycle correctly? (3) What are the characteristics of the recycling station and bins that contribute to lower levels of recycling adherence? There are obviously many others, but, assuming the problem is well-formulated, we can see how there are multiple ways to address it.

We can use generative AI tools to stress-test the data that has been gathered, by asking what the commonalities of "successful" recyclers are or inverting the question to better-understand the usual challenges faced by unsuccessful recyclers. We can ask what data might be missing from our observations so that

Table 2. Generative AI chatbot prompts to aid discovery (OpenAI, 2023)

Prompt	Explanation / Representative Result
You are a design team member working to improve coffee cup recycling adherence on a post-secondary institution campus using the Double Diamond framework. You have identified that disposable coffee cups, coffee cup lids, and cardboard sleeves are often discarded as garbage, rather than appropriately recycled. Recycling stations have either three bins (refundable beverage containers, paper, plastics and other recyclable materials, and garbage) or four bins (adding an organics bin). Bins are labeled with pictographic signage above the bin and on the bin itself.	This component of the prompt is common to each of the prompts below and clearly identifies the role ("design team member") and constraints ("post-secondary institution campus" and "Double Diamond.") This component of the prompt is common to each of the prompts below, and identifies the task context ("disposable coffee cups", "recycling stations," and "bin design").
Provide me five ways to determine whether or not we should focus on disposable coffee cups when working to improve recycling adherence.	To determine whether focusing on disposable coffee cups is the right approach to improve recycling adherence, you can employ the following five methods: Data Analysis: Analyze data on the consumption of disposable coffee cups on campus. Compare this with the overall recycling rate of these cups. If there is a high consumption but low recycling rate, it indicates a need to focus on improving adherence for coffee cups. […] [Other options include a] Waste Audit … Surveys and Interviews … [an] Observational Study … [or] Stakeholder Engagement. […] After employing these methods, you can use the insights gathered to make an informed decision on whether focusing on disposable coffee cups is the most effective strategy to improve recycling adherence on campus. Additionally, the Double Diamond framework can further assist in developing and refining solutions based on the findings.

we can formulate the problem most effectively – this is the approach taken in the preceding paragraph. Prompts to accomplish this, and representative results, are shown below in Table 2.

We have omitted prompts to evaluate what characteristics of disposable coffee cups, recycling stations, and the recycling bins proper make recycling adherence difficult, but they take the form "What are the characteristics of <x> that make it difficult to recycle them correctly / improve recycling adherence?" By coaching students to develop these prompts and iterate through information, it should help them generate more ideas, take alternative perspectives, and provide potential insights into problem constraints. This approach is in line with the discovery phase of the Double Diamond model, which emphasizes the importance of open exploration and understanding the problem space. In this phase, students are encouraged to conduct broad research and engage in divergent thinking to gather a wide range of insights and perspectives. This involves exploring the environmental, social, and practical factors influencing recycling behaviors, examining user interactions with recycling systems, and considering the design and placement of recycling bins and stations. By immersing themselves in the context of the problem, students can uncover underlying issues and opportunities that might not be immediately apparent. This thorough exploration sets a strong foundation for the subsequent stages of the Double Diamond model, where these insights are synthesized and used to inform more focused ideation and development.

Using Generative AI to Accelerate Definition

Depending on how students formulate the problem of improving recycling adherence, they may focus on the disposable coffee cups themselves, on the design, signage, and locations of recycling stations, or the characteristics of the bins themselves. It may even be possible to step back out and take a whole systems perspective. Effective discovery should generate a high volume of information that requires sift-

Table 3. Generative AI chatbot prompts to aid design (OpenAI, 2023)

Prompt	Explanation / Representative Result
You are a design team member… You have identified that disposable coffee cups, coffee cup lids, and cardboard sleeves are often discarded as garbage…	This component of the prompt is common to each of the prompts below and clearly identifies the role and constraints. This component of the prompt is common to each of the prompts below, and identifies the task context.
You have completed a data analysis that identifies that only about 30% of disposable coffee cups used on campus are found in recycling bins. You have also talked to "unsuccessful" recyclers, and they let you know that the need to rinse out the disposable coffee cups is a big barrier to recycling the coffee cups. Please suggest five ideas to improve recycling adherence, knowing these facts.	Given the insights from your data analysis and user feedback in a post-secondary institution context, here are five ideas to improve recycling adherence for disposable coffee cups: Rinse Stations: Install dedicated rinse stations near the recycling bins. These stations should be equipped with a water dispenser and a catch basin for easy rinsing of cups. Clear signage can guide users on how to quickly rinse their cups. This directly addresses the barrier of needing to rinse cups and makes it a more convenient process. Improved Signage: Revise the current pictographic signage to be more explicit about the need to rinse cups. Use clear, engaging visuals that show the separation of the cup, lid, and sleeve, and the rinsing process. Consider using humour or relatable content to engage the student population. […] [Other options include an] Educational Campaign … Recycling Ambassadors … [or a] Feedback Loop … [or] Stakeholder Engagement. […] Implementing these strategies requires a multifaceted approach, addressing both the practical barriers to recycling and the need for ongoing education and engagement within the campus community.

ing through to challenge the problem definition. Imagine that students have discovered that only about 30% of disposable coffee cups dispensed on campus are recycled, and that most "unsuccessful" recyclers ignore the need to rinse out their coffee cups before recycling them. Using generative AI tools, they may be able to do some preliminary analysis and definition of possible solutions to the problem identified. Prompts to accomplish this, and representative output, are shown below in Table 3.

We have omitted prompts to evaluate data from a waste audit, an observational study, or stakeholder interviews (from Table 2 above), but they take a similar form to the "You have…" prompts above. As part of the design phase of the Double Diamond process, teams are working through the large quantities of data and observations they have made. Generative AI prompts are instrumental in this phase, assisting teams in sifting through and making sense of the extensive information collected. They enable teams to organize and prioritize data, identify patterns and trends, and generate hypotheses about effective recycling strategies. In this phase, the focus shifts from broad exploration to converging on specific design solutions. The AI's capability to process and analyze large datasets can significantly streamline this transition, guiding teams to distil the most pertinent insights and apply them to their design thinking. This allows teams to move into the next phase of the Double Diamond model – development.

Using Generative AI to Accelerate Development and Delivery

In the development phase of the Double Diamond model, attention shifts to developing ways to pilot the identified ideas. Here, we look to define a Minimum Viable Product (MVP), which Ries (2011) defines as an innovation that gathers the maximum amount of "validated learning" about a customer with the least effort. Sketches, diagrams, and simple prototypes are the tools of choice – which does not initially seem to be the language of text-based generative AI. However, by adapting the use cases for the tools, students can both generate and critique images. For instance, the rinse stations and the improved signage ideas in Table 3 could be conceptualized through diagrams, developed using traditional tools like Adobe Illustrator or Canva, or mocked up using an AI-driven tool such as DALL-E or Midjourney. Additionally, some generative AI tools have image analysis features, enabling students to critique photographs or designs with a high degree of sophistication. Representative ChatGPT and DALL-E prompts are provided below in Table 4 and demonstrate how these tools can be effectively utilized in this phase.

We have omitted further prompts to develop the signage using generative AI tools and evaluate them in context, for example, at or near recycling stations or rinse stations, but they follow a similar structure to the previous prompts. The ability to critique imagery through generative AI tools also extends to evaluating photographs or other user-created imagery. This process allows students to refine their designs and prototypes with a critical eye, ensuring they align with the project's objectives and user needs.

As the process transitions into the delivery phase of the Double Diamond model, the focus becomes about finalizing and implementing the solutions. The delivery phase involves taking the refined prototypes and prepared designs and turning them into actionable and practical solutions. In this stage, the role of generative AI shifts from ideation and development to support in implementation.

As pilot solutions are shifted into delivery mode, generative AI becomes an invaluable tool in realizing the practical application of the project's outcomes. For instance, AI can be used to support fine-tuning the details of prototypes and designs, ensuring they are both aesthetically-pleasing and functionally effective. For example, several variations of signage can easily be created, enabling large-scale A/B testing of pilot options. As implemented solutions are deployed, we continue to evaluate user feedback to evaluate and refine them. In this way, the delivery phase is not merely the conclusion of the process

Table 4. Generative AI chatbot prompts to aid development (OpenAI, 2023)

Prompt	Explanation / Representative Result
Generate a line art drawing with an exploded view of a disposable coffee cup showing the lid, cup, and cardboard sleeve. The lid should be shown discarded into a garbage can. The rinsed cup and cardboard sleeve should be shown being placed into a recycle bin and provide the gen_id.	By defining what is to be generated in terms of style of output and the distinct components needed in the diagram, this increases the likelihood of getting usable results. The gen_id is an internal parameter that (usually) identifies a specific combination of parameters to produce a given image.
Critique the effectiveness of the line art drawing in conveying the message that the lid is garbage, the cup should be rinsed before recycling, and the cardboard sleeve should be recycled. Update the image in accordance with your critique, and provide the gen_id.	By staying within the same context window, ChatGPT can evaluate its own work and provide appropriate feedback. To critique the effectiveness of the line art drawing, I'll consider a few key aspects: Clarity of Components: The drawing effectively separates the components of the coffee cup – the lid, cup, and cardboard sleeve. This is important for understanding that each part has a different disposal method. Disposal Indicators: The image shows the lid being discarded into the garbage and the cup and sleeve being placed in a recycling bin. This visually communicates the different disposal methods. However, the action of rinsing the cup might need to be more emphasized to ensure it's clearly understood as a necessary step before recycling. Simplicity and Focus: The minimalistic style aids in focusing on the message without unnecessary distractions. However, ensuring that each action (throwing the lid away, rinsing the cup, and recycling the sleeve) is distinct and easy to interpret is crucial. Instructional Effectiveness: As an instructional tool, it's vital that each step in the process is clear and unambiguous. Adding arrows or brief text labels might enhance understanding, especially for the rinsing step. Based on this critique, I'll create an updated version of the drawing that emphasizes the rinsing of the cup more clearly and consider adding simple instructional aids like arrows or text. Let's generate the updated image.

but a gateway to continuous improvement. The Double Diamond model, therefore, does not end with delivery; instead, it cycles back to the discovery phase, where new insights and learnings inform the next iteration of the project. This cyclical nature ensures that solutions remain dynamic and responsive to evolving needs and contexts, embodying the essence of Design Thinking's adaptive and user-centred approach. In the next section, we weave together the collective impact of the full suite of pedagogical and AI interventions that will support academic integrity.

INTEGRATING AI, ITERATION, COACHING AND UNGRADING FOR ACADEMIC INTEGRITY

Much of the discussion above has focused on how artificial intelligence can support iteration velocity, brainstorming, idea evaluation, and be used to better integrate both divergent and convergent perspectives in innovation processes. However, in the absence of a framework that prioritizes student investment in achieving learning outcomes, it is likely that the use of generative AI tools will be clandestine—and, more importantly, suboptimal. Imagine planting a garden and not providing nutrients, sunlight, and water – the plants might grow, but they are not likely to reach their full potential. The new skills of prompt engineering, ethical awareness, and evaluation skills required by generative AI are distinct, and act as the nutrients, sunlight, and water for users of generative AI.

As can be seen from the representative prompts and outputs provided, a major advantage of generative AI models is iteration velocity. Some of the ideas may need to be cross-pollinated to maximize their innovative properties, and this reinforces one of the key tenets of innovation processes – that divergent thinking is inherent, and may (more than) occasionally generate a few "clunkers" of ideas. The process of learning how to use new tools that can accelerate the creation and evaluation of ideas should engender greater attachment and investment in students' ideas and show students that generative AI tools are intriguing tools that can be used for much good. This also allows instructor-coaches to more rapidly generate ideas with students and provide feedback similarly rapidly, accelerating students' learning. This enables students to shift their focus to a processual view of innovation. From there, iterative deliverables are a logical next step, and an instructor-coach perspective helps evaluate (*qua* instructor) the technical merits of a solution and guide (*qua* coach) students in their next steps. Further, given the very human limitations of an instructor-coach, having students learn to use generative AI to perform some of the evaluative functions will help hone their critical thinking skills and improve their final client-facing product.

More importantly, like any other tool, the tools' users are responsible for their usage. In order to incentivize a growth mindset in the use of the tools, the structure of the course also needs to shift. By shifting grading towards ungrading, it provides students with a measure of psychological safety to take risks, and enables them to then focus on the *process* of innovating, rather than the *results* of innovating. Ultimately, generative AI tools are accretive to existing practices, and by combining an effective instructional design and pedagogy foundation with generative AI tools, it is much easier to engender students' attachment and investment in their process, leading to a reduced likelihood of academic integrity issues.

CONCLUSION

In conclusion, the adoption of generative AI technologies in academic settings, when aligned with methodologies that support students and promote academic integrity, offers a multifaceted approach to education. This integration not only addresses known causes of academic misconduct but also provides students with invaluable practical experiences. These experiences include developing sh*tty first drafts, as described by Lamott (1995), engaging in prompt engineering, and honing skills in seeking and receiving critiques and feedback. As AI-enabled tools continue to evolve, the collaborative efforts between instructors and students in researching, evaluating, and trialing these tools will be instrumental in building students' research and evaluation skills.

From the instructors' perspective, the primary goal extends beyond merely reducing cases of academic misconduct. This initiative opens avenues for fostering stronger, more meaningful relationships with students. Instructors, alongside their students, will develop skills in prompt engineering and critiquing, enhancing their pedagogical toolkit. This process not only benefits the students but also clients who become aware of the potential of generative AI, possibly gaining skills in its use. Such an approach encourages a role reversal where students mentor clients, thereby increasing their self-efficacy. This dynamic interaction is likely to lead to a systematic, repeatable, and rapid learning process that promotes self-sufficiency and reinforces self-efficacy, a key predictor of academic honesty.

Looking ahead, the future of AI in education is one of continuous evolution and adaptation. As AI technologies advance, so too must our strategies for integrating them into educational contexts. This requires a commitment to ongoing research, interdisciplinary collaboration, and open. By staying informed and agile, we can harness the power of AI to create more engaging, inclusive, and effective learning environments.

In essence, the journey towards integrating generative AI in education is one of cautious optimism. While embracing the innovative potential of AI, we must remain steadfast in our commitment to academic integrity, ethical practice, and the holistic development of students. By doing so, we can ensure that AI serves as a catalyst for educational excellence, preparing students not only for academic success but also for the challenges and opportunities of an increasingly digital world. The ultimate outcome of this integration would likely be a transformative educational experience that emphasizes self-efficacy, practical skill development, and a deeper, more collaborative relationship between students and instructors, ultimately serving clients.

REFERENCES

Alston, E. (2023). *ChatGPT vs. Bing Chat: Which AI chatbot should you use?* Zapier. https://zapier.com/blog/chatgpt-vs-bing-chat/

Bertram Gallant, T. (2017). Academic Integrity as a Teaching & Learning Issue: From Theory to Practice. *Theory into Practice*, *56*(2), 88–94. doi:10.1080/00405841.2017.1308173

Bolton, M. K. (1999). The role of coaching in student teams: A "just-in-time" approach to learning. *Journal of Management Education*, *23*(3), 233–250. doi:10.1177/105256299902300302

Committee on Publication Ethics. (2023). *Authorship and AI Tools*. Publication Ethics. https://publicationethics.org/cope-position-statements/ai-author

Design Council. (2023a). *Framework for Innovation*. Design Council. https://www.designcouncil.org.uk/our-resources/framework-for-innovation/

Design Council. (2023b). *The Double Diamond*. Design Council. https://www.designcouncil.org.uk/our-resources/the-double-diamond/

Digging For Digits. (2023). *The Economist, 448*(9359), 57–58.

European Network for Academic Integrity (ENAI). (2022, September 20). *Academic Integrity*. ENAI. https://www.academicintegrity.eu/wp/glossary/academic-integrity/

Fu, K. W., & Tremayne, K. S. (2022). Self-efficacy and self-control mediate the relationship between negative emotions and attitudes toward plagiarism. *Journal of Academic Ethics*, *20*(4), 457–477. https://doi-org.library.smu.ca/10.1007/s10805-021-09415-3. doi:10.1007/s10805-021-09415-3

Guinness, H. (2023). *The best AI image generators in 2023*. Zapier. https://zapier.com/blog/best-ai-image-generator/

Hauhart, R. C., & Grahe, J. E. (2015). *Designing and teaching undergraduate capstone courses*. John Wiley & Sons.

Herrington, A., & Herrington, J. (2006). What is an Authentic Learning Environment? In A. Herrington & J. Herrington (Eds.), *Authentic Learning Environments in Higher Education* (pp. 1–14). Idea Group, Inc. doi:10.4018/978-1-59140-594-8.ch001

Hettich, P. I. (2010). College-to-workplace transitions: Becoming a freshman again. In T. W. Miller (Ed.), *Handbook of stressful transitions across the lifespan* (pp. 87–109). Springer. doi:10.1007/978-1-4419-0748-6_5

Hines, K. (2023, June 4). History Of ChatGPT: A Timeline Of The Meteoric Rise Of Generative AI Chatbots. *Search Engine Journal*. https://www.searchenginejournal.com/history-of-chatgpt-timeline/488370/

Johnston, S. L., & Glancey, M. (2022). Integrating Mentorship in Workplace-Integrated Learning Curriculum. *Papers on Postsecondary Learning and Teaching*, *5*, 34–41. doi:10.11575/pplt.v5i.73163

Kanewischer, B., Johnston, S. L., Lyndon, J., & Glancey, M. (2023). Emotional discomfort as a catalyst for breaking through students' self-perceived capabilities. In P. Kumar, T. Culham, R. J. Major, & R. Peregoy (Eds.), Honing self-awareness of faculty and future business leaders: Emotions connected with teaching and learning (pp. 7–21). Emerald Publishers. doi:10.1108/978-1-80262-349-920231001

Kohn, A. (2020). Foreword. In S. D. Blum (Ed.), *Ungrading: Why rating students undermines learning (and what to do instead)* (pp. xiii–xxiii). West Virginia University Press.

Kuh, G. D. (2008). *High-Impact Educational Practices: What They Are, Who Has Access to Them, and Why They Matter*. Association of American Colleges and Universities.

Lawson, R. A. (2004). Is classroom cheating related to business students' propensity to cheat in the "real world"? *Journal of Business Ethics*, *49*(2), 189–199. doi:10.1023/B:BUSI.0000015784.34148.cb

Marion, T., Cannon, D., Reid, T., & McGowan, A.-M. (2021). A conceptual model for integrating design thinking and lean startup methods into the innovation process. *Proceedings of the Design Society*, *1*, 31–40. doi:10.1017/pds.2021.4

Maurya, A. (2022). *Running Lean: Iterate from Plan A to a Plan That Works* (3rd ed.). O'Reilly.

McCabe, D. L., Butterfield, K. D., & Treviño, L. K. (2012). *Cheating in college: Why students do it and what educators can do about it*. JHU Press. doi:10.1353/book.18818

McCabe, D. L., & Treviño, L. K. (1997). Individual and contextual influences on academic dishonesty: A multicampus investigation. *Research in Higher Education*, *38*(3), 379–396. doi:10.1023/A:1024954224675

McGeeR. W. (2023). Is chat gpt biased against conservatives? An empirical study. Social Science Research Network. doi:10.2139/ssrn.4359405

MercerB.VogtL. (2022). Getting off the Beaten Path: Authentic Assessments That Enhance Teaching, Learning, and Academic Integrity. *Canadian Perspectives on Academic Integrity, 5*(1), 32. doi:10.11575/cpai.v5i1.75129

Miles, C. A., & Foggett, K. A. (2019, July 2). *Designing Authentic Assessments to Assure Student Success, Employability, and Academic Integrity*. Higher Education Research and Development Society of Australasia, Auckland, NZ. https://bpb-ap-se2.wpmucdn.com/blogs.auckland.ac.nz/dist/2/372/files/2019/02/Designing-authentic-assessments-to-assure-student-success-employability-and-academic-integrity-11roq1e.pdf

Minarcik, J., & Bridges, A. J. (2015). Psychology graduate students weigh in: Qualitative analysis of academic dishonesty and suggestion prevention strategies. *Journal of Academic Ethics*, *13*(2), 197–216. doi:10.1007/s10805-015-9230-x

MollickE. R.MollickL. (2023). Using AI to implement effective teaching strategies in classrooms: Five strategies, including prompts. Social Science Research Network. doi:10.2139/ssrn.4391243

Open A. I. (2023). ChatGPT 4.0 (September 25, 2023 version) [Large Language Model]. OPEN AI. https://chat.openai.com/?model=gpt-4

Pinsky, Y. (2023). *Bard Can Now Connect to Your Google Apps and Services*. https://blog.google/products/bard/google-bard-new-features-update-sept-2023

Ries, E. (2011). *The Lean Startup*. Crown Books.

Sahota, H. (2023). *Top 10 List of Large Language Models Reshaping the Open-Source Arena in 2023*. DECI. https://deci.ai/blog/list-of-large-language-models-in-open-source/

Southern Alberta Institute of Technology [SAIT]. (2022). *AC 3.4.3 Student Academic Conduct Schedule A - Examples of Student Academic Misconduct*. Sait. https://www.sait.ca/assets/documents/about-sait/policies-and-procedures/academic-student/ac-3-4-3-schedule-a.pdf

Southern Alberta Institute of Technology [SAIT]. (2023). Bachelor of Business Administration. https://www.sait.ca/programs-and-courses/degrees/bachelor-of-business-administration

Spurlock, S. (2023). Improving Student Motivation by Ungrading. *Proceedings of the 54th ACM Technical Symposium on Computer Science Education,* (*vol. 1*, pp. 631–637). ACM. 10.1145/3545945.3569747

Takyar, A. (2023). *Bridging the AI-Human Communication Gap: A Comprehensive Guide to Prompt Engineering*. Leeway Hertz. https://www.leewayhertz.com/prompt-engineering/

Tindall, I. K., Fu, K. W., Tremayne, K., & Curtis, G. J. (2021). Can negative emotions increase students' plagiarism and cheating? *International Journal for Educational Integrity*, *17*(1), 1–16. doi:10.1007/s40979-021-00093-7

Tranfield, D., Denyer, D., & Smart, P. (2003). Towards a methodology for developing evidence-informed management knowledge by means of systematic review. *British Journal of Management*, *14*(3), 207–222. doi:10.1111/1467-8551.00375

Williams, A., Miceli, M., & Gebru, T. (2022). The Exploited Labor Behind Artificial Intelligence. *Noema*. https://www.noemamag.com/the-exploited-labor-behind-artificial-intelligence/

Chapter 7
Exploring the Profound Impact of AI on Higher Education and Students:
Shaping Tomorrow's Workforce

Amy Emanuel
https://orcid.org/0009-0001-6077-7538
Christian Heritage College, Australia

David H. Stone
https://orcid.org/0009-0009-2911-2392
Christian Heritage College, Australia

ABSTRACT

Recent advances in artificial intelligence (AI) and generative artificial intelligence (GenAI) are beginning and will continue to have a profound impact on industry and higher education (HE). This chapter presents an overview of the relationship between AI, industry, and HE with a focus on higher education institutions (HEI) and students who are beginning to navigate the implications of AI. Following a review of global HE institution's approaches and responses to GenAI, the current impact of AI on student's education journeys and their preparedness for an AI ready world is explored through a review of the opportunities and challenges AI presents, resulting in a thematic framework for HE institution considerations for traversing this new terrain.

INTRODUCTION

Artificial intelligence (AI), or more specifically Generative Artificial Intelligence (GenAI), offers a new stratum of possibilities and challenges for our already automated and digital world. As the internet has drastically changed the speed, mobility, and accessibility of information, so too is AI changing the way we process and regenerate that information. Originally, it was thought that information technology (IT)

DOI: 10.4018/979-8-3693-0240-8.ch007

industries would be the primary beneficiaries of AI, but as AI rapidly evolves for wider applications, its impact will undoubtedly create innovative shifts to transform whole sectors of society (Rauch, 2023). With major corporations like Google, Microsoft, and Amazon investing vast amounts of finance and strategy into AI integration, it is unsurprising that many organisations, Higher Education Institutions (HEIs) and individuals are looking to better understand, upskill and utilise these tools (Leswing, 2023).

The broad aim of this chapter is to investigate the impact of AI on Higher Education (HE) and students to provide a framework (see *Figures 1 and 4*) for HEIs to better prepare wholistic responses for their organisations, staff, and students, both existing and future, for an AI integrated world. **As AI interest expands, how will HE providers adapt to meet the needs of their students? How will HE providers prepare these students for future industries and jobs that may not exist, and employers who may require graduates who can demonstrate competency with AI?**

Industry and education are inextricably linked; if there are changes to one, it follows that there will be changes to the other. A key objective of institutionalised education is to equip learners to develop life and industry skills. As a result, it can be argued that industry drives developments in education. As AI is heralding in what some are referring to as the fifth industrial revolution or at least a new aspect of the fourth (Daly, 2018), it is necessary to understand the impact on industry and therefore on education. AI related changes to industry mean that HE providers will look to tailor training, learning and graduate outcomes to serve industry needs. Likewise, when graduates develop skills in using AI, the capacity for innovation and development in these industries will continue to expand. While tertiary courses that focus on AI have historically been confined to the computer sciences, there is a growing need for students across multiple disciplines to become familiar with how AI can assist them, not only in their coursework, but in preparation for their future careers.

The impact of GenAI on HEIs and students discussed throughout this chapter is represented in the infographic below (see *Figure 1*), which lists key areas of consideration and shows the interrelationship between sectors of government, HEIs, students, and industry. While each quadrant is displayed equally in the graphic below, this framework prioritises the key areas of consideration that apply to HEIs and policy makers, as reflected in the themes discussed throughout this chapter. This infographic (*Figure 1*) is expanded further in the *Figure 4* framework, later in this chapter.

THE IMPACT OF AI ON HIGHER EDUCATION

HEIs are beginning to grapple with the crucial role they have in preparing students for their future in an AI integrated world (Klutka et al., 2018) and have begun to respond by exploring strategies and policies for its reasonable use. A review of HEIs responses concerning GenAI has been undertaken to identify existing practices, as well as discover strategies and approaches that are unique or novel. The topics below focus on some major areas within HE that have been impacted by GenAI, including: early responses and concerns for upholding academic integrity; the necessity for collaboration and open conversations between policy makers, educators and students; the role of GenAI in teaching and learning; the impact of AI on assessment design; and how HEIs can prepare graduates for an AI ready world. Understandably, this section emphasises the impacts of GenAI on teaching, learning and assessment design as these are the most significant areas of impact for HEIs.

Figure 1. A framework for higher education institutions: Key areas of GenAI impact infographic

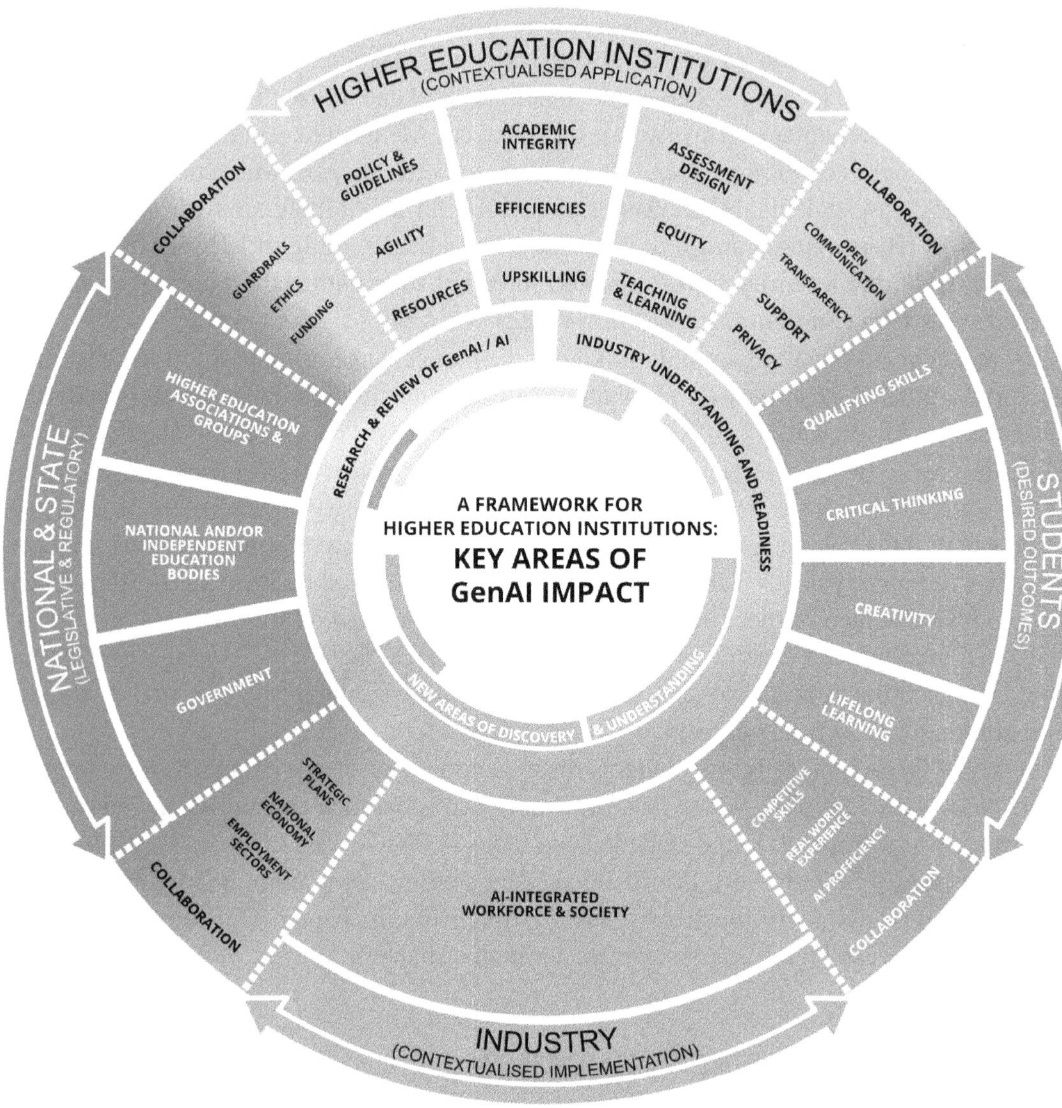

Early Responses

It felt like a crisis for HEIs: ChatGPT made a grand entrance at launch, breaking one million users within its first five days, then growing to 100 million users within its first two months (Kasneci, 2023; Diaz, 2023). Despite GenAI having garnered worldwide interest due to its potential to revolutionise global industries, it was the education sector that identified an immediate need for a response. Each stage of public and private education providers, encompassing primary, secondary, and tertiary, were compelled to choose one of four major responses to GenAI: prohibit, limit, embrace or ignore it.

It is worth noting that the first decision to outright *prohibit* GenAI tools was considered an initial response made by schools and universities globally (Leung & Niazi, 2023; Nolan, 2023; Yang, 2023). Yet, some recognised the futility of prohibiting tools that can easily be accessed by students outside of their school or university (Daly, 2023). Resigned to this realisation, many HEIs permitted GenAI, choosing to either *limit* or *embrace* it with the justification that there is nothing they can do about it (Gniel, 2023a). Among the majority of HEIs that chose to *limit* or *embrace* GenAI, the Technical University of Munich (TUM) and the University of Florida outlined clear initiatives. TUM created the Institute for Ethics in Artificial Intelligence (n.d.) in 2019 to provide a place for AI cross-disciplinary academic and practical research and to foster the ongoing conversation for how AI can transform and benefit society. Likewise, the University of Florida (n.d.), envisioned "building the Nation's First AI University" by committing to integrate AI instruction into all its disciplines across the campus (p.4).

While not all HEIs have necessarily taken such a forward approach to GenAI, many consider its impact on education a delicate balance between opportunities and threats. Grit Wolany (2023, 23:08) from Zurich University for the Arts describes this conscientious approach to GenAI as one of *critical curiosity*. This is where the choices to both *limit* and *embrace* GenAI can become one and the same as HEIs recognise both the opportunities to be embraced, as well as the risks that necessitate guardrails and limitations. This kind of critical curiosity has led Harvard University to instruct its community members to experiment with GenAI tools, whilst adhering to existing policies in information security and data privacy, compliance, copyright, and academic integrity (Hamid & Yuan, 2023).

The last identified potential way for education providers to respond to GenAI is to *ignore* it completely. This has been discouraged by academic groups who warn that a lack of guidelines and policy concerning GenAI invites breaches of academic integrity with undesirable outcomes for both students and institutions—having a documented response to GenAI is better than having none (MacLaren et al., 2023).

Protecting Academic Integrity

As a testament to GenAI's revolutionary potential, educators and those working in academic integrity quickly realised its ability to complete assessment tasks and can foresee how its growing complexity will further enable it to bypass detection software (Cassidy, 2023a). Ardea Russo from the University of Notre Dame (2023, as cited in Price & Sheikh, 2023) was one of many who shared this sentiment, stating, "the reason I wanted to start working on it right away was because I was concerned about students using it as a shortcut, rather than as a tool to their learning" (para. 11). Russo communicated two major approaches to educators: either integrate ChatGPT into classes, or (re)design assessments (Price & Sheikh, 2023). There is a vital need to ensure AI is addressed in policy and procedure to safeguard the integrity of assessment. In attempting to stay ahead, HEIs have pursued "technical solutions—digital watermarking" but this can be circumvented, "…it's an arms race that's never going to finish, and you're never going to win" (Walsh, 2023, as cited in Cassidy, 2023a, para. 19). The University of Pennsylvania's (UPenn) Centre for Teaching and Learning similarly highlight that, "at this point, there is no clearly effective automated way to detect AI-produced materials" and, like other HEIs, conclude that the most viable way to minimise the potential for academic breaches is to redesign assessment (Cassidy, 2023b).

Academic integrity detection software Turnitin, whilst controversial, is still considered a way to deter students from breaching academic integrity using GenAI. Turnitin itself has conceded that the development speed of GenAI has required it to try to keep up with the challenge—leading to what some have considered premature implementation of AI detection, resulting in contentious responses from HE providers, many of whom have ignored or treated it with extreme trepidation (Cassidy, 2023b).

Further practical ways to verify a student's originality in their work, may include confirmation checks, submitting assignment notes, drafts, or commentary on specific class content and sources used (or not used) (UPenn, 2023). Additionally, educators are encouraged to check the student's references to source material for further verification of student learning (UPenn, 2023). Another helpful option for educators is to have students work through staged assessments ensuring progress and feedback can be easily tracked, and so that students can keep at pace instead of resorting to GenAI in last-minute shortcuts (MacLaren et al., 2023). Whatever methods are chosen, it is essential that educators enforce protocols which optimise demonstratable student achievement of the learning outcomes. Students should not be expected to traverse this terrain alone. Student support services and lecturers should be well equipped to assist students in both the ethical use of GenAI as well as with strategies for helping students avoid inappropriate behaviour (MacLaren et al., 2023). This communicates a level of openness, trust and respect towards students, instead of insecurity and accusation, providing avenues to help ensure they are upholding academic integrity standards.

Government and Nationwide Collaboration and Policy

Any education provider's response to AI is also affected by whether they are subject to national or governmental regulations, policies, or strategic plans. France, Singapore, Japan, Italy, and Germany are examples of countries that appear to have taken a more nation-wide approach, with Japan openly outlining its response to AI, and Germany and Italy proactively developing strategic plans supporting the use of AI in HE to further develop their economy and industries (German Federal Government, 2020, Italian Government, 2021; Kakuchi, 2023; Kaneko, 2023; Queensland University of Technology (QUT), 2023). Other countries, including the United Kingdom (UK), the United States (US) and Australia, have seen their respective government departments offer guidelines and statements, but policy is currently actioned more at institutional levels (UK Government, 2023; U.S. Department of State, 2023; Australian Government, 2023). The argument for governmental guardrails that offer societal protection, whilst employing strategies to benefit from the innovations AI has to offer, has garnered traction (Hague, 2023; Siliezar, 2023; The White House, 2023). It is important that HEIs do not merely react to governing policy, but simultaneously collaborate with government and national bodies to institute reasonable change and establish policies and safeguards concerning the use of these new revolutionary technologies, whilst protecting the ability to innovate.

The impact of GenAI has inspired many education associations to work with their respective members to understand and develop policy, guidelines, and expectations for the responsible use of GenAI. Among the various associations collaborating to develop guidelines and policy, the Russell Group (2023), lists five principles to guide their member institutions' approach to GenAI stating:

1. Universities will support students and staff to become AI-literate.
2. Staff should be equipped to support students to use generative AI tools effectively and appropriately in their learning experience.
3. Universities will adapt teaching and assessment to incorporate the ethical use of generative AI and support equal access.
4. Universities will ensure academic rigour and integrity is upheld.

5. Universities will work collaboratively to share best practice as the technology and its application in education evolves.

(Russell Group, 2023, para. 5).

These kinds of initiatives highlight the need for a consensus response towards collaboration and the goals to support and equip students and staff in their use of GenAI, while recognising that teaching and assessment will also necessarily change to maintain good academic integrity and rigour. In Australia, universities have worked with the Tertiary Education Quality and Standards Agency (TEQSA) to share guidelines, resources, and opportunities to discuss the emergence of GenAI (Gniel, 2023b). The introduction of GenAI has brought academic institutions closer together, offering collaboration opportunities, demystify existing and potential issues, and promoting shared education and research. Exemplifying this collaborative impact of GenAI, the University of Chicago (2023) joined a group of seventeen other universities as part of a two-year research project committed to exploring the applications and impact of AI for teaching, learning and research.

Staying Relevant

Within the last decade, HEIs have worked tirelessly to adapt to changing landscapes in education and technology. The dust had barely settled from the impact of the COVID-19 pandemic, before HEIs had to face the arms race that is GenAI (Gniel, 2023a). These disruptive forces further impel HEIs to reevaluate their policies and administrative processes, particularly in delivering and approving courses. To adapt, institutions are now investigating practical ways to reduce excessive governance, streamlining years-long review cycles, and ensuring committees are more focused on their minimum viable product, while maintaining quality and governance of the process (Gniel, 2023a). Although legislation does not always allow rapid pivots in HEIs, a failure to respond in a timely manner to GenAI may result in outdated practices, higher attrition, and fewer enrolments as potential students, instead, pursue informal ways of learning. The upsurge of online video training and micro-courses is already putting pressure on formal HE and the rise of GenAI only adds to this momentum. If only for self-preservation, HEIs must work to confound any underlying perceptions that they are now, like many other industries, potential victims of irrelevance in an AI integrated world. Yet, with this pressure for more streamlined adaptability comes the consolation that "responding to generative AI is a marathon and not a sprint" (Gniel, 2023a, 15:01).

"Teachers cannot teach what they do not know" (Fyson, 2023, para. 2). It is therefore essential that educators understand the use of GenAI technology if it is to be incorporated successfully into learning and teaching. This requires knowledge in the use of GenAI technology for study and within the profession that the educator is preparing the student for (QUT, 2023). Further, the indiscriminate nature of AI proves that it will affect multiple departments within HEIs; not just educators, but administrative and general staff can also benefit from AI literacy. Upskilling may be even more necessary for general staff, as AI technology is now being embedded into major software, online services, and new apps as seen in Microsoft 365 Copilot (MacLaren, et al., 2023; Spataro, 2023). Institutional leaders must become enablers, providing staff with ongoing education, training, and support in GenAI (Gniel, 2023a).

Greater Efficiency With AI

Although GenAI impacts both academic and administration staff, it was the academic staff who felt the initial crisis and pressure, overwhelmed and uncertain with the prospect of having to re-skill (Cassidy, 2023a). Yet, research indicates that as staff become more proficient in technology they may experience a reduced workload, making them more productive (Selwood & Pilkington, 2010). GenAI task automation has the potential to: improve efficiency of administrative tasks; improve accessibility; assist with personalised learning; determine classroom vulnerabilities; create smart content; track student activity; and provide comprehensive analysis to inform AI systems (Chaudhry & Kazim, 2021; Christensen, 2023; The University of Groningen, 2023). Based on society's history of adopting revolutionary technology, what equally scares and excites us now, will eventually become mundane as it becomes more integrated in everyday use (Naughton, 2023).

Richard McInnes (2023) from the University of Adelaide, further describes how GenAI technology can assist curriculum writers, learning designers, and teachers with: creating learning artefacts; rewriting and/or translating information for different audiences; changing the tone of written works and emails; rewording course learning objectives; refining video scripts; developing rubrics; generating summaries of readings and articles; and troubleshooting technical problems; consequently freeing them to focus on more creative aspects of course creation. McInnes (2023) additionally offers reassurance that human involvement through expertise and oversight is essential, stating that the "key to unlocking the full potential of gen-AI is to strike a balance – rather than replacing educational developers and learning designers, gen-AI should be viewed as a valuable tool to complement and empower us in providing exceptional learning experiences" (para. 9).

GenAI in Teaching and Learning

Knowledge of industry AI use provides opportunities for HEIs to review and refresh course content, together with graduate and learning outcomes, to ensure that they contain contextualised elements of AI, effectively considering how it can be used in study and for relevant professional workplace application. This is important at a discipline level to determine what tools are valuable for "learning, research and professional practice" (Harper, 2023, 23:20). GenAI tools will impact conventional teaching and learning cycles for educators, affecting how they plan, implement pedagogy, and evaluate their teaching (University of Queensland, 2023a). When integrating GenAI into their classes, educators should carefully consider which phase(s) of the teaching and learning cycle are most helpful and appropriate for it to be incorporated. Furthermore, given the diverse applications of GenAI, educators should consider that students will engage with the tools in multiple ways, with some favouring it as a helpful tool for inquiry, or as a learning assistant, while others may use it in ways that constitute academic misconduct. Different functions of GenAI lend themselves to different teaching pedagogies (e.g., inquiry-based learning), and it is important to consider how these may be applied effectively, prioritising the pedagogy above the technological novelty and function of the tool (M. Rasi, personal communication, September 22, 2023).

It is important that educators identify and follow their institution's position on the use of GenAI tools and design their classes and assessments accordingly. The National Academic Integrity Network (NAIN, Ireland) encourages institutions to take a consistent approach to GenAI and present clear policies for its responsible use (MacLaren et al., 2023). But, not all HEIs have chosen to strictly mandate university-wide policy, including UPenn (2023) which provides faculty with information guides on the new tools available to them, but allow them to use their own judgement (Binday, 2023).

Johns Hopkins University (JHU) (2023) argues that as technology changes, and perspectives expand, students and staff will look for ways to use this technology thoughtfully. JHU has allowed students to use GenAI technology for class activities, but not for assessments; and, if using GenAI, require acknowledgment of use. The University of Notre Dame provides their educators with four options for using GenAI in their assessments, which includes: prohibiting (if appropriate to the context), use only with permission (specific sections assigned by the educator), use with acknowledgement (documented prompts and references), or use freely without permission (completely uninhibited) (Leary et al., 2023). Whichever boundaries educators choose for their students, Notre Dame emphasises the importance of maintaining transparency and higher-order cognition learning with a pedagogical focus.

Educators should become familiar with the emergent technologies available to them and design their classes and assessments in ways that allow exploration with these technologies while maintaining inclusivity, diversity, and privacy for students (The University of Illinois System, 2022). They should similarly review their classes and assessment tasks and redesign them to mitigate potential vulnerabilities that can be exploited by students using GenAI unethically (MacLaren et al., 2023). The Poorvu Center (2023) at Yale University openly encourages their educators to sign-up for ChatGPT to become familiar with the tool, yet they also raise the issue of privacy, cautioning that submitted information can become part of the program's development.

If GenAI tools are permitted by the institution, educators should make it a priority to clarify with their students whether, when, and how these tools can be used, specifically outlining clear expectations, boundaries, and potential issues (Cornell University, 2023). Arts colleges may have specific ways that AI image and audio generating tools such as Dall-e, or Beatoven.ai can be used. Educators can set parameters for the use of GenAI tools, for example, for inquiry, ideation, or assistance, but discontinue its use when they must explicitly measure qualifying skills and learning outcomes in assessment tasks. KU Leuven University (2023) in Belgium, attests to the learning benefits of GenAI as a language assistant, a search engine for initial data gathering, or in any way the educator has allowed it; yet they prohibit the *copy-pasting* of any content generated by AI unless it is fully acknowledged with correct citations and referencing.

Students can access GenAI tools for improved understanding of topics, creativity and brainstorming, personalised learning for themselves, and for improved accessibility for those with learning or language impairments (Leary et al., 2023). GenAI tools can also be used to analyse and reflect on AI generated works, to identify coding or information errors, to trace AI assertions back to their source, to experiment with prompts, or to discuss a course topic (UPenn, 2023). At Harvard, their computer science course (CS50) allows students to use AI to help "find bugs in their code, give feedback on the design of student programs, explain unfamiliar lines of code or error messages, and answer individual questions" (Hamid & Schisgall, 2023, para. 2).

Some education providers initially considered the impact of GenAI akin to the innovation of the calculator or the online search engine, yet this oversimplification fails to recognise its potential uses as an open and enhanced Pedagogical Conversational Agent (PCA) (Hillier, 2023a). PCAs are common in dialogical learning and GenAI allows students to engage with multiple AI agents in roleplaying scenarios with feedback (Shum, 2023). Concerning such forms of assisted learning, Stanford University's Board of Conduct Affairs (2023) has written policy that states, "AI shall be treated analogously to assistance from another person" (para. 4). Bearman and Ajjawi (2023) affirm this view to consider the wider *so-*

ciotechnical aspect of AI, since students interact with AI systems relationally, asking them to provide information, perform tasks and discuss ideas—beyond simple spelling or grammar-checking.

But even if GenAI tools can be considered as PCAs to assist in student learning, they remain subject to error. Large Language Models (LLMs) are prone to *AI hallucinations* and bias and cannot be relied upon to produce completely accurate information; they are unsuitable to take on the role of a "trusted tutor or information source", (Hillier, 2023a, para. 17) but should rather be used for brainstorming, summarising, or as a learning aide. This aspect should encourage HEIs and students to continue to emphasise the value of human evaluation (including critical thinking) and discourage blind reliance on the AI agent. If GenAI tools are to be recognised in this *sociotechnical* way, as "writing consultants" for students, they must similarly be subject to the same recognition as a cited source, and therefore still under the scrutiny of academic rigor (Hillier, 2023b; Kashani, 2023, as cited in Walker, 2023, para. 6; UPenn, 2023; Walker, 2023). Furthermore, some universities have allowed students to use GenAI with acknowledgement (Cassidy, 2023b). KU Leuven and Boston Universities require students to include their exchange with GenAI in an appendix. This promotes transparency so that teachers "can always assess…knowledge, understanding and/or skills correctly" (KU Leuven University, 2023, para. 11). Boston educators are instructed to use discernment in grading assessments, rewarding students for creative and critical thinking, while factoring in the level of assistance used (Boston University, 2023). This new consideration in marking student's work may require HEIs to change assessment rubrics or marking schematics to factor in levels of AI use.

In exploring the pedagogical considerations for the inclusion of GenAI in teaching and learning cycles, it was found that this is a developing area of knowledge that will be assisted by ongoing research. However, it is important that educators, after integrating GenAI in their classrooms, take time to review and evaluate the results and their alignment with learning outcomes (Shum, 2023).

Assessment Design

Concerns are raised over how students could use GenAI to complete assessment (Dawson, 2023; Monash University, 2023b; QUT, 2023). It is noted that there are six typical responses by education providers to GenAI in assessment design, including: *ignore, ban, invigilate, embrace, design around,* and *rethink* (Lodge et al., 2023). Assessment tasks including essays, artistic works, and coding tasks are vulnerable to academic misconduct, as these tasks can now be completed by GenAI and many, in their current state, *ignore* its use. This approach is understandably short-lived as GenAI becomes more widely used and capable. The option to *ban* GenAI is problematic as everyday applications such as Microsoft 365 and Grammarly, increasingly integrate competitive GenAI features (Harper, 2023). Despite the Russell Group's guiding principle to assist students in their AI literacy (as noted earlier), there are members that have banned the use of GenAI tools in their assessed work (Manga, 2023; Thompson & O'Brien, 2023). Other HEIs have initially chosen to ban AI use in this same way (Cassidy, 2023a). *Invigilate* is another option which essentially bypasses digital submissions, and commonly reverts to more traditional forms of assessments. Some members of the Russell Group have retained online tests for low-integrity tasks but reverted to supervised (online and on-campus) and traditional 'pen and paper' exams as a response to GAI tools (Cassidy, 2023a). This response is deemed a safe and easy remedy to contend with the technological pace of GenAI, as they work to develop the next three longer-term responses: *embrace, design around,* and *rethink.*

The option to *embrace* GenAI in assessment design involves intentionally using AI generated content as a central element within the assessment task. This may take the form of evaluation exercises in which students assess and critique the work of AI-generated artefacts themselves. If educators seek to *design around* GenAI, they may look to the work of Lodge (2023) who has developed strategies to essentially 'fool' ChatGPT; yet he concedes that this is not a long-term solution. Within this strategy, there is the option for educators to require students to refer to specific resources that are only accessible behind a paywall or membership so that they are outside of the GenAI's LLM, assisting with providing integrity in assessment (Poorvu Center, 2023).

The option to *rethink* appears to be the most sustainable model moving forward and, although it requires more time and effort, can yield the most sustainable, ethical, and creative outcomes. It is almost guaranteed that HEIs will have to *continually rethink* many of their assessment tasks given the rapid development and adoption of GenAI (Leary et al., 2023). *Rethinking* may involve one or a combination of the following:

- Incorporating GenAI into designated parts of assessment tasks (Leary et al., 2023).
- Consideration of alternative assessment design (UPenn, 2023).
- Updating assessment to target higher-order thinking, which is more difficult for GenAI technologies (Leary et al., 2023).
- Authentic assessment where students are less likely to engage in academic misconduct when they find assessment tasks personally relevant, and more readily applicable to real-world scenarios (Monash University, 2023b).
- Future-focused or 'sustainable' assessment—can help students understand how they might learn to work with new technologies like ChatGPT in ways that contribute to their personal and professional development over time (Monash University, 2023b).

As educators explore a spectrum of novel and more traditional methods to counter cheating with GenAI, forms of authentic assessment appear promising (Monash University, 2023b). Many universities promote high activity authentic assessment (Georgetown University, 2023; University of Queensland, 2023b), with some introducing more fieldwork, laboratory, oral presentation, and project-based assessment tasks (Cassidy, 2023a). When offering strategies for AI integration, teaching students how to use tools like ChatGPT for conversations on the topic, editing and drafting processes, and how to ask good questions, should be promoted (Georgetown University, 2023). Georgetown University (2023) considers only two major choices for educators: either find ways to promote creative and original student work, or have students intentionally integrate and engage with AI in their work.

Educators should be proactive and engage with their disciplinary communities and wider faculty, to redesign assessments and assessment types, to identify,

...which have a strong validity (i.e., clearly aligned with the learning outcomes and the skills which they are meant to demonstrate) and in which there is an appropriate balance of credit between the process of preparing for and undertaking the assessment and the final product, helping students to develop self-efficacy, critical thinking, and a professional disposition (MacLaren et al., 2023, p.8).

At an institutional level, academic staff should periodically review and refresh assessment design, courses, and policies, to enhance the student learning experience. If educators design clear and progressive assessment goals for their students, they may be able to mitigate stressful scenarios in which students feel tempted to resort to GenAI tools as shortcuts (MacLaren et al., 2023).

Another option that was noted in relation to assessment, is that instead of course specific assessment, HEIs implement program assessment. Harper (2023, 24:48) asserted that, "it will take a sector-level movement to enable the kind of authentic, integrative, programmatic assessments required," to ensure integrity in the longer term. Further consideration of this strategy is needed by HEIs prior to implementation, as it introduces numerous complexities.

Regardless of the strategy, assessment design proved to be a major consideration across institutions in response to GenAI. It is vital to consider: the ways in which the integrity of current assessments could be compromised using GenAI tools, the use of alternative forms of assessment, and how to clearly communicate with students the possibilities and limitations of the tools. Yet rather than fixating on technical strategies to mitigate the risk of AI breaches, educators should remember to prioritise pedagogy, qualifying skills and learning outcomes when designing assessment (Morton-Aiken, 2023). Institutions must focus on their ethos and culture, finding ways to reinforce "integrity, trust, and truthfulness as being at the heart of learning, knowledge discovery and creativity" to their students (MacLaren et al., 2023, p.9). These approaches, that afford students the opportunity to explore GenAI tools, naturally extends to them a degree of trust. Institutions will have to decide for themselves what level they believe is appropriate, but opening these avenues of learning and communication appears to be a common strategy (Boston University, 2023; KU Leuven University, 2023).

Educators are encouraged to work with their students, co-designing and collaborating throughout this process of learning (Shum, 2023). If hubris does not deter, educators should find themselves willing to share the same space with their students—as novices, learning and adapting to the new technology before them.

Ethical and Safe Use of AI

Much of the attention on GenAI tools is focussed on their responsible use, but HEIs must understand the ethical concerns and possible adverse effects of the tools, such as the technology's ability to "produce highly convincing fake images, videos, and text which could create confusion, making it challenging to differentiate between authentic and counterfeit information" (Tk, 2023, para. 2). Other concerns include privacy, security, control over personal data, and the possibility of cyberattacks (Tk, 2023, para. 2). It is important to protect staff and students from the potentially exploitative nature of these tools, ensuring their ethical and safe use mitigates some of the noted challenges of AI, including being falsely accused of cheating or of breaches of academic integrity. In addition, users should review their GenAI content critically as there also are valid concerns around the development of these tools and the information that makes up these LLMs, with issues of copyright, intellectual property, and the possible exploitation of those hired to collect and screen the data (MacLaren et al., 2023; University of Groningen, 2023).

As HEIs assist with producing tomorrow's workforce, there is a responsibility on the institution itself to understand the issues and be part of a conversation to determine appropriate and safe ways to use the tools and communicate this with their students. This may begin with facilitating training workshops and open forums to promote a healthy dialogue about GenAI (MacLaren et al.; Poorvu Center, 2023). These provide a safe space to proactively discuss the positive and negative aspects of the tools, fostering more clarity, transparency, and responsiveness than a policy document posted online.

Industry Ready Graduates

Educators are realising their responsibility for preparing students to be able to use GenAI technology in their careers and workplaces appropriately otherwise, they risk competitively disadvantaging their graduates (Morton-Aiken, 2023). Onkelejda Kasneci (2023), Professor at TUM, emphasises the need for AI literacy for a rapidly changing world, affirming that,

...to adequately equip learners for their future professional and personal goals, it is crucial to provide them with competencies in addition to basic knowledge. These competencies should enable learners to compete in an environment where numerous tasks are automated, complex cognitive processes are required, personal responsibility and interpersonal skills are increasing, and interdisciplinary collaboration is the basis for solving complicated societal problems. The mandate for education is therefore to evolve from tasks rooted in routine and impersonality to tasks that are personalized, multifaceted, and creative. We need to develop strategies that promote multiple competencies beyond traditional curricula, with an emphasis on fostering creativity, critical thinking, collaboration, and communication (translated) (para. 4).

"In essence, there is only one way to evaluate the impact of AI in Education: through learning outcomes" (Chaudhry & Kazim, 2021). Currently, it is observed that surveyed HEIs share common considerations which can assist with developing the knowledge base, empowering students, and educators, to make informed decisions. HEIs can play a role in helping students learn how to use GenAI tools which will be used increasingly inside and outside the classroom (University of Groningen, 2023). Empowering students for their future opens new windows of opportunities for graduates in a modern society reshaped by AI (Farrell, 2023).

THE IMPACT OF AI ON HE STUDENTS

Many young people preparing to leave school face decisions around whether to continue studying in preparation for a career and which career path they should focus on. This is a difficult task, given that many people will have more than one career, and AI is replacing jobs at an ever-increasing rate with some estimates as high as 40-50% (Hatzius et al., 2023; Swain, 2023). With the ever-increasing cost of HE, students need an assurance that what they study will prepare them appropriately for the workforce, but more broadly teach them skills for life that can be utilised no matter the job they undertake (Gora, 2022). This places responsibility on HEIs to ensure that the courses on offer do just this, or it could have a significant impact as students withdraw or seek alternative education methods.

For a variety of reasons, the education sector tends to lag where new technologies are concerned. "Lack of willingness to take risks, or to adopt new innovations, and lack of funding for anything different from traditional methods of teaching militate against the adoption of new technologies in all sectors of education, learning and development" (Wheeler, 2019, as cited in Bates et al., 2020, para. 29). Given the speed of technological change in AI, any lag or delay in consideration of this impact will have a detrimental effect—courses will be outdated, and students will not be prepared for the real world that is already investigating how to make jobs easier through AI (Harper, 2023). The education industry must actively consider the role of AI within their own institutions, and within the industries that their degrees service. As understanding of AI improves, it can be incorporated in meaningful and appropriate ways into teaching and learning practices.

HEIs must consider that students may have come from environments that have already established their relationship with AI. As students' experience with AI differs, education providers must recognise that any hard practices or restrictions set during their students' HE journeys may be short-lived at best (Daly, 2023). Furthermore, education providers will have to decide what restrictions on AI for students are counterintuitive to their primary aims to equip students, knowing that they may require certain aspects for their industry. AI must be acknowledged for its presence and potency as a tool for improved learning experiences for modern day students (Chen et al., 2020).

Benefits and Concerns

AI is acknowledged to present broad and promising trends and opportunities for students (Kampakis, n.d.; Noy & Zhang, 2023). It can also help to prepare them for a workforce that makes use of such tools. *Figure 2* presents an overview of the benefits/opportunities of GenAI for students.

The list of benefits is not an exhaustive list, but key items noted in literature. It is also important to remember that the benefits of AI often require at least some understanding of the tools themselves which students may not have, given the relative infancy of the technology in education. Much of the information in *Figures 2* and *3* comes from 97 submissions to the Parliament of Australia House Standing Committee on Employment, Education and Training inquiry into the use of GenAI in the Australian education system (2023). A vast majority of the submissions noted similar benefits, challenges and thoughts related to GenAI. It is worth noting that Curtin Student Guild (2023), in their response, thoughtfully considered the impact of AI on other-abled students, such as those who are visually impaired or have visual learning preferences, those who are autistic, or have ADHD.

In addition, Curtin Student Guild appeared to be the only student submission. Student voice is beginning to emerge, but is limited. Edith Cowan University (ECU) surveyed its students and found that at the time of their survey (March 2023), over half of the students surveyed had limited awareness of AI (Harper, 2023). Those that were using it identified the following as key reasons:

- For help – students made use of AI to help with writing, with research and for code creation.
- To learn – students used it for putting concepts into language that assists with learning.
- To clarify – clarification of assessment tasks or to get an idea of how to respond to questions.

Other usages noted were in relation to reducing word count, for paraphrasing or to generate an argument structure (Harper, 2023), generally things that are looked upon less favourably by HEIs. It was contended that this may lead to a "re-thinking...around what constitutes cheating" (Harper, 2023, 28:40).

Whilst the impact on students is yet to be fully recognised, the ECU survey found that overall, students appeared more excited about AI than worried, a sentiment that is echoed by Chan and Hu (2023) who note that there is an overall positive feeling towards AI in research, learning and future careers. However, they also note that students are concerned about "accuracy, transparency, privacy, and ethics… particularly plagiarism, as…determining the originality of work generated by GenAI" is difficult (para. 15). Anecdotally, students have noted being scared to use the tools for fear of doing the wrong thing, leading to being accused of academic misconduct. Over-reliance on AI and its potential impact on the value of HE, and on human jobs, were further student concerns (Chan & Hu, 2023). However, the level

Figure 2. Benefits/Opportunities of GenAI for students

Benefits/Opportunities	Source
It can assist with the development of cognitive skills, critical thinking, evaluation, and information literacy.	Australasian Academic Integrity Network (AAIN), 2023 QUT, 2023
It can assist with increased digital and AI literacy and experience in the use of generative AI tools to enhance employability.	AAIN, 2023 The University of Sydney, 2023
It can provide tailored, adaptable, personalised learning experience and feedback based on individual needs.	AAIN, 2023 Curtain Student Guild, 2023
It may provide better/faster access to feedback on learning.	AAIN, 2023 Curtain Student Guild, 2023
24/7 access to educational resources and personalised tutoring/support e.g., summaries to simplify complex concepts in documents and key texts and practice assessment questions.	AAIN, 2023 Curtain Student Guild, 2023
It provides assistive technology to enhance equity for students with diverse learning needs.	AAIN, 2023
It allows learners to feel connected.	Liu, et al., 2023
It can be used in a sociotechnical way for student learning as an effective Pedagogical Conversational Agent (PCA). It "provides a different, more conversational approach to searching online. It builds on work in searching to learn, supports knowledge creation practices" (p.1).	Shum, 2023 QUT, 2023
It helps students to overcome writer's block.	The University of Sydney, 2023
It helps students generate computer code, images, exemplars, and music.	Curtain Student Guild, 2023 The University of Sydney, 2023
AI can provide varying perspectives on specific topics.	The University of Sydney, 2023
AI allows students to learn by teaching. "When learning a new concept, students can explain the concept to ChatGPT like explaining to another student. And ChatGPT is likely to be a friendly peer because it is fine-tuned to behave in a kind and gentle way. AI improves and adapts its behaviour through learning from human feedback" (para. 15).	Liu, et al., 2023, para. 15
AI can collect and analyse data on assessment and performance, to better understand students enabling educators to make informed decisions about teaching methods and curriculum improvements which benefit students.	Greene-Harper, 2023 Curtin Student Guild, 2023
It provides learners with access to vast amounts of information as well as the ability to organise it in a variety of ways.	Greene-Harper, 2023
It can assist with reducing workload.	Greene-Harper, 2023 QUT, 2023 Curtain Student Guild, 2023
It may enhance learning experiences, course design, and teaching methods.	Greene-Harper, 2023 Curtin Student Guild, 2023
Enhanced industry cooperation.	Curtin Student Guild, 2023 The University of Sydney, 2023
Use image recognition to create visual representations allowing visually impaired, autistic students or those with visual learning preferences to get a better understanding of the material.	Curtin Student Guild, 2023
Be used for brainstorming which may "assist students with ADHD [and others] to identify and structure their ideas" (p.6).	Curtin Student Guild, 2023
Provide "lip reading, enhanced feedback, and captioning...to assist students with these specific needs" (p. 6).	Curtin Student Guild, 2023

Figure 3. Student concerns about GenAI

Concerns and Potential Challenges	Source
The reliance on GAI has the potential to reduce opportunities for independent learning, critical thinking, problem solving, independent thought, development of deep knowledge and thinking creatively.	QUT, 2023 Wogu et al., 2018, as cited in Seo et al., 2021
It may promote laziness.	Curtain Student Guild, 2023 QUT, 2023
Students may lack the confidence/knowledge to engage with GAI to further understand a topic.	QUT, 2023
GAI responses can be deceptively convincing. Students may incorrectly assume that responses generated are accurate. Students may not be able to identify structural bias, data integrity issues, misrepresentation, deception, copyright or cultural safety and bias issues.	QUT, 2023
Inappropriate use, leading to breaches in academic integrity.	Harper, 2023 Curtain Student Guild, 2023
Students' insufficient knowledge of the limitations of the technologies and LLMs that underpin GAI tools.	Cheatham et al., 2019 QUT, 2023
Disparities between students who do not understand the potential of GAI or have access/equality of access – specifically mature-age, international and other abled students.	AAIN, 2023 Southgate, 2020
Lack of social intimacy. The need for student to teacher and peer to peer interactions.	Cheatham et al., 2019 Curtain Student Guild, 2023
Students may not know if the data has been acquired ethically or if it breaches privacy.	QUT, 2023
Misuse of AI by students has the potential to damage the academic reputation of universities.	Curtin Student Guild, 2023
"Tools being used to detect the misuse of AI by students can be unreliable and might lead to students being falsely accused of cheating – especially for the international student cohort" (p.6) leading to "an erosion of trust between the students, educators and institutions" (p.3).	Curtin Student Guild, 2023, p.6. Monash University, 2023a, p.3.
Student's personal information may be used by AI companies unethically which could lead to bribery, misuse, or hacking.	Curtin Student Guild, 2023
"Environmental cost (the computational power involves significant energy and water consumption)" (p.3).	Monash University, 2023a

of concern was dependent on student experience—students who had a good understanding of the tools were generally less concerned (Chan & Hu, 2023). Aside from the benefits/opportunities, notable AI concerns and potential challenges can be seen in *Figure 3*.

HEIs can improve the experience of students and better prepare them for the workforce when knowledge of the benefits and opportunities presented by AI are clearly understood by educators and students, and appropriately facilitated and supported. However, it is essential to address the issues noted. HEIs should facilitate hands-on experience with the tools which will assist with allaying concerns and may help in enhancing students' understanding and acceptance of AI (Chan & Hu, 2023).

Critical Thinking and Creativity

Another area of concern for both students and HEIs is in relation to critical thinking and creativity—encompassing problem solving, analytical reasoning, evaluation, and communications competency. "Creativity and critical thinking are key skills for the complex and globalized economies and societies of the 21st century. There is a growing consensus that higher education…institutions should cultivate these skills with their students" (OECD, 2023, para. 1). Critical thinking and creativity are, in general, currently taught implicitly, rather than explicitly (Bellaera et al., 2021), meaning that teaching these skills happens within courses generically or broadly and that specific courses or more intentional consideration is lacking. Further research is needed to understand how these are being taught (Bellaera et al., 2021), and how they can be taught more substantially in light of AI. These skills are vital as AI makes an ever-increasing impact in current workplaces. "Not only do students need to know how to use AI, but they must also be able to analyze and identify the biases in the AI content critically" (Nguyen, 2023, para. 38). Strengthening approaches to creativity, critical thinking, and evaluation of AI generated outcomes through learning activities is essential. Without this, there is a risk of poor-quality work, less ability to solve problems effectively, recycling of thinking, and a lack of originality, both within and outside of the study environment.

Equity in Access

The topic of equity is significant to both students and HEIs. The cost of accessing GenAI tools is more problematic than previously, as free tools and software have more recently been tied to tiered subscription models, sometimes with waitlists, fostering unequal access (Harper, 2023). Additionally, student location, such as those in remote areas or studying internationally, and prior knowledge and experience or aptitude with technology, are challenges that may also result in disparity across cohorts. Strong consideration must be given to equity before integrating AI at scale (Harper, 2023). There is a risk that AI may contribute to widening the digital divide, creating a new gap in AI literacy. HEIs may need to assume responsibility for ensuring that every student can get reliable access to any tool that proves important for learning, and career development. This may require licensing at scale (Harper, 2023). It is vital that barriers to access are removed or reduced for equity and fairness, but also, so that students can take advantage of the benefits of the tools more easily.

Lifelong Learning

For education institutions, 2023 will be recognised as the year of GenAI. ChatGPT has awakened institutions to a new reality and accelerated AI adoption. As a result, it has reignited conversation around which jobs may be replaced by AI, which will become more automated, and what jobs will be created by AI (Future Learn, 2023). As jobs for life become less common, adapting to changes, upskilling, and remaining current will be essential to ensure ongoing career prospects. Ignoring the impact of AI tools may have a detrimental effect. "History has shown us time and time again that our working lives are able to withstand enormous amounts of change when we learn new skills" (Future Learn, 2023, p. 29). Lifelong learning is not just a university catchphrase to ensure students return to study; it is an essential soft skill and a way of life that will ensure longevity in the marketplace both for students and educators.

Figure 4. A framework for higher education institutions: Key areas of generative artificial intelligence (GenAI) impact

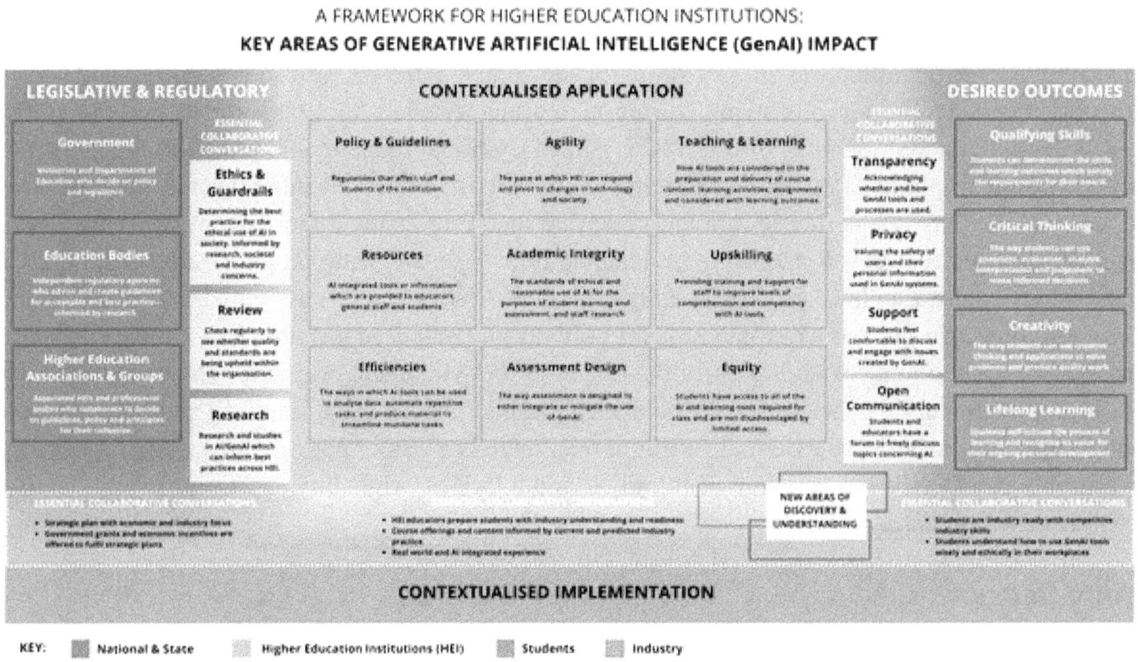

A Framework for HEIs

It is clear from the research of this chapter that HE providers must address AI with clarity, within both learning and policy, or they risk the possibility of disadvantaging and handicapping their students and their institution's relevance and longevity. The research has identified broad and specific areas that institutions should take into consideration as they review their AI strategies, including how AI is impacting educators, current students, and future graduates. Provided below is the more detailed framework (*Figure 4*) that encapsulates our research findings that may serve firstly, as a starting point for institutions who are yet to implement practical strategies for the inclusion of AI systematically across their own institutions, and secondly, a framework for institutions who have already made strides in this area for review of their current practices and responses. Below the framework, *Figure 5* presents key questions that education institutions, educators and students are asking. These can be used simultaneously with the framework to stimulate and prompt conversation regarding AI and GenAI.

FUTURE CONSIDERATIONS AND CONCLUSION

For students, HE and industry, AI exhibits many benefits, some of which are yet to be recognised; the same is true of challenges. Although some industries have mobilised with AI effortlessly, not all can adapt efficiently due to cost, organisational flexibility, size, and employee training—HE faces similar challenges. The critical response of HEIs to AI and GenAI attests to its significant impact on the educa-

Figure 5. Questions for HEIs consideration for exploring the use of AI/GenAI

Institution	Educators	Student
• Are there any pre-existing national or state policies or regulations regarding the use of GenAI—Is it banned etc.? • Are there any governmental strategic programmes that concern GenAI? • Are there any HE associations or groups that have provided policy and/or guidelines to assist? Have these changed in the past six months? How regularly are they changing? • How can we remain up to date and agile in implementing change relating to GenAI? • What is the institution's official position on AI/GenAI? • What existing policies or guidelines are provided by the institution? Are these current? Do they need to be created? • Do policies/guidelines support and encourage ethical and safe use of tools? How are we evaluating the tools? • How can the institution provide adequate and appropriate leadership in this area – what does this require? • What software or tools should be made available through the institution? • What professional development on GenAI should be provided by the institution? • How are we equipping our students with the best technology, qualifying and real-world AI skills, ready to enter their future careers? • Is there a dedicated centre for teaching and learning that is considering pedagogy and assessment design related to AI? • How are we clearly communicating to faculty and students relevant and necessary information to assist with navigating GenAI? • How are we addressing academic integrity concerns? • What resources are needed to support staff and students? • What events and forums are made available for staff and students to openly discuss GenAI's benefits and risks? • Are there collaborative opportunities for HEI to engage with shared knowledge? • Do we have a review process in place?	• How is GenAI being used in professional settings/how might it be used and how does this knowledge affect what is being taught? • What ways can/should GenAI be integrated – in curriculum, student learning, and assessment? • What is the purpose of assessment? How do we assess? • What training/professional development do educators need to adapt to using the technology and acquire the skills necessary for use and for teaching others? • How do we teach ethical and safe use of GenAI tools including the ability to critically analyse the value of the tool itself and what is produced by the tool? • How can GenAI be used within teaching pedagogy and the teaching and learning cycle? • How can we increase student understanding and skills in critical thinking, creativity, and lifelong learning?	• How does using GenAI impact me as a student and as a professional? • What software or tools are available via my institution? • What forums are available to me to discuss GenAI in my work, including study and student support? • What skills do I need to be able to use these tools appropriately and effectively? Why is this important? • How can I ensure I have current skills and knowledge for my chosen profession and for other professions I may choose to pursue? • How do I use GenAI? • How can I safely use GenAI? • How can I use GenAI for assessment? • How can I ensure that I am using GenAI appropriately in assessment so that I will not breach academic integrity?

tion sector. The rapid rise of accessible AI tools such as ChatGPT, have ensured that HEIs stand up, take notice, and approach this new age of GenAI with excitement and critical curiosity.

It is with this same attentive curiosity that this chapter considered the broad and varied responses by HEIs to AI. Upon review, many HEIs appear willing to be transparent, collaborative and explorative. HEIs are taking careful steps to walk the line between maintaining academic integrity, and considering the kinds of competitive skills and learning experiences their students might require in their future careers. Students are beginning to understand the impact of AI for study and work and are excited. Industry is already exploring integration of the tools. The key questions now are: What response will HE providers have? How can AI be appropriately used, taught, and supported in HEIs? How can HEI adequately prepare students with appropriate levels of technical and ethical knowledge to take advantage of the opportunities AI presents, and be safeguarded and equipped for their prospective careers? How should students engage with GenAI in meaningful ways, not just for the sake of technology? Answering these questions is not a simple task, but an ongoing process of discovery.

New waves of technology can present fresh reminders and opportunities for educational institutions to review their methods of preparing students for their future. As Former US Secretary of Education, Richard Riley (2004, as cited in Gunderson, 2004) states, "We are currently preparing students for jobs that don't yet exist, using technologies that haven't been invented, in order to solve problems we don't even know are problems yet" (p.90). The framework presented in this chapter may guide HEI in making informed and responsible decisions concerning the use of AI in their institutions. The impacts of GenAI on HEI, their students, and society, will have a lasting impact. And, this generation of policy makers, leaders, and members of educational institutions, are currently tasked to help guide, protect, model, educate and equip future generations to use GenAI in effective, wise, and ethical ways.

HEI are often the bridge between students and industry and, without blindly chasing after the trends of industry, must take proactive measured steps to protect the value of learning and teaching, without disadvantaging themselves or their students. In reality, we may not see the societal outcome of the impact of AI for years to come, and may not be able to fully understand the impact of GenAI on the education sector, until we have a full generation of 'AI-baptised' graduates, working and integrated in the workforce.

REFERENCES

Abd-Elaa, E. S., Gamage, S. H., & Mills, J. E. (2019). *Artificial intelligence is a tool for cheating academic integrity.* 30th Annual Conference for the Australasian Association for Engineering Education (AAEE 2019): Educators Becoming Agents of Change: Innovate, Integrate, Motivate. Montreal, Quebec, Canada. https://aaee.net.au/wp-content/uploads/2020/07/AAEE2019_Annual_Conference_paper_180.pdf

Australasian Academic Integrity Network. (2023). Submission to the House Standing Committee on employment, education and training inquiry into the use of generative artificial intelligence in the Australian education system. In *Inquiry into the use of generative artificial intelligence in the Australian education system - Submission 58.* https://www.aph.gov.au/DocumentStore.ashx?id=e5bbb538-24c1-4482-9777-12872d8a3ef7&subId=745244

Australian Government. (2023, September). *Artificial intelligence.* Australian Government. https://www.industry.gov.au/science-technology-and-innovation/technology/artificial-intelligence

Bates, T., Cobo, C., Mariño, O., & Wheeler, S. (2020). Can artificial intelligence transform higher education? *International Journal of Educational Technology in Higher Education*, *17*(42), 42. doi:10.1186/s41239-020-00218-x

Bearman, M., & Ajjawi, R. (2023). Learning to work with the black box: Pedagogy for a world with artificial intelligence. *British Journal of Educational Technology*, *00*(5), 1–14. doi:10.1111/bjet.13337

Bellaera, L., Weinstein-Jones, Y., Ilie, S., & Baker, S. T. (2021). Critical thinking in practice: The priorities and practices of instructors teaching in higher education. *Thinking Skills and Creativity*, *41*, 100856. Advance online publication. doi:10.1016/j.tsc.2021.100856

Binday, B. (2023, March 28). In absence of university-wide guidance, Penn professors vary approaches to AI in academics. *The Daily Pennsylvanian.* https://www.thedp.com/article/2023/03/penn-chat-gpt-professor-policies-future

Boston University. (2023, September). *Using generative AI in coursework.* Boston University. https://www.bu.edu/cds-faculty/culture-community/gaia-policy/#:~:text=Students%20shall&text=Not%20use%20AI%20tools%20during,work%20is%20not%20mistakenly%20flagged

Cassidy, C. (2023a, January 10). Australian universities to return to 'pen and paper' exams after students caught using AI to write essays. *The Guardian.* https://www.theguardian.com/australia-news/2023/jan/10/universities-to-return-to-pen-and-paper-exams-after-students-caught-using-ai-to-write-essays

Cassidy, C. (2023b, April 17). Australian universities split on using new tool to detect AI plagiarism. *The Guardian.* https://www.theguardian.com/australia-news/2023/apr/16/australian-universities-split-on-using-new-tool-to-detect-ai-plagiarism

Chan, C. K. Y., & Hu, W. (2023). Students' voices on generative AI: Perceptions, benefits, and challenges in higher education. *International Journal of Educational Technology in Higher Education*, *20*(43), 43. doi:10.1186/s41239-023-00411-8

Chaudhry, M. A., & Kazim, E. (2022). Artificial intelligence in education (AIEd): A high-level academic and industry note 2021. *AI and Ethics*, *2*(1), 157–165. doi:10.1007/s43681-021-00074-z PMID:34790953

Cheatham, B., Javanmardian, K., & Samandari, H. (2019, April 26). Confronting the risks of artificial intelligence. *McKinsey Quarterly.* https://www.mckinsey.com/capabilities/quantumblack/our-insights/confronting-the-risks-of-artificial-intelligence

Chen, L., Chen, P., & Lin, Z. (2020). Artificial intelligence in education: A review. *IEEE Access : Practical Innovations, Open Solutions*, *8*, 75264–75278. doi:10.1109/ACCESS.2020.2988510

Christensen, U. (2023, March 25). *How AI will revolutionize human learning – but not the way you think.* Forbes. https://www.forbes.com/sites/ulrikjuulchristensen/2023/05/25/how-ai-will-revolutionize-human-learning--but-not-the-way-you-think/?sh=2aa7080a4c65

Cochrane, T., & Ryan, T. (2023, March). *ChatGPT and Academic Integrity: Options for adapting assessment in semester 1, 2023.* Melbourne Centre for the Study of Higher Education. https://melbourne-cshe.unimelb.edu.au/__data/assets/pdf_file/0008/4533218/ChatGPT-and-Academic-Integrity.pdf

Cornell University Center for Teaching Innovation. (2023, September). *AI & academic integrity*. Cornell. https://teaching.cornell.edu/generative-artificial-intelligence/ai-academic-integrity

Curtin Student Guild. (2023). A submission to the House Standing Committee on employment, education and training inquiry into the issues and opportunities presented by generative artificial intelligence (AI). In *Inquiry into the use of generative artificial intelligence in the Australian education system - Submission 53*. https://www.aph.gov.au/DocumentStore.ashx?id=b8efd80a-5527-4151-95a9-b83c818ea36b&subId=745706

Daly, C. (2018, November 13). *AI - The fifth industrial revolution*. AI Business. https://aibusiness.com/verticals/ai-the-fifth-industrial-revolution

Daly, N. (Director). (2023). *ChatGPT could make cheating easier, but not all educators believe banning it is the solution* [Video]. ABC News. https://www.abc.net.au/news/2023-02-27/chatgpt-could-make-cheating-easier,-but-not-all/102030682

Dawson, P. (2023). *Inquiry into the use of generative artificial intelligence in the Australian education system - Submission 54*. ApH. https://www.aph.gov.au/DocumentStore.ashx?id=8ec1fbc2-72d9-4aa0-b052-d1547e71cfdc&subId=745313

Diaz, M. (2023, July 6). *ChatGPT sees its first monthly drop in traffic since launch*. ZDNet. https://www.zdnet.com/article/chatgpt-sees-its-first-monthly-drop-in-traffic-since-launch/

EDUCAUSE. (2023). *2023 EDUCAUSE horizon report - Teaching and learning edition*. EDUCAUSE. https://library.educause.edu/resources/2023/5/2023-educause-horizon-report-teaching-and-learning-edition

Farrell, T. (2023, June 27). *The impact of artificial intelligence on education (UOW)*. University of Wollongong. https://ltc.uow.edu.au/hub/page/AI-overview-impact

Future Learn. (2023, September 4). *Future-proof your career: Lifelong learning in the age of AI*. Future Learn. https://www.futurelearn.com/info/blog/lifelong-learning-in-the-age-of-ai

Fyson, S. (2023, July 24). Teachers cannot teach what they do not know. *Spectator Australia*. https://www.spectator.com.au/2023/07/teachers-cannot-teach-what-they-do-not-know/

Georgetown University. (2023, April). *Assignment design principles*. Georgetown University. https://cndls.georgetown.edu/ai/assignments/#common-questions-about-assignment-design

German Federal Government. (2020, December). *Artificial intelligence strategy of the German Federal Government – Update 2020*. German Federal Government. https://www.ki-strategie-deutschland.de/files/downloads/Fortschreibung_KI-Strategie_engl.pdf

Gniel, H. (2023a, April). *AI: A regulatory perspective*. TEQSA. https://www.teqsa.gov.au/sites/default/files/2023-04/AI-a-regulatory-perspective-2023.pdf

Gniel, H. (2023b, June 8). *AI: A regulatory perspective on what we've learnt*. ChatGPT: What have we learnt? [Online]. https://www.youtube.com/watch?v=1V0f3pw2B_0

Gora, P. (2022, March 3). *What do students expect from their universities?* https://www.universityworld-news.com/post.php?story=20220301081656159

Greene-Harper, R. T. (2023, April 27). *The pros and cons of using ai in learning: Is ChatGPT helping or hindering learning outcomes?* eLearning Industry. https://elearningindustry.com/pros-and-cons-of-using-ai-in-learning-chatgpt-helping-or-hindering-learning-outcomes#:~:text=The%20use%20of%20Artificial%20Intelligence,questions%2C%20and%20keep%20them%20motivated

Gunderson, S., Jones, R., & Scanland, K. (2004). *The jobs revolution: Changing how America works.* Copywriters Inc.

Hague, D. (2023, June 7). *What we're reading on AI regulation.* Center for Security and Emerging Technology at Georgetown University. https://cset.georgetown.edu/article/what-were-reading-on-ai-regulation/

Hamid, R., & Schisgall, E. (2023, June 21). CS50 will integrate artificial Intelligence into course instruction. *The Harvard Crimson.* https://www.thecrimson.com/article/2023/6/21/cs50-artificial-intelligence/

Hamid, R., & Yuan, C. (2023, July 14). Harvard releases first guidelines for 'responsible experimentation with generative AI tools'. *The Harvard Crimson.* https://www.thecrimson.com/article/2023/7/14/harvard-ai-guidelines/

Harper, R. (2023b, June 8). *ChatGPT: What have we learnt?* [Video]. An academic governance perspective. https://www.youtube.com/watch?v=1V0f3pw2B_0

Hatzius, J., Briggs, J., Kodnani, D., & Pierdomenico, G. (2023, March 26). *The potentially large effects of artificial intelligence on economic growth.* https://www.key4biz.it/wp-content/uploads/2023/03/Global-Economics-Analyst_-The-Potentially-Large-Effects-of-Artificial-Intelligence-on-Economic-Growth-Briggs_Kodnani.pdf

Hillier, M. (2023a, March 30). *Comparing ChatGPT to a calculator and a search engine.* Macquarie University. https://teche.mq.edu.au/2023/03/comparing-chatgpt-to-a-calculator-and-a-search-engine/

Hillier, M. (2023b, March 6). *Advising students about using and citing generative artificial intelligence for assessment.* Macquarie University. https://teche.mq.edu.au/2023/03/advising-students-about-using-and-citing-generative-artificial-intelligence-for-assessment/

Hutson, J., Jeevanjee, T., Graaf, V., Lively, J., Weber, J., Weir, G., Arnone, K., Carnes, G., Vosevich, K., Plate, D., Leary, M., & Edele, S. (2022). Artificial intelligence and the disruption of higher education: Strategies for integrations across disciplines. *Creative Education, 13*(12), 3953–3980. doi:10.4236/ce.2022.1312253

Institute of Ethics in Artificial Intelligence. (n.d.). *About IEAI.* IEAI. https://www.ieai.sot.tum.de/about-ieai/

Italian Government. (2021). *Strategic programme on artificial intelligence 2022-2024.* Italian Government. https://assets.innovazione.gov.it/1637777513-strategic-program-aiweb.pdf

Johns Hopkins University. (2023). *Student use of generative AI.* Johns Hopkins University. https://engineering.jhu.edu/cldt/chatgpt/student-use-of-generative-ai/

Kakuchi, S. (2023, July 11). New government guidelines on the use of AI in education. *University World News*. https://www.universityworldnews.com/post.php?story=20230711114553690

Kampakis, S. (n.d.). *The future of AI in education opportunities and challenges*. TheDataScientist. https://thedatascientist.com/the-future-of-ai-in-education-opportunities-and-challenges/

Kaneko, K. (2023, July 4). Japan emphasizes students' comprehension of AI in new school guidelines. *Japan Times*. https://www.japantimes.co.jp/news/2023/07/04/business/tech/schools-students-ai-guidelines/

Kasneci, O. (2023, July 25). *Generative AI for everyone? [translated]*. Technical University of Munich. https://www.tum.de/aktuelles/alle-meldungen/pressemitteilungen/details/generative-ki-fuer-alle

Klutka, J., Ackerly, N., & Magda, A. (2018). *Artificial intelligence in higher education: Current uses and future applications*. Wiley Education Services. https://universityservices.wiley.com/wp-content/uploads/2020/12/201811-AI-in-Higher-Education-TLH-with-new-bage.pdf

KU Leuven University. (2023, June 9). *Responsible use of generative artificial intelligence (2022-2023 academic year)*. KU Leuven University. https://www.kuleuven.be/english/education/student/educational-tools/generative-artificial-intelligence

Leary, A., Varela, S., Casarez, R., & Ambrose, A. (2023). *Teaching in the age of AI*. Notre Dame Learning, University of Notre Dame. https://learning.nd.edu/resources/teaching-in-the-age-of-ai/

Leswing, K. (2023, April 28). *Tech giants are pouring money into A.I. as they cut costs elsewhere*. CNBC. https://www.cnbc.com/2023/04/28/tech-earnings-calls-show-mega-cap-companies-going-big-on-ai-.html

Leung, M., & Niazi, S. (2023, February 23). Universities on alert over ChatGPT and other AI-assisted tools. *University World News*. https://www.universityworldnews.com/post.php?story=20230222132357841

Liu, D., Ho, E., Weeks, R., & Bridgeman, A. (2023, January 20). *How AI can be used meaningfully by teachers and students in 2023*. Sydney University. https://educational-innovation.sydney.edu.au/teaching@sydney/how-ai-can-be-used-meaningfully-by-teachers-and-students-in-2023/

Lodge, J. M., Howard, S., & Broadbent, J. (2023, May 2). *Assessment redesign for generative AI: A taxonomy of options and their viability*. Linkedin. https://www.linkedin.com/pulse/assessment-redesign-generative-ai-taxonomy-options-viability-lodge/

MacLaren, I., O'Brien, G., Casey, E., Clinch, G., Jackson, N., Lane, B., & Peck, C. (2023). *NAIN generative AI: Guidelines for educators*. Quality and Qualifications Ireland. https://www.qqi.ie/sites/default/files/2023-09/NAIN%20Generative%20AI%20Guidelines%20for%20Educators%202023.pdf

Manga, D. (2023, March 30). *Which UK Universities have banned ChatGPT?* Desiblitz. https://www.desiblitz.com/content/which-uk-universities-have-banned-chatgpt

McInnes, R. (2023, September 11). Embracing generative AI as a co-design partner for designing and developing courses. *Times Higher Education*. https://www.timeshighereducation.com/campus/embracing-generative-ai-codesign-partner-designing-and-developing-courses

Monash University. (2023a). Generative AI in education. In *Inquiry into the use of generative artificial intelligence in the Australian education system - Submission 3.* Monash University. https://www.aph.gov.au/DocumentStore.ashx?id=98d34f1a-1f3b-4ee1-a742-f57076f924c8&subId=745132

Monash University. (2023b). *Generative AI and assessment.* Monash. https://www.monash.edu/learning-teaching/teachhq/Teaching-practices/artificial-intelligence/generative-ai-and-assessment

Morton-Aiken, J. (2023). *Intentional pedagogy with AI technology.* Brown University and The Harriet W. Sheridan Center for Teaching and Learning. https://www.brown.edu/sheridan/teaching-learning-resources/teaching-resources/intentional-pedagogy-ai-technology

Naughton, J. (2023, January 23). The ChatGPT bot is causing panic now – but it'll soon be as mundane a tool as Excel. *The Guardian.* https://www.theguardian.com/commentisfree/2023/jan/07/chatgpt-bot-excel-ai-chatbot-tech

Nguyen, N. (2023, August 23). *AI in higher education: 8 key strategies for institutional leaders.* https://feedbackfruits.com/blog/ai-in-higher-education-8-key-strategies-for-institutional-leaders

Nolan, B. (2023, January 20). Here are the schools and colleges that have banned the use of ChatGPT over plagiarism and misinformation fears. *Insider.* https://www.businessinsider.com/chatgpt-schools-colleges-ban-plagiarism-misinformation-education-2023-1

NoyS.ZhangW. (2023, March 6). *Experimental evidence on the productivity effects of generative artificial intelligence.* http://dx.doi.org/ doi:10.2139/ssrn.4375283

OECD. (2023). *Fostering and assessing students' creative and critical thinking skills in higher education.* OECD. https://www.oecd.org/education/ceri/fostering-assessing-students-creative-and-critical-thinking-skills-in-higher-education.htm

Open A. I. (2023). *ChatGPT (Version 3) [Large language model].* Open AI. https://chat.openai.com/chat

Poorvu Center. (2023). *AI guidance.* Yale University. https://poorvucenter.yale.edu/AIguidance

Price, L., & Sheikh, I. (2023, January 30). University responds to the emergence of ChatGPT in education. *The Observer.* https://ndsmcobserver.com/2023/01/university-responds-to-emergence-of-chatgpt-in-education/

Queensland University of Technology. (2023). Queensland University of Technology response to the House of Representatives Standing Committee on employment, education and training inquiry into the use of generative artificial intelligence in the Australian education system. In *Inquiry into the use of generative artificial intelligence in the Australian education system - Submission 57.* https://www.aph.gov.au/DocumentStore.ashx?id=5b6f1c07-ae71-4187-8df3-8fd0fc059490&subId=745319

Rauch, S. (2023, August 11). *How AI is impacting industries worldwide.* Simplilearn. https://www.simplilearn.com/ai-artificial-intelligence-impact-worldwide-article

Russell Group. (2023). *Russell Group principles on the use of generative AI tools in education.* Russell Group. https://russellgroup.ac.uk/media/6137/rg_ai_principles-final.pdf

Selwood, I., & Pilkington, R. (2005). Teacher workload: Using ICT to release time to teach. *Educational Review*, *57*(2), 163–174. https://www.tandfonline.com/doi/full/10.1080/0013191042000308341 . doi:10.1080/0013191042000308341

Seo, K., Tang, J., Roll, I., Fels, S., & Yoon, D. (2021). The impact of artificial intelligence on learner–instructor interaction in online learning. *International Journal of Educational Technology in Higher Education*, *18*(54), 54. doi:10.1186/s41239-021-00292-9 PMID:34778540

Shanahan, M. (2023, February 23). *Talking about Large Language Models.* Imperial College London. https://arxiv.org/pdf/2212.03551.pdf

Shum, S. (2023b, June 8). *ChatGPT What have we learnt? What do we need to learn next?* ChatGPT: What have we learnt? https://www.youtube.com/watch?v=1V0f3pw2B_0

Siliezar, J. (2023, March 8). *Suresh Venkatasubramanian tells congress that AI guardrails are needed.* Brown University. https://cs.brown.edu/news/2023/03/08/suresh-venkatasubramanian-tells-congress-ai-guardrails-are-needed/

Southgate, E. (2020, August 12). *Artificial intelligence, ethics, equity and higher education: A 'beginning-of-the-discussion' paper.* National Centre for Student Equity in Higher Education. https://www.ncsehe.edu.au/publications/artificial-intelligence-ethics-equity-higher-education/

Spataro, J. (2023, March 16). *Introducing Microsoft 365 copilot – your copilot for work.* Microsoft. https://blogs.microsoft.com/blog/2023/03/16/introducing-microsoft-365-copilot-your-copilot-for-work/

Stanford University. (2023, February 16). *Generative AI policy guidance.* Stanford University. https://communitystandards.stanford.edu/generative-ai-policy-guidance

Swain, S. (2023, April 12). *The jobs at most risk of being replaced by artificial intelligence.* 9 News. https://www.9news.com.au/national/jobs-ai-will-replace-technology/dcaf8d90-14cb-426e-8605-712555ad4995#1

TechNews. (2023, July 7). *ChatGPT may lead to the downfall of education and critical thinking.* TechNews. https://www.techbusinessnews.com.au/blog/chatgpt-may-lead-to-the-downfall-of-eduction-and-critical-thinking/

The Whitehouse. (2023, October 30). *Fact sheet: President Biden issues executive order on safe, secure, and trustworthy artificial intelligence.* The White House. https://www.whitehouse.gov/briefing-room/statements-releases/2023/10/30/fact-sheet-president-biden-issues-executive-order-on-safe-secure-and-trustworthy-artificial-intelligence/

Thompson, S., & O'brien, K. (2023, July 18). *Russell Group Universities issue guidelines on how students can use ChatGPT in their studies.* Kingsley Napley. https://www.kingsleynapley.co.uk/insights/blogs/regulatory-blog/russell-group-universities-issue-guidelines-on-how-students-can-use-chatgpt-in-their-studies

Tk, K. (2023, March 23). *Generative AI: Exploring ethical concerns and possible adverse effects on society.* LinkedIn. https://www.linkedin.com/pulse/generative-ai-exploring-ethical-concerns-possible-adverse-tk/

UK Government Department for Education. (2023, March). *Generative artificial intelligence in education: Departmental statement.* UK Government Department for Education. https://assets.publishing.service.gov.uk/government/uploads/system/uploads/attachment_data/file/1146540/Generative_artificial_intelligence_in_education_.pdf

University of Chicago. (2023, June 5). *UChicago joins partnership to make AI generative for higher education.* University of Chicago. https://www.lib.uchicago.edu/about/news/uchicago-joins-partnership-to-make-ai-generative-for-higher-education/

University of Florida. (n.d.). *Building the nation's first AI university.* University of Florida. https://indd.adobe.com/view/99192ccb-6a52-49d9-9479-e447550d15b8

University of Groningen (Rijksuniversiteit Groningen). (2023, May 26). *Future.* University of Groningen (Rijksuniversiteit Groningen). https://edusupport.rug.nl/2430337110

University of Illinois System. (2022). *Generative AI.* University of Illinois System. https://www.vpaa.uillinois.edu/digital_risk_management/generative_ai/

University of Pennsylvania. (2023). *Generative AI and Its Implications for Your Teaching.* University of Pennsylvania. https://ctl.upenn.edu/resources/tech/generativeai/

University of Queensland. (2023a). *Planning for learning.* University of Queensland. https://itali.uq.edu.au/teaching-guidance/teaching-practices/planning-learning

University of Queensland. (2023b). *Authentic assessment.* University of Queensland. https://itali.uq.edu.au/teaching-guidance/assessment/designing-assessment/authentic-assessment#1

University of Sydney. (2023). Generative AI in education inquiry. In *Inquiry into the use of generative artificial intelligence in the Australian education system - Submission 44.* University of Sydney. https://www.aph.gov.au/DocumentStore.ashx?id=244d2db3-a7de-4631-9416-3378e1882a27&subId=745296

U.S. Department of State. (2023). *Artificial intelligence.* U.S. Department of State. https://www.state.gov/artificial-intelligence/

Walker, R. (2023, June 14). *California professors test out AI in the classroom, even as cheating debate continues.* CalMatters. https://calmatters.org/education/higher-education/2023/06/ai-classroom-california/

Wolany, G. (2023, June 23). *In curiosity we trust: AI scouting for the ZHDK* [Online]. Beyond ChatGPT - what next for generative AI in higher education? https://eua.eu/events/277:beyond-chatgpt-what-next-for-generative-ai-in-higher-education.html

Yang, M. (2023, January 7). New York City schools ban AI chatbot that writes essays and answers prompts. *The Guardian.* https://www.theguardian.com/us-news/2023/jan/06/new-york-city-schools-ban-ai-chatbot-chatgpt

Zhang, K., & Aslan, A. (2021). AI technologies for education: Recent research & future directions. *Computers and Education: Artificial Intelligence*, *2*, 100025. Advance online publication. doi:10.1016/j.caeai.2021.100025

KEY TERMS AND DEFINITIONS

AI – Artificial Intelligence: – technology or computer systems that can perform tasks that previously required human intelligence such as speech recognition and language translation.

GenAI – Generative Artificial Intelligence: – a type of artificial intelligence that can produce content (text, images, and audio etc.). In some circumstances AI and Gen AI can be used interchangeably and in the chapter the authors may have selected one over the other as a more fitting choice relating to the discussion.

HE – Higher Education: – Formal adult education.

HEI – Higher Education Institutions: - universities or collages (private or public) that provide education to generally adult students.

ChatGPT: – an artificial intelligence chatbot that uses human language to create content.

LLM – Large Language Model: – a type of artificial intelligence algorithm that uses large data sets to generate and predict new content.

PCA – Pedagogical Conversational Agent: – autonomous characters that interact with students in a learning environment.

Sociotechnical: – technology that incorporates human and social interactions.

AI Hallucinations: – responses by AI powered by LLMs in which they appear plausible and factual but are incorrect. These can be nonsensical.

Chapter 8
Reframing Assessments:
Designing Authentic Assessments in the Age of Generative AI

Peter Matheis
Navitas, Australia

Jubin Jacob John
Navitas, Australia

ABSTRACT

This study addresses the limitations of traditional assessment practices and proposes a conceptual model to reframe assessments for authenticity in the context of generative artificial intelligence (AI). Traditional assessment practices often fail to capture diverse knowledge and can be exploited by students' misuse of generative AI tools for unfair academic advantages, which underscores the need for robust assessment mechanisms. This study explores how authentic assessments can be integrated with generative AI tools to mitigate academic dishonesty and enhance the learning experience. Building on existing AI approaches in higher education, this study develops a model integrating generative AI in authentic assessments. This model can serve as a framework for incorporating authenticity in assessment practices while leveraging the capabilities of generative AI. An example illustrating the conceptual model, along with several reimagined authentic assessment types, and mitigation strategies for reframing authentic assessment design, are provided.

INTRODUCTION TO AUTHENTIC ASSESSMENT IN GENERATIVE AI

Generative AI has recently gained prominence in education and research. In academia, AI tools excel in generating literary texts (Tlili et al., 2023), aiding curriculum development (Cotton et al., 2023), promoting collaborative learning (Dwivedi et al., 2023), and enhancing student engagement (Kuhail et al., 2022). Moreover, generative AI offers personalised assistance (Farrokhnia et al., 2023) and the potential to evolve into a one-on-one personal tutor (Yeadon et al., 2022). Generative AI's diverse capabilities promise to transform education and research practices; however, students have been using generative

DOI: 10.4018/979-8-3693-0240-8.ch008

AI tools inappropriately to gain an unfair advantage in their academic pursuits (Hung & Chen, 2023). These instances of misuse often involve using such tools to generate essays, answers to assignments, or even responses during exams, which can compromise the integrity of the educational process.

Assessment plays a pivotal role in student experience and institutional administration. However, its implementation within regulatory quality frameworks has led to technological challenges and student issues associated with the integrity of the assessment (Bryant, 2023). Authentic assessments, which emphasise real-world problem-solving and critical thinking (Ashford-Rowe et al., 2014), can help address academic misconduct with generative AI tools by evaluating students' genuine understanding and application of knowledge rather than rote memorisation or plagiarism-prone tasks. An empirical study by Sotiriadou et al (2020) implemented scaffolded authentic assessments, including interactive oral examinations, to enhance academic integrity and reduce academic misconduct. These assessments were found effective in aligning with real-world scenarios, thereby diminishing misconduct tendencies while also improving students' professional identity, communication skills, and employability prospects.

This chapter aims to delineate the attributes of authentic assessment to enhance student learning in an AI-centric environment by distilling the components from the current body of literature, constructing a conceptual framework, and employing this model to maximise the benefits of generative AI in academic contexts. This framework aims to safeguard academic integrity by effectively mitigating the misuse of AI in educational settings. Although the purpose of this chapter is to conceptualise a framework that alleviates misconduct through mitigation, the term 'mitigation' in this context does not imply avoidance of AI use by staff. Rather, it refers to implementing authentic assessment as a strategy to mitigate students' potential misuse of generative AI tools. This nuanced interpretation is essential for accurately conveying the intended message within the developed academic framework.

Background and Importance of Authentic Assessment in Higher Education

Traditional assessments are typically indirect, one-shot, speed-based tests that emphasise objective measurement through standardised formats. In contrast, authentic assessments involve tasks that mirror real-world challenges, focusing on students' ability to apply knowledge and skills in practical contexts (Saher et al., 2022). Authentic assessments are seen as more effective in assessing higher-order thinking and problem-solving skills, while traditional assessments are often limited to evaluating memorisation and recall abilities (Saher et al., 2022). Authentic assessments provide an engaging alternative to traditional methods (Ashford-Rowe et al., 2014; Gulikers et al., 2008). It can complement and diversify the assessment repertoire without replacing traditional methods (Dunsmuir et al., 2017). Unlike traditional assessments, authentic assessments require tasks that evaluate understanding and application in real-life, professional contexts beyond the classroom (Ashford-Rowe et al., 2014; Janesick, 2001), fostering higher-order thinking skills (Ashford-Rowe et al., 2014). However, vague assessment criteria and their difficulty may challenge students unsure of the assessment instructions and rubrics (Hunt et al., 2012; Hunter & Docherty, 2011). The advent of new technology in educational settings has accentuated existing limitations within traditional and authentic assessment frameworks, highlighting the need for more adaptive, technologically integrated approaches to accurately evaluate students' real-world skills and competencies (Lim et al., 2022).

Before the emergence of generative AI, there were already discussions about the need to readjust higher education (HE) to emphasise authentic assessment. This is due to its ability to bridge the gap between theoretical knowledge and real-world application, enrich learning environments, and cultivate a capacity for lifelong learning. These nurture aptly equipped and adaptable individuals to fulfil contemporary professional demands (Villarroel et al., 2018) and address academic misconduct challenges (Sotiriadou et al., 2020).

Background and Importance of Generative AI in Higher Education

Generative AI, using techniques like Variational Autoencoders (VAE) and Generative Adversarial Networks (GANs), creates realistic content in various forms (e.g., text, images, sound, video, etc.), with tools like ChatGPT and Dall-E offering vast applications in sectors like healthcare, education, media, tourism, and other fields due to their advanced capabilities (Chan & Wu, 2023). Studies have explicated several benefits of using generative AI in HE, including its impact on enhancing the learning experience (Dehouche & Dehouche, 2023) and improving learning assessment (Mizumoto & Eguchi, 2023). For example, tools such as ChatGPT enrich students' learning experiences by responding to user prompts and generating original content while text-to-image generators like DALL-E are valuable for teaching technical and artistic concepts (Dehouche & Dehouche, 2023). For academics, embracing generative AI tools has been advocated to augment teaching and assessment (Jovanovic et al., 2022). ChatGPT is found to reduce grading time, ensure scoring consistency, and provide immediate feedback, potentially transforming the teaching and learning process and enhancing student outcomes in HE (Mizumoto & Eguchi, 2023).

However, from a learning perspective, there are challenges and concerns about using generative AI in HE stemming from ethical and plagiarism issues (Kumar, 2023), language proficiency requirements (Warschauer et al., 2023), use of biased, inaccurate, or harmful content (Harrer, 2023; Mogali, 2023), and challenges of academic integrity (Peres et al., 2023). While generative AI outputs are often original and relevant in the context of plagiarism, they may lack personal perspectives and contain inappropriate references (Kumar, 2023). This raises ethical concerns regarding the authenticity of student work and the potential for academic misconduct, as this can be challenging for educators to discern genuine responses and potentially undermine the integrity of higher education (Cotton et al., 2023). Moreover, an overreliance on these tools may hinder students' genuine efforts to develop writing competencies (Abd-Alrazaq et al., 2023), bypassing the learning process. In the context of academic integrity, the inability of most plagiarism checkers to detect AI-generated content complicates identifying original authorship, potentially compromising the validity of assessment practices (Khalil & Er, 2023; Peres et al., 2023; Ventayen, 2023). Therefore, students 'misusing AI' in assessments can diminish critical thinking and pose academic integrity challenges, adversely affecting student learning (Sullivan et al., 2023; Geerling et al., 2023), requiring a review of current pedagogical models to address this issue.

Advancements in AI-Integrated Assessments in Higher Education

Assessment is pivotal in HE, as it allows educators to measure the effectiveness of their teaching methods and curriculum (Ivanov & Soliman, 2023). Through diverse assessment tools like exams, projects, and assignments, educators can discern areas where students excel and pinpoint those that may warrant additional focus or refinement (Villarroel et al., 2018).

It is imperative to acknowledge that maintaining academic integrity is crucial for preserving the credibility and worth of education (Lo, 2023). Although the education sector has swiftly progressed from initially denying the impact of generative AI to experiencing feelings of anxiety, apprehension, and, in some cases, acceptance, generative AI still divides opinions within the sector. Nevertheless, many institutions have implemented policies to regulate and curb inappropriate usage by students and staff while encouraging faculty members to guide students towards responsible exploration and evaluation.

A growing body of research delves into the application of ChatGPT within diverse assessment contexts. Studies have examined both formative and summative assessment methodologies employing ChatGPT (Yeadon et al., 2023; Gilson et al., 2023). In formative assessment, scholars have probed into ChatGPT's role in providing immediate feedback to students, generating hints and elucidations, and bolstering self-assessment processes (Moqbel & Al-Kadi, 2023). On the other hand, studies on summative assessment have concentrated on leveraging ChatGPT for crafting test questions, appraising written responses, and streamlining grading procedures (Dwivedi et al., 2023; Benuyenah, 2023). Given the shortfalls of conventional assessment methods (Van Bergen & Lane, 2016), a re-evaluation and innovation in assessment strategies are crucial, moving towards more contemporary and relevant approaches. Additionally, fostering a supportive academic environment and avoiding overburdening faculty members is essential in maintaining engagement and motivation, ultimately cultivating an academic culture that is adaptable and aligned with evolving technological landscapes (Rudolph et al., 2023).

While generative AI tools hold the potential to offer numerous benefits in education, their integration into assessment practices is not without its challenges (Dwivedi et al., 2023; Geerling et al., 2023). In under a year, generative AI technologies like ChatGPT have transitioned from being on the periphery of awareness to becoming a central focus in HE (Gregorcic & Pendrill, 2023; Lo, 2023). Countless online discussions and media articles related to academic integrity and plagiarism have been initiated, including reports of incidents of students using generative AI in examinations (Farazouli et al., 2023; Kirshner, 2023; Jane, 2023), thereby necessitating a further review of the use of AI in HE.

Current tools aimed at detecting AI-generated text, such as Turnitin, OpenAI's Open Text Classifier, and HuggingFace, in their current form, have significant limitations in sophistication and accuracy, with instances of easy manipulation reported (Davis, 2023). This inadequacy has prompted educational institutions to implement varying responses, including instructional resources and comprehensive guidelines to enlighten students on responsible AI use and its implications on academic integrity and assessments (Sullivan et al., 2023). The ensuing debate and varied institutional responses underscore broader speculation about generative AI inducing fundamental reforms in educational and assessment practices (Zhai, 2022). The consensus, however, affirms the need for further empirical investigation into the associated challenges and benefits (Nikolic et al., 2023).

Adjusting assessment practices for generative AI is crucial, but HE institutions face challenges like educator workload, technology accessibility, consistent functionality, student preparation, and institutional policies affecting new assessment designs. Given these complexities, this juncture presents an opportunity for innovation in current assessment practices, urging a reconsideration and reframing of assessments to uphold authenticity and preserve the value of education.

Existent Authentic Assessment Paradigm

As explicated earlier, assessing student learning is crucial and traditional assessments tend to focus on evaluating students' knowledge through predetermined questions under time constraints. However, these assessments can be limiting as they primarily measure recall and basic understanding, often neglecting higher-order thinking skills, and in response, the authentic assessment emerges as an approach focusing on tasks that mirror real-world challenges and enhancing student learning (Frey et al., 2013; Archbald & Newmann, 1988; Newmann & Archbald, 1992).

Over time, authentic assessment evolved to emphasise *purpose*, *utility*, and *higher-order thinking* skills, including *problem-solving* and *decision-making* (Bosco & Ferns, 2014; Meisels et al., 2010). Authentic assessment is designed to align academic learning with *workplace demands* (Gulikers et al., 2004; Raymond et al., 2012), and many researchers advocate for its application using everyday scenarios and real-life cases (Ashford-Rowe et al., 2014; Iverson et al., 2008; Newmann et al., 1995). Frey et al. (2012) stress the importance of *realistic*, *cognitively complex contexts*. Assessments should, therefore, mimic the professional field of assessing *relevant skills for job performance*, including *collaborative work* (Raymond et al., 2012; Ashford-Rowe et al., 2014). This also transcends to constructivism, where participants learn through interaction and knowledge sharing (Iverson et al., 2008). Transparent assessment criteria and advanced knowledge of such criteria are essential for authenticity (Wiggins, 1990), while feedback, opportunities for re-assessment, embracing mistakes, self and peer evaluation, formative feedback, and critical reflection are pivotal for effective learning (Frey et al., 2012; Darling-Hammond & Snyder, 2000).

Mere categorisation of an assessment as either authentically aligned or not falls short. This has necessitated a thorough analysis to ascertain the presence and extent of authenticity and examine the specific elements contributing to the alignment of learning outcomes with real-world tasks. Some scholars have organised authentic assessments and their attributes into finer, more elucidating subcategories. Several systematic reviews on authentic assessment have been carried out to integrate, analyse and identify central themes, components and characteristics of authentic learning and assessment (e.g., Villarroel et al., 2017; Bosco & Ferns, 2014; Randolph, 2009; Iverson et al., 2007; Rule 2006; Gulikers et al., 2004; Renzulli et al., 2004).

Ellis and colleagues (2019) investigated the use of authentic assessment to assure academic integrity using five factors identified from the literature. The framework was adapted from both Iverson, Lewis, and Talbot (2008) and Bosco and Ferns (2014). They suggested that authentic assessment hinges on five crucial features: (1) Frequency: signifying that the task holds fundamental significance within a specific field; (2) Fidelity: ensuring a faithful representation of real-world conditions; (3) Complexity: requiring engagement with intricate, inquiry-driven challenges; (4) Impact: necessitating practical applicability beyond the confines of the educational setting; and (5) Feed Forward: entailing self-assessment and constructive feedback as integral components of a sequential task series. These features distinguish authentic assessment, highlighting its effectiveness in evaluating and fostering genuine proficiency within a given domain.

Villarroel and colleagues (2018, p. 845) conducted a systematic review to conceptualise the term authentic assessment to inform assessment design and identified three conceptual dimensions: (1) Realism: distinguishes authentic assessment, understood as representing something that might be encountered in the world beyond the classroom; (2) Cognitive challenge: represents a challenge whereby students use higher-order cognitive skills related to using, modifying, or rebuilding knowledge into something new, and (3) Evaluative judgement: necessary capability of graduates to make decisions about the quality of work of oneself and others (Villarroel et al., 2018, p. 845). It allows students to anticipate, monitor and improve the quality of their work and that of others. These dimensions can define and evaluate the quality of assessments designed to reflect real-world tasks and promote deeper learning.

Iverson, Lewis, & Talbot's (2008) framework for determining the authenticity of tasks explicates five criteria for authenticity: (1) Alignment with professional activity: the task mirrors the activities performed by professionals in the field of study; (2) Authentic environment and audience: the task is performed and assessed in an authentic environment; (3) Development of higher-order thinking: the task develops and stimulates higher-order thinking within students through complex challenges; (4) Self-reflection: the task involves students engaging in self-reflection; (5) Formative and forward-feeding: the task is formative and provides feedback for improving subsequent tasks. The framework can be used to evaluate the authenticity of instructional tasks to improve current practices.

The three frameworks converge on authentic assessment, each offering distinct but complementary perspectives. They all emphasise the importance of designing assessments that reflect real-world settings, involve higher-order thinking, provide an authentic environment and audience, promote self-reflection, and offer formative feedback for improvement. Together, these frameworks enrich the understanding and application of authentic assessment, providing a comprehensive guide for designing assessments that mirror real-world contexts and foster deeper learning. The dimensions and criteria will be adopted as foundational models in conceptualising reframing authentic assessment.

Conceptual Model of Authentic Assessment

Based on an extensive review of authentic assessment literature, the following model serves as a framework for incorporating authenticity in assessment practices while leveraging the capabilities of generative AI and, in turn, mitigating the academic integrity risks associated with the misuse of generative AI by students. Before applying the model, it is necessary to ensure that assessments align with the learning outcomes (Lasen et al., 2018) and comply with the Australian Higher Education Standards Framework 2021 legislation (specifically Part A Section 1.4 clauses 3 and 4). Furthermore, the model incorporates graduate qualities that are essential for human skills that are not replaceable by AI. It also employs the Structure of the Observed Learning Outcome (SOLO) and Bloom's Taxonomies to promote deep and higher-order learning in authentic task design (Biggs & Collins, 1982; Anderson & Krathwohl, 2001).

The proposed **Comprehensive Authentic Assessment Model (CAAM)** is a holistic framework that integrates the key components and elements from the following three authentic assessment models: Villarroel and colleagues (2017), Iverson, Lewis, & Talbot (2008), and Ellis and colleagues (2019). CAAM is intended to inform the design and evaluation of realistic and reflective assessments of real-world tasks, promote higher-order cognitive skills, encourage evaluative judgment, and provide a comprehensive learning experience.

The model incorporates four dimensions - Authenticity in Task Design, Cognitive Engagement, Critical Reflection, and Formative Feedback. Each dimension and component serve a distinct purpose and contributes to the framework for creating authentic assessments (refer to Appendix 1 caveat). The components are designed to work together synergistically to ensure that assessments are realistic, cognitively challenging, and promote evaluative judgment while also providing opportunities for self-reflection, formative feedback, and future growth. The dimensions and components of CAAM are explicated below:

Dimension 1: Authenticity in Task Design

- *Relevance to Professional Activity:* The assessment task aligns with real-world professional activities, making it relevant and meaningful to learners (Iverson et al., 2008; Bosco & Ferns, 2014; Wiggins, 1999).

- *Commonality in Practice:* The task is common or fundamental to the discipline, profession, or workplace, ensuring its authenticity in context (Ellis et al., 2019).
- *Reflective Fidelity:* The task accurately reflects the conditions and constraints of the discipline, profession, or workplace where it would typically be performed (Ellis et al., 2019; Wiggins & McTighe, 2006).

Dimension 2: Cognitive Engagement

- *Contextual Immersion:* The assessment task requires learners to perform in an environment and for an audience that closely resembles real-world scenarios (Iverson et al., 2008; Wiggins, 1999).
- *Higher-Order Thinking:* The task not only mirrors professional practice but also demands critical thinking, problem-solving, and application of knowledge to solve complex, systemic problems (Iverson et al., 2008; Zessoules & Gardner, 1991).
- *Inquiry-Based Complexity:* The task involves complex, inquiry-based challenges that encourage students to explore and develop contingent solutions (Ellis et al., 2019; Wiggins, 1999).

Dimension 3: Critical Reflection

- *Critical Self-Reflection:* The assessment process includes opportunities for students to self-reflect. It also involves teachers continuously evaluating their learning and teaching methods, fostering a deeper understanding of their actions' impacts, and encouraging a sense of responsibility in learning and assessment processes (Iverson et al., 2008; Darling-Hammond & Snyder, 2000).
- *Evaluative Judgement:* The assessment process includes opportunities for students to regulate and evaluate their learning and make judgements about the quality of their work and others, encouraging them to assess their work critically and identify areas for improvement, fostering a sense of responsibility for quality and continuous improvement (Villarroel et al., 2017; Tai et al., 2016; Boud & Molloy, 2013).
- *Impact Assessment:* The task has a real-world impact, involving participation, sharing, delivery, or use in a real-world setting, which requires students to consider the broader consequences of their actions (Ellis et al., 2019).

Dimension 4: Formative Feedback and Opportunities for Future Growth

- *Provision of Formative Feedback:* Assessors provide constructive feedback that guides students in improving their work and understanding (Iverson et al., 2008).
- *Feed Forward:* The assessment is part of a sequential set of tasks encouraging students to reflect on their performance and plan for future growth and development (Ellis et al., 2019).

By incorporating these dimensions and features into CAAM, educators and institutions can create assessments that prepare students for success in their chosen professions and beyond within the age of generative AI. The Appendix 1 table distils the opportunities to leverage generative AI and mitigate potential risks associated with academic integrity.

Illustrating Conceptual Model Efficacy in Modern Higher Education

This newly developed model adopts previously proposed frameworks to improve tasks' authenticity by including generative AI capabilities. The dimensions identified through the empirical review are foundational to consider in assessment design, thus the following section explores the applications of authentic assessment in AI with case studies and real-world examples with the model. The following sections illustrate the application of the model in the context of medical education and clinical management. However, it's important to note that the model and the principles of authentic assessment using AI can be applied across various disciplines and contexts.

Authenticity in Task Design

Generative AI can design tasks that accurately simulate the work undertaken by professionals, thereby meeting the criterion of relevance to **professional activity**. As Khan et al. (2023) demonstrated, tools like ChatGPT can craft case studies and scenarios that are invaluable for medical students in refining their diagnostic and treatment planning competencies. Through the integration of generative AI, educators can augment clinical reasoning skills and more effectively equip students for actual clinical encounters. Generative AI not only bolsters clinical reasoning for students but, with its pattern recognition and content creation abilities, is essential for applications ranging from code writing to customer interactions (Ellingrud et al., 2023). The influence of automation, facilitated by such advanced tools, is pervasive in roles that demand expertise, creativity, and human engagement.

Moreover, the **criterion of commonality** in practice is addressed by focusing on fundamental and prevalent tasks in the relevant profession or discipline. By selecting such tasks, the authenticity of the assessment is increased, as it reflects practices that are routine or core to the discipline or profession. The wide-ranging applications of generative AI in business are examples of common tasks in practice, ensuring that students are prepared to handle the practical aspects of their respective fields. Therefore, **leveraging** AI through authentic assessments can address the **criterion of commonality.** The **reflective fidelity** of assessment tasks is achieved by designing tasks that genuinely replicate the conditions, constraints, and context of the professional environment (Khan et al. (2023). This can be exemplified by ensuring that the generative AI-created tasks closely mirror the complexities and challenges in real-world professional settings, preparing students to adapt and apply their knowledge in actual professional scenarios. For example, as Khan et al. (2023) exemplify, AI-generated case studies and scenarios refine their diagnostic and treatment planning competencies of medical students can replicate the conditions, constraints, and context of the professional environment, thereby addressing **reflective fidelity**. Understanding the potential and capabilities of generative AI is instrumental in elevating their relevance to professional activities, aligning the learning experience closely with professional requirements and expectations. By doing so, assessments can reflect professional activity, align with standard practices, and maintain fidelity to the professional context, enhancing their authenticity in task design.

Similarly, Rencic et al. (2020) explored the influence of authentic assessments using the theoretical lens of situated cognition theory (SCT) in medical education. The SCT suggests that a clinician's cognitive abilities, such as clinical reasoning, are influenced by their interactions with situational and contextual factors. It highlights the potential for studying these interactions to understand clinical reasoning performance and its assessment better. By creating authentic scenarios, based on Rencic et al.'s (2020) conceptualisation of the SCT, generative AI can benefit in better aligning the student with an authentic environment, thereby addressing the **representation of an authentic environment and audience.** Generative AI tools, such as GitHub Copilot and ChatGPT, can compromise the authenticity of programming assessments, raising concerns about maintaining genuine assessment environments amid AI-generated code assistance (Russell, Caton, & Becker, 2023). However, employing SCT in the context of medical education and creating scenarios through generative AI addresses relevance to **professional activity** and **reflective fidelity**, ensuring that tasks mirror professional situations and incorporate interactions with situational and contextual factors, hence fostering a deeper understanding and enhancement of clinical reasoning abilities in an authentic environment. Furthermore, the impacts of tools like GitHub Copilot and ChatGPT on programming assessments allude to **commonality in practice** and the challenges in maintaining the authenticity and academic integrity in assessments, emphasising the need for vigilance and adaptability in task design to preserve the alignment with actual professional activities and contexts.

Cognitive Engagement

By presenting complex challenges, authentic assessments can stimulate **higher-order thinking** skills, allowing students to delve into critical thinking, problem-solving, analysis, and synthesis within intricate scenarios (Mohamed & Lebar, 2017). However, the rise of AI in education also beckons a re-evaluation of conventional assessments, questioning the validity of traditional methods in appraising the competencies of healthcare professionals in complex decision-making, technology adaptation, and patient interaction. The challenges and ethical concerns regarding the accuracy and dependency on NLP models like ChatGPT and Google Bard underscore the importance of competence development for academic and professional prosperity (Fuchs, 2022; Sok & Heng, 2023). Thus, while integrating innovative assessment methods and technology is crucial in preparing students for **real-world scenarios**, it necessitates a balanced approach and conscientious design to maintain academic integrity and foster analytical and decision-making processes within the student body. Authentic assessments, if contextualised based on real-world scenarios, can profoundly influence **contextual immersion**, **higher-order thinking**, and **inquiry-based complexity** by compelling students to operate in realistic environments and engage with content at an advanced cognitive level, thereby promoting critical analysis, problem-solving, and adaptive learning while exploring diverse, intricate inquiries and proposing contingent solutions.

Critical Reflection

Generative AI, like ChatGPT, can play a pivotal role in crafting cases that incite such cognitive engagement, although it inherently lacks the capacity for **'self-reflection'**. Consequently, educators hold a pivotal role in guiding students toward self-reflection and heightened awareness of their learning strategies, compensating for the current limitations of AI generators (Currie et al., 2023). The integration of technologies like ChatGPT in fields such as medical education requires new authentic assessments that promote practical knowledge and critical thinking (Khan et al., 2023) but these tools cannot foster **critical self-reflection**, emphasising the educator's role in guiding this essential aspect (Currie et al., 2023).

Integrating AI necessitates a balanced approach to maintain academic integrity and **stimulate critical thinking** and **judicious evaluation**, enabling students to make informed judgments about their work and its real-world impact. This can be achieved through the design of authentic assessments (Ashford-Rowe et al., 2014). However, the use of AI necessitates the consideration of concerns raised by Elyoseph & Levkovich (2023) regarding AI's limitations in evaluating critical mental health conditions, for example, and its potential impact on students' higher-order thinking abilities. Given AI's potential inaccuracies and underestimations in high-stakes assessments, students must not rely **solely on AI tools for critical thinking** and **decision-making**, reinforcing the importance of human engagement and critical reflection in assessments. However, it's important to recognise that generative AI, when used appropriately, can be a valuable aid in the learning process. It is also pivotal that educators continually foster self-reflection and judicious evaluation to mitigate the dependency on AI and to nurture innovation, analytical, and decision-making processes within students.

Formative Feedback and Opportunities for Future Growth

Integrating AI tools can substantially enhance the dimension of "Formative Feedback and Opportunities for Future Growth" within the authentic assessment model, addressing both the provision of **formative feedback** and **feed-forward** criteria. Providing **formative feedback** by AI can be invaluable, offering constructive feedback that guides students in refining their understanding and improving their work, a concept illustrated by the personalised learning experiences facilitated by ChatGPT (Baidoo-anu & Owusu Ansah, 2023). Further, addressing the **feed-forward** criterion, the assessment is ideally structured as a sequence of tasks, encouraging students to reflect on their performance and make plans for future growth and development, a process enhanced by the continuous, adaptive feedback and learning experiences offered by ChatGPT. While generative AI cannot replace academics in educational settings, incorporating AI in designing authentic assessments is noteworthy, allowing a collaborative approach to fostering learning and improvement. Particularly in services industries, the real-time decision-making feedback and customised experiences provided by ChatGPT are pivotal, addressing the need to equip students with essential critical thinking skills and confidence required for effective decision-making (Songwei & Yang, 2023). This amalgamation of AI in educational **feedback systems** ultimately improves the learning impact, equipping students with robust, holistic learning experiences.

Reframing Assessment Design for Mitigation

The increasing prevalence of AI in generating assignments has prompted concerns over their impact on education. There are two potential scenarios. One, where the value of HE is questioned as students, assisted by AI, perform equally well in their jobs as if they did the coursework themselves, prompting a re-evaluation and potential reformation of educational focuses and outcomes (Scott, 2023). The alternative scenario suggests serious repercussions, especially for students in online classes, where AI could hinder genuine engagement and learning, potentially leading to the failure of students to engage in the learning process actively. The focus here is the seemingly widespread dependence and integration of AI in education and how it may reduce the value and essence of learning (Scott, 2023).

Based on the review, several assessment characteristics were identified as indicators to mitigate the misuse of generative AI by students. These indicators act as a foundation for assessment design that were incorporated in the conceptual model as key criteria for reducing risk: (1) diversify assessment formats; (2) assessing product versus process; and (3) forms of knowledge. By considering these additional criteria alongside the CAAM, educators can develop comprehensive assessment tasks that reduce the risk of inappropriate use of generative AI by students and mitigate academic integrity concerns, thereby enabling students to engage in a more meaningful style of assessment and learning process.

The potential misuse of generative AI in assessments necessitates promoting responsible AI use and reevaluating assessment purposes, criteria, and evidence-gathering methods. Integrating existing dimensions of authentic assessment, several academic guidelines are proposed for modifying and overhauling assessments to examine students' learning effectively.

Diversify Assessment Formats

Assessments should explicitly require engagement with **paywalled** sources to safeguard against generative AI's potential misuse (Anderson et al., 2023). These premium resources, such as subscription-based journal articles, are often excluded from the datasets used to train generative AI models. Students demonstrate their ability to access and evaluate credible, authentic information by necessitating interaction with these specialised materials. Academics can ensure tasks are significant and related to **professional tasks** and **real-world problems** by incorporating current events and recent research to make assignments more relevant to professional activity (Rudolph et al., 2023).

Employing a **multimodal** approach in assessments is a key strategy to counter the influence of generative AI. This entails combining various forms of information, such as text, images, videos, animations, and infographics (and/or a combination) (Rudolph et al., 2023). This diverse format challenges students to present information and/or create content uniquely and integrated. It poses a considerable obstacle for generative AI models replicating such diverse content.

Real-time assessment, where a student's performance is observed as it happens, provides an effective deterrent against generative AI interference. Activities like live medical examinations, musical performances, or assessments conducted in the physical presence of the assessor, such as presentations, offer assessments that are inherently challenging for generative AI to replicate accurately (Chaudhry et al., 2023). A **longitudinal** assessment, spanning over time with multiple connected submissions, introduces a substantial complexity that counters generative AI's proficiency. Portfolio-based assessments thoroughly represent a student's learning path as a longitudinal assessment. They document advancement over time and exhibit the student's competence across various tasks and settings (Paulson et al., 1991). Their individualised and longitudinal nature inherently introduces complexity to the assessment process, making them more resilient against AI-driven cheating (Barrett, 2007).

Furthermore, portfolios can offer a multi-faceted perspective of student learning, capturing not only their factual knowledge but also their cognitive processes over time (Ifelebuegu, 2023; Barrett, 2007). This format allows for ongoing progress tracking and feedback, making it harder for generative AI models to predict or replicate future submissions. These activities can be **supervised** (discussed in the F2F environment) and **small-scale** assessments to ensure authenticity and decrease risks of AI-generated academic misconduct.

Engaging students in a **dialogic dialogue** with the assessor forms a robust defence against generative AI's attempts to mimic authentic interactions. Tasks that involve responding to the assessor's questions, prompts, and interactions over a period, such as viva voce tasks and staged components of a larger project with opportunities for iterative feedback after submission, pose a significant challenge for generative AI models.

Assessing Product vs. Process

Emphasising the **evaluation of the process** alongside the final product ensures a comprehensive assessment that is less susceptible to generative AI influence. Requiring students to document and reflect on their thought processes, iterations, and decision-making provides valuable insights that generative AI models cannot replicate. Academics should also allow students to assess their learning process through self-evaluation and reflection on AI usage and involve students in discussions about academic integrity and the impact of AI on their learning and writing processes. These strategies can be encapsulated in authentic assessments that are **personalised** to each cohort, **requiring students to reflect on their experiences, opinions, and learning progressions**. Granting the **assessor visibility** into the student's work process is a critical safeguard against generative AI manipulation. This can be achieved by submitting drafts, sketches, reflective accounts, or other evidence of the development process. This transparency ensures that the authentic effort and thought put into the assessment are evident.

Encouraging **teamwork and collaborative** efforts in assessments, where each team member's contribution is interdependent on others, establishes a dynamic that is inherently resistant to generative AI replication. This cooperative approach underscores the importance of shared contributions, making assessments more resilient to generative AI manipulation. Fostering collaborative efforts through social constructivism among students, where each team member's contribution is interdependent on others, creates a synergistic learning environment (Vygotsky, 1978). Collaborative assessments can take on diverse formats, including team-based assignments, peer evaluations, and joint problem-solving endeavours (Ifelebuegu, 2023). Engaging in collaborative assessments in AI chatbots introduces an added level of intricacy. This collaborative undertaking entails negotiating concepts, empathy, conflict resolution, and shared participation – aspects where AI chatbots presently face limitations (Wooldridge, 2018).

Forms of Knowledge

Designing questions and tasks that demand critical thinking, synthesis of information, complex judgment, and applying creative or novel ideas presents a formidable challenge for generative AI (Rasul et al., 2023; Pellegrino & Quellmalz, 2010). By assessing **higher-order cognitive processes**, educators create assessments resistant to generative AI's attempts at mimicry. Conventional assessments often emphasise basic cognitive skills like memory recall and understanding, which are now more vulnerable to intervention by AI chatbots. Assessments of higher-order cognitive skills prove to be an effective remedy for this challenge. They emphasise skills such as analysis, synthesis, evaluation, and creation, which are fundamental according to Bloom's revised taxonomy (Anderson & Krathwohl, 2001). These skills necessitate active engagement with the learning material, thereby promoting deep learning (Marton & Säljö, 1976). Academics can design authentic assessments to encourage students to make connections between different ideas or concepts and to apply knowledge in new contexts. Such assessments align more closely, intending to equip students for a world that is both complex and rapidly evolving (Reimers & Chung, 2018). Essentially, academics should leverage AI's limitations in contextual thinking by focusing on assignments requiring deep understanding and original thinking rather than recall and knowledge regurgitation.

Designing assessments that assess **contextualised and personalised knowledge** and require the application of concepts to specific settings or personal contexts would ensure a level of individualised thought that generative AI struggles to achieve (Currie et al., 2023). By contextualising knowledge, assessments become less amenable to replication by generative AI models, as they require a nuanced understanding of specific scenarios. For instance, assessments based on real-world problems demand that students link theoretical knowledge with hands-on application, underscoring the need for a thorough and sophisticated grasp of the subject matter. Therefore, problem-based assessment is critical in preserving integrity (Ifelebuegu, 2023).

The Future of Authentic Assessments in AI

The evolving landscape of generative AI demands an adaptive approach to authentic assessment design. This responsibility lies with educators, institutions, and AI developers to cultivate a harmonious ecosystem where technology empowers learning without hindering it and serves as an enabler (Ifelebuegu, 2023). Institutions must provide educators with training and resources to seamlessly adapt assessment strategies in this rapidly changing context. Simultaneously, AI developers must consider educational imperatives and ethical considerations in creating generative AI tools for educational purposes (Zhao et al., 2021).

As technology evolves, so must our understanding of learning and evaluation processes. Relying on rote memorisation for assessments is transitioning towards authentic evaluations, emphasising critical thinking, problem-solving, creativity, and collaborative skills (Binkley et al., 2012). Adapting curriculum and teaching methods for AI integration can enhance learning experiences, automate tasks, and assess complex assignments. Still, viewing AI as a complement to human judgment is vital, not a replacement (George & Wooden, 2023).

Future skills like AI literacy and prompt engineering will be crucial for meaningful interactions with AI and for students to delve deeper into subjects. Educators will assess students' ability to engage effectively with AI and their contribution to AI-generated outputs. However, educators face challenges in maintaining academic integrity, addressing the digital divide, and staying abreast of evolving AI technologies while teaching students about the associated limitations, biases, and ethical considerations (Lacey & Smith, 2023).

Ellis et al. (2019) empirically proved that relying solely on authentic assessment does not guarantee academic integrity. However, it is essential to note that this does not diminish the recognised educational value of authentic assessment design. Our model advocates for the continued incorporation of authentic assessment in HE pedagogy as such authentic assessments can, to a degree, combat the escalating problem of contract cheating. The application of authentic assessment in AI-based learning environments, where students use AI tools, raises a parallel concern. Our current model mitigates AI misuse by students but questions if authentic assessment alone upholds academic integrity. As generative AI evolves, the limitations of such assessments might be more evident, making further research vital to safeguard educational integrity.

Conclusion

The model incorporating generative AI in authentic assessments proposed in this study offers educators and researchers a framework to enhance task authenticity, develop higher-order thinking skills, align students with authentic environments, encourage self-reflection, and facilitate formative feedback and growth. It bridges the gap between academic learning and real-world application, benefiting students' educational experiences and preparing them for professional challenges. Additionally, utilising generative AI in this context opens new avenues for education research, enabling investigations into the effectiveness and impact of authentic assessments on learning outcomes and the development of cognitive abilities. Considering academic integrity concerns, generative AI can be used to improve authentic assessment task design and provide opportunities for its use in assessing and mitigating generative AI misuse.

REFERENCES

Abd-Alrazaq, A., AlSaad, R., Alhuwail, D., Ahmed, A., Healy, P. M., Latifi, S., & Sheikh, J. (2023). Large language models in medical education: Opportunities, challenges, and future directions. *JMIR Medical Education*, *9*(1), e48291. doi:10.2196/48291 PMID:37261894

Anderson, L. W., Krathwohl, D. R., & Associates. (2001). A taxonomy for learning, teaching, and assessing: A revision of Bloom's taxonomy of educational objectives. Allyn & Bacon/Pearson Education Group, Boston, MA.

Anderson, N., Belavy, D. L., Perle, S. M., Hendricks, S., Hespanhol, L., Verhagen, E., & Memon, A. R. (2023). AI did not write this manuscript, or did it? Can we trick the AI text detector into generated texts? The potential future of ChatGPT and AI in sports & exercise medicine manuscript generation. *BMJ Open Sport & Exercise Medicine*, *9*(1), e001568. doi:10.1136/bmjsem-2023-001568 PMID:36816423

Archbald, D. A., & Newmann, F. M. (1988). *Beyond standardized testing: Assessing authentic academic achievement in the secondary school*. Office of Educational Research and Improvement.

Ashford-Rowe, K., Herrington, J., & Brown, C. (2014). Establishing the critical elements that determine authentic assessment. *Assessment & Evaluation in Higher Education*, *39*(2), 205–222. doi:10.1080/02602938.2013.819566

Aydın, Ö., & Karaarslan, E. (2023). Is ChatGPT leading generative AI? What is beyond expectations? *Academic Platform Journal of Engineering and Smart Systems*, *11*(3), 118–134. doi:10.21541/apjess.1293702

Baidoo-anu, D., & Owusu Ansah, L. (2023). Education in the era of generative artificial intelligence (AI): Understanding the potential benefits of ChatGPT in promoting teaching and learning. *Journal of AI*, *7*(1), 52–62. https://dergipark.org.tr/en/pub/jai/issue/77844/1337500. doi:10.61969/jai.1337500

Barrett, H. C. (2007). Researching electronic portfolios and learner engagement: The REFLECT initiative. *Journal of Adolescent & Adult Literacy*, *50*(6), 436–449. doi:10.1598/JAAL.50.6.2

Benner, P., Sutphen, M., Leonard, V., & Day, L. (2009). *Educating nurses: A call for radical transformation*. Jossey-Bass.

Benuyenah, V. (2023). Commentary: ChatGPT use in higher education assessment: Prospects and epistemic threats. *Journal of Research in Innovative Teaching and Learning*, *16*(1), 134–135. doi:10.1108/JRIT-03-2023-097

Biggs, J. B., & Collis, K. F. (1982). *Evaluating the quality of learning: The SOLO taxonomy*. Academic Press.

Binkley, M., Erstad, O., Herman, J., Raizen, S., Ripley, M., & Rumble, M. (2012). Defining twenty-first century skills. In P. Griffin, B. McGaw, & E. Care (Eds.), *Assessment and teaching of 21st century skills* (pp. 17–66). Springer. doi:10.1007/978-94-007-2324-5_2

Bosco, A. M., & Ferns, S. (2014). Embedding of authentic assessment in work-integrated learning curriculum. *Asia Pacific Journal of Cooperative Education, 15*(4), 281–290.

Boud, D., & Molloy, E. (2013). Rethinking models of feedback for learning: The challenge of design. *Assessment & Evaluation in Higher Education, 38*(6), 698–712. doi:10.1080/02602938.2012.691462

Bryant, P. (2023). *Navigating the dissonances of authenticity in assessment: (Re)defining authentic assessment in business education.* Retrieved from https://diberg.blog/2023/09/20/navigating-the-dissonances-of-authenticity-in-assessment-redefining-authentic-assessment-in-business-education-part-2

Chan, C. K. Y., & Hu, W. (2023). Students' voices on generative AI: Perceptions, benefits, and challenges in higher education. arXiv preprint arXiv:2305.00290.

Chaudhry, I. S., Sarwary, S. A. M., El Refae, G. A., & Chabchoub, H. (2023). Time to revisit existing student's performance evaluation approach in higher education sector in a new era of ChatGPT—A case study. *Cogent Education, 10*(1), 2210461. doi:10.1080/2331186X.2023.2210461

Cotton, D. R. E., Cotton, P. A., & Shipway, J. R. (2023). Chatting and cheating: Ensuring academic integrity in the era of ChatGPT. *Innovations in Education and Teaching International, 0*(0), 1–12. doi: 10.1080/14703297.2023.2190148

Currie, G., Singh, C., Nelson, T., Nabasenja, C., Al-Hayek, Y., & Spuur, K. (2023). ChatGPT in medical imaging higher education. *Radiography, 29*(4), 792–799. doi:10.1016/j.radi.2023.05.011 PMID:37271011

Darling-Hammond, L., & Snyder, J. (2000). Authentic assessment of teaching in context. *Teaching and Teacher Education, 16*(5–6), 523–545. doi:10.1016/S0742-051X(00)00015-9

Davis, A. K. (2023, Feb 08). 'Pay attention to it, ignore it or push back on it': Brown professors discuss AI's impact on academic integrity. *The Brown Daily Herald.* https://www.proquest.com/wire-feeds/pay-attention-ignore-push-bac

Dehouche, N., & Dehouche, K. (2023). *What's in a text-to-image prompt: The potential of stable diffusion in visual arts education.*

Dunsmuir, S., Atkinson, C., Lang, J., Warhurst, A., & Wright, S. (2017). Objective structured professional assessments for trainee educational psychologists: An evaluation. *Educational Psychology in Practice, 33*(4), 418–434. doi:10.1080/02667363.2017.1352490

Dwivedi, Y. K., Kshetri, N., Hughes, L., Slade, E. L., Jeyaraj, A., Kar, A. K., Baabdullah, A. M., Koohang, A., Raghavan, V., Ahuja, M., Albanna, H., Albashrawi, M. A., Al-Busaidi, A. S., Balakrishnan, J., Barlette, Y., Basu, S., Bose, I., Brooks, L., Buhalis, D., & Wright, R. (2023). "So what if ChatGPT wrote it?" Multidisciplinary perspectives on opportunities, challenges, and implications of generative conversational AI for research, practice, and policy. *International Journal of Information Management, 71*, 102642. doi:10.1016/j.ijinfomgt.2023.102642

Ellingrud, K., Sanghvi, S., Dandona, G. S., Madgavkar, A., Chui, M., White, O., & Hasebe, P. (2023). *Which jobs will be in demand? Which ones are shrinking? And which ones could be hardest to fill?* McKinsey & Company.

Ellis, C., Van Haeringen, K., Harper, R., Bretag, T., Zucker, I., McBride, S., Rozenberg, P., Newton, P., & Saddiqui, S. (2020). Does authentic assessment assure academic integrity? Evidence from contract cheating data. *Higher Education Research & Development*, *39*(3), 454–469. doi:10.1080/07294360.2019.1680956

Elyoseph, Z., & Levkovich, I. (2023). Beyond human expertise: The promise and limitations of ChatGPT in suicide risk assessment. *Frontiers in Psychiatry*, *14*, 14. doi:10.3389/fpsyt.2023.1213141 PMID:37593450

Farazouli, A., Cerratto-Pargman, T., Bolander-Laksov, K., & McGrath, C. (2023). Hello GPT! Goodbye home examination? An exploratory study of AI chatbots impact on university teachers' assessment practices. *Assessment & Evaluation in Higher Education*, 1–13. doi:10.1080/02602938.2023.2241676

Farrokhnia, M., Banihashem, S. K., Noroozi, O., & Wals, A. (2023). *A SWOT analysis of ChatGPT: Implications for educational practice and research*. Innovations in Education and Teaching International.

Frey, B. B. (2013). *Modern classroom assessment*. SAGE Publications.

Fuchs, K. (2022). The importance of competency development in higher education: Letting go of rote learning. *Frontiers in Education*, *7*, 1004876. doi:10.3389/feduc.2022.1004876

Geerling, W., Mateer, G. D., Wooten, J., & Damodaran, N. (2023). ChatGPT has Aced the Test of Understanding in College Economics: Now What? *The American Economist*, *68*(2), 233–245. doi:10.1177/05694345231169654

George, B., & Wooden, O. (2023). Managing the strategic transformation of higher education through artificial intelligence. *Administrative Sciences*, *13*(9), 196. doi:10.3390/admsci13090196

Gilson, A., Safranek, C. W., Huang, T., Socrates, V., Chi, L., Taylor, R. A., & Chartash, D. (2023). How Does ChatGPT Perform on the United States Medical Licensing Examination? The Implications of Large Language Models for Medical Education and Knowledge Assessment. *JMIR Medical Education*, *9*, 9. doi:10.2196/45312 PMID:36753318

Gregorcic, B., & Pendrill, A. M. (2023). ChatGPT and the frustrated Socrates. *Physics Education*, 58.

Gulikers, J. M., Bastiaens, T. J., & Kirshner, P. A. (2004). A Five-Dimensional Framework for Authentic Assessment. *Educational Technology Research and Development*, *52*(3), 67–87. doi:10.1007/BF02504676

Gulikers, J. T. M., Kester, L., Kirschner, P. A., & Bastiaens, T. J. (2008). The effect of practical experience on perceptions of assessment authenticity, study approach, and learning outcomes. *Learning and Instruction*, *18*(2), 172–186. doi:10.1016/j.learninstruc.2007.02.012

Harrer, S. (2023). Attention is not all you need: The complicated case of ethically using large language models in healthcare and medicine. *EBioMedicine*, *90*, 90. doi:10.1016/j.ebiom.2023.104512

Higher education standards framework (threshold standards) 2021. (n.d.). Retrieved from https://www.legislation.gov.au/Details/F2022C00105/Html/Text#_Toc67664713

Hmelo-Silver, C. E. (2004). Problem-based learning: What and how do students learn? *Educational Psychology Review*, *16*(3), 235–266. doi:10.1023/B:EDPR.0000034022.16470.f3

Hung, J., & Chen, J. (2023). The benefits, risks and regulation of using ChatGPT in Chinese academia: A content analysis. *Social Sciences (Basel, Switzerland)*, *12*(7), 380. doi:10.3390/socsci12070380

Hunt, L. A., McGee, P., Gutteridge, R., & Hughes, M. (2012). Assessment of student nurses in practice: A comparison of theoretical and practical assessment results in England. *Nurse Education Today*, *32*(4), 351–355. doi:10.1016/j.nedt.2011.05.010 PMID:21640448

Hunter, K., & Docherty, P. (2011). Reducing variation in the assessment of student writing. *Assessment & Evaluation in Higher Education*, *36*(1), 109–124. doi:10.1080/02602930903215842

Ifelebuegu, A. (2023). Rethinking online assessment strategies: Authenticity versus AI chatbot intervention. *JALT, 6.* . doi:10.37074/jalt.2023.6.2.2

Ivanov, S. & Soliman, M. (2023). Game of algorithms: ChatGPT implications for the future of tourism education and research. *Journal of Tourism Futures*.

Iverson, H. L., Lewis, M. A., & Talbot, R. M. III. (2008). Building a framework for determining the authenticity of instructional tasks within teacher education programs. *Teaching and Teacher Education*, *24*(2), 290–302. doi:10.1016/j.tate.2007.09.003

Jane, E. (2023, July 19). *"CheatGPT?"* Openforum (blog). https://www.openforum.com.au/cheatgpt-2/

Janesick, V. J. (2001). *The assessment debate: A reference handbook*.

Jopp, R. (2019). A case study of a technology enhanced learning initiative that supports authentic assessment. *Teaching in Higher Education*, 1–17.

Jovanovic, M., & Campbell, M. (2022). Generative Artificial Intelligence: Trends and Prospects. *Computer*, *55*(10), 107–112. doi:10.1109/MC.2022.3192720

KhalilM.ErE. (2023). Will ChatGPT Get You Caught? Rethinking of Plagiarism Detection. arXiv:2302.04335. doi:10.1007/978-3-031-34411-4_32

Khan, R. A., Jawaid, M., Khan, A. R., & Sajjad, M. (2023). ChatGPT-Reshaping medical education and clinical management. *Pakistan Journal of Medical Sciences*, *39*(2), 605. doi:10.12669/pjms.39.2.7653 PMID:36950398

Kirshner, S. (2023, June 15). *Education in the Age of ChatGPT.* Openforum. https://www.openforum.com.au/education-in-the-age-of-chatgpt/

Kuhail, M. A., Alturki, N., Alramlawi, S., & Alhejori, K. (2022). Interacting with educational chatbots: A systematic review. *Education and Information Technologies*, *28*, 1–46.

Kumar, A. H. S. (2023). Analysis of ChatGPT tool to assess the potential of its utility for academic writing in biomedical domain. *BEMS Reports*, *9*(1), 24–30. doi:10.5530/bems.9.1.5

Lacey, M. M., & Smith, D. P. (2023). Teaching and assessment of the future today: Higher education and AI. *Microbiology Australia*, *44*(3), 124–126. doi:10.1071/MA23036

Lasen, M., Evans, S., Tsey, K., Campbell, C., & Kinchin, I. (2018). Quality of WIL assessment design in higher education: A systematic literature review. *Higher Education Research & Development*, *37*(4), 788–804. doi:10.1080/07294360.2018.1450359

Lim, T., Gottipati, S., & Cheong, M. (2022). Authentic Assessments for Digital Education: Learning Technologies Shaping Assessment Practices. In Proceedings of the 30th International Conference on Computers in Education. Asia-Pacific Society for Computers in Education. Iyer, S. et al.(Eds.). November 28 - December 2. 587-592.

Lo, C. K. (2023). What Is the Impact of ChatGPT on Education? A Rapid Review of the Literature. *Education Sciences*, *13*(4), 13. doi:10.3390/educsci13040410

Marton, F., & Säljö, R. (1976). On qualitative differences in learning: I—Outcome and process. *The British Journal of Educational Psychology*, *46*(1), 4–11. doi:10.1111/j.2044-8279.1976.tb02980.x

Meisels, S. J., Wen, X., & Beachy-Quick, K. (2010). Authentic Assessment for Infants and Toddlers: Exploring the Reliability and Validity of the Ounce Scale. *Applied Developmental Science*, *14*(2), 55–71. doi:10.1080/10888691003697911

Mizumoto, A., & Eguchi, M. (2023). *Exploring the potential of using an AI language model for automated essay scoring*.

Mogali, S. R. (2023). Initial Impressions of ChatGPT for Anatomy Education. *Anatomical Sciences Education*, 1–4. doi:10.1002/ase.2261 PMID:36749034

Mohamed, R., & Lebar, O. (2017). Authentic assessment in assessing higher order thinking skills. *International Journal of Academic Research in Business & Social Sciences*, *7*(2), 466–476.

Moqbel, M. S. S., & Al-Kadi, A. M. T. (2023). Foreign language learning assessment in the age of ChatGPT: A theoretical account. *Journal of English Studies in Arabia Felix*, *2*(1), 71–84. doi:10.56540/jesaf.v2i1.62

Newman, F., Bryk, A., & Nagaoka, J. (2001). *Authentic Intellectual Work and Standardized Test: Conflict or Coexistence?* Consortium on Chicago School Research.

Newmann, F. M., & Archbald, D. A. (1992). The nature of authentic academic achievement. In H. Berlak, F. M. Newmann, E. Adams, D. A. Archbald, T. Burgess, J. Raven, & T. A. Romberg (Eds.), *Toward a new science of educational testing and assessment* (pp. 71–84). State University of New York Press.

Newmann, F. M., Secada, W., & Wehlage, G. G. (1995). Authentic assessment tasks. In *A guide to authentic instruction and assessment: Vision, standards, and scoring*. WCER.

Nikolic, S., Daniel, S., Haque, R., Belkina, M., Hassan, G. M., Grundy, S., Lyden, S., Neal, P., & Sandison, C. (2023). ChatGPT versus Engineering Education Assessment: A multidisciplinary and multi-institutional benchmarking and analysis of this generative artificial intelligence tool to investigate assessment integrity. *European Journal of Engineering Education*, *48*(4), 559–614. doi:10.1080/03043797.2023.2213169

Ohaja, M., Dunlea, M., & Muldoon, K. (2013). Group marking and peer assessment during a group poster presentation: The experiences and views of midwifery students. *Nurse Education in Practice*, *13*(5), 466–470. doi:10.1016/j.nepr.2012.11.005 PMID:23265913

Paulson, F. L., Paulson, P. R., & Meyer, C. (1991). What makes a portfolio a portfolio? *Educational Leadership*, *48*(5), 60–63.

Pellegrino, J. W., & Quellmalz, E. S. (2010). Perspectives on the integration of technology and assessment. *Journal of Research on Technology in Education*, *43*(2), 119–134. doi:10.1080/15391523.2010.10782565

Peres, R., Shreier, M., Schweidel, D., & Sorescu, A. (2023). On ChatGPT and beyond: How generative artificial intelligence may affect research, teaching, and practice. *International Journal of Research in Marketing*, *40*(2), 269–275. doi:10.1016/j.ijresmar.2023.03.001

Rasul, T., Nair, S., Kalendra, D., Robin, M., de Oliveira Santini, F., Ladeira, W. J., & Heathcote, L. (2023). The role of ChatGPT in higher education: Benefits, challenges, and future research directions. *Journal of Applied Learning and Teaching*, *6*(1), 41–56.

Raymond, J., Homer, C., Smith, R., & Gray, J. (2012). Learning through authentic assessment: An evaluation of a new development in the undergraduate midwifery curriculum. *Nurse Education in Practice*, *13*(5), 471–476. doi:10.1016/j.nepr.2012.10.006 PMID:23140801

Rencic, J., Schuwirth, L. W., Gruppen, L. D., & Durning, S. J. (2020). Clinical reasoning performance assessment: Using situated cognition theory as a conceptual framework. *Diagnosis (Berlin, Germany)*, *7*(3), 241–249. doi:10.1515/dx-2019-0051 PMID:32031971

Renzulli, J. S., Gentry, M., & Reis, S. M. (2004). A time and a place for authentic learning. *Educational Leadership*, *62*(1), 73–77.

Rudolph, J., Tan, S., & Tan, S. (2023). ChatGPT: Bullshit spewer or the end of traditional assessments in higher education? *Journal of Applied Learning and Teaching*, *6*(1).

Rule, A. C. (2006). The components of authentic learning. *Journal of Authentic Learning*, *3*(1), 1–10.

Russell, S., Caton, S., & Becker, B. A. (2023). Online programming exams-an experience report. In *Proceedings of the 2023 Conference on Innovation and Technology in Computer Science Education* V. 1 (pp. 436-442).

Scott, I. (2023). Yes, we are in a (ChatGPT) crisis. Inside Higher Ed.

SokS.HengK. (2023). ChatGPT for education and research: A review of benefits and risks. SSRN. doi:10.2139/ssrn.4378735

Sotiriadou, P., Logan, D., Daly, A., & Guest, R. (2020). The role of authentic assessment to preserve academic integrity and promote skill development and employability. *Studies in Higher Education*, *45*(11), 2132–2148.

Sullivan, M., Kelly, A., & McLaughlan, P. (2023). ChatGPT in higher education: Considerations for academic integrity and student learning. *Journal of Applied Learning & Teaching*, *6*(1), 1–10.

Tai, J., Canny, B. J., Haines, T. P., & Molloy, E. K. (2016). The Role of Peer-assisted Learning in Building Evaluative Judgement: Opportunities in Clinical Medical Education. *Advances in Health Sciences Education: Theory and Practice*, *21*(3), 659–676. doi:10.1007/s10459-015-9659-0 PMID:26662035

Tlili, A., Shehata, B., Adarkwah, M. A., Bozkurt, A., Hickey, D. T., Huang, R., & Agyemang, B. (2023). What if the devil is my guardian angel: ChatGPT as a case study of using chatbots in education. *Smart Learning Environments*, *10*(1), 1–24. doi:10.1186/s40561-023-00237-x

Van Bergen, P., & Lane, R. (2016, November 30). Should we do away with exams altogether? No, but we need to rethink their design and purpose. *The Conversation*. https:// theconversation.com/should-we-do-away-with-examsaltogether-no-but-we-need-to-rethink-their-design-andpurpose-67647

Ventayen, R. J. M. (2023). OpenAI ChatGPT Generated Results: Similarity Index of Artificial Intelligence-Based Contents. *SSRN*, *4332664*. https://ssrn.com/abstract=4332664

Villarroel, V., Bloxham, S., Bruna, D., Bruna, C., & Herrera, C. (2018). Authentic assessment: Creating a blueprint for course design. *Assessment & Evaluation in Higher Education*, *43*(5), 840–854. doi:10.1080/02602938.2017.1412396

Warschauer, M., Tseng, W., Yim, S., Webster, T., Jacob, S., Du, Q, & Tate, T. (2023). *The affordances and contradictions of AI-generated text for second language writers*.

Wiggins, G. (1990). The Case for Authentic Assessment. *Practical Assessment, Research & Evaluation*, *2*(2), 28–37.

Wiggins, G. (1993). *Assessing Student Performance*. Jossey-Bass.

Wiggins, G. (1999). *Assessing student performance: Exploring the purpose and limits of testing*. Jossey-Bass Publishers.

Wiggins, G., & McTighe, J. (2006). Examining the Teaching Life. *Educational Leadership*, *63*(6), 26–29.

Wooldridge, M. (2018). The road to conscious machines: The story of AI. Penguin UK.

Yeadon, W., Inyang, O. O., Mizouri, A., Peach, A., & Testrow, C. P. (2023). The death of the short-form physics essay in the coming AI revolution. *Physics Education*, *58*(3), 58. doi:10.1088/1361-6552/acc5cf

Zessoules, R., & Gardner, H. (1991). Authentic assessment: Beyond the buzzword and into the classroom. In V. Perrone (Ed.), *Expanding student assessment* (pp. 47–71). ASCD.

Zhai, X. (2022). *ChatGPT user experience: Implications for education*.

Zhao, Y., Ni, L., & Li, D. (2021). Unpacking AI education for K–12: Comprehensive, equitable, and effective. *Educational Technology Research and Development*, *69*(3), 953–976.

KEY TERMS AND DEFINITIONS

Academic Integrity: Adherence to ethical principles and standards in academic work, including proper citation, avoiding plagiarism, and respecting intellectual property rights.

Authentic Assessment: An evaluation method that requires students to apply their knowledge and skills in real-world, meaningful contexts, reflecting actual tasks they might encounter in their professional or personal lives.

Deep Learning: A subset of machine learning that uses artificial neural networks with multiple layers to analyse and process complex patterns in data.

Dialogic: Learning approaches that emphasise open, interactive, and collaborative communication, allowing learners to engage in meaningful conversations and discussions.

Generative Adversarial Networks (GANs): A machine learning framework involving two neural networks, a generator and a discriminator, that work together in a competitive manner to create, refine, and evaluate synthetic data.

Generative Artificial Intelligence: AI systems capable of generating new, original content or responses, as opposed to simply processing and providing predefined information.

Higher-Order Thinking: Advanced cognitive processes like critical thinking, analysis, synthesis, and evaluation that involve deeper levels of understanding and application.

Multimodal: In education, this refers to the use of multiple forms of media (e.g., text, images, audio, video) to enhance learning and communication.

Variational Autoencoders (VAE): A type of artificial neural network used in machine learning, particularly for generative tasks, that learns to encode and decode data in a probabilistic manner.

APPENDIX

While generative AI can be a powerful tool in task design, it may have limitations in replicating certain nuanced, context-specific elements that require human judgment, creativity, or interpretation. Additionally, the effectiveness of the feedback generated by AI may vary depending on the sophistication of the model and the specificity of the task criteria.

Table 1. Opportunities to leverage generative AI and mitigate potential risks

Dimension	Criterion	Operationalisation (Authentic Task Design)	Authenticity	Concepts & Characteristics	Leverage (Generative AI)	Mitigation (Against Generative AI)	Limitation(s)
Authenticity in Task Design	Relevance to Professional Activity	Align assessment tasks with actual professional activities within the chosen field of study.	Ensures tasks directly mirror real-world professional practices.	Professional Relevance, Practical Application, Skill Transferability, Performance, Practical Mastery	Generative AI can assist in simulating specific professional scenarios or tasks to increase realism.	Include elements that require personal reflection, interpretation, and application of knowledge.	It may be challenging to replicate highly specialised professional activities in some fields.
	Commonality in Practice	Select tasks that are common or fundamental in the discipline, profession, or workplace.	Ensures tasks are commonplace and relevant within the chosen field.	Common Practice, Foundational Knowledge, Standard Procedures	Generative AI can assist in generating tasks representative of common professional activities.	Incorporate elements that require domain-specific knowledge and skills that may be hard to generate.	Availability of authentic tasks may vary depending on the discipline or profession.
	Reflective Fidelity	Design tasks to accurately reflect the conditions, constraints, and context of the discipline or profession.	Ensures tasks mirror the real-world conditions of the chosen field.	Environmental Accuracy, Contextual Fidelity, Work Setting Realism, Context	Generative AI can help in simulating specific environmental conditions or constraints.	Include elements that require context-specific understanding or adaptation, which may be hard to generate.	It may be challenging to replicate certain unique aspects or constraints of specific professions.
Cognitive Engagement	Contextual Immersion	Require students to perform in an environment and for an audience that closely resembles real-world scenarios.	Ensures tasks replicate authentic contexts and audiences.	Audience Familiarity, Role Authenticity, Real-World Situation, Engagement, Adaptation	Generative AI can assist in creating realistic scenarios and audiences for tasks.	Incorporate elements that require nuanced understanding or adaptation to specific contexts.	Some fields may have highly specialised environments or audiences that are difficult to replicate.
	Higher-Order Thinking	Design tasks that demand critical thinking, problem-solving, and application of knowledge to solve complex problems.	Pushes students to higher levels of understanding and application.	Critical Thinking, Problem-Solving, Knowledge Synthesis, Creative Solution Development, Complex Challenges	Generative AI can generate tasks that require complex thinking and problem-solving skills.	Include elements that necessitate personal interpretation and application of knowledge.	It may be challenging to generate tasks that truly demand higher-order cognitive skills.
	Inquiry-Based Complexity	Involve students in complex, inquiry-based challenges that call for inquiry-based approaches and contingent solutions.	Engages students in messy, complex problems with no clear-cut answers.	Inquiry-Based Learning, Contingent Problem-Solving, Ambiguity Tolerance, Analytical Thinking, Multidimensionality	Generative AI can help create intricate, multifaceted tasks that involve contingent solutions.	Incorporate elements that require creative thinking and adaptability, which may be challenging to generate.	Generating tasks with sufficient complexity and variability may be computationally intensive.

Dimension	Criterion	Operationalisation (Authentic Task Design)	Authenticity	Concepts & Characteristics	Leverage (Generative AI)	Mitigation (Against Generative AI)	Limitation(s)
Critical Reflection	Critical Self-Reflection	Provide opportunities for students to engage in self-reflection. It also involves teachers continuously evaluating their own learning and teaching methods, fostering a deeper understanding of their actions' impacts.	Encourages students and teachers to critically assess and improve their work and teaching methods.	Self-Assessment, Reflective Practice, Self-Improvement, Empowerment & Choice	Generative AI can assist in generating prompts or questions for self-reflection.	Include elements that necessitate personal reflection and interpretation, which are hard to automate.	The depth and quality of self-reflection may vary depending on the individual student or teacher.
	Evaluate Judgement	Require students to make judgments about the quality of their own work and the work of others. Encouraging them to evaluate	Develops students' capability to evaluate work, fostering responsibility for quality.	Critical Evaluation, Quality Assessment, Peer Review, Feedback Analysis, Performance Review	Generative AI can help in generating evaluation criteria or prompts for judging work.	Incorporate elements that necessitate subjective judgment and interpretation, which may be hard to automate.	Ensuring consistent and fair evaluation judgments can be challenging, especially in subjective tasks.
	Impact Assessment	Involve tasks evaluating real-world impact, requiring participation, sharing, delivery, or use in a real-world setting.	Demonstrates the broader consequences and significance of students' work.	Stakeholder Involvement, Practical Application, Consequence, Significance, Influence	Generative AI can help simulate real-world contexts and stakeholders for tasks.	Include elements that require consideration of broader consequences and stakeholders.	Measuring and assessing real-world impact can be subjective and context-dependent.
Formative Feedback and Opportunities for Future Growth	Provision of Formative Feedback	Provide constructive feedback that guides students in improving their work and understanding.	Facilitates ongoing learning and improvement based on feedback.	Constructive Critique, Performance Evaluation, Enhancement of student skills	Generative AI can assist in generating tailored feedback based on specific task criteria.	Include elements that necessitate personalised feedback and interpretation, which may be challenging to automate.	The quality and effectiveness of formative feedback may depend on the proficiency of the feedback generation model.
	Feed Forward	The assessment is part of a sequential set of tasks that encourage students to reflect on their performance and plan for future growth and development.	Fosters a forward-looking approach to learning and improvement.	Planning for Growth, Future Development, Sequential Task Integration	Generative AI can assist in generating tasks that incorporate elements of future planning and development.	Include elements that require forward-thinking and strategic planning, which may be challenging to automate.	Ensuring consistent implementation of feed-forward strategies may require human judgment and expertise.

Caveat - the dimensions and criteria within this model are not all mutually exclusive and there may be overlap among them.

Chapter 9
AI as an Accessibility Tool:
Using Generative AI to Support Universal Design for Learning Approach

Brenda McDermott
https://orcid.org/0009-0007-5547-3357
University of Calgary, Canada

ABSTRACT

While generative AI is often discussed in terms of challenging notions of academic integrity, it is increasingly looked at as a potential tool to break down barriers in post-secondary education. In particular, this chapter considers how generative artificial intelligence technologies could be leveraged to provide multiple means of engagement, representation and expression (CAST, n.d.). In other words, how can the use of generative AI support social justice in higher education. An ethical approach to generative AI requires respect for the diversity among learners. An ethical approach to generative AI must reflect fairness, which requires recognizing the inherent biases built into the post-secondary learning environments. Using generative AI to support universal design for learning shifts this narrative, considering how technology acceptance could support social justice in post-secondary learning.

INTRODUCTION

In 2022, the emergence of the commonly available Generative Artificial Intelligence (Gen AI) challenged post-secondary education, particularly sparking discussion around the ethics of using these technologies. In particular, several discussions have emerged about the ethics of students using technology and whether that impacts the quality of the assessment or authorship (Eke, 2023; Godwin-Jones, 2022; Xiao et al., 2023). These discussions overlooked the importance of these emerging technologies in addressing existing inequities or gaps. Using a social justice approach to education, this chapter proposes how Gen AI can help address systemic inequity in educational practices by supporting a Universal Design for Learning (UDL). It articulates how current Gen AI tools and future developments can be used by faculty

DOI: 10.4018/979-8-3693-0240-8.ch009

to support student engagement in course material, provide a variety of representations of the content, and facilitate diversity in assessment.

A SOCIAL JUSTICE APPROACH TO GENERATIVE ARTIFICIAL INTELLIGENCE

A social justice approach to education starts with the awareness of how embedded practices and educational traditions have privileged particular learners over others (Evans et al., 2018; Hanesworth et al., 2019). For example, Domage (2017), in his analysis of post-secondary educational institutions, highlights how these institutions have been developed to meet the needs of certain learners, based on gender, racial, class and ability lines. Learners who differ from these norms do not have the privilege of assuming their needs will be met in these settings. As a result, non-normative learners are not given the same opportunity for success. In the context of individuals with disabilities, Domage highlights that these students have to work through an accommodation model to address their needs; in contrast, normative students can meet their needs without this labour.

The rise of machine learning and Gen AI has created new concerns regarding equity in education. One of the common concerns is the use of student data to determine educational approaches and placement decisions. Braun and others (2023) highlight how many of the decision-making associations with AI involve the recognition of variation. In this way, machine learning products often result in an invisibility or hypervisibility of difference. In the education context, the outcomes of both models may continue perpetuating existing biases towards these groups. In addition to perpetuating existing harms, these tools may create new harms by not providing equal benefits from the new technology. For example, benefits based on machine learning in education may only provide positive results for normative learners as the models don't address the marginalized learners because of data bias or lack of data (Baker & Hawn, 2022; Pessach & Shmueli, 2023; Zajko, 2022).

In contrast to concerns about the unexpected bias within machine learning tools, other authors highlight how these models can also be used to identify inequalities. Graham and Hopkins (2022) note how machine learning can also counter the oppression of statistical data by providing new ways to code and understand patterns in data. In this way, they position AI as a tool to reveal oppression that might otherwise be implicit or overlooked.

Another emerging use of AI in education has been machine learning to provide customized learning experiences for students. Integrating AI into the tutoring systems has been seen as a critical element of the personalization of education (Alasadi & Baiz, 2023; Lytvyn, 2023; Wald, 2021) . However, concerns emerge about AI driven personalized education creating the assumption that AI is the solution to inequity in education. If AI is used to personalize education experiences, Katz and others (2022) comments that the tool may not give all students full access to the curriculum, as the AI system may gatekeep access to educational opportunities based on poor performance in particular areas. Berendt and others (2020) notes a difference between the use of learning analytics for customization versus customization by learner choices. The limitation of learning analytics is tied to the samples used in machine learning. McIntrye (2023) highlights that studies on machine learning to customize education experience have focused on affluent populations. She highlights how these applications have not addressed how different access to technology and the infrastructure impacts their functionality. Holstein and Doroudi's (2021) review of AI models in education notes that working on AI personalized feedback and tutoring systems without human oversight is problematic and likely to result in a model that overlooks socio-cultural factors.

UNIVERSAL DESIGN FOR LEARNING

In contrast to the literature highlighting the limitations of Gen AI and machine learning to address marginalization in education, these approaches have not considered Gen AI in the context of Universal Design of Learning (UDL). UDL has gained prominence during the pandemic educational practices as a framework to address the variation in the students' lived reality (Nave, 2020). In this way, UDL is commonly evoked as a way to counter the normative privileges embedded in education, particularly within the post-secondary context, including a more cultural response approach (Westine et al., 2019). UDL is often considered in contrast to accommodations or retrofits, in which the needs of learners are added after the final design is completed. With accommodation, the needs of students with disabilities are treated as an afterthought, reinforcing ableism within the education practices (Dolmage, 2017).

Universal Design for Learning emerges out of the Universal Design movements. Universal Design's roots originate in building and landscape design, where they considered the accessibility of space by design rather than retrofitting afterwards (Basham et al., 2020). One of the benefits of this approach was how accessible design has unintended positive effects that increase access for all users. The most common example is the curb cut effect, in which sidewalks contain small ramps at intersections to improve access for wheelchair users; however, the curb cut benefits a wide range of unanticipated users, strollers, walkers, and those pulling suitcases – creating a broader impact of improved experiences.

Moreover, through a UDL approach to learning, the benefits of designing for diversity resonates for a wide group of non-dominant learners. A similar spread of benefit is associated with UDL in supporting mature learners, additional language learners and others. Through this benefit, UDL is often considered a tool for addressing inequity in the educational landscape beyond a focus on those with disabilities. In other words, it looks to remove barriers built into the educational environment (Davies et al., 2013). In education, Universal Design for Learning originated as an approach to embed the needs of cognitively diverse learners into educational practices. In particular, the model proposed by CAST (n.d.) examines three common cognitive networks involved in education to connect brain science and educational practices, aiming to better meet students' needs.

Despite the benefits of the UDL, several barriers exist to its widespread implementation. There have been concerns about how a UDL model would require additional labour from instructors, and that limits its implementation (Westine et al., 2019). In a post-secondary context, significant concerns have been associated with time and labour. Singleton and others (2019) identified several barriers to the UDL, often including a discussion of the additional labour involved. In the context of course development, the integration of the UDL elements would require action on the part of the instructor to provide options for the students to engage with the content in different ways.

One of the benefits of using Gen AI to support UDL is that it requires less labour on the instructor's part to implement UDL. Gen AI-related tools can help students to interact with the course materials and learning experiences in different ways, driven by student choice. This emphasis on student choice supports alternative learning methods and helps avoid concerns regarding AI's uses in educational customization. Students have full access to the course curriculum and can select how to engage and develop their knowledge and skills.

Using UDL principles to apply Gen AI helps position AI as a tool for societal benefits. In particular, UDL helps to focus on the use of Gen AI associated with its ethical use and development (Paraman & Anamalah, 2023). UDL's emphasis on student choice aligns with the importance of human agency in Gen AI uses. Similarly, its uses to support diversity in education align to increase social capital through

AI use. UDL's emphasis on planning for diversity and creating an opportunity for student choices helps to align AI tools within a social justice perspective. In particular, it solves the problem of personalized learning by having the individual dictate the content engaged with rather than the AI tools. The Gen AI tools support multiple ways of engaging and expressing the content.

UNIVERSAL DESIGN FOR LEARNING AND GENERATIVE AI

By reviewing the UDL principles articulated by CAST (n.d.), this paper provides examples of how features of current and future Gen AI can support the implementation of these principles. In turn, the UDL framework helps to address concerns around AI education by emphasizing elements of ethical AI uses, particularly human agency and prevention of harm (through bias).

CAST's UDL framework is based on the notion of the three neural networks involved in learning – the recognition, strategic, and affective (Rose et al., 2006). The affective network refers to the why of learning. It includes designing learning experiences that address motivation, persistence, and self-regulation. The recognition network focuses on how the content or what is learned is presented. It considers the importance of multiple forms of engagement with the learning materials across different senses. Lastly, the strategic network focuses on the demonstration of the learning; this includes approaches to assessments and reflection on learning.

Affective Network: Why of Learning Through Generative AI

The first element of the affective network involves several actions to create engagement or interest in the subject. This includes providing students with options, authentic learning, and reducing distractions (Campbell, 2004). There are several ways in which Gen AI can support this engagement in learning. Gen AI facilitates engagement by supporting multiple pathways to explore content rather than in a traditional linear fashion.

For example, the Gen AI tool *Ask your pdf* (Block Technology OU, 2023) allows readers to ask a series of questions about a particular document. Rather than requiring the students to read from start to finish, the students can explore the text by asking questions about the tool. For example, Sharples (2023) describes the potential for Gen AI tools that support the development of the articles by providing counterarguments to statements from the students' learning. In using Gen AI as a Socratic questioning tool, the students can engage in debate to refine their understanding of the text. These interactions help maintain student choice and direct their learning based on their interests in the topic. Similarly, Gen AI can support the creation of networked or mapped learning tools, where students can explore the content in various pathways rather than a linear structure.

In addition to providing tools for engaging interest in learning, Gen AI tools help manage distractions. Early AI tools for text-reading software have a long history of reducing distraction. For example, text-reading software has been used to support the attention of learners with disabilities in reading, attention, or English as an additional language (Harvey et al., 2013; Wood et al., 2018). Similarly, Gen AI can limit distraction by chunking the content provided into sections to reduce distraction. Several existing tools, such as Genei (2021) and Jasper (2023), offer text summarization and reformat existing textual documents by creating headings and subheadings. This reformatting of text can help maintain attention by providing chunks rather than full text, which can help students maintain motivation through the documents.

The second element of the affective network emphasizes keeping students engaged throughout the learning process. This engagement is maintained by emphasizing goal-oriented learning, scaffolding, and collaboration. These elements of design support student persistence throughout the learning activity. Gen AI can support various aspects of resilience by supporting goal-oriented learning, providing scaffolding for multiple skills, and feedback on elements of progress. Several Gen AI writing assistants, such as *Grammarly Go (2023),* offer customized outlines for writing documents in response to prompts. Through an interactive process, the students can customize the level of the guidance or steps based on their understanding of the section. Using Gen AI tools, students can get customized step-by-step instructions down to the level of detail they need. Rather than relying on the assignment outline provided by the instructor, students can use Gen AI to explain critical steps, develop timelines, and seek out additional resources for key elements. Students can break down steps into increased details through an interactive process based on their experience and needs.

Building on the idea of authentic learning, goal-oriented learning focuses on the benefits of learning to the students' lived experience. Goal-oriented learning is often defined in contrast to performance-based learning, which focuses on the final grade achieved (Alhadabi & Karpinski, 2020). Performance-focussed learners struggle to make learning-oriented goals. Gen AI could support the brainstorming of these goals. Students can generate goals based on the course content and customize them by including their current degree or career aspirations. Sharples (2023) notes that Gen AI can take on various roles, such as an AI coach that supports students in completing assignments through goal setting and designs. Pocket Confidant (2020) and Plaito (2023) provides computer-based human coaching as a substitute for traditional human-to-human coaching to support student development.

Moreover, feedback, as a way of allowing students to shift and adapt as part of the learning process, is a key component of this network as a way of allowing students to shift and adapt as part of the learning process. Gen AI tools that provide feedback on learning are developing quickly, and the field of products is shifting. While new products and features are emerging, the potential of the tools can be seen in the advancement of AI to provide feedback on writing. Nieminen and Tuohilampi, (2020) notes that AI feedback may support student agency in their learning as students and support student feedback literacy. AI feedback, like any, still requires the student to consider how they would include feedback in their work. However, AI feedback could be more iterative as the student could ask for rephrasing or further explanations of the feedback provided. For example, Feedback Fruit (2023) allows instructors to set parameters for the formative feedback to integrate the instructor's pedagogical experience, with the AI ability to analyze based on criteria. Using more generalized AI tools, AI feedback can also be customized through prompt design to reflect the stages and type of feedback the learner is ready for.

The last step section of the affective network highlights the internalization of this engagement and persistence by building toward a self-regulated learner. In particular, this step involves the ability to reflect and evaluate the learning. Gen AI can be used to support self-evaluation through the development of self-testing questions and supporting evaluative judgements. Furthermore, Gen AI tools can provide samples of self-testing questions in various forms. Cope and other (2021) highlights that one of the strengths of AI tools is how they support measurability, such as students measuring their learning through feedback. Several tools promote their ability to design multi-choice tests or cue cards based on uploaded materials, such as Quizbot (2023) and Revisely (2023). Even non-specialized tools can create review questions for students to check for understanding. Similarly, Gen AI can provide sample responses or drafts of tasks for students to evaluate based on the course rubrics. Using Gen AI examples for evaluations, students better understand the evaluative standards of the discipline. This allows students to internalize feedback that they might receive on their assignments.

Recognition Network: What of Learning Through Generative AI

The recognition network focuses on how the course learning experiences are represented. A key consideration of this network is the shift away from unimodal learning experiences to those with a choice of modalities. This network is rooted in understanding that some modalities may privilege certain learners, because of cognitive functions or cultural tradition.

Gen AI's ability to provide multiple representations of the same content is often discussed as a strength of the tool and its support of accessibility education. The role of Gen AI and Natural Language Processes has allowed support for the shifting between spoken and written language, allowing users to interact with content in different formats (Brewer et al., 2022). Similarly, Gen AI is seen as a support for shifting content between visual representation and textual representation, such as using these tools for generative content description or alternative text for images.

The first element of the recognition network is ensuring that information is provided in multiple models. In particular, the model challenges how materials have been traditionally shown in the visual (typically textual format) or solely in auditory forms. It aims to allow students choices in how information is shared based on their needs. Gen AI has already demonstrated a strong capacity to support the multimodality of information. Audio-captioning tools based on AI models have become mainstays in video conference tools such as those embedded in *Zoom* and *Teams*. Moreover, AI-based note-taking services are becoming more affordable and can provide an alternative representation of lectures, providing more contextualized and chunked information than a straight transcript, such as Glean (2023).

Textual information continues to be more commonly available as auditory with the increased improvements in OCR, NLP, and Gen AI tools. Screen readers have more natural speaking voices, —more than just the transfer of textual to auditory information (Kumar et al., 2023). Generative AI is moving to provide textual information in an alternative visual format. Tools will create images, charts, and PowerPoints based on users' prompts. This suggests the ability for textual information to be represented in new ways as technology emerges.

AI produced alternative text for images continues to improve, with the ability to use contextual cues from the surrounding text. With increasing accuracy expected over the coming years, alternative text for images may become as standard as captioning in meetings. However, in its current state, image analysis is one of the weakest areas of AI analysis (Edwards et al., 2023). As Gen AI tools continue to develop, they will likely increase their ability to support visual descriptions.

The second element of the representation network is tied to the cognitive accessibility of the content presented. Rather than solely looking at a modality, this area considers the impact of language, symbols, and syntax on the learner's access to the material. In particular, it highlights how different linguistic experiences, such as multiple language speakers, may face challenges accessing content (Boals et al., 2018) . In a post-secondary context, students need to become familiar with disciplinary terminology and patterns of expression. As experts who have been socialized in the field, instructors may have difficulty identifying areas challenging for the student population. Several Gen AI tools, such as Paraphraser (n.d.) and Quillbot (n.d.) have been developed to paraphrase or use synonyms in content. While these tools are often marketed as circumventing plagiarism detections, their foundation skills could increase the decoding of the textbooks and other resources for learners. Using a similar pattern, Gen AI could support readers to customize the language or simplify syntax in a reading. Gen AI's ability for pattern recognition could also support the development of glossaries and other tools for students to support the acquisition of this disciplinary knowledge.

As multilingual tools, Gen AI and NLP have been supporting a variety of text translation options. As these modules improve, they can also provide the option of supporting language acquisition skills. Alasadi and Baiz (2023) note that AI tools have been keyed to create a global exchange of ideas by providing transition and composition tools. They note that when used in an instructional context, they can support the creation of multi-lingual learning materials.

The last element of the representation network looks at comprehension from the macro levels, considering how the learners are primed to engage with the material and are supported to understand the material. This includes access to background information on the topics and mapping or relationships. This model of UDL recognizes that not all students have the same lived experience or shared background knowledge before entering the classes. Gen AI provides a tool to support students by ensuring all students have the same background knowledge. This could be done through the interactive model that provides supplemental materials to the learner or as simple as creating hyperlinks in a summary that learners can navigate, such those in Perplexity (n.d.). Gen AI's ability to summarize and rephrase existing knowledge can be leveraged to support the variability in learners.

Gen AI strength in summary and representing existing knowledge can allow it to support the creation or mapping of key ideas and concepts. In this way, Gen AI can support students to understand the interconnection of ideas and the recognition of patterns. Cope and others (2021) describe this as AI's ability to name and identify information, allowing for the search and presentation of the information in alternative ways, such as concept maps. Tools that support the visualization of textual information are one element of Gen AI that can support knowledge mapping. Similarly, Gen AI can be used to chunk information for learning to help the transfer of information. For example, Gen AI can create headings and outlines for documents that don't already have such indications, making it easier for students to see the object. Returning to the idea of the demonstration of learning and transfer, Gen AI can help students consider new cases for application to shift from the comprehension of the information to exploring the application.

Strategic Network: How of Learning Through Generative AI

The last network in CAST's UDL model focuses on how students demonstrate their learning (CAST, n.d.). In this way, it addresses the students' actions and expressions as indicator of learning. One of the key considerations of these practices is recognizing that certain ways of doing or expression learning have tended to be prioritized or emphasized over others; as a result, some learners were privileged by these practices.

The first part of the patterns looks at what physical actions students require to complete the task and where tools and options can be used to allow variation within these actions. Typically, tools include screen readers, dictation software and word protection to support the needs for textual responses. These tools use NLP or AI to recognize language and represent it. Gen AI supports the students to externalize their thinking through tools that help them represent their ideas through AI images (Vartiainen & Tedre, 2023).

The second aspect of the network moves beyond the physical actions required to demonstrate the learning to how it is communicated and expressed. Rather than limiting the options to use tools areas for the multiway of expressing learning, which is no medium-specific requirement. In other words, this looks like a move away from methods of assessment that specify how the learning is demonstrated by allowing for choices. Instructors with a traditional focus on specific mediums of learning expression could look to Gen AI as a tool to support the creation of UDL-style assignments. Gen AI could evaluate and adapt existing assignments to allow for multiple modalities (Cardona et al., 2023). A critical Gen AI tool can provide sample rubrics for evaluation that shift away from medium-specific language.

The second aspect of the strategic network also considers the need for multiple tools to be involved in the building and creating these tools. It highlights the aim of improving performance through practices and different levels of support. This aspect of the UDL corresponds with the notion of considering Gen AI as a teaching tool. By recognizing the need for the tools to support future fluency, Gen AI uses in this context to support future achievement (Koltovskaia, 2020; Shin & Kim, 2022). It could parallel how patchwriting can be seen as a transition step within English as an additional language learning (Leu & Neumann, 2023).

Cope and others (2021) expand this idea to consider how AI can support the deconstruction and reconstruction of learning. They presented that this process highlights how learning is presented in new ways, rather than traditional assessment in which learning had to be inferred. This deconstruction process can be reflected in how prompt crafting provides an interactive process similar to scaffolding (Vartiainen & Tedre, 2023). As the student engages in the prompting process and reflects on the response, they start to understand the impact of their choices on the output provided, particularly the choices that help to reach the designed output.

Lastly, this section highlights the aim of recognizing the role of the executive function in the how of learning. This section includes ways in which instructors need to support goal-setting and planning skills in students. Similarly, it highlights the need for learners to develop ways of managing information and resources. At the same time, it highlights the need for students to monitor along the way. This way, the final aspect of the strategic network has strong ties to the last element of the affective network. Chan & Hu (2023) highlights when students struggle with assignments, Gene AI can act as a virtual tutor, providing personalized learning support and answering their questions immediately. Moreover, Chan (2023) notes that AI not only provides content but also provides ways of processing the information and a mnemonic study approach as well.

Goal setting and planning potential of Gen AI have already been discussed; however, Gen AI tools can also support the more integrative approach to study skill development through Gen AI calendars and reminders. Students could use a Gen AI tool to create a schedule incorporating existing events, lifestyle activities, and specific assignment activities. These tools, such as Reclaim (n.d.) then create calendar entries that sync with other tools and create reminders and ways of tracking process. By building around existing activities and considering students' reported productive times, the customized calendar can become a tool for creating habits and practices.

Gen AI is also increasingly moving into the research spaces where it demonstrates its ability to source and cross-reference information. As research tools, Gen AI can create suggested reading lists for topics, draft literature reviews and support the coding of information. These tools provide starting points for students to understand patterns and potential organizations of information. In this way, Gen AI's ability to label and organization information supports the learner as they look to create models and schemas from this data (Cope et al., 2021.)

CONCLUSION

While Generative AI provides various opportunities to support the consistent integration of the UDL, privacy consideration around the use of the tool remains. Many of the current generative applications gather the information provided to them and use it as part of the ongoing development of these tools. To ensure students' privacy, the Gen AI tools used to support UDL should be constitutional. AI doesn't use the user's information to train the model. Privacy policies and data usage will be key to ensuring that this use of Gen AI does not repeat earlier concerns about personalized learning, such as restricting access to content or inappropriate information sharing (Hsu & Ching, 2023).

Gen AI has the potential to help post-secondary instructors operationalize the promise of the UDL. As an interactive tool that the learners use, Gen AI can customize content to reflect the experience and interests of the learners. Moreover, tools, such as *Slatebox*, (n.d.) and *Stretch* (n.d.) allows for new ways for learners to actively engage in traditional static content, such as text. Similarly, the engagement with the material can be networking or non-linear as students can move around and over content through Gen AI's ability to build links and context to material. This supports the students' affective network and ongoing engagement with the material.

In these ways, Gen AI's strength in representing content in multiple formats helps to align with UDL principles of representation of content while avoiding additional work on the part of the instructors. In addition to supporting multiple modalities, Gen AI can help socialize students into disciplinary knowledge. As Gen AI increasingly supports data visualization and learning, it provides ways of modelling schemata and structures.

In addition to Gen AI's support for the implementation of UDL, UDL also provides a framework to think about how Gen AI can function as a tool for learning. In the strategic network, UDL highlights the roles of technology to enable learners to demonstrate their learning, particularly in ways not limited to particular ways of doing. Gen AI, whether text-based or through visual input, can support the externalization of the thinking. Through its interactive prompt process, Gen AI requires the student to self-reflect on their prompts and the generative content.

Considering the expected improvement of Generative AI and its application in additional learning areas, the applicability to support Universal Design for Learning is only likely to increase. In this way, Gen AI could be integrated into post-secondary as a tool for good. Importantly, the UDL framework does not suggest limiting students' access to content based on their current performance, a recognized problem with using AI in personalized learning. In contrast, AI for UDL would emphasize the multiplicity of access and access in the context of the individual's lived experience. The concern regarding privacy and AI tools would remain but could be mitigated by expanding and adopting constitutional AI that incorporates user interaction into the model.

REFERENCES

Alasadi, E. A., & Baiz, C. R. (2023). Generative AI in education and research: Opportunities, concerns, and solutions. *Journal of Chemical Education*, *100*(8), 2965–2971. doi:10.1021/acs.jchemed.3c00323

Alhadabi, A., & Karpinski, A. C. (2020). Grit, self-efficacy, achievement orientation goals, and academic performance in university students. *International Journal of Adolescence and Youth, 25*(1), 519–535. doi:10.1080/02673843.2019.1679202

Baker, R. S., & Hawn, A. (2022). Algorithmic bias in education. *International Journal of Artificial Intelligence in Education, 32*(4), 1052–1092. doi:10.1007/s40593-021-00285-9

Basham, J. D., Blackorby, J., & Marino, M. T. (2020). Opportunity in crisis: The role of Universal Design for Learning in educational redesign. *Learning Disabilities (Weston, Mass.), 18*(1), 71–91. https://www.ldw-ldcj.org/

Berendt, B., Littlejohn, A., & Blakemore, M. (2020). AI in education: Learner choice and fundamental rights. *Learning, Media and Technology, 45*(3), 312–324. doi:10.1080/17439884.2020.1786399

Block TechnologyO. U. (2023). *Ask for PDF*. www.askyourpdf.com

Boals, T., Castro, M., & Shafer Willner, L. (2018). Moving beyond assumptions of cultural neutrality to improve accessibility and opportunity to learn for English Language Learners. In S. N. Elliott, R. J. Kettler, P. A. Beddow, & A. Kurz (Eds.), *Handbook of accessible instruction and testing practices: Issues, innovations, and applications* (pp. 119–134). Springer International Publishing. doi:10.1007/978-3-319-71126-3_8

Braun, M., Bleher, H., Hille, E. M., & Krutzinna, J. (2023). Tackling structural injustices: On the entanglement of visibility and justice in emerging technologies. *The American Journal of Bioethics, 23*(7), 100–102. doi:10.1080/15265161.2023.2207514 PMID:37339313

Brewer, J., Gerard, C., & Hakkinen, M. (2022, June 3). 3 ways AI can help students with disabilities. *EDUCAUSE Review*. https://er.educause.edu/articles/2022/6/3-ways-ai-can-help-students-with-disabilities

Campbell, D. M. (2004). Assistive technology and Universal Instructional Design: A postsecondary perspective. *Equity & Excellence in Education, 37*(2), 167–173. doi:10.1080/10665680490454057

Cardona, M. A., Rodríguez, R. J., & Ishmael, K. (2023). *Artificial Intelligence and the future of teaching and learning*. Office of Educational Technology, United States of America https://tech.ed.gov

CAST. (n.d.). *The UDL Guidelines*. CAST. https://udlguidelines.cast.org/

Chan, C. (2023, March 9). *AI will transform teaching and learning*. Stanford University. https://hai.stanford.edu/news/ai-will-transform-teaching-and-learning-lets-get-it-right

Chan, C. K. Y., & Hu, W. (2023). Students' voices on generative AI: Perceptions, benefits, and challenges in higher education. *International Journal of Educational Technology in Higher Education, 20*(43), 43. doi:10.1186/s41239-023-00411-8

Cope, B., Kalantzis, M., & Searsmith, D. (2021). Artificial intelligence for education: Knowledge and its assessment in AI-enabled learning ecologies. *Educational Philosophy and Theory, 53*(12), 1229–1245. doi:10.1080/00131857.2020.1728732

Davies, P., Schelly, C., & Spooner, C. (2013). Measuring the effectiveness of Universal Design for Learning intervention in postsecondary education. *Journal of Postsecondary Education and Disability*, *26*(3), 195–220. www.ahead.org

Dolmage, J. (2017). *Academic ableism: Disability and higher education*. University of Michigan Press. http://www.jstor.org.ezproxy.lib.ucalgary.ca/stable/j.ctvr33d50

Edwards, E. J., Gilbert, M., Blank, E., & Branham, S. M. (2023). How the alt text gets made: What roles and processes of Alt text creation can teach us about inclusive imagery. *ACM Transactions on Accessible Computing*, *16*(2), 1–28. doi:10.1145/3587469 PMID:37427355

Eke, D. O. (2023). ChatGPT and the rise of generative AI: Threat to academic integrity? *Journal of Responsible Technology*, *13*, 100060. doi:10.1016/j.jrt.2023.100060

Evans, N., Broido, E., Brown, K., Wilke, A., & Herriott, T. (2018). *Disability in higher education: A social justice approach*. John Wiley & Sons, Ltd.

Feedback Fruits. (2023). *Automated feedback*. Feedback Fruits. www.feedbackfruits.com/automated-feedback

Genei. (2021). *Summary tool*. Genei. www.genei.io

Glean. (2023). *Personal study tool*. Glean. www.glean.co

Godwin-Jones, R. (2022). Partnering with AI: Intelligent writing assistance and instructed language learning. *Language Learning & Technology*, *26*(2), 5–24. 10125/73474

Graham, S. S., & Hopkins, H. R. (2022). AI for social justice: New methodological horizons in technical communication. *Technical Communication Quarterly*, *31*(1), 89–102. doi:10.1080/10572252.2021.1955151

Grammarly Inc. (2023). *Grammarly fo*. www.grammarly.com/ai

Hanesworth, P., Bracken, S., & Elkington, S. (2019). A typology for a social justice approach to assessment: Learning from universal design and culturally sustaining pedagogy. *Teaching in Higher Education*, *24*(1), 98–114. doi:10.1080/13562517.2018.1465405

Harvey, J., Hux, K., Scott, N., & Snell, J. (2013). Text-to-speech technology effects on reading rate and comprehension by adults with traumatic brain injury. *Brain Injury : [BI]*, *27*(12), 1388–1394. doi:10.3109/02699052.2013.823649 PMID:24102239

HolsteinK.DoroudiS. (2021). Equity and artificial intelligence in education: Will "AIEd" amplify or alleviate inequities in education? https://arxiv.org/abs/2104.12920

Hsu, Y.-C., & Ching, Y.-H. (2023). Generative Artificial Intelligence in dducation. *TechTrends*. Advance online publication. doi:10.1007/s11528-023-00863-9

Jasper. (2023). *Text summarizer*. www.jasper.ai

Katz, D., Huggins-Manley, A. C., & Leite, W. (2022). Personalized online learning, test fairness, and educational measurement: Considering differential content exposure prior to a high stakes end of course exam. *Applied Measurement in Education*, *35*(1), 1–16. doi:10.1080/08957347.2022.2034824

Koltovskaia, S. (2020). Student engagement with automated written corrective feedback (AWCF) provided by Grammarly: A multiple case study. *Assessing Writing*, *44*, 100450. doi:10.1016/j.asw.2020.100450

Kumar, Y., Koul, A., & Singh, C. (2023). A deep learning approaches in text-to-speech system: A systematic review and recent research perspective. *Multimedia Tools and Applications*, *82*(10), 15171–15197. doi:10.1007/s11042-022-13943-4

Leu, S., & Neumann, H. (2023). Patchwriting: Co-opting a transgressive practice for pedagogical purposes. In Teaching and Learning Source-Based Writing: Current Perspectives and Future Directions (pp. 80–93). Taylor and Francis.

Lytvyn, M. (2023, June 7). *A framework for responsible AI in education*. Grammarly. https://www.grammarly.com/blog/responsible-ai-education/

McIntyre, N. A. (2023). Access to online learning: Machine learning analysis from a social justice perspective. *Education and Information Technologies*, *28*(4), 3787–3832. doi:10.1007/s10639-022-11280-5 PMID:36210911

Nave, L. (2020). UDL in Online Environments: The Why of Learning. *Journal of Developmental Education*, *44*(1), 30–31. https://www.jstor.org/stable/45381107

Nieminen, J. H., & Tuohilampi, L. (2020). 'Finally studying for myself' – examining student agency in summative and formative self-assessment models. *Assessment & Evaluation in Higher Education*, *45*(7), 1031–1045. doi:10.1080/02602938.2020.1720595

Paraman, P., & Anamalah, S. (2023). Ethical artificial intelligence framework for a good AI society: Principles, opportunities and perils. *AI & Society*, *38*(2), 595–611. doi:10.1007/s00146-022-01458-3

Paraphraser.io. (n.d.). *Text summarizer*. Paraphraser.io. https://www.paraphraser.io/

PerplexityA. I. (n.d.). *Perplexity*. Perplexity A. I. www.perplexity.ai

Pessach, D., & Shmueli, E. (2023). A Review on fairness in machine learning. *ACM Computing Surveys*, *55*(3), 1–44. doi:10.1145/3494672

Plaito. (2023). *Your personal AI tutor*. Plaito. www.plaito.ai

Pocket Confidant, A. I. SAS. (2020). *Pocket Confidant*. www.pocketconfidant.comv

Quillbot. (n.d.). *Paraphraser*. Quillbot. https://quillbot.com/

Quizbot. (2023). *AI question generator*. Quillbot. www.quizbot.ai/

Reclaim A. I. (n.d.). *Smart AI scheduling*. Reclaim A. I. www.reclaim.ai

Revisely. (2023). *AI flash card generator*. Revisely. www.revisely.com/flashcard-generator

Rose, D. H., Harbour, W., Johnston, C. S., Daley, S. G., & Abarbanell, L. (2006). Universal Design for Learning in postsecondary education: Reflections on principles and their application. *Journal of Postsecondary Education and Disability, 19*(2), 135–151. www.ahead.org

SharplesM. (2023). *Towards social generative AI for education: theory, practices and ethics.* https://arxiv.org/abs/2306.10063

Shin, Y., & Kim, G. (2022). The effect of automated written feedback through Grammarly. *Multimedia-Assisted Language Learning, 25*(2), 84–102. www.doi.org/10.15702/mall.2022.25.2.84

Singleton, K., Evmenova, A., Jerome, M., & Clark, K. (2019). Integrating UDL strategies into the online course development process. *Online Learning : the Official Journal of the Online Learning Consortium, 23*(1), 206–235. doi:10.24059/olj.v23i1.1407

Vartiainen, H., & Tedre, M. (2023). Using artificial intelligence in craft education: Crafting with text-to-image generative models. *Digital Creativity (Exeter), 34*(1), 1–21. doi:10.1080/14626268.2023.2174557

Wald, M. (2021). AI data-driven personalisation and disability inclusion. *Frontiers in Artificial Intelligence, 3*, 571955. doi:10.3389/frai.2020.571955 PMID:33733215

Westine, C., Oyarzun, B., Ahlgrim-Delzell, L., Casto, A., Okraski, C., Park, G., Person, J., & Steele, L. (2019). Familiarity, current use, and interest in Universal Design for Learning among online university instructors. *International Review of Research in Open and Distance Learning, 20*(5), 21–41. doi:10.19173/irrodl.v20i5.4258

Wood, S. G., Moxley, J. H., Tighe, E. L., & Wagner, R. K. (2018). Does use of text-to-speech and related read-aloud tools improve reading comprehension for students with reading disabilities? A meta-analysis. *Journal of Learning Disabilities, 51*(1), 73–84. doi:10.1177/0022219416688170 PMID:28112580

XiaoP.ChenY.BaoW. (2023). *Waiting, banning, and embracing: An empirical analysis of adapting policies for Generative AI in higher education.* https://arxiv.org/abs/2305.18617

Zajko, M. (2022). Artificial intelligence, algorithms, and social inequality: Sociological contributions to contemporary debates. *Sociology Compass, 16*(3), e12962. doi:10.1111/soc4.12962

Chapter 10
The Inherent Uncertainties of AI-Text Detection and the Implications for Education Institutions:
An Overview

Robin Crockett
https://orcid.org/0000-0002-8047-5182
University of Northampton, UK

Robert Howe
https://orcid.org/0000-0002-1344-5530
University of Northampton, UK

ABSTRACT

This chapter focuses on the implications of the improving generative-AI 'chatbot' technologies and the inevitable unreliability of attendant AI-text detection technologies. The goal of generative-AI programmers is to design AIs which produce text indistinguishable from typical human-written text: an eventuality that will render AI-text detectors redundant. The authors outline the underpinning mathematics of AI-generated and human-written text as the basis of AI-text detection, and how this leads to inherent inaccuracies and uncertainties in AI-text detection. The chapter proceeds to overview on how institutions will have to work with both the growth in use of AI and the unreliability of AI-text detection: institutions cannot avoid AI and cannot rely on 'tech' to police it. Students need to be taught how to use AIs ethically with integrity and insight and sanctioned when they do not. At the same time, institutions need to resource people to investigate students suspected of false authorship, whether commissioning a human ghost-writer or using an AI inappropriately.

DOI: 10.4018/979-8-3693-0240-8.ch010

INTRODUCTION

This chapter considers the detection and classification of text produced by generative artificial intelligences (i.e., generative AIs, gAIs), with some extension into other generative AI capabilities (Ibrahim et al, 2023; New Scientist, 2023). It does not consider artificial general intelligence (AGI). A "generative" AI is one that humans can instruct and interrogate. Generative AI supports the creation of text, images and other media using existing sources and rules by which this knowledge may be combined in new ways giving new insights. Due to the wide range of sources which are aggregated, current and emerging AI systems are impacting on many areas of society. There is a range of literature (Lim et al, 2023; Yu and Guo, 2023; Nah et al., 2023), which provides a comprehensive background to gAI but it should be noted that a detailed understanding of these systems is not needed to appreciate the detection processes – and problems therewith – covered in this chapter. Jisc (2023c) has also developed an introduction to gAI to help institutions better understand the current range of tools which are categorised as gAI. The issue being covered in this chapter is the fact that some students are using gAI tools to create some or all of the content for their assignments, sometimes in ways which constitute academic misconduct, and the inherent unreliability of AI-text detectors in the academic integrity context. For clarity to avoid confusion with use of the verb "to generate" and the noun "generation", all references to AIs hereinafter are to generative AIs.

The problem of students submitting unauthorised AI-generated text first manifested in any significant way with OpenAI's launch of GPT-3 in 2020 (Brown et al., 2020; Crompton & Burke, 2023) and the subsequent appearance of numerous essay bots (Crockett, 2023a), many operated by essay mills, that explicitly targeted students seeking to cheat assignments. However, the problem became immeasurably bigger and more significant with OpenAI's release of ChatGPT in November 2022 (OpenAI, 2022), with its vastly improved user interface, e.g., the capability to "chat", as well as its improved and refined algorithms and larger training datasets. That has been followed by, for example, OpenAI's GPT-4 and Google's Bard in March 2023, Anthropic's Claude-2 in July 2023 (OpenAI, 2023b; Google, 2023a&b; Anthropic, 2023).

In response to these technological developments, numerous AI-text detectors/classifiers have been released by a variety of technology and educational technology companies (for example, not an exclusive list: Copyleaks, 2023; Crossplag, 2023; OpenAI, 2023a; Tayeb, 2023 (Draft & Goal); Tian, 2023a (GPTZero); Turnitin, 2023). These all work using essentially the same underpinning mathematics and rely on the intrinsic stylistic differences between typical human-written text and typical AI-generated text. Those differences arise from the intrinsic differences between the ways which human writers actually write and the ways AIs generate text according to their programming.

AIs programmed to generate text, such as ChatGPT, Bard and Claude, sometimes referred to as "chatbots", are based on large language models (LLMs), and the chapter opens with a brief introduction into the way those work. That is followed by a consideration of the differences between AI-generated and human-written text that underpin AI-text detection, including a brief outline of the underpinning mathematics to introduce the terminology commonly encountered on websites, in the academic literature and other reporting. That leads directly to the core of the chapter: i.e., the functionality of AI-text detectors/classifiers and the inherent uncertainties that give rise to the observed and reported unreliabilities (Anderson, 2023; Chakraborty et al., 2023; Ibrahim et al., 2023; Liang et al., 2023; Sadasivan et al., 2023; Weber-Wulff et al., 2023). The chapter concludes with an overview of the challenges all this poses for course and assessment design, and challenges faced by learning technologists in trying to meet the emerging and sometimes conflicting demands.

GENERATIVE AIS AND LARGE LANGUAGE MODELS

The AIs in question are based on large language models (LLMs) (Shanahan, 2023). A language model can be defined as a mathematical/statistical/probability model of natural language, i.e., human-written, texts (DeepLearningAI, 2023). Those texts can be modelled in terms of individual words or phrases or, indeed, parts of words (e.g., stems and affixes) and punctuation, i.e., what are referred to as "tokens". An LLM, such as used by OpenAI for its GPT variants (Generative Pre-trained Transformer), Google for Bard (LaMDA, Language Model for Dialogue Applications; PaLM, Pathways Language Model) and Anthropic for its Claude variants, is a (very) large version of the above, typically using vast numbers of texts scraped from the Internet (Anthropic, 2023; Google, 2023a&b; OpenAI, 2022 & 2023b).

For an individual AI, its artificial-intelligence machine-learning algorithms analyse its LLM dataset to determine patterns of language usage and characterise relationships between words/phrases and the ideas and concepts that it "sees" these as being semantically and/or syntactically linked to (DeepLearningAI, 2023; Hahn, 2023; Havlik, 2023). From there, according to its programming, an artificial neural network (ANN) is constructed: it is that ANN that is at the core of the predictive and generative capabilities.

There is a variety of definitions for AI but a helpful definition in the current context is "the branch of computer science involved with the design of computers or other programmed mechanical devices having the capacity to imitate human intelligence and thought" (Dictionary.com, 2023). However, let us be clear: current AIs (latter half of 2023) are not intelligent in a human-like way and whilst AIs are programmed to generate text that appears human-like, and do so increasingly successfully, the text-generation process does not (currently) resemble a typical human writing process, see the illustrative analogy in this section.

If you ask a human to write an answer to a question, they typically think about what they are writing as they write, whereas if you prompt an AI to generate some text or ask it a question, it does not think about and write an answer. Instead, it parses the prompt/question and searches for the most probable, most commonly-occurring words in its dataset and joins those together to generate grammatically correct but not necessarily subject-fluent text, all according to its programming (Heikkila, 2022; Shanahan, 2023). Every word in the generated text depends on the prompt(s) and the preceding generated words. Every word, every punctuation mark in the generated text occurs somewhere in the LLM dataset, with sentence and paragraph breaks determined algorithmically.

Thus, if you ask an AI a question, what you are in effect doing is giving the LLM software an instruction along the lines (quoting Shanahan, 2023): "Here's a fragment of text. Tell me how this fragment might go on. According to your model of the statistics of human language, what words are likely to come next?" For example, if you enter "Humpty Dumpty" then you are effectively asking the software which words commonly associate with "Humpty Dumpty" in its model, and the expectation is that the LLM will return "sat on a wall", possibly followed by the remainder of the nursery rhyme.

That is very different to how a human typically writes text. In essence, when a human writes, they express their thoughts in the best way for the task in hand, choosing the best vocabulary and phrase/sentence/paragraph structure etc. according to the subject matter and their personal stylistic preferences, often reviewing and editing as they write. The resulting text reflects that individuality of writing style:

indeed, such considerations with regard to individual writing style lie at the core of stylometry (Crockett, 2023a; Crockett & Best, 2020; Fox et al., 2012; Juola, 2013). In contrast, because of the way AIs work in always supplying high-probability previously written text that aligns with the prompts, AI generated text is predictable, with sentence and paragraph breaks determined algorithmically and not necessarily according to immediate changes in subject emphasis, lacking individuality and generally bland, monotone and unvaried in comparison to typical human-written text (Goom, 2023; Reed, 2023). That can sometimes be easy to observe but not always, hence the initial stimulus for the development of AI-text detectors/classifiers. Subsequently, human-observation has generally been becoming more difficult as the AIs improve, also posing increasing challenges for AI-text detectors/classifiers. Furthermore, AIs generally have an element of randomisation coded-in such that if a user clicks to regenerate the text, or another user enters the same prompt, the AI outputs further text that describes the same content in the same underlying way as the previous output, but with different wording, phrasing, sentences, and sometimes different content-precedence. That, coupled with continuing improvements in the AIs, makes it increasingly impossible for tutors, for example, to reproduce AI-text even if they know the specific AI used by a student in question, and the specific prompts used.

In order to help illustrate the AI text generation process, consider the loose analogy described as follows. A person who knows how to write grammatically correct text is tasked with writing about a subject of which they have no knowledge, according to the following method:

i. Search the Internet for the most common opening phrase associated with the subject.
ii. Search the Internet for the words/phrases that most commonly follow that.
iii. Repeat (ii), incorporating grammatically correct punctuation, until the opening sentence is grammatically complete.
iv. Search the Internet for the most common opening phrase for a following sentence.
v. Search the Internet for the words/phrases that most commonly follow that.
vi. Repeat (v), incorporating grammatically correct punctuation, until that sentence is grammatically complete.
vii. Repeat (iv)-(vi), without reviewing previously written sentences, until the body of text is complete in grammatical terms even if not in subject terms, separating groups of sentences into paragraphs at grammatically appropriate points.

A process such as this is very different to normal human writing but it would yield a body of text that is grammatically correct. However, because the writer is inferring correctness and consistency of content as aligning with the most commonly associated words/phrases that appear on the Internet, it would not necessarily be correct or consistent with regard to the specified subject. Also, that reliance on the most commonly associated words/phrases will result in an absence of individuality (Heikkila, 2022).

Further illustration was obtained by providing Claude-2 (Anthropic, 2023) with the user-prompt "Describe ChatGPT's writing style". The output is [verbatim]:

I don't actually have detailed insights into ChatGPT's writing style, since I'm a different AI created by Anthropic. However, from what I've seen, ChatGPT tends to produce very natural and human-like responses by training on a massive dataset of online dialog. It aims to sound conversational and articulate while providing useful information to users. Some key aspects of its style seem to be:

- *Uses common speech patterns and informal language*
- *Varies sentence structure and length to sound more natural*
- *Incorporates facts and data seamlessly into fluent explanations*
- *Adapts tone based on the prompt and conversation context*
- *Avoids overtly sounding like a bot through the use of opinions, quirky remarks etc.*
- *Seeks to continue conversations and engage users through follow-up questions and remarks*

Of course, this is just my impression based on limited interactions and observations. ChatGPT's capabilities and output will likely continue evolving over time as Anthropic refines its model. But overall it tends to exhibit a flexible, human-like narrative voice in service of delivering informative and satisfying responses. (Anthropic, 2023)

Briefly interpreting Claude-2's output. First, there is the "hallucination" that ChatGPT will evolve as Anthropic refines its model, which is not correct: ChatGPT is OpenAI, not Anthropic. An AI hallucination is text (in this context, but also potentially images etc.) that does not reflect reality, arising from the AI addressing a user prompt according to its programming, and joining sections of high-probability text but without any understanding or subject-related error-checking (Bender et al., 2021; Ji et al., 2023). This highlights an important aspect of AIs' programming, at least with the current generation of AIs (latter half of 2023): in essence, AIs conflate correctness with the (high) probability of occurrence in their datasets and so can erroneously link incorrect and/or individually correct but inconsistent sections of text in their outputs. Second, the statements regarding "massive dataset", "common speech patterns", are basic statements reflecting the design and programming as are, to varying extents, the references to fluency and varying sentence structure. Third, it includes the statement "incorporation of facts and data" but does not state that those are necessarily appropriate, correct or consistent and are not hallucinatory: even "opinions" and "quirky remarks" will be generated from the dataset according to the programming, with no guarantee of correctness.

In a different context, there is a good illustration of the pitfalls of uninsightful use of AIs and AI hallucinations reported in July 2023 by Retraction Watch concerning a pre-print posted on Preprints.org (Retraction Watch, 2023). This appears to be research fraud rather than academic misconduct, but it nevertheless illustrates what can happen if a determined user is prepared to prompt and re-prompt an AI in order to obtain highly detailed text, but then not to check in sufficient detail before proceeding, and the Retraction-Watch narrative is informative with regard to several aspects of misuse of AIs.

In summary, an AI outputs the most probable words/phrases according to its programming, and there is no guarantee that facts, data, information, opinions or remarks are relevant or correct in context, and there is no guarantee that the text will not contain hallucinations. AIs are not currently programmed to either understand the text they generate or to error-check for veracity (Heikkila, 2022). In contrast, human writers can typically vary their writing based on their knowledge and understanding of the subject (noting that there are atypical human writers who do not do this (Liang et al., 2023)) and, importantly, can check and verify that facts, data, information, opinions and remarks are relevant and correct in context as their subject knowledge and understanding develop during the writing process.

Thus, hallucinations can be very reliable tell-tales of AI-generated text, and a common and easily-detectable type of hallucination is invented/faked citations and references (where the AI has been tasked to generate referenced text). In the academic integrity context, hallucinations are examples of fabrication/

falsification of data/information and thus represent serious academic misconduct irrespective of whether the fabrication/falsification is attributable to AI text generation or human writing. Furthermore, it must be remembered that it is probable that some hallucinations in AI-generated text will propagate. This is because some hallucinations will appear in documents that are collated for the AI training datasets when those datasets are updated. This will have the unfortunate consequence that, for example, a fabricated citation/reference currently identifiable using text-matching software, which will not flag that citation as similar as it is not present in the software's database, could be incorporated into an updated database. That, in turn, will mean that both staff and students will have to be more careful in their checking of data and information as they undertake research.

Finally, before considering AI-text detection/classification, it is possible to prompt AIs to produce more human-like text, i.e., "smart prompting" (Lu et al., 2023; Sadavisan et al., 2023) and it is also possible to "watermark" AI-generated text by programming the AI with whitelists and blacklists of words to use frequently and infrequently respectively. Whilst watermarking itself is detectable, Sadasivan et al. (2023) and others have shown that putting such text through a paraphrasing or rewriting tool can very effectively reduce or remove the watermarking tell-tales: this is in addition to the documented use of such tools to reduce evidence of "ordinary" plagiarism (Rogerson & McCarthy, 2017). Thus, all that someone trying to render AI-generated less detectable has to do is put the AI-generated text through a readily available paraphrasing/rewriting tool, and then perhaps check with one or more online AI-text detectors/classifiers (noting that AI-text detectors/classifiers are inherently unreliable, see following sections). In that context, Phrasly (2023) explicitly targets students with the lure "Transform AI-generated content into undetectable text with Phrasly. Save time on your assignments, boost grades, and easily bypass AI detectors like TurnItIn and GPTZero". Consequently, AI-text detectors/classifiers that rely on watermarking are particularly vulnerable to paraphrasing/rewriting tools. However, it should be noted that as well as reducing/removing watermarking, putting AI-generated text through such tools can change the style and use-of-language, e.g., grammar and vocabulary, meaning that all AI-text detectors/classifiers have some degree of vulnerability to such tools. Furthermore, this situation will not improve: the next generation(s) of AI-equipped paraphrasing/rewriting tools will produce text that is more human-like and more effectively stripped of watermarking than the current/preceding generations of such tools.

AI-TEXT DETECTION/CLASSIFICATION

Leaving hallucinations and watermarking aside, it is these inherent stylistic differences that underpin the functionality of AI-text detectors/classifiers, but that functionality is clearly not definitive, and never can be. For example, some humans sometimes write in AI like ways (Liang et al., 2023). Conversely, a careful AI user with subject knowledge can smart-prompt an AI to vary its default output style, and putting AI-generated text through a paraphrasing or rewriting tool can reduce its "AI-ness" thereby obfuscating the evidence. However, over-riding all such individual factors is the ongoing improvement of the AIs: each new AI generation produces text that is more human-like than the previous generation, further blurring the distinctions between AI-generated and human-written text, thereby increasing the uncertainty of AI-text detection.

There is subject jargon in the AI-text detection context with some commonly encountered terms it is useful to be aware of. The stylistic factors outlined in the preceding section can be characterised via the text "entropy" (or "information entropy" – broadly, the unpredictability of the words, see next section), which can be quantified in various ways (Brownlee, 2019; Snow et al., 2016; Tian, 2023b). The basic underpinning quantity is the (information) entropy, but natural language processing (NLP) programmers designing the AI-text generators and detectors/classifiers generally use the related quantity of "perplexity" (Bernstein, 2021; Tian, 2023b). Both of these are related to the "surprisal" of words, i.e., how unpredictable or surprising they are. In outline, words that occur frequently (common, unsurprising words) are low-surprisal and words that occur infrequently (uncommon, surprising words) are high-surprisal, and entropy and perplexity are measures of average surprisal (Crockett, 2023a; Rogers, 2023). There is also "burstiness": there are several definitions of this but, broadly, it is a measure of the variation of entropy over a whole document, often quantified in terms of variations over sentences (or other "chunks" of text), and is also related to surprisal (Tian, 2023b).

Underpinning Mathematics

The details of the mathematics that underpins the functionality of AI-text detectors/classifiers are beyond the scope of this chapter, and it is not necessary to understand the mathematics in order to appreciate the problems inherent to AI-text detection/classification, but it is useful to develop a little of the theory in order to establish the context of the terms and concepts commonly encountered on AI-text detector/classifier and related websites and in the literature, as introduced in the preceding section.

In his landmark analyses, Shannon (1948, 1951) set out the framework for information entropy and defined the entropy of (a body of) text as the expectation of the surprisal of the symbols (i.e., words in the current context) used to represent that text. Surprisal (self-information, Shannon information) is a key quantity which has useful mathematical properties in the context of information theory and natural language processing.

Therefore, customising Shannon's definitions and notation for the current context, the surprisal, *SI*, of a word *x* in a (body of) text, *X*, is defined as

$$SI(x) = log_2\left(\frac{1}{p(x)}\right) = -log_2(p(x))$$

where p(*x*) is the probability of *x* occurring in *X*.

Thus, surprisal as the negative log-probability is an inverse measure of probability, i.e., it increases as probability decreases and thus is a measure of unpredictability or surprise.

From there, the entropy, *H*, of the overall (body of) text *X* is defined as

$$H(X) = \sum\nolimits_{x \in X} p(x) SI(x)$$

i.e., the entropy is the expectation of the surprisal.

For surprisal and entropy as above, the perplexity, *PP*, is

$$PP(X) = 2^{H(X)}$$

There are various definitions of burstiness but the most accessible one is the Fano factor. For a sentence, or other chunk of text, *X*, the Fano factor, *F*, is the ratio of the variance to the mean of the word surprisals, SI_x, i.e.

$$F(X) = \frac{\sigma_{SIx}^2}{\mu_{SIx}}$$

These are core definitions which should help with interpreting material on and about detector websites. However, it should be noted that different programmers use variations of these basic quantities in trying to develop effective and reliable AI detectors/classifiers, and, thus, different but related statements and definitions might be encountered with regard to specific detectors/classifiers depending on their programming.

Relating this to linguistics, there are two basic categories of words, i.e., content words (also referred to as lexical or open-class words, e.g., words such as main nouns and adjectives, main verbs and adverbs) and stop words (also referred to as function or closed-class words, e.g., structural/grammatical words such as articles, conjunctions, prepositions, pronouns, particles, helping verbs). Content words carry the subject content and are generally high-surprisal, whereas stop words carry the grammar between the content words and are generally low-surprisal (Kermes & Teich, 2017; Lancaster University, n.d.; UCL, n.d.). Thus, text containing relatively high and low proportions of stop-words and content-words respectively, as typifies AI-generated text, will be relatively low-entropy, low-perplexity. Conversely, text containing relatively low and high proportions of stop-words and content-words respectively, as typifies human-written text, will be relatively high-entropy, high-perplexity. Extending this reasoning, text consisting of relatively uniformly structured sentences containing a relatively high proportion of stop words plus commonly-used "everyday" content words, as typifies AI-generated text, will be relatively low-burstiness, whereas text consisting of more variably structured sentences containing a relatively low proportion of stop words plus a relatively varied set of content words, as typifies human-written text, will be relatively high-burstiness.

Thus, human-written text, with its innate stylistic individuality, is typically relatively high-surprisal, high-entropy, high-perplexity, high-burstiness. Conversely, AI-generated text, due to an AI being programmed to select the most probable words/phrases from its dataset, i.e., the most commonly used, most everyday words/phrases, and to generate sentences and paragraphs algorithmically rather than according to the immediate subject matter, is typically relatively low-surprisal, low-entropy, low-perplexity, low-burstiness (Anderson, 2023).

Illustrative AI-Text Classification

For clarity, in this section, the term "entropy" is used to include entropy, perplexity, burstiness and any related/derived quantities that are used in AI-text detection/classification.

The detection/classification of a text as "AI" or "human" (sometimes expressed as, in terms, "not-AI") depends (a) on that text being either a typical AI text or a typical human text and the less typical in either sense, the less reliable the classification, and (b) on typical AI texts being distinguishable from typical human texts. However, those dependencies cannot be guaranteed: some AI-generated texts are more human-like, i.e., with higher-than-typical entropy compared to the majority of AI-generated text, and some human-written texts are more AI-like, i.e., with lower-than-typical entropy compared to the majority of human-written text. This is a real concern: Snow et al. (2016) observe that lower-proficiency students write with more rigidity and less flexibility, which manifests as lower text-entropy, i.e., text that is more AI-like. Thus, in general, there are systematic overlaps between the statistical distributions of entropy statistics from AI-generated and human-written texts. That overlap means that there is always a systematic uncertainty in AI-text detection/classification because an AI-text detector/classifier cannot simply make a determination with reference to an AI-entropy distribution but must also take account of a human-entropy distribution. In essence, it is not a simple case of determining how typically AI-like a piece of text is because any determination also has to account for how typically human-like that piece of text is.

As a consequence of this, AI-text detectors/classifiers are generally configured with detection thresholds, and those detection thresholds are generally set to minimise false-positive probabilities (rates). A false positive is human-written text incorrectly classified as AI-generated; a false negative is AI-generated text incorrectly classified as human-written. It is not possible to set a detection threshold to minimise both the false-positive and false-negative rates simultaneously: indeed, minimising one necessarily maximises the other and, therefore, AI-text detectors/classifiers configured with minimised false-positive rates effectively have maximised false-negative rates (Anderson, 2023; Crockett, 2023b). The small-scale false-negatives investigation reported by Crockett (2023b) demonstrates two important aspects of AI-text detector/classifier performance. First, a detector/classifier only achieves its claimed accuracies for text obtained from an AI-text generator that is explicitly listed by that detector, and even then only if the AI generator was not smart-prompted: accuracies for other categories of AI-generated text are significantly worse. Second, and only for an AI text generator that is explicitly named/listed, a detector/classifier that is "tuned" to minimise its false-positive rate necessarily has a significantly worse false-negative rate with observed false-negative rates of ca. 1-in-4 corresponding to claimed false-positive rates of ca. 1-in-100. That is important: in terms of academic misconduct, any false-negative is potentially a cheated student submission going undetected – "slipping under the radar" – which compromises our abilities to (a) help any such student study with integrity, and (b) protect our institutional integrity and reputation.

Whether explicitly or implicitly, whether as a direct statistical evaluation or as an indirect AI-enabled evaluation where the AI's training – calibration – has taken account of the necessary statistical criteria, AI-text detection/classification involves a complex assessment of entropy. However, a loose but nonetheless informative analogy is to think of AI classification in terms of a Mann-Whitney U-test (McClenaghan, 2022), as follows. A hypothetical AI-text detector has very large reference samples of entropy statistics from both AI-generated and human-written texts and it U-tests the entropy statistics sample from the text in question against its reference samples. That will yield two p-values, one for "AI-ness" and one for "human-ness". Thus, and noting "strong" in the following will depend on the setting of the detection threshold:

- if the AI p-value is strong null-hypothesis and the human p-value is strong alternative hypothesis, then the text in question is classified as "AI-generated";
- if the human p-value is strong null-hypothesis and the AI p-value is strong alternative hypothesis, then the text in question is classified as "human written";
- if one or both of the p-values is insufficiently strong, the classification is determined by the threshold and is not a simple "which p-value is stronger" decision and, for example, if the threshold is set to minimise the false-positive rate, the classification will be "human written".

Figure 1. Illustrative entropy distributions. The AI distribution is shown as a solid/red line, the human distribution is shown as a dashed/blue line.

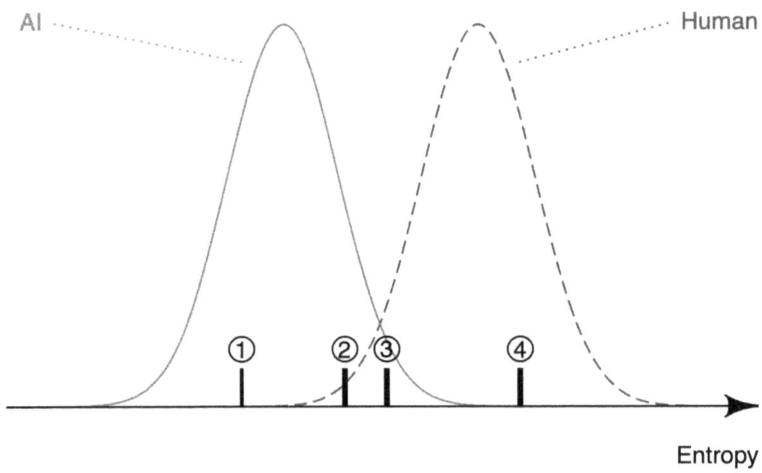

This is illustrated in Figures 1, 2 and 3. In these figures:

- the shapes of the AI-generated and human-written entropy distributions are arbitrary and are chosen for clarity and should not be interpreted as actual entropy distributions;
- the AI-generated and human-written entropy distributions overlap, reflecting the reality that some AI-generated text is atypically human-like, and some human-written text is atypically AI-like.

The basic situation is illustrated in Figure 1.

Figure 1 shows four hypothetical entropy statistics (solid vertical bars, labelled 1-4) in relation to the entropy distributions for AI-generated and human-written text. With regard to Figure 1:

- statistic 1 is central within the AI-text entropy distribution (i.e., high probability), and a long way along the tail of the human-text entropy distribution (i.e., low probability), and is therefore classified as "AI-generated" with a high degree of confidence;
- statistic 4 is a long way along the tail of the AI-text entropy distribution (i.e., low probability), and central within the human-text entropy distribution (i.e., high probability), and is therefore classified as "human-written" with a high degree of confidence;
- statistics 2 and 3 are ambiguous, falling in the overlap regions of the two distributions.

In order to classify statistics 2 and 3, a threshold is required as described in the preceding section. This is illustrated in Figure 2.

Figure 2 clearly shows that there is more of the AI-distribution area (probability) on the human side of threshold than there is human-distribution area (probability) on the AI side of the threshold, clearly illustrating that minimising the false-positive probability maximises the false-negative probability, and vice-verse if the threshold had been set to minimise the false-negative probability. With regard to Figure 2:

Figure 2. Illustrative entropy distributions, as Figure 1, with classification threshold set to minimise false-positive rate (probability). The false-positive and false-negative probabilities are shown as shaded areas: false positive shaded leftwards-up/blue, false negative shaded rightwards-up/red.

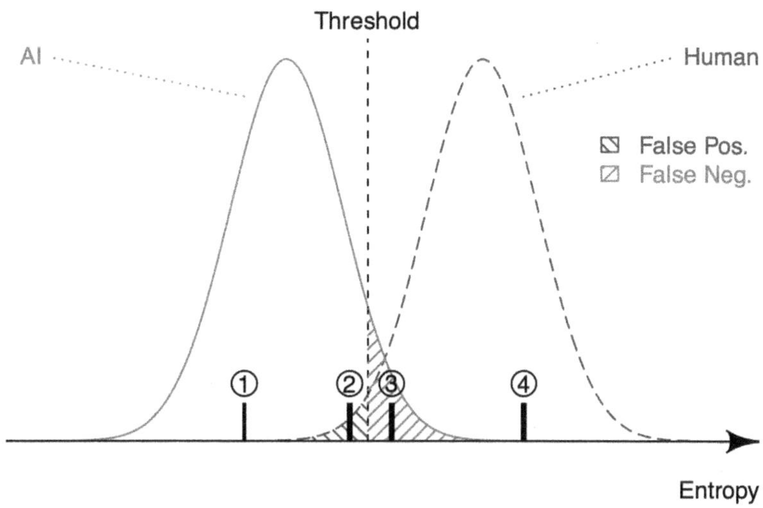

- statistic 2 is on the AI side (left) of the threshold, so is classified as "AI-generated" but clearly with less confidence than statistic 1;
- statistic 3 is on the human side (right) of the threshold, so is classified as "human-written" but clearly with less confidence than statistic 4.

Thus, if statistic 2 arises from AI-generated text, it is classified correctly, however if it arises from human-written text, it is incorrectly classified and is a false positive. Similarly, if statistic 3 arises from human-written text, it is classified correctly, however if it arises from AI-generated text, it is incorrectly classified and is a false negative.

This illustrates the fundamental uncertainty inherent to AI-text detection/classification. Furthermore, if Figures 1 and 2 are regarded as reflecting the current situation with the current generation of AIs, the next generation of AIs will mean that AI-generated text entropies further overlap with human-written text entropies and the AI-text entropy distribution will overlap the human-text entropy distribution to greater extent. This is shown in Figure 3.

Interpreting Figure 3, it is clear that as AI-generated text becomes more human-like, the overlap between the entropy distributions increases, meaning fewer distinguishable differences. It is also clear that keeping the same classification threshold to maintain the same false-positive probability (area shaded leftwards-up/blue) necessitates an increased false-negative probability (area shaded rightwards-up/red). Also consider that if the previous example statistic 3 were to arise in conjunction with this future generation of AIs, it would again be classified as "human-written" despite falling close to the centre of the AI distribution and, therefore, having greater actual probability of being AI-generated than in Figure 2.

Thus, however reliable the current generation of AI-text detectors/classifiers becomes with improved programming and larger datasets (as more people use AI-text generators and thus provide data), these detectors/classifiers will still be less reliable with the next generation of AIs that will produce more

Figure 3. Illustrative entropy distributions: future AI. Future AI distribution shown as a solid/red line, human distribution (same as Figures 1, 2) as a dashed/blue line, current AI entropy distribution (same as Figures 1, 2) shown in grey for comparison

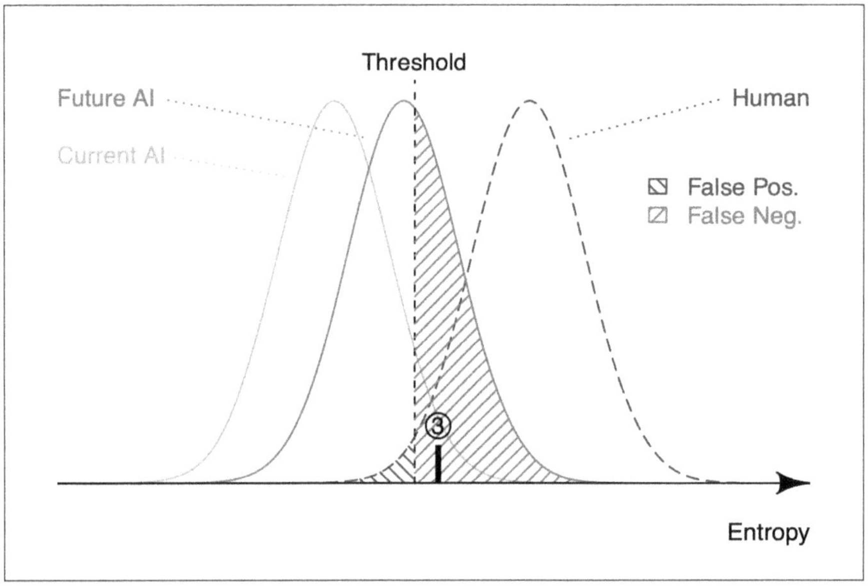

human-like text than the current generation (AI Writing Check, 2023; Anderson, 2023). Also, while custom, focused tools such as that reported by Desaire et al. (2023) for chemistry can perform better than general AI-text detectors in narrowly specified contexts, the probable overfitting and/or overtraining involved significantly constrain the applicability. Furthermore, such focused tools do not address the fundamental issues associated with AIs continuing to improve and produce ever more human-like text.

Even if it transpires that AI-text detectors/classifiers continue to improve (Chakraborty et al., 2023), both within AI-generations and from AI-generation to AI-generation, the goal of (many) AI designers and programmers is to produce AIs that generate text that is indistinguishable from human-written text (Nvidia, 2023). In that eventuality, AI-text detectors will become redundant. Even with the current generation of AIs (latter half of 2023), AI-text detection/classification is unreliable (Crockett, 2023b; Orenstrakh et al., 2023; Sadasivan et al., 2023; Weber-Wulff et al., 2023). Also, OpenAI withdrew their AI-text classifier on 20 July 2023, stating:

As of July 20, 2023, the AI classifier is no longer available due to its low rate of accuracy. We are working to incorporate feedback and are currently researching more effective provenance techniques for text, and have made a commitment to develop and deploy mechanisms that enable users to understand if audio or visual content is AI-generated. (OpenAI, 2023c).

That action by OpenAI explicitly raises the question that if OpenAI – the designers of ChatGPT, with all their (inside) knowledge of AI-functionality – cannot make a reliable AI-text detector, even for their own AI, is it reasonable to expect other AI-text detectors/classifiers to be any more accurate and reliable? Also, there is OpenAI's FAQ which in response to the listed question "Do AI detectors work?", states "In short, no. While some (including OpenAI) have released tools that purport to detect AI-generated content, none of these have proven to reliably distinguish between AI-generated and human-generated content" before further statements which augment and clarify that statement (OpenAI, 2023d).

IMPLICATIONS FOR ACADEMIC INTEGRITY AND TEACHING

To summarise, AI-text detection/classification is currently inherently unreliable (Al-Sibai, 2023; Anderson, 2023; Crockett, 2023b; Tangermann, 2023; Williams, 2023). Furthermore, this inherent unreliability will become increasingly significant as AIs improve and AI-generated text becomes more human-like with (possibly) fewer hallucinations (Bender et al., 2021). In that context, Atleson (2023) on the USA Federal Trade Commission's business blog has written:

If you're interested in tools to help detect if you're getting the good turtle soup or merely the mock, take claims about those tools with a few megabytes of salt. Overconfidence that you've caught all the fakes and missed none can hurt both you and those who may be unfairly accused, including job applicants and students.

Also, even if watermarking becomes more robust, paraphrasing and rewriting tools will also improve and will more effectively alter the text vocabulary and structure, obfuscating the evidence by reducing and possibly completely removing the watermarking, as well as altering the entropy-related properties. Coupled with that, it is safe to observe that as people discover ways of disguising AI-generated text, "How to beat AI detectors" webpages will proliferate, similar to the proliferation of "How to beat text-matching software" webpages some years ago. Such webpages already exist, and not all necessarily contain reliable advice, just as not all advice with regard to beating text-matching software was reliable. Without making any judgement or endorsement on either of these see, for example, articles by Gluska (2023) and Khan (2023) as indicators of what is already available to students and others who search the Internet for advice. Lastly, there is recent legal opinion from Gaumann and Veale (2023) with regard to the legal position of generative AIs in the context of academic integrity and whether such AIs can be regarded as essay mills.

The consequence of this is that education institutions cannot rely on AI-text detectors/classifiers to (help) police academic integrity (Chan, 2023; Wilhelm, 2023): simply, for the reasons outlined above, AI detectors are not reliable for such purposes and never will be. It should also be noted that expert human "classifiers" cannot reliably detect AI-generated text either (Casal & Kessler, 2023). Thus, it is not meaningful for education institutions to announce bans on the use of AIs for assessments where the students control the environments in which they prepare their submissions.

Therefore, the role of the tutors will be key, but also very difficult at least in the next few years while institutions are establishing their policies and guidance and individual tutors experiment with and assess AI capabilities. However, it is already clear that assessments where use of AIs is not permitted will need to be conducted in institutionally-controlled environments, such as in-class assessments and formal examinations, and a degree of redesign of assessments is probable. Conversely, in this new environment, education institutions need to teach their students how to use AIs ethically, with integrity and insight, but cannot rely on AI-text detectors/classifiers to ensure that students actually use AI text generators for assessments where use of AIs is mandated. Consequently, there is need for assessment strategies to be reviewed, including the balance between subject understanding and evaluation on the one hand and abilities to access, collate and present information on the other. One possibility with regard to assessment design, in overview, is to actively encourage the use of AI tools but with an assessment focus on how the tools contribute to knowledge and understanding, i.e., learning outcomes that explicitly require students to critically evaluate and analyse subject material rather than more straightforward collation and presentation, because collation and presentation are easily achieved via AI. Thus, as a summary overview statement, institutions should ensure that they are not setting assignments which mean that simple, basic "thought-free" use of an AI tool can reliably meet the learning outcomes (AdvanceHE, 2023; Bowditch, 2023; Jisc, 2023d).

The development of AI tools presents education institutions with opportunities and positive challenges: it is far from being all negative, but it is going to be challenging. Let us consider the reality that current and future students are going to graduate into workplaces and environments where use of such AIs is increasingly the norm (Sabzalieva & Valentini, 2023; Salvagno et al., 2023). Therefore, students who have not been taught how to use AIs ethically, with insight and integrity, might well find themselves at a disadvantage compared to those who have (Jisc, 2023a; Lancaster, 2023; Wang et al., 2023). Therefore, education institutions need to incorporate use of generative AIs into their syllabuses so as not to disadvantage their students. That itself presents a major challenge for many education staff who up to this point have been little if no more familiar – indeed, possibly less familiar – with these AIs than their students: that is a major challenge that it is not going to be possible to avoid.

Lastly, given the potential for AI-misuse and academic misconduct on a par with contract cheating, education institutions are going to have to adequately resource their staff who advise students and enforce academic integrity and misconduct policies. However, whilst a major issue to address, it might not turn out to be as daunting a task as initially anticipated by some (Akbari, 2023; Eaton, 2023; Namik et al., 2023; Susnjak, 2022).

Stylometry

Up to this point, the focus has been the unreliability of AI-text detectors and the implications of that. However, there are alternative approaches to assessing authorship of student submissions. One such approach, although it is time and resource intensive, is stylometry (Crockett, 2023a; Juola, 2017). Stylometry means, reasonably literally, "measurement of style". A more informative definition is statistical analysis of variation of (writing) style with authorship (Eder et al., 2016).

In outline in the academic integrity context, using stylometry to investigate authorship involves the comparison of a suspect submission to other submissions by an individual student in question, i.e., investigation of a portfolio of submissions by an individual student in question for consistency of writing style. The objective in the academic integrity context is to identify inconsistencies in authorship and not necessarily identify specific authors (who are often unidentifiable assignment ghost-writers working for essay-mills), whereas in literary contexts, the objective of stylometry is to identify specific authors. Thus, the objective is to identify two or more subsets of submissions according to writing style that when considered on balance of probabilities, do not align with having been written by a single individual and so align with being written by multiple authors of which the student is, at most, one (Crockett, 2023a).

That objective is superficially similar to using an AI-text detector/classifier as part of an academic integrity investigation: if an AI-text detector/classifier indicates "AI generated" then an investigator has to determine, on balance of probabilities, whether or not that submission was written by the student in question and not simply rely on what is an unreliable classification.

Thus, while the problems associated with AI-text detectors/classifiers as outlined in the preceding sections also apply to stylometry, they do not do so to the same extent. This is because stylometry focuses on the uniqueness of the individual whereas AI-text detectors/classifiers sacrifice individuality in effectively comparing text to a typical aggregate human (who doesn't actually exist). Furthermore, an AI-text detector/classifier might return an "AI-generated" result for a student in question whose natural writing style is AI-like but who has not used an AI (Liang et al., 2023), or even an apparently random "AI-generated" result due to an unfortunate coincidence between something a mainstream student has written and an undocumented feature of the AI-detector's model fitting and training (Al-Sibai, 2023). This would obviously have negative consequences if that determination were to be accepted unquestioningly, or even weighted too highly, by a tutor or institution placing too much faith in what is deeply unsound software (Al-Sibai, 2023).

An AI-text detector takes one document at a time with no individual context, no consideration of an individual's writing style. Conversely stylometry, because it can evaluate an entire portfolio of student submissions, has the demonstrated potential to confirm consistency of an individual student's natural writing style, thereby establishing an impacted student's natural "AI-ness", including where misuse of AI is suspected (Sokol, 2023). Thus, stylometry has at least the potential to be a more reliable and accurate means of assessing whether a student is the writer of (all) the assignments they submit and whether or not they have misused an AI, or contract cheated, but it is time-consuming, requires expertise and needs to be resourced.

It is true that as AIs improve, and AI-generated text becomes more human-like, stylometry will become more difficult, particularly with regard to students who write in more AI-like ways. However, until AIs are programmed with the capability to imitate arbitrary individual-user writing styles "on-the-fly", there will still be differences between AI-generated text and text written by an individual student, with the potential for those differences to be sufficiently significant to provide evidence for an academic integrity disciplinary process (Crockett, 2023a).

IMPLICATIONS FOR LEARNING TECHNOLOGY

As well as posing problems for academic staff, the recent rapid developments in AI technologies pose problems for those who provide the technological support for those staff – and students – and learning technologists are at the forefront of this. Even prior to these developments, learning technology teams had been becoming increasingly central components of educational institutions (Walker & Voce, 2023). In addition to working with staff and students to assess and test the suitability of new technology products, they also have to be alert to any emerging technologies which may impact – negatively as well as positively – learning and teaching.

Whilst AI is not new, the extraordinarily rapid pace of developments and the accompanying intense media attention ("hype") since the release of ChatGPT has made adhering to established procurement processes more complicated. A procurement process typically involves identification of an institutional need, development of a formal specification for a new system, checking that any new systems fulfils the identified needs and does not unnecessarily duplicate existing systems or does not confound existing systems, and some form of bidding/tendering process. Within such processes, there will need to be data-protection and equality-impact assessments, according to institutional and legal requirements, to ensure, for example, that users' confidentiality is not compromised and that identifiable groups of users are not disadvantaged or excluded. Institutions are currently in the position that their staff and students can access a variety of AIs, including AI-text detectors and paraphrasing and rewriting tools, simply by signing-up with an email address, effectively bypassing formal procurement processes due to the need to keep up-to-date with developments. For example, students are seeing the need to meet employers' expectations and, consequently, signing-up to AI tools to gain the experience and expertise they consider they need ahead of institutional options, advice and guidelines. Similarly, staff out of their own curiosity plus, of course, the need to keep up-to-date with their students and what their students can do with these new tools. Furthermore, those AI tools have much unknown functionality and, despite being procured informally by individuals, those individuals still expect support from learning technologists and others, for example, with regard to ethics and academic integrity. That situation is becoming further complicated by AI tools being increasingly integrated into mainstream products such as Microsoft Office and web-browsers, meaning that that it can be possible for individuals to use AIs without being aware of so doing. This means that many institutions are "playing catchup" with regards to their policies and guidance, as well as procurement, due to having to deal with this unprecedented release of uncontrolled products.

Some institutions initially declared bans on generative AIs, bans which were never credible – because institutions do not control students' out-of-institution study environments and access to online tools/ resources. Such bans rapidly proved fruitless because there were too many technical and policy loopholes and, as discussed in the preceding sections, the inherent inaccuracy and unreliability of AI-text detectors/ classifiers (Wood, 2023). Subsequently, more realistic attitudes have generally prevailed and institutions have increasingly recognised that such AI tools would be part of a longer-term future (Russell Group, 2023). Institutional student surveys during 2023 picked up that students were often far more aware of the implications of AI on academia than many had originally thought (Jisc, 2023b; Lea, 2023). Rather than being seen as a tool which would allow them to have assignments automatically created, many students recognised the impact of the tool on academic integrity and qualifications. As a result, some students actively avoided the use of the AI tools and discouraged others from using them (Charnovsky, 2023; Hough, 2023; Jisc, 2023a). Lea (2023) noted that the number of students adopting AI tools in their studies was in a surprising minority (during the middle of 2023), and also noted that many of the students who had not adopted tools were very ethically aware – "citing concerns of cheating as the main reason they were not using AI tools". Lea (2023) also noted that some students did not have the skills to use AI or did not feel the need to use them, and sometimes considered their use unfair. As institutions moved to the latter part of 2023, they were increasingly starting to see the benefit of the tools in certain situations and are working to improve staff and student AI skill-sets and confidence (Diplo, 2023; Hough, 2023). From the student perspective, this means that they have clear guidance on when, where and how they should and should not be using AI tools, and who they can approach for guidance – with enquiries often being passed to learning technologists (Hough, 2023; Jisc, 2023b).

In addition to the student perspective, staff are also becoming more aware of the potential of using AI in their own work (Hurix, 2023, Pine Cove, 2023). Those conducting research now have a wide range of tools which allow them to analyse data, conduct literature reviews and assist with the writing of articles. Those staff needing help with creating teaching resources now have access to systems that start to cross over with the role of course and assessment designers (Hurix, 2023). Furthermore, senior and professional services staff now have access to tools that will assist with the production and analysis of, for example, planning documents and institutional reports, and learning technologists need to be able to meet those demands.

The availability of these tools means that responsibility for AI goes far beyond that of a single learning technology team. Wider teams including learning designers, ethics and academic integrity staff, learning developers, academic librarians, academic support teams, as well as academic staff, senior managers and students will all need to be involved in the ethical roll out of systems. Institutions – with learning technologists at the forefront – need to ensure that they maintain full awareness of the implications of AI for both themselves and the wider sector, and need to address the potentially dangerous implications of some AI systems bypassing any form of formal procurement. In addition, relevant policies and procedures need to be regularly reviewed in the light of new technologies.

CONCLUSION

This chapter has outlined the basic operation of generative AIs and presented an overview of the underlying principles of AI-text detection in an effort to de-mystify the many claims and assertions that higher education staff and others have been exposed to – and will continue to be exposed to.

It is not going to be easy: to use a phrase, it is going to be a "bumpy ride" over the next several years as individual institutions and the sector as a whole progress through interim policies and regulations to more considered positions in the "brave new world" we find ourselves in. However, the key is to avoid panicking and avoid being panicked by the hype. We need to move quickly to embrace the new AI technologies, but not so quickly that we circumvent established good practices (Webb, 2023).

To put all this in context, institutions are currently dealing with a previously unencountered situation which will have implications far in excess of those which arose during the covid-19 pandemic. Whilst covid-19 alerted many institutions to gaps and shortcomings in their current teaching and assessment policies and procedures, the recent rapid – and almost certainly ongoing – developments in AI technologies will take education in new, previously unforeseeable directions. It will take effort, perseverance and drive from those inside learning technology teams and beyond to ensure that institutions maintain their position on the "crest of the wave" rather than get left behind.

Lastly, and by way of a little speculation, how long will it take for (some) students to realise that AIs – or at least the current generation thereof – are not "silver bullets"? (Marshall, 2023) As well as its programming, an AI is dependent on its dataset: if that is incomplete, out-of-date, or contains biased or widely-propagated misinformation/disinformation etc., that is reflected in the text it generates. Consequently, a student requires an appropriate degree of subject knowledge to use a generative AI to fulfil an assignment brief to an acceptable standard, noting they will generally have to revise/refine their side of the "chat" a few times in order to obtain acceptable text and not simply enter an assignment title and accept the first version the AI generates. That takes time and effort and then, ideally, the "final" text should be checked and verified (as per ethical use, insight and integrity). Thus, it is possible that after an initial flurry of activity, (some) students will largely revert to creating assignments without AI assistance or, perhaps, using AI solely for "routine" tasks such as initial information-scoping and essay-planning? Time – or, perhaps, the next generation of AIs – will tell...

ETHICS DECLARATION

The authors have not received any payment/reward/support/incentive of any kind from any artificial intelligence or educational technology companies or organisations with regard to this research.

Except for the single referenced section of text obtained from Claude-2, no generative AI was used in the writing of this chapter.

ACKNOWLEDGEMENT

The authors wish to thank their colleagues both within and outwith the University of Northampton for their support and encouragement in the preparation of this chapter.

REFERENCES

AdvanceHE. (n.d.) *Authentic Assessment in the era of AI*. AdvanceHE. https://www.advance-he.ac.uk/membership/all-member-benefit-projects/Authentic-Assessment-in-the-era-of-AI

AI Writing Check. (2023, August) *August 2023 Update – AI Writing Check is no longer available* [Press release]. AI Writing Check. https://aiwritingcheck.org/

Akbari, N. (2023, July 14) *Academic Integrity in the age of AI: Approaching Apocalypse or Achievable Equilibrium?* Linkedin. https://www.linkedin.com/pulse/academic-integrity-age-ai-approaching-apocalypse-achievable

Al-Sibai, N. (2023, June 06). *AI Plagiarism Detection Software Keeps Falsely Accusing Students of Cheating*. Futurism. https://futurism.com/ai-plagiarism-software-false-accusing-students

Anderson, C. (2023, June 01) *The False Promise of AI Writing Detectors*. Linkedin. https://www.linkedin.com/pulse/false-promise-ai-writing-detectors-carol-anderson

Anthropic. (2023, July 14) *Claude 2* [Press release]. Anthropic PBC. https://www.anthropic.com/index/claude-2

Atleson, M. (2023, July 06). *Watching the detectives: Suspicious marketing claims for tools that spot AI-generated content*. USA Federal Trade Commission. https://www.ftc.gov/business-guidance/blog/2023/07/watching-detectives-suspicious-marketing-claims-tools-spot-ai-generated-content

Bender, E. M., Gebru, T., McMillan-Major, A., & Shmitchell, S. (2021) On the Dangers of Stochastic Parrots: Can Language Models Be Too Big? *Proceedings of the 2021 ACM Conference on Fairness, Accountability, and Transparency*, (pp. 610–623). Association for Computing Machinery. 10.1145/3442188.3445922

Bernstein, M. N. (2021, October 08) *Perplexity: a more intuitive measure of uncertainty than entropy*. Github. https://mbernste.github.io/posts/perplexity/

Bowditch, E. (2023, September 12). *Assessment Menu: Designing assessment in an AI enabled world*. Jisc. https://nationalcentreforai.jiscinvolve.org/wp/2023/09/12/designing-assessment-in-an-ai-enabled-world/

Brown, T. B., Mann, B., Ryder, N., Subbiah, M., Kaplan, J., Dhariwal, P., Neelakantan, A., Shyam, P., Sastry, G., Askell, A., Agarwal, S., Herbert-Voss, A., Krueger, G., Henighan, T., Child, R., Ramesh, A., Ziegler, D. M., Wu, J., Winter, C., & Amodei, D. (2020) Language Models are Few-Shot Learners. arXiv. https://doi.org//arXiv.2005.14165 doi:10.48550

Brownlee, J. (2019, October 14) *A Gentle Introduction to Information Entropy*. Machine Learning Mastery. https://machinelearningmastery.com/what-is-information-entropy/

Casal, J. E., & Kessler, M. (2023). Can linguists distinguish between ChatGPT/AI and human writing?: A study of research ethics and academic publishing. *Research Methods in Applied Linguistics*, *2*(3), 1–12. doi:10.1016/j.rmal.2023.100068

Chakraborty, S., Bedi, A. S., Zhu, S., An, B., Manocha, D., & Huang, F. (2023). *On the Possibilities of AI-Generated Text Detection*. arXiv. https://doi.org//arXiv.2304.04736 doi:10.48550

Chan, C. K. Y. (2023) *Is AI Changing the Rules of Academic Misconduct? An In-depth Look at Students' Perceptions of 'AI-giarism'*. arXiv. https://doi.org//arXiv.2306.03358 doi:10.48550

Charnosky, C. (2023, October 02). *Pre-Law Students Avoid Using AI for Admissions*. ALM Global LLC. https://www.law.com/2023/10/02/pre-law-students-nix-using-ai-for-admissions-kaplan-survey-reports/

Copyleaks. (2023, January 12) *Copyleaks Officially Launches First-Of-Its-Kind Multi-Language AI Content Detection Solution with 99 Percent Accuracy* [Press release]. Copyleaks Ltd. https://copyleaks.com/about-us/media/copyleaks-launches-ai-content-detector

Crockett, R. (2023a). Forensic Assignment Stylometry. In S. E. Eaton (Ed.), *Handbook of Academic Integrity* (pp. 1–19). Springer. doi:10.1007/978-981-287-079-7_154-1

Crockett, R. (2023b, November 20) Testing the AI detectors Part 2. University of Northampton. North-Hampton. https://blogs.northampton.ac.uk/learntech/2023/11/20/testing-the-ai-detectors-part-2/

Crockett, R., & Best, K. (2020). Stylometric Comparison Of Professionally Ghost-Written And Student-Written Assignments. In Z. R. Khan, C. Hill, & T. Foltynek (Eds.), *Integrity in Education for Future Happiness* (pp. 35–49). Mendel University Press. doi:10.11118/978-80-7509-772-9-0035

Crompton, H., & Burke, D. (2023). Artificial intelligence in higher education: The state of the field. *International Journal of Educational Technology in Higher Education*, *20*(1), 1–22. doi:10.1186/s41239-023-00392-8

Crossplag. (2023, July 31) *AI Content Detector* [Press release]. Inspera AS. https://crossplag.com/ai-content-detector/

DeepLearningAI. (2023, January 11). *A Complete Guide to Natural Language Processing*. DeepLearning.AI LLC. https://www.deeplearning.ai/resources/natural-language-processing/

Desaire, H., Chua, A. E., Kim, M.-G., & Hua, D. (2023). Accurately detecting AI text when ChatGPT is told to write like a chemist. *Cell Reports. Physical Science*, *4*(11), 1–13. doi:10.1016/j.xcrp.2023.101672 PMID:38078148

Diplo. (2023, September 24) *Universities stop using AI detection tool such as Turnitin.*. Diplo Foundation. https://www.diplomacy.edu/updates/universities-stop-using-ai-detection-tool-such-as-turnitin/

Eaton, S. E. (2023, March 04) Artificial intelligence and academic integrity, post-plagiarism. *University World News*. https://www.universityworldnews.com/post.php?story=20230228133041549

Fox, N. P., & Ehmoda, O. (2012). *Statistical Stylometrics and the Marlowe-Shakespeare Authorship Debate*. Brown University. https://cs.brown.edu/research/pubs/theses/masters/2012/ehmoda.pdf

GaumannN.VealeM. (2023) AI Providers as Criminal Essay Mills? Large Language Models meet Contract Cheating Law. socarXiv. https://osf.io/preprints/socarxiv/cpbfd doi:10.31235/osf.io/cpbfd

Gluska, J. (2023, August 09). *How to Bypass ChatGPT Writing Detection Tools With Other Tools*. Gold Penguin. https://goldpenguin.org/blog/avoiding-ai-detection-for-chatgpt-writing/

Google. (2023a, February 06) *An important next step on our AI journey* [Press release]. Google LLC. https://blog.google/technology/ai/bard-google-ai-search-updates

Google. (2023b, March 21). *Try Bard and share your feedback* [Press release]. Google LLC. https://blog.google/technology/ai/try-bard

Goom, H. (2023, July 12). *AI-Generated vs. Human-Written Text: Technical Analysis*. Artmap Inc. https://hackernoon.com/ai-generated-vs-human-written-text-technical-analysis

Hahn, W. W. (2023, September 15). *ChatGPT and Large Language Models: Syntax and Semantics*. CFA Institute. https://blogs.cfainstitute.org/investor/2023/09/25/chatgpt-and-large-language-models-syntax-and-semantics/

Havlik, V. (2023) Meaning and understanding in large language models. arXiv. https://doi.org//arXiv.2310.17407 doi:10.48550

Heikkila, M. (2022, December 19). How to spot AI-generated text. *MIT Technology Review*. https://www.technologyreview.com/2022/12/19/1065596/how-to-spot-ai-generated-text/

Hough, D. (2023, October 10). *Student guidance for the responsible use of AI*. Association for Learning Technology. https://altc.alt.ac.uk/blog/2023/10/student-guidance-for-the-responsible-use-of-ai/

Ibrahim, H., Liu, F., Asim, R., Battu, B., Benabderrahmane, S., Alhafni, B., Adnan, W., Alhanai, T., AlShebli, B., Baghdadi, R., Bélanger, J., Beretta, E., Celik, K., Chaqfeh, M., Daqaq, M., El Bernoussi, Z., Fougnie, D., Garcia de Soto, B., Gandolfi, A., & Zaki, Y. (2023) Perception, performance, and detectability of conversational artificial intelligence across 32 university courses. *Scientific Reports, 13*, 1–13. Nature Publishing. doi:10.1038/s41598-023-38964-3

Ji, Z., Lee, N., Frieske, R., Yu, T., Su, D., Xu, Y., Ishii, E., Bang, Y. J., Madotto, A., & Fung, P. (2023). Survey of Hallucination in Natural Language Generation. *ACM Computing Surveys*, *55*(12), 1–38. doi:10.1145/3571730

Jisc. (2023a). *Artificial intelligence (AI) in tertiary education*. 3rd edition. Joint Information Systems Committee (JISC). https://beta.jisc.ac.uk/reports/artificial-intelligence-in-tertiary-education

Jisc. (2023b). *Student perceptions of generative AI*. Joint Information Systems Committee (JISC). https://beta.jisc.ac.uk/reports/student-perceptions-of-generative-ai

Jisc. (2023c). Generative AI – a primer. Version 1.1. Joint Information Systems Committee (JISC). https://repository.jisc.ac.uk/9182/1/generative-ai-a-primer.pdf

Jisc. (2023d, July 31). How UCL is redesigning assessment for the AI age. Joint Information Systems Committee (JISC). Retrieved, January 05, 2024, from https://www.jisc.ac.uk/member-stories/how-ucl-is-redesigning-assessment-for-the-ai-age

Juola, P. (2013, August 20). How a Computer Program Helped Show J. K. Rowling wrote A Cuckoo's Calling. *Scientific American*. https://www.scientificamerican.com/article/how-a-computer-program-helped-show-jk-rowling-write-a-cuckoos-calling/

Juola, P. (2017). Detecting Contract Cheating via Stylometric Methods. *Proceedings Plagiarism across Europe and Beyond*, 187–198. Mendel University Press. https://academicintegrity.eu/conference/proceedings/2017/Juola_Detecting.pdf

Kermes, H., & Teich, E. (2017). Average surprisal of parts-of-speech. *Proceedings Corpus Linguistics 2017*, 1–6. University of Birmingham. https://www.birmingham.ac.uk/Documents/college-artslaw/corpus/conference-archives/2017/general/paper207.pdf

Khan, U. (2023, May 16). How To Bypass AI Content Detectors: Remove AI Detection. Linkedin. https://www.linkedin.com/pulse/how-bypass-ai-content-detectors-uzair-khan

Lancaster, T. (2022, December 04). Artificial Intelligence, Generated Text and Academic Integrity: Navigating the Ethics of AI in Academia. Thomas Lancaster's Blog. Retrieved, January 05, 2024, from https://thomaslancaster.co.uk/blog/artificial-intelligence-generated-text-and-academic-integrity-navigating-the-ethics-of-ai-in-academia/

Lancaster University. (n.d.). Ling 131 – Language & Style. Department of Linguistics and English Language (LAEL), Lancaster University. Retrieved, January 05, 2024, from https://www.lancaster.ac.uk/fass/projects/stylistics/index.htm

Lea, K. (2023, November 24). Students are still confused about AI. WonkHE. Retrieved, January 05, 2024, from https://wonkhe.com/blogs-sus/students-are-still-confused-about-ai/

Liang, W., Yuksekgonul, M., Mao, Y., Wu, E., & Zou, J. (2023). GPT detectors are biased against non-native English writers. *Patterns (New York, N.Y.)*, *4*(7), 1–4. doi:10.1016/j.patter.2023.100779 PMID:37521038

Lim, W. M., Gunasekara, A., Pallant, J. L., Pallant, J. I., & Pechenkina, E. (2023). Generative AI and the future of education: Ragnarok or reformation? A paradoxical perspective from management educators. *International Journal of Management Education*, *21*(2), 1–13. doi:10.1016/j.ijme.2023.100790

Lu, N., Liu, S., He, R., Wang, Q., & Tang, K. (2023). Large Language Models can be Guided to Evade AI-Generated Text Detection. arXiv. https://doi.org//arXiv.2305.10847 doi:10.48550

Marshall, A. J. (2023, July 17). AI: There Is No Such Thing As A Silver Bullet. Linkedin. https://www.linkedin.com/pulse/ai-thing-silver-bullet-alexander-james-marshall

McClenaghan, E. (2022, July 06). *Mann-Whitney U Test: Assumptions and Example*. Labx Media Group Inc. https://www.technologynetworks.com/informatics/articles/mann-whitney-u-test-assumptions-and-example-363425

Namik, H., Sims, A., & Withy, A. (2023, May 22). Can academic integrity prevail when AI is so good? *Ingenio*. University of Auckland. https://www.auckland.ac.nz/en/news/2023/05/22/ingenio-taking-issue-opinion-chatgpt.html

New Scientist. (2023, July 29). How To Think About AI... And How To Live With It. *New Scientist, 259*, 32–40. https://www.sciencedirect.com/science/article/pii/S0262407923014276. doi:10.1016/S0262-4079(23)01427-6

Nvidia. (2023, March 20). *What is Generative AI?* Nvidia Corporation. https://www.nvidia.com/en-us/glossary/data-science/generative-ai/

OpenAI. (2022, November 30) *Introducing ChatGPT* [Press release]. OpenAI LLC. https://openai.com/blog/chatgpt

OpenAI. (2023a, January 31). *New AI classifier for indicating AI-written text.* [Press release]. OpenAI LLC. https://openai.com/blog/new-ai-classifier-for-indicating-ai-written-text

OpenAI. (2023b, March 14). *GPT-4*. [Press release]. OpenAI LLC. https://openai.com/research/gpt-4

OpenAI. (2023c, July 20). *As of July 20, 2023, the AI classifier is no longer available...* [Press release] OpenAI LLC. https://openai.com/blog/new-ai-classifier-for-indicating-ai-written-text

OpenAI. (2023d, September 22). *How can educators respond to students presenting AI-generated content as their own?* OpenAI LLC. https://help.openai.com/en/articles/8313351-how-can-educators-respond-to-students-presenting-ai-generated-content-as-their-own

Orenstrakh, M. S., Karnalim, O., Suarez, C. A., & Liut, M. (2023). Detecting LLM-Generated Text in Computing Education: A Comparative Study for ChatGPT Cases. arXiv. https://doi.org//arXiv.2307.07411 doi:10.48550

Phrasly. (2023, September 21). *AI Powered Writing for...* Phrasly LLC. https://phrasly.ai/?gclid=EAIaIQobChMIk_-J6puxgQMVi_ftCh0rugu0EAMYASAAEgIgQ_D_BwE

Pine Cove Consulting. (2023, April 07). *How Can an Educator Can Prevent Students from Using AI Writers? Pine Cove Consulting*. Pine Cove Consulting. https://marketing.pinecc.com/blog/how-can-an-educator-can-prevent-students-from-using-ai-writers

Reed, T. (2023, March 20). *Decoding Humanity: How to Differentiate Between AI and Human Writing*. Linkedin. https://www.linkedin.com/pulse/decoding-humanity-how-differentiate-between-ai-human-writing-reed

Retraction Watch. (2023, July 07). *Publisher blacklists authors after preprint cites made-up studies.* Center for Scientific Integrity. https://retractionwatch.com/2023/07/07/publisher-blacklists-authors-after-preprint-cites-made-up-studies/

Rogers, R. (2023, February 08). *How to Detect AI-Generated Text, According to Researchers.* Advance Magazine Publishers Inc. https://www.wired.com/story/how-to-spot-generative-ai-text-chatgpt/

Rogerson, A. M., & McCarthy, G. (2017). Using Internet based paraphrasing tools: Original work, patchwriting or facilitated plagiarism? *International Journal for Educational Integrity, 13*(1), 1833–2595. doi:10.1007/s40979-016-0013-y

Russell Group. (2023, July 04). *New principles on use of AI in education.* The Russell Group. https://russellgroup.ac.uk/news/new-principles-on-use-of-ai-in-education/ -:~:text=

Sabzalieva, E., & Valentini, A. (2023). *ChatGPT and artificial intelligence in higher education: Quick start guide.* UNESCO. https://www.iesalc.unesco.org/wp-content/uploads/2023/04/ChatGPT-and-Artificial-Intelligence-in-higher-education-Quick-Start-guide_EN_FINAL.pdf

Sadasivan, V. S., Kumar, A., Balasubramanian, S., Wang, W., & Feizi, S. (2023) Can AI-Generated Text be Reliably Detected? arXiv. https://doi.org//arXiv.2303.11156 doi:10.48550

Salvagno, M., Taccone, F. S., & Gerli, A. G. (2023). Can artificial intelligence help for scientific writing? *Critical Care, 27*(1), 75–79. doi:10.1186/s13054-023-04380-2 PMID:36841840

Shanahan, M. (2023) Talking About Large Language Models. arXiv. https://doi.org//arXiv.2212.03551 doi:10.48550

Shannon, C. E. (1948). A Mathematical Theory of Communication. *The Bell System Technical Journal, 27*(3), 379–423. doi:10.1002/j.1538-7305.1948.tb01338.x

Shannon, C. E. (1951). Prediction and entropy of printed English. *The Bell System Technical Journal, 30*(1), 50–64. doi:10.1002/j.1538-7305.1951.tb01366.x

Snow, E. L., Allen, L. K., Jacovina, M. E., Crossley, S. A., Perret, C. A., & McNamara, D. S. (2016). Keys to Detecting Writing Flexibility Over Time: Entropy and Natural Language Processing. *Journal of Learning Analytics, 2*(3), 40–54. doi:10.18608/jla.2015.23.4

Sokol, D. (2023, July 10) It is too easy to falsely accuse a student of using AI: a cautionary tale. *Times Higher Education (THE).* https://www.timeshighereducation.com/blog/it-too-easy-falsely-accuse-student-using-ai-cautionary-tale

Susnjak, T. (2022). ChatGPT: The End of Online Exam Integrity? arXiv. https://doi.org//arXiv.2212.09292 doi:10.48550

Tangermann, V. (2023, January 09). There's a Problem With That App That Detects GPT-Written Text: It's Not Very Accurate. Futurism. https://futurism.com/gptzero-accuracy

Tayeb, N. (2023, January 23). *Today we are launching our #chatgpt Detector* [Press Release]. Linkedin. https://www.linkedin.com/posts/nabil-tayeb_chatgpt-schools-universities-activity-7021140020723933184-YZcB

Tian, E. (2023a, January 03). *I spent New Years building GPTZero…* [Press release]. X/Twitter https://twitter.com/edward_the6/status/1610067688449007618?s=20&t=KgkIlG9q3Zkw_AeyXQMRVA

Tian, E. (2023b, June 01). *A Statistical Defence for AI Detection*. GPTZero LLC. https://gptzero.me/blogs/statistical-approach

Turnitin. (2023, April 04). *The launch of Turnitin's AI writing detector and the road ahead* [Press release]. Turnitin LLC. https://www.turnitin.com/blog/the-launch-of-turnitins-ai-writing-detector-and-the-road-ahead

UCL. (n.d.). *The Internet Grammar of English. The Survey of English Usage, University College London 1996-1998 & Jisc*. University College London. https://www.ucl.ac.uk/internet-grammar/home.htm

Walker, R., & Voce, J. (2023). Post-Pandemic Learning Technology Developments in UK Higher Education: What Does the UCISA Evidence Tell Us? *Sustainability (Basel)*, *15*(17), 1–16. doi:10.3390/su151712831

Wang, W., Wang, G., Marivate, V., & Hufton, A. L. (2023). On the transparency of large AI models. *Patterns (New York, N.Y.)*, *4*(7), 1–2. doi:10.1016/j.patter.2023.100797 PMID:37521049

Webb, M. (2023, September 18). *AI Detection – Latest Recommendations. Jisc National Centre for AI in Tertiary Education*. National Center for Education. https://nationalcentreforai.jiscinvolve.org/wp/2023/09/18/ai-detection-latest-recommendations/

Weber-Wulff, D., Anohina-Naumeca, A., Bjelobaba, S., Foltynek, T., Guerrero-Dib, J., Popoola, O., Sigut, P., & Waddington, L. (2023) Testing of Detection Tools for AI-Generated Text. arXiv. https://doi.org//arXiv.2306.15666 doi:10.48550

Wilhelm, I. (2023, June 12). Nobody Wins in an Academic-Integrity Arms Race: How artificial intelligence is changing the way colleges think about cheating. *The Chronicle of Higher Education*. Retrieved, January 05, 2024, from https://www.chronicle.com/article/nobody-wins-in-an-academic-integrity-arms-race

Williams, R. (2023, July 07). AI-text detection tools are really easy to fool. *MIT Technology Review*. https://www.technologyreview.com/2023/07/07/1075982/ai-text-detection-tools-are-really-easy-to-fool/

Wood, P. (2023, February 28). Oxford and Cambridge ban ChatGPT over plagiarism fears but other universities choose to embrace AI bot. *iNews*. https://inews.co.uk/news/oxford-cambridge-ban-chatgpt-plagiarism-universities-2178391

Yu, H., & Guo, Y. (2023). Generative artificial intelligence empowers educational reform: Current status, issues, and prospects. *Frontiers in Education*, *8*, 1–10. doi:10.3389/feduc.2023.1183162

Chapter 11
AI Detection's High False Positive Rates and the Psychological and Material Impacts on Students

Whitney Gegg-Harrison
https://orcid.org/0009-0008-4258-2834
University of Rochester, USA

Claire Quarterman
Independent Researcher, USA

ABSTRACT

This chapter, per the authors, explains the inherent impossibility of "AI detection," and explores the material and psychological impacts of AI detection false positives on students. A small corpus study is presented demonstrating much higher than advertised rates of false positives across a range of popular "AI detection" tools. Based on this study along with news reports and first-person testimony from affected students, the chapter presents the possibility that neurodivergent writers, along with L2 writers, are more likely to be impacted by false positives. Given the current rates of mental health challenges on college campuses and the likelihood of a disproportionate impact on students who already face marginalization, the use of these AI detection tools is argued to be unethical. The chapter closes with recommendations for writing teachers.

INTRODUCTION

The release of ChatGPT in November, 2022 came towards the end of what was, for most college instructors, the fifth straight semester of disruption due to the COVID-19 pandemic. Instructors saw magazine headlines like "The College Essay is Dead" (Marche, 2022), and were left to wonder whether the work students submitted at the end of the semester was actually their own, and what they should do to best

DOI: 10.4018/979-8-3693-0240-8.ch011

prepare for the next semester, when ChatGPT and other tools would be in their classrooms whether they wanted them there or not. Professors face an increasing challenge: how to know whether a text was actually written by the student who submitted it?

The remote learning that took place during the pandemic had already led many schools, fearing rampant cheating, towards using automated surveillance tools, with predictably terrible impacts on the stress levels of student test-takers (Harwell, 2022). So it is not surprising that the release of ChatGPT also stoked fears about cheating, and alongside those fears, an impulse towards banning the use of ChatGPT and other similar tools (Johnson, 2023; Yang, 2023). Capitalizing on this impulse, developers like Edward Tian of GPTZero and companies like Turnitin raced to create tools that would "detect" the use of tools like ChatGPT. It has always been possible for students to turn in work that is not their own, e.g. through contract-cheating. What AI text-generators have changed is primarily due to their accessibility and speed relative to human writers, which likely changes the calculus for students considering passing off AI-generated text as their own.

In this chapter, we argue that automated detection tools are not the answer to this problem. Large Language Models (LLMs) that power tools like ChatGPT are designed to produce text that is plausibly human, and because of this, there will always be the risk of both false positives and false negatives when tools are used to determine whether the text was produced by a human or by an LLM[1]. Both of the authors of this text have had their own writing falsely flagged as "AI-generated"; this informs the position we take in this chapter.

THE FUNDAMENTAL IMPOSSIBILITY OF "AI-DETECTION" FOR WRITING

We begin by breaking down the "GPT" in ChatGPT, which stands for "Generative Pre-trained Transformer". The word "transformer" refers to a type of neural network architecture first introduced by the famous paper "*Attention is all you need*" (Vaswani et al., 2017). Models using transformer architectures can learn about what words are likely in various contexts by processing sequences of text; the model can attend not just to the immediately preceding word, but to words in other positions in the sequence, and even to intermediate representations in other layers of the neural network.

The learning occurs during "pre-training". In essence, the model learns by playing a "fill in the blank" game: given a sequence of text with a mask in place of one of the words, it predicts what word should replace the mask, and updates its parameters to account for how close or not the guess was to the actual masked word. "Closeness" is based on the representations within the neural network, which are called "embeddings". A word embedding is a vector of values representing information about the contexts in which that word appears, which can be thought of as representing coordinates in a massively multidimensional space. For any pair of words, their "embedding" vectors can be compared to generate a measurement of how "similar" they are. While there is good reason to be skeptical about precisely how much world knowledge is actually captured in these word embeddings (Bender & Koller, 2020), some cognitive scientists argue that word embeddings closely align with human conceptual knowledge (Piantadosi & Hill, 2022). Research suggests that transformer models can predict nearly all of the variance in human neural responses to sentences (Schrimpf et al., 2021), and that alignment with humans at both the neural and behavioral level is possible even with "developmentally-realistic" amounts of training data (Hosseini et al., 2022). To be clear, this does not mean that LLMs are equivalent to human minds, but it does suggest that we should not be surprised when the output of an LLM is indistinguishable from human writing.

This brings us to the word "generative": GPT models generate text using the prompt provided by the user as the context, and from there, predicting words that would be a plausible continuation or response to the content of the prompt. And while there are obviously very important differences between LLMs and humans, we know that human language processing is also incremental and rooted in prediction (Altmann & Steedman, 1988; Chambers et al., 2004; Martin et al., 2018; McRae & Matsuki, 2013); we use what we've already heard or read, along with knowledge about the broader linguistic context, about the world, about the likely intentions of the person communicating with us, and so on, to predict what is likely to come next. When what comes next aligns with that prediction, we are able to process or produce it more efficiently. The knowledge that informs these predictions is inherently probabilistic and associative in nature; it is learned from our experience as users of the language and as experiencers of the world (Clark, 2013).

Unlike LLMs, humans have intentions, goals, personal experiences, desires, and senses, and we are interacting in and can act upon the physical world in ways that LLMs cannot. But the ways that LLMs generate text and humans generate language are both fundamentally rooted in prediction, and thus if we imagine that the "predictability" of a text will give us clues as to its provenance, we are likely to be misled. The patterns in choices humans make about what word to use next are precisely the patterns picked up on by LLMs trained on massive amounts of human output. Thus, if we are trying to decide, purely on the basis of a piece of text, whether that text was generated by a person or by an LLM, we are inherently likely to fall victim to both false positives and false negatives. Indeed, recent research shows that even linguists, who we might expect to have greater sensitivity to patterns in language than the general population, cannot successfully distinguish human-generated from AI-generated text (Casal & Kessler, 2023).

TESTING AI-DETECTION TOOLS

There were good reasons to hope that automatic AI-detection tools could work, even outside of concerns about academic dishonesty: reliable automatic detection would enable synthetic text to be quickly identified and flagged as such, which would help in the fight against automatically-generated disinformation or spam. Automated detection tools are designed to pick up on certain "signatures" of LLM-generated text, either those that are supposed artifacts of the prediction-driven LLM text-generation process described above, or those that could be superimposed on the text in the form of a "watermark" that would be required for all LLM text-generators to add to their output. However, researchers at the University of Maryland showed that both empirically and theoretically, neither approach is reliable in practical scenarios (Sadasivan et al., 2023). Importantly, they also show that these "signature" or "watermark" patterns could be inferred by a malicious actor who then adds them to human-generated text, in what is called a "spoofing attack," to cause those texts to be flagged as AI-generated. As the authors point out, these kinds of attacks could cause reputational damage to writers who did not actually use LLM-generated text. While our focus in this chapter is not on false positives caused by spoofing attacks, but rather on those caused by the reliance on statistics that cannot reliably distinguish between human-written and LLM-generated text, we think this point about reputational damage is important, as it shows what is at stake when we claim to be able to detect "AI-generated" text.

AI-detection tools vary in their implementation, but all attempt to classify texts as either human-produced or AI-produced based on statistical analysis of the features of the writing. GPTZero, for example, relies primarily on measures of "perplexity" and "burstiness". Perplexity is a measure of how predictable a word is in context, based on a particular language model; low perplexity means that, across the sample, the words are highly predictable in context. Burstiness measures the variance in the length and structure of sentences; lower burstiness indicates that a sample contains sentences that are generally similar to each other in length and structure. In essence, these two measures aim to detect the "signature" of an LLM, based on the fact that LLMs are predictive models; the assumption is that LLM-generated text should be lower than human-generated text in both perplexity and burstiness, and that humans should be "more random" than LLMs.

However, as noted above, human language production is also rooted in prediction, and the assumption that humans will necessarily be more random than LLMs in any given example of writing is not valid. Perplexity and burstiness in human writing are affected by genre (some genres are more constrained than others in terms of word choices and sentence structures), the goals of the writer (e.g. prioritizing clarity and ease of reading will often result in lower perplexity and burstiness), and by the individual writer's facility with language. For example, Liang et al. (2023) demonstrated that AI-detection tools were biased against TOEFL writers, whose native language is not English, due to the more limited variability in sentence structure and word choice in these writers' texts. They then asked ChatGPT to "improve" the word choices in these texts to sound "more like a native speaker," and found that the perplexity and burstiness of the resulting texts went up to the point where the texts were no longer likely to be flagged by detectors; when they asked ChatGPT to "simplify the word choices" in texts written by native English speakers, the resulting texts had reduced perplexity and burstiness similar to that of the TOEFL essays. One takeaway from this research is that LLMs can be used to either increase or decrease the perplexity and burstiness of a given text before submitting it, and a text with increased perplexity and burstiness produced via this method is likely to evade detection. Thus, the idea that the detectors are picking up on anything like a "signature" of LLM usage seems quite implausible.

Companies like GPTZero and Turnitin claim to have extremely high accuracy rates, with GPTZero claiming that their "improved" model as of January 5th, 2023 had a ">2% false positive rate" (Tian, 2023a), and Turnitin claiming a false positive rate of "under 1%" in their FAQ (Turnitin, 2023a). However, the cited rates are implausible in terms of signal detection theory, which allows us to analyze the detectors in terms of a "Receiver Operating Characteristic" (ROC) curve[2]. In evaluating the overall accuracy of a classifier, what we are interested in is the *sensitivity* (corresponding to the rate of true positives) and the *specificity* (corresponding to the rate of false positives). A good classifier should have a very sharp ROC curve, such that the detector is both highly sensitive, correctly identifying true positives, and highly specific, correctly rejecting true negatives. We do have numbers that can help us estimate the ROC curve for at least one AI-detection tool: namely, OpenAI's now-withdrawn detection tool (Kirchner et al., 2023). When OpenAI tuned their detector to have 91% specificity (meaning that it identified human-written texts as AI-generated 9% of the time, a higher false positive rate than either GPTZero or Turnitin claim), they were only able to achieve a sensitivity of 26% (meaning that they accurately identified AI-generated texts as AI-generated only 26% of the time). In other words, the ROC is not the sharp curve that allows reliable classification, and it is for this reason that OpenAI withdrew their tool. Given that GPTZero and Turnitin are attempting the same classification task (though perhaps using different metrics), if they are correct in claiming a specificity of 98-99%, it seems incredibly unlikely that they could simultaneously achieve a sensitivity that is so much higher than what OpenAI achieved with an even lower specificity. Without a high sensitivity, these tools would not be useful as detectors, as they would allow far too many false negatives - in other words, these tools would fail to detect true positives, allowing AI-generated text to be falsely declared to be human-generated, undermining the very purpose of AI-detection.

The science fiction magazine Clarkesworld's attempts to ensure that human writers are able to submit their work for potential publication shows us a potential harm that results from failure to detect true positives: given the speed with which AI-generated text can be generated, it has the potential to completely overwhelm the submissions of stories written by human authors, making it even harder for those authors to have their work seen (Clarke, 2023). In education contexts, this has the potential to create a perverse system in which students speedily and illicitly submitting AI-generated text find themselves rewarded for their lack of effort while those who spend the time and energy required to truly learn fall behind. However, in the work we present in this chapter, we focus on the harms of false positives, where human-produced text is falsely identified as AI-generated, because it is in this situation where we see the largest potential for harm to individual writers.

Unsurprisingly, real world application of these tools has shown them to be far less reliable than the marketing would have us believe, as has now been documented in numerous news articles (Fowler, 2023b, 2023a; Gluska, 2023; D'Agostino, 2023; Edwards, 2023a; Jimenez, 2023). As mentioned above, OpenAI quietly closed down their own AI-detector on July 20th, 2023 due to poor performance (Edwards, 2023b; Epstein-Gross, 2023). But while GPTZero claims to have never had the intention to be a "plagiarism-detection" company (Tian, 2023b), it is still being widely used for the purpose of determining whether a text was AI-generated for the purpose of academic honesty proceedings. And while Turnitin recently made it possible for users to opt-out of AI Writing Detection, as of the time of writing, it is still on by default (Turnitin, 2023b). In what follows, we present the results of a small corpus-based study demonstrating significantly higher false positive rates than those claimed by GPTZero and other companies.

Method

Corpus

Our corpus consists of a collection of 186 documents written by the two authors of this chapter, as well as those donated to the cause by friends and family members, representing a number of different genres: term papers, application essays, homework assignments, letters of recommendation, handouts, and even some social media posts. While there are larger, more representative corpora of undergraduate writing[3], we did not feel that it was appropriate to use those corpora in our study, as none of the students whose writing is included in those corpora consented to having their writing submitted to an AI-detection tool.

Detectors Used

Because GPTZero was the AI-detector that first caught our interest, we originally focused our efforts there. However, after Turnitin enabled its AI-detection feature and many other AI-detectors were marketed to educators, employers, and other professionals, we felt compelled to test a selection. Along with GPTZero and Turnitin, we tested four other AI-detectors: ZeroGPT, GPTKit, Originality.AI, and Passed.AI.

Explanation of Method for GPTZero

In March of 2023, Author-2 tested 92 texts written by herself, her brother, and two other people who wish to remain anonymous. Between June 21 and July 21, we retested GPTZero with the updated dataset of 186 texts. However, on July 19, GPTZero updated its model, so we retested it.

After GPTZero analyzes a text, it delivers a verdict, and if it believes that any part of the text was generated by an LLM, it highlights that portion of text (GPTZero, 2023):

- "Your text is likely to be written entirely by AI"
- "Your text may include parts written by AI"
- "Your text is most likely human written but there are some sentences with low perplexities"
- "Your text is most likely human written"
- "Your text is likely to be written entirely by a human"

We condensed these into two categories:

- False positive: Combines the verdicts "written entirely by AI" and "parts written by AI".
- True negative: Combines the two "human written" verdicts and the "low perplexities" verdict, though some sections of these texts were highlighted as being "more likely to be written by AI"

Explanation of Method for the Other AI-detectors

Most of the AI-detectors we tested highlight text they believe were generated by AI, and include an "AI score". On their website, Originality.AI claims that "a score of 60% Original and 40% AI, if you know the content was 100% created by you, is not a false positive" (Gillham, 2023). However, most people using AI-detectors do so because they do *not* know if a text was generated by an LLM. In addition, based on reports from students, many teachers consider it cheating if even one sentence is flagged as AI-generated (Bobertsmith1928, 2023; Glaze-Wolf, 2023; The-Rice-Boi, 2023b). As a result, we defined a false positive as any text with at least one sentence flagged as generated by an LLM, in order to more accurately capture the way these tools are currently used in educational settings.

The Character Limit Issue

GPTZero had a limit of 50,000 characters while ZeroGPT had a limit of 15,000 characters. Texts with character counts just exceeding those limits were truncated to the last complete sentence. The others were split into roughly equivalent blocks of texts, which were then passed through individually. Finally, Turnitin had a minimum character count, so many of the texts we could process on other AI-detectors were not processed by Turnitin. We have elected to calculate Turnitin's false positive rate from the 109 texts that were processed.

Figure 1. A comparison of the tests run on GPTZero

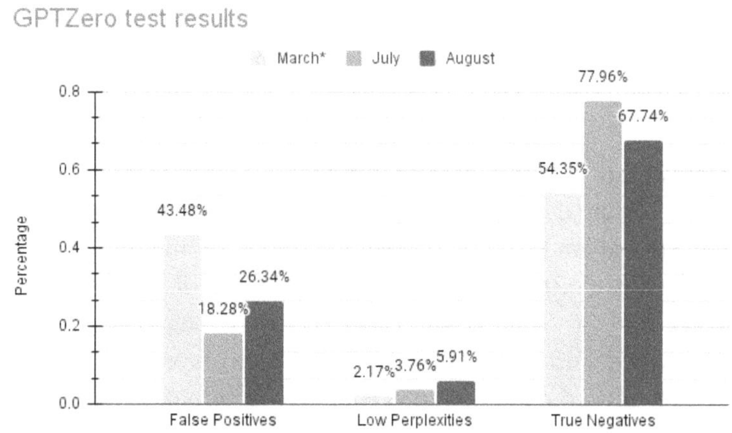

RESULTS

We first show the results of the tests run on GPTZero in March, June/July, and August of 2023. Note that in March of 2023, the dataset passed through GPTZero consisted of only 92 texts.

While the false positive rate decreased between March and July, it increased after GPTZero's July 19 update. In that update, GPTZero claims to have "tuned our deep learning model to improve its performance on ESL writing, and generally" (GPTZero Release Notes, 2023).

We found that there was considerable variation between detectors. Of the 109 texts properly processed by all AI-detectors tested, only 26 texts were not falsely identified as AI by any. In other words, only 23.85% of our smaller corpus was consistently correctly identified as human.

Figure 2. AI detector false positives

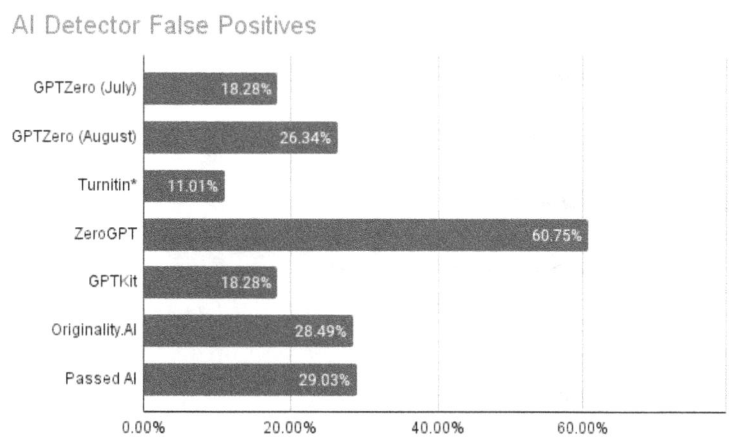

The provenance of our corpus means we can be certain that all of the writing included is human-generated, and thus all the "AI-generated" flags are indeed false. The size of the corpus means that we cannot make claims about the *true* false positive rates of these AI-detection tools, as our corpus is not representative. Our results do suggest at least one of three things, none of which are something we should hope to be true if these detection tools are widely used:

(1) The true false positive rate is higher than advertised,
(2) Creators of AI-detectors are defining false positives inconsistently with how consumers do, OR
(3) The false positives are not randomly distributed, and affect some writers more than others. Figure 3 illustrates the wide range of false positive rates between different authors in our corpus.

There is already research supporting the idea that false positives are not randomly distributed. Recall the previously mentioned study from Liang et al. (2023)[4], which found that TOEFL writing is far more likely to be falsely flagged as "AI-generated" due to lower perplexity and burstiness. However, the contributors to our corpus are all native English speakers. Is there anything else that most of these authors have in common that could potentially explain why their writing is so often flagged as AI-generated? It turns out that there is: *neurodivergence*.

Neurodivergence is a catch-all term that includes many diagnoses (Cleveland Clinic, n.d.-a); for the contributors to our corpus, the relevant diagnoses are ADHD and/or autism. While we cannot make any sweeping claims about the relationship between neurodivergence and AI-detection false positives on the basis of our very small corpus, further anecdotal evidence suggests that this may indeed be a real issue. Several students and freelance writers have reached out to the authors of this chapter to share the experiences they had with being accused of using AI to generate their writing on the basis of AI-detection tools

Figure 3. AI detector false positives, author comparison

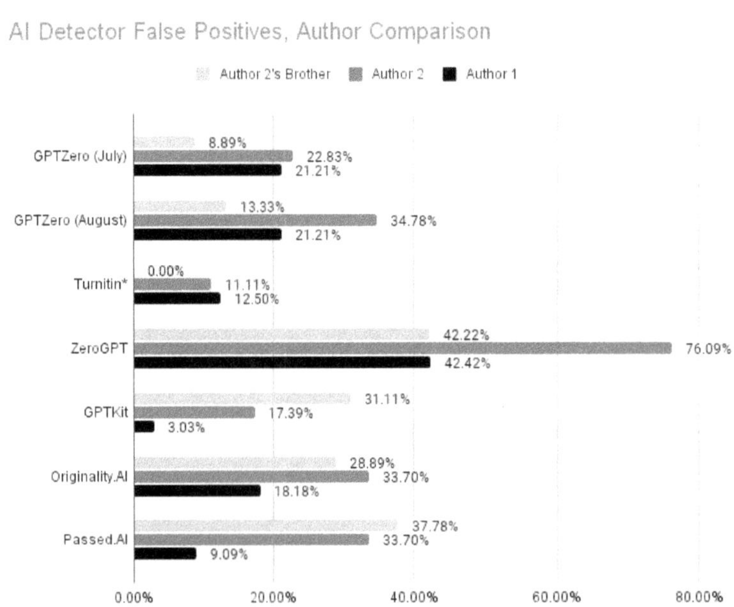

used by their school or their employers; a disproportionate number of those individuals also identified themselves as neurodivergent, many hypothesizing that neurodivergence may be the reason their writing is flagged as AI-generated.

This possibility has also been noted in cases where "AI-detection" was performed by a human, rather than a tool, as in the recent case of the autistic Purdue professor Rua Williams, whose email was accused of being AI-generated because it supposedly "lacked warmth" (Pollina, 2023). In a subsequent Mastodon post, Williams elaborates on their motivation for sharing their experience, pointing out that "The panic over what generated text means for society has made people suspicious, and without proof they label anything that feels different as fake. But there's a huge diversity in linguistic expression and fear of difference leads to discrimination." (Williams, 2023). We are ushering in a world in which everyone is under suspicion, leaving those like Williams and the neurodivergent authors of the texts in our small corpus without any way of proving our humanity via the very medium in which many of us feel most like ourselves: writing. There is unfortunately little research on the writing processes of neurodivergent writers (Gillespie-Lynch et al., 2020), and most of the existing research on neurodivergent writers approaches the question with a focus on remediating deficits (e.g. Zajic et al., 2018), though many of the neurodivergent writers whose writing is flagged in this way report viewing writing as a particularly strong skill. More research is needed here in order to understand whether neurodivergent writing is truly more likely to be flagged as "AI-generated", and why.

What we are most concerned about in the arguments we make in this chapter is the impact false positives have on students. While any student is likely to be harmed by a false accusation of "AI-plagiarism", there is also good reason to believe that neurodivergent writers are more likely to experience the worst harms. We will explore this issue further in the next section.

What Is the Impact on Students?

Academic honesty policies have always needed to recognize the possibility of false accusations, and most academic honesty policies do claim to include protections and support for accused students. Even prior to the release of ChatGPT, students could be (and were) accused of submitting work that was not their own, and some were eventually exonerated and thus understood to be innocent of the charges against them. Pitt et al. (2021) interviewed students who had experienced an accusation (whether proven or not) of contract cheating; this is the type of cheating that bears the closest resemblance to the type of "AI-plagiarism" faculty are most concerned about. In this study, researchers found that significant consequences of the contract cheating allegation process affected both those students whose cases were "proven" and those whose cases were "not proven" (understood to be falsely accused). They found 5 key themes in the interviews with students:

1. The most challenging experience of the student's life
2. Not telling their family about the allegation and managing any financial impact themselves
3. Stress and hypervigilance around future assignment submission
4. Rumours and reputational damage: changed relationships with academics and peers
5. Staying on track and guiding other students to practice academic integrity

(Pitt et al., 2021)

Students whose cases were not proven agree that the experience rates as one of the most challenging of their lives, and report a great deal of stress and hypervigilance around future assignment submission, with specific fears around how they will be able to prove that their writing is their own. This last point echoes the experiences we find in reporting about accusations resulting from AI-detection false positives. In what follows, we explore the specific material and psychological impacts on students who are falsely accused of AI-plagiarism.

Material Impacts

One of the most severe material impacts for students falsely accused of AI-plagiarism is that they may be prevented from graduating, or at least from graduating on time. Reporting on an especially problematic case at Texas A&M describes "a panic in the class, with some students fearful their diplomas were at risk", though the article later quotes a statement from a Texas A&M spokesman pointing out that "several students have been exonerated and their grades have been issued" and "no students failed [the] class or were barred from graduating" (Verma, 2023a). While the worst outcome seems to have been averted here, the fears expressed by students do point to a real potential material harm. Depending on when an accusation is made, students may be left without a true grade in the course during the period when they need to register for next semester's classes. If required coursework needs to be delayed because of this due to rules around prerequisites, this can impact the timing of their graduation, even if they are eventually exonerated.

This points to another material impact: the amount of time and energy required to exonerate oneself in the face of a false accusation. A recent news article describes the experience of Louise Stivers, a college senior falsely accused of AI-plagiarsm, as "a bureaucratic nightmare lasting more than two weeks"; Stivers "was expected to parse the school's dense cheating policies and mount a formal defense of her work, with little institutional support and while facing the ordinary pressures of senior year," and "because of this split focus, she says, her grades began to slide" (Klee, 2023b). Time lost to defending oneself against false accusations of cheating cannot be gotten back, and if students' grades in their other classes drop because of the amount of time they are spending working on defending themselves, this will have a permanent impact on their GPA regardless of whether they are eventually exonerated.

Many international students and students on scholarships are required to maintain a certain minimum GPA, and a false accusation in a class in which the student was otherwise performing well may leave them unable to count that class towards their GPA at the time when they must demonstrate they meet minimum GPA-requirements, potentially resulting in a loss of scholarship funding or enrollment status for the next semester. One student facing a false accusation of submitting AI-generated work expressed this fear in a post on Reddit seeking advice: "If I can't fight this, I can't get an A in this class, and I might lose my scholarship. PLEASE HELP" (GlaireWolf, 2023). Even if these cases are eventually resolved in the student's favor, this may not happen quickly enough to avert at least a temporary loss in scholarship funding. If these cases are not resolved in the students' favor, then they may receive penalties that lower their GPAs permanently, eliminating any potential for the scholarship to be reinstated.

Even in those cases where students are exonerated, the negative material impact of the *accusation* is significant. False accusations of "AI-plagiarism" can also impact the future opportunities of students, particularly those who intend to go into professional training in fields that require self-disclosure of all disciplinary procedures at their college. For example, applicants to law school and to state bars are advised to proactively disclose any such proceedings, even if exonerated, since they can show up in background checks (Klee, 2023b). This adds to the material impacts for students like Stivers who are applying to law school, complicating their application process and possibly placing them at a disadvantage compared to students who do not have anything to report.

Psychological Impacts

Stress is the first and most obvious psychological impact of being accused of AI-plagiarism, and is mentioned in every news article describing a case of AI-detection false positives (Fowler, 2023b, 2023a; D'Agostino, 2023; Edwards, 2023a; Jimenez, 2023; Klee, 2023b, 2023a). We have already discussed the amount of time that students must devote to the process of clearing their names, but the cost here is not just lost time: the stress involved in navigating dense academic honesty policies also significantly impacts students, creating distraction from other course work (Klee, 2023b) and in at least some cases, even provoking the first panic attack experience of a student's life (Jimenez, 2023). We know that many university academic honesty offices are structured to be biased in favor of university faculty (Kara & MacAlister, 2010). When students feel helpless to defend themselves, they understandably panic about the potential impact these false accusations can have on their reputation, standing as students, and future goals.

A sense of helplessness pervades reporting from students on their experiences with AI-detection false positives. Many say that when they attempted to demonstrate their innocence by providing access to their version history, their notes, previous documents they've written in the same voice, and so forth, the response from their professors and those responsible for adjudicating the academic dishonesty process was one of disbelief, or at least indifference. In some cases, teachers reportedly dismiss the evidence provided by students as not outweighing the determination of the AI-detection tool, as described by one Reddit user seeking advice (The-Rice-Boi, 2023a); in others, the evidence simply goes unacknowledged, as in the case of a student who reported pleading her case up the institutional hierarchy, all "to no avail" (Verma, 2023b). Students report feeling particular distress about the fact that the teachers who accused them of AI-plagiarism will be assessing their work for the rest of the semester, leaving them feeling both helpless and hopeless; the dismissal of exonerating evidence destroys the trust that students have in their teachers, leaving them fearful that future writing will also be subject to suspicion.

AI-detection false positives seem to evoke stress, helplessness, and fear regardless of whether students are finding out due to an accusation from a teacher or from testing AI-detection tools on their own writing. For example, one Reddit user, in the r/OpenAI forum, describes finding out through their own testing that GPTZero said some of their homework answers are "completely generated by AI", and states, "I'm scared I'll be falsely accused" (ElevenBurnie, 2023). Another Reddit user, in the r/autism forum, describes "freaking out" upon testing various AI-detectors on their own writing and finding that it is frequently flagged as AI-generated (NeetMastery, 2023). Heartbreakingly, this user seems to question whether it is even possible for them to write well "without sounding like an AI" (NeetMastery, 2023).

The worry about "sounding like an AI" points to a further potential psychological impact of AI-detection false positives: these false positives tell a writer that they do not sound human, but instead sound "like an AI". No student wants to hear that they don't sound human, but this accusation almost certainly hits harder when levied against neurodivergent students, who have typically experienced accusations of being "robotic" or "alien" throughout their life (Merrick, 2023; Pollina, 2023; Stagg & Belcher, 2019). It's worth considering the impact this kind of othering language might have on a student who tests their own writing using the AI-Detector from Content @ Scale, which offers this message when identifying a text as AI-generated: "Did you write this yourself? Unfortunately, it reads very machine-like. If you write like a robot, you're going to get graded like a robot" (Content @ Scale, 2023). Not only does the message blame false positives on the writer's lack of skill, rather than on the detection tool, it also suggests that what they call "machine-like" writing deserves to receive poor grades. This is compounded by the critical rhetoric that surrounds "AI-generated" text; it is rightfully described as "bullshit" (Bergstrom & Ogbuno, 2023), but also typically identified as "terrible", "generic", and "voiceless," and while these latter descriptions may or may not be fair as descriptions of at least some of the output of LLMs, knowing that false positives are possible, we have to consider how this discourse impacts students whose own work is falsely flagged as "AI-generated" and said to be indistinguishable from work that is terrible, generic, voiceless bullshit.

Many neurodivergent individuals, especially those with ADHD, also experience Rejection Sensitive Dysphoria (RSD). Individuals with RSD experience "severe emotional pain because of a failure or feeling rejected" (Cleveland Clinic, n.d.-b). The emotional dysregulation that is typical of ADHD leads those who experience RSD to react intensely to perceived failure or rejection, even in situations that others might describe as neutral. Thus, when faculty raise questions about the provenance of a students' writing and suggest that unauthorized use of AI is suspected, students with RSD are likely to experience this as an extremely emotionally destabilizing event. Research suggests that students with RSD are also more likely than their neurotypical peers to consider self-harm as a reaction to their intense emotional response to rejection (Bedrossian, 2021).

Both authors of this chapter experience RSD. Neither of us is currently a student, and as such, we are less likely to experience the material harms we've described above. But given the frequency with which our own writing is flagged as "AI-generated" by automated detection tools, it is not impossible that either or both of us could face professional repercussions should our employers, academic conferences, or publishers decide to rely upon these tools for enforcing a ban on the use of generative AI (Harker, 2023). And we can attest that even as experienced writers who were testing these tools on ourselves, seeing our own writing flagged as "AI-generated" produced feelings of helplessness and a sense of dehumanization; it is all too easy for us to imagine how our younger selves might have responded to a situation like those the students whose cases we've covered here faced. Given the ways in which RSD manifests for us, what we can imagine is nothing good. The psychological impact of AI-detection false positives leaves us deeply concerned for the welfare of those who are currently students, particularly those students who share our neurotypes.

The students who are now at risk of being falsely accused of submitting AI-generated work have already lived through the COVID-19 pandemic, one of the most disruptive periods in education, and reported mental health challenges on college campuses have been rising for quite some time. The most recent surveys suggest that measures of student flourishing have dropped 32.5% between 2013 and 2021; in the same time span, rates depression amongst all students have risen 134.6%, rates of anxiety have risen 110%, and rates of suicidal ideation have risen 64.0% (Lipson et al., 2022). Given these troubling statistics, automated AI-detection tools are effectively throwing a match into gasoline.

Turnitin, in particular, initially made it impossible for users to opt-out of their AI Writing Detection tool. Given Turnitin's claim that over 16,000 institutions rely on their services (Turnitin, 2023c), their decision knowingly exposed an enormous amount of student work to an imperfect AI-detection tool. As of July 25, 2023, Turnitin announced that more 65 million papers had been reviewed in the time since AI Writing Detection was turned on (Turnitin, 2023d); even if the false positive rate is as low as the 1% that was originally claimed, a 1% false positive rate on 65 million papers would mean 650,000 falsely-flagged papers.

Even if students successfully demonstrate that they truly are the authors of their own texts, the process is stressful, and students enter into it knowing that despite all their efforts, they may fail to be heard, and may face academic penalties that could derail their plans for the future. Some portion of these students are likely to be neurodivergent; based on the evidence so far, it seems quite possible that such students are actually overrepresented amongst those falsely accused of AI-plagiarism, which suggests that higher than average rates of RSD are also likely. Given the mixture of stress, helplessness, and fear experienced by those falsely accused of AI-plagiarism, would it be any surprise if at some point, these kinds of false accusations lead to a suicide attempt? In our current campus climate, in which 27.6% of US college students report having considered suicide (American College Health Association, 2022), this is not something we should be willing to risk.

What Can Faculty Do?

At this point, we hope that it is clear to readers that "AI-detection" is not viable. It would be unethical to continue to use tools that claim to be able to detect AI, given the fundamental limitations we've discussed, and given that false positives can lead to harms both material and psychological. There is cause for hope here. Universities in the UK opted out of Turnitin's AI-detection tool (University of Greenwich, 2023). In the United States, some universities opted out of Turnitin's AI-detection tool early (UC Berkeley, 2023) with more joining their ranks in the new school year (Coley, 2023; University of Pittsburgh, 2023).

The concept of an "Algorithmic Imprint" (Ehsan et al., 2022) is important to consider here. Even if we continue to abandon the use of these tools, and even if these tools are eventually removed from the market (as OpenAI's detector was), this does not necessarily mean that we will no longer be affected by them. Instead, these tools will have left many people with the impression that AI-detection is something that is possible (Ehsan, 2023), but as we have already seen in the case of professor Rua Williams (Pollina, 2023), replacing automatic AI-detection tools with human intuition does not eliminate the possibility of harm, since human intuition is also unreliable (Casal & Kessler, 2023), and likely to be subject to many of the same biases as the automated tools.

But the impossibility of reliably detecting AI-generated text should not lead faculty to abandon the goal of ensuring that students are learning fundamental writing skills. It is possible, even probable, that much of the learning and writing that students do in the future will involve collaborating with AI systems, but as Oravec (2023) points out, without careful pedagogical planning, "students might feel it less necessary to learn and practice basic writing and design skills, focusing rather on the kinds of skills involved in editing and revising ChatGPT or Bard results so as to appear like their original productions." While many articles highlight the ways in which generative AI will make us more productive by eliminating "busywork" and automating "boring" repetitive tasks (Mollick, 2023; Noy & Zhang, 2023; Peng et al., 2023), it is worth thinking about whether some of what is considered "busywork" by experienced professionals is actually important practice for students who are still developing their skills as writers.

The problem that educators now face is ensuring that the practice we know students need for skill development does not feel like the kind of "busywork" best handed over to ChatGPT. We can find a hopeful perspective in James Lang's 2013 book, "Cheating Lessons: Learning from Academic Dishonesty." This book, written well before the release of ChatGPT, offers a promising argument: the pedagogical changes that reduce the likelihood of cheating are those which promote the best, deepest learning. Lang emphasizes frequent, shorter, scaffolded assignments where much of the work is done with faculty coaching during class time instead of outside of class, and advises ensuring that assignments are grounded in issues that students care about, which increases students' motivation to do the work themselves. These recommendations would also make it harder for students to rely on LLMs for their work.

If institutions decide to continue using AI-detection tools, knowing that false positives are possible, we owe it to students to help them understand what they would need to do to verify their innocence if accused of AI-plagiarism (Fowler, 2023c), and to give them access to tools for documenting their own writing process and opportunities to practice using those tools in a positive setting. In particular, we should help students practice using reference managers (such as Zotero, Endnote, or Mendeley) and word processors that provide some kind of *Version history* (such as Google Docs, Microsoft Word, or LibreOffice).

Generating citations is for many students a source of confusion and stress (Adam, 2016). Reference managers allow for students to keep track of notes about their sources as well as easily generate citations for their papers. Thus, teaching students how to effectively use reference managers is likely to improve their learning experience, but if accused of AI-plagiarism, students can also use the notes they kept in their Zotero folder to demonstrate that the references are genuine, and that they really did read and engage with the sources that are cited. LLMs are notorious for "confabulating" non-existent references when asked to produce a paper with citations (Welborn, 2023), and this is something we should ensure that students know. Helping students understand the importance of verifying references and teaching them strategies keeping good track of their own references is an excellent way to emphasize academic literacy while also discouraging reliance on LLMs.

Several students whose experiences we covered earlier in this chapter mentioned using a tool like Google Docs, which allows for users to view earlier states of a document via the *Version history*. Related tools like *Track Changes* in Microsoft Word and in the free, open-source LibreOffice also allow for the history of a document to be viewed. These tools offer a picture of the process through which the final text came to be, showing all of the changes, restarts, reorganizations, and deletions that took place as the text moved from early draft to finished piece. However, many students routinely write significant portions of their text in various "notes" apps, pasting large blocks of text from those apps into what becomes the final draft. Unfortunately, this pattern of large blocks of text pasted into a document is precisely what would be seen if the student asked ChatGPT to generate text that was then added to the final draft. For this reason, it is worthwhile to teach students to write using tools that allow them to access their version history, or to use other strategies (e.g. reflective writing, screenshots with timestamps) to document their own process.

However, it is worth noting that as of the time of writing, AI-text generation is now built into Google Docs (in the form of the *Help me write* button) and at least some versions of Microsoft Word (in the form of *Copilot*). This potentially complicates the picture in terms of students being able to demonstrate that they are the author of their own work via the version history. It also complicates the picture when we consider what it is that we mean by "submitting AI-generated text". Even text submitted long prior to the release of ChatGPT may well have been shaped in some way by AI, since AI-informed tools like autocomplete and Grammarly have been around for quite some time. We agree with Conrad (2023) that it is deeply problematic for the developers of the standard tools that educators and students use to add generative AI capability without full consideration of the impact this would have on teaching and learning, and yet, it is now our reality. This should ideally lead us away from a focus on whether a text was produced by a human or an LLM (since most texts, going forward, will likely be produced through a hybrid process), and towards a focus on whether students are actually learning what they need to learn through the process of writing. Documenting the writing process has many benefits for developing writers (Council of Writing Program Administrators, 2019), and is a worthwhile approach even if future developments in AI-assisted writing continue (Mills, 2023).

We emphasize that our recommendations are *not* intended to suggest that instructors should be constantly surveilling students' writing and research processes. We agree with Oravec (2023), who says, "the current forms of student surveillance may make educational administrators believe that 'something is being done about cheating' but also introduce new possibilities for bias and personal disempowerment." Instead, we should give students the tools and knowledge they need to advocate for themselves if faced with an instructor who accuses them of AI-plagiarism, and we intentionally focus on suggestions that have the added benefit of improving students' own learning regardless of whether AI tools are further integrated into the process.

CONCLUSION

Reliably detecting AI-generated text, whether through an automated tool or the use of our human intuitions, is a fool's errand. Treating it otherwise is harmful to students as learners and as humans. While some examples are "obviously" the work of an LLM or a human, there are also plenty of examples that could plausibly be the work of either, and neither AI-detection tools nor human judgment can reliably tell the difference. When we try to guess whose writing was generated by AI and whose was generated by a human, we are likely to reinforce existing biases, particularly against students who already face marginalization, like multilingual students and neurodivergent students.

False positives harm students, in ways both material and psychological, and are likely to intersect in dangerous ways with existing high rates of mental health challenges on college campuses. While the concerns about students submitting work that was entirely produced by an AI text-generator are valid, the answer is not to use AI-detection tools to police student writing. Instead, we should work to create writing assignments that are meaningful to our students, ensuring that we use more frequent but lower-stakes assignments, and helping our students learn to document their own writing process; all of of these approaches are likely to reduce the chances that a student will turn to an AI-text generator instead of doing the work themselves, but more importantly, all of these approaches will also lead to better, deeper learning for students.

REFERENCES

Adam, L. (2016). Student Perspectives on Plagiarism. In T. Bretag (Ed.), *Handbook of Academic Integrity* (pp. 519–535). Springer. doi:10.1007/978-981-287-098-8_67

Altmann, G., & Steedman, M. (1988). Interaction with context during human sentence processing. *Cognition*, *30*(3), 191–238. doi:10.1016/0010-0277(88)90020-0 PMID:3215002

American College Health Association. (2022). *American College Health Association: National College Health Assessment III Fall 2022 Reference Group Executive Summary*. American College Health Association. https://www.acha.org/documents/ncha/NCHA-III_FALL_2022_REFERENCE_GROUP_EXECUTIVE_SUMMARY.pdf

Bedrossian, L. (2021). Understand and address complexities of rejection sensitive dysphoria in students with ADHD. *Disability Compliance for Higher Education*, *26*(10), 4–4. doi:10.1002/dhe.31047

Bender, E. M., & Koller, A. (2020). Climbing towards NLU: On Meaning, Form, and Understanding in the Age of Data. *Proceedings of the 58th Annual Meeting of the Association for Computational Linguistics*, (pp. 5185–5198). ACL. 10.18653/v1/2020.acl-main.463

Bergstrom, C. T. (2023, May 18). *Numerous sources claim that TurnItIn has a generative AI detector with something like 98% sensitivity and 99% specificity. For example, the…* [Mastodon post]. Mastodon. https://fediscience.org/@ct_bergstrom/110391417412257374

Berkeley. (2023, May 1). *Availability of Turnitin Artificial Intelligence Detection*. Berkley. https://rtl.berkeley.edu/news/availability-turnitin-artificial-intelligence-detection

Bobertsmith1928. (2023, May). *Falsely accused of ai written essay, what should i do?* [Reddit Post]. R/College. https://www.reddit.com/r/college/comments/12j0073/falsely_accused_of_ai_written_essay_what_should_i/

Casal, J. E., & Kessler, M. (2023). Can linguists distinguish between ChatGPT/AI and human writing?: A study of research ethics and academic publishing. *Research Methods in Applied Linguistics*, *2*(3), 100068. doi:10.1016/j.rmal.2023.100068

Chambers, C. G., Tanenhaus, M. K., & Magnuson, J. S. (2004). Actions and affordances in syntactic ambiguity resolution. *Journal of Experimental Psychology. Learning, Memory, and Cognition*, *30*(3), 687–696. doi:10.1037/0278-7393.30.3.687 PMID:15099136

Clark, A. (2013). Expecting the World: Perception, Prediction, and the Origins of Human Knowledge. *The Journal of Philosophy*, *110*(9), 469–496. https://www.jstor.org/stable/43820791. doi:10.5840/jphil2013110913

Clarke, N. (2023, February 15). A Concerning Trend [Blog]. *Neil Clarke Blog*. http://neil-clarke.com/a-concerning-trend/

Cleveland Clinic. (n.d.-a). *Neurodivergent: What It Is, Symptoms & Types*. Cleveland Clinic. https://my.clevelandclinic.org/health/symptoms/23154-neurodivergent

Cleveland Clinic. (n.d.-b). *Rejection Sensitive Dysphoria (RSD): Symptoms & Treatment*. Cleveland Clinic. https://my.clevelandclinic.org/health/diseases/24099-rejection-sensitive-dysphoria-rsd

Coley, M. (2023, August 16). *Guidance on AI Detection and Why We're Disabling Turnitin's AI Detector*. Vanderbilt University Brightspace. https://www.vanderbilt.edu/brightspace/2023/08/16/guidance-on-ai-detection-and-why-were-disabling-turnitins-ai-detector/

Conrad, K. (2023, July 17). *SNEAK PREVIEW: A Blueprint for an AI Bill of Rights for Education*. Critical AI. https://criticalai.org/2023/07/17/a-blueprint-for-an-ai-bill-of-rights-for-education-kathryn-conrad/

Content @ Scale. (2023). *AI Content Detector Checks GPT-4, ChatGPT, Bard, & More*. Content @ Scale. https://contentatscale.ai/ai-content-detector/

Council of Writing Program Administrators. (2019). *WPA Outcomes Statement for First-Year Composition (3.0), Approved July 17, 2014*. WPA Council. https://wpacouncil.org/aws/CWPA/pt/sd/news_article/243055/_PARENT/layout_details/false

D'Agostino, S. (2023, June 1). *Turnitin's AI Detector: Higher-Than-Expected False Positives*. Inside Higher Ed. https://www.insidehighered.com/news/quick-takes/2023/06/01/turnitins-ai-detector-higher-expected-false-positives

Edwards, B. (2023a, July 14). *Why AI detectors think the US Constitution was written by AI*. Ars Technica. https://arstechnica.com/information-technology/2023/07/why-ai-detectors-think-the-us-constitution-was-written-by-ai/

Edwards, B. (2023b, July 26). *OpenAI discontinues its AI writing detector due to "low rate of accuracy."* Ars Technica. https://arstechnica.com/information-technology/2023/07/openai-discontinues-its-ai-writing-detector-due-to-low-rate-of-accuracy/

Ehsan, U. (2023, August 1). *1/OpenAI quietly shut down its "AI" detector. Did shutting it down undo the harms? No, its Algorithmic Imprint lives on. Here's how #AI #ML...* [Mastodon post]. Mastodon. https://hci.social/@upol/110815089962878235

Ehsan, U., Singh, R., Metcalf, J., & Riedl, M. (2022). The Algorithmic Imprint. *2022 ACM Conference on Fairness, Accountability, and Transparency*, (pp. 1305–1317). ACM. 10.1145/3531146.3533186

ElevenBurnie. (2023, May 5). *Professor using GPTZero to accuse students of cheating* [Reddit Post]. R/OpenAI. www.reddit.com/r/OpenAI/comments/138ayhf/professor_using_gptzero_to_accuse_students_of/

Epstein-Gross, C. (2023, July 26). OpenAI Abruptly Shuts Down ChatGPT Plagiarism Detector—And Educators Are Worried. *Observer*. https://observer.com/2023/07/openai-shut-ai-classifier/

Fowler, G. A. (2023a, April 14). Analysis | We tested a new ChatGPT-detector for teachers. It flagged an innocent student. *Washington Post*. https://www.washingtonpost.com/technology/2023/04/01/chatgpt-cheating-detection-turnitin/

Fowler, G. A. (2023b, June 2). Analysis | Detecting AI may be impossible. That's a big problem for teachers. *Washington Post*. https://www.washingtonpost.com/technology/2023/06/02/turnitin-ai-cheating-detector-accuracy/

Fowler, G. A. (2023c, August 14). How to prove your innocence after a false positive from Turnitin, GPTZero—The Washington Post. *Washington Post*. https://www.washingtonpost.com/technology/2023/08/14/prove-false-positive-ai-detection-turnitin-gptzero/

Gillespie-Lynch, K., Hotez, E., Zajic, M., Riccio, A., DeNigris, D., Kofner, B., Bublitz, D., Gaggi, N., & Luca, K. (2020). Comparing the writing skills of autistic and nonautistic university students: A collaboration with autistic university students. *Autism*, *24*(7), 1898–1912. doi:10.1177/1362361320929453 PMID:32640841

Gillham, J. (2023). *AI Content Detector False Positives – Accused Of Using Chat GPT Or Other AI?* Originality.Ai. https://originality.ai/blog/ai-content-detector-false-positives

GlaireWolf. (2023, April 18). *False accusation of cheating* [Reddit Post]. R/UofArizona. www.reddit.com/r/UofArizona/comments/12qsp4b/false_accusation_of_cheating/

Glaze-Wolf. (2023, May). *I was falsely accused of using a AI to write my final paper* [Reddit Post]. R/College. https://www.reddit.com/r/college/comments/138ug6h/i_was_falsely_accused_of_using_a_ai_to_write_my/

Gluska, J. (2023, April 14). *Are Innocent Students Paying the Price for Turnitin's AI Detection Flaws?* Gold Penguin. https://goldpenguin.org/blog/turnitin-ai-detection-concerns/

GPTZero. (2023). *GPTZero | FAQ*. GPTZero. https://gptzero.me/

GPTZero Release Notes. (2023). *GPT Release Notes (Model and API)*. https://gptzero.notion.site/GPTZero-Release-Notes-Model-and-API-6f58686f6381498baef35212463b7da6

Harker, J. (2023, March). *Science journals set new authorship guidelines for AI-generated text*. National Institute of Environmental Health Sciences. https://factor.niehs.nih.gov/2023/3/feature/2-artificial-intelligence-ethics

Harwell, D. (2022). Cheating-detection companies made millions during the pandemic. Now students are fighting back. In *Ethics of data and analytics*. Auerbach Publications. doi:10.1201/9781003278290-60

HosseiniE. A.SchrimpfM.ZhangY.BowmanS.ZaslavskyN.FedorenkoE. (2022). Artificial neural network language models align neurally and behaviorally with humans even after a developmentally realistic amount of training (p. 2022.10.04.510681). bioRxiv. doi:10.1101/2022.10.04.510681

Jimenez, K. (2023, April 12). Professors are using ChatGPT detector tools to accuse students of cheating. But what if the software is wrong? *USA Today*. https://www.usatoday.com/story/news/education/2023/04/12/how-ai-detection-tool-spawned-false-cheating-case-uc-davis/11600777002/

Johnson, A. (2023, January 18). ChatGPT In Schools: Here's Where It's Banned—And How It Could Potentially Help Students. *Forbes*. https://www.forbes.com/sites/ariannajohnson/2023/01/18/chatgpt-in-schools-heres-where-its-banned-and-how-it-could-potentially-help-students/

Kara, F., & MacAlister, D. (2010). Responding to academic dishonesty in universities: A restorative justice approach. *Contemporary Justice Review*, *13*(4), 443–453. https://www.msudenver.edu/wp-content/uploads/2022/12/Responding-to-Academic-Dishonesty-RJ.pdf. doi:10.1080/10282580.2010.517981

Kirchner, J. H., Ahmad, L., Aaronson, S., & Leike, J. (2023, July 20). *New AI classifier for indicating AI-written text*. Open AI. https://openai.com/blog/new-ai-classifier-for-indicating-ai-written-text

Klee, M. (2023a, May 17). *Texas A&M Professor Wrongly Accuses Class of Cheating With ChatGPT*. Rollingstone. https://www.rollingstone.com/culture/culture-features/texas-am-chatgpt-ai-professor-flunks-students-false-claims-1234736601/

Klee, M. (2023b, June 6). *She Was Falsely Accused of Cheating With AI -- And She Won't Be the Last*. Rolling Stone. https://www.rollingstone.com/culture/culture-features/student-accused-ai-cheating-turnitin-1234747351/

Lang, J. M. (2013). *Cheating Lessons: Learning from Academic Dishonesty*. Harvard University Press. doi:10.4159/harvard.9780674726239

Liang, W., Yuksekgonul, M., Mao, Y., Wu, E., & Zou, J. (2023). GPT detectors are biased against non-native English writers. *Patterns (New York, N.Y.)*, *4*(7), 100779. doi:10.1016/j.patter.2023.100779 PMID:37521038

Lipson, S. K., Zhou, S., Abelson, S., Heinze, J., Jirsa, M., Morigney, J., Patterson, A., Singh, M., & Eisenberg, D. (2022). Trends in college student mental health and help-seeking by race/ethnicity: Findings from the national healthy minds study, 2013–2021. *Journal of Affective Disorders*, *306*, 138–147. doi:10.1016/j.jad.2022.03.038 PMID:35307411

Marche, S. (2022, December 6). The College Essay is Dead. *The Atlantic*. https://www.theatlantic.com/technology/archive/2022/12/chatgpt-ai-writing-college-student-essays/672371/

Martin, C. D., Branzi, F. M., & Bar, M. (2018). Prediction is Production: The missing link between language production and comprehension. *Scientific Reports*, *8*(1), 1. doi:10.1038/s41598-018-19499-4 PMID:29348611

McRae, K., & Matsuki, K. (2013). Constraint-based models of sentence processing. In *Sentence processing* (pp. 51–77). Psychology Press.

Merrick, J. (2023). *A narrative inquiry of life stories told by women with ADHD.* [Master's thesis, University of Calgary, Calgary, Canada].

MICUSP. (2009). *Michigan Corpus of Upper Level Student Papers* [dataset]. https://elicorpora.info/main

Mills, A. (2023, March 23). Advice | ChatGPT Just Got Better. What Does That Mean for Our Writing Assignments? *The Chronicle of Higher Education*. https://www.chronicle.com/article/chatgpt-just-got-better-what-does-that-mean-for-our-writing-assignments

Mollick, E. (2023, July 15). *In Praise of Boring AI*. https://www.oneusefulthing.org/p/in-praise-of-boring-ai

NeetMastery. (2023, April 16). *Have any of you learned to write well? My friend told me my writing style was similar to AI's, and I am now finding that detectors constantly flag me.* [Reddit Post]. R/Autism. www.reddit.com/r/autism/comments/12nuvfz/have_any_of_you_learned_to_write_well_my_friend/

Noy, S., & Zhang, W. (2023). *Experimental Evidence on the Productivity Effects of Generative Artificial Intelligence* [MIT Economics Working Paper]. https://economics.mit.edu/sites/default/files/inline-files/Noy_Zhang_1.pdf

Oravec, J. A. (2023). Artificial Intelligence Implications for Academic Cheating: Expanding the Dimensions of Responsible Human-AI Collaboration with ChatGPT and Bard. *Journal of Interactive Learning Research*, *34*(2), 213–237.

Peng, S., Kalliamvakou, E., Cihon, P., & Demirer, M. (2023). *The Impact of AI on Developer Productivity: Evidence from GitHub Copilot* (arXiv:2302.06590). arXiv. http://arxiv.org/abs/2302.06590

Piantadosi, S. T., & Hill, F. (2022). *Meaning without reference in large language models* (arXiv:2208.02957). arXiv. https://doi.org//arXiv.2208.02957 doi:10.48550

Pitt, P., Dullaghan, K., & Sutherland-Smith, W. (2021). 'Mess, stress and trauma': Students' experiences of formal contract cheating processes. *Assessment & Evaluation in Higher Education*, *46*(4), 659–672. doi:10.1080/02602938.2020.1787332

Pollina, R. (2023, July 21). Autistic Purdue professor accused of being AI for lacking "warmth" in email. *New York Post*. https://nypost.com/2023/07/21/autistic-purdue-professor-accused-of-being-ai-for-lacking-warmth-in-email/

Sadasivan, V. S., Kumar, A., Balasubramanian, S., Wang, W., & Feizi, S. (2023). *Can AI-Generated Text be Reliably Detected?* (arXiv:2303.11156). arXiv. http://arxiv.org/abs/2303.11156

Schrimpf, M., Blank, I. A., Tuckute, G., Kauf, C., Hosseini, E. A., Kanwisher, N., Tenenbaum, J. B., & Fedorenko, E. (2021). The neural architecture of language: Integrative modeling converges on predictive processing. *Proceedings of the National Academy of Sciences of the United States of America*, *118*(45), e2105646118. doi:10.1073/pnas.2105646118 PMID:34737231

Stagg, S. D., & Belcher, H. (2019). Living with autism without knowing: Receiving a diagnosis in later life. *Health Psychology and Behavioral Medicine*, *7*(1), 348–361. doi:10.1080/21642850.2019.1684920 PMID:34040855

Staples, S., & Dilger, B. (2018). *Corpus and repository of writing [Learner corpus articulated with repository]* [dataset]. https://elicorpora.info/main

The-Rice-Boi. (2023a, April 17). *My teacher has falsely accused me of using ChatGPT to use an assignment.* [Reddit Post]. R/ChatGPT. www.reddit.com/r/ChatGPT/comments/12ppt5w/my_teacher_has_falsely_accused_me_of_using/

The-Rice-Boi. (2023b, June). *I was falsely accused of using ChatGPT after my teacher used some online detectors and 3 sentences of a 6 page essay got flagged as AI. My superintendent won't listen. What are my options?* [Reddit Post]. R/Legaladvice. https://www.reddit.com/r/legaladvice/comments/14eof13/i_was_falsely_accused_of_using_chatgpt_after_my/

Tian, E. (2023a, January 5). Gptzero update v1 [Substack newsletter]. *GPTZero*. https://gptzero.substack.com/p/gptzero-update-v1

Tian, E. (2023b, April 28). *GPTZero | GPTZero vs Turnitin*. GPTZero. https://gptzero.me/blogs/gptzero-vs-turnitin

Turnitin. (2023a). *AI Writing Detection Frequently Asked Questions*. Turnitin. https://www.turnitin.com/products/features/ai-writing-detection/faq

Turnitin. (2023b). *AI Writing Settings*. Turnitin AI Writing Settings. https://help.turnitin.com/integrity/administrator/settings/ai-writing-settings.htm

Turnitin. (2023c, April 4). *Turnitin turns on AI writing detection capabilities for educators and institutions (NA and EMEA)*. https://www.turnitin.com/press/turnitin-turns-on-ai-writing-detection-capabilities-for-educators-and-institutions

Turnitin. (2023d, July 25). *Turnitin AI detection feature reviews more than 65 million papers*. https://www.turnitin.com/press/turnitin-ai-detection-feature-reviews-more-than-65-million-papers

University of Greenwich. (2023, March 31). *Our decision to opt-out of using Turnitin's AI detection tool | Articles*. University of Greenwich. https://www.gre.ac.uk/articles/public-relations/our-decision-to-opt-out-of-using-turnitins-ai-detection-tool

University of Pittsburgh. (2023, June 22). *Teaching Center doesn't endorse any generative AI detection tools*. https://www.utimes.pitt.edu/news/teaching-center-doesn-t

Vaswani, A., Shazeer, N., Parmar, N., Uszkoreit, J., Jones, L., Gomez, A. N., Kaiser, Ł., & Polosukhin, I. (2017). Attention is All you Need. In I. Guyon, U. V. Luxburg, S. Bengio, H. Wallach, R. Fergus, S. Vishwanathan, & R. Garnett (Eds.), *Advances in Neural Information Processing Systems* (Vol. 30). Curran Associates, Inc. https://proceedings.neurips.cc/paper_files/paper/2017/file/3f5ee243547dee91fbd053c1c4a845aa-Paper.pdf

Verma, P. (2023a, May 19). A professor accused his class of using ChatGPT, putting diplomas in jeopardy. *Washington Post*. https://www.washingtonpost.com/technology/2023/05/18/texas-professor-threatened-fail-class-chatgpt-cheating/

Verma, P. (2023b, August 13). Professors have a summer assignment: Prevent ChatGPT chaos in the fall. *Washington Post*. https://www.washingtonpost.com/technology/2023/08/13/ai-chatgpt-chatbots-college-cheating/

Welborn, A. (2023, March 9). ChatGPT and Fake Citations. *Duke University Libraries Blogs*. https://blogs.library.duke.edu/blog/2023/03/09/chatgpt-and-fake-citations/

Williams, R. M. (@FractalEcho@kolektiva. social). (2023, July 29). *I shared "the email" because it was interesting to me that this happened to me when it's actually something I write about academically* ... [Mastodon post]. Mastodon. https://kolektiva.social/@FractalEcho/110800085168655662

Yang, M. (2023, January 6). New York City schools ban AI chatbot that writes essays and answers prompts. *The Guardian*. https://www.theguardian.com/us-news/2023/jan/06/new-york-city-schools-ban-ai-chatbot-chatgpt

Zajic, M. C., McIntyre, N., Swain-Lerro, L., Novotny, S., Oswald, T., & Mundy, P. (2018). Attention and written expression in school-age, high-functioning children with autism spectrum disorders. *Autism*, *22*(3), 245–258. doi:10.1177/1362361316675121 PMID:27940570

ENDNOTES

1 And of course, much of the text that writers have produced in the last decade has already been shaped in some fashion through the precursors to today's AI tools: autocomplete and automated grammar checkers like Grammarly. Thus, even what most people would currently feel comfortable calling "human-produced" text is already in many cases a kind of hybrid text.

2 This is an observation originally made by Carl Bergstrom on Mastodon (Bergstrom, 2023)

3 e.g. MICUSP (2009) and CROW (Staples & Dilger, 2018)

4 A note about consent: there is no indication in this paper that the researchers sought explicit consent for the use of AI-detectors from the students whose writing is represented in the corpora they used.

Chapter 12
Detecting Is Just the Start:
Deciding Whether to Take Action and Generating Evidence Is Harder

Irene Glendinning
https://orcid.org/0000-0001-9967-351X
Coventry University, UK

ABSTRACT

When students submit work for assessment that that they did not create themselves, unless this can be both identified and proven, the students will unfairly gain credits towards their qualification. For text-based plagiarism or collusion, even if the student has tried to disguise it, it is likely to be detected and evidenced if text matching software is used systematically to check all submissions. If it is original work that has been created for the student, typically contract cheating or use of generative AI, then it is less straightforward. The first challenge is detecting a potential breach of integrity. The second challenge is for the marker to have both the time and the will to report it. Next, the marker needs to know what evidence is needed and how to report it. There are many reasons why a marker may decide not to raise allegations. Addressing doubts and concerns like these can make a huge difference to how many cases of conduct are reported and investigated. This chapter suggests what actions can be taken within institutions to ensure that fairness and integrity prevail.

BACKGROUND

Educational institutions that are serious about academic integrity will already have invested substantial resources into designing, maintaining and operating policies for encouraging an institutional culture of integrity. Those institutions that have not made that investment, place themselves at risk of poor academic quality and standards and reputational damage by lax attention to academic integrity breaches.

Many ideas in this chapter come from the author's experience of conducting research into academic integrity policies in 38 countries, across Europe and parts of Eurasia (Glendinning, 2016; Foltýnek et al., 2017; Glendinning et al., 2021; Foltýnek & Glendinning, 2023). Additional contributions come from

DOI: 10.4018/979-8-3693-0240-8.ch012

a global research project exploring how quality assurance and accreditation bodies are responding to corruption in education (Glendinning et al., 2019). The author's own experiences of teaching, external examining and oversight of academic integrity, in the UK and elsewhere, also contributes to her ideas and views, which naturally predisposes the content of this chapter towards a UK perspective.

The focus is very much on ensuring that operational practices for deterring, detecting and managing academic integrity breaches are effective, rather than exploring strategy, policy design, review and revision. Considering different approaches to handling academic integrity breaches, readers are reminded about the advantages of having of a consistent institution-wide approach (Park, 2004; Carroll, 2005; Macdonald & Carroll, 2006; Bretag et al, 2011; Bretag & Mahmud, 2016; Morris & Carroll, 2011). Taking the perspective of academics, this chapter presents a range of reasons why some integrity breaches are not reported, together with suggestions of how to improve the rate of reporting and evidencing of cases. To reduce the number of academic integrity breaches, there is need to better understand the scale of the problem (Curtis et al., 2021) and the underlying reasons for academic misconduct, which in turn should result in a more targeted approach to deterrence (Glendinning & Orim, 2023).

Inclusive approaches to managing change are proposed as a means of ensuring that institutional policies for academic integrity remain up to date, fit for purpose and owned by the community that they are designed to serve (Glendinning, 2023b).

Dimensions of Academic Integrity Policies

Given limited resources available in an institution, policies and procedures need to maintain the balance between investment in deterrence measures, efforts to detect misconduct and adjudication of decisions and consequences students face if a case is upheld. If this mix works, then they will together serve to generate a culture of integrity, keep the number of cases low, but ensure that the vast majority of cases are detected and dealt with consistently, proportionately and fairly.

As Figure 1 illustrates, institutional policies can be considered in terms of four dimensions: deterrence, detection, decisions and documentation.

Each of these four dimensions will now be discussed in turn.

Deterring

All institutions should have measures in place for deterring breaches of academic and research integrity, whether deliberate or accidental. Deterrence can take various forms, the main approaches are: education and training for everyone, not just students; innovative approaches to pedagogy and design of assessment; regular communication about academic integrity; and improving the number of breaches detected and sanctioned through a robust approach (Figure 2). Each of these elements will now be explored in more detail.

A comprehensive programme of education and support should be available for all students in the institution, to ensure they develop appropriate skills and knowledge to reach their full potential, both on their chosen study programme and for their future workplace or on-going study. Education, guidance and support can help to reduce accidental breaches, especially plagiarism and collusion. Formative use of text matching software can help students to improve their academic writing, use of sources and referencing (Davis, 2007). It is not enough just to provide an hour of induction when students first arrive.

Figure 1. Four overlapping, interdependent dimensions of policies for academic and research integrity (source, author)

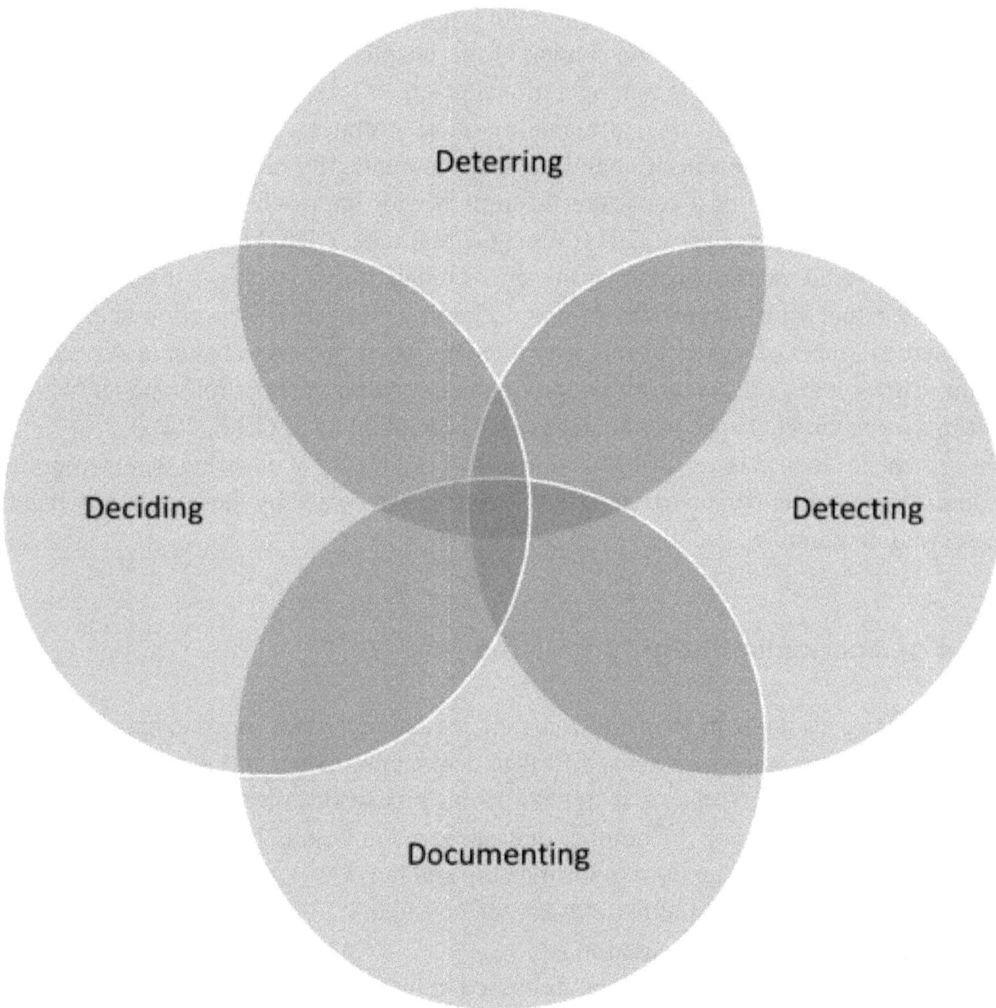

Students have many other things on their mind at that time in their lives and some students may join the course late. Guidance and training for students on integrity needs to be developed throughout the student journey as part of the core curriculum (Glendinning, 2022, 2023a), and important information readily accessible at all times.

Who should deliver training? Ideally the course director should orchestrate the scheduling of the development for students and if needed bring in specialists to deliver materials at different stages. For this to work all academic staff need to develop and maintain their own skills and knowledge, which necessitates providing a range of professional development for staff, ideally facilitated by specialists in this field. There is also need for considerable provision of specific training and support for all staff associated with handling and making decisions about allegations of academic integrity breaches. Regular updates are needed for both staff and students to ensure any changes are disseminated and consistently applied across the institution.

Figure 2. Elements for deterring academic integrity breaches
(source: author)

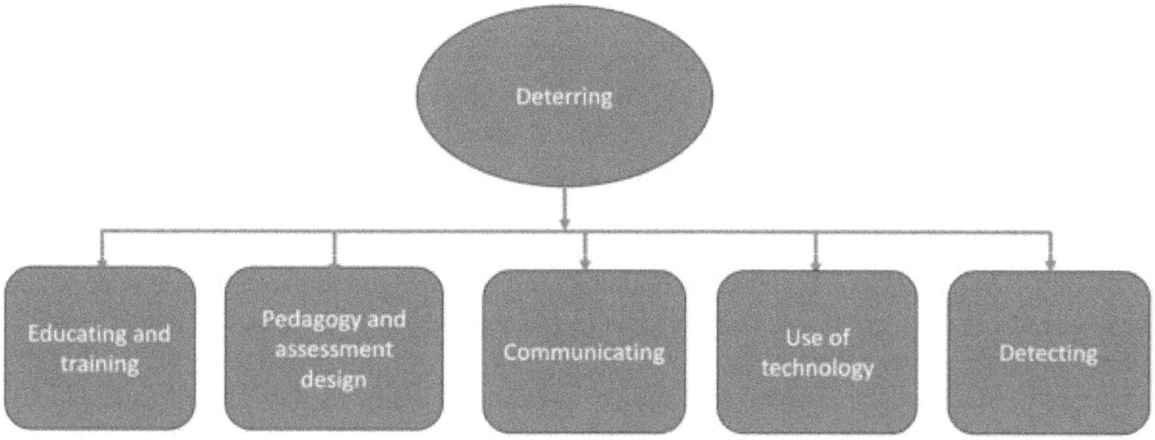

One of the most powerful deterrence responses to academic integrity breaches is through pedagogy and assessment design (Bowditich, 2023; QAA, 2023). The same assessment approaches are applicable to contract cheating and misuse of AI tools (JISC, 2023a, 2023b). Adopting an active learning approach almost compels students to engage with the learning process. While it is technically still possible for students to avoid doing the activity themselves, for example, by freeloading on team members, engaging a ghost-writer to help, or using generative AI to assist, carefully designed individual assessments, applying and extending what has been learnt, involving some direct contact with the student to defend their work, are ways to expose any deficits in understanding.

There may be reluctance to change teaching and learning methods when there are very large cohorts of students, in the belief that these pedagogical approaches are resource intensive and will not scale well (Dawson, 2020). However, in the longer term, with fewer misconduct cases, the reduction in resource allocation for managing allegations should make the transition worthwhile and cost-effective. The argument is that it is worth the short-term pain of allocating more resources to measures that reduce the overall number of breaches in a cohort and in the institutional as a whole in the longer term.

The need for strong and regular communication about academic integrity, expectations, requirements, verbal and written, with colleagues and students, cannot be overemphasised. However, if the same message is repeated too many times, then students will switch off and the opportunity will be lost. To be seen as valuable, any communication needs to be purposeful, supportive, informative and timely. Depending on the demographics and diversity of the student population, the institution, and individual academics, may also need to manage students' expectations as well as sharing learning requirements of the institution, to ensure they understand that learning is an active, participatory process, rather than largely passive "edutainment" or rote learning. Communications with students should include information about the joy of learning, the purpose of education, what assessment is for, as well as acquainting students with the need to develop appropriate skills and knowledge for use in their future career or for further study.

Detection as an Element of Deterrence

Detection is an important dimension of policies in its own right, but effective approaches to detection also contribute to deterring integrity breaches.

Strong focus on detection and management of allegations serves to negate any possible unfair advantage gained by a student. If students believe dishonest actions are more likely than not to be detected and if detection carries serious consequences, then it becomes less attractive for students to resort to deliberate academic dishonesty. For this approach to be an effective deterrent, there must be a good track record of detecting, reporting, evidencing and then applying effective sanctions to the majority of integrity breaches. Conversely, if there is awareness among students that many student colleagues are successfully evading detection for integrity breaches, or if the sanctions are not imposed or considered to be trivial, then any deterrence effect from having strong policies will be seriously undermined. Unchecked cheating is contagious.

In any student population, there are always students that would never knowingly breach integrity. At the opposite end of the spectrum are students who are intent on academic dishonesty, irrespective of deterrence measures deployed. Between these two extremes, the remaining, students can be assumed to be at some risk of breaching integrity. Actions can and should be taken to address all three of these categories.

Understanding the underlying reasons for the conduct of those intent on deliberate cheating can help to reduce the number of academic integrity breaches. These students may have

- a history of cheating from their previous studies, resulting in undeserved admission;
- falsified their entry qualifications or received help from a corrupt agent;
- fabricated evidence of their language competency;
- no interest in studying, just gaining the qualification;
- the intention to earn money rather than study, whether or not this is legal;
- applied for education to gain access to a visa to enter the country of study.

Ideally unqualified or bogus students need to be identified at the earliest opportunity and the institution should either ensure they are enrolled on and pass a suitable remedial programme before they are admitted to their intended study programme, withdraw their acceptance offer or expel the student for presenting fraudulent credentials. The reality is that students admitted to a study programme without the necessary prerequisites or capacity to succeed will be destined to fail unless they have help in completing their assessments. A diagnostic writing exercise conducted on arrival under controlled conditions is useful for identifying students who have misrepresented their language or skills competences during the application process. If persistent integrity problems come to light after enrolment, for example, serial use of essay mills, then the academic conduct procedures should allow for immediate expulsion.

As all students are potentially at risk of accidentally breaching integrity if they lack skills and knowledge relating to academic integrity (Borg, 2009; Ireland & English, 2011), the need for an on-going programme of training and education, throughout the student journey, is further reinforced. Students must become fully equipped to meet the challenges they will face with integrity and continue to develop skills and knowledge relating to academic integrity throughout their studies.

Students can be open to persuasion to take short-cuts in their assessments if they face any adversity or pressure. These are the students who particularly need to be targeted by initiatives and persuaded to behave with integrity. Understanding the reasons, motivations and pressures they face is key to reducing the number of cases of integrity breaches.

If a student perceives that other students are cheating and there are no effective measures to address this, then they may believe that *not* cheating will be disadvantageous for them. It stands to reason that if they do not observe other students cheating, or if they are aware of cases of student cheating being detected, then leading to serious consequences, they will be less likely to cheat. Students facing pressures, including personal problems, health, financial, relationship issues, poor time management, may breach integrity by cutting corners in panic or desperation. Clearly signposted, welcoming and easy to access (ideally, free) support services, combined with effective and timely procedures to identify and respond compassionately to genuine extenuating circumstances, allowing extensions, late submission or deferral of the assessment, can also help to reduce integrity breaches.

The Detection Dimension

The detection process itself requires that a potential breach is first identified, typically by the person grading or marking the student's work, or by the academic supervisor of a project or dissertation. Supporting evidence then needs to be generated, before communicating and reporting the allegation according to institutional procedures (Figure 3). The last element of this dimension is presenting the allegation, at the appropriate forum, which may range from an informal meeting with the student to a formal panel or committee (Figure 3).

There are many reasons why a tutor, marker or supervisor may not detect a breach, particularly if their first language is not the study language, if the integrity breach involves contract cheating or content inappropriately generated by an AI tool. Even if the breach is detected, there are many very solid reasons why the marker may decide not to raise this as an allegation of an integrity breach.

If the academic community is vigilant and committed, particularly aided by systematic use of reputable and effective text matching software (Foltýnek et al., 2020), detecting and evidencing routine cases of plagiarism and inappropriate collusion by students, should be relatively straightforward. The challenge is then to ensure that academic staff know how and when to raise allegations of potential misconduct and are committed to doing so. Training and support for academic staff can help to improve detection and evidencing (Dawson & Sutherland-Smith, 2018). However, in the author's experience, it is often the "worried well" who regularly attend training, rather than those academics who are less well informed and have most to benefit from training. Whether staff decide to invest time and effort to generate evidence and formally report a case, is a different but related problem that we will consider shortly.

Integrity breaches involving disguised plagiarism, contract cheating, translation plagiarism or including unacknowledged content from generative artificial intelligence tools as their own work, any breaches that involve deceit and fraud, all of which by definition, involve very serious, deliberate and premeditated corruption of educational processes, are particularly problematic and time-consuming to detect and evidence (Glendinning et al., 2019). Deterrence and detection measures targeting these very serious forms of breaches can make a huge difference to the rate of academic misconduct and the workload of staff involved in evidencing and adjudicating such cases.

In contrast to cases of plagiarism, if a student submits a piece of original work that they did not create, typically resorting to contract cheating (essay mill or other ghost-writer) or use of a generative AI tool, then detecting it is not easy. The first challenge is for the marker to recognise the signs that something may not be right. The second challenge is for the marker to have both the time and the motivation to do

Figure 3. Elements for detecting academic integrity breaches
(source: author)

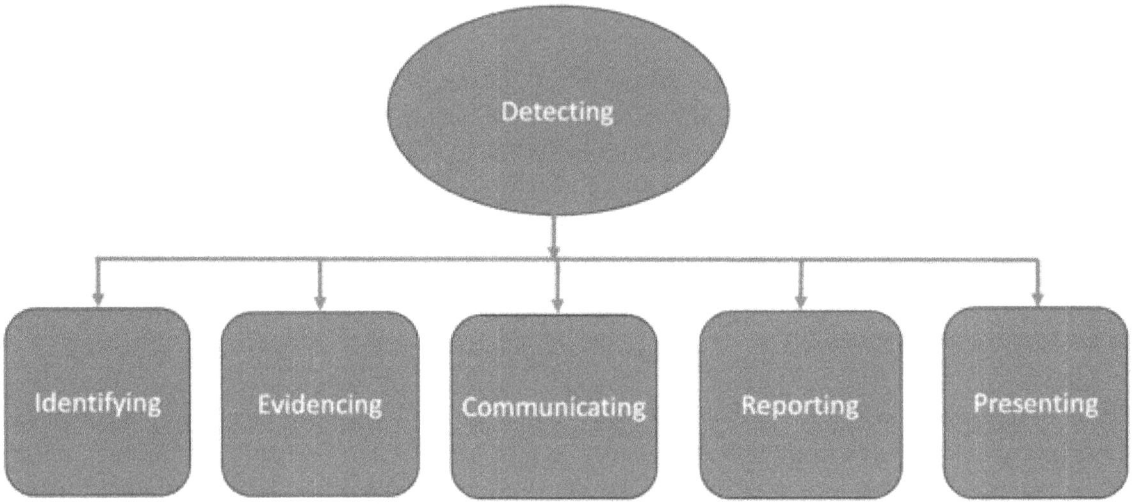

something about it, which is not always the case. Next, there is the need for the marker to know how to respond, understand what procedures they should follow, how to report their suspicions, what evidence they need to generate, how to submit this and being aware of what will happen next.

There are many reasons for academics not reporting suspected misconduct, including:

- Serious pressure to complete academic grading or marking of student assessments, perhaps constrained by a very tight deadline, with a very large number of assessments to mark;
- Reluctance to raise any potential cases of misconduct that are going to prove time-consuming to report, especially the more serious and deliberate types of misconduct, such as contract cheating and unauthorised and unacknowledged use of generative AI tools;
- Belief that no one else will notice or care about this case and no action will result;
- Unclear procedures for how to report and what evidence is needed;
- Fear of being viewed as out of line with colleagues who rarely or never report their suspicions;
- When it is uncommon for anyone to report such cases in the subject area, faculty or institution;
- Being seen as a troublemaker for raising allegations;
- Being deterred by previous experiences of similar cases being rejected because the evidence was not considered to be strong enough;
- Demands from the academic conduct adjudication process requiring students to admit to the allegation before a case is considered proven;
- Requirements for evidence of "intent" to deceive before a case can be raised;
- Being discouraged by the complexity or workload involved in the process of reporting, generating evidence and then supporting or presenting the allegations in an academic conduct meeting;
- Fear of being given a poor teacher evaluation by the student and their colleagues as a result of reporting the case;

- Fear of being investigated and blamed for causing student cheating, leading to dismissal or not being considered for pay rise or promotion;
- Fear of being sued by the student for false allegations or defamation;
- Other priorities, typically family or work duties may preclude the use of time to generate the evidence;
- When adjunct or casual staff are only paid for time spent in the classroom; raising a case of academic misconduct must be in their own time;
- If academics are poorly remunerated they may need to have multiple jobs to make a living; academic integrity is not their first priority;
- Knowing that if the case is raised and upheld the penalties will be too lenient to deter further misconduct, for example, the student given a verbal warning not to do it again;
- Knowing that if the case is raised and upheld, then the process and penalties will be disproportional, very arduous, for example the student may face a judicial-style committee and then be expelled;
- Belief that it is better not to report the allegations, but instead to deal with the situation by reducing the student's mark and/or failing the student;
- Being put under pressure by managers to meet targets, affecting league tables and metrics for high pass rates.

This list was compiled using examples from the author's personal experience, combined with data collected during four different research studies (Glendinning, 2013; Glendinning, 2016; Foltýnek et al., 2017; Glendinning et al., 2019; Glendinning et al., 2021; Foltýnek & Glendinning, 2023).

When designing and revising institutional policies and procedures all the above reasons need to be taken into account and addressed. Some of the above reasons are side effects or unintended consequences of initiatives to improve institutional reputation or league table position. There are ways that most, or perhaps all these reasons can be mitigated, if there is awareness of the underlying causes.

One further consideration that can cause problems in some countries is the burden of proof. In most parts of the world even deliberate academic integrity breaches are not classified as criminal acts, although there have been reports of several recent cases resulting in criminal convictions (for example: BBC News, 2021; Norman, 2018). Academic misconduct is certainly viewed as ethically and morally inappropriate conduct in almost all educational circles and conduct such as plagiarism is generally considered to be socially inappropriate when happening outside education (Webber-Wulff, 2014). Taking into account the educational basis of academic integrity, unless there is evidence of criminal behaviour (such as fraud or hacking), the appropriate burden of proof for academic breaches should be "on balance of probability" (QAA, 2022; OIAHE, 2018), following what normally applies for civil law cases.

As found by Dawson and Sutherland-Smith (2017), training for academic staff can improve their ability to detect contract cheating cases. Training and guidance are also needed to improve ability for detecting inappropriate use by students of generative AI tools, such as ChatGPT and using transformative AI tools, such as Google Translate and Grammarly to disguise plagiarism or other forms of misconduct. Providing checklists of features that characterise misuse of these tools, and work not written by the student, can aid detection and evidencing of inauthentic work. The author has created a checklist of indicators to help to detect when that AI software tools have been used in student assessments without authorisation or acknowledgement (see Appendix 1), which could be added to existing checklists on contract cheating (for example, OutLiar, n.d.), to create a combined checklist for supporting detection of inauthenticity.

Referring to Figure 3, despite all the reasons to avoid it, when a marker decides to raise an allegation, the next stages are to first generate, then assemble the evidence to support the allegation. If it is solely the responsibility of the academic marker or examiner to do this, then this introduces another barrier in the process, especially for the more complex cases, including contract cheating and inappropriate use of AI tools. Making it as easy as possible for the marker or supervisor to report an allegation can make a huge difference to the rate of reporting. Providing expert support to generate good quality and useful evidence is an obvious way to ease the burden and ensure the case is well supported.

Once the evidence is ready, the person raising or processing the allegation must know what process to follow to formally report their suspicions. Asking them to complete and submit a formal report or form containing data that they don't have access to, can present yet another barrier. The ideal situation is to have a system integrated with the student record system that automatically completes all the necessary background details, based on the student's name or ID and specific details of the assessment being investigated. Automatic population of data fields, or drop-down list boxes, with overrides to allow for exceptions, can help with ease of data entry plus improve consistency of data collection. In addition, having an early triaging process, for someone with expertise to check whether the evidence indicates that there is a case to answer, can save everyone time and effort. These are not new concepts: Access, Responsibility and Support are three of the five core elements of the exemplar academic integrity policy framework proposed more than a decade ago (Bretag et al., 2011).

The final element of the detecting dimension is presenting the allegation and supporting evidence. How and when this happens and who is responsible for presenting and explaining the evidence varies greatly, depending on institutional preferences and procedures. It can be very useful for the subject expert who set the assignment to be involved in presenting the evidence and advising the decision-makers about subject-specific details and issues, but this also carries some disadvantages, especially in terms of increased workloads and potential conflicts of interest for the subject expert. This may or may not be the same person that raised the allegation. As this element crosses over into the deciding dimension, this will be considered next, together with other elements of that dimension.

The Deciding Dimension

The third dimension in Figure 1 refers to the adjudication process where crucial decisions are made about allegations raised. The process needs to be transparent, consistent and fair. The decisions made also need to be considerate, fair, consistent and in proportion with the level of severity of the integrity breach. Many people may be involved in the process of reaching a fair decision on an allegation. Considerable resources, time and effort can be involved in this dimension. It can also be a very stressful time for students facing allegations and for other people involved in the decision-making process.

The deciding dimension can be divided into six elements: hearing evidence; deliberating; deciding the severity level; examining the student's situation, background and history; deciding what outcomes should be applied and, most importantly, communication (Figure 4).

Although judicial terms and negative language are often used when talking about integrity breaches, (e.g. offence, case, penalty), it is the author's belief that this dimension should be viewed principally as a supportive educational and learning opportunity for everyone involved, rather than a judicial process. However, can be difficult to maintain that ethos if those involved find it stressful and feel personally targeted. It also becomes very challenging when dealing with students who persistently and serially, deliberately engage in serious forms of academic misconduct.

Figure 4. Elements for deciding outcomes of academic integrity breaches
(source: author)

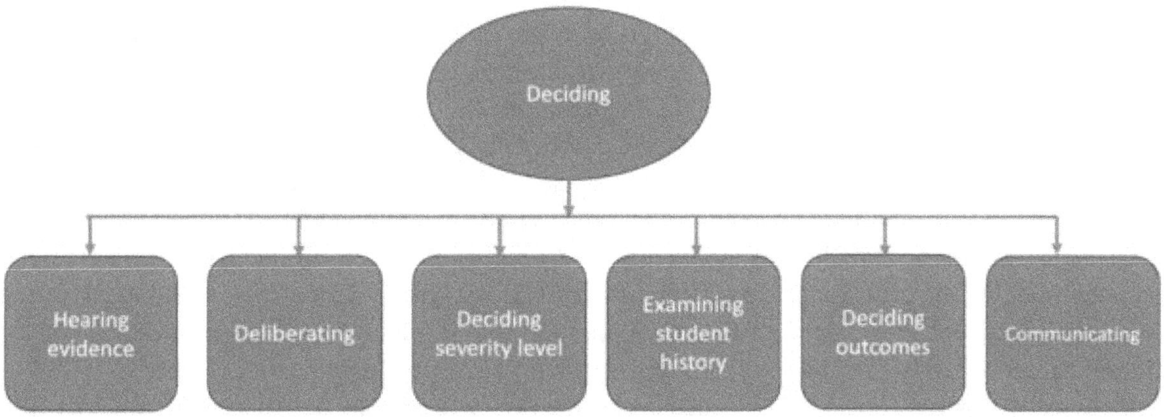

The process will certainly become judicial if students ask to be accompanied by a lawyer to help them to challenge the allegations. This should be discouraged, if at all possible, because it does not contribute anything educationally and it certainly raises the level of anxiety for everyone involved. Some institutions simply refuse to allow legal representation; others may allow representation, but set constraints. When legal representation is permitted, a team of experienced panellists should be appointed to adjudicate and the institution should always have their own legal representative in the meeting to provide balance and allow legal arguments to be raised and challenged by both sides.

Ideally, a student facing allegations of misconduct will have access to constructive and helpful support to guide them before, during and after any process they face, by someone independent who is knowledgeable about the student's rights, the institutional procedures and possible outcomes. Typically, a student association may provide this type of support. This is one aspect of the communication element, but effective communication between all parties is essential to all four dimensions and all elements.

In many European and Eurasian countries the responsibility for making decisions about whether there is a case to answer and, if so, what outcomes should apply, lies with a manager, typically a dean (Glendinning, 2016). In some countries, it is common for individual professors to have responsibility for making these decisions (Glendinning, 2016; Foltýnek et al., 2017; Glendinning et al., 2021; Foltýnek & Glendinning, 2023). An institutional panel that convenes to make decisions is another option, for example in Sweden, where the procedures are defined nationally, for a panel chaired by the rector, with external judicial membership (Glendinning, 2013). In the UK it is common for trained academic Integrity Officers to handle routine cases, with panels appointed to deal with more serious cases (Carroll, 2005). Whatever procedures are adopted and responsibilities assigned, the important factors are to ensure that there is fairness, proportionality, consistency, transparency and accountability in both processes and decisions. Where individuals rather than panels make the decisions, it is more difficult to maintain fairness, consistency and accountability, therefore additional measures need to be added to ensure equable experiences and to counter any for conflicts of interest and potential for corruption and intimidation, from either direction (Glendinning et al., 2021).

Considering the UK approach, for routine cases, one trained academic integrity officer (AIO), with no conflicts of interest, following a set of clear procedures and rules, is a more efficient use of resources (Carroll, 2005). This can be especially effective for large institutions with relatively high caseloads. The AIO, ideally accompanied by the subject expert or a colleague, is empowered to chair a meeting with the student and possibly one independent supporter, hear the evidence, allow the student respond and allow controlled questioning. If managed by an experienced AIO, this lighter touch approach can be less threatening to the student facing allegations and can even be a positive experience that helps students to develop a more ethical approach. For cases that are complex or likely to lead to career-changing outcomes, it is not a good idea for one person, however senior or experienced, to be responsible for the decision. Instead, an experienced and well-trained panel of experts is needed. Whether it is an AIO or a panel making the decisions, hearing evidence should be a balanced process, with the allegations presented objectively, the student given every opportunity to respond and question the allegations. In addition, attention to the student's welfare must be paramount throughout.

An objective approach is needed for considering the evidence presented. In particular, the individual or panel members involved in hearing the evidence and making the decision must have no conflicts of interest. This includes initially having no prior knowledge of any previous allegations faced by the student (OIAHE, 2018). As already mentioned, applying "on balance of probability" as the burden of proof is appropriate for an educational setting (QAA, 2022). The first stage is to determine whether there is a case to answer; if so, the level of severity of the breach needs to be determined. There are various approaches that can be taken to ensure consistency of decisions (Glendinning & Orim, 2023; QAA, 2021), some of which will be discussed next.

Following a decision on the level of severity of the breach, ideally, the background and history of the student should be revealed before the sanctions or outcomes are decided. As depicted in Figure 5, these should be separate processes, to negate the potential for the decision on the current case to be influenced by knowledge of the student's previous conduct (OIAHE, 2018).

Again for the UK, the AMBeR (Academic Misconduct Benchmarking Research) project proposed using a metrics approach to determining both severity level and sanctions (Tennant & Duggan, 2008; Tennant & Rowell, 2010), which has been adopted and adapted and is still used by many institutions in the UK and in other parts of the world. At a major policy review in 2010, the working group in my own institution decided not to adopt a metrics-based approach and instead developed a 2-D table, with rows containing level of severity and columns used for number of repeat cases for that student. The body of the table shows what sanctions should apply, with increased sanctions for repeated and persistent breaches. At the latest institutional review in 2019-20, which this author led, a mandatory training element was added to each sanction and the table became known as the "Scale of Outcomes Table", to reflect the positive educational aspects of the sanctions.

There should be some scope for an AIO or panel to vary the outcomes in response to evidence of extenuating circumstances, but when this happens, for accountability, the justification for changes must be documented and the level of severity should be recorded unchanged, to reflect the true gravity of the breach. If a student persistently breaches integrity, or has a history of other types of misconduct, such as breaches of disciplinary, ethical or research conduct, then these factors should be taken into account when deciding what outcomes / sanctions to apply. The ultimate sanction for academic misconduct by students is expulsion from the institution without graduating, but in research conducted across parts of Europe and Eurasia it was found that this sanction was rarely applied (Glendinning & Orim, 2023). Clearly, this need for documentation and accountability discussed here overlaps with the next dimension.

Whatever procedures are followed, where possible, the timescale of the investigation should be as short as possible, certainly no more than two weeks. Ideally the outcomes should be communicated to the student immediately after the case is discussed and decisions made, or as soon as possible after that time. Advising the student in the meeting provides the opportunity for a supportive discussion about what education and support they need and/or is required to undertake and how to access this. All the communication and recording elements of the deciding dimension overlap with the next dimension, which involves documenting, monitoring and tracking of the whole process.

The Documenting Dimension

Documenting the processes followed for handling and managing all allegations of academic integrity breaches, tracking and recording progress and decisions are essential components of any academic integrity policies and procedures (Bretag et al., 2011). It important to keep a record of the allegations, evidence provided, what happened at each stage and when and to follow the progress of an allegation through the different stages of the process (Figure 5). The documentation should describe what actions and decisions were taken and justify why each was deemed to be appropriate. The accuracy and completeness of the recorded information is vital for auditing, accountability and consistency-checking. Any communications about each case should be maintained as part of the evidence to ensure that compliance with procedures and requirements can be demonstrated if needed (OIAHE, 2018).

If anyone involved in the case, typically the student or other contributors, lodges a complaint or appeal, then scrutiny of the documentation will provide supportive evidence. If the case was dealt with according to the correct institutional procedures, if progress and outcomes have been appropriately recorded, with input from the student and due consideration for the student's situation, then it is unlikely there would be grounds for challenging the outcome or process. However, should the documentation be incomplete, inaccurate or otherwise defective, then there could be a strong case for overturning or changing the decisions (OIAHE, 2018).

Figure 5. Elements of documenting progress of academic integrity breaches
(source: author)

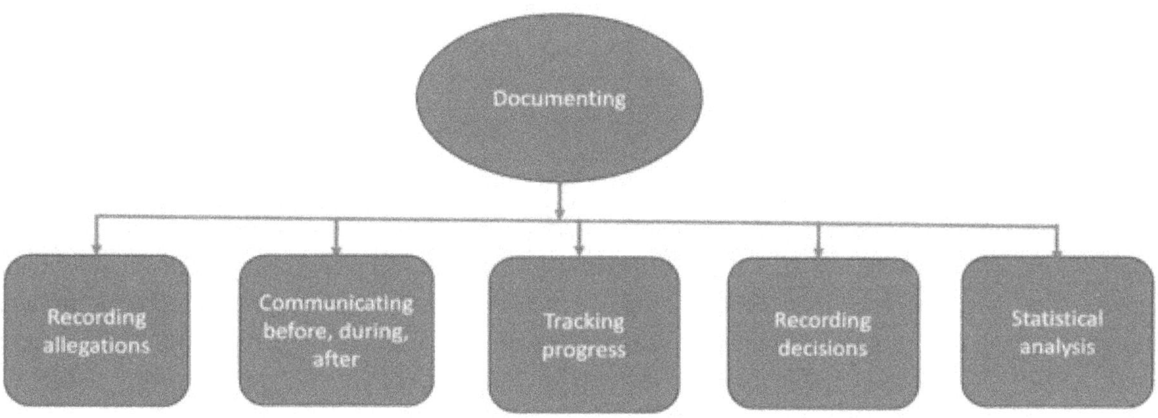

In some parts of the world there are ombudspersons, either appointed by the institution, state or nationally, to independently mediate on disagreement, complaints and appeals. In the UK after all internal processes within an institution have been completed, if a student is still dissatisfied with the process or outcomes, then they may submit an appeal to the national Office of the Independent Adjudicator (OIA), which provides an ombud service to consider any irregularities in the student's evidence and experiences in such cases. If the OIA finds in favour of the student, then the institution will be asked to respond accordingly. Although it is not a binding requirement, the findings of all cases are public information and institutions almost always comply with the recommendations (OIAHE, 2018; OIA, 2023). Substantial financial compensation payments from the institution to the student can result when the OIA supports a student's complaint. For this reason, all higher education institutions in the UK pay careful attention to any guidance, rulings or decisions taken by the OIA, irrespective of the institution involved.

If a student complains about their experience or outcomes after facing an academic conduct allegation, then the internal institutional documentation is the main evidence that an institutional or national ombud, such as the OIA, will use to make their decision. This factor seriously influences attention to compliance with policies and procedures in all UK higher education institutions and demands careful completion of associated records and other documentary evidence.

Maintaining records of cases and outcomes has other important purposes. If no formal records are kept, ideally by a central office within an institution, then it is not possible to identify (or respond to) cases of serial or habitual academic integrity breaches by the same student. In addition, analysis of data about cases arising can provide very useful information that can help to improve policies, pedagogy and assessment practices. It can also be used to inform training for both staff and students as a means of improving deterrence, detection and decision-making.

Importantly, annual statistics, based on in-depth analysis of data from academic conduct and integrity cases and processes, provide essential key performance indicators (KPI) and other evidence. These statistics should be carefully scrutinised by academic leaders and institutional governing bodies (Andrews & Glendinning, 2023), to evaluate the efficacy of institutional policies and procedures. Governing bodies and institutional leaders have an obligation to ensure all essential services are adequately resourced and operating as intended. If systems, policies and procedures associated with maintaining academic integrity are not adequately supported and resourced, then the institution places itself of risk of reputational damage, through poor academic standards and quality, as evidenced by the capabilities and skills of graduates (Andrews & Glendinning, 2023).

Lessons learned from tracking and analysis of case data and other documentary sources should be applied to the other three dimensions, especially deterrence measures, operational efficiency and overall strategic thinking about academic integrity.

RECOMMENDATIONS

The 4-D dimensions in Figure 1 provide novel a way to categorise what different elements academic integrity policies should contain, how these dimensions overlap and why all are important. Central to the Venn diagram, applying to all four dimensions (Figures 2, 3, 4 and 5) is the need for effective communication. Recording progress, education and tracking the case also implicitly link each of the dimensions.

The following recommendations on how to address the challenges identified are not new and they will come as no surprise to most readers, but they are still worth setting out in the light of the proposals and supporting evidence presented in this chapter.

Deterring is often mistakenly called preventing – the author thanks researcher Cath Ellis for pointing out that anomaly, several years ago. We can take steps to minimise accidental breaches and make it as difficult as possible for determined students to deliberately cheat, but educators should never expect to be able to eliminate academic integrity breaches altogether (Carroll, 2005). The obvious pedagogical and assessment measures involve careful attention to assessment design and assessment criteria, such as not setting the same assessments, authentic assessment, using active learning, including problem-based learning and learning by doing, setting individual or specific assessments, typically requiring application rather than recall of knowledge, knowing and engaging your students, assessment criteria requiring critical thinking and deep learning (for example, see University of Sydney, 2023; Bowditch, 2023; QAA, 2023). However, this approach can prove difficult, maybe impossible to implement, especially for large cohorts of students, in poorly resourced institutions and in cultures where rote learning is the expectation. Redesigning teaching and learning approaches, setting different assessments for every cohort, and applying innovative approaches is a huge investment for individual academic staff, especially adjunct staff, those poorly paid and those working part-time. On-going institutional investment in resources is essential for providing training and support for all student-facing staff in order to introduce these approaches and sustain the changes in the longer term. Failure to invest in approaches and initiatives for deterring academic integrity breaches will result in the need for further expenses being required to support the other three dimensions. The alternative is to ignore academic misconduct altogether, undermining the institutional quality, standards and reputation (QAA, 2023).

Working with students as partners is an essential factor in responding to threats to academic integrity. Individual students and student organisations can help to ensure that any messages to students are accessible and appropriate. Student representatives can help with the design, formulation and delivery of deterrence initiatives and advise on details, including the format, use of vocabulary and via which channels and media students are most likely to receive the information.

Understanding why students breach integrity is the first stage in addressing the causes. The concept of viewing the institutional student population in terms of their susceptibility for breaching integrity can help to put things into perspective. If a high and growing number of breaches are being detected within an institution, then it is likely that only the "tip of the iceberg" of cases are being reported (Curtis et al., 2021). If cases are not reported, if reported cases are not processed as required, or if genuine cases of misconduct are rejected during the decision-making process, either due to poor evidence or lack of understanding of the significance of the evidence, perhaps the decision-makers' perceptions of the necessary burden of proof may be too high, then students will assume cheating is condoned or not taken seriously. If this happens, it will fuel more misconduct, especially in the "middle group" of students who are susceptible to following the perceived prevailing culture. At least some of these students are more likely to accept inappropriate offers of help or take other short-cuts to complete their assessments if they believe it is normal to do so.

To address this situation, more resources should be allocated to deterrence and detection in order to persuade the at-risk students that academic dishonesty is unacceptable, it is more likely than not to be detected and they will face sanctions. This shift in focus should help to reduce the perceived level of complacency among students. In the short term the number of reported and recorded cases may increase significantly, but in the longer term the number of cases should gradually decrease as the culture of academic dishonesty begins to decline.

Essentially, education is a global marketplace. It should never be assumed that any student brings with them all the necessary basic skills and knowledge to enable them to succeed. Students arriving from different cultures and educational settings, even within the same country, will need information and time to adjust to the new study requirements. They may not appreciate what their new institution expects of them unless this is made clear. However, bombarding students with facts and demands when they first arrive can be counterproductive. A programme of education and skills development should be integrated with subject-based studies, carefully staged, delivered throughout the student journey, ideally by tutors who are experts and enthusiasts about the specific topics (Glendinning, 2023b).

It is clear from the long, bulleted list included earlier, that there are many disincentives that can deter academic staff from investigating, collecting evidence and reporting suspicions of academic integrity breaches. These disincentives can and should be addressed by understanding and negating or removing each of the underlying reasons that apply in that specific institutional setting. One approach would be to provide resources to support academic staff to generate evidence, to remove the additional workload burden. Where there is an institutional culture of academics not reporting cases, or where there is a stigma attached to reporting cases, changing that culture will not be easy, it may take some time, but with strong leadership and determination, it can be achieved. The Westen Balkans country Montenegro provides an example that others can learn from (Foltýnek & Glendinning, 2023). The Montenegrin government transformed their higher education sector's approach to academic integrity, using the results from the SEEPPAI project (Foltýnek et al., 2017) as a guide to develop a national legal framework relating to ethics and academic integrity (Kurpejović, 2019), which is having a substantial impact on practices in their higher education sector.

To help to improve both detection and reporting of integrity breaches, all staff involved in teaching, assessment and research should receive regular training on how to identify different types of academic integrity breaches, how to ask for help and what evidence they need to provide to raise an allegation. Their role should be as light-touch as possible, to ensure that all potential cases are reported, then they can focus on their main duties. If dedicated and experienced support staff are available to take cases forward and ensure good evidence is generated, the majority of cases should be reported and appropriately progressed.

The processing of cases can be improved by having clear and transparent, uncomplicated, easy to follow procedures, for all staff. Anyone involved in deliberating and decision-making, which may include student representatives, needs to be regularly trained in conducting meetings, asking appropriate questions, understanding what evidence is relevant and indicative of different types of misconduct and how to interpret and make sense of the evidence presented. Critically, all people making decisions need a clear understanding of what is meant by "on balance of probabilities" and how to apply and interpret this when deliberating on real cases and the associated evidence.

When any policies and procedures are under review, it is important to consult widely, to understand different perspectives, and to get buy-in from staff, student representatives and students involved in these operations, before any changes are finalised. This is especially important when reviewing policies relating to academic integrity, because academic integrity policies can be complex and they usually involve and affect a wide range of different people and roles within and, sometimes, external to the institution (Glendinning, 2023b). Failure to understand and factor in the different roles and how they interact with others, can lead to unforeseen problems. If people who are impacted by any changes are not consulted, or their views not listened to, then this is likely to lead to lack of ownership, which could result in unworkable stalemate, delays in processing cases and a rise in non-reporting of allegations (Glendinning, 2023b).

Documenting cases has much wider implications than use in tracking progress and monitoring cases. The accuracy, quality and completeness of case records is crucial evidence available for auditing and appeal processes. Careful design of data entry documents, integration with student records systems, combined with training and guidance for those responsible, are measures that will help to improve the quality of what is recorded. Those completing case records need to know how to write objectively, what level of detail is required and the nature, vocabulary and expressions that should be used, and what to avoid, when completing different types of documentation.

Although transparency is important, in the author's view, the data associated with academic conduct and integrity should be reserved for internal use rather than released as public information. There are several reasons for taking this stance: data relating to misconduct cases is very sensitive; it can easily be misinterpreted by people who do not understand internal processes in educational institutions; different institutions have different ways of recording data and classifying breaches, therefore statistical information cannot be compared across institutions – for example to create a league table of cheating (The Sunday Telegraph, 2011); a low number of recorded cases does not necessarily mean a low amount of academic dishonesty – it could mean that cases are not being reported or recorded; a high number of cases has to be put into the context of the size of the institution and the nature of the cases reported.

All the above recommendations here are intended as guidance on what actions could be taken to overcome possible barriers to maintaining academic integrity, but, clearly, very much biased towards the author's view of a UK culture. Importantly, when designing and reviewing institutional strategies and policies, a consultative and inclusive approach towards the local culture and ethos is needed. Blindly adopting what has been recommended from a different setting is likely to result in unworkable policies (Glendinning, 2023b).

CONCLUSION

It is hoped that the 4-D model presented here will inspire and guide others when considering the big picture of academic integrity. As the rise in misuse of AI tools by students demonstrates, academic integrity is not a static area for study. This dynamic landscape is part of its appeal to researchers who choose to devote a substantial part of their lives and careers to working on potential solutions to "wicked problems" and complex situations. The author's idea of educational nirvana is a scenario where all students arrive ready to and willing to learn, understand our expectations and aspirations, follow the institutional rules and requirements, and continue to absorb themselves into enjoying and fulfilling all aspects of their learning throughout their studies. Even if the majority of students fit that scenario, or aspire to do so, a substantial minority of students arrive with less desirable intentions, as evidenced by the more serious and deliberate forms of academic integrity breaches that arise, despite deterrence measures and educational initiatives to deter inappropriate conduct.

The on-going challenges of students who plagiarise, try to disguise plagiarism, submit work as their own that was acquired, generated by an AI tool, or commissioned by or for them, are not going to go away any time soon. Effectively managing such conduct absorbs a huge amount of time and human resources that should be focused on education and support. Although there are no silver bullets, it is hoped that the suggestions, recommendations and ideas in this chapter will serve as an inspiration for other people and institutions facing the same challenges.

REFERENCES

Andrews, S., & Glendinning, I. (2023). Governing academic integrity: Conceptualizing the assurance and efficacy of strategies and outcomes. Eaton, S. (Ed), Handbook for Academic Integrity, 2nd Edition. Springer. doi:10.1007/978-981-287-079-7_185-1

BBC News. (2021). *University of South Wales: Hacker jailed for selling exam answers*. BBC News. https://www.bbc.co.uk/news/uk-wales-58502963

Borg, E. (2009, August). Local Plagiarisms. *Assessment & Evaluation in Higher Education, 34*(4), 415–426. doi:10.1080/02602930802075115

Bowditich, I. (2023). Assessment Menu: Designing assessment in an AI enabled world. *JISC*. https://nationalcentreforai.jiscinvolve.org/wp/2023/09/12/designing-assessment-in-an-ai-enabled-world/

Bretag, T., & Mahmud, S. (2016). A conceptual framework for implementing exemplary academic integrity policy in Australian higher education. Handbook of academic integrity, 463-480.

Bretag, T., Mahmud, S., Wallace, M., Walker, R., James, C., Green, M., East, J., McGowan, U., & Partridge, L. (2011). Core elements of exemplary academic integrity policy in Australian higher education. *International Journal for Educational Integrity*, *7*(2), 3–12. doi:10.21913/IJEI.v7i2.759

Carroll, J. (2005). Handling Student Plagiarism: Moving to Mainstream. Brookes eJournal of Learning and Teaching, 1(2).

Curtis, G. C., McNeill, M., Slade, C., Tremayne, K., Harper, R., Rundle, K., & Greenaway, R. (2021). Moving beyond self-reports to estimate the prevalence of commercial contract cheating: An Australian study. *Studies in Higher Education*. Advance online publication. doi:10.1080/03075079.2021.1972093

Davis, M. (2007). *The role of Turnitin within the formative proves of academic writing: a tool for learning and unlearning*. Research Gate. https://www.researchgate.net/publication/281848114_The_role_of_Turnitin_within_the_formative_process_of_academic_writing_a_tool_for_learning_and_unlearning/comments#fullTextFileContent

Dawson, P. (2020). *Defending Assessment Security in a Digital World*. Routledge. doi:10.4324/9780429324178

Dawson, P. & Sutherland-Smith, W. (2018) Can markers detect contract cheating? Results from a pilot study. *Assessment & Evaluation in Higher Education, 43*. doi:10.1080/02602938.2017.1336746

Foltýnek, T., Dlabolová, D., Anohina-Naumeca, A., Razi, S., Kravjar, J., Kamzola, L., Guerrero-Dib, J., Celek, O., & Weber-Wulff, D. (2020). Testing of support tools for plagiarism detection. *International Journal of Educational Technology in Higher Education*, *17*(1), 46. doi:10.1186/s41239-020-00192-4

Foltýnek, T., Dlabolová, D., Glendinning, I., Lancaster, T., & Linkeschová, D. (2017). *South-East European Project on Policies for Academic Integrity, Project report*. Council of Europe. http://www.plagiarism.cz/seeppai/Final-report_SEEPPAI.pdf

Foltýnek, T., & Glendinning, I. (2023). European Cooperation in Academic Integrity. Eaton, S. (Ed), Handbook for Academic Integrity, 2nd Edition, Springer. doi:10.1007/978-981-287-079-7_176-1

Glendinning, I. (2016). European perspectives of academic integrity. In T. Bretag (Ed.), Handbook of Academic Integrity (pp. 55–74). Springer. doi:10.1007/978-981-287-098-8_3

Glendinning, I. (2022). Aligning academic quality and standards with academic integrity. In S. E. Eaton, G. Curtis, B. M. Stoesz, K. Rundle, J. Clare, & J. Seeland (Eds.), Contract cheating in higher education: Global perspectives on theory, practice, and policy. Palgrave Macmillan. doi:10.1007/978-3-031-12680-2_14

Glendinning, I. (2023a). Linking quality, standards and Integrity. Eaton, S. (Ed), Handbook for Academic Integrity, 2nd Edition, Springer. On-line. doi:10.1007/978-981-287-079-7_117-1

Glendinning, I. (2023b Forthcoming). Developing and implementing policies for academic Integrity – management of change. In G. J. Curtis (Ed.), *Academic Integrity in the Social Sciences*. Springer. doi:10.1007/978-3-031-43292-7_6

Glendinning, I., Foltýnek, T., Dlabolová, D., Dannhoferová, J., Králíková, V., Michalska, A., Orim, S.-M., & Turčínek, P. (2021). *Project on academic integrity in Armenia, Azerbaijan, Georgia, Kazakhstan and Turkey*. ETINED, Council of Europe Platform on Ethics, Transparency and Integrity in Education. https://book.coe.int/en/education-policy/10662-pdf-etined-council-of-europe-platform-on-ethics-transparency-and-integrity-in-education-volume-6-project-on-academic-integrity-in-armenia-azerbaijan-georgia-kazakhstan-and-turkey.html

Glendinning, I., Orim, S., & King, A. (2019). *Policies and Actions of Accreditation and Quality Assurance Bodies to Counter Corruption in Higher Education*. CHEA / CIQG 2019. https://www.chea.org/quality-assurance-combatting-academic-corruption-resources

Glendinning, I., & Orim, S. M. (2023). Comparison of Institutional Strategies for Academic Integrity in Europe and Eurasia. Bjelobaba, S., Foltýnek, T., Glendinning, I., Králíková, V., Dlabolová, D. (Eds) (2023). Academic Integrity: Broadening Practices, Technologies, and the Role of Students. Springer series: Ethics and Education in Educational Contexts. Springer. doi:10.1007/978-3-031-16976-2_3

Ireland, C., & English, J. (2011). Let them plagiarise: Developing Academic Writing in a Safe Environment. *Journal of Academic Writing*, *1*(1), 165–172. doi:10.18552/joaw.v1i1.10

JISC. (2023a). AI in Tertiary education. *JISC*. https://beta.jisc.ac.uk/reports/artificial-intelligence-in-tertiary-education report to download first published 26/04/21 updated 06/09/2023

JISC. (2023b) Generative AI – a primer. *JISC*. https://beta.jisc.ac.uk/reports/generative-ai-a-primer

Kurpejović, M. (2019). Montenegro just made plagiarism illegal. What does it hope to achieve? *RetractionWatch*. https://retractionwatch.com/2019/03/25/montenegro-just-made-plagiarism-illegal-what-does-it-hope-to-achieve/

Macdonald, R., & Carroll, J. (2006). Plagiarism: A Complex Issue Requiring a Holistic Institutional Approach. *Assessment & Evaluation in Higher Education*, *31*(2), 233–245. doi:10.1080/02602930500262536

McCabe, D. (2016). Cheating and honor: Lessons from a long-term research project. In T. Bretag (Ed.), *Handbook of Academic Integrity* (pp. 187–198). Springer. doi:10.1007/978-981-287-098-8_35

Morris, E., & Carroll, J. (2011). *Policy Works*. Higher Education Academy for England. https://www.advance-he.ac.uk/knowledge-hub/policy-works-recommendations-reviewing-policy-manage-unacceptable-academic-practice

Norman, G. (2018). Chinese Student to be deported after paying $3,000 to imposter. *Fox News*. https://www.foxnews.com/us/2018/04/05/chinese-student-to-be-deported-after-paying-3000-to-impostor-to-help-her-get-into-american-university.html

OIA. (2023). *Casework Note: Complaints relating to academic misconduct*. OIA. https://www.oiahe.org.uk/resources-and-publications/casework-note-complaints-relating-to-academic-misconduct/

OIAHE. (2018). *Good Practice Framework – Disciplinary Procedures* OIAHE. https://www.oiahe.org.uk/media/2045/good-practice-framework-disciplinary-procedures-section.pdf

OutLiar. (n.d.). *Resources for detecting Contract Cheating*. OutLiar. https://outliar.blog/2021/10/19/resources-for-detecting-contract-cheating

Park, C. (2004, August). Rebels without a Clause: Towards an institutional framework for dealing with plagiarism by students. *Journal of Further and Higher Education*, *28*(3), 291–306. doi:10.1080/0309877042000241760

QAA. (2021). *Exploring QAA Members' Approach to Academic Conduct Cases and Use of Penalties*. QAA.

QAA. (2022). *Contracting to Cheat in Higher Education*. QAA. https://www.qaa.ac.uk/docs/qaa/guidance/contracting-to-cheat-in-higher-education-third-edition.pdf?sfvrsn=2fbfa581_14

QAA. (2023). *Maintaining quality and standards in the ChatGPT era*. QAA. https://www.qaa.ac.uk/docs/qaa/members/maintaining-quality-and-standards-in-the-chatgpt-era.pdf released 8th May 2023

Tennant, P., & Duggan, F. (2008). *Academic Misconduct Benchmarking Research Project: Part 2. The Recorded Incidence of Student Plagiarism and the Penalties Applied*. UK: The Higher Education Academy and JISC. https://www.plagiarism.org/paper/academic-misconduct-benchmarking-research-project-part-2

Tennant, P., & Rowell, G. (2010). *Benchmark Plagiarism Tariff for the Application of Penalties for Student Plagiarism and the Penalties Applied*. UK: Plagiarismadvice.org https://www.plagiarism.org/paper/benchmark-plagiarism-tariff

The Sunday Telegraph. (2011). The cheating epidemic at Britain's Universities. *The Sunday Telegraph*. https://www.telegraph.co.uk/education/educationnews/8363345/The-cheating-epidemic-at-Britains-universities.html

University of Sydney. (2023). ChatGPT is old news: How do we assess in the age of AI-writing copilots? University of Sydney. https://educational-innovation.sydney.edu.au/teaching@sydney/chatgpt-is-old-news-how-do-we-assess-in-the-age-of-ai-writing-co-pilots/?fbclid=IwAR1JSRu8bjMo8H8zX5VJl-BjqyArQxikEpM898MVCLPm_cU3vblLgNE7GpQ_aem_AV28MDpP_1nOo4_m4IJFhy0EyKy3u-N2YBFO4BIms8g7O507zESUxe5fznU4W-JE7T9k

Weber-Wulff, D. (2014). *False Feathers: A Perspective on Academic Plagiarism*. Springer. doi:10.1007/978-3-642-39961-9

Weber-WulffD.Anohina-NaumecaA.BjelobabaS.FoltýnekT.Guerrera-DibJ.PopoolaO.ŠigutP.WaddingtonL. (2023). Testing detection tools for AI-Generated Text. https://arxiv.org/abs/2306.15666

APPENDIX ONE: CHECKLIST FOR AIDING DETECTION OF INAPPROPRIATE USE OF AI TOOLS

- Lack of critical thinking, largely factual content
- Repetition of content
- Inaccuracies and completely made up "facts"
- References irrelevant / unavailable / old / fabricated / copied – but some genuine
- Check the similarity report for unmatched references – they may be fake
- Content generic, off the point – but it is getting better
- Vocabulary, spelling (US/UK)
- Sentence length relatively uniform – no variability or "burstiness"
- Knowing the student:
  - Grammar is just too perfect
  - Could this student have written this?
  - Writing, content too advanced
- Could it have been translated? – check the language of references
- Could it be translation plagiarism? – does reference list match in similarity report?
- Fabrication of data, references, facts – does it look genuine, repurposed, fake?
- Strange synonyms – a paraphrasing tool or word spinning could have been used
- Graphics, artwork: inaccurate portrayal of physical objects and anatomical features, details (eg hands, fingers)

Some of these could also be signs of contract cheating
Essay mills and ghost writers also make use of these tools

Chapter 13
Harnessing the Power of Generative Artificial Intelligence to Promote Academic Integrity

Nadia Koren
TAFE NSW, Australia

Brent A. Anders
TAFE NSW, Australia

ABSTRACT

This chapter explores how generative artificial intelligence, which poses a threat to academic integrity, can also be used to address some of the root causes of breaches in academic integrity. The root causes discussed are primarily derived from the largest self-reported academic integrity survey conducted across Australia's leading universities. Some of these root causes that the chapter will address include dissatisfaction with the teaching and learning environment, challenges related to English as an additional language, and the perception of easy access to cheating opportunities. By embracing generative artificial intelligence and incorporating it into the classroom, educators are afforded the opportunity to discuss its acceptable use in assessments and to bring attention to the academic integrity policies and procedures of the institution.

INTRODUCTION

The academic community has been in a state of excitement, uncertainty, and stress due to concerns about the potential increase in academic integrity issues since the explosive growth and popularity of Generative Artificial Intelligence (AI), highlighted by the release OpenAI's ChatGPT in November 2022. One of the reasons behind academic integrity breaches, as identified in a large survey encompassing 14,086 Australian Higher Education students, is the abundance of cheating opportunities (Bretag et al., 2018). This has become an even more pressing reality with the now free and easy access to tools like OpenAI's ChatGPT, Bing Chat, Google Bard and GitHub Co-pilot. This heightened risk to academic

DOI: 10.4018/979-8-3693-0240-8.ch013

integrity has caused a panic among academics. Instead of implementing a ban, many academics have engaged in ongoing webinars, discussions, and collaborative efforts to support one another and adopt a positive stance (Banerji, 2023; Dukewich & Larsen, 2023; Muscanell & Robert, 2023). Even though it led to a ban on ChatGPT in all Australian state schools (except for South Australia) and other countries/regions, not everyone reacted in the same way (Duffy, 2023; Nolan, 2023). Australian federal education minister announced the lifting of the ban of Generative AI in state schools starting from 2024, adopting a framework for the use of such technology (Cassidy, 2023).

This chapter assumes a proactive and inclusive approach aimed at addressing the challenges posed by the release of Generative AI, like ChatGPT, while embracing its potential benefits to enhance student learning and help directly prevent breaches of academic integrity. We will explore how harnessing Generative AI's power can effectively address the root causes of academic integrity breaches which include: students that struggle when English is an additional language (not their native language), dissatisfaction with the teaching and learning environment, lack of clarification of assessment and content, poor time management and procrastination, perception of easy access to cheating opportunities, and providing meaningful and timely feedback on assessments (Awdry & Ives, 2022; Bretag et al., 2019; Miles et al., 2022). Specific prompts and detailed instructions are provided on how the power of Generative AI can be harnessed to better address these issues.

FOR EQUITY REASONS, ALL EXAMPLES INCLUDED IN THIS CHAPTER ARE FROM FREE GENERATIVE AI TOOLS

Students With English as an Additional Language

Increased international student intakes and migrant intakes in countries where English is the main language demands extra support for students with English as an Additional Language (EAL). An article from *Frontiers in Education* (Russell et al., 2022) on post-secondary education in Canada sought to understand the academic experiences of international students and faculty members' perspectives on their language needs. Their findings add further responsibility on education providers to support students with language barriers as English language tests like International English Language Testing System (IELTS) may not fully represent the language demands in an academic setting (Russell et al., 2022). Sawir's 2010 research paper, based on interviews with students from five Asian countries, states that students' prior learning focused on the rules of grammar for written text rather than on conversational English. This focus leads them to become passive learners who are less likely to engage in class discussions or express their need for support. Given these challenges, to improve support and confidence for EAL students, Generative AI provides more accessible and user-friendly methods of support. (Ortiz, 2023).

With Generative AI, EAL students could obtain assistance whenever needed without concern of being embarrassed by seeking repeated clarification their lecturer or tutor. Examples of how these tools can be used for EAL students are show below.

- **Make topics covered more relatable to student's country of origin.**

Prompt ChatGPT: Assume the role of a university lecturer and explain real estate business principles to an international student from Pakistan who has been learning English only for 4 years. Compare and contrast with examples from Australia and Pakistan.

Generated Response: ChatGPT (OpenAI, 2023):

Of course, I'd be happy to help explain real estate business principles to an international student from Pakistan who has been learning English for four years. Let's start by breaking down some key concepts and then comparing them with examples from both Australia and Pakistan.

Examples to compare and contrast real estate in the two countries are generated (see reference for link to the entire chat)

- **Summarise**: To summarise lengthy papers in simple English to save time for EAL students who may be slower in reading. Additionally, they can interact with further prompts to ask additional questions on the paper.

Prompt Bard: Assume the role of a university tutor, summarise the content of https://journals.physiology.org/doi/full/10.1152/physrev.00010.2018 to your EAL student.

Generated Response: Bard (Google, 2023).

Sure, here is a summary of the article for you: [...]

Here are some specific examples from the article: [. . .]

Five examples from the articles in short sentences is generated (see reference for link to entire chat).

- **Translation for EAL students**: Encouraging contributions of EAL students to tutorial discussion. These students can first submit their thoughts or questions into Generative AI tools for rephrasing. This may boost their confidence levels, allowing for more active participation in discussion. Importantly, this does not imply that only those with flawless English should engage; the objective is inclusive participation.

Prompt ChatGPT: Take the role of an international student from Nepal studying a Nursing degree, contributing to a tutorial discussion on mental health. How would you say it in English keeping in mind the sensitive nature of the topic and cultural diversity in the class?: "नमस्ते, म तपाईंसँग [तपाईंको नाम] भनेर परचिति गराउँदैछु, एक अन्तर्राष्ट्रयि वद्यिार्थी नेपालबाट। मैले हाम्रो देशमा मानसकि स्वास्थ्यको दृष्टकिोणको बारेमा थोडै जानकारी दनि चाहन्छु। नेपालमा मानसकि स्वास्थ्यलाई धेरै नकारात्मक रूपमा हेरन्छि, मानसिहरू यसलाई श्राप वा भूत-प्रेतको प्रवेशको रूपमा हेर्छन्। यसै कारणले धेरै मानसिहरू चकित्सिालाई टाउको मारेर धार्मकि वा परम्परागत उपचारको साथमा जान्छन्। हाम्रो सांस्कृतकि दृष्टकिोणहरूलाई ठीक रूपमा बुझ्न मानसकि स्वास्थ्यको सम्पूर्ण दृष्टकिोणको लाग मिहत्त्वपूर्ण छ। धन्यवाद।"

Generated Response: ChatGPT (OpenAI, 2023a)

Hello, I would be happy to help you phrase that in English for your tutorial discussion on mental health, considering the sensitive nature of the topic and the cultural diversity in the class:

"Hello, I'd like to introduce myself as [Your Name], an international student from Nepal. I have some knowledge about the perspective on mental health in our country that I'd like to share. In Nepal, mental health is often viewed negatively, and some people associate it with curses or supernatural influences. This can lead many individuals to seek traditional or religious remedies alongside medical treatment. Understanding our cultural perspectives is crucial for a comprehensive view of mental health. Thank you."

This way, you address your background and intention to contribute to the discussion while sensitively explaining the cultural context related to mental health in Nepal.

- **Proofreading and learning grammar**: Students can submit their writing for scrutiny to correct their grammar, learn from their errors and request exercises to improve their recurrent mistakes. Students can also translate the content they wrote in English to their most proficient language to verify if their intended message has been conveyed.

Prompt ChatGPT: Take the role of a tutor, correct the grammar and explain the grammar rules which were broken: It is important to spend a considerable time on the requirement analysis phase of a system development. This often can lead to failed systems or constant updates as the needs of the user and how the current system (manual or automated) operates. It also makes the user feel heard and understood and it is more likely that the new system will be accepted more positively. Explanation of grammar rules:

Generated Response: ChatGPT (OpenAI, 2023b):

Certainly, let's correct the grammar in the provided text and explain the grammar rules that were broken:

Original Text: [...]

Corrected Text: [...]

Explanation of Grammar Corrections: [...]

Prompt continued: Provide some practice exercises specifically targeting the grammar errors made.

Generated Response:

Certainly, here are some practice exercises focusing on the grammar errors made in the original text: [...]

Each original sentence, corrected sentence and the explanation are generated. In response to continued prompt, four exercises are generated for the student to practice on their weak areas of grammar (see reference for link to the entire chat). Student can continue to interact by answering the questions and asking for further feedback.

- **Active learning in lectures**: To actively engage in lectures, live, with the permission of the lecturer, the student can input content the instructor is speaking to better understand the class material. This can help the student to pose additional questions related to the class content or request explanations in a simplified manner. If still unclear the student can request clarification in the language they are most fluent in. Although, this should ideally be done as the last option to gain more language proficiency in English, the medium of study.

Prompt ChatGPT mobile app: Take the role of a university tutor and answer questions on the following content presented by the lecturer:

Generated Response: ChatGPT mobile app (OpenAI, 2023c).

Of course, I can help answer questions on the content presented by the lecturer. Please provide the specific topic or questions you have in mind and I will do my best to assist.

Prompt continued: [voice input] and [tap when finished]

Generated Response: [output]

Prompt continued: [ask any questions on the topic covered]

It is important for EAL students to strike a balance and not rely too heavily on using Generative AI for translation, due to possible inaccuracies and as it may hinder the development of their English language skills. Actively engaging in writing and speaking in English, even if it means using imperfect English at times, is crucial for practice and improvement. Learning in an English-speaking environment carries the dual aspiration of gaining academic credentials while also demonstrating proficiency in the English language. Consequently, a key educational goal is the enhancement of language proficiency.

While encouraging the use of these tools for EAL students, students need to be made aware of the expectations of assessments to maintain academic integrity, as in some cases, language and academic writing skills may be part of the learning outcome. For example, University of Melbourne general guidance instructions on Generative AI clarifies to students that acceptable use may vary depending on the learning outcomes.

Learning to do this well is an important part of developing your academic skills. Expression or language use may be a learning outcome in your subjects or course. These tools can be used to the extent that the expression is no longer your own or you gain an unfair advantage over other students who have not used these tools. (Academic Integrity, University of Melbourne, n.d., para. 11)

While our focus has primarily revolved around harnessing the capabilities of Generative AI for EAL students, it is crucial to recognise that proficiency in spoken English, even among native speakers, does not necessarily translate to confident and grammatically correct written expression. Therefore, Generative AI tools can play a pivotal role in assisting these students in creating written content with confidence and precision.

DISSATISFACTION WITH TEACHING AND LEARNING ENVIRONMENT

Multiple factors determine student satisfaction with the learning environment. In the survey conducted by Bretag et al (2019), the students were posed with ten questions that were related to dissatisfaction with the teaching and learning environment. In the cheating group there was a marked difference in the responses to four perceptions compared to the non-cheating group. These four student perceptions will be reviewed in the light of how the power of Generative AI can be harnessed to address them.

- **"I have opportunities to approach my lecturers and tutors for assistance when needed"** (Bretag et al., 2019, p.9)

Generative AI tools can now assume the role of an ever-accessible, 24/7 personal tutor, readily available to students. These tools help clarify lecture content and simplify complex topics as needed by students even when there are limited opportunities to approach the academic staff. Moreover, they foster interactive engagement by encouraging further exploration through targeted questions. The use of Generative AI for assessment clarification with examples is covered later in the chapter.

Additionally, it is imperative for students to adhere diligently to the assessment specifications, particularly in relation to the permissible extent of Generative AI use. While an academic staff member would know the acceptable assistance to be given in assessments, Generative AI, if not used judiciously, runs the risk of completing assessments on behalf of the student, thereby compromising academic integrity. Nevertheless, when assessments are re-designed to align with the era of Generative AI, the associated risks can be significantly minimised.

- "**My lecturers and tutors ensure that I understand what is required on assignments**" (Bretag et al., 2019, p.9)

This issue may be stemming from lack of clarity in assessment requirements and lack of discussions in the lecture or tutorial about the assessment. Generative AI can be used by academic staff when writing assessment requirements and rubrics to ensure clarity and that it is written at a level preferred by most people, which is at a level of a 7th grader - around the age of a 12-year-old (Australian Government Style Manual, 2023). Flesch-Kincaid readability analysis is widely used to assess readability of documents in English speaking environments and ideal recommended is 9th grade or lower and it a requirement across many (Wylie 2018). For example, a prompt such as "Rewrite the following to Flesch-Kincaid readability scale 9th grade: [enter the content]", will be a very efficient way to ensure the level is met. Even though we expect students to have a certain level of English when entering tertiary education, it would better if the assessments specifications met this standard too. Therefore, Generative AI can be promoted among educators to ensure the assessments are written at a certain level. Written at this level or in clear, concise, and simple language, which will also help EAL students. Note that this does not mean lowering any assessment standards but stating the requirements in clear and simple language.

Generative AI can also be employed to clarify assessment tasks, but there are guardrails to be considered. It is not acceptable for staff and students to submit assessments which are copyrighted material of the university, in that these materials could be used for the future training of Large Language Learning Models (LLMs). However, in cases where institutions have their own Generative AI models, trained on their specific datasets, such concerns dissipate, and the tool can offer more robust support to students.

- "**My lecturers and tutors spend class time teaching me how to engage in scholarship in my discipline** (i.e., research, read, critically analyse and discuss discipline material)" (Bretag et al., 2019, p.10)

This need is best left for lecture/tutorial discussions rather than rely on Generative AI. However, as Generative AI is used to save staff/student time, it can free up more time during a lecture/tutorial for the guidance and discussion of how to engage in discipline specific scholarship. Academics can also use Generative AI to generate discipline specific scenarios and topics for debates.

Prompt Bing Chat: Take the role of a Civil Engineering lecturer. Create specific scenarios in Australian context to create discussion among students on important aspects to consider when designing bridges such as Sydney Harbour Bridge. Also provide some related topics for a debate.

Generated Response: (Microsoft, 2023)

Sure, here are some scenarios and related debate topics: [...]

Four scenarios and corresponding debate topics are generated (see reference for link to the entire chat).

- "**I receive sufficient feedback to ensure that I learn from the work I do**" (Bretag et al., 2019, p.10)

Students have the option, to use these tools to generate feedback for themselves, as they are able to upload their own content which is their intellectual property. It is worth noting that while students should be aware that these AI systems are not completely reliable, this accessible 24/7 interactive feedback remains a valuable resource. This approach serves as a constructive means of reviewing and receiving feedback before submitting an assessment, potentially prompting further queries for the tutor based on the insights gained from Generative AI feedback.

On the other hand, academics need to take care not to submit student work into Generative AI for assessing and generating feedback due to privacy (in case of identifiable data) and as it the student's own intellectual property. However, this view or acceptable use may vary from institute to institute. This would not be a concern when the institution has their own Generative AI and if students, upon enrollment, are informed and agree that their work will be submitted to these LLMs. Therefore, when it is acceptable to submit student work, the academics can save an immense amount of their time and generate feedback for student assessments. However, it is the combination of Generative AI feedback with human review that can provide the most meaningful feedback to students. Academics who rely heavily on Generative AI for assessment without manual review may face multiple challenges. These can include unfair evaluations due to inaccuracies in the generated feedback. Additionally, the lack of review can result in academics being unaware of the content of student submissions, which may further reduce opportunities for personal interaction and discussion about the assessment. Where institute's own Generative AI is not available or they are advised not to submit student work into Generative AI, academics can still harness the power of Generative AI by, listing feedback in a rough format and asking Generative AI to re-write to suit a particular student giving some context about the student (while avoiding personal data).

In a study published in JAMA Internal Medicine that submitted 200 patient questions for ChatGPT to generate responses, evaluators preferred ChatGPT's responses nearly 80% of the time over the responses of human doctors (Reed, 2023). Though there were no similar studies in an educational setting at the time of writing, it is highly likely that that academic's feedback can be enhanced and written in a more empathetic, engaging way by Generative AI.

The burden of an academic's marking workload can sometimes lead to diminished feedback quality, but the integration of Generative AI can enable tutors to craft high-quality, positive, and encouraging feedback while providing constructive suggestions for improvement.

Some examples of how Generative AI can be used to generate feedback in creative and engaging ways:

Prompt ChatGPT: Rewrite the following feedback on a student assessment with more empathy and to inspire them to improve in the next assessment: "limited research, need to look at the other side of the argument, no sound argument, your voice does not come through"

Generated Response: ChatGPT (OpenAI, 2023d).

I understand that receiving feedback on your assessment can be a valuable opportunity for growth and improvement. In your recent assessment, there are some areas where you can further enhance your work: [...]

Prompt ChatGPT continued: write the same feedback with humour but not sarcasm - must still be with much empathy.

Generated Response:

I can understand that feedback can sometimes feel like a serious business, but let's try to add a touch of humor while still being empathetic. Here's a lighter take on your recent assessment:

[...]

Prompt ChatGPT continued: could you write the original response as a poem?

Generated Response:

Of course! Here's the original feedback transformed into a poem with empathy:

[...]

Responses of feedback that is humorous and a poem, both with empathy is generated (see reference for link to the entire chat).

In addition to the four specific questions mentioned earlier, which are used to measure satisfaction with the teaching and learning environment, it is essential to explore other strategies for enhancing this satisfaction and examining how Generative AI can support and, in turn, minimise academic integrity breaches. An illustrative example of this is the flipped classroom model, where students are required to engage with the lecture material before the class, ensuring they come prepared to discuss it with their peers and the lecturer/tutor. One of the reasons flipped classroom model has gained much attention is because of the possibility to increase student engagement. A study conducted by Zainuddin and Halili (2016), reviewed 20 articles between 2013 and 2015 on the flipped classroom. Their conclusion was that "Analysis of the impacts showed that flipped classroom brought positive impacts toward students' learning activities such as achievement, motivation, engagement, and interaction." (Zainuddin & Halili, 2016, p.1)

Even though the flipped classroom model is very effective, researchers, Diwanji, P., Hinkelmann, K., and Witschel, H. F. (2018), revealed through a student survey in a Business School in Switzerland that only 7% always prepared for the class and nearly 88% students ascribed to lack of time as the main reason students, particularly those who lack sufficient time and/or are slow readers did not prepare. The paper proposes an application based on AI and data analytics to intrinsically motivate students. Therefore, Generative AI could come to the rescue in saving time in pre-reading very effectively and efficiently and Generative AI developed especially for personalised learning may even enhance it further. The students can request Generative AI to summarise and carry out an interactive session with further probing on the content. They can learn, critically analyse, research further and come prepared for the class with content to contribute and/or discuss with other students or the tutor. Diwanji et al., (2018) looked further into how AI Chat Bots (on the e-learning platform) motivated students to complete their pre-class material and help provide educators with data analysis of student pre-class engagement. Generative AI can enhance the performance of the AI Chat Bots and thus may create more engagement with the pre-class material.

Bockmier-Sommers and co-researchers (2017) brought a multidisciplinary lens to their study, incorporating insights from psychology, educational theory and technology and explored how teacher-student interactions influence student engagement. It states how Rogers' Person-Centred Theory suggests core conditions of empathy, genuineness, and unconditional positive regard can create an environment conducive to learning, where students feel emotionally sage and more engaged. Educators that lack empathy can use Generative AI to guide them on how to communicate with more empathy. Generative AI can be used to ask how to say something in a respectful way in the class or in an email. Words alone will not be sufficient as this would have to be come intrinsically, but Generative AI can help improve these skills by interacting and asking how to treat students in various situations.

Empathy: The following are several prompt examples that can be used with Generative AI to assist with more empathic reactions/engagements:

Prompt ChatGPT: I am a university lecturer. Suggest ways I can show empathy towards my students and that I care about them.

Generated Response: ChatGPT (OpenAI, 2023e)

It's wonderful that you want to show empathy and care for your students as a university lecturer. Demonstrating empathy can create a more supportive and engaging learning environment. Here are some ways you can do that: [12 tips are given]

Prompt ChatGPT (continued): There is a student that always disrupts the lecture and distracts other students. How can I solve the issue and respond to the student with empathy?

Generated Response: Dealing with a disruptive student while maintaining empathy is essential for creating a positive and inclusive learning environment. Here are steps you can take to address the issue: [...]

Prompt ChatGPT Continued: Do you recommend that I stop the lecture and walk over to the student? This may embarrass the student. Suggest what I can say over the mic without walking over.

Generate response: [...]

Prompt ChatGPT continued: Draft an email to the student to meet me to discuss the issue.

Generated response: [...]

More advice on how to tackle with disruptive students with respect and empathy, whether to approach them in the lecture or not and a polite email to request the student to meet for further discussion is generated (see reference for the link to the entire chat).

Lastly, a survey of 266 Hungarian University students surveyed indicated a correlation between teacher enthusiasm and self-reported academic integrity breaches, though underlying reasons is yet to be analysed (Gábor Orosz et al., 2015). Generative AI may add to teacher enthusiasm because of potential to develop creative ways to teach, ideas for games for learning, having a virtual teaching assistant, generating fun and engaging feedback on assessments and excitement about possibilities of increased student engagement. Furthermore, a survey of 710 students and 31 teachers from a French speaking college in Canada found that educator autonomy-supportive practices had their students self-reported more honesty and less premediated cheating, less likelihood and magnitude of cheating (Bureau et al 2021). Autonomy-supportive practice is to give students as much control as possible of their learning and offer trust (Bureau et al 2021). Generative AI can therefore be used to provide this opportunity to students in an effective way, once again to address potential root causes of academic integrity breaches.

CLARIFICATION OF ASSESSMENT AND CONTENT

Students that do not fully understand the course content or the specifics of a given assignment (in multiple ways) can resort to academic dishonesty. In addition to this aspect being identified by an Australian survey of almost 1000 higher education students (Bretag et al., 2019), this was also highlighted by North-West University humanities professors Anne H. Verhoef's and Yolandi M. Coetser's phenomenological research (2021). Verhoef and Coetser research was obtained through a forum held directly with university students and is well expressed by one of the student's comments "when they [students] don't understand the work, they tend to ask friends for help, and this can often lead to cheating" (2021, p. 5). A literature review by Australian and American researchers Rebecca Awdry and Bob Ives, in their article "International Predictors of Contract Cheating in Higher Education" also identified a lack of understanding of the topic as a reason why students commit academic dishonesty (2022).

Lack of understanding can occur when students simply don't comprehend the content to be learned, as Verhoef and Yolandi study expressed that "Academic inexperience seems to be a telling reason why students resort to dishonesty" (2021, p.6). Additionally, psychology and neuroscience researchers from the University of St Andrews, Scotland, identified that "lack of understanding of what constitutes academic misconduct" can be a major reason why some students commit academic dishonesty (Miles et al., 2022).

Multiple research has shown that use of Generative AI technology can be used to help students across different fields better comprehend instructional material (Liu & Ma, 2023; Qureshi, 2023; Rodrigues Vasconcelos & dos Santos, 2023; Shoufan, 2023). This can be accomplished in many ways in that use of Generative AI such as ChatGPT, Microsoft Bing Chat, or Google Bard is very flexible and capable. One powerful technique is the implementation of scaffolding.

Scaffolding, dealing with the instructional design concept of supportive mechanisms/processes/materials to help students comprehend, is an important instructional method that AI can help facilitate. Some examples of scaffolding include practice worksheets, assistive handouts that help students follow along with a presentation and then fill in key portions to important notes about the topic, practice quizzes/tests, and simulations so that students can go over the material or learning even as many times as needed.

A well-formed prompt, to be used with a Generative AI, can help with each of the scaffolding examples presented.

Practice Worksheet:

Prompt ChatGPT: Please assume the role of an intro to college algebra mathematics instructor. Create a worksheet for my students that have 12 math problems for them to complete that deals with absolute value and polynomial functions.

Generated Response: ChatGPT (OpenAI, 2023f):

Certainly! Here's a worksheet with 12 problems covering absolute value and polynomial functions for your students:

Worksheet: Absolute Value and Polynomial Functions

Problem 1: Absolute Value Basics

Simplify the following absolute value expressions:

$|3x-7|$

$|2-4y|$

Problem 2: Absolute Value Inequalities

Solve the following absolute value inequalities:

$|2x-5|<3$

$|3y+1|\geq 7$

Problem 3: Absolute Value Equations

Solve the following absolute value equations:

$|4x-3|=9$

$|2y+6|=-8$

More math problems provided by the Generative AI (see reference for link to the entire chat)

Prompt ChatGPT: Please assume the role of a university philosophy instructor. Create an assistive 1- page handout dealing with Plato's Allegory of the Cave with the main outline in bold, but leave some of the key words/phrases of the subsections out so that students will have to fill it in (fill in the blank) as they follow along with the presentation. This is to help students pay attention and to go through the process of identifying the key information to learn the material.

Generated Response: ChatGPT (OpenAI, 2023g):

Understanding Plato's Allegory of the Cave

Introduction:

- Plato's Allegory of the Cave is a metaphorical story found in Book VII of "The Republic."
- It explores the nature of reality, knowledge, and the journey of enlightenment.

An additional 1-page hand-out is generated (see reference for link to the entire chat).

Practice Quizzes/Tests

Prompt Bing: Assume the role of a university history teacher. Create a 10 question practice quiz on the American revolution. Include some multiple choice, true/false, and fill in the blank questions.

Generated Response: Bing Chat (Microsoft, 2023a):

Here is a 10-question practice quiz on the American Revolution:

1. Who was the first president of the United States?

    A. George Washington
    B. Thomas Jefferson
    C. John Adams
    D. Benjamin Franklin

Nine other quiz questions were generated (see reference for link to the entire chat).

Prompt ChatGPT: Assume the role of a high school Principal who is interviewing me for the position of a high school English teacher at a prominent high school. Please ask me one interview question at a time, and wait for my response before asking the next one. After you ask me five questions, give me feedback on how well I answered the questions and tell me if you would hire me.

Generated Response: ChatGPT (OpenAI, 2023h)

Of course, I'd be happy to conduct this mock interview with you. Let's begin.

1. Could you please tell me about your experience and background in teaching English at the high school level?

Subsequent questions would then follow after student's input.

In addition to the use of Generative AI as a mechanism to help students understand content. It can also be used in different ways to help students understand the concept of academic integrity itself.

Generative AI as a Discussion Point

The Generative AI and reality of Generative AI itself could be used as a discussion starting point to talk about what Generative AI is, policies surrounding Generative AI use, how Generative AI can be used to help with teaching and learning, as well as how someone could use Generative AI in an academically dishonest way. As an example, the American University of Armenia has a policy on AI use within its Students Code of Ethics that states,

Cheating. Cheating includes but is not limited to: 6.4.2.1. using or referring to notes, books, devices or other sources of information, including advanced Artificial Intelligence (AI) tools, such as ChatGPT, in completing an Academic Evaluation or Assignment, when such use has not been expressly allowed by the faculty member who is conducting the examination. (AUA, 2023, para. 6.4.2.1)

By discussing the Generative AI policy with students, they will gain a better understanding of what is allowed at the educational institution. Faculty can additionally go over do's and don't regarding how AI would be used in the course as well as other aspects of academic misconduct.

AI can also be used to create scenarios with associated questions and answers for students to answer so that they can gain greater clarification, knowledge, and even experience regarding what consists of an academic integrity breach and how to avoid it.

Prompt Bard: Create a scenario regarding a university student and academic misconduct. Please present the scenario and ask me questions about it so that I can better understand what academic dishonesty is and how I can best avoid it.

Generated Response: Bard (Google, 2023a):

Scenario:

Sarah is a university student who is struggling in her economics class. She has a lot of other commitments, and she doesn't have enough time to study as much as she would like. One day, she's feeling particularly overwhelmed, and she decides to cheat on her upcoming exam. She finds a copy of the exam online and memorises the answers.

On the day of the exam, Sarah sits down and looks at the questions. She knows all of the answers, and she easily finishes the exam. She's relieved that she cheated and that she doesn't have to worry about failing the class.

Questions:

- Do you think Sarah's actions constitute academic dishonesty?
- Why or why not?
- What are some other examples of academic dishonesty?
- What are the consequences of academic dishonesty?
- How can students best avoid academic dishonesty?

Answers also given to the scenario questions, generated (see reference for link to the entire chat).

AI's increasing capabilities and flexibility allows it to be a uniquely effective tool to help address and prevent issues regarding a lack of understanding of assessments and content which can lead to academic dishonesty.

POOR TIME MANAGEMENT AND PROCRASTINATION

The issue of poor time management skills and procrastination is another major reason given regarding why students resort to some form of cheating. A research study, presented at the World Conference on Educational Sciences, once again found this aspect to be a major reason for breaches of academic integrity,

Furthermore, the current study, similar to the study of Beasley (2014) and the results of others (Comas-Forgas & Sureda-Negre, 2010; Heckler & Forde, 2014; Honsy & Fatima, 2014) have found that students lack time management skills, and this is often considered the reason why students engage in academic dishonesty. (Lepp, 2017, p. 49)

Additionally, research conducted on higher education engineering students found that "The students, however, considered the lack of time to complete assignments or study for exams as the main reason for violating academic integrity regulations" (Tabsh et al., 2017, p. 387). Other, more modern research and reports have identified similar findings with time management and procrastination as causes of cheating (Grenness, 2022; Murdiana et al., 2023; Mukasa et al., 2023; Shepherd, 2022).

Using AI can greatly assist students with issues of poor time management and procrastination in multiple ways. AI can provide direct instruction to students to help them learn about different aspects regarding time management and how to overcome procrastination, it can assist with creating tools to assist with time management, and AI can help faculty learn about different ways that they can also help students overcome issues with time management and procrastination.

AI Direct Instruction to Students

Prompt Bard: Please assume the role of a professional university life coach. Help me learn about different aspects regarding improving my time management and how to overcome procrastination in order to be the best university student possible.

Generated Response: Bard (Google, 2023b):

As a professional university life coach, I can help you learn about different aspects regarding improving your time management and how to overcome procrastination in order to be the best university student possible.

Time management is the process of planning and controlling how you spend your time. It is an essential skill for university students, who often have to juggle multiple assignments, deadlines, and extracurricular activities.

More explanation on time management along with tips and a conclusion were generated (see reference for link to the entire chat).

Help With Time Management

Prompt ChatGPT: Please assume the role of a professional life coach. I have problems with time management and procrastination. Help me create a full weekly schedule so that I can succeed in getting my university degree. I go to sleep at 11:00 PM and wake up at 7:30 AM. I have two classes every Monday, Wednesday, and Friday, my Advanced marketing class from 10:00 AM until 10:50 AM, and College Algebra from 2:00 PM until 2:50 PM. I have two classes every Tuesday and Thursday, my Professional Communication class from 12:00 PM until 1:15 PM, and my Creative Writing class from 2:00 PM until 3:15 PM. I also work Monday through Friday from 4 PM until 10 PM. Make a schedule that includes time for classes, studying, assignments, healthy exercising (before breakfast), and other activities. Be sure to add in breaks and time for relaxation.

Generated Response: ChatGPT (OpenAI, 2023i):

[...]

A full detailed schedule each day is provided by the generative AI (see reference for link to the entire chat)

This can be taken even deeper by asking the AI for further assistance.

Prompt continued ChatGPT: What additional tools can you make for me to assist me with time management and/or procrastination?

Generated Response:

Certainly! Here are some additional tools and techniques that can help you with time management and overcoming procrastination:

A listing of 15 tools to help with is issue is provided by the generative AI (see reference for link to the entire chat)

It is important to remember that interacting with Generative AI is a conversation, so again, the interaction can go even deeper for further assistance:

Prompt continued ChatGPT: I like the idea of Self-Reflection and Goal Setting Worksheets. Please create these worksheets for me.

Generated Response: […]

Two full worksheets are provided by the generative AI (see reference for link to the entire chat)

How to help students: AI can also be used by instructors to learn about different ways that they can directly help students overcome issues with time management and procrastination.

Prompt Llama 2.0: Teach me what I can do as a professor to directly help students overcome issues with time management and procrastination.

Generated Response: Llama 2.0 (Meta, 2023):

As a professor, there are several ways you can help your students overcome issues with time management and procrastination. Here are some suggestions:

A listing of 10 different courses of action are provided by the generative AI (see reference for link to the entire chat)

Many students lack sufficient time management skills and have issues with procrastination. This can lead to students resorting to actions that can lead to breaches of academic integrity. Yet through the use of Generative AI, students can not only learn about ways to improve these issues, but can also use the AI to directly help them via different tools, such as the creation of an actual schedule or worksheets to help them with time management and procrastination.

PERCEPTION OF EASY ACCESS TO CHEATING OPPORTUNITIES

Many students reported that they were drawn to contract cheating due to the perception that opportunities to cheat were abundant and the risks of getting caught were low (Bretag et al., 2018). Factors contributing to this perception included the ease of accessing cheating services, affordability or even free availability, and the belief that there were insufficient penalties for such actions.

Free and easy access to Generative AI will contribute to the perception of easy access to cheating opportunities. KMPG Canada (2023) surveyed 5140 students aged 18 and over. More than 52% of students aged 18+ in Canada are using Generative AI to help them in their schoolwork and 68% saying their grades improved, despite 60% of them believing that it was cheating (KMPG Canada, 2023). Perception of easy access to cheating opportunities that were identified in Bretag and researchers was regards to contract cheating (2018). However, this can also be applied to Generative AI which is even easier to access to because it is free and has quicker response time. Tertiary Education Quality and Standards Agency (TEQSA), Australia's regulator for Higher Education, advises that substantial use of content generated by AI be considered as Contract Cheating (TEQSA, 2023). The opportunities for students to engage in "outsourcing" the completion of assessments has only gotten easier. CNBC news recently reported that the popular Chegg homework-help website recently experienced a drop of more than 50%

in the value of its company's shares, which may also be an indication of students using Generative AI to outsource this help (Min, 2023).

Free and easy access to Generative AI could be perceived as an invitation to cheat in that students who had no intention of cheating might feel tempted if the ease of access means their peers are likely doing the same. However, if educators integrate Generative AI into their teaching, they can use this as an opportunity to not only highlight but also actively discuss the institution's academic integrity policies and procedures. Educators can clarify that using generated content and presenting it as one's own is a breach of academic standards, and they can specify the acceptable uses of Generative AI in assessments. Importantly, peer-to-peer discussions can serve as a powerful tool for reinforcing these messages. High-achieving students who are intrinsically motivated often find it unfair when others cheat, and their perspectives can lead to meaningful conversations about the reasons for maintaining academic integrity. Coming from peers, these discussions are likely to have a greater influence on those who might be tempted to cheat.

As the use of Generative AI in the classroom, brings an opportunity for discussions, the educator can use the tools to generate engaging discipline or even subject specific scenarios.

PROVIDING MEANINGFUL AND TIMELY FEEDBACK ON ASSESSMENTS

Students that don't receive feedback that is both meaningful and timely may resort to academic dishonesty. This phenomenon has been identified across multiple higher education domains such as within business (Von Dran et al., 2001), health sciences (Poulos & Mahony, 2008), as well as generally within higher education (Bozok, 2023; Bretag et al., 2019; Getachew et al., 2020; Goodboy, 2011). Similarly, author and academic, Cris Tovani, in an Educational Leadership article titled How We Drive Students to Cheat expressed that "Students who cheat lack something. Usually they lack a sense of the relevance of what they're learning, or know-how, or timely feedback" (2014, p. 1). Additionally, qualitative interview research on undergraduate students have found that not having this type of usable feedback can lead to a reduction in student motivation which can also lead to academic dishonesty (Lepp, 2017).

Generative AI can assist with feedback in multiple ways to help the students obtain comments or critiques regarding their ideas, writing, or work. This can be done by students interacting with the AI directly or by faculty working with AI as a tool to help in providing feedback to the student.

Students Directly Obtaining AI Feedback

Students can receive meaningful and timely feedback on their written assignments at any time from an AI. This is especially valuable when they complete a rough draft or final version of an essay in the middle of the night and don't have a friend or family member to help provide feedback or review it as a second pair of eyes. Additionally, there may not be enough time for the document to be reviewed by an instructor due to timing/completion issues. In this case a student could provide some or all of their written essay to obtain appropriate feedback. "Appropriate" is the key word in this example in that if a student has not developed a suitable level of AI Literacy, then they could very easily accidentally commit academic dishonesty.

Prompt ChatGPT: help me improve the following essay.

Generated Response: ChatGPT (OpenAI, 2023j):

Of course, I'd be happy to help you improve your essay. Please provide the essay or the specific parts you'd like assistance with, and let me know what kind of feedback or suggestions you're looking for.

[essay provided]

You've presented a well-structured argument with strong citations to support your points. However, I do have a few suggestions to help improve the flow and clarity of your essay:

[…]

[The essay was then completely rewritten by the AI to include the indicated suggestions for overall improvement]

In this realistic example the student would have fed in their essay to the AI and the AI would have provided some general feedback, but would have also completely given a fully rewritten and improved essay to the student, providing a very tempting option to commit academic dishonesty. Instead, instructors need to help students use the AI appropriately when using it to obtain feedback by explaining how it works and by offering more advanced prompts. To effectively use the AI in providing generalised feedback, the following advanced prompt can be used:

Prompt ChatGPT: Please act as a professional university writing tutor. Use your college-level abilities to provide useful feedback on how to improve writing composition. Use your advanced experience in higher education and knowledge dealing with effective writing techniques to suggest specific ways to best express thoughts and ideas through writing. Do not provide a revised version of the writing provided. Do you understand?

Notice how a more advanced prompt formula is used to give the AI context, a role to play, and more specific instructions. The AI is specifically told "Do not provide a revised version of the writing provided" in order to help ensure that academic integrity is not violated. For assignments/situations where the students need more advanced feedback, the following prompt can be provided:

Prompt ChatGPT: Please act as a professional university writing tutor. Use your college-level abilities to provide useful feedback on how to improve the essay that I will provide. Give me specific guidance on the following rubric variables for this assignment: organisation (thesis and main points properly presented), academic integrity (proper citations and quotations used), flow (essay is well structured with transitions sentences and logical delivery of content), and language and mechanics (proper sentence structure, grammar, and vocabulary used). Be sure to highlight any issue that needs to be improved. Do not provide a revised version of the writing provided. Do you understand?

Generated Response: ChatGPT (OpenAI, 2023k):

Yes, I understand. Please provide the essay you would like me to review, and I will provide feedback based on the rubric variables you mentioned: organisation, academic integrity, flow, and language and mechanics.

Prompt continued ChatGPT*: [essay provided]*

Generated response: Thank you for providing your essay. I'll go through it and offer feedback based on the rubric variables you mentioned. […]

Notice the differences between the two prompts and how the second more advanced prompt provides the student with greater detail and personalisation, specific to the essay and the rubric that will eventually be used to grade the assignment.

Faculty Using AI to Assist With Student Feedback

To help faculty provide feedback to students, AI could be used to help the instructors learn/know about the best way to provide actionable feedback to students.

Prompt Bard: I am a university professor. Tell me the best ways that I should be providing timely and actionable feedback to my students.

An instructor could also use an AI to help articulate proper verbiage to present feedback in a more friendly and usable tone to help ensure that student will accept and use the feedback provided.

Prompt continued Bard: Please act as a university professor. Give me specific guidance on how I can best provide feedback in a more friendly and usable tone so that my student will accept the feedback and improve. How can I best express to my student that they did very poorly on an essay assignment? They did poorly on all parts of the rubric: organisation (thesis and main points properly presented), academic integrity (proper citations and quotations used), flow (essay is well structured with transitions sentences and logical delivery of content), and language and mechanics (proper sentence structure, grammar, and vocabulary used).

Generated Response: Bard (Google, 2023c):

Specific guidance and detailed examples are generated (see reference for link to the entire chat).

Educators to generate feedback: In a similar manner to the example of how a student could use AI on their own to obtain feedback, faculty can also use AI in this way to obtain feedback on the students writing. It is important to note that faculty must also develop AI Literacy, not only to know about AI and how to use it, but to critically evaluate AI processes and responses and to ensure ethical utilisation such as to protect students' information (Anders, 2023). Students' names, other personal information, or sensitive writings should never be fed into an AI. Additionally, faculty should make sure that they are using an AI that specifically states that they will not be reselling any submitted user content.

Faculty could submit a portion of or a complete assignment along with the rubric to obtain direct feedback on the students' writing. This would save a lot of time but additional aspects need to be considered. In addition to ensuring protection of students data, faculty should also consider what might be lost if they are partially or fully removed from the evaluation/review of students' writings. They may not completely know the students or their development if they are not fully engaged in the writing evaluation process. Additionally, Generative AI can produce false (hallucinated) responses and could give incorrect feedback (Fui-Hoon Nah et al., 2023; OpenAI, 2023j).

Given the expressed issues of concern, it is recommended that faculty's use of AI to create direct student feedback be used only as an assistive tool and not as a replacement for instructor review. Time would still be saved by creating a once over review and by providing an initial framework for the feedback to be provided for the student, but in this way an instructor would still review the findings, make any needed modifications, and be more aware of the student's progress/development.

In this case the type of advanced prompt used would be something like this:

Prompt Bard: Please act as a professional university professor. Use your college-level abilities to provide useful feedback on how to improve the essay that I will provide. Give me specific guidance on the following rubric variables for this assignment: organisation (thesis and main points properly presented), academic integrity (proper citations and quotations used), flow (essay is well structured with transitions sentences and logical delivery of content), and language and mechanics (proper sentence structure, grammar, and vocabulary used). Be sure to highlight any issue that needs to be improved. Do not provide a revised version of the writing provided. Do you understand?

Additionally, note that using AI in this way is never an all or nothing. An instructor could use the AI to assist with providing feedback for only a portion of the essays, maybe just for the intros, or the conclusions. The instructor could also use the AI to assist with "tricky" essays where an additional point of view might assist the instructor with their overall assessment and feedback.

By using AI as an assistive tool in the different ways presented, meaningful and timely feedback on assessment can be accomplished. This will then help students to understand what they need to do to improve and help motivate them to not only succeed, but to avoid the temptation of violating academic integrity.

SUMMARY

There are many important issues and aspects regarding why students breach academic integrity, yet by properly using Generative AI, these issues can be addressed and better mitigated. The preceding chapter identified some of the main causes of these academic integrity issues as self-reported by students and presented detailed instructions and usable examples so that faculty at any educational institution can harness the capabilities of AI to help address this issue. This topic helps to illustrate that AI Literacy is an important issue that both instructors and students must develop to use Generative AI effectively and ethically to improve teaching and learning without breaching academic integrity. It is important for institutions to invest in professional development for educators who may be hesitant or lack confidence in using Generative AI for various reasons. In fact, the absence of its use by educators could potentially lead to an increase in breaches of academic integrity. This is because the aforementioned methods to support students may not be employed, especially with the surge in freely available Generative AI tools. Additionally, such breaches may go undetected as educators might not be aware of the capabilities of these tools. Finally, educators need to be enthusiastic about embracing Generative AI and see how the very tool that was feared for potential academic integrity breaches could indeed be used to address root causes of academic integrity breaches. As a result of Generative AI, educators can save time, create an engaging teaching and learning environment, and have a teaching assistant which can support students because they cannot be with students 24/7.

CONTRIBUTIONS

Nadia Koren: Students with English as an Additional Language, Dissatisfaction with Teaching and Learning Environment, Perception of Easy Access to Cheating Opportunities.

Brent A. Anders: Clarification of Assessment and Content, Poor Time Management and Procrastination, Providing Meaningful and Timely Feedback on Assessments,

REFERENCES

University of Melbourne. (n.d.). *Advice for students regarding translation and editing tools.* Universiyt of Melbourne. https://academicintegrity.unimelb.edu.au/plagiarism-and-collusion/advice-for-students-regarding-translation-and-editing-tools

Anders, B. (2023). *The AI literacy imperative: Empowering instructors & students*. Sovorel.

AUA. (2023). *Student code of ethics*. American University of Armenia. https://policies.aua.am/policy/10

Australian Government. (2022). *Literacy and access | Style Manual*. Australian Government. Www.stylemanual.gov.auCommonwealth of Australia. https://www.stylemanual.gov.au/accessible-and-inclusive-content/literacy-and-access

Awdry, R., & Ives, B. (2022). International predictors of contract cheating in higher education. *Journal of Academic Ethics*, 1–20. PMID:35431710

Banerji, O. (2023, August 3). *How schools are coaching — or coaxing — teachers to use ChatGPT*. EdSurge. https://www.edsurge.com/news/2023-08-03-how-schools-are-coaching-or-coaxing-teachers-to-use-chatgpt

Bockmier-Sommers, D., Chen, C., & Martsch, M. (2017). Student Perception of Teacher Empathy, High Regard and Genuineness and the Impact on Student Engagement. *E-Mentor*, *2017*(70(3)), 66–72. doi:10.15219/em70.1310

Bozok, D. (2023). Attitudes of students towards violations of academic integrity in online English courses. *Journal of Learning and Teaching in Digital Age*, *8*(2), 209–220. doi:10.53850/joltida.1177949

Bretag, T., Harper, R., Burton, M., Ellis, C., Newton, P., Rozenberg, P., Saddiqui, S., & van Haeringen, K. (2018). Contract cheating: A survey of Australian university students. *Studies in Higher Education*, 1–20.

Bretag, T., Harper, R., Rundle, K., Newton, P. M., Ellis, C., Saddiqui, S., & van Haeringen, K. (2019). Contract cheating in Australian higher education: A comparison of non-university higher education providers and universities. *Assessment & Evaluation in Higher Education*, 1–15. doi:10.1080/02602938.2019.1614146

Bureau, J. S., Gareau, A., Guay, F., & Mageau, G. A. (2021). Investigating how autonomy-supportive teaching moderates the relation between student honesty and premeditated cheating. *The British Journal of Educational Psychology*, *92*(1), 175–193. doi:10.1111/bjep.12444 PMID:34236697

Cassidy, C. (2023, October 6). Artificial intelligence such as ChatGPT to be allowed in Australian schools from 2024. *The Guardian*. https://www.theguardian.com/australia-news/2023/oct/06/chatgpt-ai-allowed-australian-schools-2024

Chen, K., Monrouxe, L. V., Lu, Y., Jenq, C., Chang, Y., Chang, Y., & Chai, P. Y. (2018). Academic outcomes of flipped classroom learning: A meta-analysis. *Medical Education*, *52*(9), 910–924. doi:10.1111/medu.13616 PMID:29943399

Diwanji, P., Knut, H., & Hans, F. W. (2018, March). *Enhance classroom preparation for flipped classroom using AI and analytics*. 20th International Conference on Enterprise Information Systems (ICEIS 2018) [Presentation], Madeira, Portugal. https://pdfs.semanticscholar.org/2a4a/4b44c369b872b4f62915f5df56acba188632.pdf

Duffy, C. (2023, May 25). ChatGPT's class divide: Are public school bans on the AI tool giving private school kids an unfair edge? *ABC News*. https://www.abc.net.au/news/2023-05-26/artificial-intelligence-chatgpt-classrooms-schools/102356926

Dukewich, K., & Larsen, C. (2023). *How are faculty reacting to ChatGPT?* Curriculum Research Collaborative. https://files.eric.ed.gov/fulltext/ED627303.pdf

Getachew, A., Tekle, T., & Bayisa, K. (2020). Nature and causes of students' misbehaviour as perceived by Ambo University teachers. *Journal of Social Sciences*, *48*(2), 762–771.

Goodboy, A. K. (2011). Instructional dissent in the college classroom. *Communication Education*, *60*(3), 296–313. doi:10.1080/03634523.2010.537756

Google. (2023). *Googe Bard [AI model].* Google. https://g.co/bard/share/62a1ab50ef60

Google. (2023a). *Google Bard [AI model].* Google. https://g.co/bard/share/81836b07a821

Google. (2023b). *Google Bard [AI model].* Google. https://g.co/bard/share/ba507c1d022a

Google. (2023c). *Google Bard [AI model].* Google. https://g.co/bard/share/cc37d8ff0536

KMPG Canada. (2023, August 30). *Despite popularity, six in 10 students consider generative AI cheating - KPMG Canada.* KMPG. https://kpmg.com/ca/en/home/media/press-releases/2023/08/six-in-ten-students-consider-generative-ai-cheating.html

Lepp, L. (2017). Undergraduate students' views on academic dishonesty. *New Trends and Issues Proceedings on Humanities and Social Sciences*, *3*(1), 41–51. doi:10.18844/prosoc.v3i1.1728

Liu, G., & Ma, C. (2023). Measuring EFL learners' use of ChatGPT in informal digital learning of English based on the technology acceptance model. *Innovation in Language Learning and Teaching*, 1–14. doi:10.1080/17501229.2023.2240316

Microsoft. (2023). *Bing Chat* [AI model]. The New Bing.

Microsoft. (2023a). *Bing Chat* [AI model]. The New Bing.

Miles, P. J., Campbell, M., & Ruxton, G. D. (2022). Why students cheat and how understanding this can help reduce the frequency of academic misconduct in higher education: A literature review. *Journal of Undergraduate Neuroscience Education*, *20*(2), A150–A159.

Min, S. (2023, May 2). *Chegg shares drop more than 40% after company says ChatGPT is killing its business.* CNBC. https://www.cnbc.com/2023/05/02/chegg-drops-more-than-40percent-after-saying-chatgpt-is-killing-its-business.html

Muscanell, N., & Robert, J. (2023, February 14). *EDUCAUSE quickpoll results: Did ChatGPT write this report?* Educause. https://er.educause.edu/articles/2023/2/educause-quickpoll-results-did-chatgpt-write-this-report

Nolan, B. (2023, January 30). *Here are the schools and colleges that have banned the use of ChatGPT over plagiarism and misinformation fears.* Business Insider. https://www.businessinsider.com/chatgpt-schools-colleges-ban-plagiarism-misinformation-education-2023-1

Open A. I. (2023). ChatGPT (Aug 3 version) [Large language model]. https://chat.openai.com/share/2004efe2-9066-4606-908c-c4d8e7460eac

Open A. I. (2023a). ChatGPT (Aug 3 version) [Large language model]. https://chat.openai.com/share/a70f7367-26be-4905-8c28-817783dae23a

Open A. I. (2023b). ChatGPT (Aug 3 version) [Large language model]. https://chat.openai.com/share/84ce0eca-1e42-4746-92c2-484b17c668d2

Open A. I. (2023c). ChatGPT (Aug 3 version) [Large language model]. https://apps.pple.com/us/app/chatgpt/id6448311069

Open A. I. (2023d). ChatGPT (Sept 25 version) [Large language model]. https://chat.openai.com/share/6741a04e-16c1-4509-9724-b54d204709f0

Open A. I. (2023e). ChatGPT (Sept 25 version). [Large language model]. https://chat.openai.com/share/973ce815-766e-438d-b398-4fa8a2dc91bf

Open A. I. (2023f). ChatGPT (Sept 25 version). [Large language model]. https://chat.openai.com/share/532900f0-26c5-4050-90a6-3fddd9e8f347

Open A. I. (2023g). ChatGPT (Sept 25 version). [Large language model]. https://chat.openai.com/share/973ce815-766e-438d-b398-4fa8a2dc91bf

Open A. I. (2023h). ChatGPT (Sept 25 version). [Large language model]. https://chat.openai.com/share/463aa99f-75bb-4dd3-b779-9e435c2715a7

Open A. I. (2023i). ChatGPT (Sept 25 version). [Large language model]. https://chat.openai.com/share/e83bf50a-899d-4403-b962-8cc1b0648d67

Open A. I. (2023j). ChatGPT (Sept 25 version). [Large language model]. https://chat.openai.com

Open A. I. (2023k). ChatGPT (Sept 25 version). [Large language model]. https://chat.openai.com

Open A. I. (2023l). *GPT-4 technical report*. arXiv, 2303-08774. https://cdn.openai.com/papers/gpt-4.pdf

Orosz, Gã., TÃ3th-KirÃ¡ly, I., BÅ‘the, B., Kusztor, A., KovÃ¡cs, Z. Ã., & JÃ¡nvÃ¡ri, M. (. (2015). Teacher enthusiasm: A potential cure of academic cheating. *Frontiers in Psychology*, *6*. doi:10.3389/fpsyg.2015.00318 PMID:25873903

Orosz, G., Tóth-Király, I., Bőthe, B., Kusztor, A., Kovács, Z., & Jánvári, M. (2015). Teacher enthusiasm: A potential cure of academic cheating. *Frontiers in Psychology*, *6*. doi:10.3389/fpsyg.2015.00318 PMID:25873903

Ortiz, S. (2023, September 15). *What is ChatGPT and why does it matter? Here's what you need to know.* ZDNet. https://www.zdnet.com/article/what-is-chatgpt-and-why-does-it-matter-heres-everything-you-need-to-know/

Poulos, A., & Mahony, M. J. (2008). Effectiveness of feedback: The students' perspective. *Assessment & Evaluation in Higher Education*, *33*(2), 143–154. doi:10.1080/02602930601127869

Qureshi, B. (2023). *Exploring the use of chatgpt as a tool for learning and assessment in undergraduate computer science curriculum: Opportunities and challenges*. arXiv preprint arXiv:2304.11214.

Reed, T. (2023, May 1). ChatGPT might show more empathy than docs, study finds. *AXIOS*. https://www.axios.com/2023/05/01/chatgpt-empathy-better-than-doctors

Rodrigues Vasconcelos, M. A., & P dos Santos, R. (2023). Enhancing STEM learning with ChatGPT and Bing Chat as objects-to-think-with: A Case Study. Rodrigues Vasconcelos, Marco Antonio and P dos Santos, Renato, *Enhancing STEM Learning with ChatGPT and Bing Chat as Objects-to-Think-With: A Case Study* (May 1, 2023). *SSRN*. . doi:10.2139/ssrn.4434060

Russell, B., Barron, C., Kim, H., & Jang, E. E. (2022). A mixed-method investigation into international university students' experience with academic language demands. *Frontiers in Education*, *7*, 934692. doi:10.3389/feduc.2022.934692

Shoufan, A. (2023). Exploring students' perceptions of CHATGPT: Thematic analysis and follow-up survey. *IEEE Access : Practical Innovations, Open Solutions*, *11*, 38805–38818. doi:10.1109/ACCESS.2023.3268224

Tertiary Education & Quality and Standards Agency. (2023, January 18). *Sector update: Maintaining up to date academic integrity policies and procedures | Tertiary Education Quality and Standards Agency*. Teqsa.gov.au.

Tovani, C. (2014). How we drive students to cheat. *Educational Leadership*, *71*(6), 50–53.

Verhoef, A. H., & Coetser, Y. M. (2021). Academic integrity of university students during emergency remote online assessment: An exploration of student voices. *Transformation in Higher Education*, *6*(0), a132. doi:10.4102/the.v6i0.132

Von Dran, G. M., Callahan, E. S., & Taylor, H. V. (2001). Can students' academic integrity be improved? Attitudes and behaviors before and after implementation of an academic integrity policy. *Teaching Business Ethics*, *5*(1), 35–58. doi:10.1023/A:1026551002367

Wylie, A. (2018, February 22). Flesch-Kincaid Grade Level: How hard is it? Master the art of readable writing. *Medium*. https://medium.com/@annwylie/flesch-kincaid-grade-level-how-hard-is-it-ebb0bfcdfa87

Zainuddin, Z., & Halili, S. H. (2016). Flipped Classroom Research and Trends from Different Fields of Study. *International Review of Research in Open and Distance Learning*, *17*(3). doi:10.19173/irrodl.v17i3.2274

Chapter 14
Empowering Students From Assumptions to Knowledge: Making Integrity Everyone's Business

Lynn C. Gribble
https://orcid.org/0000-0002-3012-4798
University of New South Wales, Australia

Janis E. Wardrop
University of New South Wales, Australia

ABSTRACT

The arrival of 'free to access' generative AI platforms in late 2022 has irrevocably changed the educational landscape. Of concern to many is how to uphold academic integrity in assessments ensuring students are able to demonstrate their learning in this new environment where a 'machine' can research and write for you. In this chapter, the authors present a process which is designed to uncover the true nature of the 'work' expected to be performed by students during assessment, which then allows GenAI tools to be knowingly used by students as just another research tool. While it is still early days, changing our understanding that what should be assessed is 'the work' expected of students rather than the 'output' suggests that all is not lost when it comes to academic integrity.

INTRODUCTION

This chapter seeks to support teaching academics with a process to design assessment that addresses some of the integrity concerns that have been raised due to the 'explosion' in access to, and use of, generative forms of artificial intelligence (GenAI) since late 2022. The widespread availability of GenAI has left many in higher education concerned about issues such as the authorship of assessment, academic integrity and the impact on student learning and knowledge acquisition. While GenAI will and does impact other areas of education such as admissions, student support services, research and scholarship, this chapter exclusively considers assessment design and academic integrity concerns. It should be noted that it only

DOI: 10.4018/979-8-3693-0240-8.ch014

briefly touches upon a student view, noting that students may be less aware of when and how they are using GenAI products and the importance of demonstrating their academic ability along with mastery of knowledge remains central to their success at university and beyond.

The reach and impact of artificial intelligence (AI) extends well beyond learning environments, with a growing acceptance that AI will also impact the world of work and society more broadly (Bannon, 2023). In this uncertain environment, fundamental to all these concerns is the question of trust: how do we have trust in who 'did the work' and how 'the work' was undertaken or produced? In higher education, questions such as how do we ensure that students have done the work being submitted for assessment, and therefore have the level of knowledge and skills we are 'certifying' have been keeping many awake at night since the advent of the internet (Hinman, 2002*).* Our discussions with students tell us, they also care about ensuring no student is awarded or rewarded unfairly. This becomes even more important when the course is a means of credentialing professional expertise for example for lawyers, doctors, engineers, and accountants. In academia at the end of 2023, it is GenAI that is attracting most attention because GenAI can produce a largely fully formed output as would be written by a person.

The advent of the internet changed access to information (Fuller and Kuromiya 1981, Luo, et al., 2018); no longer is education (particularly higher education) meant to be the mere transfer of knowledge from expert to student. In part this is a result of the acceptance of employability as a central outcome of a university education (Prokou, 2008; Collini, 2012; Wheaton, 2020). The ideal of 'learning for learning's sake' has been replaced (if it did ever truly exist) with the idea of learning as a means to improve personal futures through access to professional careers, and higher paid jobs. At the same time, the rise of student fees and loans in systems that previously offered 'free' higher education, as well as changing economic conditions more broadly mean that students often approach higher education as a transaction or task to be completed. Competing demands on student's time can create pressure on students to be more strategic learners, trying to minimise efforts while still wanting to maximise outcomes. The broad access to GenAI which is now available requires us to reimagine both teaching and learning approaches as well as associated assessment practices (OECD, 2023a) to measure learning outcomes. This chapter proposes a model to support academics to explore what may be appropriate assessment in the face of GenAI while at the same time informing students of their responsibilities in using such tools.

Academic integrity matters and according to the Australian Tertiary Education Quality and Standards Agency (TEQSA) who both govern and oversee educational standards in Australia, academic integrity is "the expectation that teachers, students, researchers and all members of the academic community act with: honesty, trust, fairness, respect and responsibility" (TEQSA, 2022). The ever-changing landscape means constantly updated resources and in November 2023, Lodge et al. note in TEQSA's "Assessment reform for the age of artificial intelligence" that:

Good assessment design that allows for 'rich portrayals' of student learning is critical. Thus, we take as given that assessment should engage students in learning, provide a partnership between teachers and students, and promote student participation in feedback. These key elements of assessment can then guide how best to consider the role of AI in assessment design.

When academics talk of 'integrity' in student learning and assessment it is often a term used as shorthand to describe whether a student has done the work on their own without assistance. Hence, this chapter recognizes that to design appropriate assessments in the face of GenAI one requires a clear understanding of what learning is being assessed and what academic integrity would look like in that 'space'. The mapping we propose supports changes with practical considerations for the classroom and students in a world where access to GenAI is both ubiquitous but also unequal.

BACKGROUND AND LITERATURE

In order to suggest practical strategies for the classroom and assessment while considering academic integrity, we explore the literature to set a foundation of collective understanding. Commencing with academic integrity, this section also looks at the purpose of assessment, the responsibility of the students in undertaking assessment, the need for both academics and students to understand GenAI relative to the discipline of study, along with resultant issues of authorship, ownership and responsibility, and truth of the generated output.

Academic Integrity

In order to explore academic integrity, the history and evolution of the term must be explored. Originally the term 'academic integrity' focused on the conduct and character of students, however this has shifted over time to include student learning behaviour (Bertram Gallant, 2008). Anderman et al. (2009) categorized cheating four ways: information transfer between individuals; the use of assisting tools; exploitation of weakness; and copying answers or information. In exploring how GenAI is impacting HE, GenAI clearly falls under 'use of assisting tools', as well as it also provides for information transfer although the individual is replaced in this instance by a machine or individuals unknown. Teachers want to know the student 'did' the work and 'can do' the work on their own or as prescribed as a group task. Academic integrity concerns about written assessments focus on students cheating by submitting work that they have had assistance in producing. Using a previous student's work or paying a person to assist or outsourcing the work to another person and submitting it as one's own are all seen as 'fraudulent' practices. It is the academic equal of the legal issue of 'passing off' (representing the good as one's own). While using another student's work is plagiarism, the outsourcing is considered contract cheating and occasionally misnamed as ghost writing such as might be seen used to write a memoir. Such forms of misconduct are also seen as egregious as they are deliberate and seek to deceive. Where the use of GenAI may not necessarily be an act to deceive, students are gaining assistance which if not appropriately acknowledged is an act of deception.

Over the past 20 years, software responses such as those provided by TurnitinÒ and GrammarlyÒ have been able to access large databases of previously submitted and published works providing students and academics alike a visible means of knowing when work was a direct text match or likely plagiarism. In instances of plagiarism, students would often still 'author' the submitted work but do so by cobbling together unattributed extracts from others work. The internet has provided much greater access to not only scholarly works, but also to the work of fellow students across the globe. Platforms such as Course Hero® provide a space to share previously submitted work (coursehero.com, 2023) in exchange to access other's previously submitted work and as such are able to provide 'assistance' to students. The rise of GenAI platforms such as Quillbot®, through their association with Course Hero®, means that the reach of this assistance has grown exponentially, as students now have access to thousands of previously submitted student papers. The platform draws on their textual database and can paraphrase significantly enough to read as original work. This practice also falls under the scrutiny of academic integrity as the student has gained an 'unfair advantage' and is known as 'assignment spinning.'

The issue of academic integrity has long been a concern to the higher education sector. Contract cheating is not new and was first coined by Clarke & Lancaster in 2006. It is defined as "when a student submits work that has been completed for them by a third party" (Harper et al., 2018). Studies (Bretag et al., 2018; see also Bretag et al., 2019; Rigby et al., 2015) suggest between 7 - 9% of students will 'cheat', meaning they will outsource some or all of their assessment items to a third party as a means of gaining a qualification. They are most likely to do so where the risk of being caught or the penalties are low. Beyond such blatant fraudulent practice there is also the concern of unfair advantage. This form of advantage is often considered less egregious and might include accessing another's work and sufficiently changing it to represent original work where clearly there has been advantage gained. It could also be gaining advantage through a well-meaning parent or friend assisting in the development of the assessment item without commercial exchange for the assistance provided (TEQSA, 2023). These two concepts are critical when discussing academic integrity in general and with GenAI in particular as the student remains at responsible for the action.

Technological Support for Assessment

When considering assessment (both formative and summative) the purpose is important. Usually, the task is designed to ensure that a student has met course and/or program learning outcomes. Where graded assessment is used, students are differentiated by levels of attainment in that outcome (OECD, ND). Over the past 15 years, tools freely available in word processors and internet-based document repositories have provided grammar and spell checkers based on natural language processing rules. This has meant that most students should be able to produce written work that is free of spelling errors and largely free of grammar errors. Such tools have also enabled Non-English-Speaking Background or English as a Second Language students and those with neuro diverse needs such as dyslexia to be able to produce written work to an acceptable professional standard. These tools are based upon Machine Learning (ML) rules and these days are considered requisite use rather than optional. The 'norm' has arisen that the acknowledgement of the use of these tools has not been required. As these tools assist 'better' or 'error free' writing, they are seen as extensions to using dictionaries, thesauruses, and an extension of basic language learning. These tools are a type of 'digital editor'. They correct and enhance what has been written. However, slowly and ubiquitously, GenAI has been embedded in places such as GrammarlyGo® and Google Documents® whereby instead of supporting the student to write they suggest what to write. Where previously students were doing the work of curating and producing information, now GenAI can provide a fully formed written output that can meet knowledge output requirements (Kelly et al., 2023).

Student Responsibility in Assessment

The issue of student responsibility with assessment must also be explored in relation to academic integrity and as a bridge to the problem with GenAI use. It is often assumed that students understand their responsibility with assessment (Kwong et al., 2010). However, as stated at the outset, gaining an advantage in any manner lacks integrity, and students may unwittingly accept advice, assistance or more from family or friends. If they are struggling, they may employ an external tutor who does more than support them offering what to write over how to do it. Platforms such as ChatGPT® are being promoted as a similar type of support. A 'digital online tutor' of sorts. However, academe and institutions are concerned as to how students are using this 'digital tutor' and thus it is therefore critical that students understand their responsibility to complete the assessment on their own without assistance unless it is acknowledged. There can be accepted distinctions between the intellectual work to produce the output and the writing, grammar, or other editorial work. For example, the use of editors for large submissions such as PhDs, books and longer papers is widely accepted. Editors play the role of ensuring the work is clear and concise, they are language experts. They may ask clarifying questions, but they are not the content producers. This point highlights the commencement question for all assessments; what is the knowledge over the form, or more simply what is 'the work' that is required for submission?

In the social sciences and humanities, we require students to read broadly, to consult multiple sources and to critically analyse the knowledge and data that is available to them. Students are required to cite these sources as the foundation of their own thinking and the evidence they are drawing on. For time immemorial, some students have looked to find sources that provide easy access to fundamental knowledge, whether that be 'Cliff notes' used in studies of literature, or sites like Wikipedia®. In these instances, students understand they are taking a 'short cut' and hence the norm has been to not disclose their use. However, it should also be noted that such practices often relinquish the responsibility of doing the work in the face of expediency or surface learning. The recent rise of GenAI means that students may equate these tools with these earlier sources of foundational knowledge failing to recognize the advantage GenAI provides as a form of research assistant and therefore not recognize the need to cite it. Further, for students studying in a second or third language, they may see GenAI as a tool to overcome language problems rather than understanding that the ability to produce 'the work' in the required language could be fundamental to meeting the course/ program learning outcomes.

Understanding AI, its Place in Higher Education and the Problems it Poses

To address the concerns of integrity and assessment it is important to explore what AI is, if it has a place in higher education and how the problems it poses might be resolved. As stated, AI has been incorporated in many of the most used software programs (supporting grammar and word choice in word processing and designers in PowerPoint in recent years). It can be difficult for users to recognize where AI is helping. Rarely is the use of these types of tools acknowledged and, more readily it is expected that it will be used and is seen as integral to produce an appropriate and 'professional' standard of work. The ready availability of GenAI has put a writing assistant, a research assistant, and a scribe, front and centre of every student's computer. The easy access to this multifaceted 'assistant,' may, in part, blind students to the real issue of academic integrity. This creates a scenario in which breaches in academic integrity are not specific and purposeful acts to deceive the institution and others as to one's abilities, but rather the result of students normalizing the use of these GenAI 'assistants'.

GenAI goes beyond correcting or supporting the editing of an originally produced piece of work, using both natural language processing and large language models (LLMS) to both produce and create work for and on behalf of the person based on the prompts provided. The recent release of GenAI platforms to the public has enabled a no to low-cost model for producing written work. Given the pressures felt by many students, it is no surprise the use of these platforms and tools can be highly tempting. These LLMs are 'trained' on vast quantities of publicly available data and sources drawn from websites. As it can only use previously produced knowledge GenAI is itself a plagiarist! In the case of Chat GPT3/3.5 it draws on data that was available prior to 2021. Newer models such as ChatGPT4, Bard and Bing have had more recent sources added and are more regularly updated, but they are still not able to generate new knowledge. The NY Times recently considered its works being used as a breach of copyright (Allyn, 2023), no doubt there are more of these suits to come.

A further issue arises in that the much of the data GenAI is trained upon draws from biased and discriminatory information (Alba, 2022). As much information stored on the internet favors a white Anglo-Saxon male perspective, so too does GenAI. At present GenAI platforms are generally limited to publicly available information as opposed to information held behind any type of paywall (such as many academic journals, although Elicit.org does access journal articles). Importantly, with the right prompting, GenAI can provide information and answers drawn from a vast array of sources and many more than any individual student could reasonably be expected to consult in the given timeframe. Students may see these platforms as merely a more modern 'Wikipedia' – a source to consult which has consolidated vast amounts of information into an easy to read and understand form. Therefore, they are also seen as 'somewhat' legitimate sources, meaning that for some, 'consulting' a computer to 'assist' in the development of a paper/presentation etc may not be considered or recognized by the student as fraudulent or gaining unfair advantage.

With good prompt engineering and a critical read of what is produced, ChatGPT has been able to produce work that can pass 'the Bar' (US Legal practicing entrance examinations) (Cassens Weiss, 2023) and the Harvard admissions test (Grassini, 2023). ChatGPT has also been able to successfully earn an MBA! (Terweisch, 2023). Therefore, the time has come when we need to acknowledge that all submitted work, may have been produced with significant input from a GenAI platform. The focus of assessment needs to move beyond the final 'product' to the process of doing the work, applying knowledge, and demonstrating the skills and knowledge use in practical situations.

Issues of Authorship, Ownership and Responsibility, and Truth

When considering the use of GenAI the first issue to arise is authorship. As GenAI moves beyond editorial assistance (suggesting words) to now producing content there is a fundamental question over the integrity of who produced or wrote the assessment. Does the student still have 'authorship' of the work given their agency in prompting 'the machine'? Or is the 'machine' the author, having pulled together vast resources in response to the prompts to produce a textual answer to these prompts? Actually neither: the prompts tell the machine what to find, it finds other people's information and the output is a collection of information it scrapped from various sources. GenAI creatively seeks to provide plausible information based upon its large scrape of publicly available (including published) work.

Courts have already determined that a machine cannot claim ownership or copyright nor a moral right (Arts Law Centre, 2023). It has also been acknowledged that a machine cannot take responsibility for its actions as it does so at the request of a human (although some AI has been producing its own language which we humans do not understand yet). Therefore, the responsibility for what is used and how it is used sits with the GenAI user rather than the GenAI owner such as OpenAI (the owner of ChatGPT). The (human) user is responsible to ensure the technology is used ethically and in a manner that aligns with what is deemed acceptable. Consequently, it would seem, regardless of the use the technology for now, any user must acknowledge the input of GenAI as a source.

Other legal, ethical, and moral issues arise as the information provided has not been attributed and may be more than general knowledge, hence some form of moral right has been infringed. Further, the responsibility in terms of any output used or relied upon may be factually incorrect, biased, or discriminatory will be the responsibility of the user or author not the machine that provided it. For these reasons, in higher education, it is incumbent on the student to acknowledge their use of GenAI as a source when submitting assessments (McAdoo, 2023).

Beyond the problems already mentioned the technology has been programmed to create plausible but not truthful answers. In GenAI this is called the temperature. For example, ChatGPT has this (temperature) parameter set at 0.7. "The default setting of OpenAI's ChatGPT creativity level aims to strike a balance between providing helpful and informative responses while also introducing a moderate level of creativity and novelty. Therefore, while the plausibility factor means what it produces could be true, and sounds true, any critical thinking applied to most AI answers will highlight generative AI's flaws." (Gribble and Wardrop 2023). If this were research, this level of confidence would render the information at substantial risk of being inaccurate; the use of this data result would be reported noting such limitations making sure the reader knew the flaws and constraints of what was being reported. However, output produced by GenAI platforms do not provide this note of caution in the output. While it is possible to prompt ChatGPT to use a lower temperature setting (that is to 'turn down' the creativity), to date, it appears few users are doing so, mainly because they are unaware of the existence of such settings.

Despite these problems, technology can provide many benefits such as making narrow specialised skill sets accessible for all. For example, the widespread use of SPSS (Statistical Package for Social Sciences) software in higher education has saved many hours of statistical analysis producing statistical results that can be interpreted by the author/researcher without needing to be a statistician. Academically, such use is publicly acknowledged in the write up of the methodology in the subsequent produced papers. Similarly access to, or use of editorial assistance would be expected to be disclosed. Perhaps then, the most key place to launch our investigations is based upon the capabilities and limitations of the technology, informed use, and acknowledgement, along with student understanding of integrity.

Opportunities, Innovations, and Positive Visions for GenAI in Education

Despite the issues and challenges presented, Gen AI offers opportunities for HE including but not limited to reducing mundane tasks, curating large amounts of information at record speed, supporting those with neuro diverse learning needs, providing and offering learning support 24/7 (Chan & Hu, 2023). Many innovations have already been seen such as universities creating their own 'skins' on ChatGPT to provide personalized support based on specific course information (pers comm, ISSOTL, 2023). Hence, while there are concerns there are also positive visions for GenAI in education for the future and it is the role of educators to ensure these are capitalized.

METHOD

Given the new landscape of easy to access GenAI and the articulated concerns, and with the teaching session about to commence, for our investigation we turned to action learning as both a problem-solving method and a process to reflect upon actions in an iterative and concurrent manner as a means to improve practice (Leitch & Day, 2000). Action learning is used as a method to solve organizational problems as well as manage change (Garratt, 2011). Further, as it does not require a separation of the phases of action and reflection, action learning was and remains a fitting practice. This method also aligns to our disciplinary practice as it is taught to business and management students as a means of continuous personal, professional, and organizational learning and improvement. The action learning cycle phases includes theorize, plan, action and reflect steps (Garratt, 2011). As the use of AI had not yet been encountered in our teaching and assessment practices our launch point in the cycle was to theorize. Action learning also supported us to engage in reflective practice to explore change. We were able to implement two full iterations of the action learning cycle. The first, as an initial response to the changed educational landscape. The second iteration allowed us to act on the lessons uncovered and learnt in the reflection step of the first cycle. In the second iteration, the action phase incorporated some teaching about GenAI ethics to broaden student's conceptual use of GenAI as a tool. This clearly demonstrates the cyclical and 'ongoing' principles of this method – it has no fixed end, rather it is an approach that supports a mindset of continuous development and improvement.

Irrespective of method, to commence any enquiry, a question is helpful as the departure point for action. Our question to be addressed was:

Can the student write to a professional standard on their own, using the course concepts and materials in an applied manner, that enables us to attest they have the level of knowledge and skills we are 'certifying'?

Theorizing this problem became a process of creating a duo-ethnographic account as formed through recursive discussions (Brailas & Sotiropoulou, 2023). It was through probing and challenging each other and our assumptions that we could theorize the problem of ensuring assessments had been completed by the student and were designed to assess the skills and competences that the course was expected to 'certify'. Faced with the impending start of a new academic year, and a vastly different AI informed educational landscape, we needed to theorize the problem we had, by exploring what the technology could do, we then quickly moved to consider the impact of its potential use by students. With the problem firmly understood, our theorizing concluded with determining what the work was.

Entering into the planning phase we designed a process of mapping the course to determine 'the work' expected of students to produce the assessment outcome. In order to create meaningful assessments, we firstly asked, what is 'the work' we are expecting of students when completing course assessment? and how could or might GenAI technology impact the production of 'this work'? The fundamental statement of "what is the work expected to be performed by students" guided our actions and enabled us to provide clear guidelines of acceptable use of GenAI technology in an evolving higher education landscape.

The action phase focused on implementing changed assessments for the course including allowing declared use of the technology. Reflections were undertaken after each assessment item. This process enabled us to remain agile in our actions.

Two full action learning cycles were undertaken across two separate teaching terms. This involved close to 1900 individual students producing approximately 7,600 pieces of written submitted work. Marking tutors are asked to note patterns occurring in submissions each term and as such they undertook the process of highlighting anomalies in submissions, or any occurrences that differed from what the submissions would usually contain. These observations were collated from across the tutor team and analysed thematically as would be done in qualitative research. These themes were feedback to the tutor team who confirmed the findings. Identified issues were further explored through textual analysis.

Any method has limitations and action learning is not immune to problems such as incorrect theorizing of the problem or failure to deeply reflect and enact necessary changes, however, given the time constraints, action learning supported problem focused change to be enabled and ongoing opportunities to adapt quickly to a rapidly evolving higher education landscape with concerns about assessment and integrity.

Defining the Work: The Model and the Mapping

To determine 'the work to be performed,' we recognized that our own growing understanding of GenAI was instrumental in our ability to conceptualize our response to the concerns being raised and to differentiate the actions and outcome of 'the work.' Therefore, we created a map as would be designed to implement a strategy (Ferraro et al., 2018). To undertake the process of mapping, steps must be defined. The first step in this map is for the academic is to audit their AI knowledge. This allows consideration how might Gen AI be integrated or excluded, it also reduces assumptions and difficulties in designing an integrated GenAI assessment as it considers how the students may use it as a tool in their work. Developing an understanding of how AI works, will enable consideration the potential uses and problems of use within a specific disciplinary area. Focused curiosity (Andriopoulos, 2022) can help here. There is an assumption that students and academics understand GenAI, yet in our experience, the knowledge is varied. Taking time to 'play' with GenAI provides a sense of what it can produce. Do you and your students understand temperature, prompt engineering, LLMs (Large Language Models)? What level of confidence does everyone have with the technology? Making sure you understand this and what it means for how information is provided will set a baseline upon which to build changes for your course along with supporting the notion of integrity as it is interpreted both in higher education and in specific discipline-based learning. It will also support your students to understand what can be used and the rationale informing these practices.

The Mapping

Once the level of GenAI knowledge is deemed as sufficient to determine what might be acceptable use, the mapping can begin in earnest. As the awarding of a degree is public recognition that a student has achieved a prescribed level of achievement, assessment must include some measure of knowledge and the skill to utilise that knowledge in situ. Consequently, allowing students to use GenAI to fully produce the 'work' of their degree, even if correctly attributed, calls into question their level of attainment. Therefore, we must look at ways to assess students on their mastery of knowledge and skills which can incorporate the use of GenAI into their creation. To do so, we propose engaging in a deliberate process of constructive alignment to develop a clear understanding of the meaning and purpose of the 'work' required to complete an assessment. We refer to this process as 'mapping the work.'

In order to 'map the work' of assessment, we considered:

- The course and program learning outcomes (CLOs and PLOs);
- The relationship of this course to others (for example is this a compulsory core course and hence needing to provide certain fundamental or threshold concepts to 'conscripted' students, or an elective course with a self-selecting cohort?);
- the graduate attributes (or skills) that students will learn, practice and/or be assessed on in the course;
- The course syllabus in terms of the level of knowledge you would expect each student to demonstrate;

- The student cohort – their context (i.e., what brings them to study), the level of study (undergraduate/ postgraduate), their experience in the program (e.g., first year, later years), and other contextual factors that may affect learning (second language, low SES (Socio Economic Status), Indigenous);
- For each learning outcome what you expect to see and hear when certifying their abilities;
- How will this knowledge and/or skill need to be used by the student in their future roles (in situ in the workplace)?

Armed with this information step two was complete and we could move to step three which was to identify the actions students are expected to perform for each assessment task, to ensure knowledge has not only been made available to them, but that actual learning has been 'tested' in some manner to ascertain knowledge and skill acquisition.

Applying Model and Mapping: The Process

To apply our model and the mapping process, we mapped a large (approximately 1000+ students) compulsory core post graduate course taught to mainly an international cohort. These students were considered 'participants' of the study, however it was the tutors' observations of these students that informed the reflections and next stages of each action learning cycle. Important information in undertaking the mapping process are the course aims which are to introduce students to business ethics and the United Nation's Sustainability Development Goals. In the process, students explore their agency to act, personal leadership development and explore their personal values as a means of experiencing a transformational learning experience.

Our first action step was to define acceptable use of GenAI, considering the constraints or implications of the PLOs for this course which are: Business Communication, Responsible Business Practice, Global and Cultural Competence and Leadership Development. In this course, assessment must include an evaluation the student's ability to communicate effectively in 'professional English' both written and oral. As such, the use of GenAI to fully write or translate any submitted work was deemed unacceptable – as this would not demonstrate the student's own skill and abilities to communicate effectively. There are forms of AI used to translate word for word such as found in products such as DeepL® or Google translate®, that use Artificial Neural Networks replacing a 'like for like' word, which may result in a loss of meaning during translation. The use of such AI results in it being impossible to correctly assess the student's own communication skills. They were excluded in this course.

Another skill expected in doing 'the work' was to be able to research academic literature and develop an informed opinion based on this research. The availability of GenAI platforms has changed the way research can be done. In this unfamiliar environment research is has expanded beyond the use of library tools or Google Scholar alone. Some GenAI platforms such tools as Elicit® (elicit.org) Scite® (scite.ai) and research rabbit® (researchrabbit.ai) to name a few, incorporate peer reviewed 'academic' sources in their LLM, and thus go beyond the general knowledge sources used by ChatGPT and others. Hence, students need to be able to articulate their research strategies and acknowledge any tools utilized.

As a result of the mapping exercise, we identified that 'the work' to be undertaken was to apply knowledge developed during the course to demonstrate a systems approach to the interconnectedness of the economic, political, ecological, and social spheres of human activity. As a management subject, writing and presenting are core communication skills. Thus, the student demonstrates their acquired skills and expertise through four assessment tasks: a short written 'memo', a written business report, written weekly reflections and a recorded video presentation. The recorded videos were not part of the data considered as textual analysis was part of our process of data collection for reflection.

The articulation of the actions required to produce these tasks also meant previous grading standards, such as submitting descriptions of information rather than critical analysis to achieve a minimum pass no longer applied. Students would no longer be 'rewarded' for submitting descriptive or generic responses. Hence, work a machine could do would fail, regardless of if a human or machine did it. Students preparing for a world of work needed to demonstrate their 'value add.' These actions provided the basis for our reflections which are reported under observations.

THE OBSERVATIONS

Utilizing the map enabled us to make observations both of how our students approached their studies and the subsequent outcomes. While not a pure research study, the term results through observing student submissions and comparing previous term results proved insightful.

Term one: Despite our instructions to use and acknowledge GenAI technology in the production of their work, markers reported fewer than 1% of students did so. Textual analysis of the work submitted showed an irregular pattern. There were also a higher number of fails. In previous course offerings, fails (2022) were quite low at approximately 5%, this term the failure rate hit approximately 23% for a single assessment task. When exploring why students had failed this time, graders reported discriminatory and biased answers along with factually incorrect information being applied. This aligns with the known biases in the developed LLM of GenAI platforms. We had not experienced this in prior submissions and the task had not substantially changed. Therefore, a consistent pattern which was not aligned to anything taught or omitted from the course was noted. This feedback was provided to the students as a group, and the reactions made it clear that perhaps there had been little or no human oversight or consideration on the output submitted. When noted to the students specifically, that their answers contained discriminatory or biased information (such as women were not capable of certain tasks or that only women were affected by caring responsibilities) they often offered explanations such as "this is what I think" but upon questioning they acknowledged they had sourced it through GenAI. We had uncovered a level of student overconfidence in using GenAI as a research tool. Of note is also that we also uncovered a further 5% submitted papers that were either fully translated or largely GenAI created. This resulted in academic integrity breaches being recorded and upheld as they had failed to meet the learning outcomes, but more importantly this highlighted our academic integrity concerns were, at least founded.

By our second term, both awareness and use of GenAI technology had broadened, along with our experience. The world responded to the broad concerns with parliamentary enquiries, national standards, ethical standards, protocols, lawsuits and even citation structure. These along with the insights from our first round of implementation guided a different approach. We sought to engage students in applied ethics to consider GenAI technology as the subject of the assessment. The students were provided with codes of ethics specifically about GenAI on issues such as writing, responsibility, and appropriate attribution. Class discussions were held about what does their degree 'certify' and mean inside and outside of the university. This was offered as a means to upskill students but also engage them in some critical thinking about GenAI as a tool and its use.

With clear guidelines on citation when used, and explanation of acceptable use we saw student awareness increase as to why full translation was unacceptable. Few students used full translation software seeing only approximately 1% of students doing so, however it was the increase in other GenAI breaches found that were more serious often uncovering larger integrity issues such as contract cheating. In terms of students failing assessments, the numbers dropped to approximately 17%. Textual analysis showed the primary reason for these failures, was the use of outdated or incorrect information suggesting ongoing use of GenAI platforms and a lack of understanding of the limitations of these. Again, student reactions to this feedback were insightful and uncovered student's inability to use GenAI effectively, or a general lack of understanding as to its use, or a belief that the use would not be uncovered.

As we enter the third term of teaching and assessing with this technology freely available, we have focused the student's attention on both the rationale of acceptable use but have also been explicit in the weaknesses of the technology highlighting the information it provides is often outdated and potentially discriminatory and biased and such submissions are unacceptable. The shift to engage students with a critique of the technology fully aware of its limitations seeks to focus the student back to seeing and using it as a tool that requires their expertise.

DISCUSSION

As educators grapple with a GenAI informed learning environment, some argue that if GenAI is used in the process of writing an assignment, it should be acknowledged as a tool of assistance or source similar to the use of SPSS for analysing data, or a reference like any other cited when producing the work (McAdoo, 2023). While important in terms of academic practice, this approach still does not address the question of certifying a student's abilities and capabilities inherent to the awarding of a degree. It is critical that the student can demonstrate proficiency with course and program outcomes. Quite simply, the student must be able to do the work reasonably expected of someone who has undertaken the prescribed learning.

While there may be a time when the use of GenAI will be an integral part of our study (and working) life, for now, at the end of 2023, we suggest a model of explicitly defining what 'the work' is to support academics in creating and implementing learning and assessment that both integrates and specifically calls upon the use of GenAI with integrity. To do this, we must support students to understand what integrity looks like and how to complete their 'work' with integrity.

As educators, we need to recognize the lure of GenAI may be strong for students. The realities of being a student including multiple assessment deadlines, competing, and conflicting pressures and priorities (juggling studies with paid work and family responsibilities) and the expense of their studies makes the risk of 'failing' an additional financial burden which can lead to lapses in judgement (Rigby et al., 2015). These pressures may lead to unintentional inappropriate use. Students with a focus on grades over learning, the lack of language and writing skills, a desire to excel in assignments as a mean to protect self-esteem, or even being tasked with compulsory core units that they see little value in, may all lead to unintentional misuse or an overconfidence when using GenAI. TEQSA (2023) acknowledges that while most students commence their studies with a strong intention to learn, time pressures along with learning efficacy may tempt a student to 'cheat.'

We propose that to combat the challenge to academic integrity presented by the rise of GenAI platforms, educators must clearly define 'the work' that is to be performed by students, explicitly identifying the degree to which GenAI can be used in the process. For example, can GenAI be used as an extension of existing 'research' practices in place of or in addition to academic research, Wikipedia or a google search? Or may it to be used to as a tool to edit the work produced by the student (as a 'professional polish')? Either way, the use of the GenAI tool should be acknowledged. Given these parameters, GenAI as a technology is not the problem but rather it is the use to substitute the expected 'work' of the student that is misleading.

WHAT NOW AND NEXT?

In higher education, acceptable use must be explored as prohibition has never worked (Reuter, 1997). Hence, commencing by exploring the complexity of what is 'acceptable use' (of AI) in higher education provides a launch point to uphold integrity. Incorporating discussions with students about the CLOs and PLOs supports them to engage with GenAI as a tool and highlights the value of their degrees, qualification, and the subsequent value they can add to their prospective employers and organizations as well as society at large. By supporting students to understand how to use and integrate AI as a tool, a community that upholds academic integrity is built and maintained. Further, integrating GenAI use in higher education develops students to appraise future technology as tools to be both used and exploited.

Adjusting Assessment

There are many types of assessment that may be successfully used to measure student mastery in the new educational landscape. Consideration of course or program learning outcomes along with any certification (explicit or implied) will impact what can be deemed as acceptable, such as where a student's communication skills are assessed or asserted. There is certainly no need to rush back to invigilated exams done by paper and pen under a watchful pair of eyes. However, consideration of all forms of assessments is useful. GenAI has perhaps heightened the need to explore the inherent problems with written submissions produced outside of invigilated exams. While these have long been under scrutiny, unfair advantage in terms of editing or written assistance can now be assumed. Therefore, the use of GenAI as a tool should be considered to be part of the work.

Authentic assessment enables students to use their knowledge and undertake actions in a practical and applied manner. Designed to encourage students to engage with tasks ('the work') that replicate conditions and outputs that will be expected of them in their chosen career, some have argued that this addresses the concerns raised in relation to the technology enabling the student to complete an assessment. However, other studies to date have shown that GenAI with some human oversight can score well even in authentic assessment tasks.

Other forms of assessment may include critiquing AI generated outputs to enable the student to show how they used course knowledge to correct and edit the output to demonstrate critical thinking (Gribble & Wardrop in Press). Assessment of presentation skills should focus on the student's presentation 'performance,' rather than the content delivered. Newer approaches such as interactive orals which follow a conversation as one might have with their manager or peer (Ward et al., 2023) are both authentic and robust in terms of assessment of and for learning. Meanwhile, Viva Voce are being used to 'test' or explore the student's understanding of the work submitted and has been useful to evaluate a student's learning.

FURTHER CONSIDERATIONS TO INTEGRATE GenAI

Before expecting wide use or integration of GenAI it must be noted that there is a vast difference between the free access and paid premium GenAI tools. While much has been written about unequal access to technology and its impact on student equity (Pedro et al., 2019), GenAI platforms have been quick to provide 'open access' to anyone with what is considered 'basic' access to technology (at least in developed economies and the higher education systems within). ChatGPT 3/3.5 has been freely available for anyone with internet access since October 2022, and as of April 2023 it supports several languages, including English, Spanish, French, German, Portuguese, Italian, Dutch, Russian, Arabic, and Chinese. Other products such as Google's Bard® allows the user/student to feel they are in a conversation which can then 'lull them into a false security' about its capability. Named after the Celtic notion of a 'storyteller,' it was launched in March 2023, in beta form it has been available to all since May and is often called a 'co-pilot' but appears to lack the brand awareness of OpenAI's ChatGPT. Microsoft's Bing® became available to anyone with a Microsoft account around the same time and is also freely accessible. Like all technology, some are easier to use, with better functionality, but only time will tell as to what models expand or become extinct.

Beyond the free models, the premium product, ChatGPT4 has been available since March 2023 and has an improved LLM source underpinning it, with more up to date data. Its output is considered superior but at a cost, which limits access to those with the financial resources to gain access. At our university, there are discussions surrounding the need to provide access to these premium versions to all students to ensure equal access for and by all. At the beginning of 2024 it is expected that organizations and institutions will pay a subscription model akin to that of Office365 for GenAI access in an enterprise wide solution. Once this occurs, some of the equity issues will have been addressed for students enrolled at an institution, but will not, of course, stop students with the financial resources to 'go beyond' and access yet other sources. For now, any use must recognize the divide between the 'haves and have nots' in terms of those who can afford to pay for a premium model over those limited to using the free access and now less developed versions. If we are to accept or expect its use to produce academic work, then all students must have the same level of access to the same technology at a similar level. and how the lack of equal access might further disadvantage those students from low SES backgrounds. At the same time those with neuro diverse learning needs, learning difficulties or disabilities may also benefit from such access enabling greater participation and access to education for all. While GenAI has been criticized for its impact on energy consumption, it may also move UN Sustainability Development Goal 4 "Ensure inclusive and equitable quality education and promote lifelong learning opportunities for all" to more possible.

KEY TAKEAWAYS AND RECOMMENDATIONS

We encourage all academics to undertake the basics of mapping the work that is being credentialed. At the beginning of 2024, GenAI knowledge needs to be explicitly stated and explored both for faculty and students. Where there is no enterprise solution provided issues such as privacy and access must be addressed.

Academics must continue to outline what academic integrity is and demonstrate its importance. Further, assessments will need continual adjustments and updating, and this must be recognized as part of the academic workload. At the same time vigilance in educating students on integrity as well as ensuring integrity is upheld will require attention by all teaching and grading staff. This way, students and academics can uphold the values that have held in the face of GenAI.

CONCLUSION

By determining the work that students are required to perform to produce assessment tasks, as well as focusing on ethical use of it as a tool there is not really any greater risk to academic integrity than has previously existed. Both academics and students alike can embrace GenAI for what it is, as a new piece of technology that can support student learning and student output reducing the more 'administrative tasks' (basic research, grammar, and spell checking) to allow more time to focus on the more intellectually demanding process of producing the work. For this to happen academics and students alike must focus clearly on what 'the work is' and that this is produced truthfully and without unfair advantage.

REFERENCES

Alba, D. (2022, December 8). OpenAI Chatbot Spits Out Biased Musings, Despite Guardrails. *Bloomberg*. https://www.bloomberg.com/news/newsletters/2022-12-08/chatgpt-open-ai-s-chatbot-is-spitting-out-biased-sexist-results accessed September 20

Allyn, B. (2023, August 16). 'New York Times' considers legal action against OpenAI as copyright tensions swirl. *New York Times*. https://www.npr.org/2023/08/16/1194202562/new-york-times-considers-legal-action-against-openai-as-copyright-tensions-swirl

Anderman, M., Cupp, K., & Lane, D. (2009). Impulsivity and academic cheating. *Journal of Experimental Education*, *78*(1), 135–150. doi:10.1080/00220970903224636

Andriopoulos, C. (2022). *Purposeful Curiosity*. Hachette.

APDR Staff (2023, August 14). Organisations in Australia set to ban ChatGPT and generative AI apps on work devices. https://asiapacificdefencereporter.com/organisations-in-australia-set-to-ban-chatgpt-and-generative-ai-apps-on-work-devices/

Arts Law Centre. (2023). *Artificial Intelligence (AI) and Copyright*. Arts Law Centre. https://www.artslaw.com.au/information-sheet/artificial-intelligence-ai-and-copyright/

Bannon, M. T. (2023, June 22). How AI Is Changing The Future Of Work. *Forbes Magazine*. https://www.forbes.com/sites/marenbannon/2023/06/22/how-ai-is-changing-the-future-of-work/?sh=624cfccf72e0

Bertram Gallant., T. (2017). Academic Integrity as a Teaching & Learning Issue: From Theory to Practice. *Theory Into Practice*, *56*(2), 88-94. doi:10.1080/00405841.2017.1308173

Brailas, A., & Sotiropoulou, C. (2023). *Relational, Appreciative, and Process-oriented Digital Storytelling: A Duoethnography*. Hu Arenas. doi:10.1007/s42087-023-00337-7

Bretag, T., Harper, R., Burton, M., Ellis, C., Newton, P., Rozenberg, P., Saddiqui, S., & van Haeringen, K. (2018). Contract cheating: A survey of Australian university students. *Studies in Higher Education*, *44*(11), 1837–1856. doi:10.1080/03075079.2018.1462788

Bretag, T., Harper, R., Rundle, K., Newton, P. M., Ellis, C., Saddiqui, S., & van Haeringen, K. (2019). Contract cheating in Australian higher education: A comparison of non-university higher education providers and universities. *Assessment & Evaluation in Higher Education*, *45*(1), 125–139. doi:10.1080/02602938.2019.1614146

Cassens Weiss, D. (2023, March 16). Latest version of ChatGPT aces bar exam with score nearing 90th percentile. *ABA Journal*. https://www.abajournal.com/web/article/latest-version-of-chatgpt-aces-the-bar-exam-with-score-in-90th-percentile

Chan, C. K. Y., & Hu, W. (2023). Students' voices on generative AI: Perceptions, benefits, and challenges in higher education. *International Journal of Educational Technology in Higher Education*, *20*(43), 1–18. doi:10.1186/s41239-023-00411-8

Clarke, R., & Lancaster, T. (2006). Eliminating the successor to plagiarism? Identifying the usage of contract cheating sites. In *Proceedings of 2nd international plagiarism conference*.

Collini, S. (2012). *What are Universities for?* Penguin.

Columbia weighs an honor system: Students request pledges from new freshmen. (1963, September 24). *New York Times*. https://www.nytimes.com/1963/09/24/archives/columbia-weighs-an-honor-system-students-request-pledges-from-new.html

Crush, P. (2023). *Most workers would still use AI – even if their workplace banned it*. TLNT. https://www.tlnt.com/articles/staff-would-still-use-ai-at-work-even-if-it-was-banned-workplace-rules-can-be-challenge August 4

Ferraro, F., Ferraro, A., Massimo, J., & Massimo, M. (2018, March 20). A Road Map for Successful Strategy Execution: Strategic Leadership. *IESE INSIGHT*. https://www.iese.edu/insight/articles/strategy-successful-execution-road-map/

Fuller, R. B., & Kuromiya, K. (1981). *Critical path*. Macmillan.

Garratt, B. (2011). The Power of Action Learning. In M. Pedler (Ed.), *Action Learning in Practice* (4th ed.). Routledge. doi:10.4324/9781315565521

Grassini, S. (2023). Shaping the Future of Education: Exploring the Potential and Consequences of AI and ChatGPT in Educational Settings. *Education Sciences*, *13*(7), 692–704. doi:10.3390/educsci13070692

Gribble, L., & Wardrop, J. (2023, August 2). Incorporating Generative AI in Authentic Assessments. *Disruptive Innovations in Business Education Research Group*. https://diberg.blog/2023/08/02/incorporating-generative-ai-in-authentic-assessments

Gribble, L., & Wardrop J. (in press). Building AI literacy: Assessment as a process to navigate the future. *Advance HE*. United Kingdom.

Hinman, L. M. (2002). Academic integrity and the World Wide Web. *Computers & Society, 32*(1), 33–42. doi:10.1145/511134.511139

Kelly, A., Sullivan, M., & Strampel, K. (2023). Generative artificial intelligence: University student awareness, experience, and confidence in use across disciplines. *Journal of University Teaching & Learning Practice, 20*(6). doi:10.53761/1.20.6.12

Kwong, T., Ng, H., Mark, K., & Wong, E. (2010). Students' and faculty's perception of academic integrity in Hong Kong. *Campus-Wide Information Systems, 27*(5), 341–355. doi:10.1108/10650741011087766

Leitch, R., & Day, C. (2000). Action research and reflective practice: Towards a holistic view. *Educational Action Research, 8*(1), 179–193. doi:10.1080/09650790000200108

Lodge, J., Howard, S., Bearman, M., & Dawson, P. (2023, November). Assessment reform for the age of artificial intelligence. *TEQSA*. https://www.teqsa.gov.au/guides-resources/resources/corporate-publications/assessment-reform-age-artificial-intelligence

Luo, B., Lui, S., Lui, C., & Zhang, R. (2018). Knowledge exploration and innovation: A review and inverse S-curve proposition. *Journal of Management & Organization, 24*(6), 870–892. doi:10.1017/jmo.2016.39

Maybee, C., Bruce, C. S., Lupton, M., & Pang, M. F. (2019). Informed learning design: Teaching and learning through engagement with information. *Higher Education Research & Development, 38*(5), 579–593. doi:10.1080/07294360.2018.1545748

McAdoo, T. (2023, April 7). How to cite ChatGPT. *APA Style.* https://apastyle.apa.org/blog/how-to-cite-chatgpt

OECD. (2023, July 20). Generative AI in the classroom: From hype to reality? *Launch meeting of the Schools+ Network 22-23 May 2023,* Boulogne. https://one.oecd.org/document/EDU/EDPC(2023)11/en/pdf accessed Sept 10 2023

OECD. (n.d.). *AE Assessment for Learning - OECD*. OECD. https://www.oecd.org/site/educeri21st/40600533.pdf

Open A. I. (2023). *Introducing ChatGPT Enterprise. Get enterprise-grade security & privacy and the most powerful version of ChatGPT yet.* Open AI. https://openai.com/blog/introducing-chatgpt-enterprise

Pedró, F., Subosa, M., Rivas, A., & Valverde, P. (2019). Artificial intelligence in education: challenges and opportunities for sustainable development. *Working papers on education policy, 07.* UN. https://unesdoc.unesco.org/ark:/48223/pf0000366994.locale=en

Prokou, E. (2008). The Emphasis on Employability and the Changing Role of the University in Europe. *Higher Education in Europe, 33*(4), 387–394. doi:10.1080/03797720802522593

Reuter, P. (1997). Why Can't We Make Prohibition Work Better? Some Consequences of Ignoring the Unattractive. *Proceedings of the American Philosophical Society, 141*(3), 262–275. https://www.jstor.org/stable/987202 PMID:11619507

Rigby, D., Burton, M., Balcombe, K., Bateman, I., & Mulatu, A. (2015). Contract cheating & the market in essays. *Journal of Economic Behavior & Organization, 111*, 23–37. doi:10.1016/j.jebo.2014.12.019

TEQSA. (2019). *Guidance note: Academic integrity Tertiary Education Quality and Standards Agency*. TEQSA. https://www.teqsa.gov.au/guides-resources/resources/guidance-notes/guidance-note-academic-integrity

Terwiesch, C. (2023). *Would Chat GPT Get a Wharton MBA? A Prediction Based on Its Performance in the Operations Management Course*. Mack Institute for Innovation Management at the Wharton School, University of Pennsylvania. https://mackinstitute.wharton.upenn.edu/wp-content/uploads/2023/01/Christian-Terwiesch-Chat-GTP.pdf

Ward, M., O'Riordan, F., Logan-Fleming, D., Cooke, D., Concannon-Gibney, T., Efthymiou, M., & Watkins, N. (2023, August 29). Interactive oral assessment case studies: An innovative, academically rigorous, authentic assessment approach. *Innovations in Education and Teaching International*, 1–18. doi:10.1080/14703297.2023.2251967

Wheaton, A. (2020). Shift happens; moving from the ivory tower to the mushroom factory. *Higher Education Research & Development*, *39*(1), 67–80. doi:10.1080/07294360.2019.1670145

Chapter 15
New Innovations in Higher Education's Academic Integrity and Classroom Strategies

Maya Jaber
University of Wisconsin-Platteville, USA

ABSTRACT

In recent decades, technology has advanced exponentially, ushering in the widespread integration of artificial intelligence (AI) to daily life. AI is now omnipresent, from smart home devices to autonomous vehicles, and it has gained significant traction across various industries. In higher education, educators must adapt to this cultural shift by revising curriculum, learning environments, and teaching methods. AI has the potential to revolutionize higher education but raises concerns about academic integrity. This chapter explores AI's impact on global society, discusses AI-related academic integrity issues, proposes a redefined concept of academic integrity, and offers practical strategies for nurturing students' evolving thinking processes.

INTRODUCTION

Technology has dramatically progressed during the last few decades, and subsequently, Artificial Intelligence (AI) is becoming increasingly prevalent in daily lives. From smart home appliances to self-driving cars, Artificial Intelligence is everywhere. AI is pertinently being used in the workplace, irrespective of the field (Dwivedi et al., 2021). AI has seen massive growth, for example, in the fields of healthcare, finance, management, real estate development, and so much more. Educators in higher education need to embrace the nuances of AI applications in the workplace, which is a major cultural shift in a global society. With this paradigm shift, educators in higher education must bring changes to their curriculum, learning environment, as well as instructional and teaching strategies (Francesc, 2019). As educators in all fields are training the new generation of workers, it is imperative that they introduce this innovative mindset to classrooms. This would involve constructing practical approaches and techniques aimed at transforming students' approaches to learning.

DOI: 10.4018/979-8-3693-0240-8.ch015

AI has the potential to revolutionize higher education, but it also carries concerns like academic integrity. With this global societal reform, educators should redefine academic integrity. In this chapter, the proposal is to present concrete evidence of the cultural evolution that AI is bringing to our global society. Later, the discussion about the concerns of AI to traditional higher education's academic integrity. Then, the chapter will present a new definition of academic integrity for these institutions. Finally, the author will present practical strategies that can be utilized by educators to aid in the evolution of students' ways of thinking.

AI USE IN SOCIETY

AI is being seen as the next disruptive innovation and will revolutionize the workplaces of the future (Păvăloaia & Necula, 2023). AI has seen massive growth, for example, in the fields of healthcare, finance, management, real estate development, and so much more. It is viewed as an integral driver of the fourth industrial revolution (Zhai et al., 2021). Across all sectors, AI has already improved efficiency, increased accuracy, and reduced costs.

This transformative technology is no longer limited to the realm of futurology but has become an integral part of many organizations' business models and strategic plans across various sectors. AI's impact has sparked academic interest, with studies focusing on its consequences and implications rather than just performance (Dwivedi et al., 2021). AI is defined as systems that mimic human cognitive functions like learning, speech, and problem-solving, and it has the potential to replace or augment human tasks and activities in industries such as finance, healthcare, manufacturing, retail, and more (Păvăloaia & Necula, 2023).

AI has been a major influence in the transformation of current society. It has enabled sectors to collect, process, and analyze large amounts of data at a much faster rate. It has affected all industries and enabled innovations in areas such as technology, business processes, manufacturing, and communication (Francesc, 2019). It has come into all aspects of societal life, for example, the use of AI in smartphone technology with personal assistance such as Google Assistant, Siri, to smart home systems. These AI-powered technologies and others are being enhanced to offer more personalized recommendations and services and improve user experience.

While AI presents numerous opportunities, there are also challenges and considerations to address. Society is still grappling with the ethical and economic implications of AI and big data, including their impact on human life, culture, sustainability, and technological transformation. The World Economic Forum predicts that AI technologies could impact up to 20% of existing jobs in the UK and even more in emerging economies like China and India (Dwivedi et al., 2021). However, AI is also expected to drive innovation, economic growth, and the creation of new jobs globally.

In essence, AI has infiltrated all aspects of contemporary society, revolutionizing the way people live, work, and interact with technology (Peeters et al., 2021). Its influence extends from personal assistants in our pockets to smart systems in our homes and permeates critical industries. As AI continues to advance, it will undoubtedly shape the future of society in even more profound ways, pushing the boundaries of what is possible in the realms of technology, business, and daily life.

AI holds immense potential for further adoption and research. By 2030, it is estimated that 70% of businesses will have incorporated some form of AI technology into their processes (Dwivedi et al., 2021). Ensuring the safety of AI systems and protecting against their misuse is a significant challenge.

The unpredictable consequences of AI systems that learn on their own through reinforcement learning can be a cause for concern. Preventing the misuse of AI technology for destructive goals, similar to the challenges faced from the internet and cybercrime, is a complex task. The potential for AI systems to be used by criminal organizations or dictatorial governments highlights the need for robust safety standards and regulations (Păvăloaia & Necula, 2023).

AI has been utilized to simulate human intelligence for decision-making or problem-solving. It has been utilized in fields such as economics, manufacturing, law, medicine, and engineering (Mellit & Kalogirou, 2008). For example, AI can potentially revolutionize the medical field in many ways. It can help in the early detection and diagnosis of diseases, assist in personalized treatment plans, and improve patient outcomes. AI can also help in drug discovery, medical imaging analysis, and predicting patient outcomes. Additionally, AI can help reduce healthcare costs and improve healthcare systems' efficiency. Overall, AI has the potential to transform the medical field and improve the quality of healthcare for patients (Rangarajan & Ramachandran, 2021).

The dynamic nature of the global market, driven by the swift evolution of emerging markets and the advent of cutting-edge technologies, has significantly hastened a wide array of industries. This accelerated pace encompasses everything from creating innovative products to analyzing consumer input (Krasavina, 2019). Information Technology (IT) and AI are now being used in tandem for the creation of a 'Smart' economy that is helping to create trends in businesses globally (Matyushok et al., 2021). AI is playing a pivotal role in the transformation of business and business management. It is becoming an essential tool for organizations to remain competitive globally. Organizational leaders and managers will need to understand how to utilize these tools to streamline processes and advance their organization. Educators, who are the pillars of the future workforce, will need to comprehend these transformations and build this knowledge into their curriculum and student foundations.

AI USE IN EDUCATION

As it is observed, AI has and continues to have transformative effects on societal and business behaviors. Educators, as the trainers of the future workforce, will be obliged to understand these mechanisms and tools to identify possible pathways to optimize learning. AI has been recognized as having strategic educational value and a tool for teachers and students (Seldon & Abidoye, 2018) (Loeckx, 2016). The pandemic has drastically shifted the education landscape, opened the virtual learning environment, and embedded technology as a core part of education.

The application of artificial intelligence in education, commonly referred to as AIED, has been a focal point in academic research for over three decades. This field delves into the study of learning in various settings, be it within traditional classrooms or professional environments, with the aim of bolstering not just formal education but also continuous lifelong learning. It fuses the interdisciplinary nature of AI with the learning sciences encompassing education, psychology, neuroscience, linguistics, sociology, and anthropology (Luckin & Holmes, Intelligence Unleashed: An argument for AI in Education, 2016). This union is intended to foster the creation of adaptive learning environments and diverse AIED tools that prioritize flexibility, inclusivity, personalization, engagement, and efficacy. Artificial intelligence involves computer software designed to interact with the world in a manner that typically demands human intelligence. This underscores the reliance of AI on both comprehensive knowledge about the world and sophisticated algorithms that intelligently process this information.

AI in Education (AIED) research focuses on directly and instantaneously aiding the learning and teaching process across all fields and environments. Underwood and Luckin discuss that AIED techniques can be applied to various areas of education, including but not limited to K-12 education, higher education, vocational training, and lifelong learning. AIED can deliver more flexible, inclusive, personalized, effective, and engaging learning experiences throughout life and in formal and informal settings (Underwood & Luckin, 2011). Some AIED tools that are being used in learning environments are ChatGPT, ChatPDF, Dall-E, Scholarcy, YouTubeDigest, Dall-E, Elicit, and Copy.ai. For example, these tools aid in answering questions, summarizing PDF information, finding research papers, helping summarize article and video information. AI in Education (AIED) research focuses on directly and instantaneously aiding the learning and teaching process across all fields and environments (Păvăloaia & Necula, 2023).

AI has the capability to optimize both learning and teaching. There are many opportunities for the development of AI applications in education connected with current education developments, such as digitization of education resources, gamification, and personalized learning experiences (Boulay, 2016). For students, AI can be used as a **universal 24/7 access to learning.** Online AI-powered learning tools open access to all students and work with their learning levels to help them achieve their goals and grow through their own capabilities. This also helps bring equity to those who are less fortunate to close the gap that exists because of location or economic challenges. Furthermore, AI **tutoring** and chatbots give students first-hand information and the ability to break down information for them to make it more understandable at a much faster rate than an educator with limited time. These tools can assist learners in perfecting their skills and improving weak points outside the classroom.

As students' learning capabilities are vast, AI can help students find answers to their most asked questions in seconds. It provides **quick responses** and a one-on-one learning experience without having teachers there to answer questions, therefore accelerating the learning process. It is a continuous learning tool; it learns users' preferences, styles, and needs. AI can adapt to each student's familiarity level of knowledge, speed of learning, and desired goals for optimized learning (Francesc, 2019). It can also identify and analyze students' previous learning histories, identify limitations, and offer courses best suited for improvement. It is imperative, though, for educators to teach students how to use these tools and help them identify how to find relevant and accurate information from these tools, as information produced by these programs is not always correct or what is required for their needs.

AI, as a tool, can help free up educators' time by automating tasks, analyzing student performance, and closing educational gaps. Educators want to focus on the education of their students, dive into research, and continue their own education. They struggle with time management as juggling a multitude of tasks leaves them short on time. For educators, AI can aid them in administrative tasks, such as grading papers, assessing, replying to generated questions, assessing learning patterns, and more. Through these **task automation** tools, educators can automate manual processes, leaving them more time to focus on teaching core competencies (Chen et al., 2020). It can also aid educators in **brainstorming ideas and lesson planning**. AI can help in breaking down projects for different learning levels for easier delivery for special needs students. AI can give educators a clear picture of which subjects and lessons need to be reevaluated or reviewed as student assessments are analyzed. It can also discover the educator's style to deliver information and adapt to their preferences.

A study done by McKinsey & Company (2020) shows that 20 to 40% of educators' time is spent on activities that can be automated using existing technology; this equates to 13 hours per week being redirected to teaching and student wellbeing. They have concluded that existing technologies, AI, and emerging technologies can help educators streamline their processes and become more efficient and effective educators.

As the industry moves forward, it is crucial for educators and educational institutions to embrace AI as a valuable ally in the pursuit of better learning outcomes. By understanding the mechanisms and tools AI offers, educators can harness its potential to optimize learning and teaching, ultimately shaping a brighter future for education. The journey of AI in education is ongoing, and with continued innovation and collaboration, it holds the promise of transforming education for generations to come. As this moves forward, there are societal and ethical concerns that should be addressed when implementing AI in education (Francesc, 2019). Some of these concerns include AI systems discriminating unfairly, taking life-impacting decisions non-transparently, and AI's potential to take over human control.

In the context of education, there are concerns about the ethical implications of collecting and mining data from learners, and any policy framework regarding the use of AI in education needs to address this issue. Additionally, using Machine Learning algorithms to accept or reject students can lead to lack of explain ability and unfair discrimination. Therefore, it is important to consider these ethical implications and work towards addressing them when implementing AI in education.

AI FEARS AND CONCERNS IN EDUCATION

In the dynamic landscape of higher education, the integration of artificial intelligence (AI) presents transformative opportunities but also triggers significant concerns, particularly regarding academic integrity. Addressing these concerns is vital, encompassing liability, workforce impact, ethical considerations, technology dependency, lack of regulation, and accessibility (Francesc, 2019). Overall, while AI has the potential to improve education, some potential risks and challenges need to be addressed to ensure that AI is used responsibly and ethically.

The accountability for AI-driven decisions guiding students remains ambiguous, sparking questions about responsibility for educational outcomes. This uncertainty raises concerns about liability and the implications for the consequences of AI-empowered education. Moreover, the increasing automation of tasks traditionally performed by educators may potentially displace jobs, negatively impacting the teaching profession and educational quality.

Ethical implications as relevant in the use of AI in education, encompassing worries about data privacy, algorithmic bias, and the transparency of decision-making processes (Păvăloaia & Necula, 2023). The risk of students overly relying on technology at the expense of crucial social and emotional skills developed through human interaction is a pressing concern.

Additionally, the current absence of robust regulations and guidelines for AI in education poses risks of unintended consequences and adverse outcomes. The implementation of AI systems could also exacerbate inequalities by creating disparities in access to quality education among institutions with varying financial capabilities. Addressing these concerns is pivotal to ensuring the responsible and ethical integration of AI in the educational sphere.

REDEFINING ACADEMIC INTEGRITY

In the ever-evolving landscape of higher education, the advent of artificial intelligence (AI) brings forth transformative possibilities. However, it also raises significant concerns, particularly in the realm of academic integrity. Academic integrity, characterized by values such as trust, respect, responsibility, fairness, courage, and honesty, stands as a cornerstone of educational excellence. Typical guidelines require students and staff to uphold academic integrity codes of ethics, setting out procedures to follow if they have been breached (Bretag, et al., 2011). This section delves into the redefinition of academic integrity within the context of AI in higher education, highlighting the challenges and opportunities it presents.

Academic integrity is important for maintaining the credibility and reputation of educational institutions, as well as for ensuring that students develop the skills and knowledge necessary for success in their chosen fields (Sefcik et al., 2020). It refers to the ethical and moral principles of honesty, trust, fairness, respect, and responsibility that are fundamental to the educational process. It involves upholding high standards of academic honesty, avoiding plagiarism, cheating, and other forms of academic misconduct, and ensuring that all work submitted is original and properly cited.

In the realm of academic writing, there exists a growing apprehension regarding the potential misapplication of AI tools, particularly exemplified by chatbots like ChatGPT-3. This concern pivots on two key facets, both of which underscore anxieties about the erosion of academic integrity. First and foremost, a prominent apprehension arises from the possibility that students might resort to these AI tools to fabricate entire papers or assignments instead of personally undertaking the requisite work. Such a course of action could precipitate a decline in the standards of academic integrity. The source of this concern lies in the fact that the output produced by AI tools can be exceptionally challenging to differentiate from human-generated content. Consequently, the conventional methods of detection, primarily reliant on text-matching software, may prove ineffectual in identifying instances of AI-generated content.

Furthermore, it is worth noting that there are reservations about the efficacy of existing plagiarism detection software, such as Turnitin, in correctly identifying content generated by AI. Consequently, a pressing need emerges for educators to modernize their academic integrity policies and allocate resources toward the acquisition of tools and technologies capable of detecting the surreptitious utilization of chatbots in academic undertakings (Perkins, 2023).

AI and academic integrity can work collaboratively to detect plagiarism, ensure fair assessment, and provide personalized learning experiences and enhance student engagement (Francesc, 2019). By tailoring educational content and support based on individual needs, AI can foster active participation and a deeper connection to the learning process while maintaining the ethical standards essential for academic integrity.

The integration of AI into higher education introduces both challenges and opportunities for academic integrity. By embracing AI ethically, educating students about its role, providing human oversight, and fostering critical thinking, educators can create a balanced approach that maximizes the benefits of AI while preserving the core values of academic integrity. This ensures that technology enhances, rather than undermines, the educational journey, allowing students to thrive with integrity in an increasingly AI-driven world.

Addressing academic integrity and AI issues requires careful consideration of ethics, transparency, and the responsible use of AI in higher education. Institutions and educators must strike a balance between the benefits AI can bring to academic integrity and the potential risks it poses to students' privacy and fairness in education. Educators can take several proactive steps to address the issues related to academic integrity and the use of AI in higher education.

Educators should familiarize themselves with the AI tools and systems being used in their educational institutions. This includes understanding the capabilities, limitations, and potential biases of these tools. They should encourage ethical AI use by advocating for transparency, fairness, and privacy. Work with institutions to ensure that AI tools used for academic integrity adhere to strict ethical guidelines. They should educate students about the use of AI in academic integrity measures (Hollman et al., 2021). Explain how AI is used, the importance of maintaining ethical standards, and how AI can be a valuable tool for both students and educators.

Also, when AI systems flag potential violations, educators should provide context and allow students to explain their work. AI may not always understand the nuances of academic assignments, so human judgment is essential. Institutions should supplement AI with human oversight, as they use AI as a tool to support, not replace, human judgment. Maintain human oversight in grading and addressing academic misconduct cases to ensure fairness and understanding of context. Educators should foster critical thinking and academic integrity discussions in the classroom. Encourage students to reflect on the importance of honesty and ethical conduct in their academic work. By taking these steps, educators can help create a balanced and responsible approach to using AI to maintain academic integrity while addressing potential issues and concerns. This ensures that the benefits of AI are maximized while preserving the integrity of the educational process.

Considering the evolving educational landscape, it becomes evident that academic institutions must embark on a journey of redefining Academic Integrity within the context of their respective establishments. The integration of AI into the educational process, encompassing both instructional methodologies and institutional operations, emerges as an imperative step in this transformative process.

In essence, the redefinition of academic integrity aligns with the broader mission of academic institutions — to prepare individuals for the challenges and opportunities of an ever-evolving world. By embracing AI as an integral component of this mission, institutions not only preserve the integrity of education but also empower their students with the skills and insights necessary to lead and innovate in the future. This harmonious fusion of tradition and technology heralds a new era in academia, one where the foundations of academic integrity remain unshaken, while the horizons of educational excellence continue to expand.

PRACTICAL STRATEGIES IN THE CLASSROOM

In today's rapidly evolving world, the integration of technology into education has become more than a trend; it's a necessity. As classrooms adapt to the digital age, educators and students alike are faced with the exciting prospect of harnessing the potential of Artificial Intelligence (AI) to enhance teaching and learning experiences (Francesc, 2019). From personalized learning pathways to automating administrative tasks, AI offers a myriad of practical strategies that can revolutionize the modern classroom.

As AI continues to evolve and influence the world around us, it will be crucial for educators to consider, discuss, and maintain academic integrity in their classrooms. They will need to clearly communicate what constitutes academic integrity, explaining plagiarism, proper citation, and ethical academic behavior. They will need to set clear guidelines for assignments and assessments, detailing what is allowed and what isn't. They will have to design assessments that deter cheating by focusing on critical thinking, application, and individualized responses. They should foster an open dialogue about the importance of academic integrity and the consequences of academic dishonesty. They will need to engage students in creating a culture of integrity as they offer resources and support for students, such as writing centers or tutoring, to assist in understanding proper citation and academic writing.

This section will explore some practical strategies for integrating AI into educational settings, empowering educators with innovative tools and techniques to engage students, improve outcomes, and streamline their workload (Păvăloaia & Necula, 2023). Whether an educator is looking to enhance their teaching methods or an education enthusiast curious about the future of learning, the following section will discuss some strategies to harness AI's potential for the betterment of education.

Educators can utilize AI to develop **personalized learning pathways for their students** (Bertolini et al., 2022). By utilizing and implementing AI-driven platforms and software that adapt to individual student needs. These tools can analyze each student's learning style, progress, strengths, and weaknesses to provide customized lessons and assignments. To follow this context, **AI-powered tutoring** is a highly effective tool. Educators can utilize AI chatbots and virtual tutors to offer students immediate assistance outside of classroom hours. These AI-driven systems can answer questions, provide explanations, and help with problem-solving. Educators employing this method must comprehensively grasp its integration with learning objectives, educate students on its utilization, and conduct multifaceted assessments to gauge students' learning progress effectively (Leary et al., 2021). Educators who implement these foundations would aid in upholding the academic integrity of their institution.

To aid educators and cut down on their administrative time, **automated grading** platforms can be used and added as part of their teaching strategies. By using AI to grade assignments, quizzes, and tests, allows educators to focus more on providing feedback and addressing specific learning needs. The use of **data-driven insights** can also be a great asset to educators and help them design their classes for their students' needs (Franzoni et al., 2020). By leveraging AI analytics to gain insights into student performance, educators can identify areas where students may be struggling and intervene with targeted support and resources. Educators can use AI for **content curation,** AI algorithms can recommend textbooks, articles, videos, and other materials tailored to each student's interests and learning goals. It can also help educators brainstorm ideas and develop needed content for their specified subject matter, minimizing the amount of time in content creation and more focused on the delivery of the material and student engagement.

To enhance student learning, the integration of **Virtual Reality (VR) and Augmented Reality (AR)** applications into lessons for immersive learning experiences (Beck, 2019). These technologies can transport students to historical events, remote locations, or simulated scientific experiments. Also, AI-powered **language translation** tools can be utilized to break down language barriers in diverse classrooms. These tools can facilitate communication and inclusivity among students who speak different languages. To add to this, **Natural Language Processing (NLP)** technologies can be incorporated to improve language arts instruction. AI can analyze students' writing and provide suggestions for grammar, style, and vocabulary enhancements (Meurers, 2020).

AI technologies, such as **student engagement analytics,** can help monitor student engagement during online classes or lectures, help identify when students are most attentive, and allow for adjusting teaching methods accordingly. **AI-enhanced assessments** can create interactive and adaptive assessments that challenge students at their individual skill levels. AI can adjust the difficulty of questions based on students' performance. Implementing these tools can create AI-driven early warning systems that flag at-risk students who may need additional support. This allows educators to intervene and provide timely assistance (Bertonini et al., 2022). AI can also be used for professional development for educators by recommending relevant training courses and resources to enhance their teaching skills.

In the classroom, educators can facilitate collaborative projects among students with AI-supported tools that help them work together efficiently, even in virtual or remote settings, to support **collaborative learning**. To make learning more engaging and enjoyable, **gamification** learning experiences that use AI to adapt game elements can be incorporated into individual students' education (Bennani et al., 2021). It will also be essential to teach students about the ethical implications of AI, including bias, privacy, and responsible use, to ensure they become informed digital citizens. These practical strategies showcase the versatility and potential of AI in education. Educators can tailor these approaches to suit their teaching style, subject matter, and students' needs, ultimately creating more effective and engaging learning environments. Top of that educators will need to diversify teaching to incorporate other skills with the use of AI to tackle the

Furthermore, educators will need to differentiate their teaching in the classroom to include critical thinking, experiential learning, creative thinking, problem-solving tools, and soft skills development in teaching. These are needed skills for all students as AI is further developed and becomes integrated into the framework of current society. A combination of these skills with AI integration can greatly enrich the educational experience. The following section will discuss some strategies and activities that align with these goals.

Educators can encourage critical thinking by using AI chatbots or virtual assistants to facilitate **Socratic questioning** sessions (Guo et al., 2023). These sessions can stimulate thoughtful discussions and promote a deeper understanding of topics. They can leverage AI-powered simulations and virtual labs that allow students to gain practical experience in various fields. For instance, in science classes, students can conduct virtual experiments to explore concepts, which can harness **experiential learning.** To help develop students' problem-solving skills, **AI-enhanced case studies** can be incorporated into learning tools. These are AI-driven data analysis tools that analyze real-world case studies as students explore solutions based on data-driven insights.

Creative thinking is vital as it drives innovation, problem-solving, and adaptability, fostering progress in both personal and professional realms (Nadjafikhaha & Yaftian, 2013). Educators can assign creative projects that require students to use AI tools to generate innovative solutions. For example, students can design AI-driven applications, write AI-generated poetry, or create art with AI algorithms to enhance **creative project-based learning**. To aid in this process, AI brainstorming tools can be utilized to assist students in generating and organizing ideas (Figoli et al., 2022). AI can suggest creative prompts, identify patterns, and help students explore different angles of a problem. To build on the collaborative process that Design Thinking and creative problem-solving depict, educators can assign group projects where students must work together to design and implement AI-driven solutions. An example of this can be presenting students with real-world problems that AI can help address. Encourage them to collaborate and use AI tools to find innovative solutions. This approach fosters and promotes problem-solving skills, teamwork, and enhances students' technological proficiency.

Educators can also utilize AI to build on students' **soft skills development** (Luckin & Holmes, 2016). They can organize AI-assisted debates or discussions on important social, ethical, or global topics. This encourages students to develop soft skills such as communication, persuasion, and empathy.

To build on their **critical analysis**, educators can engage students in critical discussions about AI's impact on society, ethics, and biases. Encourage them to analyze AI-related news, research, and developments, fostering critical thinking. AI can also be utilized as a self-assessment tool for reflection. For example, the use of AI-based assessments to evaluate and provide feedback on students' soft skills, such as adaptability, leadership, and problem-solving. This helps them recognize areas for improvement. Another example would be to ask students to maintain reflective journals and use AI language analysis tools to gain insights into their thought processes and emotional states. This can also promote self-awareness and emotional intelligence. Finally, AI can provide opportunities for creative writing, storytelling, and cultural exploration, by integrating AI language learning platforms that adapt to students' proficiency levels, educators can aid their students' learning challenges and bring more equity into their classrooms.

These strategies not only align with AI integration but also cultivate essential 21st-century skills, nurturing students' abilities in critical thinking, creative problem-solving, collaboration, and emotional intelligence (Luckin & Holmes, 2016). By combining these approaches, educators can create well-rounded learning experiences that prepare students for the complex challenges of the future.

SAMPLE PRACTICAL STRATEGIES IN THE CLASSROOM

In an ever-evolving world where technology continuously shapes the landscape of education, the importance of soft skills cannot be overstated. These skills encompass a wide range of human qualities, from effective communication and teamwork to emotional intelligence and adaptability. They form the foundation upon which success in both personal and professional realms is built, and they are in high demand in today's job market.

The classroom, as a vessel of learning and personal growth, plays a pivotal role in nurturing these essential soft skills. It is within these classrooms that students not only acquire knowledge but also refine their abilities to collaborate, communicate persuasively, and navigate the complex landscape of human emotions and relationships. Educators bear the responsibility of equipping students with the skills they need to thrive in an increasingly interconnected and dynamic world. The following section explores innovative strategies and tools that harness the potential of AI to foster the development of soft skills in the classroom.

Critical Thinking

Critical thinking is the cornerstone of informed decision-making, problem-solving, and intellectual growth. It is the ability to analyze, evaluate, and synthesize information, allowing individuals to make reasoned judgments and develop well-rounded perspectives (Shidqiyah et al., 2023). In an ever-changing world filled with complex issues, the significance of critical thinking cannot be overstated. It empowers individuals to question assumptions, seek evidence, and think beyond the surface, ultimately fostering intellectual independence. This skill transcends academic boundaries, permeating all aspects of life, from personal relationships to professional endeavors. Here are three sample activities that can promote critical thinking skills among general education students using AI:

These activities empower general education students to think critically about various aspects of AI, including its impact on information credibility, its role in creativity, and its potential as a problem-solving tool. They provide opportunities for students to engage with AI technology while honing their critical thinking skills, a valuable asset in today's information-rich world.

Critical thinking serves as a cornerstone in both the workforce and in addressing academic integrity in AI. In the workforce, critical thinking is the cornerstone of problem-solving, innovation, and decision-

Table 1. AI-Enhanced news analysis

AI-Enhanced News Analysis:	
Activity Description: Assign students to analyze news articles or social media posts related to a current event or issue. Introduce them to AI tools that can help fact-check information, detect bias, and analyze sentiment. Students must critically evaluate the credibility of sources, identify potential biases, and discern between facts and opinions.	Objectives: • Develop critical thinking by assessing the reliability of information. • Encourage media literacy and the ability to differentiate between reliable and unreliable sources. • Promote discussion on the role of AI in combating misinformation.

Table 2. AI-Driven creative writing

AI-Driven Creative Writing:	
Activity Description: Challenge students to write short stories, poems, or essays using AI-generated prompts or themes. AI algorithms can suggest creative ideas, characters, or settings. Students must critically evaluate and expand upon these prompts to develop unique and engaging narratives.	**Objectives:** • Cultivate critical thinking skills by assessing and enhancing AI-generated content. • Encourage creativity and originality in storytelling. • Promote reflection on the creative collaboration between humans and AI.

Table 3. AI-Assisted problem solving

AI-Assisted Problem Solving:	
Activity Description: Provide students with a complex problem or puzzle and introduce AI-driven problem-solving tools or algorithms. Students must work collaboratively to devise strategies, apply critical thinking, and use AI assistance to explore potential solutions. Encourage them to evaluate the effectiveness of AI in problem-solving.	**Objectives:** • Develop critical thinking and problem-solving abilities. • Promote teamwork and collaboration. • Encourage reflection on the role of AI as a problem-solving tool.

making. Employees equipped with strong critical thinking skills can analyze complex situations, identify potential issues, and devise effective solutions. They're adept at evaluating information, discerning biases, and making sound judgments. In a rapidly evolving landscape where job roles continuously shift, individuals with robust critical thinking abilities adapt more readily, contributing to creativity, efficiency, and strategic planning.

When combating academic integrity issues in AI, critical thinking becomes essential to discern the ethical implications of AI implementation. With critical thinking, stakeholders can anticipate the challenges and implications of integrating AI in education, thereby making informed decisions to preserve academic integrity. Critical thinking prompts individuals to scrutinize the use of AI tools for plagiarism detection or exam invigilation. It helps in distinguishing between enhancing learning experiences and compromising student privacy or fostering a culture of distrust.

Experiential Learning

Experiential learning is a dynamic educational approach that emphasizes hands-on experiences as a primary method of learning (Bradberry & Maio, 2019). In contrast to traditional classroom instruction,

Table 4. AI-Enhanced virtual field trips

AI-Enhanced Virtual Field Trips:	
Activity Description: Organize virtual field trips using AI-guided tours or explorations. For example, students can "visit" historical landmarks, art museums, or ecosystems through AI-enhanced virtual tours. AI can provide contextual information, answer questions, and make the experience interactive.	**Objectives:** • Facilitate experiential learning by immersing students in real-world environments. • Encourage critical thinking and observation skills during virtual explorations. • Foster cultural and historical awareness through AI-guided experiences.

Table 5. AI-Driven data analysis projects

AI-Driven Data Analysis Projects:	
Activity Description: Assign students data analysis projects that involve real datasets obtained from various sources (e.g., government databases, research institutions). Students use AI tools and machine learning algorithms to analyze the data, draw conclusions, and make data-driven recommendations.	**Objectives:** • Promote experiential learning through hands-on data analysis. • Develop critical thinking skills by interpreting complex datasets. • Encourage problem-solving and decision-making based on AI-driven insights.

Table 6. AI-Powered business consultations

AI-Powered Business Consultations:	
Activity Description: Partner with local businesses or organizations and assign student teams to act as AI-driven consultants. Students analyze the business's data, operations, or marketing strategies using AI tools. They then present recommendations for improving efficiency or solving specific business challenges.	**Objectives:** • Create experiential learning opportunities through real-world consulting experiences. • Develop critical thinking skills by identifying business opportunities and challenges. • Encourage teamwork and collaboration in solving practical problems with AI support.

experiential learning encourages students to actively engage with concepts, theories, and real-world problems through direct encounters. Whether it involves field trips, internships, simulations, or practical projects, experiential learning immerses students in authentic experiences that promote deeper understanding and skill development. This approach not only enhances retention but also cultivates critical thinking, problem-solving, and adaptability. Here are three experiential learning activities:

These experiential learning activities immerse students in real-world scenarios, providing opportunities to apply AI technology and critical thinking skills to authentic situations (Beckem & Watkins, 2012). They enable students to gain practical experience and insights while preparing them for future challenges in a variety of fields.

Experiential learning holds significance in both the workforce and the realm of academic integrity in AI. In the workforce, experiential learning allows individuals to apply theoretical knowledge in practical settings. This hands-on approach fosters skill development, enhances problem-solving abilities, and encourages innovation. Employees engage in real-world scenarios, honing their critical thinking and decision-making skills. This practical experience equips them with a deeper understanding of their roles and the challenges they might encounter, making them more adaptable and resourceful in addressing complex, real-time situations.

When addressing academic integrity concerns in AI, experiential learning can play a crucial role. By incorporating hands-on experiences with AI tools and systems, students can understand the ethical implications of these technologies (Borbajo et al., 2023). They can witness firsthand the potential biases in algorithms or the challenges of ensuring fairness and transparency in automated decision-making. Experiential learning allows students to explore the limitations and capabilities of AI systems, encouraging critical thinking about the ethical use of AI in educational settings. in combating academic integrity issues related to AI, experiential learning can help students understand the potential risks associated with technology, such as plagiarism detection software or automated grading systems. By actively engaging with these tools, students gain a deeper comprehension of their capabilities and limitations, fostering a more ethical use of AI in their academic work.

Creative Thinking and Problem-Solving Tools and Activities

Creative thinking and problem-solving are indispensable skills in an ever-evolving world. They empower individuals to confront complex challenges with imaginative solutions, fostering adaptability and resilience (Bishan, 2015). This succinct exploration delves into the realm of creative thinking and problem-solving tools and activities. From brainstorming sessions that ignite inventive ideas to AI-powered algorithms that offer innovative insights, these tools and activities unveil new avenues for innovation. Here are three examples of creative thinking and problem-solving tools and activities that can be implemented in the classroom:

These creative thinking and problem-solving tools and activities not only inspire innovation but also provide students with practical experiences in applying AI to solve real challenges. They encourage students to think outside the box, collaborate effectively, and leverage AI technology as a tool for creative problem-solving.

Table 7. Design thinking workshops

Design Thinking Workshops:	
Activity Description: Organize design thinking workshops where students collaborate to address complex challenges. Using design thinking methodologies, students empathize with end-users, define problems, ideate solutions, create prototypes, and test their ideas. AI can assist in the ideation phase by generating innovative concepts or analyzing user data to inform design choices.	**Objectives:** • Cultivate creative thinking by encouraging students to brainstorm and generate unconventional ideas. • Develop problem-solving skills as students tackle real-world problems through a human-centered approach. • Integrate AI-driven brainstorming tools or predictive analytics to enhance idea generation and solution development.

Table 8. AI-Enhanced hackathons

AI-Enhanced Hackathons:	
Activity Description: Host hackathons that focus on solving specific challenges using AI technologies. Students form teams and work intensively to develop AI-driven solutions, such as mobile apps, chatbots, or data-driven models. AI mentors and resources can be provided to guide students during the event.	**Objectives:** • Foster creative problem-solving by encouraging students to innovate with AI. • Promote teamwork and collaboration in creating practical AI solutions. • Provide a platform for students to explore AI's potential in addressing real-world issues.

Table 9. AI art and music generation

AI Art and Music Generation:	
Activity Description: Explore the intersection of AI and creativity by engaging students in art and music projects. Students can use AI tools to generate art, music compositions, or poetry. They can experiment with AI algorithms that can suggest artistic styles, harmonies, or themes, serving as creative prompts.	**Objectives:** • Cultivate creative thinking by challenging students to create unique artworks with AI assistance. • Encourage exploration of AI's role in artistic expression. • Promote reflection on the collaboration between human creativity and AI technology.

Creative thinking, problem-solving tools, and activities hold substantial value in both the workforce and in addressing academic integrity concerns in AI (Xie et al., 2023). In the workforce, these skills foster innovation and adaptability. Employees adept in creative thinking can propose novel solutions to complex issues, promoting innovation and advancement within their roles and organizations. Problem-solving tools enable individuals to navigate challenges, fostering resilience and agility in dynamic work environments. These skills encourage a proactive approach to tackling issues, enhancing productivity and efficiency in problem resolution.

When addressing academic integrity concerns in AI, creative thinking and problem-solving tools aid in developing ethical AI systems and practices. These skills empower educators, developers, and policymakers to ideate innovative solutions to mitigate the biases in AI algorithms and enhance transparency in decision-making processes. Innovative problem-solving helps anticipate and address ethical dilemmas surrounding AI implementation in education, ensuring a balanced and ethical integration that upholds academic integrity. Also, creative thinking and problem-solving activities can aid in designing AI tools that actively promote academic integrity. These skills and tools encourage individuals to think outside the box, fostering creative, ethical, and innovative solutions. They are crucial in navigating the challenges of AI integration in education and promoting academic integrity by developing ethical and effective AI systems.

Soft Skills Development

Soft skills are interpersonal, communication, and personal attributes that enable individuals to interact effectively with others and succeed in various aspects of life, including education, work, and personal relationships (Asefer & Abidin, 2021). These skills are often intangible and include qualities like communication, teamwork, adaptability, empathy, problem-solving, and emotional intelligence. In the student context, soft skills are essential for effective learning, collaboration, and personal growth. They enable students to communicate clearly, work well in teams, handle challenges, and navigate diverse social and academic environments. In the business world, soft skills are highly prized by employers as they contribute to a productive and harmonious work environment. Employees with strong soft skills excel in areas such as leadership, customer service, teamwork, and conflict resolution, ultimately driving business success. These skills are increasingly important in today's global and interconnected workplace, where effective communication and interpersonal relationships are crucial for career advancement and organizational growth. Here are three examples of activities and tools that can be used to develop soft skills in students:

These soft skills development activities and tools leverage AI to provide students with valuable insights and practical experiences in areas such as communication, leadership, teamwork, and emotional

Table 10. AI-Enhanced communication workshops

AI-Enhanced Communication Workshops	
Activity Description: Organize communication workshops where students engage in AI-mediated communication exercises. For instance, students can practice delivering persuasive speeches or engaging in difficult conversations with AI-driven virtual conversational partners. AI can provide instant feedback on communication style, tone, and effectiveness.	**Objectives:** • Develop effective communication skills, including active listening and empathetic communication. • Cultivate self-awareness by receiving feedback from AI on communication strengths and areas for improvement. • Encourage students to adapt their communication style to different contexts and audiences.

Table 11. AI-Powered leadership and teamwork assessments

AI-Powered Leadership and Teamwork Assessments:	
Activity Description: Implement AI-driven leadership and teamwork assessments where students participate in group projects. AI tools can collect data on individual and team behaviors, leadership styles, and collaboration dynamics. Students receive AI-generated reports that highlight their leadership and teamwork strengths and suggest areas for growth.	**Objectives:** • Foster leadership and teamwork skills by providing students with actionable feedback. • Encourage self-reflection and self-improvement in leadership roles. • Promote effective collaboration and conflict resolution in team environments.

Table 12. AI-Enhanced emotional intelligence training

AI-Enhanced Emotional Intelligence Training:	
Activity Description: Offer emotional intelligence training sessions where students use AI applications to assess and enhance their emotional intelligence (EQ). AI can guide students through exercises that help them recognize and manage emotions, empathize with others, and develop emotional resilience.	**Objectives:** • Develop emotional intelligence by increasing self-awareness and empathy. • Encourage students to recognize and regulate emotions effectively. • Provide AI-guided tools and resources for ongoing EQ development.

intelligence. They equip students with essential interpersonal and self-awareness skills that are crucial for success in various personal and professional contexts.

Soft skills development is crucial in both the workforce and addressing academic integrity concerns in AI. In the workforce, soft skills such as communication, teamwork, adaptability, and emotional intelligence are highly valued. They complement technical competencies, enabling employees to collaborate effectively, communicate ideas, and navigate diverse work environments. These skills foster a harmonious workplace, enhancing teamwork, productivity, and overall job performance (Meeks, 2017). Employees with strong soft skills are better equipped to handle challenges and adapt to changes, promoting a positive work culture.

In combating academic integrity issues in AI, soft skills play a pivotal role. Effective communication and collaboration skills are essential in fostering ethical discussions and decision-making around the integration of AI in education. Educators, developers, and policymakers need to work together, leveraging their communication and teamwork abilities to address the ethical implications of AI tools effectively. Likewise, emotional intelligence plays a critical role in understanding the ethical considerations and implications of AI in education. It helps individuals discern the potential biases in AI algorithms and fosters empathy toward the impact of technology on students' learning experiences and privacy.

Soft skills are also essential in promoting a culture of academic integrity in the context of AI. Educators need to communicate effectively with students about the ethical use of AI tools, ensuring that they understand the importance of academic honesty and the responsible utilization of technology. Overall, soft skills development fosters a beneficial work environment and aids in ethical decision-making around AI implementation in education. These skills are fundamental in promoting a culture of academic integrity and ensuring the responsible integration of AI in the educational sphere.

CONCLUSION

In conclusion, the chapter offers a comprehensive overview of the transformative impact of Artificial Intelligence (AI) in higher education, with a specific focus on its implications for academic integrity and classroom strategies. The analysis begins by acknowledging AI's pervasive influence across diverse sectors, extending from healthcare to finance, and underscores its pivotal role as a driving force behind the fourth industrial revolution. As AI continues to permeate contemporary society, it becomes imperative for educators in higher education to adapt to this profound cultural shift, as educators are the front-line developers of the future workforce, helping them build their knowledge of each industry and building strategies for their success in that dominion.

The chapter further reveals how AI has emerged as a game-changer within the realm of industry, elevating productivity, refining decision-making processes, creating new avenues of employment, enhancing the customer experience, and mitigating risks. The evolving dynamics of the global market and the rapid evolution of emerging technologies underscore the irreplaceable role of AI in reshaping the landscape of business management and bolstering competitiveness. This transformation is evident through the convergence of information technology (IT) and operational activities, the implementation of data-driven strategies, and the integration of fifth generation (5G) mobile technology.

Within the sphere of education, the chapter accentuates AI's potential to optimize both teaching and learning experiences. AI offers students unrestricted access to learning materials, personalized tutoring, swift responses to inquiries, and tailored learning experiences. Simultaneously, educators benefit from AI through the automation of administrative tasks, support in lesson planning, and insights into student performance, allowing for the allocation of more time to teaching and student well-being.

It delves into the critical issue of academic integrity in the era of AI. It emphasizes the enduring significance of traditional academic integrity principles, including honesty, trust, fairness, respect, and responsibility, as foundational to the educational process. In this context, AI is presented as a valuable ally, equipped to detect plagiarism, ensure equitable assessments, and provide personalized learning experiences while upholding ethical standards.

The information also addresses the imperative of redefining academic integrity in higher education, highlighting the necessity of striking a balance between the advantages of AI and the potential risks to privacy and fairness. Educators are encouraged to acquaint themselves with AI tools, champion ethical AI usage, and educate students about AI's role in upholding academic integrity. Human oversight is deemed essential, particularly in the context of grading and addressing instances of academic misconduct, to ensure fairness and contextual understanding. Lastly, the chapter underscores the importance of nurturing critical thinking and fostering discussions on academic integrity within the classroom, promoting a judicious and responsible approach to AI integration. It serves as a guiding framework for educators and educational institutions to embrace AI as a potent tool for elevating the quality of teaching and learning while maintaining the core principles of academic integrity.

REFERENCES

Asefer, A., & Abidin, Z. (2021, December). Soft skills and graduates'employability in the 21st century - from employers' perspectives: A review of literature. *International Journal of Infrastructure Research and Management*, *9*(2), 44–59. https://iukl.edu.my/rmc/wp-content/uploads/sites/4/2022/02/5.-Al-Asefer_compressed.pdf

Beck, D. (2019). Special Issue: Augmented and Virtual Reality in Education: Immersive Learning Research. *Journal of Educational Computing Research*, *57*(7), 1619–1625. Advance online publication. doi:10.1177/0735633119854035

Beckem, J., & Watkins, M. (2012, October). Bringing Life to Learning: Immersive Experiential Learning Simulations for Online and Blended Courses. *Journal of Asynchronous Learning Networks*, *16*(5), 61–70. https://files.eric.ed.gov/fulltext/EJ1000091.pdf

Bennani, S., Maalel, A., & Ghezala, H. (2021, December 01). Adaptive gamification in E-learning: A literature review and future challenges. *Computer Applications in Engineering Education*, *30*(2), 628–642. doi:10.1002/cae.22477

Bertolini, R., Finch, S., & Nehm, R. (2022). Quantifying variability in predictions of student performance: Examining. *Computers and Education: Artificial Intelligence*, *3*, 100067. doi:10.1016/j.caeai.2022.100067

Bishan, G. (2015). Cultivating Critical Thinking Skills in the Classroom. *Global International Research Thoughts (GIRT), 3*(1). https://girt.shodhsagar.com/index.php/j/article/view/14/15

Borbajo, M., Malbas, M., & Dacanay, L. (2023). Reforming Education: The Global Impact of Integrating Artificial Intelligence in the Classroom Environment. *American Journal of Language, Literacy and Learning in STEM Education (2993-2769), 1*(5), 16–27. https://grnjournal.us/index.php/STEM/article/view/356

Boulay, B. (2016). Artificial intelligence as an effective classroom assistant. *IEEE Intelligent Systems*, *31*(6), 76–81. doi:10.1109/MIS.2016.93

Bradberry, L., & Maio, J. (2019). Learning By Doing: The Long-Term Impact of Experiential Learning Programs on Student Success. *Journal of Political Science Education*, *15*(1), 94–111. doi:10.1080/15512169.2018.1485571

Bretag, T., Mahmud, S., Wallace, M., Walker, R., James, C., Green, M., & Partridge, L. (2011, December). Core elements of exemplary academic integrity. *International Journal for Educational Integrity*, *7*(2), 3-12. file:///C:/Users/maya3/Downloads/ojsadmin,+Bretag+et+al+Oct+11.pdf

Chen, L., Chen, P., & Lin, Z. (2020). Artificial Intelligence in Education: A Review. *IEEE Access : Practical Innovations, Open Solutions*. Retrieved November 2023, from

Dwivedi, Y., Hughes, L., Ismagilova, E., Aarts, G., Coombs, C., Crick, T., & Janssen, M. (2021). Artificial Intelligence (AI): Multidisciplinary perspectives on emerging challenges, opportunities, and agenda for research, practice and policy. *International Journal of Information Management*, *57*, 101994. Advance online publication. Retrieved November 2023, from. doi:10.1016/j.ijinfomgt.2019.08.002

Figoli, F., Mattioli, F., & Rampino, L. (2022). *Artificial intelligence in the design process - The Impact on Creativity and Team Collaboration.* Milan: FrancoAngeli. https://library.oapen.org/handle/20.500.12657/53627

Francesc, P. (2019). Artificial intelligence in education: challenges and opportunities for sustainable development. *Working Papers on Education Policy*. Respositorio. https://repositorio.minedu.gob.pe/bitstream/handle/20.500.12799/6533/Artificial%20intelligence%20in%20education%20challenges%20and%20opportunities%20for%20sustainable%20development.pdf?sequence=1&isAllowed=y

Franzoni, V., Milani, A., Mengoni, P., & Piccinatio, F. (2020). Artificial Intelligence Visual Metaphors in E-Learning Interfaces for Learning Analytics. *Applied Sciences (Basel, Switzerland)*, *10*(20), 7195. doi:10.3390/app10207195

Guo, K., Zhong, Y., Li, D., & Chu, S. (2023, October). Effects of chatbot-assisted in-class debates on students'. *Computers & Education*, *203*(104862), 104862. doi:10.1016/j.compedu.2023.104862

Hollman, T., Palmer, N., Chaffin, D., & Luthans, K. (2021). Lying, Cheating, & Stealing: Strategies for Mitigating Technology-Driven Academic Dishonesty in Collegiate Schools of Business. *Mountain Plains Journal of Business and Technology*. https://openspaces.unk.edu/mpjbt/vol22/iss1/

Krasavina, V. (2019). Current trends in the IT services market. *E3S Web of Conferences*. https://www.e3s-conferences.org/articles/e3sconf/abs/2019/61/e3sconf_itese18_04039/e3sconf_itese18_04039.html

Leary, M., Tylka, A., Corsi, V., & Bryner, B. (2021). The Effect of First-Year Seminar Classroom Design on Social Integration and Retention of STEM First-Time, Full-Time College Freshmen. *Education Research International*, *2021*(4262905), 9. https://www.hindawi.com/journals/edri/2021/4262905/. doi:10.1155/2021/4262905

Loeckx, J. (2016). Blurring boundaries in education: context and impact of MOOCs. *International Review of Research in Open and Distributed Learning*.

Luckin, R., & Holmes, W. (2016). Intelligence Unleashed: An argument for AI in Education. *UCL Knowledge Lab*. https://www.pearson.com/content/dam/corporate/global/pearson-dot-com/files/innovation/Intelligence-Unleashed-Publication.pdf

Luckin, R., & Holmes, W. (2016). *Intelligence Unleashed: An argument for AI in Education.* UCL Discovery. London: Pearson. https://www.pearson.com/content/dam/corporate/global/pearson-dot-com/files/innovation/Intelligence-Unleashed-Publication.pdf

Matyushok, V., Krasavina, V., Berezin, A., & García, J. (2021). The global economy in technological transformation conditions: A review of modern trends. *Economic Research-Ekonomska Istraživanja*. https://www.tandfonline.com/doi/full/10.1080/1331677X.2020.1844030

Meeks, G. (2017). *Critical Soft Skills to Achieve Success in the Workplace*. Walden University ProQuest Dissertations Publishing.

Mellit, A., & Kalogirou, S. (2008). Artificial Intelligence Techniques for Photovoltaic Applications: A Review. *Progress in Energy and Combustion Science*, *34*(5), 574–632. doi:10.1016/j.pecs.2008.01.001

Meurers, D. (2020). Natural Language Processing and Language. *The Concise Encyclopedia of Applied Linguistics*. https://www.sfs.uni-tuebingen.de/~dm/papers/Meurers-20.pdf

Nadjafikhaha, M., & Yaftian, N. (2013). The frontage of Creativity and Mathematical Creativity. *ScienceDirect*, *90*, 344 – 350. https://pdf.sciencedirectassets.com/277811/1-s2.0-S1877042813X00230/1-s2.0-S1877042813019897/main.pdf?X-Amz-Security-Token=IQoJb3JpZ2luX2VjEHEaCXVzLWVhc3QtMSJIMEYCIQC6MnNKqE8vWm1Unf6yKMi4r5t6JOyfBP6p%2BpYIQNedGAIhAKdYMG3RLDGIgCow9xHAFv%2B64zCwdyWtzOiqn91b

Păvăloaia, V., & Necula, S. (2023). *Artificial Intelligence as a Disruptive Technology—A Systematic Literature Review*. Basel: MDPI. https://www.mdpi.com/2079-9292/12/5/1102

Peeters, M. M., Diggelen, J., Bosch, K., Bronkhorst, A., Neerincx, M., Schraagen, J., & Raaijmakers, S. (2021). Hybrid collective intelligence in a human–AI society. *AI & Society*. https://link.springer.com/article/10.1007/s00146-020-01005-y

Perkins, M. (2023). Academic Integrity considerations of AI Large Language Models in the post-pandemic era: ChatGPT and beyond. *Journal of University Teaching & Learning Practice*. https://ro.uow.edu.au/jutlp/vol20/iss2/07/

Rangarajan, A. K., & Ramachandran, H. K. (2021). A preliminary analysis of AI based smartphone application for diagnosis of COVID-19 using chest X-ray images. *Expert systems with applications*.

Sefcik, L., Striepe, M., & Yorke, J. (2020). Mapping the landscape of academic integrity education programs: what approaches are effective? Sefcik, Lesley; Striepe, Michelle; Yorke, Jonathan, 2020, Mapping the landscape of academic integrity education programs: what approaches are effective? *Journal of Asynchronous Learning Networks*, *16*(5), 61–71. https://files.eric.ed.gov/fulltext/EJ1000091.pdf

Seldon, A., & Abidoye, O. (2018). The fourth education revolution: will artificial intelligence liberate or infantilise humanity. *Higher Education*. Springer. https://link.springer.com/article/10.1007/s10734-020-00506-5

Shidqiyah, S., Thalib, B., Wiratama, R., Alam, S., & Riyanto, R. (2023, December). DEVELOPMENT OF THE LATEST CURRICULUM-BASED LEARNING MODEL TO IMPROVE STUDENTS' DIGITAL LITERACY AND CRITICAL THINKING SKILLS IN THE INFORMATION TECHNOLOGY ERA. [INJOTEL]. *International Journal of Teaching and Learning*, *1*(4), 412–425. https://injotel.org/index.php/12/article/view/36/55

Underwood, J., & Luckin, R. (2011). What is AIED and why does Education need it? A report for the UK's TLRP Technology Enhanced Learning - Artificial Intelligence in Education Theme. *The London Knowledge Lab*. https://www.researchgate.net/profile/Joshua-Underwood-3/publication/241698223_What_is_AIED_and_why_does_Education_need_it/links/56e519d508ae68afa11068a7/What-is-AIED-and-why-does-Education-need-it.pdf

Xie, Y., Wu, S., & Chakravarty, S. (2023, October 2023). AI Meets AI: Artificial Intelligence and Academic Integrity - A Survey on Mitigating AI-Assisted Cheating in Computing Education. *ACM*, 79-83. doi:10.1145/3585059.3611449

Zhai, X., Chu, X., Chai, C., Jong, M., Istenic, A., Spector, M., & C, N. (2021). *A Review of Artificial Intelligence (AI) in Education from 2010 to 2020.* New York City: Hoboken: Hindawi Coplexity.

KEY TERMS AND DEFINITIONS

Academic Integrity: Upholding honesty and ethical conduct in academic work, including proper citation, originality, and avoiding plagiarism.

Artificial Intelligence: Refers to the development of computer systems and software that can perform tasks that typically require human intelligence.

Collaborative Teams: Groups of individuals working together to achieve common goals, share ideas, and leverage collective expertise to solve problems or complete tasks.

Creative Thinking: The ability to generate innovative ideas, approaches, and solutions by thinking outside traditional boundaries and embracing originality.

Critical Thinking: The capacity to analyze, evaluate, and synthesize information and ideas systematically, enabling effective problem-solving and decision-making.

Experiential learning: An educational approach that emphasizes hands-on, practical experiences as a primary method of Learning, promoting active engagement and skill development.

Soft Skills: Interpersonal and personal attributes, including communication, teamwork, adaptability, empathy, and problem-solving, that enhance interactions and effectiveness in both academic and professional contexts.

Compilation of References

Abd-Alrazaq, A., AlSaad, R., Alhuwail, D., Ahmed, A., Healy, P. M., Latifi, S., & Sheikh, J. (2023). Large language models in medical education: Opportunities, challenges, and future directions. *JMIR Medical Education*, *9*(1), e48291. doi:10.2196/48291 PMID:37261894

Abd-Elaa, E. S., Gamage, S. H., & Mills, J. E. (2019). *Artificial intelligence is a tool for cheating academic integrity.* 30th Annual Conference for the Australasian Association for Engineering Education (AAEE 2019): Educators Becoming Agents of Change: Innovate, Integrate, Motivate. Montreal, Quebec, Canada. https://aaee.net.au/wp-content/uploads/2020/07/AAEE2019_Annual_Conference_paper_180.pdf

Adam, L. (2016). Student Perspectives on Plagiarism. In T. Bretag (Ed.), *Handbook of Academic Integrity* (pp. 519–535). Springer. doi:10.1007/978-981-287-098-8_67

Adiguzel, T., Kaya, M. H., & Cansu, F. K. (2023). Revolutionizing education with AI: Exploring the transformative potential of ChatGPT. *Contemporary Educational Technology*, *15*(3), ep429.AdvanceHE. (n.d.) *Authentic Assessment in the era of AI.* AdvanceHE. https://www.advance-he.ac.uk/membership/all-member-benefit-projects/Authentic-Assessment-in-the-era-of-AI

AI Writing Check. (2023, August) *August 2023 Update – AI Writing Check is no longer available* [Press release]. AI Writing Check. https://aiwritingcheck.org/

Akbari, N. (2023, July 14) *Academic Integrity in the age of AI: Approaching Apocalypse or Achievable Equilibrium?* Linkedin. https://www.linkedin.com/pulse/academic-integrity-age-ai-approaching-apocalypse-achievable

Alam, A. (2022). Employing adaptive learning and intelligent tutoring robots for virtual classrooms and smart campuses: Reforming education in the age of artificial intelligence. In *Advanced Computing and Intelligent Technologies Proceedings of ICACIT.* Springer.

Alasadi, E. A., & Baiz, C. R. (2023). Generative AI in education and research: Opportunities, concerns, and solutions. *Journal of Chemical Education*, *100*(8), 2965–2971. doi:10.1021/acs.jchemed.3c00323

Alba, D. (2022, December 8). OpenAI Chatbot Spits Out Biased Musings, Despite Guardrails. *Bloomberg.* https://www.bloomberg.com/news/newsletters/2022-12-08/chatgpt-open-ai-s-chatbot-is-spitting-out-biased-sexist-results accessed September 20

Alhadabi, A., & Karpinski, A. C. (2020). Grit, self-efficacy, achievement orientation goals, and academic performance in university students. *International Journal of Adolescence and Youth*, *25*(1), 519–535. doi:10.1080/02673843.2019.1679202

Alkhaqani, A. L. (2023). ChatGPT and Nursing Education: Challenges and Opportunities. *Al-Rafidain Journal of Medical Sciences (ISSN 2789-3219)*, *4*, 50-51.

Allyn, B. (2023, August 16). 'New York Times' considers legal action against OpenAI as copyright tensions swirl. *New York Times.* https://www.npr.org/2023/08/16/1194202562/new-york-times-considers-legal-action-against-openai-as-copyright-tensions-swirl

Al-Sibai, N. (2023, June 06). *AI Plagiarism Detection Software Keeps Falsely Accusing Students of Cheating.* Futurism. https://futurism.com/ai-plagiarism-software-false-accusing-students

Alston, E. (2023). *ChatGPT vs. Bing Chat: Which AI chatbot should you use?* Zapier. https://zapier.com/blog/chatgpt-vs-bing-chat/

Altmann, G., & Steedman, M. (1988). Interaction with context during human sentence processing. *Cognition, 30*(3), 191–238. doi:10.1016/0010-0277(88)90020-0 PMID:3215002

Alvero, R. (2023). ChatGPT: Rumors of human providers' demise have been greatly exaggerated. *Fertility and Sterility, 119*(6), 930–931. doi:10.1016/j.fertnstert.2023.03.010 PMID:36921837

American College Health Association. (2022). *American College Health Association: National College Health Assessment III Fall 2022 Reference Group Executive Summary.* American College Health Association. https://www.acha.org/documents/ncha/NCHA-III_FALL_2022_REFERENCE_GROUP_EXECUTIVE_SUMMARY.pdf

Amzalag, M., Shapira, N., & Dolev, N. (2021). Two Sides of the Coin: Lack of Academic Integrity in Exams During the Corona Pandemic, Students' and Lecturers' Perceptions. *Journal of Academic Ethics, 20*(2), 243–263. https://doi-org.ezproxy.derby.ac.uk/10.1007/s10805-021-09413-5. doi:10.1007/s10805-021-09413-5 PMID:33846681

Anderman, M., Cupp, K., & Lane, D. (2009). Impulsivity and academic cheating. *Journal of Experimental Education, 78*(1), 135–150. doi:10.1080/00220970903224636

Anders, B. (2023). *The AI literacy imperative: Empowering instructors & students.* Sovorel.

Anderson, C. (2023, June 01) *The False Promise of AI Writing Detectors.* Linkedin. https://www.linkedin.com/pulse/false-promise-ai-writing-detectors-carol-anderson

Anderson, L. W., Krathwohl, D. R., & Associates. (2001). A taxonomy for learning, teaching, and assessing: A revision of Bloom's taxonomy of educational objectives. Allyn & Bacon/Pearson Education Group, Boston, MA.

Anderson, N., Belavy, D. L., Perle, S. M., Hendricks, S., Hespanhol, L., Verhagen, E., & Memon, A. R. (2023). AI did not write this manuscript, or did it? Can we trick the AI text detector into generated texts? The potential future of ChatGPT and AI in Sports & Exercise Medicine manuscript generation. *BMJ Open Sport & Exercise Medicine, 9*(1), e001568. doi:10.1136/bmjsem-2023-001568 PMID:36816423

Andrews, S., & Glendinning, I. (2023). Governing academic integrity: Conceptualizing the assurance and efficacy of strategies and outcomes. Eaton, S. (Ed), Handbook for Academic Integrity, 2nd Edition. Springer. doi:10.1007/978-981-287-079-7_185-1

Andrews, S., Bare, L., Bentley, P., Goedegebuure, L., Pugsley, C., & Rance, B. (2016). *Contingent academic employment in Australian universities.* LH Martin Institute.

Andriopoulos, C. (2022). *Purposeful Curiosity.* Hachette.

Anohina-Naumeca, A., Tauginienė, L., & Odineca, T. (2018). Academic integrity policies of Baltic state-financed universities in online public spaces. *International Journal for Educational Integrity, 14*(1), 8. doi:10.1007/s40979-018-0031-z

Anson, C. M., & Kruse, O. (2023). Plagiarism Detection and Intertextuality Software. In O. Kruse, C. Rapp, C. M. Anson, K. Benetos, E. Cotos, A. Devitt, & A. Shibani (Eds.), *Digital Writing Technologies in Higher Education: Theory, Research, and Practice* (pp. 231–243). Springer International Publishing. doi:10.1007/978-3-031-36033-6_15

Anthropic. (2023, July 14) *Claude 2* [Press release]. Anthropic PBC. https://www.anthropic.com/index/claude-2

APDR Staff (2023, August 14). Organisations in Australia set to ban ChatGPT and generative AI apps on work devices. https://asiapacificdefencereporter.com/organisations-in-australia-set-to-ban-chatgpt-and-generative-ai-apps-on-work-devices/

Arantes, J. A. (2022). Personalization in Australian K-12 classrooms: How might digital teaching and learning tools produce intangible consequences for teachers' workplace conditions? *Australian Educational Researcher*, 1–18. doi:10.1007/s13384-022-00530-7 PMID:35505893

Archbald, D. A., & Newmann, F. M. (1988). *Beyond standardized testing: Assessing authentic academic achievement in the secondary school*. Office of Educational Research and Improvement.

Arts Law Centre. (2023). *Artificial Intelligence (AI) and Copyright*. Arts Law Centre. https://www.artslaw.com.au/information-sheet/artificial-intelligence-ai-and-copyright/

Asefer, A., & Abidin, Z. (2021, December). Soft skills and graduates' employability in the 21st century - from employers' perspectives: A review of literature. *International Journal of Infrastructure Research and Management*, *9*(2), 44–59. https://iukl.edu.my/rmc/wp-content/uploads/sites/4/2022/02/5.-Al-Asefer_compressed.pdf

Ashford-Rowe, K., Herrington, J., & Brown, C. (2014). Establishing the critical elements that determine authentic assessment. *Assessment & Evaluation in Higher Education*, *39*(2), 205–222. doi:10.1080/02602938.2013.819566

Atleson, M. (2023, July 06). *Watching the detectives: Suspicious marketing claims for tools that spot AI-generated content*. USA Federal Trade Commission. https://www.ftc.gov/business-guidance/blog/2023/07/watching-detectives-suspicious-marketing-claims-tools-spot-ai-generated-content

AUA. (2023). *Student code of ethics*. American University of Armenia. https://policies.aua.am/policy/10

Australasian Academic Integrity Network. (2023). Submission to the House Standing Committee on employment, education and training inquiry into the use of generative artificial intelligence in the Australian education system. In *Inquiry into the use of generative artificial intelligence in the Australian education system - Submission 58*. https://www.aph.gov.au/DocumentStore.ashx?id=e5bbb538-24c1-4482-9777-12872d8a3ef7&subId=745244

Australasian Academic Integrity Network. (2023). *Summary of institutional responses to the use of generative artificial intelligence*. AAIN. https://wordpress-ms.deakin.edu.au/academicintegrity/wp-content/uploads/sites/290/2023/06/AAIN-Institutional-Responses-to-the-use-of-Generative-Artificial-Intelligence-V1.1.pdf

Australian Catholic University. (2023, July 25). *Artificial intelligence (AI) tools*. ACU. https://libguides.acu.edu.au/referencing/artificial-intelligence-tools

Australian Federal Police. (2022). *Identity crime*. AFP. https://www.afp.gov.au/what-we-do/crime-types/fraud/identity-crime

Australian Government Department of Education. (2021). *Higher education standards framework (threshold standards) 2021*. Legislation. https://www.legislation.gov.au/Details/F2022C00105

Australian Government Tertiary Education Quality and Standards Agency. (TEQSA). (2023). *TEQSA module 3 — Policies and procedures*. TEQSA. https://learning.teqsa.gov.au/mod/scorm/player.php?a=3&currentorg=TEQSA_Module_3_-_Policies_and_procedures_ORG&scoid=12

Australian Government. (2022). *Literacy and access | Style Manual*. Australian Government. Www.stylemanual.gov.auCommonwealth of Australia. https://www.stylemanual.gov.au/accessible-and-inclusive-content/literacy-and-access

Australian Government. (2023, September). *Artificial intelligence*. Australian Government. https://www.industry.gov.au/science-technology-and-innovation/technology/artificial-intelligence

Australian Qualifications Framework Council. (2013). *Australian qualifications framework second edition January 2013*. AFQ. https://www.aqf.edu.au/framework/australian-qualifications-framework

Awdry, R., & Ives, B. (2022). International predictors of contract cheating in higher education. *Journal of Academic Ethics*, 1–20. PMID:35431710

Aydın, Ö., & Karaarslan, E. (2023). Is ChatGPT leading generative AI? What is beyond expectations? *Academic Platform Journal of Engineering and Smart Systems*, *11*(3), 118–134. doi:10.21541/apjess.1293702

Baartman, L., Baukema, H., & Prins, F. (2023). Exploring students' feedback seeking behavior in the context of programmatic assessment. *Assessment & Evaluation in Higher Education*, *48*(5), 598–612. doi:10.1080/02602938.2022.2100875

Baartman, L., van Schilt-Mol, T., & van der Vleuten, C. (2022). Programmatic assessment design choices in nine programs in higher education. *Frontiers in Education*, *7*, 931980. doi:10.3389/feduc.2022.931980

Baidoo-anu, D., & Owusu Ansah, L. (2023). Education in the era of generative artificial intelligence (AI): Understanding the potential benefits of ChatGPT in promoting teaching and learning. *Journal of AI*, *7*(1), 52–62. https://dergipark.org.tr/en/pub/jai/issue/77844/1337500. doi:10.61969/jai.1337500

Baidoo-AnuD.Owusu AnsahL. (2023). Education in the era of generative artificial intelligence (AI): Understanding the potential benefits of ChatGPT in promoting teaching and learning. SSRN 4337484. doi:10.2139/ssrn.4337484

Baker, R. S., & Hawn, A. (2022). Algorithmic bias in education. *International Journal of Artificial Intelligence in Education*, *32*(4), 1052–1092. doi:10.1007/s40593-021-00285-9

Banerji, O. (2023, August 3). *How schools are coaching — or coaxing — teachers to use ChatGPT*. EdSurge. https://www.edsurge.com/news/2023-08-03-how-schools-are-coaching-or-coaxing-teachers-to-use-chatgpt

Bannon, M. T. (2023, June 22). How AI Is Changing The Future Of Work. *Forbes Magazine*. https://www.forbes.com/sites/marenbannon/2023/06/22/how-ai-is-changing-the-future-of-work/?sh=624cfccf72e0

Barrett, H. C. (2007). Researching electronic portfolios and learner engagement: The REFLECT initiative. *Journal of Adolescent & Adult Literacy*, *50*(6), 436–449. doi:10.1598/JAAL.50.6.2

Basham, J. D., Blackorby, J., & Marino, M. T. (2020). Opportunity in crisis: The role of Universal Design for Learning in educational redesign. *Learning Disabilities (Weston, Mass.)*, *18*(1), 71–91. https://www.ldw-ldcj.org/

Bates, T., Cobo, C., Mariño, O., & Wheeler, S. (2020). Can artificial intelligence transform higher education? *International Journal of Educational Technology in Higher Education*, *17*(42), 42. doi:10.1186/s41239-020-00218-x

Bauschard S, Rao A, Shah P, and Shryock C (2023) *Chat(GPT): Navigating the Impact of Generative AI Technologies on Educational Theory and Practice: Educators Discuss ChatGPT and other Artificial Intelligence Tools*. Independently published.

BBC News. (2021). *University of South Wales: Hacker jailed for selling exam answers*. BBC News. https://www.bbc.co.uk/news/uk-wales-58502963

Bearman, M., & Luckin, R. (2020). Preparing university assessment for a world with AI: Tasks for human intelligence. *Re-imagining university assessment in a digital world*, 49-63.

Bearman, M., & Ajjawi, R. (2023). Learning to work with the black box: Pedagogy for a world with artificial intelligence. *British Journal of Educational Technology*, *00*(5), 1–14. doi:10.1111/bjet.13337

Bearman, M., & Luckin, R. (2020). Preparing university assessment for a world with AI: Tasks for human intelligence. In M. Bearman, P. Dawson, R. Ajjawi, J. Tai, & D. Boud (Eds.), *Re-imagining university assessment in a digital world* (pp. 49–63). Springer. doi:10.1007/978-3-030-41956-1_5

Bearman, M., Nieminen, J. H., & Ajjawi, R. (2023). Designing assessment in a digital world: An organising framework. *Assessment & Evaluation in Higher Education*, *48*(3), 291–304. doi:10.1080/02602938.2022.2069674

Beck, D. (2019). Special Issue: Augmented and Virtual Reality in Education: Immersive Learning Research. *Journal of Educational Computing Research*, *57*(7), 1619–1625. Advance online publication. doi:10.1177/0735633119854035

Beckem, J., & Watkins, M. (2012, October). Bringing Life to Learning: Immersive Experiential Learning Simulations for Online and Blended Courses. *Journal of Asynchronous Learning Networks*, *16*(5), 61–70. https://files.eric.ed.gov/fulltext/EJ1000091.pdf

Bedrossian, L. (2021). Understand and address complexities of rejection sensitive dysphoria in students with ADHD. *Disability Compliance for Higher Education*, *26*(10), 4–4. doi:10.1002/dhe.31047

Bellaera, L., Weinstein-Jones, Y., Ilie, S., & Baker, S. T. (2021). Critical thinking in practice: The priorities and practices of instructors teaching in higher education. *Thinking Skills and Creativity*, *41*, 100856. Advance online publication. doi:10.1016/j.tsc.2021.100856

Bender, E. M., Gebru, T., McMillan-Major, A., & Shmitchell, S. (2021) On the Dangers of Stochastic Parrots: Can Language Models Be Too Big? *Proceedings of the 2021 ACM Conference on Fairness, Accountability, and Transparency*, (pp. 610–623). Association for Computing Machinery. 10.1145/3442188.3445922

Bender, E. M., & Koller, A. (2020). Climbing towards NLU: On Meaning, Form, and Understanding in the Age of Data. *Proceedings of the 58th Annual Meeting of the Association for Computational Linguistics*, (pp. 5185–5198). ACL. 10.18653/v1/2020.acl-main.463

Bennani, S., Maalel, A., & Ghezala, H. (2021, December 01). Adaptive gamification in E-learning: A literature review and future challenges. *Computer Applications in Engineering Education*, *30*(2), 628–642. doi:10.1002/cae.22477

Benner, P., Sutphen, M., Leonard, V., & Day, L. (2009). *Educating nurses: A call for radical transformation*. Jossey-Bass.

Benuyenah, V. (2023). Commentary: ChatGPT use in higher education assessment: Prospects and epistemic threats. *Journal of Research in Innovative Teaching and Learning*, *16*(1), 134–135. doi:10.1108/JRIT-03-2023-097

Berendt, B., Littlejohn, A., & Blakemore, M. (2020). AI in education: Learner choice and fundamental rights. *Learning, Media and Technology*, *45*(3), 312–324. doi:10.1080/17439884.2020.1786399

Bergstrom, C. T. (2023, May 18). *Numerous sources claim that TurnItIn has a generative AI detector with something like 98% sensitivity and 99% specificity. For example, the…* [Mastodon post]. Mastodon. https://fediscience.org/@ct_bergstrom/110391417412257374

Berkeley. (2023, May 1). *Availability of Turnitin Artificial Intelligence Detection*. Berkley. https://rtl.berkeley.edu/news/availability-turnitin-artificial-intelligence-detection

Bernstein, M. N. (2021, October 08) *Perplexity: a more intuitive measure of uncertainty than entropy*. Github. https://mbernste.github.io/posts/perplexity/

Bertolini, R., Finch, S., & Nehm, R. (2022). Quantifying variability in predictions of student performance: Examining. *Computers and Education: Artificial Intelligence*, *3*, 100067. doi:10.1016/j.caeai.2022.100067

Bertram Gallant, T. & Drinan, P. (2008) Toward a Model of Academic Integrity Institutionalization: Informing Practice in Postsecondary Education. *Canadian journal of higher education (1975) 38* (2), 25-43.

Bertram Gallant, T. (2017). Academic Integrity as a Teaching & Learning Issue: From Theory to Practice. *Theory into Practice*, *56*(2), 88–94. doi:10.1080/00405841.2017.1308173

Bertram Gallant, T. (2020). Leveraging the teachable moment: What, if anything, can students learn from cheating? In T. Bretag (Ed.), *A Research Agenda for Academic Integrity* (pp. 55–68). Edward Elgar Publishing Ltd. doi:10.4337/9781789903775.00011

Bertram-Gallant, T. (Ed.). (2011). *Creating the ethical academy: A systems approach to understanding misconduct and empowering change*. Routledge. doi:10.4324/9780203840481

Biggs, J. B., & Collis, K. F. (1982). *Evaluating the quality of learning: The SOLO taxonomy*. Academic Press.

Binday, B. (2023, March 28). In absence of university-wide guidance, Penn professors vary approaches to AI in academics. *The Daily Pennsylvanian.* https://www.thedp.com/article/2023/03/penn-chat-gpt-professor-policies-future

Binkley, M., Erstad, O., Herman, J., Raizen, S., Ripley, M., & Rumble, M. (2012). Defining twenty-first century skills. In P. Griffin, B. McGaw, & E. Care (Eds.), *Assessment and teaching of 21st century skills* (pp. 17–66). Springer. doi:10.1007/978-94-007-2324-5_2

Birkbeck, University of London (2023). *Appendix 1: AI (AI) and academic integrity*. BBK. https://www.bbk.ac.uk/downloads/registry/student-policies-2022-23/ai-and-academic-integrity-appendix.pdf

Bishan, G. (2015). Cultivating Critical Thinking Skills in the Classroom. *Global International Research Thoughts (GIRT), 3*(1). https://girt.shodhsagar.com/index.php/j/article/view/14/15

Block TechnologyO. U. (2023). *Ask for PDF*. www.askyourpdf.com

Bloom, B. S. (1968). Learning for Mastery. Instruction and Curriculum. *Evaluation Comment, 1*(2).

Boals, T., Castro, M., & Shafer Willner, L. (2018). Moving beyond assumptions of cultural neutrality to improve accessibility and opportunity to learn for English Language Learners. In S. N. Elliott, R. J. Kettler, P. A. Beddow, & A. Kurz (Eds.), *Handbook of accessible instruction and testing practices: Issues, innovations, and applications* (pp. 119–134). Springer International Publishing. doi:10.1007/978-3-319-71126-3_8

Bobertsmith1928. (2023, May). *Falsely accused of ai written essay, what should i do?* [Reddit Post]. R/College. https://www.reddit.com/r/college/comments/12j0073/falsely_accused_of_ai_written_essay_what_should_i/

Bockmier-Sommers, D., Chen, C., & Martsch, M. (2017). Student Perception of Teacher Empathy, High Regard and Genuineness and the Impact on Student Engagement. *E-Mentor*, *2017*(70(3)), 66–72. doi:10.15219/em70.1310

Boehm, P. J., Justice, M., & Weeks, S. (2009). Promoting academic integrity in higher education. *The Community College Enterprise*, *15*(1), 45–61.

Bolton, M. K. (1999). The role of coaching in student teams: A "just-in-time" approach to learning. *Journal of Management Education*, *23*(3), 233–250. doi:10.1177/105256299902300302

Borbajo, M., Malbas, M., & Dacanay, L. (2023). Reforming Education: The Global Impact of Integrating Artificial Intelligence in the Classroom Environment. *American Journal of Language, Literacy and Learning in STEM Education (2993-2769), 1*(5), 16–27. https://grnjournal.us/index.php/STEM/article/view/356

Borg, E. (2009, August). Local Plagiarisms. *Assessment & Evaluation in Higher Education*, *34*(4), 415–426. doi:10.1080/02602930802075115

Bosco, A. M., & Ferns, S. (2014). Embedding of authentic assessment in work-integrated learning curriculum. *Asia Pacific Journal of Cooperative Education*, *15*(4), 281–290.

Boston University. (2023, September). *Using generative AI in coursework*. Boston University. https://www.bu.edu/cds-faculty/culture-community/gaia-policy/#:~:text=Students%20shall&text=Not%20use%20AI%20tools%20during,work%20is%20not%20mistakenly%20flagged

Boud, D., & Molloy, E. (2013). Rethinking models of feedback for learning: The challenge of design. *Assessment & Evaluation in Higher Education*, *38*(6), 698–712. doi:10.1080/02602938.2012.691462

Boulay, B. (2016). Artificial intelligence as an effective classroom assistant. *IEEE Intelligent Systems*, *31*(6), 76–81. doi:10.1109/MIS.2016.93

Bowditch, E. (2023, September 12). *Assessment Menu: Designing assessment in an AI enabled world.* Jisc. https://nationalcentreforai.jiscinvolve.org/wp/2023/09/12/designing-assessment-in-an-ai-enabled-world/

Bowditich, I. (2023). Assessment Menu: Designing assessment in an AI enabled world. *JISC*. https://nationalcentreforai.jiscinvolve.org/wp/2023/09/12/designing-assessment-in-an-ai-enabled-world/

Bowers, W. J. (1964). *Student dishonesty and its control in college*. Bureau of Applied Social Research, Columbia University.

Bozok, D. (2023). Attitudes of students towards violations of academic integrity in online English courses. *Journal of Learning and Teaching in Digital Age*, *8*(2), 209–220. doi:10.53850/joltida.1177949

Bradberry, L., & Maio, J. (2019). Learning By Doing: The Long-Term Impact of Experiential Learning Programs on Student Success. *Journal of Political Science Education*, *15*(1), 94–111. doi:10.1080/15512169.2018.1485571

Brailas, A., & Sotiropoulou, C. (2023). *Relational, Appreciative, and Process-oriented Digital Storytelling: A Duoethnography*. Hu Arenas. doi:10.1007/s42087-023-00337-7

Brainard, J. (2023). Journals take up arms against AI-written text. *Science*, *379*(6634), 740–741. doi:10.1126/science.adh2762 PMID:36821673

Braun, M., Bleher, H., Hille, E. M., & Krutzinna, J. (2023). Tackling structural injustices: On the entanglement of visibility and justice in emerging technologies. *The American Journal of Bioethics*, *23*(7), 100–102. doi:10.1080/15265161.2023.2207514 PMID:37339313

Braun, V., & Clarke, V. (2006). Using Thematic Analysis in Psychology. *Qualitative Research in Psychology*, *3*(2), 77–101. doi:10.1191/1478088706qp063oa

Bretag, T. (2017). *Good practice note: Addressing contract cheating to safeguard academic integrity*. Australian Government Tertiary Education Quality and Standards Agency (TEQSA). https://www.teqsa.gov.au/sites/default/files/good-practice-note-addressing-contract-cheating.pdf?v=1507082628

Bretag, T., & Mahmud, S. (2013). *Academic integrity standards: Aligning policy and practice in Australian universities*. Australian Government Office for Learning and Teaching. https://ltr.edu.au/resources/PP10_1783_Bretag_report_2013.pdf

Bretag, T., & Mahmud, S. (2014). *Embedding and extending exemplary academic integrity policy and support frameworks across the higher education sector*. A. Government. https://ltr.edu.au/resources/SP12_2327_Bretag_Report_2014.pdf

Bretag, T., & Mahmud, S. (2016). A conceptual framework for implementing exemplary academic integrity policy in Australian higher education. Handbook of academic integrity, 463-480.

Bretag, T., Mahmud, S., East, J., Green, M., James, C., McGowan, U., Partridge, L., Walker, R. G., & Wallace, M. (2011). Academic integrity standards: A preliminary analysis of the academic integrity policies at Australian Universities. In *Proceedings of AuQF 2011 Demonstrating Quality* (pp. 48–53). AuQF. https://ro.uow.edu.au/asdpapers/323/

Bretag, T., Mahmud, S., Wallace, M., Walker, R., James, C., Green, M., & Partridge, L. (2011, December). Core elements of exemplary academic integrity. *International Journal for Educational Integrity, 7*(2), 3-12. file:///C:/Users/maya3/Downloads/ojsadmin,+Bretag+et+al+Oct+11.pdf

Bretag, T. (Ed.). (2016). *Handbook of academic integrity*. Springer Singapore. doi:10.1007/978-981-287-098-8

Bretag, T., Harper, R., Burton, M., Ellis, C., Newton, P., Rozenberg, P., Saddiqui, S., & van Haeringen, K. (2019). Contract cheating: A survey of Australian university students. *Studies in Higher Education, 44*(11), 1837–1856. doi:10.1080/03075079.2018.1462788

Bretag, T., Harper, R., Rundle, K., Newton, P. M., Ellis, C., Saddiqui, S., & van Haeringen, K. (2019). Contract cheating in Australian higher education: A comparison of non-university higher education providers and universities. *Assessment & Evaluation in Higher Education*, 1–15. doi:10.1080/02602938.2019.1614146

Bretag, T., Mahmud, S., Wallace, M., Walker, R., James, C., Green, M., East, J., McGowan, U., & Patridge, L. (2011). Core elements of exemplary academic integrity policy in Australian higher education. *International Journal for Educational Integrity, 7*(2). doi:10.21913/IJEI.v7i2.759

Bretag, T., Mahmud, S., Wallace, M., Walker, R., McGowan, U., East, J., Green, M., Partridge, L., & James, C. (2014). 'Teach us how to do it properly!' An Australian academic integrity student survey. *Studies in Higher Education, 39*(7), 1150–1169. doi:10.1080/03075079.2013.777406

Brewer, J., Gerard, C., & Hakkinen, M. (2022, June 3). 3 ways AI can help students with disabilities. *EDUCAUSE Review*. https://er.educause.edu/articles/2022/6/3-ways-ai-can-help-students-with-disabilities

Brown, T. B., Mann, B., Ryder, N., Subbiah, M., Kaplan, J., Dhariwal, P., Neelakantan, A., Shyam, P., Sastry, G., Askell, A., Agarwal, S., Herbert-Voss, A., Krueger, G., Henighan, T., Child, R., Ramesh, A., Ziegler, D. M., Wu, J., Winter, C., & Amodei, D. (2020) Language Models are Few-Shot Learners. arXiv. https://doi.org//arXiv.2005.14165 doi:10.48550

Brownlee, J. (2019, October 14) *A Gentle Introduction to Information Entropy*. Machine Learning Mastery. https://machinelearningmastery.com/what-is-information-entropy/

Bryant, P. (2023). *Navigating the dissonances of authenticity in assessment: (Re)defining authentic assessment in business education*. Retrieved from https://diberg.blog/2023/09/20/navigating-the-dissonances-of-authenticity-in-assessment-redefining-authentic-assessment-in-business-education-part-2

Bureau, J. S., Gareau, A., Guay, F., & Mageau, G. A. (2021). Investigating how autonomy-supportive teaching moderates the relation between student honesty and premeditated cheating. *The British Journal of Educational Psychology, 92*(1), 175–193. doi:10.1111/bjep.12444 PMID:34236697

Caldas, I. M., Pereira, M. L., Azevedo, R., & Madureira-Carvalho, Á. (2022). Self-Report of Academic Misconduct Practices Among University Students in Portugal. In S. Bjelobaba, T. Foltýnek, I. Glendinning, V. Krásničan, & D. H. Dlabolová (Eds.), *Academic Integrity: Broadening Practices, Technologies, and the Role of Students. Ethics and Integrity in Educational Contexts* (Vol. 4). Springer. https://doi-org.ezproxy.derby.ac.uk/10.1007/978-3-031-16976-2_13

Campbell, D. M. (2004). Assistive technology and Universal Instructional Design: A postsecondary perspective. *Equity & Excellence in Education, 37*(2), 167–173. doi:10.1080/10665680490454057

Canterbury Christ Church University. (2023). *Generative AI (AI): Guidance for Staff*. Canterbury Christ Church University. https://www.canterbury.ac.uk/learning-and-teaching-enhancement/resources-for-academics/Docs/Generative-Artificial-Intelligence-AI-Guidance-for-Staff.pdf

Cardona, M. A., Rodríguez, R. J., & Ishmael, K. (2023). *Artificial Intelligence and the future of teaching and learning*. Office of Educational Technology, United States of America https://tech.ed.gov

Carroll, J. (2005). Handling Student Plagiarism: Moving to Mainstream. Brookes eJournal of Learning and Teaching, 1(2).

Carroll, J., & Development, O. C. f. S. (2002). *A handbook for deterring plagiarism in higher education*. Oxford Centre for Staff and Learning Development Oxford.

Carter, S. (2022). *Academic integrity and testing: Digging deeper into impersonation*. International Center for Academic Integrity. https://academicintegrity.org/resources/blog/99-2022/may-2022/370-academic-integrity-and-testing-digging-deeper-into-impersonation

Casal, J. E., & Kessler, M. (2023). Can linguists distinguish between ChatGPT/AI and human writing?: A study of research ethics and academic publishing. *Research Methods in Applied Linguistics*, *2*(3), 1–12. doi:10.1016/j.rmal.2023.100068

Cassens Weiss, D. (2023, March 16). Latest version of ChatGPT aces bar exam with score nearing 90th percentile. *ABA Journal*. https://www.abajournal.com/web/article/latest-version-of-chatgpt-aces-the-bar-exam-with-score-in-90th-percentile

Cassidy, C. (2023, October 6). Artificial intelligence such as ChatGPT to be allowed in Australian schools from 2024. *The Guardian*. https://www.theguardian.com/australia-news/2023/oct/06/chatgpt-ai-allowed-australian-schools-2024

Cassidy, C. (2023a, January 10). Australian universities to return to 'pen and paper' exams after students caught using AI to write essays. *The Guardian*. https://www.theguardian.com/australia-news/2023/jan/10/universities-to-return-to-pen-and-paper-exams-after-students-caught-using-ai-to-write-essays

Cassidy, C. (2023b, April 17). Australian universities split on using new tool to detect AI plagiarism. *The Guardian*. https://www.theguardian.com/australia-news/2023/apr/16/australian-universities-split-on-using-new-tool-to-detect-ai-plagiarism

CAST. (n.d.). *The UDL Guidelines*. CAST. https://udlguidelines.cast.org/

Central Queensland University. (2023). *Student academic integrity policy and procedure*. CQU. https://delivery-cqucontenthub.stylelabs.cloud/api/public/content/student-academic-integrity-policy-and-procedure.pdf

Chambers, C. G., Tanenhaus, M. K., & Magnuson, J. S. (2004). Actions and affordances in syntactic ambiguity resolution. *Journal of Experimental Psychology. Learning, Memory, and Cognition*, *30*(3), 687–696. doi:10.1037/0278-7393.30.3.687 PMID:15099136

Chan, C. (2023, March 9). *AI will transform teaching and learning*. Stanford University. https://hai.stanford.edu/news/ai-will-transform-teaching-and-learning-lets-get-it-right

Chan, C. K. Y., & Hu, W. (2023). Students' voices on generative AI: Perceptions, benefits, and challenges in higher education. arXiv preprint arXiv:2305.00290.

Chan, C. K. Y., & Hu, W. (2023). Students' voices on generative AI: Perceptions, benefits, and challenges in higher education. *International Journal of Educational Technology in Higher Education*, *20*(43), 43. doi:10.1186/s41239-023-00411-8

Charnosky, C. (2023, October 02). *Pre-Law Students Avoid Using AI for Admissions*. ALM Global LLC. https://www.law.com/2023/10/02/pre-law-students-nix-using-ai-for-admissions-kaplan-survey-reports/

Chaudhry, I. S., Sarwary, S. A. M., El Refae, G. A., & Chabchoub, H. (2023). Time to Revisit Existing Student's Performance Evaluation Approach in Higher Education Sector in a New Era of ChatGPT—A Case Study. *Cogent Education*, *10*(1), 2210461. doi:10.1080/2331186X.2023.2210461

Chaudhry, M. A., & Kazim, E. (2022). Artificial intelligence in education (AIEd): A high-level academic and industry note 2021. *AI and Ethics*, *2*(1), 157–165. doi:10.1007/s43681-021-00074-z PMID:34790953

Cheatham, B., Javanmardian, K., & Samandari, H. (2019, April 26). Confronting the risks of artificial intelligence. *McKinsey Quarterly*. https://www.mckinsey.com/capabilities/quantumblack/our-insights/confronting-the-risks-of-artificial-intelligence

Chen, J. (2023). Four directions for assessment redesign in the age of generative AI. *The Times Higher Education*. https://www.timeshighereducation.com/campus/four-directions-assessment-redesign-age-generative-ai

Chen, K., Monrouxe, L. V., Lu, Y., Jenq, C., Chang, Y., Chang, Y., & Chai, P. Y. (2018). Academic outcomes of flipped classroom learning: A meta-analysis. *Medical Education*, *52*(9), 910–924. doi:10.1111/medu.13616 PMID:29943399

Chen, L., Chen, P., & Lin, Z. (2020). Artificial intelligence in education: A review. *IEEE Access : Practical Innovations, Open Solutions*, *8*, 75264–75278. doi:10.1109/ACCESS.2020.2988510

Chen, L., Chen, P., & Lin, Z. (2020). Artificial Intelligence in Education: A Review. *IEEE Access : Practical Innovations, Open Solutions*. Retrieved November 2023, from

Christensen, U. (2023, March 25). *How AI will revolutionize human learning – but not the way you think*. Forbes. https://www.forbes.com/sites/ulrikjuulchristensen/2023/05/25/how-ai-will-revolutionize-human-learning--but-not-the-way-you-think/?sh=2aa7080a4c65

Clark, A. (2013). Expecting the World: Perception, Prediction, and the Origins of Human Knowledge. *The Journal of Philosophy*, *110*(9), 469–496. https://www.jstor.org/stable/43820791. doi:10.5840/jphil2013110913

Clarke, N. (2023, February 15). A Concerning Trend [Blog]. *Neil Clarke Blog*. http://neil-clarke.com/a-concerning-trend/

Clarke, R., & Lancaster, T. (2006). Eliminating the successor to plagiarism? Identifying the usage of contract cheating sites. In *Proceedings of 2nd international plagiarism conference*.

Cleveland Clinic. (n.d.-a). *Neurodivergent: What It Is, Symptoms & Types*. Cleveland Clinic. https://my.clevelandclinic.org/health/symptoms/23154-neurodivergent

Cleveland Clinic. (n.d.-b). *Rejection Sensitive Dysphoria (RSD): Symptoms & Treatment*. Cleveland Clinic. https://my.clevelandclinic.org/health/diseases/24099-rejection-sensitive-dysphoria-rsd

Cochrane, T., & Ryan, T. (2023, March). *ChatGPT and Academic Integrity: Options for adapting assessment in semester 1, 2023*. Melbourne Centre for the Study of Higher Education. https://melbourne-cshe.unimelb.edu.au/__data/assets/pdf_file/0008/4533218/ChatGPT-and-Academic-Integrity.pdf

Cole, M. T., Shelley, D. J., & Swartz, L. B. (2019). *Re launching a new vision in education and e-learning: Fostering a culture of academic integrity in e-learning. In Smart Education and e-Learning*. Springer.

Coley, M. (2023, August 16). *Guidance on AI Detection and Why We're Disabling Turnitin's AI Detector*. Vanderbilt University Brightspace. https://www.vanderbilt.edu/brightspace/2023/08/16/guidance-on-ai-detection-and-why-were-disabling-turnitins-ai-detector/

Collini, S. (2012). *What are Universities for?* Penguin.

Columbia weighs an honor system: Students request pledges from new freshmen. (1963, September 24). *New York Times*. https://www.nytimes.com/1963/09/24/archives/columbia-weighs-an-honor-system-students-request-pledges-from-new.html

Committee on Publication Ethics. (2023). *Authorship and AI Tools*. Publication Ethics. https://publicationethics.org/cope-position-statements/ai-author

Conrad, K. (2023, July 17). *SNEAK PREVIEW: A Blueprint for an AI Bill of Rights for Education*. Critical AI. https://criticalai.org/2023/07/17/a-blueprint-for-an-ai-bill-of-rights-for-education-kathryn-conrad/

Content @ Scale. (2023). *AI Content Detector Checks GPT-4, ChatGPT, Bard, & More*. Content @ Scale. https://contentatscale.ai/ai-content-detector/

Cooper, G. (2023). Examining Science Education in ChatGPT: An Exploratory Study of Generative Artificial Intelligence. *Journal of Science Education and Technology*, *32*(3), 1–9. doi:10.1007/s10956-023-10039-y

Cope, B., Kalantzis, M., & Searsmith, D. (2021). Artificial intelligence for education: Knowledge and its assessment in AI-enabled learning ecologies. *Educational Philosophy and Theory*, *53*(12), 1229–1245. doi:10.1080/00131857.2020.1728732

Copyleaks. (2023, January 12) *Copyleaks Officially Launches First-Of-Its-Kind Multi-Language AI Content Detection Solution with 99 Percent Accuracy* [Press release]. Copyleaks Ltd. https://copyleaks.com/about-us/media/copyleaks-launches-ai-content-detector

Cornell University Center for Teaching Innovation. (2023, September). *AI & academic integrity*. Cornell. https://teaching.cornell.edu/generative-artificial-intelligence/ai-academic-integrity

Cotton, D., Cotton, P., & Shipway, J. R. (2023) Chatting and Cheating: Ensuring academic integrity in the era of ChatGPT. *Innovations in education and teaching international*. https://www-tandfonline-com.ezproxy.derby.ac.uk/doi/full/10.1080/14703297.2023.2190148

Cotton, D. R., Cotton, P. A., & Shipway, J. R. (2023). Chatting and cheating: Ensuring academic integrity in the era of ChatGPT. *Innovations in Education and Teaching International*, 1–12. doi:10.1080/14703297.2023.2190148

Council of Writing Program Administrators. (2019). *WPA Outcomes Statement for First-Year Composition (3.0), Approved July 17, 2014*. WPA Council. https://wpacouncil.org/aws/CWPA/pt/sd/news_article/243055/_PARENT/layout_details/false

Coverstone, A. (2023) Generative AI and Teaching Students to Think Critically. In Bauschard S, Rao A, Shah P and Shryock C (Eds.) (2023) Chat(GPT): Navigating the Impact of Generative AI on Education theory and Practice. Great Britain: Pedagogy Ventures.

Crockett, R. (2023b, November 20) Testing the AI detectors Part 2. University of Northampton. NorthHampton. https://blogs.northampton.ac.uk/learntech/2023/11/20/testing-the-ai-detectors-part-2/

Crockett, R. (2023a). Forensic Assignment Stylometry. In S. E. Eaton (Ed.), *Handbook of Academic Integrity* (pp. 1–19). Springer. doi:10.1007/978-981-287-079-7_154-1

Crockett, R., & Best, K. (2020). Stylometric Comparison Of Professionally Ghost-Written And Student-Written Assignments. In Z. R. Khan, C. Hill, & T. Foltynek (Eds.), *Integrity in Education for Future Happiness* (pp. 35–49). Mendel University Press. doi:10.11118/978-80-7509-772-9-0035

Crompton, H., & Burke, D. (2023). Artificial intelligence in higher education: The state of the field. *International Journal of Educational Technology in Higher Education*, *20*(1), 1–22. doi:10.1186/s41239-023-00392-8

Crossplag. (2023, July 31) *AI Content Detector* [Press release]. Inspera AS. https://crossplag.com/ai-content-detector/

Crush, P. (2023). *Most workers would still use AI – even if their workplace banned it.* TLNT. https://www.tlnt.com/articles/staff-would-still-use-ai-at-work-even-if-it-was-banned-workplace-rules-can-be-challenge August 4

Currie, G., Singh, C., Nelson, T., Nabasenja, C., Al-Hayek, Y., & Spuur, K. (2023). ChatGPT in medical imaging higher education. *Radiography, 29*(4), 792–799. doi:10.1016/j.radi.2023.05.011 PMID:37271011

Curtin Student Guild. (2023). A submission to the House Standing Committee on employment, education and training inquiry into the issues and opportunities presented by generative artificial intelligence (AI). In *Inquiry into the use of generative artificial intelligence in the Australian education system - Submission 53.* https://www.aph.gov.au/DocumentStore.ashx?id=b8efd80a-5527-4151-95a9-b83c818ea36b&subId=745706

Curtis, G. C., McNeill, M., Slade, C., Tremayne, K., Harper, R., Rundle, K., & Greenaway, R. (2021). Moving beyond self-reports to estimate the prevalence of commercial contract cheating: An Australian study. *Studies in Higher Education.* Advance online publication. doi:10.1080/03075079.2021.1972093

D'Agostino, S. (2023, June 1). *Turnitin's AI Detector: Higher-Than-Expected False Positives.* Inside Higher Ed. https://www.insidehighered.com/news/quick-takes/2023/06/01/turnitins-ai-detector-higher-expected-false-positives

Dai, Y., Liu, A., & Lim, C. P. (2023) Reconceptualizing ChatGPT and generative AI as a student-driven innovation in higher education. *Procedi 33rd CIRP*, 119. https://www.sciencedirect.com/science/article/pii/S2212827123004407

Daly, C. (2018, November 13). *AI - The fifth industrial revolution.* AI Business. https://aibusiness.com/verticals/ai-the-fifth-industrial-revolution

Daly, N. (Director). (2023). *ChatGPT could make cheating easier, but not all educators believe banning it is the solution* [Video]. ABC News. https://www.abc.net.au/news/2023-02-27/chatgpt-could-make-cheating-easier,-but-not-all/102030682

Dans, E. (2019, February 6). Meet Bertie, Heliograf and Cyborg, the new journalists on the block. *Forbes.* https://www.forbes.com/sites/enriquedans/2019/02/06/meet-bertie-heliograf-and-cyborg-the-new-journalists-on-the-block/?sh=669bf965138d

Darling-Hammond, L., & Podolsky, A. (2019). Breaking the cycle of teacher shortages: What kind of policies can make a difference? *Education Policy Analysis Archives, 27*, 34–34. doi:10.14507/epaa.27.4633

Darling-Hammond, L., & Snyder, J. (2000). Authentic assessment of teaching in context. *Teaching and Teacher Education, 16*(5–6), 523–545. doi:10.1016/S0742-051X(00)00015-9

Davenport, T. H. (2018). *The AI advantage: How to put the artificial intelligence revolution to work.* MIT Press. doi:10.7551/mitpress/11781.001.0001

Davies, P., Schelly, C., & Spooner, C. (2013). Measuring the effectiveness of Universal Design for Learning intervention in postsecondary education. *Journal of Postsecondary Education and Disability, 26*(3), 195–220. www.ahead.org

Davis, A. K. (2023, Feb 08). 'Pay attention to it, ignore it or push back on it': Brown professors discuss AI's impact on academic integrity. *The Brown Daily Herald.* https://www.proquest.com/wire-feeds/pay-attention-ignore-push-bac

Davis, M. (2007). *The role of Turnitin within the formative proves of academic writing: a tool for learning and unlearning.* Research Gate. https://www.researchgate.net/publication/281848114_The_role_of_Turnitin_within_the_formative_process_of_academic_writing_a_tool_for_learning_and_unlearning/comments#fullTextFileContent

Dawson, P. & Sutherland-Smith, W. (2018) Can markers detect contract cheating? Results from a pilot study. *Assessment & Evaluation in Higher Education, 43.* doi:10.1080/02602938.2017.1336746

Dawson, P. (2023). *Inquiry into the use of generative artificial intelligence in the Australian education system - Submission 54.* ApH. https://www.aph.gov.au/DocumentStore.ashx?id=8ec1fbc2-72d9-4aa0-b052-d1547e71cfdc&subId=745313

Dawson, P. (2020). *Defending assessment security in a digital world: preventing e-cheating and supporting academic integrity in higher education.* Routledge. doi:10.4324/9780429324178

Dawson, P. (2021). *Defending assessment security in a digital world: Preventing e-cheating and supporting academic integrity in higher education.* Routledge.

Dawson, P., Nicola-Richmond, K., & Partridge, H. (2023). Beyond open book versus closed book: A taxonomy of restrictions in online examinations. *Assessment & Evaluation in Higher Education*, 1–13. doi:10.1080/02602938.2023.2209298

DeepLearningAI. (2023, January 11). *A Complete Guide to Natural Language Processing.* DeepLearning.AI LLC. https://www.deeplearning.ai/resources/natural-language-processing/

Dehouche, N., & Dehouche, K. (2023). *What's in a text-to-image prompt: The potential of stable diffusion in visual arts education.*

Delisio, L. A., & Butaky, C. A. (2019). UDL and assistive technology. In W. W. Murawski & K. L. Scott (Eds.), *What really works With Universal Design for Learning* (pp. 157–172). Corwin.

deMontigny, D. (2022). Managing academic integrity in Canadian engineering schools. In S. E. Eaton & J. Christensen Hughes (Eds.), *Academic integrity in Canada: Ethics and integrity in educational contexts* (pp. 291–306). Springer International Publishing. doi:10.1007/978-3-030-83255-1_15

Desaire, H., Chua, A. E., Kim, M.-G., & Hua, D. (2023). Accurately detecting AI text when ChatGPT is told to write like a chemist. *Cell Reports. Physical Science*, *4*(11), 1–13. doi:10.1016/j.xcrp.2023.101672 PMID:38078148

Design Council. (2023a). *Framework for Innovation.* Design Council. https://www.designcouncil.org.uk/our-resources/framework-for-innovation/

Design Council. (2023b). *The Double Diamond.* Design Council. https://www.designcouncil.org.uk/our-resources/the-double-diamond/

Devlin, M. (2006). Policy, preparation, and prevention: Proactive minimization of student plagiarism. *Journal of Higher Education Policy and Management*, *28*(1), 45–58. doi:10.1080/13600800500283791

Di Vaio, A., Palladino, R., Hassan, R., & Escobar, O. (2020). AI and business models in the sustainable development goals perspective: A systematic literature review. *Journal of Business Research*, *121*, 283–314. doi:10.1016/j.jbusres.2020.08.019

Diaz, M. (2023, July 6). *ChatGPT sees its first monthly drop in traffic since launch.* ZDNet. https://www.zdnet.com/article/chatgpt-sees-its-first-monthly-drop-in-traffic-since-launch/

Digging For Digits. (2023). *The Economist, 448*(9359), 57–58.

Diplo. (2023, September 24) *Universities stop using AI detection tool such as Turnitin..* Diplo Foundation. https://www.diplomacy.edu/updates/universities-stop-using-ai-detection-tool-such-as-turnitin/

Ditto Music. (2023 v). AI for music production: 10 tools to produce like a pro. *Unsigned Advice.* Retrieved July 30, 2023, from https://dittomusic.com/en/blog/ai-for-music-production-tools-for-musicians/

Diwanji, P., Knut, H., & Hans, F. W. (2018, March). *Enhance classroom preparation for flipped classroom using AI and analytics.* 20th International Conference on Enterprise Information Systems (ICEIS 2018) [Presentation], Madeira, Portugal. https://pdfs.semanticscholar.org/2a4a/4b44c369b872b4f62915f5df56acba188632.pdf

Dolmage, J. (2017). *Academic ableism: Disability and higher education.* University of Michigan Press. http://www.jstor.org.ezproxy.lib.ucalgary.ca/stable/j.ctvr33d50

Drinan, P. M., & Bertram Gallant, T. (2008). Plagiarism and Academic Integrity Systems. *Journal of Library Administration, 47*(3-4), 3–4, 125–140. doi:10.1080/01930820802186472

Drozdowski, M. J. (2023, April 23). *Testing Turnitin's New AI Detector: How Accurate I sit?* Best Colleges. https://www.bestcolleges.com/news/analysis/testing-turnitin-new-ai-detector/

Duffy, C. (2023, May 25). ChatGPT's class divide: Are public school bans on the AI tool giving private school kids an unfair edge? *ABC News.* https://www.abc.net.au/news/2023-05-26/artificial-intelligence-chatgpt-classrooms-schools/102356926

Duin, A. H., & Pedersen, I. (2021). *Writing futures: Collaborative, algorithmic, autonomous.* Springer. doi:10.1007/978-3-030-70928-0

Dukewich, K., & Larsen, C. (2023). *How are faculty reacting to ChatGPT?* Curriculum Research Collaborative. https://files.eric.ed.gov/fulltext/ED627303.pdf

Dumin, L. (2023) Developing Acceptable Use Policies for the College Classroom. In Bauschard S, Rao A, Shah P and Shryock C (Eds.) (2023) Chat(GPT): Navigating the Impact of Generative AI on Education theory and Practice. Great Britain: Pedagogy Ventures.

Dunsmuir, S., Atkinson, C., Lang, J., Warhurst, A., & Wright, S. (2017). Objective structured professional assessments for trainee educational psychologists: An evaluation. *Educational Psychology in Practice, 33*(4), 418–434. doi:10.1080/02667363.2017.1352490

Dwivedi, Y. K., Kshetri, N., Hughes, L., Slade, E. L., Jeyaraj, A., Kar, A. K., Baabdullah, A. M., Koohang, A., Raghavan, V., Ahuja, M., Albanna, H., Albashrawi, M. A., Al-Busaidi, A. S., Balakrishnan, J., Barlette, Y., Basu, S., Bose, I., Brooks, L., Buhalis, D., & Wright, R. (2023). "So what if ChatGPT wrote it?" Multidisciplinary perspectives on opportunities, challenges, and implications of generative conversational AI for research, practice, and policy. *International Journal of Information Management, 71*, 102642. doi:10.1016/j.ijinfomgt.2023.102642

Dwivedi, Y., Hughes, L., Ismagilova, E., Aarts, G., Coombs, C., Crick, T., & Janssen, M. (2021). Artificial Intelligence (AI): Multidisciplinary perspectives on emerging challenges, opportunities, and agenda for research, practice and policy. *International Journal of Information Management, 57*, 101994. Advance online publication. Retrieved November 2023, from. doi:10.1016/j.ijinfomgt.2019.08.002

Eaton, S. E. (2023, March 04) Artificial intelligence and academic integrity, post-plagiarism. *University World News.* https://www.universityworldnews.com/post.php?story=20230228133041549

Eaton, S. E., Mindzak, M., & Morrison, R. (2021). *The impact of text-generating technologies on academic integrity: AI & AI.* Paper presented at the Canadian Association for the Study of Educational Administration (CASEA), University of Alberta. http://hdl.handle.net/1880/113569

Eaton, S. E. (2021). *Plagiarism in higher education: Tackling tough topics in academic integrity.* ABC-CLIO. doi:10.5040/9798400697142

Eaton, S. E., Carmichael, J. J., & Pethrick, H. (Eds.). (2023). *Fake degrees and fraudulent credentials in higher education.* Springer Cham., doi:10.1007/978-3-031-21796-8

EatonS. E.KumarR. (Eds.). 2023 Academic Integrity Lessons: Practical Ideas for Teaching, Learning, and Assessment. University of Calgary. Calgary, Canada. https://dx.doi.org/ doi:10.11575.PRISM/42226

EDUCAUSE. (2023). *2023 EDUCAUSE horizon report - Teaching and learning edition.* EDUCAUSE. https://library.educause.edu/resources/2023/5/2023-educause-horizon-report-teaching-and-learning-edition

Edwards, B. (2023a, July 14). *Why AI detectors think the US Constitution was written by AI.* Ars Technica. https://arstechnica.com/information-technology/2023/07/why-ai-detectors-think-the-us-constitution-was-written-by-ai/

Edwards, B. (2023b, July 26). *OpenAI discontinues its AI writing detector due to "low rate of accuracy."* Ars Technica. https://arstechnica.com/information-technology/2023/07/openai-discontinues-its-ai-writing-detector-due-to-low-rate-of-accuracy/

Edwards, B. I., & Cheok, A. D. (2018). Why not robot teachers: Artificial intelligence for addressing teacher shortage. *Applied Artificial Intelligence*, *32*(4), 345–360. doi:10.1080/08839514.2018.1464286

Edwards, E. J., Gilbert, M., Blank, E., & Branham, S. M. (2023). How the alt text gets made: What roles and processes of Alt text creation can teach us about inclusive imagery. *ACM Transactions on Accessible Computing*, *16*(2), 1–28. doi:10.1145/3587469 PMID:37427355

Ehsan, U. (2023, August 1). *1/OpenAI quietly shut down its "AI" detector. Did shutting it down undo the harms? No, its Algorithmic Imprint lives on. Here's how #AI #ML…* [Mastodon post]. Mastodon. https://hci.social/@upol/110815089962878235

Ehsan, U., Singh, R., Metcalf, J., & Riedl, M. (2022). The Algorithmic Imprint. *2022 ACM Conference on Fairness, Accountability, and Transparency*, (pp. 1305–1317). ACM. 10.1145/3531146.3533186

Eke, D. O. (2023). ChatGPT and the rise of generative AI: Threat to academic integrity? *Journal of Responsible Technology*, *13*, 1–4. https://www.sciencedirect.com/science/article/pii/S2666659623000033. doi:10.1016/j.jrt.2023.100060

ElevenBurnie. (2023, May 5). *Professor using GPTZero to accuse students of cheating* [Reddit Post]. R/OpenAI. www.reddit.com/r/OpenAI/comments/138ayhf/professor_using_gptzero_to_accuse_students_of/

Elkhatat, A. M., Elsaid, K., & Almeer, S. (2023). Evaluating the efficacy of AI content detection tools in differentiating between human and AI-generated text. *International Journal for Educational Integrity*, *19*(1), 17. doi:10.1007/s40979-023-00140-5

Ellingrud, K., Sanghvi, S., Dandona, G. S., Madgavkar, A., Chui, M., White, O., & Hasebe, P. (2023). *Which jobs will be in demand? Which ones are shrinking? And which ones could be hardest to fill?* McKinsey & Company.

Ellis, C., Van Haeringen, K., Harper, R., Bretag, T., Zucker, I., McBride, S., Rozenberg, P., Newton, P., & Saddiqui, S. (2020). Does authentic assessment assure academic integrity? Evidence from contract cheating data. *Higher Education Research & Development*, *39*(3), 454–469. doi:10.1080/07294360.2019.1680956

Elyoseph, Z., & Levkovich, I. (2023). Beyond human expertise: The promise and limitations of ChatGPT in suicide risk assessment. *Frontiers in Psychiatry*, *14*, 14. doi:10.3389/fpsyt.2023.1213141 PMID:37593450

Epstein-Gross, C. (2023, July 26). OpenAI Abruptly Shuts Down ChatGPT Plagiarism Detector—And Educators Are Worried. *Observer*. https://observer.com/2023/07/openai-shut-ai-classifier/

European Network for Academic Integrity (ENAI). (2022, September 20). *Academic Integrity*. ENAI. https://www.academicintegrity.eu/wp/glossary/academic-integrity/

European Network for Academic Integrity (ENAI). (2023) *Glossary: Academic Integrity*. ENAI. https://www.academicintegrity.eu/wp/

Evans, N., Broido, E., Brown, K., Wilke, A., & Herriott, T. (2018). *Disability in higher education: A social justice approach*. John Wiley & Sons, Ltd.

Exemplary Academic Integrity Project. (n.d.-a). *Academic integrity policy toolkit*. APP. https://app.secure.griffith.edu.au/policy-form/index.php?pageno=2

Exemplary Academic Integrity Project. (n.d.-b). *Academic integrity policy toolkit*. Griffith. https://app.secure.griffith.edu.au/policy-form/

Farazouli, A., Cerratto-Pargman, T., Bolander-Laksov, K., & McGrath, C. (2023). Hello GPT! Goodbye home examination? An exploratory study of AI chatbots impact on university teachers' assessment practices. *Assessment & Evaluation in Higher Education*, 1–13. doi:10.1080/02602938.2023.2241676

Farrell, T. (2023, June 27). *The impact of artificial intelligence on education (UOW)*. University of Wollongong. https://ltc.uow.edu.au/hub/page/AI-overview-impact

Farrokhnia, M., Banihashem, S. K., Noroozi, O., & Wals, A. (2023). *A SWOT analysis of ChatGPT: Implications for educational practice and research*. Innovations in Education and Teaching International.

Feedback Fruits. (2023). *Automated feedback*. Feedback Fruits. www.feedbackfruits.com/automated-feedback

Ferraro, F., Ferraro, A., Massimo, J., & Massimo, M. (2018, March 20). A Road Map for Successful Strategy Execution: Strategic Leadership. *IESE INSIGHT*. https://www.iese.edu/insight/articles/strategy-successful-execution-road-map/

Figoli, F., Mattioli, F., & Rampino, L. (2022). *Artificial intelligence in the design process - The Impact on Creativity and Team Collaboration*. Milan: FrancoAngeli. https://library.oapen.org/handle/20.500.12657/53627

Fitzpatrick, D., Fox, A., & Weinstein, B. (2023). *The AI Classroom: The Ultimate Guide to Artificial Intelligence in Education*. TeacherGoals Publishing.

Flanagin, A., Bibbins-Domingo, K., Berkwits, M., & Christiansen, S. L. (2023). Nonhuman "authors" and implications for the integrity of scientific publication and medical knowledge. *Journal of the American Medical Association*, *329*(8), 637–639. doi:10.1001/jama.2023.1344 PMID:36719674

Foltýnek, T., & Glendinning, I. (2023). European Cooperation in Academic Integrity. Eaton, S. (Ed), Handbook for Academic Integrity, 2nd Edition, Springer. doi:10.1007/978-981-287-079-7_176-1

Foltýnek, T., Dlabolová, D., Glendinning, I., Lancaster, T., & Linkeschová, D. (2017). *South-East European Project on Policies for Academic Integrity, Project report*. Council of Europe. http://www.plagiarism.cz/seeppai/Final-report_SEEPPAI.pdf

Foltynek, T., Bjelobaba, S., Glendinning, I., Khan, Z. R., Santos, R., Pavletic, P., & Kravjar, J. (2023). ENAI Recommendations on the ethical use of Artificial Intelligence in Education. *International Journal for Educational Integrity*, *19*(1), 12. doi:10.1007/s40979-023-00133-4

Foltýnek, T., Dlabolová, D., Anohina-Naumeca, A., Razi, S., Kravjar, J., Kamzola, L., Guerrero-Dib, J., Celek, O., & Weber-Wulff, D. (2020). Testing of support tools for plagiarism detection. *International Journal of Educational Technology in Higher Education*, *17*(1), 46. doi:10.1186/s41239-020-00192-4

Foltýnek, T., & Glendinning, I. (2015). Impact of Policies for Plagiarism in Higher Education Across Europe: Results of the Project. *Acta Universitatis Agriculturae et Silviculturae Mendelianae Brunensis*, *63*(1), 207–216. doi:10.11118/actaun201563010207

Foltýnek, T., Meuschke, N., & Gipp, B. (2019). Academic plagiarism detection: A systematic literature review. *ACM Computing Surveys*, *52*(6), 1–42. doi:10.1145/3345317

Fowler, G. A. (2023a, April 14). Analysis | We tested a new ChatGPT-detector for teachers. It flagged an innocent student. *Washington Post.* https://www.washingtonpost.com/technology/2023/04/01/chatgpt-cheating-detection-turnitin/

Fowler, G. A. (2023b, June 2). Analysis | Detecting AI may be impossible. That's a big problem for teachers. *Washington Post.* https://www.washingtonpost.com/technology/2023/06/02/turnitin-ai-cheating-detector-accuracy/

Fowler, G. A. (2023c, August 14). How to prove your innocence after a false positive from Turnitin, GPTZero—The Washington Post. *Washington Post.* https://www.washingtonpost.com/technology/2023/08/14/prove-false-positive-ai-detection-turnitin-gptzero/

Fox, N. P., & Ehmoda, O. (2012). *Statistical Stylometrics and the Marlowe-Shakespeare Authorship Debate.* Brown University. https://cs.brown.edu/research/pubs/theses/masters/2012/ehmoda.pdf

Francesc, P. (2019). Artificial intelligence in education: challenges and opportunities for sustainable development. *Working Papers on Education Policy.* Respositorio. https://repositorio.minedu.gob.pe/bitstream/handle/20.500.12799/6533/Artificial%20intelligence%20in%20education%20challenges%20and%20opportunities%20for%20sustainable%20development.pdf?sequence=1&isAllowed=y

Franzoni, V., Milani, A., Mengoni, P., & Piccinatio, F. (2020). Artificial Intelligence Visual Metaphors in E-Learning Interfaces for Learning Analytics. *Applied Sciences (Basel, Switzerland), 10*(20), 7195. doi:10.3390/app10207195

Frey, B. B. (2013). *Modern classroom assessment.* SAGE Publications.

Fuchs, K. (2022). The importance of competency development in higher education: Letting go of rote learning. *Frontiers in Education, 7*, 1004876. doi:10.3389/feduc.2022.1004876

Fu, K. W., & Tremayne, K. S. (2022). Self-efficacy and self-control mediate the relationship between negative emotions and attitudes toward plagiarism. *Journal of Academic Ethics, 20*(4), 457–477. https://doi-org.library.smu.ca/10.1007/s10805-021-09415-3. doi:10.1007/s10805-021-09415-3

Fuller, R. B., & Kuromiya, K. (1981). *Critical path.* Macmillan.

Future Learn. (2023, September 4). *Future-proof your career: Lifelong learning in the age of AI.* Future Learn. https://www.futurelearn.com/info/blog/lifelong-learning-in-the-age-of-ai

Fyson, S. (2023, July 24). Teachers cannot teach what they do not know. *Spectator Australia.* https://www.spectator.com.au/2023/07/teachers-cannot-teach-what-they-do-not-know/

Gao, A. K. (2023). *Go to Google Scholar and look up 'As an AI language model" -"ChatGPT"'* [Tweet]. Twitter [X]. https://twitter.com/itsandrewgao/status/1689634145717379074

García, S. B., & Guerra, P. L. (2004). Deconstructing Deficit Thinking: Working with Educators to Create More Equitable Learning Environments. *Education and Urban Society, 36*(2), 150–168. doi:10.1177/0013124503261322

Garratt, B. (2011). The Power of Action Learning. In M. Pedler (Ed.), *Action Learning in Practice* (4th ed.). Routledge. doi:10.4324/9781315565521

GaumannN.VealeM. (2023) AI Providers as Criminal Essay Mills? Large Language Models meet Contract Cheating Law. socarXiv. https://osf.io/preprints/socarxiv/cpbfd doi:10.31235/osf.io/cpbfd

Geerling, W., Mateer, G. D., Wooten, J., & Damodaran, N. (2023). ChatGPT has Aced the Test of Understanding in College Economics: Now What? *The American Economist, 68*(2), 233–245. doi:10.1177/05694345231169654

Gegg-Harrison, W. (2023) Against the use of GPTZero and other LLM-output Detection Tool. In Bauschard S, Rao A, Shah P and Shryock C (Eds.) (2023) Chat(GPT): Navigating the Impact of Generative AI on Education theory and Practice. Great Britain: Pedagogy Ventures.

Genei. (2021). *Summary tool*. Genei. www.genei.io

George, B., & Wooden, O. (2023). Managing the strategic transformation of higher education through artificial intelligence. *Administrative Sciences*, *13*(9), 196. doi:10.3390/admsci13090196

Georgetown University. (2023, April). *Assignment design principles*. Georgetown University. https://cndls.georgetown.edu/ai/assignments/#common-questions-about-assignment-design

German Federal Government. (2020, December). *Artificial intelligence strategy of the German Federal Government – Update 2020*. German Federal Government. https://www.ki-strategie-deutschland.de/files/downloads/Fortschreibung_KI-Strategie_engl.pdf

Getachew, A., Tekle, T., & Bayisa, K. (2020). Nature and causes of students' misbehaviour as perceived by Ambo University teachers. *Journal of Social Sciences*, *48*(2), 762–771.

Gibson, J. J. (1979). *The ecological approach to visual perception*. Houghton, Mifflin and Company.

Gillespie-Lynch, K., Hotez, E., Zajic, M., Riccio, A., DeNigris, D., Kofner, B., Bublitz, D., Gaggi, N., & Luca, K. (2020). Comparing the writing skills of autistic and nonautistic university students: A collaboration with autistic university students. *Autism*, *24*(7), 1898–1912. doi:10.1177/1362361320929453 PMID:32640841

Gillham, J. (2023). *AI Content Detector False Positives – Accused Of Using Chat GPT Or Other AI?* Originality.Ai. https://originality.ai/blog/ai-content-detector-false-positives

Gilson, A., Safranek, C. W., Huang, T., Socrates, V., Chi, L., Taylor, R. A., & Chartash, D. (2023). How Does ChatGPT Perform on the United States Medical Licensing Examination? The Implications of Large Language Models for Medical Education and Knowledge Assessment. *JMIR Medical Education*, *9*, 9. doi:10.2196/45312 PMID:36753318

GlaireWolf. (2023, April 18). *False accusation of cheating* [Reddit Post]. R/UofArizona. www.reddit.com/r/UofArizona/comments/12qsp4b/false_accusation_of_cheating/

Glaze-Wolf. (2023, May). *I was falsely accused of using a AI to write my final paper* [Reddit Post]. R/College. https://www.reddit.com/r/college/comments/138ug6h/i_was_falsely_accused_of_using_a_ai_to_write_my/

Glean. (2023). *Personal study tool*. Glean. www.glean.co

Glendinning, I. (2016). European perspectives of academic integrity. In T. Bretag (Ed.), Handbook of Academic Integrity (pp. 55–74). Springer. doi:10.1007/978-981-287-098-8_3

Glendinning, I. (2022). Aligning academic quality and standards with academic integrity. In S. E. Eaton, G. Curtis, B. M. Stoesz, K. Rundle, J. Clare, & J. Seeland (Eds.), Contract cheating in higher education: Global perspectives on theory, practice, and policy. Palgrave Macmillan. doi:10.1007/978-3-031-12680-2_14

Glendinning, I. (2023). *Academic integrity: Responding to advances in artificial intelligence* [Video presentation]. Aga Khan University. https://www.youtube.com/watch?app=desktop&v=JGxtHxXH79I

Glendinning, I. (2023a). Linking quality, standards and Integrity. Eaton, S. (Ed), Handbook for Academic Integrity, 2nd Edition, Springer. On-line. doi:10.1007/978-981-287-079-7_117-1

Glendinning, I., & Orim, S. M. (2023). Comparison of Institutional Strategies for Academic Integrity in Europe and Eurasia. Bjelobaba, S., Foltýnek, T., Glendinning, I., Králíková, V., Dlabolová, D. (Eds) (2023). Academic Integrity: Broadening Practices, Technologies, and the Role of Students. Springer series: Ethics and Education in Educational Contexts. Springer. doi:10.1007/978-3-031-16976-2_3

Glendinning, I., Foltýnek, T., Dlabolová, D., Dannhoferová, J., Králíková, V., Michalska, A., Orim, S.-M., & Turčínek, P. (2021). *Project on academic integrity in Armenia, Azerbaijan, Georgia, Kazakhstan and Turkey*. ETINED, Council of Europe Platform on Ethics, Transparency and Integrity in Education. https://book.coe.int/en/education-policy/10662-pdf-etined-council-of-europe-platform-on-ethics-transparency-and-integrity-in-education-volume-6-project-on-academic-integrity-in-armenia-azerbaijan-georgia-kazakhstan-and-turkey.html

Glendinning, I., Orim, S., & King, A. (2019). *Policies and Actions of Accreditation and Quality Assurance Bodies to Counter Corruption in Higher Education*. CHEA / CIQG 2019. https://www.chea.org/quality-assurance-combatting-academic-corruption-resources

Glendinning, I. (2014). Responses to student plagiarism in higher education across Europe. *International Journal for Educational Integrity*, *10*(1). doi:10.21913/IJEI.v10i1.930

Glendinning, I. (2023). Educational Integrity in Schools: A Framework for Young Learners. In S. E. Eaton & Z. R. Khan (Eds.), *Ethics and Integrity in Teacher Education. Ethics and Integrity in Educational Contexts* (Vol. 3). Springer. doi:10.1007/978-3-031-16922-9_11

Glendinning, I. (2023b Forthcoming). Developing and implementing policies for academic Integrity – management of change. In G. J. Curtis (Ed.), *Academic Integrity in the Social Sciences*. Springer. doi:10.1007/978-3-031-43292-7_6

Gluska, J. (2023, April 14). *Are Innocent Students Paying the Price for Turnitin's AI Detection Flaws?* Gold Penguin. https://goldpenguin.org/blog/turnitin-ai-detection-concerns/

Gluska, J. (2023, August 09). *How to Bypass ChatGPT Writing Detection Tools With Other Tools*. Gold Penguin. https://goldpenguin.org/blog/avoiding-ai-detection-for-chatgpt-writing/

Gniel, H. (2023a, April). *AI: A regulatory perspective*. TEQSA. https://www.teqsa.gov.au/sites/default/files/2023-04/AI-a-regulatory-perspective-2023.pdf

Gniel, H. (2023b, June 8). *AI: A regulatory perspective on what we've learnt.* ChatGPT: What have we learnt? [Online]. https://www.youtube.com/watch?v=1V0f3pw2B_0

Godwin-Jones, R. (2022). Partnering with AI: Intelligent writing assistance and instructed language learning. *Language Learning & Technology*, *26*(2), 5–24. 10125/73474

Goodboy, A. K. (2011). Instructional dissent in the college classroom. *Communication Education*, *60*(3), 296–313. doi:10.1080/03634523.2010.537756

Google. (2023). *Googe Bard [AI model].* Google. https://g.co/bard/share/62a1ab50ef60

Google. (2023a). *Google Bard [AI model].* Google. https://g.co/bard/share/81836b07a821

Google. (2023a, February 06) *An important next step on our AI journey* [Press release]. Google LLC. https://blog.google/technology/ai/bard-google-ai-search-updates

Google. (2023b). *Google Bard [AI model].* Google. https://g.co/bard/share/ba507c1d022a

Google. (2023b, March 21). *Try Bard and share your feedback* [Press release]. Google LLC. https://blog.google/technology/ai/try-bard

Google. (2023c). *Google Bard [AI model]*. Google. https://g.co/bard/share/cc37d8ff0536

Goom, H. (2023, July 12). *AI-Generated vs. Human-Written Text: Technical Analysis*. Artmap Inc. https://hackernoon.com/ai-generated-vs-human-written-text-technical-analysis

Gora, P. (2022, March 3). *What do students expect from their universities?* https://www.universityworldnews.com/post.php?story=20220301081656159

GPTZero Release Notes. (2023). *GPT Release Notes (Model and API)*. https://gptzero.notion.site/GPTZero-Release-Notes-Model-and-API-6f58686f6381498baef35212463b7da6

GPTZero. (2023). *GPTZero | FAQ*. GPTZero. https://gptzero.me/

Graham, S. S., & Hopkins, H. R. (2022). AI for social justice: New methodological horizons in technical communication. *Technical Communication Quarterly*, *31*(1), 89–102. doi:10.1080/10572252.2021.1955151

Grammarly Inc. (2023). *Grammarly fo*. www.grammarly.com/ai

Grassini, S. (2023). Shaping the Future of Education: Exploring the Potential and Consequences of AI and ChatGPT in Educational Settings. *Education Sciences*, *13*(7), 692–704. doi:10.3390/educsci13070692

Greene-Harper, R. T. (2023, April 27). *The pros and cons of using ai in learning: Is ChatGPT helping or hindering learning outcomes?* eLearning Industry. https://elearningindustry.com/pros-and-cons-of-using-ai-in-learning-chatgpt-helping-or-hindering-learning-outcomes#:~:text=The%20use%20of%20Artificial%20Intelligence,questions%2C%20and%20keep%20them%20motivated

Gregorcic, B., & Pendrill, A. M. (2023). ChatGPT and the frustrated Socrates. *Physics Education*, 58.

Gribble, L., & Wardrop J. (in press). Building AI literacy: Assessment as a process to navigate the future. *Advance HE*. United Kingdom.

Gribble, L., & Wardrop, J. (2023, August 2). Incorporating Generative AI in Authentic Assessments. *Disruptive Innovations in Business Education Research Group*. https://diberg.blog/2023/08/02/incorporating-generative-ai-in-authentic-assessments

Grobe, C. (2023). Why I'm Not Scared of ChatGPT. [+ https://www.chronicle.com/article/why-im-not-scared-of-chatgpt]. *The Chronicle of Higher Education*, *69*(11), 32.

Group, R. (2023). *New principles on use of AI in education*. Russell Group. https://russellgroup.ac.uk/news/new-principles-on-use-of-ai-in-education/

Gruetzemacher, R., & Whittlestone, J. (2022). The transformative potential of artificial intelligence. *Futures*, *135*, 102884. doi:10.1016/j.futures.2021.102884

Guinness, H. (2023). *The best AI image generators in 2023*. Zapier. https://zapier.com/blog/best-ai-image-generator/

Gulikers, J. M., Bastiaens, T. J., & Kirshner, P. A. (2004). A Five-Dimensional Framework for Authentic Assessment. *Educational Technology Research and Development*, *52*(3), 67–87. doi:10.1007/BF02504676

Gulikers, J. T. M., Kester, L., Kirschner, P. A., & Bastiaens, T. J. (2008). The effect of practical experience on perceptions of assessment authenticity, study approach, and learning outcomes. *Learning and Instruction*, *18*(2), 172–186. doi:10.1016/j.learninstruc.2007.02.012

Gunderson, S., Jones, R., & Scanland, K. (2004). *The jobs revolution: Changing how America works*. Copywriters Inc.

Guo, K., Zhong, Y., Li, D., & Chu, S. (2023, October). Effects of chatbot-assisted in-class debates on students'. *Computers & Education, 203*(104862), 104862. doi:10.1016/j.compedu.2023.104862

Hague, D. (2023, June 7). *What we're reading on AI regulation.* Center for Security and Emerging Technology at Georgetown University. https://cset.georgetown.edu/article/what-were-reading-on-ai-regulation/

Hahn, W. W. (2023, September 15). *ChatGPT and Large Language Models: Syntax and Semantics.* CFA Institute. https://blogs.cfainstitute.org/investor/2023/09/25/chatgpt-and-large-language-models-syntax-and-semantics/

Hamid, R., & Schisgall, E. (2023, June 21). CS50 will integrate artificial Intelligence into course instruction. *The Harvard Crimson.* https://www.thecrimson.com/article/2023/6/21/cs50-artificial-intelligence/

Hamid, R., & Yuan, C. (2023, July 14). Harvard releases first guidelines for 'responsible experimentation with generative AI tools'. *The Harvard Crimson.* https://www.thecrimson.com/article/2023/7/14/harvard-ai-guidelines/

Hanesworth, P., Bracken, S., & Elkington, S. (2019). A typology for a social justice approach to assessment: Learning from universal design and culturally sustaining pedagogy. *Teaching in Higher Education, 24*(1), 98–114. doi:10.1080/13562517.2018.1465405

Harker, J. (2023, March). *Science journals set new authorship guidelines for AI-generated text.* National Institute of Environmental Health Sciences. https://factor.niehs.nih.gov/2023/3/feature/2-artificial-intelligence-ethics

Harper, R. (2023b, June 8). *ChatGPT: What have we learnt?* [Video]. An academic governance perspective. https://www.youtube.com/watch?v=1V0f3pw2B_0

Harrer, S. (2023). Attention is not all you need: The complicated case of ethically using large language models in healthcare and medicine. *EBioMedicine, 90*, 90. doi:10.1016/j.ebiom.2023.104512

Harvey, J., Hux, K., Scott, N., & Snell, J. (2013). Text-to-speech technology effects on reading rate and comprehension by adults with traumatic brain injury. *Brain Injury : [BI], 27*(12), 1388–1394. doi:10.3109/02699052.2013.823649 PMID:24102239

Harwell, D. (2022). Cheating-detection companies made millions during the pandemic. Now students are fighting back. In *Ethics of data and analytics.* Auerbach Publications. doi:10.1201/9781003278290-60

Hatzius, J., Briggs, J., Kodnani, D., & Pierdomenico, G. (2023, March 26). *The potentially large effects of artificial intelligence on economic growth.* https://www.key4biz.it/wp-content/uploads/2023/03/Global-Economics-Analyst_-The-Potentially-Large-Effects-of-Artificial-Intelligence-on-Economic-Growth-Briggs_Kodnani.pdf

Hauhart, R. C., & Grahe, J. E. (2015). *Designing and teaching undergraduate capstone courses.* John Wiley & Sons.

Heffernan, A., Bright, D., Kim, M., Longmuir, F., & Magyar, B. (2022). 'I cannot sustain the workload and the emotional toll': Reasons behind Australian teachers' intentions to leave the profession. *Australian Journal of Education, 66*(2), 196–209. doi:10.1177/00049441221086654

Heikkila, M. (2022, December 19). How to spot AI-generated text. *MIT Technology Review.* https://www.technologyreview.com/2022/12/19/1065596/how-to-spot-ai-generated-text/

Herrington, A., & Herrington, J. (2006). What is an Authentic Learning Environment? In A. Herrington & J. Herrington (Eds.), *Authentic Learning Environments in Higher Education* (pp. 1–14). Idea Group, Inc. doi:10.4018/978-1-59140-594-8.ch001

Hettich, P. I. (2010). College-to-workplace transitions: Becoming a freshman again. In T. W. Miller (Ed.), *Handbook of stressful transitions across the lifespan* (pp. 87–109). Springer. doi:10.1007/978-1-4419-0748-6_5

Higher education standards framework (threshold standards) 2021. (n.d.). Retrieved from https://www.legislation.gov.au/Details/F2022C00105/Html/Text#_Toc67664713

Hillier, M. (2023a, March 30). *Comparing ChatGPT to a calculator and a search engine*. Macquarie University. https://teche.mq.edu.au/2023/03/comparing-chatgpt-to-a-calculator-and-a-search-engine/

Hillier, M. (2023b, March 6). *Advising students about using and citing generative artificial intelligence for assessment*. Macquarie University. https://teche.mq.edu.au/2023/03/advising-students-about-using-and-citing-generative-artificial-intelligence-for-assessment/

Hines, K. (2023, June 4). History Of ChatGPT: A Timeline Of The Meteoric Rise Of Generative AI Chatbots. *Search Engine Journal*. https://www.searchenginejournal.com/history-of-chatgpt-timeline/488370/

Hinman, L. M. (2002). Academic integrity and the World Wide Web. *Computers & Society*, *32*(1), 33–42. doi:10.1145/511134.511139

Hmelo-Silver, C. E. (2004). Problem-based learning: What and how do students learn? *Educational Psychology Review*, *16*(3), 235–266. doi:10.1023/B:EDPR.0000034022.16470.f3

Hollman, T., Palmer, N., Chaffin, D., & Luthans, K. (2021). Lying, Cheating, & Stealing: Strategies for Mitigating Technology-Driven Academic Dishonesty in Collegiate Schools of Business. *Mountain Plains Journal of Business and Technology*. https://openspaces.unk.edu/mpjbt/vol22/iss1/

Holmes, W., Bialik, M., & Fadel, C. (2023). Artificial intelligence in education. Globethics Publications.

HolsteinK.DoroudiS. (2021). Equity and artificial intelligence in education: Will "AIEd" amplify or alleviate inequities in education? https://arxiv.org/abs/2104.12920

Hosseini, M., Rasmussen, L. M., & Resnik, D. B. (2023) Using AI to write scholarly publications. *Accountability in Research*. Taylor and Francis. https://www.tandfonline.com/doi/full/10.1080/08989621.2023.2168535

HosseiniE. A.SchrimpfM.ZhangY.BowmanS.ZaslavskyN.FedorenkoE. (2022). Artificial neural network language models align neurally and behaviorally with humans even after a developmentally realistic amount of training (p. 2022.10.04.510681). bioRxiv. doi:10.1101/2022.10.04.510681

Hough, D. (2023, October 10). *Student guidance for the responsible use of AI*. Association for Learning Technology. https://altc.alt.ac.uk/blog/2023/10/student-guidance-for-the-responsible-use-of-ai/

Howard, R. M. (1995). Plagiarisms, authorships, and the academic death penalty. *College English*, *57*(7), 788–806. doi:10.2307/378403

Howard, R. M. (2007). Understanding "internet plagiarism". *Computers and Composition*, *24*(1), 3–15. doi:10.1016/j.compcom.2006.12.005

Hrastinski, S., Olofsson, A. D., Arkenback, C., Ekström, S., Ericsson, E., Fransson, G., Jaldemark, J., Ryberg, T., Öberg, L.-M., Fuentes, A., Gustafsson, U., Humble, N., Mozelius, P., Sundgren, M., & Utterberg, M. (2019). Critical Imaginaries and Reflections on Artificial Intelligence and Robots in Postdigital K-12 Education. *Postdigital Science and Education*, *1*(2), 427–445. doi:10.1007/s42438-019-00046-x

Hsu, Y.-C., & Ching, Y.-H. (2023). Generative Artificial Intelligence in dducation. *TechTrends*. Advance online publication. doi:10.1007/s11528-023-00863-9

Huggins-Manley, A. C., Booth, B. M., & D'Mello, S. K. (2022). Toward Argument-Based Fairness with an Application to AI-Enhanced Educational Assessments. *Journal of Educational Measurement*, *59*(3), 362–388. doi:10.1111/jedm.12334

Hughes, M. L. (1997). Technorisk: Who's responsible? *Risk Management*, *44*(11), 20–24.

Hung, J., & Chen, J. (2023). The benefits, risks and regulation of using ChatGPT in Chinese academia: A content analysis. *Social Sciences (Basel, Switzerland)*, *12*(7), 380. doi:10.3390/socsci12070380

Hunter, K., & Docherty, P. (2011). Reducing variation in the assessment of student writing. *Assessment & Evaluation in Higher Education*, *36*(1), 109–124. doi:10.1080/02602930903215842

Hunt, L. A., McGee, P., Gutteridge, R., & Hughes, M. (2012). Assessment of student nurses in practice: A comparison of theoretical and practical assessment results in England. *Nurse Education Today*, *32*(4), 351–355. doi:10.1016/j.nedt.2011.05.010 PMID:21640448

Hutson, J., Jeevanjee, T., Graaf, V., Lively, J., Weber, J., Weir, G., Arnone, K., Carnes, G., Vosevich, K., Plate, D., Leary, M., & Edele, S. (2022). Artificial intelligence and the disruption of higher education: Strategies for integrations across disciplines. *Creative Education*, *13*(12), 3953–3980. doi:10.4236/ce.2022.1312253

Ibrahim, H., Liu, F., Asim, R., Battu, B., Benabderrahmane, S., Alhafni, B., Adnan, W., Alhanai, T., AlShebli, B., Baghdadi, R., Bélanger, J., Beretta, E., Celik, K., Chaqfeh, M., Daqaq, M., El Bernoussi, Z., Fougnie, D., Garcia de Soto, B., Gandolfi, A., & Zaki, Y. (2023) Perception, performance, and detectability of conversational artificial intelligence across 32 university courses. *Scientific Reports, 13*, 1–13. Nature Publishing. doi:10.1038/s41598-023-38964-3

ICAI. (2021). *The Fundamental Values of Academic Integrity* (3 ed.). International Center for Academic Integrity. https://academicintegrity.org/images/pdfs/20019_ICAI-Fundamental-Values_R12.pdf

Ifelebuegu, A. (2023). Rethinking online assessment strategies: Authenticity versus AI chatbot intervention. *JALT, 6*. . doi:10.37074/jalt.2023.6.2.2

Illia, L., Colleoni, E., & Zyglidopoulos, S. (2023). Ethical implications of text generation in the age of artificial intelligence. *Business Ethics, the Environment & Responsibility*, *32*(1), 201–210. doi:10.1111/beer.12479

Insights, C. (2013). The value of Google result positioning. Westborough: Chitika Inc, 0-10.

Institute of Ethics in Artificial Intelligence. (n.d.). *About IEAI.* IEAI. https://www.ieai.sot.tum.de/about-ieai/

International Center for Academic Integrity. (2014). *The fundamental values of academic integrity*. Second Edition. https://academicintegrity.org/wp- content/uploads/2017/12/Fundamental-Values-2014.pdf

Ireland, C., & English, J. (2011). Let them plagiarise: Developing Academic Writing in a Safe Environment. *Journal of Academic Writing*, *1*(1), 165–172. doi:10.18552/joaw.v1i1.10

Ison, D. C. (2015). The influence of the Internet on plagiarism among doctoral dissertations: An empirical study. *Journal of Academic Ethics*, *13*(2), 151–166. doi:10.1007/s10805-015-9233-7

Italian Government. (2021). *Strategic programme on artificial intelligence 2022-2024.* Italian Government. https://assets.innovazione.gov.it/1637777513-strategic-program-aiweb.pdf

ITVnews. (2023, 28 February). Oxford and Cambridge ban ChatGPT over plagiarism fears, but other universities choose to embrace AI bot. *ITVNews.* https://inews.co.uk/news/oxford-cambridge-ban-chatgpt-plagiarism-universities-2178391

Ivanov, S. & Soliman, M. (2023). Game of algorithms: ChatGPT implications for the future of tourism education and research. *Journal of Tourism Futures.*

Iverson, H. L., Lewis, M. A., & Talbot, R. M. III. (2008). Building a framework for determining the authenticity of instructional tasks within teacher education programs. *Teaching and Teacher Education*, *24*(2), 290–302. doi:10.1016/j.tate.2007.09.003

Jane, E. (2023, July 19). *"CheatGPT?"* Openforum (blog). https://www.openforum.com.au/cheatgpt-2/

Janesick, V. J. (2001). *The assessment debate: A reference handbook.*

Jasper. (2023). *Text summarizer.* www.jasper.ai

Jimenez, K. (2023, April 12). Professors are using ChatGPT detector tools to accuse students of cheating. But what if the software is wrong? *USA Today*. https://www.usatoday.com/story/news/education/2023/04/12/how-ai-detection-tool-spawned-false-cheating-case-uc-davis/11600777002/

JISC. (2023a). AI in Tertiary education. *JISC.* https://beta.jisc.ac.uk/reports/artificial-intelligence-in-tertiary-education report to download first published 26/04/21 updated 06/09/2023

Jisc. (2023a). *Artificial intelligence (AI) in tertiary education.* 3rd edition. Joint Information Systems Committee (JISC). https://beta.jisc.ac.uk/reports/artificial-intelligence-in-tertiary-education

JISC. (2023b) Generative AI – a primer. *JISC.* https://beta.jisc.ac.uk/reports/generative-ai-a-primer

Jisc. (2023b). *Student perceptions of generative AI.* Joint Information Systems Committee (JISC). https://beta.jisc.ac.uk/reports/student-perceptions-of-generative-ai

Jisc. (2023c). Generative AI – a primer. Version 1.1. Joint Information Systems Committee (JISC). https://repository.jisc.ac.uk/9182/1/generative-ai-a-primer.pdf

Jisc. (2023d, July 31). How UCL is redesigning assessment for the AI age. Joint Information Systems Committee (JISC). Retrieved, January 05, 2024, from https://www.jisc.ac.uk/member-stories/how-ucl-is-redesigning-assessment-for-the-ai-age

Ji, Z., Lee, N., Frieske, R., Yu, T., Su, D., Xu, Y., Ishii, E., Bang, Y. J., Madotto, A., & Fung, P. (2023). Survey of Hallucination in Natural Language Generation. *ACM Computing Surveys*, *55*(12), 1–38. doi:10.1145/3571730

Johns Hopkins University. (2023). *Student use of generative AI.* Johns Hopkins University. https://engineering.jhu.edu/cldt/chatgpt/student-use-of-generative-ai/

Johnson, A. (2023, January 18). ChatGPT In Schools: Here's Where It's Banned—And How It Could Potentially Help Students. *Forbes*. https://www.forbes.com/sites/ariannajohnson/2023/01/18/chatgpt-in-schools-heres-where-its-banned-and-how-it-could-potentially-help-students/

Johnston, S. L., & Glancey, M. (2022). Integrating Mentorship in Workplace-Integrated Learning Curriculum. *Papers on Postsecondary Learning and Teaching*, *5*, 34–41. doi:10.11575/pplt.v5i.73163

Jopp, R. (2019). A case study of a technology enhanced learning initiative that supports authentic assessment. *Teaching in Higher Education*, 1–17.

Jovanovic, M., & Campbell, M. (2022). Generative Artificial Intelligence: Trends and Prospects. *Computer*, *55*(10), 107–112. doi:10.1109/MC.2022.3192720

Juola, P. (2013, August 20). How a Computer Program Helped Show J. K. Rowling wrote A Cuckoo's Calling. *Scientific American*. https://www.scientificamerican.com/article/how-a-computer-program-helped-show-jk-rowling-write-a-cuckoos-calling/

Juola, P. (2017). Detecting Contract Cheating via Stylometric Methods. *Proceedings Plagiarism across Europe and Beyond*, 187–198. Mendel University Press. https://academicintegrity.eu/conference/proceedings/2017/Juola_Detecting.pdf

Justo-Hanani, R. (2022). The politics of Artificial Intelligence regulation and governance reform in the European Union. *Policy Sciences*, *55*(1), 137–159. doi:10.1007/s11077-022-09452-8

Kakuchi, S. (2023, July 11). New government guidelines on the use of AI in education. *University World News*. https://www.universityworldnews.com/post.php?story=20230711114553690

Kampakis, S. (n.d.). *The future of AI in education opportunities and challenges*. TheDataScientist. https://thedatascientist.com/the-future-of-ai-in-education-opportunities-and-challenges/

Kaneko, K. (2023, July 4). Japan emphasizes students' comprehension of AI in new school guidelines. *Japan Times*. https://www.japantimes.co.jp/news/2023/07/04/business/tech/schools-students-ai-guidelines/

Kanewischer, B., Johnston, S. L., Lyndon, J., & Glancey, M. (2023). Emotional discomfort as a catalyst for breaking through students' self-perceived capabilities. In P. Kumar, T. Culham, R. J. Major, & R. Peregoy (Eds.), Honing self-awareness of faculty and future business leaders: Emotions connected with teaching and learning (pp. 7–21). Emerald Publishers. doi:10.1108/978-1-80262-349-920231001

Kara, F., & MacAlister, D. (2010). Responding to academic dishonesty in universities: A restorative justice approach. *Contemporary Justice Review*, *13*(4), 443–453. https://www.msudenver.edu/wp-content/uploads/2022/12/Responding-to-Academic-Dishonesty-RJ.pdf. doi:10.1080/10282580.2010.517981

Kasneci, O. (2023, July 25). *Generative AI for everyone? [translated]*. Technical University of Munich. https://www.tum.de/aktuelles/alle-meldungen/pressemitteilungen/details/generative-ki-fuer-alle

Katz, D., Huggins-Manley, A. C., & Leite, W. (2022). Personalized online learning, test fairness, and educational measurement: Considering differential content exposure prior to a high stakes end of course exam. *Applied Measurement in Education*, *35*(1), 1–16. doi:10.1080/08957347.2022.2034824

Kelly, A., Sullivan, M., & Strampel, K. (2023). Generative artificial intelligence: University student awareness, experience, and confidence in use across disciplines. *Journal of University Teaching & Learning Practice*, *20*(6). doi:10.53761/1.20.6.12

Kermes, H., & Teich, E. (2017). Average surprisal of parts-of-speech. *Proceedings Corpus Linguistics 2017*, 1–6. University of Birmingham. https://www.birmingham.ac.uk/Documents/college-artslaw/corpus/conference-archives/2017/general/paper207.pdf

Khalil, M., & Er, E. (2023). Will ChatGPT get you caught? Rethinking of plagiarism detection. *arXiv preprint arXiv:2302.04335*. doi:10.1007/978-3-031-34411-4_32

Khan, U. (2023, May 16). How To Bypass AI Content Detectors: Remove AI Detection. Linkedin. https://www.linkedin.com/pulse/how-bypass-ai-content-detectors-uzair-khan

Khan, R. A., Jawaid, M., Khan, A. R., & Sajjad, M. (2023). ChatGPT-Reshaping medical education and clinical management. *Pakistan Journal of Medical Sciences*, *39*(2), 605. doi:10.12669/pjms.39.2.7653 PMID:36950398

Khan, Z. R., Sivasubramaniam, S., Anand, P., & Hysaj, A. (2021).. . *International Journal for Educational Integrity*, *17*, 1–27. doi:10.1007/s40979-020-00063-5

Kibler, W. L. (1993). Academic Dishonesty: A Student Development Dilemma. *NASPA Journal*, *30*(4), 252–267. doi:10.1080/00220973.1993.11072323

Kirchner, J. H., Ahmad, L., Aaronson, S., & Leike, J. (2023, July 20). *New AI classifier for indicating AI-written text*. Open AI. https://openai.com/blog/new-ai-classifier-for-indicating-ai-written-text

Kirshner, S. (2023, June 15). *Education in the Age of ChatGPT*. Openforum. https://www.openforum.com.au/education-in-the-age-of-chatgpt/

Klee, M. (2023a, May 17). *Texas A&M Professor Wrongly Accuses Class of Cheating With ChatGPT*. Rollingstone. https://www.rollingstone.com/culture/culture-features/texas-am-chatgpt-ai-professor-flunks-students-false-claims-1234736601/

Klee, M. (2023b, June 6). *She Was Falsely Accused of Cheating With AI -- And She Won't Be the Last*. Rolling Stone. https://www.rollingstone.com/culture/culture-features/student-accused-ai-cheating-turnitin-1234747351/

Klutka, J., Ackerly, N., & Magda, A. (2018). *Artificial intelligence in higher education: Current uses and future applications*. Wiley Education Services. https://universityservices.wiley.com/wp-content/uploads/2020/12/201811-AI-in-Higher-Education-TLH-with-new-bage.pdf

KMPG Canada. (2023, August 30). *Despite popularity, six in 10 students consider generative AI cheating - KPMG Canada*. KMPG. https://kpmg.com/ca/en/home/media/press-releases/2023/08/six-in-ten-students-consider-generative-ai-cheating.html

Kohn, A. (2020). Foreword. In S. D. Blum (Ed.), *Ungrading: Why rating students undermines learning (and what to do instead)* (pp. xiii–xxiii). West Virginia University Press.

Koltovskaia, S. (2020). Student engagement with automated written corrective feedback (AWCF) provided by Grammarly: A multiple case study. *Assessing Writing*, *44*, 100450. doi:10.1016/j.asw.2020.100450

Kortemeyer, G. (2023). Could an artificial-intelligence agent pass an introductory physics course? *Physical Review. Physics Education Research*, *19*(1), 010132. doi:10.1103/PhysRevPhysEducRes.19.010132

Krakowski, S., Luger, J., & Raisch, S. (2023). Artificial intelligence and the changing sources of competitive advantage. *Strategic Management Journal*, *44*(6), 1425–1452. doi:10.1002/smj.3387

Krasavina, V. (2019). Current trends in the IT services market. *E3S Web of Conferences*. https://www.e3s-conferences.org/articles/e3sconf/abs/2019/61/e3sconf_itese18_04039/e3sconf_itese18_04039.html

KU Leuven University. (2023, June 9). *Responsible use of generative artificial intelligence (2022-2023 academic year)*. KU Leuven University. https://www.kuleuven.be/english/education/student/educational-tools/generative-artificial-intelligence

Kuhail, M. A., Alturki, N., Alramlawi, S., & Alhejori, K. (2022). Interacting with educational chatbots: A systematic review. *Education and Information Technologies*, *28*, 1–46.

Kuh, G. D. (2008). *High-Impact Educational Practices: What They Are, Who Has Access to Them, and Why They Matter*. Association of American Colleges and Universities.

Kumar, A. H. S. (2023). Analysis of ChatGPT tool to assess the potential of its utility for academic writing in biomedical domain. *BEMS Reports*, *9*(1), 24–30. doi:10.5530/bems.9.1.5

Kumar, R., Eaton, S. E., Mindzak, M., & Morrison, R. (2023). Academic Integrity and Artificial Intelligence: An Overview. In S. E. Eaton (Ed.), *Handbook of Academic Integrity*. Springer. doi:10.1007/978-3-031-39989-3_153

Kumar, Y., Koul, A., & Singh, C. (2023). A deep learning approaches in text-to-speech system: A systematic review and recent research perspective. *Multimedia Tools and Applications*, *82*(10), 15171–15197. doi:10.1007/s11042-022-13943-4

Kurpejović, M. (2019). Montenegro just made plagiarism illegal. What does it hope to achieve? *RetractionWatch*. https://retractionwatch.com/2019/03/25/montenegro-just-made-plagiarism-illegal-what-does-it-hope-to-achieve/

Kwong, T., Ng, H., Mark, K., & Wong, E. (2010). Students' and faculty's perception of academic integrity in Hong Kong. *Campus-Wide Information Systems*, *27*(5), 341–355. doi:10.1108/10650741011087766

La Trobe University. (2022). *Student academic misconduct policy*. La Trobe University. https://policies.latrobe.edu.au/document/view.php?id=221

Lacey, M. M., & Smith, D. P. (2023). Teaching and assessment of the future today: Higher education and AI. *Microbiology Australia*, *44*(3), 124–126. doi:10.1071/MA23036

Lancaster University. (n.d.). Ling 131 – Language & Style. Department of Linguistics and English Language (LAEL), Lancaster University. Retrieved, January 05, 2024, from https://www.lancaster.ac.uk/fass/projects/stylistics/index.htm

Lancaster, T. (2020a). *Academic integrity 2020 – Keynote presentation slides* [Blog]. https://thomaslancaster.co.uk/blog/academic-integrity-2020-keynote-presentation-slides/

Lancaster, T. (2020b). *Contract cheating in the context of Covid-19: Five key ideas to consider* [Slideshare presentation]. https://www.slideshare.net/ThomasLancaster/contract-cheating-in-the-context-of-covid19-five-key-ideas-to-consider

Lancaster, T. (2022, December 04). Artificial Intelligence, Generated Text and Academic Integrity: Navigating the Ethics of AI in Academia. Thomas Lancaster's Blog. Retrieved, January 05, 2024, from https://thomaslancaster.co.uk/blog/artificial-intelligence-generated-text-and-academic-integrity-navigating-the-ethics-of-ai-in-academia/

Lancaster, T., & Clarke, R. (2016). Contract cheating: The outsourcing of assessed student work. Handbook of academic integrity, 1, 639-654.

Lang, J. M. (2013). *Cheating Lessons: Learning from Academic Dishonesty*. Harvard University Press. doi:10.4159/harvard.9780674726239

Lasen, M., Evans, S., Tsey, K., Campbell, C., & Kinchin, I. (2018). Quality of WIL assessment design in higher education: A systematic literature review. *Higher Education Research & Development*, *37*(4), 788–804. doi:10.1080/07294360.2018.1450359

Latif, E., Mai, G., Nyaaba, M., Wu, X., Liu, N., Lu, G., Li, S., Liu, T., & Zhai, X. (2023). Artificial general intelligence (AGI) for education. *arXiv preprint arXiv:2304.12479.*

Lawson, R. A. (2004). Is classroom cheating related to business students' propensity to cheat in the "real world"? *Journal of Business Ethics*, *49*(2), 189–199. doi:10.1023/B:BUSI.0000015784.34148.cb

Lea, K. (2023, November 24). Students are still confused about AI. WonkHE. Retrieved, January 05, 2024, from https://wonkhe.com/blogs-sus/students-are-still-confused-about-ai/

Leary, A., Varela, S., Casarez, R., & Ambrose, A. (2023). *Teaching in the age of AI.* Notre Dame Learning, University of Notre Dame. https://learning.nd.edu/resources/teaching-in-the-age-of-ai/

Leary, M., Tylka, A., Corsi, V., & Bryner, B. (2021). The Effect of First-Year Seminar Classroom Design on Social Integration and Retention of STEM First-Time, Full-Time College Freshmen. *Education Research International*, *2021*(4262905), 9. https://www.hindawi.com/journals/edri/2021/4262905/. doi:10.1155/2021/4262905

Lee, E., & Hannafin, M. J. (2016) A design framework for enhancing engagement in student-centered learning: own it, learn it, and share it. *Educational technology research and development.* [Online] *64*(4), 707–734. https://link.springer.com/article/10.1007/s11423-015-9422-5

Leitch, R., & Day, C. (2000). Action research and reflective practice: Towards a holistic view. *Educational Action Research*, *8*(1), 179–193. doi:10.1080/09650790000200108

Lepp, L. (2017). Undergraduate students' views on academic dishonesty. *New Trends and Issues Proceedings on Humanities and Social Sciences*, *3*(1), 41–51. doi:10.18844/prosoc.v3i1.1728

Leswing, K. (2023, April 28). *Tech giants are pouring money into A.I. as they cut costs elsewhere.* CNBC. https://www.cnbc.com/2023/04/28/tech-earnings-calls-show-mega-cap-companies-going-big-on-ai-.html

Leu, S., & Neumann, H. (2023). Patchwriting: Co-opting a transgressive practice for pedagogical purposes. In Teaching and Learning Source-Based Writing: Current Perspectives and Future Directions (pp. 80–93). Taylor and Francis.

Leung, M., & Niazi, S. (2023, February 23). Universities on alert over ChatGPT and other AI-assisted tools. *University World News*. https://www.universityworldnews.com/post.php?story=20230222132357841

Liang, W., Yuksekgonul, M., Mao, Y., Wu, E., & Zou, J. (2023). GPT detectors are biased against non-native English writers. *Patterns (New York, N.Y.)*, *4*(7), 1–4. doi:10.1016/j.patter.2023.100779 PMID:37521038

Lim, T., Gottipati, S., & Cheong, M. (2022). Authentic Assessments for Digital Education: Learning Technologies Shaping Assessment Practices. In Proceedings of the 30th International Conference on Computers in Education. Asia-Pacific Society for Computers in Education. Iyer, S. et al.(Eds.). November 28 - December 2. 587-592.

Lim, W. M., Gunasekara, A., Pallant, J. L., Pallant, J. I., & Pechenkina, E. (2023). Generative AI and the future of education: Ragnarok or reformation? A paradoxical perspective from management educators. *International Journal of Management Education*, *21*(2), 1–13. doi:10.1016/j.ijme.2023.100790

Lipson, S. K., Zhou, S., Abelson, S., Heinze, J., Jirsa, M., Morigney, J., Patterson, A., Singh, M., & Eisenberg, D. (2022). Trends in college student mental health and help-seeking by race/ethnicity: Findings from the national healthy minds study, 2013–2021. *Journal of Affective Disorders*, *306*, 138–147. doi:10.1016/j.jad.2022.03.038 PMID:35307411

Liu, D., Ho, E., Weeks, R., & Bridgeman, A. (2023, January 20). *How AI can be used meaningfully by teachers and students in 2023.* Sydney University. https://educational-innovation.sydney.edu.au/teaching@sydney/how-ai-can-be-used-meaningfully-by-teachers-and-students-in-2023/

Liu, G., & Ma, C. (2023). Measuring EFL learners' use of ChatGPT in informal digital learning of English based on the technology acceptance model. *Innovation in Language Learning and Teaching*, 1–14. doi:10.1080/17501229.2023.2240316

Lo, C. K. (2023). What is the impact of ChatGPT on education? A rapid review of the literature. *Education Sciences*, *13*(4), 410. doi:10.3390/educsci13040410

Lodge, J. M., Howard, S., & Broadbent, J. (2023, May 2). *Assessment redesign for generative AI: A taxonomy of options and their viability.* Linkedin. https://www.linkedin.com/pulse/assessment-redesign-generative-ai-taxonomy-options-viability-lodge/

Lodge, J., Howard, S., Bearman, M., & Dawson, P. (2023, November). Assessment reform for the age of artificial intelligence. *TEQSA*. https://www.teqsa.gov.au/guides-resources/resources/corporate-publications/assessment-reform-age-artificial-intelligence

Lodge, J. M., Thompson, K., & Corrin, L. (2023). Mapping out a research agenda for generative artificial intelligence in tertiary education. *Australasian Journal of Educational Technology*, *39*(1), 1–8. doi:10.14742/ajet.8695

Loeckx, J. (2016). Blurring boundaries in education: context and impact of MOOCs. *International Review of Research in Open and Distributed Learning*.

Löfström, E., & Kupila, P. (2013). The instructional challenges of student plagiarism. *Journal of Academic Ethics*, *11*(3), 231–242. doi:10.1007/s10805-013-9181-z

London Metropolitan University. (2023). *Guidance on the use of AI.* London Metropolitan University. https://student.londonmet.ac.uk/your-studies/student-administration/guidance-on-the-use-of-artificial-intelligence/

Love, T. S., & Love, Z. J. (2023). The teacher recruitment crisis: Examining influential recruitment factors from a United States technology and engineering teacher preparation program. *International Journal of Technology and Design Education*, *33*(1), 105–121. doi:10.1007/s10798-022-09727-4

Luckin, R., & Holmes, W. (2016). *Intelligence Unleashed: An argument for AI in Education.* UCL Discovery. London: Pearson. https://www.pearson.com/content/dam/corporate/global/pearson-dot-com/files/innovation/Intelligence-Unleashed-Publication.pdf

Luckin, R., & Holmes, W. (2016). Intelligence Unleashed: An argument for AI in Education. *UCL Knowledge Lab.* https://www.pearson.com/content/dam/corporate/global/pearson-dot-com/files/innovation/Intelligence-Unleashed-Publication.pdf

Lund, B. D., Wang, T., Mannuru, N. R., Nie, B., Shimray, S., & Wang, Z. (2023). ChatGPT and a new academic reality: Artificial Intelligence-written research papers and the ethics of the large language models in scholarly publishing. *Journal of the Association for Information Science and Technology*, *74*(5), 570–581. doi:10.1002/asi.24750

Luo, B., Lui, S., Lui, C., & Zhang, R. (2018). Knowledge exploration and innovation: A review and inverse S-curve proposition. *Journal of Management & Organization*, *24*(6), 870–892. doi:10.1017/jmo.2016.39

Lytvyn, M. (2023, June 7). *A framework for responsible AI in education.* Grammarly. https://www.grammarly.com/blog/responsible-ai-education/

Macdonald, R., & Carroll, J. (2006). Plagiarism—A complex issue requiring a holistic institutional approach. *Assessment & Evaluation in Higher Education*, *31*(2), 233–245. doi:10.1080/02602930500262536

Macfarlane, B., Zhang, J., & Pun, A. (2014). Academic integrity: A review of the literature. *Studies in Higher Education*, *39*(2), 339–358. doi:10.1080/03075079.2012.709495

MacLaren, I., O'Brien, G., Casey, E., Clinch, G., Jackson, N., Lane, B., & Peck, C. (2023). *NAIN generative AI: Guidelines for educators.* Quality and Qualifications Ireland. https://www.qqi.ie/sites/default/files/2023-09/NAIN%20Generative%20AI%20Guidelines%20for%20Educators%202023.pdf

Mahmud, S., & Ali, I. (2023). Evolution of research on honesty and dishonesty in academic work: A bibliometric analysis of two decades. *Ethics & Behavior*, *33*(1), 55–69. doi:10.1080/10508422.2021.2015598

Ma, K., & Cavanagh, M. S. (2018). Classroom ready?: Pre-service teachers' self-efficacy for their first professional experience placement. *The Australian Journal of Teacher Education*, *43*(7), 134–151. doi:10.14221/ajte.2018v43n7.8

Manga, D. (2023, March 30). *Which UK Universities have banned ChatGPT?* Desiblitz. https://www.desiblitz.com/content/which-uk-universities-have-banned-chatgpt

Manly, T. S., Leonard, L. N., & Riemenschneider, C. K. (2015). Academic integrity in the information age: Virtues of respect and responsibility. *Journal of Business Ethics*, *127*(3), 579–590. doi:10.1007/s10551-014-2060-8

Marche, S. (2022, December 6). The College Essay is Dead. *The Atlantic.* https://www.theatlantic.com/technology/archive/2022/12/chatgpt-ai-writing-college-student-essays/672371/

Marion, T., Cannon, D., Reid, T., & McGowan, A.-M. (2021). A conceptual model for integrating design thinking and lean startup methods into the innovation process. *Proceedings of the Design Society*, *1*, 31–40. doi:10.1017/pds.2021.4

Marshall, A. J. (2023, July 17). AI: There Is No Such Thing As A Silver Bullet. Linkedin. https://www.linkedin.com/pulse/ai-thing-silver-bullet-alexander-james-marshall

Martin, C. D., Branzi, F. M., & Bar, M. (2018). Prediction is Production: The missing link between language production and comprehension. *Scientific Reports*, *8*(1), 1. doi:10.1038/s41598-018-19499-4 PMID:29348611

Marton, F., & Säljö, R. (1976). On qualitative differences in learning: I—Outcome and process. *The British Journal of Educational Psychology*, *46*(1), 4–11. doi:10.1111/j.2044-8279.1976.tb02980.x

Matyushok, V., Krasavina, V., Berezin, A., & García, J. (2021). The global economy in technological transformation conditions: A review of modern trends. *Economic Research-Ekonomska Istraživanja*. https://www.tandfonline.com/doi/full/10.1080/1331677X.2020.1844030

Maurya, A. (2022). *Running Lean: Iterate from Plan A to a Plan That Works* (3rd ed.). O'Reilly.

Maybee, C., Bruce, C. S., Lupton, M., & Pang, M. F. (2019). Informed learning design: Teaching and learning through engagement with information. *Higher Education Research & Development*, *38*(5), 579–593. doi:10.1080/07294360.2018.1545748

McAdoo, T. (2023, April 7). How to cite ChatGPT. *APA Style*. https://apastyle.apa.org/blog/how-to-cite-chatgpt

McCabe, D. (2016). Cheating and honor: Lessons from a long-term research project. In T. Bretag (Ed.), *Handbook of Academic Integrity* (pp. 187–198). Springer. doi:10.1007/978-981-287-098-8_35

McCabe, D. L., Butterfield, K. D., & Trevino, L. K. (2012). *Cheating in college: Why students do it and what educators can do about it*. JHU Press. doi:10.1353/book.18818

McCabe, D. L., & Makowski, A. L. (2001). Resolving Allegations of Academic Dishonesty: Is There a Role for Students to Play? *About Campus: Enriching the Student Learning Experience*, *6*(1), 17–21. doi:10.1177/108648220100600104

McCabe, D. L., & Trevino, L. K. (1993). Academic dishonesty: Honor codes and other contextual influences. *The Journal of Higher Education*, *64*(5), 522–538. doi:10.1080/00221546.1993.11778446

McCabe, D. L., & Treviño, L. K. (1997). Individual and contextual influences on academic dishonesty: A multicampus investigation. *Research in Higher Education*, *38*(3), 379–396. doi:10.1023/A:1024954224675

McCabe, D. L., Trevino, L. K., & Butterfield, K. D. (2001). Cheating in Academic Institutions: A Decade of Research. *Ethics & Behavior*, *11*(3), 219–232. doi:10.1207/S15327019EB1103_2

McCabe, D., & Pavela, G. (2000). Some Good News About Academic Integrity, Change. *Change*, *32*(5), 32–38. doi:10.1080/00091380009605738

McCarthy, J., Minsky, M. L., Rochester, N., & Shannon, C. E. (2006). A proposal for the dartmouth summer research project on artificial intelligence, august 31, 1955. *AI Magazine*, *27*(4), 12–12.

McClenaghan, E. (2022, July 06). *Mann-Whitney U Test: Assumptions and Example*. Labx Media Group Inc. https://www.technologynetworks.com/informatics/articles/mann-whitney-u-test-assumptions-and-example-363425

McGeeR. W. (2023). Is chat gpt biased against conservatives? An empirical study. Social Science Research Network. doi:10.2139/ssrn.4359405

McInnes, R. (2023, September 11). Embracing generative AI as a co-design partner for designing and developing courses. *Times Higher Education*. https://www.timeshighereducation.com/campus/embracing-generative-ai-codesign-partner-designing-and-developing-courses

McIntyre, N. A. (2023). Access to online learning: Machine learning analysis from a social justice perspective. *Education and Information Technologies*, *28*(4), 3787–3832. doi:10.1007/s10639-022-11280-5 PMID:36210911

McKillup, S., & McKillup, R. (2007). An assessment strategy that pre-empts plagiarism. *International Journal for Educational Integrity*, *3*(2). doi:10.21913/IJEI.v3i2.163

McMurtrie, B. (2023) Teaching: Will ChatGPT change the way you teach? *The Chronicle of Higher Education*. https://www.chronicle.com/newsletter/teaching/2023-01-05

McMurtrie, B. (2022, December). AI and the future of undergraduate writing. [Online] [Available at: https://www.chronicle.com/article/ai-and-the-future-of-undergraduate-writing]. *The Chronicle of Higher Education, 13.*

McRae, K., & Matsuki, K. (2013). Constraint-based models of sentence processing. In *Sentence processing* (pp. 51–77). Psychology Press.

Meeks, G. (2017). *Critical Soft Skills to Achieve Success in the Workplace*. Walden University ProQuest Dissertations Publishing.

Meisels, S. J., Wen, X., & Beachy-Quick, K. (2010). Authentic Assessment for Infants and Toddlers: Exploring the Reliability and Validity of the Ounce Scale. *Applied Developmental Science*, *14*(2), 55–71. doi:10.1080/10888691003697911

Mellit, A., & Kalogirou, S. (2008). Artificial Intelligence Techniques for Photovoltaic Applications: A Review. *Progress in Energy and Combustion Science*, *34*(5), 574–632. doi:10.1016/j.pecs.2008.01.001

MercerB.VogtL. (2022). Getting off the Beaten Path: Authentic Assessments That Enhance Teaching, Learning, and Academic Integrity. *Canadian Perspectives on Academic Integrity, 5*(1), 32. doi:10.11575/cpai.v5i1.75129

Merrick, J. (2023). *A narrative inquiry of life stories told by women with ADHD.* [Master's thesis, University of Calgary, Calgary, Canada].

Metz, C., & Weise, K. (2023). Microsoft bets big on the creator of ChatGPT in race to dominate A.I. *The New York Times.* https://www.nytimes.com/2023/01/12/technology/microsoft-openai-chatgpt.html

Meurers, D. (2020). Natural Language Processing and Language. *The Concise Encyclopedia of Applied Linguistics.* https://www.sfs.uni-tuebingen.de/~dm/papers/Meurers-20.pdf

Microsoft. (2023). *Bing Chat* [AI model]. The New Bing.

MICUSP. (2009). *Michigan Corpus of Upper Level Student Papers* [dataset]. https://elicorpora.info/main

Mijwil, M. M., Hiran, K. K., Doshi, R., Dadhich, M., Al-Mistarehi, A.-H., & Bala, I. (2023). ChatGPT and the future of academic integrity in the artificial intelligence era: A new frontier. *Al-Salam Journal for Engineering and Technology*, *2*(2), 116–127. doi:10.55145/ajest.2023.02.02.015

Milan, S. (2020). Techno-solutionism and the standard human in the making of the COVID-19 pandemic. *Big Data & Society*, *7*(2), 2053951720966781. doi:10.1177/2053951720966781

Miles, C. A., & Foggett, K. A. (2019, July 2). *Designing Authentic Assessments to Assure Student Success, Employability, and Academic Integrity*. Higher Education Research and Development Society of Australasia, Auckland, NZ. https://bpb-ap-se2.wpmucdn.com/blogs.auckland.ac.nz/dist/2/372/files/2019/02/Designing-authentic-assessments-to-assure-student-success-employability-and-academic-integrity-11roq1e.pdf

Miles, P. J., Campbell, M., & Ruxton, G. D. (2022). Why students cheat and how understanding this can help reduce the frequency of academic misconduct in higher education: A literature review. *Journal of Undergraduate Neuroscience Education*, *20*(2), A150–A159.

Mills, A. (2023). AI Text Generators: Sources to Stimulate Discussion Among Teachers. Google Docs. https://docs.google.com/document/d/1V1drRG1XlWTBrEwgGqd-cCySUB12JrcoamB5i16-Ezw/edit#heading=h.sot8caygc8jr

Mills, A. (2023, March 23). Advice | ChatGPT Just Got Better. What Does That Mean for Our Writing Assignments? *The Chronicle of Higher Education.* https://www.chronicle.com/article/chatgpt-just-got-better-what-does-that-mean-for-our-writing-assignments

Min, S. (2023, May 2). *Chegg shares drop more than 40% after company says ChatGPT is killing its business*. CNBC. https://www.cnbc.com/2023/05/02/chegg-drops-more-than-40percent-after-saying-chatgpt-is-killing-its-business.html

Minarcik, J., & Bridges, A. J. (2015). Psychology graduate students weigh in: Qualitative analysis of academic dishonesty and suggestion prevention strategies. *Journal of Academic Ethics*, *13*(2), 197–216. doi:10.1007/s10805-015-9230-x

Miron, J., McKenzie, A., Eaton, S. E., Stoesz, B., Thacker, E., Devereaux, L., Persaud, N., Steeves, M., & Rowbotham, K. (2021). Academic integrity policy analysis of publicly-funded universities in Ontario, Canada: A focus on contract cheating. *Canadian Journal of Educational Administration and Policy*, *197*(197), 62–75. https://files.eric.ed.gov/fulltext/EJ1316334.pdf. doi:10.7202/1083333ar

Mirshekary, S., & Lawrence, A. D. (2009). Academic and business ethical misconduct and cultural values: A cross national comparison. *Journal of Academic Ethics*, *7*(3), 141–157. doi:10.1007/s10805-009-9093-0

Mizumoto, A., & Eguchi, M. (2023). *Exploring the potential of using an AI language model for automated essay scoring*.

Mockler, N. (2022). *Constructing Teacher Identities: How the Print Media Define and Represent Teachers and Their Work*. Bloomsbury Publishing., doi:10.5040/9781350132917

Mogali, S. R. (2023). Initial Impressions of ChatGPT for Anatomy Education. *Anatomical Sciences Education*, 1–4. doi:10.1002/ase.2261 PMID:36749034

Mohamed, R., & Lebar, O. (2017). Authentic assessment in assessing higher order thinking skills. *International Journal of Academic Research in Business & Social Sciences*, *7*(2), 466–476.

Mohd, C. K. N. C. K., Shahbodin, F., Mohd, S., Nor, A. M., Mohamad, S. N., & Saaya, Z. (2020). Educational technologies in a personalised learning environment (PLE): An overview. *World Transactions on Engineering and Technology Education*, *18*(4), 485–490.

Möller, A. (2023). An analysis of university academic integrity policies in New Zealand. *Journal of Further and Higher Education*, *47*(3), 338–350. doi:10.1080/0309877X.2022.2130195

Mollick, E. (2023, July 15). *In Praise of Boring AI*. https://www.oneusefulthing.org/p/in-praise-of-boring-ai

MollickE. R.MollickL. (2023). Using AI to implement effective teaching strategies in classrooms: Five strategies, including prompts. Social Science Research Network. doi:10.2139/ssrn.4391243

Monash University. (2023a). Generative AI in education. In *Inquiry into the use of generative artificial intelligence in the Australian education system - Submission 3*. Monash University. https://www.aph.gov.au/DocumentStore.ashx?id=98d34f1a-1f3b-4ee1-a742-f57076f924c8&subId=745132

Monash University. (2023b). *Generative AI and assessment*. Monash. https://www.monash.edu/learning-teaching/teachhq/Teaching-practices/artificial-intelligence/generative-ai-and-assessment

Moqbel, M. S. S., & Al-Kadi, A. M. T. (2023). Foreign language learning assessment in the age of ChatGPT: A theoretical account. *Journal of English Studies in Arabia Felix*, *2*(1), 71–84. doi:10.56540/jesaf.v2i1.62

Morgan, D. (2023). An autoethnography and analysis of Australian academic integrity policies amidst emerging threats. In U. G. Singh, C. S. Nair, & R. Watson (Eds.), *Academic integrity and quality assurance in the new digital higher education environment* (pp. 1–21). Elsevier. https://www.sciencedirect.com/book/9780323954235/academic-quality-and-integrity-in-the-new-higher-education-digital-environment

Morozov, E. (2013). *To save everything, click here: The folly of technological solutionism*. Public Affairs.

Morris, E., & Carroll, J. (2011). *Policy Works*. Higher Education Academy for England. https://www.advance-he.ac.uk/knowledge-hub/policy-works-recommendations-reviewing-policy-manage-unacceptable-academic-practice

Morris, E. J. (2018). Academic integrity matters: Five considerations for addressing contract cheating. *International Journal for Educational Integrity*, *14*(1), 15. doi:10.1007/s40979-018-0038-5

Morris, E. J. (2023). Integrating Academic Integrity: An Educational Approach. In S. E. Eaton (Ed.), *Handbook of Academic Integrity*. Springer. doi:10.1007/978-981-287-079-7_96-1

Morton-Aiken, J. (2023). *Intentional pedagogy with AI technology*. Brown University and The Harriet W. Sheridan Center for Teaching and Learning. https://www.brown.edu/sheridan/teaching-learning-resources/teaching-resources/intentional-pedagogy-ai-technology

Munoz, A., Wilson, A., Pereira Nunes, B., Del Medico, C., Slade, C., Bennett, D., Tyler, D., Seymour, E., Hepplewhite, G., & Randell-Moon, H. (2023). *AAIN Generative Artificial Intelligence Guidelines*.

Muscanell, N., & Robert, J. (2023, February 14). *EDUCAUSE quickpoll results: Did ChatGPT write this report?* Educause. https://er.educause.edu/articles/2023/2/educause-quickpoll-results-did-chatgpt-write-this-report

N., S. M. S. (2013, April 29). *Weak methods*. Psychology Dictionary. https://psychologydictionary.org/weak-methods/

Nadjafikhaha, M., & Yaftian, N. (2013). The frontage of Creativity and Mathematical Creativity. *ScienceDirect, 90*, 344 – 350. https://pdf.sciencedirectassets.com/277811/1-s2.0-S1877042813X00230/1-s2.0-S1877042813019897/main.pdf?X-Amz-Security-Token=IQoJb3JpZ2luX2VjEHEaCXVzLWVhc3QtMSJIMEYCIQC6MnNKqE8vWm1Unf6yKMi4r5t6JOyfBP6p%2BpYIQNedGAIhAKdYMG3RLDGIgCow9xHAFv%2B64zCwdyWtzOiqn91b

Namik, H., Sims, A., & Withy, A. (2023, May 22). Can academic integrity prevail when AI is so good? *Ingenio*. University of Auckland. https://www.auckland.ac.nz/en/news/2023/05/22/ingenio-taking-issue-opinion-chatgpt.html

Naughton, J. (2023, January 23). The ChatGPT bot is causing panic now – but it'll soon be as mundane a tool as Excel. *The Guardian*. https://www.theguardian.com/commentisfree/2023/jan/07/chatgpt-bot-excel-ai-chatbot-tech

Nave, L. (2020). UDL in Online Environments: The Why of Learning. *Journal of Developmental Education*, *44*(1), 30–31. https://www.jstor.org/stable/45381107

NeetMastery. (2023, April 16). *Have any of you learned to write well? My friend told me my writing style was similar to AI's, and I am now finding that detectors constantly flag me.* [Reddit Post]. R/Autism. www.reddit.com/r/autism/comments/12nuvfz/have_any_of_you_learned_to_write_well_my_friend/

Nejati, M., Shafaei, A., Salamzadeh, Y., & Daraei, M. (2011). Corporate social responsibility and universities: A study of top 10 world universities' websites. *African Journal of Business Management*, *5*(2), 440–447.

NeumannM.RauschenbergerM.SchönE.-M. (2023) "We Need To Talk About ChatGPT": The Future of AI and Higher Education. 2023:4. doi:10.1109/SEENG59157.2023.00010

New Scientist. (2023, July 29). How To Think About AI... And How To Live With It. *New Scientist, 259*, 32–40. https://www.sciencedirect.com/science/article/pii/S0262407923014276. doi:10.1016/S0262-4079(23)01427-6

Newman, F., Bryk, A., & Nagaoka, J. (2001). *Authentic Intellectual Work and Standardized Test: Conflict or Coexistence?* Consortium on Chicago School Research.

Newmann, F. M., & Archbald, D. A. (1992). The nature of authentic academic achievement. In H. Berlak, F. M. Newmann, E. Adams, D. A. Archbald, T. Burgess, J. Raven, & T. A. Romberg (Eds.), *Toward a new science of educational testing and assessment* (pp. 71–84). State University of New York Press.

Newmann, F. M., Secada, W., & Wehlage, G. G. (1995). Authentic assessment tasks. In *A guide to authentic instruction and assessment: Vision, standards, and scoring*. WCER.

Ng, D. T. K., Leung, J. K. L., Chu, S. K. W., & Qiao, M. S. (2021). Conceptualizing AI literacy: An exploratory review. *Computers and Education: Artificial Intelligence*, *2*, 100041. doi:10.1016/j.caeai.2021.100041

Nguyen, N. (2023, August 23). *AI in higher education: 8 key strategies for institutional leaders*. https://feedbackfruits.com/blog/ai-in-higher-education-8-key-strategies-for-institutional-leaders

Nieminen, J. H., & Tuohilampi, L. (2020). 'Finally studying for myself' – examining student agency in summative and formative self-assessment models. *Assessment & Evaluation in Higher Education*, *45*(7), 1031–1045. doi:10.1080/02602938.2020.1720595

Nikolic, S., Daniel, S., Haque, R., Belkina, M., Hassan, G. M., Grundy, S., Lyden, S., Neal, P., & Sandison, C. (2023). ChatGPT versus Engineering Education Assessment: A multidisciplinary and multi-institutional benchmarking and analysis of this generative artificial intelligence tool to investigate assessment integrity. *European Journal of Engineering Education*, *48*(4), 559–614. doi:10.1080/03043797.2023.2213169

Nolan, B. (2023, January 20). Here are the schools and colleges that have banned the use of ChatGPT over plagiarism and misinformation fears. *Insider*. https://www.businessinsider.com/chatgpt-schools-colleges-ban-plagiarism-misinformation-education-2023-1

Nolan, B. (2023, January 30). *Here are the schools and colleges that have banned the use of ChatGPT over plagiarism and misinformation fears*. Business Insider. https://www.businessinsider.com/chatgpt-schools-colleges-ban-plagiarism-misinformation-education-2023-1

Norman, G. (2018). Chinese Student to be deported after paying $3,000 to imposter. *Fox News*. https://www.foxnews.com/us/2018/04/05/chinese-student-to-be-deported-after-paying-3000-to-impostor-to-help-her-get-into-american-university.html

Nowik, C. (2022, December 17). The robots are coming! The robots are coming! Nah, the robots are here. *Substack*. https://christinenowik.substack.com/p/the-robots-are-coming-the-robots#detail

Noy, S., & Zhang, W. (2023). *Experimental Evidence on the Productivity Effects of Generative Artificial Intelligence* [MIT Economics Working Paper]. https://economics.mit.edu/sites/default/files/inline-files/Noy_Zhang_1.pdf

NoyS.ZhangW. (2023, March 6). *Experimental evidence on the productivity effects of generative artificial intelligence*. http://dx.doi.org/ doi:10.2139/ssrn.4375283

Nvidia. (2023, March 20). *What is Generative AI?* Nvidia Corporation. https://www.nvidia.com/en-us/glossary/data-science/generative-ai/

OECD. (2023). *Fostering and assessing students' creative and critical thinking skills in higher education*. OECD. https://www.oecd.org/education/ceri/fostering-assessing-students-creative-and-critical-thinking-skills-in-higher-education.htm

OECD. (2023, July 20). Generative AI in the classroom: From hype to reality? *Launch meeting of the Schools+ Network 22-23 May 2023,* Boulogne. https://one.oecd.org/document/EDU/EDPC(2023)11/en/pdf accessed Sept 10 2023

OECD. (n.d.). *AE Assessment for Learning - OECD*. OECD. https://www.oecd.org/site/educeri21st/40600533.pdf

Ohaja, M., Dunlea, M., & Muldoon, K. (2013). Group marking and peer assessment during a group poster presentation: The experiences and views of midwifery students. *Nurse Education in Practice*, *13*(5), 466–470. doi:10.1016/j.nepr.2012.11.005 PMID:23265913

OIA. (2023). *Casework Note: Complaints relating to academic misconduct.* OIA. https://www.oiahe.org.uk/resources-and-publications/casework-note-complaints-relating-to-academic-misconduct/

OIAHE. (2018). *Good Practice Framework – Disciplinary Procedures* OIAHE. https://www.oiahe.org.uk/media/2045/good-practice-framework-disciplinary-procedures-section.pdf

Open A. I. (2023). ChatGPT (Aug 3 version) [Large language model]. https://chat.openai.com/share/2004efe2-9066-4606-908c-c4d8e7460eac

Open A. I. (2023). *ChatGPT (Version 3) [Large language model].* Open AI. https://chat.openai.com/chat

Open A. I. (2023). ChatGPT 4.0 (September 25, 2023 version) [Large Language Model]. OPEN AI. https://chat.openai.com/?model=gpt-4

Open A. I. (2023). *Introducing ChatGPT Enterprise. Get enterprise-grade security & privacy and the most powerful version of ChatGPT yet.* Open AI. https://openai.com/blog/introducing-chatgpt-enterprise

Open A. I. (2023a). ChatGPT (Aug 3 version) [Large language model]. https://chat.openai.com/share/a70f7367-26be-4905-8c28-817783dae23a

Open A. I. (2023b). ChatGPT (Aug 3 version) [Large language model]. https://chat.openai.com/share/84ce0eca-1e42-4746-92c2-484b17c668d2

Open A. I. (2023c). ChatGPT (Aug 3 version) [Large language model]. https://apps.pple.com/us/app/chatgpt/id6448311069

Open A. I. (2023d). ChatGPT (Sept 25 version) [Large language model]. https://chat.openai.com/share/6741a04e-16c1-4509-9724-b54d204709f0

Open A. I. (2023e). ChatGPT (Sept 25 version). [Large language model]. https://chat.openai.com/share/973ce815-766e-438d-b398-4fa8a2dc91bf

Open A. I. (2023f). ChatGPT (Sept 25 version). [Large language model]. https://chat.openai.com/share/532900f0-26c5-4050-90a6-3fddd9e8f347

Open A. I. (2023g). ChatGPT (Sept 25 version). [Large language model]. https://chat.openai.com/share/973ce815-766e-438d-b398-4fa8a2dc91bf

Open A. I. (2023h). ChatGPT (Sept 25 version). [Large language model]. https://chat.openai.com/share/463aa99f-75bb-4dd3-b779-9e435c2715a7

Open A. I. (2023i). ChatGPT (Sept 25 version). [Large language model]. https://chat.openai.com/share/e83bf50a-899d-4403-b962-8cc1b0648d67

Open A. I. (2023j). ChatGPT (Sept 25 version). [Large language model]. https://chat.openai.com

Open A. I. (2023k). ChatGPT (Sept 25 version). [Large language model]. https://chat.openai.com

Open A. I. (2023l). *GPT-4 technical report.* arXiv, 2303-08774. https://cdn.openai.com/papers/gpt-4.pdf

OpenAI. (2022, November 30) *Introducing ChatGPT* [Press release]. OpenAI LLC. https://openai.com/blog/chatgpt

OpenAI. (2023a, January 31). *New AI classifier for indicating AI-written text.* [Press release]. OpenAI LLC. https://openai.com/blog/new-ai-classifier-for-indicating-ai-written-text

OpenAI. (2023b, March 14). *GPT-4.* [Press release]. OpenAI LLC. https://openai.com/research/gpt-4

OpenAI. (2023c, July 20). *As of July 20, 2023, the AI classifier is no longer available…* [Press release] OpenAI LLC. https://openai.com/blog/new-ai-classifier-for-indicating-ai-written-text

OpenAI. (2023d, September 22). *How can educators respond to students presenting AI-generated content as their own?* OpenAI LLC. https://help.openai.com/en/articles/8313351-how-can-educators-respond-to-students-presenting-ai-generated-content-as-their-own

Oravec, J. A. (2023). Artificial Intelligence Implications for Academic Cheating: Expanding the Dimensions of Responsible Human-AI Collaboration with ChatGPT and Bard. *Journal of Interactive Learning Research*, *34*(2), 213–237.

Orosz, Gã., TÃ3th-KirÃ¡ly, I., BÅ'the, B., Kusztor, A., KovÃ¡cs, Z. Ã., & JÃ¡nvÃ¡ri, M. (. (2015). Teacher enthusiasm: A potential cure of academic cheating. *Frontiers in Psychology*, *6*. doi:10.3389/fpsyg.2015.00318 PMID:25873903

Ortiz, S. (2023, September 15). *What is ChatGPT and why does it matter? Here's what you need to know.* ZDNet. https://www.zdnet.com/article/what-is-chatgpt-and-why-does-it-matter-heres-everything-you-need-to-know/

OutLiar. (n.d.). *Resources for detecting Contract Cheating*. OutLiar. https://outliar.blog/2021/10/19/resources-for-detecting-contract-cheating

Oxford Brookes University. (2023). *AI*. Oxford Brookes University. https://www.brookes.ac.uk/students/academic-development/online-resources/artificial-intelligence

Padillah, R. (2023). Ghostwriting: A reflection of academic dishonesty in the AI era. *Journal of Public Health*. doi:10.1093/pubmed/fdad169

Palinkas, L. A., Horwitz, S. M., Green, C. A., Wisdom, J. P., Duan, N., & Hoagwood, K. (2015). Purposeful sampling for qualitative data collection and analysis in mixed method implementation research. *Administration and Policy in Mental Health*, *42*(5), 533–544. doi:10.1007/s10488-013-0528-y PMID:24193818

Paraman, P., & Anamalah, S. (2023). Ethical artificial intelligence framework for a good AI society: Principles, opportunities and perils. *AI & Society*, *38*(2), 595–611. doi:10.1007/s00146-022-01458-3

Paraphraser.io. (n.d.). *Text summarizer*. Paraphraser.io. https://www.paraphraser.io/

Park, C. (2004, August). Rebels without a Clause: Towards an institutional framework for dealing with plagiarism by students. *Journal of Further and Higher Education*, *28*(3), 291–306. doi:10.1080/0309877042000241760

Paulson, F. L., Paulson, P. R., & Meyer, C. (1991). What makes a portfolio a portfolio? *Educational Leadership*, *48*(5), 60–63.

Păvăloaia, V., & Necula, S. (2023). *Artificial Intelligence as a Disruptive Technology—A Systematic Literature Review.* Basel: MDPI. https://www.mdpi.com/2079-9292/12/5/1102

Pavletić, P., & Hammerbauer, M. (2022). The Role of Students in the Preservation of Academic Integrity. In S. Bjelobaba, T. Foltýnek, I. Glendinning, V. Krásničan, & D. H. Dlabolová (Eds.), *Academic Integrity: Broadening Practices, Technologies, and the Role of Students. Ethics and Integrity in Educational Contexts* (Vol. 4). Springer. https://doi-org.ezproxy.derby.ac.uk/10.1007/978-3-031-16976-2_18

Pedró, F., Subosa, M., Rivas, A., & Valverde, P. (2019). Artificial intelligence in education: challenges and opportunities for sustainable development. *Working papers on education policy, 07.* UN. https://unesdoc.unesco.org/ark:/48223/pf0000366994.locale=en

Peeters, M. M., Diggelen, J., Bosch, K., Bronkhorst, A., Neerincx, M., Schraagen, J., & Raaijmakers, S. (2021). Hybrid collective intelligence in a human–AI society. *AI & Society*. https://link.springer.com/article/10.1007/s00146-020-01005-y

Pellegrino, J. W., & Quellmalz, E. S. (2010). Perspectives on the integration of technology and assessment. *Journal of Research on Technology in Education*, *43*(2), 119–134. doi:10.1080/15391523.2010.10782565

Peng, S., Kalliamvakou, E., Cihon, P., & Demirer, M. (2023). *The Impact of AI on Developer Productivity: Evidence from GitHub Copilot* (arXiv:2302.06590). arXiv. http://arxiv.org/abs/2302.06590

Peres, R., Shreier, M., Schweidel, D., & Sorescu, A. (2023). On ChatGPT and beyond: How generative artificial intelligence may affect research, teaching, and practice. *International Journal of Research in Marketing*, *40*(2), 269–275. doi:10.1016/j.ijresmar.2023.03.001

Perkins, M. (2023). Academic Integrity considerations of AI Large Language Models in the post-pandemic era: ChatGPT and beyond. *Journal of University Teaching & Learning Practice, 20*(2), 07.

Perkins, M. (2023). Academic Integrity considerations of AI Large Language Models in the post-pandemic era: ChatGPT and beyond. *Journal of University Teaching & Learning Practice*. https://ro.uow.edu.au/jutlp/vol20/iss2/07/

Perkins, M., Gezgin, U. B., & Roe, J. (2020). Reducing plagiarism through academic misconduct education. *International Journal for Educational Integrity*, *16*(1), 3. doi:10.1007/s40979-020-00052-8

Perkins, M., & Roe, J. (2023). Decoding academic integrity policies: A corpus linguistics investigation of AI and other technological threats. *Higher Education Policy*. Advance online publication. doi:10.1057/s41307-023-00323-2

PerplexityA. I. (n.d.). *Perplexity*. Perplexity A. I. www.perplexity.ai

Perrotta, C., Selwyn, N., & Ewin, C. (2022). Artificial intelligence and the affective labour of understanding: The intimate moderation of a language model. *New Media & Society*, *14614448221075296*. doi:10.1177/14614448221075296

Pessach, D., & Shmueli, E. (2023). A Review on fairness in machine learning. *ACM Computing Surveys*, *55*(3), 1–44. doi:10.1145/3494672

Phrasly. (2023, September 21). *AI Powered Writing for...* Phrasly LLC. https://phrasly.ai/?gclid=EAIaIQobChMIk_-J6puxgQMVi_ftCh0rugu0EAMYASAAEgIgQ_D_BwE

Picciano, A. G. (2019). Artificial Intelligence and the Academy's Loss of Purpose. *Online Learning : the Official Journal of the Online Learning Consortium*, *23*(3), 270–284. doi:10.24059/olj.v23i3.2023

Pickler, R. H. (2023). Artificial "Intelligence" and Scientific Integrity, *72*(3), 165-166.

Pine Cove Consulting. (2023, April 07). *How Can an Educator Can Prevent Students from Using AI Writers? Pine Cove Consulting*. Pine Cove Consulting. https://marketing.pinecc.com/blog/how-can-an-educator-can-prevent-students-from-using-ai-writers

Pinsky, Y. (2023). *Bard Can Now Connect to Your Google Apps and Services*. https://blog.google/products/bard/google-bard-new-features-update-sept-2023

Pitt, P., Dullaghan, K., & Sutherland-Smith, W. (2021). Mess, stress and trauma': Students' experiences of formal contract cheating processes. *Assessment & Evaluation in Higher Education*, *46*(4), 659–672. doi:10.1080/02602938.2020.1787332

Plaito. (2023). *Your personal AI tutor*. Plaito. www.plaito.ai

Pocket Confidant, A. I. SAS. (2020). *Pocket Confidant*. www.pocketconfidant.comv

Pollina, R. (2023, July 21). Autistic Purdue professor accused of being AI for lacking "warmth" in email. *New York Post*. https://nypost.com/2023/07/21/autistic-purdue-professor-accused-of-being-ai-for-lacking-warmth-in-email/

Polytechnic Institute Australia. (2023). *Academic integrity and misconduct policy*. PIA. https://docs.pia.edu.au/wp-content/uploads/Academic-Integrity-and-Misconduct-Policy.pdf

Poorvu Center. (2023). *AI guidance.* Yale University. https://poorvucenter.yale.edu/AIguidance

Popenici, S. A., & Kerr, S. (2017). Exploring the impact of artificial intelligence on teaching and learning in higher education. *Research and Practice in Technology Enhanced Learning, 12*(1), 1–13. doi:10.1186/s41039-017-0062-8 PMID:30595727

Poulos, A., & Mahony, M. J. (2008). Effectiveness of feedback: The students' perspective. *Assessment & Evaluation in Higher Education, 33*(2), 143–154. doi:10.1080/02602930601127869

Price, L., & Sheikh, I. (2023, January 30). University responds to the emergence of ChatGPT in education. *The Observer.* https://ndsmcobserver.com/2023/01/university-responds-to-emergence-of-chatgpt-in-education/

Prokou, E. (2008). The Emphasis on Employability and the Changing Role of the University in Europe. *Higher Education in Europe, 33*(4), 387–394. doi:10.1080/03797720802522593

QAA. (2021). *Exploring QAA Members' Approach to Academic Conduct Cases and Use of Penalties*. QAA.

QAA. (2022). *Contracting to Cheat in Higher Education*. QAA. https://www.qaa.ac.uk/docs/qaa/guidance/contracting-to-cheat-in-higher-education-third-edition.pdf?sfvrsn=2fbfa581_14

QAA. (2023). *Maintaining quality and standards in the ChatGPT era*. QAA. https://www.qaa.ac.uk/docs/qaa/members/maintaining-quality-and-standards-in-the-chatgpt-era.pdf released 8th May 2023

Queensland University of Technology. (2023). Queensland University of Technology response to the House of Representatives Standing Committee on employment, education and training inquiry into the use of generative artificial intelligence in the Australian education system. In *Inquiry into the use of generative artificial intelligence in the Australian education system - Submission 57.* https://www.aph.gov.au/DocumentStore.ashx?id=5b6f1c07-ae71-4187-8df3-8fd0fc059490&subId=745319

Quillbot. (n.d.). *Paraphraser*. Quillbot. https://quillbot.com/

Quizbot. (2023). *AI question generator*. Quillbot. www.quizbot.ai/

Qureshi, B. (2023). *Exploring the use of chatgpt as a tool for learning and assessment in undergraduate computer science curriculum: Opportunities and challenges*. arXiv preprint arXiv:2304.11214.

Rangarajan, A. K., & Ramachandran, H. K. (2021). A preliminary analysis of AI based smartphone application for diagnosis of COVID-19 using chest X-ray images. *Expert systems with applications*.

Rasul, T., Nair, S., Kalendra, D., Robin, M., de Oliveira Santini, F., Ladeira, W. J., & Heathcote, L. (2023). The role of ChatGPT in higher education: Benefits, challenges, and future research directions. *Journal of Applied Learning and Teaching, 6*(1), 41–56.

Rauch, S. (2023, August 11). *How AI is impacting industries worldwide*. Simplilearn. https://www.simplilearn.com/ai-artificial-intelligence-impact-worldwide-article

Raymond, J., Homer, C., Smith, R., & Gray, J. (2012). Learning through authentic assessment: An evaluation of a new development in the undergraduate midwifery curriculum. *Nurse Education in Practice, 13*(5), 471–476. doi:10.1016/j.nepr.2012.10.006 PMID:23140801

Reclaim A. I. (n.d.). *Smart AI scheduling*. Reclaim A. I. www.reclaim.ai

Reed, T. (2023, March 20). *Decoding Humanity: How to Differentiate Between AI and Human Writing*. Linkedin. https://www.linkedin.com/pulse/decoding-humanity-how-differentiate-between-ai-human-writing-reed

Reed, T. (2023, May 1). ChatGPT might show more empathy than docs, study finds. *AXIOS*. https://www.axios.com/2023/05/01/chatgpt-empathy-better-than-doctors

Rencic, J., Schuwirth, L. W., Gruppen, L. D., & Durning, S. J. (2020). Clinical reasoning performance assessment: Using situated cognition theory as a conceptual framework. *Diagnosis (Berlin, Germany)*, *7*(3), 241–249. doi:10.1515/dx-2019-0051 PMID:32031971

Renzulli, J. S., Gentry, M., & Reis, S. M. (2004). A time and a place for authentic learning. *Educational Leadership*, *62*(1), 73–77.

Retraction Watch. (2023, July 07). *Publisher blacklists authors after preprint cites made-up studies*. Center for Scientific Integrity. https://retractionwatch.com/2023/07/07/publisher-blacklists-authors-after-preprint-cites-made-up-studies/

Reuter, P. (1997). Why Can't We Make Prohibition Work Better? Some Consequences of Ignoring the Unattractive. *Proceedings of the American Philosophical Society*, *141*(3), 262–275. https://www.jstor.org/stable/987202 PMID:11619507

Revisely. (2023). *AI flash card generator*. Revisely. www.revisely.com/flashcard-generator

Ries, E. (2011). *The Lean Startup*. Crown Books.

Rigby, D., Burton, M., Balcombe, K., Bateman, I., & Mulatu, A. (2015). Contract cheating & the market in essays. *Journal of Economic Behavior & Organization*, *111*, 23–37. doi:10.1016/j.jebo.2014.12.019

Rodrigues Vasconcelos, M. A., & P dos Santos, R. (2023). Enhancing STEM learning with ChatGPT and Bing Chat as objects-to-think-with: A Case Study. Rodrigues Vasconcelos, Marco Antonio and P dos Santos, Renato, *Enhancing STEM Learning with ChatGPT and Bing Chat as Objects-to-Think-With: A Case Study* (May 1, 2023). *SSRN*. . doi:10.2139/ssrn.4434060

Rogers, R. (2023, February 08). *How to Detect AI-Generated Text, According to Researchers*. Advance Magazine Publishers Inc. https://www.wired.com/story/how-to-spot-generative-ai-text-chatgpt/

Rogerson, A. M., & McCarthy, G. (2017). Using Internet based paraphrasing tools: Original work, patchwriting or facilitated plagiarism? *International Journal for Educational Integrity*, *13*(1), 1833–2595. doi:10.1007/s40979-016-0013-y

Rose, D. H., Harbour, W., Johnston, C. S., Daley, S. G., & Abarbanell, L. (2006). Universal Design for Learning in postsecondary education: Reflections on principles and their application. *Journal of Postsecondary Education and Disability*, *19*(2), 135–151. www.ahead.org

Rospigliosi, P. (2023). Artificial intelligence in teaching and learning: What questions should we ask of ChatGPT? *Interactive Learning Environments*, *31*(1), 1–3. https://www.tandfonline.com/doi/full/10.1080/10494820.2023.2180191. doi:10.1080/10494820.2023.2180191

Rudolph, J., Tan, S., & Tan, S. (2023). ChatGPT: Bullshit spewer or the end of traditional assessments in higher education? *Journal of Applied Learning and Teaching*, *6*(1).

Rule, A. C. (2006). The components of authentic learning. *Journal of Authentic Learning*, *3*(1), 1–10.

Russell Group. (2023). *Russell Group principles on the use of generative AI tools in education*. Russell Group. https://russellgroup.ac.uk/media/6137/rg_ai_principles-final.pdf

Russell Group. (2023, July 04). *New principles on use of AI in education*. The Russell Group. https://russellgroup.ac.uk/news/new-principles-on-use-of-ai-in-education/ -:~:text=

Russell, B., Barron, C., Kim, H., & Jang, E. E. (2022). A mixed-method investigation into international university students' experience with academic language demands. *Frontiers in Education*, *7*, 934692. doi:10.3389/feduc.2022.934692

Russell, S., Caton, S., & Becker, B. A. (2023). Online programming exams-an experience report. In *Proceedings of the 2023 Conference on Innovation and Technology in Computer Science Education* V. 1 (pp. 436-442).

Sabzalieva, E., & Valentini, A. (2023). *ChatGPT and artificial intelligence in higher education: Quick start guide.* UNESCO. https://www.iesalc.unesco.org/wp-content/uploads/2023/04/ChatGPT-and-Artificial-Intelligence-in-higher-education-Quick-Start-guide_EN_FINAL.pdf

Sadasivan, V. S., Kumar, A., Balasubramanian, S., Wang, W., & Feizi, S. (2023). *Can AI-Generated Text be Reliably Detected?* (arXiv:2303.11156). arXiv. http://arxiv.org/abs/2303.11156

Safón, V. (2019). Inter-ranking reputational effects: An analysis of the Academic Ranking of World Universities (ARWU) and the Times Higher Education World University Rankings (THE) reputational relationship. *Scientometrics*, *121*(2), 897–915. doi:10.1007/s11192-019-03214-9

Sahota, H. (2023). *Top 10 List of Large Language Models Reshaping the Open-Source Arena in 2023*. DECI. https://deci.ai/blog/list-of-large-language-models-in-open-source/

Salvagno, M., Taccone, F. S., & Gerli, A. G. (2023). Can artificial intelligence help for scientific writing? *Critical Care*, *27*(1), 75–79. doi:10.1186/s13054-023-04380-2 PMID:36841840

Satariano, A. (2023). Europeans Take a Major Step Toward Regulating A.I. *New York Times.* https://www.nytimes.com/2023/06/14/technology/europe-ai-regulation.html

Schrimpf, M., Blank, I. A., Tuckute, G., Kauf, C., Hosseini, E. A., Kanwisher, N., Tenenbaum, J. B., & Fedorenko, E. (2021). The neural architecture of language: Integrative modeling converges on predictive processing. *Proceedings of the National Academy of Sciences of the United States of America*, *118*(45), e2105646118. doi:10.1073/pnas.2105646118 PMID:34737231

Scott, I. (2023). Yes, we are in a (ChatGPT) crisis. Inside Higher Ed.

See, B. H., Gorard, S., Morris, R., & Ventista, O. (2022). Rethinking the complex determinants of teacher shortages. The Palgrave Handbook of Teacher Education Research, 1-28. doi:10.1007/978-3-030-59533-3_2-1

Sefcik, L., Striepe, M., & Yorke, J. (2019). Mapping the landscape of academic integrity education programs: What approaches are effective? *Assessment & Evaluation in Higher Education.*

Sefcik, L., Striepe, M., & Yorke, J. (2020). Mapping the landscape of academic integrity education programs: what approaches are effective? Sefcik, Lesley; Striepe, Michelle; Yorke, Jonathan, 2020, Mapping the landscape of academic integrity education programs: what approaches are effective? *Journal of Asynchronous Learning Networks*, *16*(5), 61–71. https://files.eric.ed.gov/fulltext/EJ1000091.pdf

Seldon, A., & Abidoye, O. (2018). The fourth education revolution: will artificial intelligence liberate or infantilise humanity. *Higher Education.* Springer. https://link.springer.com/article/10.1007/s10734-020-00506-5

Selwood, I., & Pilkington, R. (2005). Teacher workload: Using ICT to release time to teach. *Educational Review*, *57*(2), 163–174. https://www.tandfonline.com/doi/full/10.1080/0013191042000308341. doi:10.1080/0013191042000308341

Selwyn, N. (2009). The digital native - myth and reality. [Online]. *Aslib Proceedings*, *61*(4), 364–379. doi:10.1108/00012530910973776

Seo, K., Tang, J., Roll, I., Fels, S., & Yoon, D. (2021). The impact of artificial intelligence on learner–instructor interaction in online learning. *International Journal of Educational Technology in Higher Education, 18*(54), 54. doi:10.1186/s41239-021-00292-9 PMID:34778540

Shanahan, M. (2023, February 23). *Talking about Large Language Models.* Imperial College London. https://arxiv.org/pdf/2212.03551.pdf

Shannon, C. E. (1948). A Mathematical Theory of Communication. *The Bell System Technical Journal, 27*(3), 379–423. doi:10.1002/j.1538-7305.1948.tb01338.x

Shannon, C. E. (1951). Prediction and entropy of printed English. *The Bell System Technical Journal, 30*(1), 50–64. doi:10.1002/j.1538-7305.1951.tb01366.x

Sharples, M. (2022). Automated essay writing: An AIED opinion. *International Journal of Artificial Intelligence in Education, 32*(4), 1119–1126. https://link.springer.com/article/10.1007/s40593-022-00300-7. doi:10.1007/s40593-022-00300-7

SharplesM. (2023). *Towards social generative AI for education: theory, practices and ethics*. https://arxiv.org/abs/2306.10063

Sheikh, H., Prins, C., & Schrijvers, E. (2023). Artificial Intelligence: Definition and Background. In Mission AI: The New System Technology (pp. 15-41). Springer.

Shidqiyah, S., Thalib, B., Wiratama, R., Alam, S., & Riyanto, R. (2023, December). DEVELOPMENT OF THE LATEST CURRICULUM-BASED LEARNING MODEL TO IMPROVE STUDENTS' DIGITAL LITERACY AND CRITICAL THINKING SKILLS IN THE INFORMATION TECHNOLOGY ERA. [INJOTEL]. *International Journal of Teaching and Learning, 1*(4), 412–425. https://injotel.org/index.php/12/article/view/36/55

Shin, Y., & Kim, G. (2022). The effect of automated written feedback through Grammarly. *Multimedia-Assisted Language Learning, 25*(2), 84–102. www.doi.org/10.15702/mall.2022.25.2.84

Shoufan, A. (2023). Exploring students' perceptions of CHATGPT: Thematic analysis and follow-up survey. *IEEE Access : Practical Innovations, Open Solutions, 11*, 38805–38818. doi:10.1109/ACCESS.2023.3268224

Shum, S. (2023b, June 8). *ChatGPT What have we learnt? What do we need to learn next?* ChatGPT: What have we learnt? https://www.youtube.com/watch?v=1V0f3pw2B_0

Siliezar, J. (2023, March 8). *Suresh Venkatasubramanian tells congress that AI guardrails are needed.* Brown University. https://cs.brown.edu/news/2023/03/08/suresh-venkatasubramanian-tells-congress-ai-guardrails-are-needed/

Singh, T., Goel, R., & Baral, S. K. (2022). A Study on Big Data Privacy in Cross-Industrial Challenges and Legal Implications. In *Cross-Industry Applications of Cyber Security Frameworks* (pp. 112–123). IGI Global. doi:10.4018/978-1-6684-3448-2.ch006

Singleton, K., Evmenova, A., Jerome, M., & Clark, K. (2019). Integrating UDL strategies into the online course development process. *Online Learning : the Official Journal of the Online Learning Consortium, 23*(1), 206–235. doi:10.24059/olj.v23i1.1407

Slade, C., Rowland, S., & McGrath, D. (2016). *Student dishonesty in assessment: Issues paper for UQ assessment subcommittee. Institute for Teaching and Learning Innovation.* The University of Queensland. uq.edu.au

Sliter, J. (2004). "Techno risk"-technology and intelligence data need to be pushed. *Journal of Financial Crime, 11*(4), 322–324. doi:10.1108/13590790410809266

Snow, E. L., Allen, L. K., Jacovina, M. E., Crossley, S. A., Perret, C. A., & McNamara, D. S. (2016). Keys to Detecting Writing Flexibility Over Time: Entropy and Natural Language Processing. *Journal of Learning Analytics*, *2*(3), 40–54. doi:10.18608/jla.2015.23.4

Sokol, D. (2023, July 10) It is too easy to falsely accuse a student of using AI: a cautionary tale. *Times Higher Education (THE)*. https://www.timeshighereducation.com/blog/it-too-easy-falsely-accuse-student-using-ai-cautionary-tale

SokS.HengK. (2023). ChatGPT for education and research: A review of benefits and risks. SSRN. doi:10.2139/ssrn.4378735

Sotiriadou, P., Logan, D., Daly, A., & Guest, R. (2020). The role of authentic assessment to preserve academic integrity and promote skill development and employability. *Studies in Higher Education*, *45*(11), 2132–2148.

Sotiriadou, P., Logan, D., Daly, A., & Guest, R. (2020). The role of authentic assessment to preserve academic integrity and promote skill development and employability. *Studies in Higher Education*, *45*(11), 2132–2148. doi:10.1080/03075079.2019.1582015

Southern Alberta Institute of Technology [SAIT]. (2022). *AC 3.4.3 Student Academic Conduct Schedule A - Examples of Student Academic Misconduct*. Sait. https://www.sait.ca/assets/documents/about-sait/policies-and-procedures/academic-student/ac-3-4-3-schedule-a.pdf

Southern Alberta Institute of Technology [SAIT]. (2023). Bachelor of Business Administration. https://www.sait.ca/programs-and-courses/degrees/bachelor-of-business-administration

Southgate, E. (2020, August 12). *Artificial intelligence, ethics, equity and higher education: A 'beginning-of-the-discussion' paper.* National Centre for Student Equity in Higher Education. https://www.ncsehe.edu.au/publications/artificial-intelligence-ethics-equity-higher-education/

Sparrow, J. (2022). The machines are learning: How artificial intelligence is already affecting journalism education. *Australian Journalism Review*, *44*(2), 163–169. doi:10.1386/ajr_00101_7

Spataro, J. (2023, March 16). *Introducing Microsoft 365 copilot – your copilot for work.* Microsoft. https://blogs.microsoft.com/blog/2023/03/16/introducing-microsoft-365-copilot-your-copilot-for-work/

Spurlock, S. (2023). Improving Student Motivation by Ungrading. *Proceedings of the 54th ACM Technical Symposium on Computer Science Education, (vol. 1*, pp. 631–637). ACM. 10.1145/3545945.3569747

Stagg, S. D., & Belcher, H. (2019). Living with autism without knowing: Receiving a diagnosis in later life. *Health Psychology and Behavioral Medicine*, *7*(1), 348–361. doi:10.1080/21642850.2019.1684920 PMID:34040855

Stanford University. (2023, February 16). *Generative AI policy guidance.* Stanford University. https://communitystandards.stanford.edu/generative-ai-policy-guidance

Staples, S., & Dilger, B. (2018). *Corpus and repository of writing [Learner corpus articulated with repository]* [dataset]. https://elicorpora.info/main

Stephen, G. L., & Jummai, N. M. (2022). Information Ownership and Privacy Control in Information Society. [IJSRM]. *International Journal of Scientific Research and Management*, *10*(06), 25–33. doi:10.18535/ijsrm/v10i6.lis01

Stoesz, B. M., & Eaton, S. E. (2022). Academic integrity policies of publicly funded universities in western Canada. *Educational Policy*, *36*(6), 1529–1548. doi:10.1177/0895904820983032

Stokel-Walker C (2022) AI bot ChatGPT writes smart essays — Should professors worry? *Nature*. doi:10.1038/d41586-022-04397-7

Su, J., & Yang, W. (2023) Unlocking the Power of ChatGPT: A Framework for Applying Generative AI in Education. *ECNU review of education, 6*(3), 355–366. https://journals.sagepub.com/doi/full/10.1177/20965311231168423

Su, J., Ng, D. T. K., & Chu, S. K. W. (2023). Artificial intelligence (AI) literacy in early childhood education: The challenges and opportunities. *Computers and Education: Artificial Intelligence*, *4*, 100124. doi:10.1016/j.caeai.2023.100124

Su, J., Zhong, Y., & Ng, D. T. K. (2022). A meta-review of literature on educational approaches for teaching AI at the K-12 levels in the Asia-Pacific region. *Computers and Education: Artificial Intelligence*, *3*, 100065. doi:10.1016/j.caeai.2022.100065

Sullivan, M., Kelly, A., & McLaughlan, P. (2023). ChatGPT in higher education: Considerations for academic integrity and student learning. *Journal of Applied Learning & Teaching*, *6*(1), 1–10.

Sullivan, M., Kelly, A., & McLaughlan, P. (2023). ChatGPT in higher education: Considerations for academic integrity and student learning. *Journal of Applied Learning and Teaching*, *6*(1), 31–40. https://journals.sfu.ca/jalt/index.php/jalt/article/view/731

Sutherland-Smith, W. (2010). Retribution, deterrence and reform: The dilemmas of plagiarism management in universities. *Journal of Higher Education Policy and Management*, *32*(1), 5–16. doi:10.1080/13600800903440519

Swain, S. (2023, April 12). *The jobs at most risk of being replaced by artificial intelligence.* 9 News. https://www.9news.com.au/national/jobs-ai-will-replace-technology/dcaf8d90-14cb-426e-8605-712555ad4995#1

Sweeney, S. (2023). Who wrote this? Essay mills and assessment–Considerations regarding contract cheating and AI in higher education. *International Journal of Management Education*, *21*(2), 100818. doi:10.1016/j.ijme.2023.100818

Tai, J., Canny, B. J., Haines, T. P., & Molloy, E. K. (2016). The Role of Peer-assisted Learning in Building Evaluative Judgement: Opportunities in Clinical Medical Education. *Advances in Health Sciences Education: Theory and Practice*, *21*(3), 659–676. doi:10.1007/s10459-015-9659-0 PMID:26662035

Takyar, A. (2023). *Bridging the AI-Human Communication Gap: A Comprehensive Guide to Prompt Engineering.* Leeway Hertz. https://www.leewayhertz.com/prompt-engineering/

Tangermann, V. (2023, January 09). There's a Problem With That App That Detects GPT-Written Text: It's Not Very Accurate. Futurism. https://futurism.com/gptzero-accuracy

Tayeb, N. (2023, January 23). *Today we are launching our #chatgpt Detector* [Press Release]. Linkedin. https://www.linkedin.com/posts/nabil-tayeb_chatgpt-schools-universities-activity-7021140020723933184-YZcB

TechNews. (2023, July 7). *ChatGPT may lead to the downfall of education and critical thinking.* TechNews. https://www.techbusinessnews.com.au/blog/chatgpt-may-lead-to-the-downfall-of-eduction-and-critical-thinking/

TEMAG. (2014). *Action Now: Classroom Ready Teachers – Report of the Teacher Education Ministerial Advisory Group (TEMAG).* Australian Government Department of Education.

Tennant, P., & Duggan, F. (2008). *Academic Misconduct Benchmarking Research Project: Part 2. The Recorded Incidence of Student Plagiarism and the Penalties Applied.* UK: The Higher Education Academy and JISC. https://www.plagiarism.org/paper/academic-misconduct-benchmarking-research-project-part-2

Tennant, P., & Rowell, G. (2010). *Benchmark Plagiarism Tariff for the Application of Penalties for Student Plagiarism and the Penalties Applied.* UK: Plagiarismadvice.org https://www.plagiarism.org/paper/benchmark-plagiarism-tariff

TEQSA. (2019). *Guidance note: Academic integrity Tertiary Education Quality and Standards Agency.* TEQSA. https://www.teqsa.gov.au/guides-resources/resources/guidance-notes/guidance-note-academic-integrity

TEQSA. (2023a). *Artificial Intelligence*. TEQSA. https://www.teqsa.gov.au/guides-resources/higher-education-good-practice-hub/artificial-intelligence

TEQSA. (2023b). *Protecting sector integrity: Assessment reform and AI*. TESQA. https://www.teqsa.gov.au/about-us/news-and-events/latest-news/protecting-sector-integrity-assessment-reform-and-ai

Tertiary Education & Quality and Standards Agency. (2023, January 18). *Sector update: Maintaining up to date academic integrity policies and procedures | Tertiary Education Quality and Standards Agency*. Teqsa.gov.au.

Terwiesch, C. (2023). *Would Chat GPT Get a Wharton MBA? A Prediction Based on Its Performance in the Operations Management Course*. Mack Institute for Innovation Management at the Wharton School, University of Pennsylvania. https://mackinstitute.wharton.upenn.edu/wp-content/uploads/2023/01/Christian-Terwiesch-Chat-GTP.pdf

The International Centre for Academic Integrity (ICAI). (1999). Fundamental values project. Academic Intregity. http://www.academicintegrity.org/icai/resources-2.php

The Sunday Telegraph. (2011). The cheating epidemic at Britain's Universities. *The Sunday Telegraph*. https://www.telegraph.co.uk/education/educationnews/8363345/The-cheating-epidemic-at-Britains-universities.html

The Whitehouse. (2023, October 30). *Fact sheet: President Biden issues executive order on safe, secure, and trustworthy artificial intelligence*. The White House. https://www.whitehouse.gov/briefing-room/statements-releases/2023/10/30/fact-sheet-president-biden-issues-executive-order-on-safe-secure-and-trustworthy-artificial-intelligence/

The-Rice-Boi. (2023a, April 17). *My teacher has falsely accused me of using ChatGPT to use an assignment*. [Reddit Post]. R/ChatGPT. www.reddit.com/r/ChatGPT/comments/12ppt5w/my_teacher_has_falsely_accused_me_of_using/

The-Rice-Boi. (2023b, June). *I was falsely accused of using ChatGPT after my teacher used some online detectors and 3 sentences of a 6 page essay got flagged as AI. My superintendent won't listen. What are my options?* [Reddit Post]. R/Legaladvice. https://www.reddit.com/r/legaladvice/comments/14eof13/i_was_falsely_accused_of_using_chatgpt_after_my/

Thomas, M. (Ed.). (2011). *Deconstructing digital natives: young people, technology and the new literacies* [Online]. Routledge. https://ebookcentral.proquest.com/lib/derby/reader.action?docID=684081 doi:10.4324/9780203818848

Thompson, S., & O'brien, K. (2023, July 18). *Russell Group Universities issue guidelines on how students can use ChatGPT in their studies*. Kingsley Napley. https://www.kingsleynapley.co.uk/insights/blogs/regulatory-blog/russell-group-universities-issue-guidelines-on-how-students-can-use-chatgpt-in-their-studies

Thurzo, A., Strunga, M., Urban, R., Surovková, J., & Afrashtehfar, K. I. (2023). Impact of artificial intelligence on dental education: A review and guide for curriculum update. *Education Sciences*, *13*(2), 150. doi:10.3390/educsci13020150

Tian, E. (2023a, January 03). *I spent New Years building GPTZero…* [Press release]. X/Twitter https://twitter.com/edward_the6/status/1610067688449007618?s=20&t=KgkIlG9q3Zkw_AeyXQMRVA

Tian, E. (2023a, January 5). Gptzero update v1 [Substack newsletter]. *GPTZero*. https://gptzero.substack.com/p/gptzero-update-v1

Tian, E. (2023b, April 28). *GPTZero | GPTZero vs Turnitin*. GPTZero. https://gptzero.me/blogs/gptzero-vs-turnitin

Tian, E. (2023b, June 01). *A Statistical Defence for AI Detection*. GPTZero LLC. https://gptzero.me/blogs/statistical-approach

Tierney, W. G., & Almeida, D. J. (2017). Academic responsibility: Toward a cultural politics of integrity. *Discourse (Abingdon)*, *38*(1), 97–108. doi:10.1080/01596306.2015.1104855

Times Higher Education. (2023, 13 March). Keep calm and carry on: ChatGPT doesn't change a thing for academic integrity. *Times Higher Education*. https://www.timeshighereducation.com/campus/keep-calm-and-carry-chatgpt-doesnt-change-thing-academic-integrity

Tindall, I. K., Fu, K. W., Tremayne, K., & Curtis, G. J. (2021). Can negative emotions increase students' plagiarism and cheating? *International Journal for Educational Integrity*, *17*(1), 1–16. doi:10.1007/s40979-021-00093-7

Tk, K. (2023, March 23). *Generative AI: Exploring ethical concerns and possible adverse effects on society*. LinkedIn. https://www.linkedin.com/pulse/generative-ai-exploring-ethical-concerns-possible-adverse-tk/

Tlili, A., Shehata, B., Adarkwah, M. A., Bozkurt, A., Hickey, D. T., Huang, R., & Agyemang, B. (2023). What if the devil is my guardian angel: ChatGPT as a case study of using chatbots in education. *Smart Learning Environments*, *10*(1), 1–24. doi:10.1186/s40561-023-00237-x

Tovani, C. (2014). How we drive students to cheat. *Educational Leadership*, *71*(6), 50–53.

Tranfield, D., Denyer, D., & Smart, P. (2003). Towards a methodology for developing evidence-informed management knowledge by means of systematic review. *British Journal of Management*, *14*(3), 207–222. doi:10.1111/1467-8551.00375

Turner, S. P., & Beemsterboer, P. L. (2003). Enhancing academic integrity: Formulating effective honor codes. *Journal of Dental Education*, *67*(10), 1122–1129. doi:10.1002/j.0022-0337.2003.67.10.tb03705.x PMID:14587677

Turnitin. (2023, April 04). *The launch of Turnitin's AI writing detector and the road ahead* [Press release]. Turnitin LLC. https://www.turnitin.com/blog/the-launch-of-turnitins-ai-writing-detector-and-the-road-ahead

Turnitin. (2023a). *AI Writing Detection Frequently Asked Questions*. Turnitin. https://www.turnitin.com/products/features/ai-writing-detection/faq

Turnitin. (2023b). *AI Writing Settings*. Turnitin AI Writing Settings. https://help.turnitin.com/integrity/administrator/settings/ai-writing-settings.htm

Turnitin. (2023c, April 4). *Turnitin turns on AI writing detection capabilities for educators and institutions (NA and EMEA)*. https://www.turnitin.com/press/turnitin-turns-on-ai-writing-detection-capabilities-for-educators-and-institutions

Turnitin. (2023d, July 25). *Turnitin AI detection feature reviews more than 65 million papers*. https://www.turnitin.com/press/turnitin-ai-detection-feature-reviews-more-than-65-million-papers

U.S. Department of State. (2023). *Artificial intelligence*. U.S. Department of State. https://www.state.gov/artificial-intelligence/

UCL. (n.d.). *The Internet Grammar of English. The Survey of English Usage, University College London 1996-1998 & Jisc*. University College London. https://www.ucl.ac.uk/internet-grammar/home.htm

UK Government Department for Education. (2023, March). *Generative artificial intelligence in education: Departmental statement*. UK Government Department for Education. https://assets.publishing.service.gov.uk/government/uploads/system/uploads/attachment_data/file/1146540/Generative_artificial_intelligence_in_education_.pdf

Underwood, J., & Luckin, R. (2011). What is AIED and why does Education need it? A report for the UK's TLRP Technology Enhanced Learning - Artificial Intelligence in Education Theme. *The London Knowledge Lab*. https://www.researchgate.net/profile/Joshua-Underwood-3/publication/241698223_What_is_AIED_and_why_does_Education_need_it/links/56e519d508ae68afa11068a7/What-is-AIED-and-why-does-Education-need-it.pdf

UNESCO. (2022). *Transforming teaching from within – Current trends in the status and development of teachers*. United Nations Educational, Scientific and Cultural Organization. https://unesdoc.unesco.org/ark:/48223/pf0000383002.

University of Birmingham. (2023). *Generative AI and its Role Within Teaching, Learning and Assessment*. University of Birmingham. https://www.birmingham.ac.uk/university/hefi/gai/index.aspx

University of Chicago. (2023, June 5). *UChicago joins partnership to make AI generative for higher education*. University of Chicago. https://www.lib.uchicago.edu/about/news/uchicago-joins-partnership-to-make-ai-generative-for-higher-education/

University of Florida. (n.d.). *Building the nation's first AI university*. University of Florida. https://indd.adobe.com/view/99192ccb-6a52-49d9-9479-e447550d15b8

University of Greenwich. (2023, March 31). *Our decision to opt-out of using Turnitin's AI detection tool | Articles*. University of Greenwich. https://www.gre.ac.uk/articles/public-relations/our-decision-to-opt-out-of-using-turnitins-ai-detection-tool

University of Groningen (Rijksuniversiteit Groningen). (2023, May 26). *Future*. University of Groningen (Rijksuniversiteit Groningen). https://edusupport.rug.nl/2430337110

University of Illinois System. (2022). *Generative AI*. University of Illinois System. https://www.vpaa.uillinois.edu/digital_risk_management/generative_ai/

University of Melbourne. (n.d.). *Advice for students regarding translation and editing tools*. Universiyt of Melbourne. https://academicintegrity.unimelb.edu.au/plagiarism-and-collusion/advice-for-students-regarding-translation-and-editing-tools

University of Pennsylvania. (2023). *Generative AI and Its Implications for Your Teaching*. University of Pennsylvania. https://ctl.upenn.edu/resources/tech/generativeai/

University of Pittsburgh. (2023, June 22). *Teaching Center doesn't endorse any generative AI detection tools*. https://www.utimes.pitt.edu/news/teaching-center-doesn-t

University of Queensland. (2023a). *Planning for learning*. University of Queensland. https://itali.uq.edu.au/teaching-guidance/teaching-practices/planning-learning

University of Queensland. (2023b). *Authentic assessment*. University of Queensland. https://itali.uq.edu.au/teaching-guidance/assessment/designing-assessment/authentic-assessment#1

University of South Australia. (2013). *The exemplary academic integrity project*. https://www.unisa.edu.au/EAIP

University of Sydney. (2023). ChatGPT is old news: How do we assess in the age of AI-writing copilots? University of Sydney. https://educational-innovation.sydney.edu.au/teaching@sydney/chatgpt-is-old-news-how-do-we-assess-in-the-age-of-ai-writing-co-pilots/?fbclid=IwAR1JSRu8bjMo8H8zX5VJl-BjqyArQxikEpM898MVCLPm_cU3vblLgNE7G-pQ_aem_AV28MDpP_1nOo4_m4IJFhy0EyKy3uN2YBFO4BIms8g7O507zESUxe5fznU4W-JE7T9k

University of Sydney. (2023). Generative AI in education inquiry. In *Inquiry into the use of generative artificial intelligence in the Australian education system - Submission 44*. University of Sydney. https://www.aph.gov.au/DocumentStore.ashx?id=244d2db3-a7de-4631-9416-3378e1882a27&subId=745296

Vaccino-Salvadore, S., & Hall Buck, R. (2021). Moving from plagiarism police to integrity coaches: Assisting novice students in understanding the relationship between research and ownership. *International Journal for Educational Integrity*, *17*(20), 1–18. doi:10.1007/s40979-021-00085-7

Van Bergen, P., & Lane, R. (2016, November 30). Should we do away with exams altogether? No, but we need to rethink their design and purpose. *The Conversation*. https:// theconversation.com/should-we-do-away-with-examsaltogether-no-but-we-need-to-rethink-their-design-andpurpose-67647 van Dis, E A M., Bollen, J., Zuidema, W., van Rooij, R., & Bockting, C. L. (2023) ChatGPT: five priorities for research. *Nature, 614* (7947), 224–226. https://www.nature.com/articles/d41586-023-00288-7.pdf

Varsha, P. (2023). How can we manage biases in artificial intelligence systems–A systematic literature review. *International Journal of Information Management Data Insights*, *3*(1), 100165.

Vartiainen, H., & Tedre, M. (2023). Using artificial intelligence in craft education: Crafting with text-to-image generative models. *Digital Creativity (Exeter)*, *34*(1), 1–21. doi:10.1080/14626268.2023.2174557

Vaswani, A., Shazeer, N., Parmar, N., Uszkoreit, J., Jones, L., Gomez, A. N., Kaiser, Ł., & Polosukhin, I. (2017). Attention is All you Need. In I. Guyon, U. V. Luxburg, S. Bengio, H. Wallach, R. Fergus, S. Vishwanathan, & R. Garnett (Eds.), *Advances in Neural Information Processing Systems* (Vol. 30). Curran Associates, Inc. https://proceedings.neurips.cc/paper_files/paper/2017/file/3f5ee243547dee91fbd053c1c4a845aa-Paper.pdf

VentayenR. J. M. (2023). OpenAI ChatGPT generated results: Similarity index of artificial intelligence-based contents. *Advances in Intelligent Systems and Computing*.

Ventayen, R. J. M. (2023). OpenAI ChatGPT Generated Results: Similarity Index of Artificial Intelligence-Based Contents. *SSRN*, *4332664*. https://ssrn.com/abstract=4332664

Verhoef, A. H., & Coetser, Y. M. (2021). Academic integrity of university students during emergency remote online assessment: An exploration of student voices. *Transformation in Higher Education*, *6*(0), a132. doi:10.4102/the.v6i0.132

Verma, P. (2023a, May 19). A professor accused his class of using ChatGPT, putting diplomas in jeopardy. *Washington Post*. https://www.washingtonpost.com/technology/2023/05/18/texas-professor-threatened-fail-class-chatgpt-cheating/

Verma, P. (2023b, August 13). Professors have a summer assignment: Prevent ChatGPT chaos in the fall. *Washington Post*. https://www.washingtonpost.com/technology/2023/08/13/ai-chatgpt-chatbots-college-cheating/

Victorian Legislation. (2023). *Crimes act 1958*. https://www.legislation.vic.gov.au/in-force/acts/crimes-act-1958/299

Villarroel, V., Bloxham, S., Bruna, D., Bruna, C., & Herrera, C. (2018). Authentic assessment: Creating a blueprint for course design. *Assessment & Evaluation in Higher Education*, *43*(5), 840–854. doi:10.1080/02602938.2017.1412396

Von Dran, G. M., Callahan, E. S., & Taylor, H. V. (2001). Can students' academic integrity be improved? Attitudes and behaviors before and after implementation of an academic integrity policy. *Teaching Business Ethics*, *5*(1), 35–58. doi:10.1023/A:1026551002367

Wald, M. (2021). AI data-driven personalisation and disability inclusion. *Frontiers in Artificial Intelligence*, *3*, 571955. doi:10.3389/frai.2020.571955 PMID:33733215

Walker, R. (2023, June 14). *California professors test out AI in the classroom, even as cheating debate continues.* CalMatters. https://calmatters.org/education/higher-education/2023/06/ai-classroom-california/

Walker, R., & Voce, J. (2023). Post-Pandemic Learning Technology Developments in UK Higher Education: What Does the UCISA Evidence Tell Us? *Sustainability (Basel)*, *15*(17), 1–16. doi:10.3390/su151712831

Wang, W., Wang, G., Marivate, V., & Hufton, A. L. (2023). On the transparency of large AI models. *Patterns (New York, N.Y.)*, *4*(7), 1–2. doi:10.1016/j.patter.2023.100797 PMID:37521049

Ward, M., O'Riordan, F., Logan-Fleming, D., Cooke, D., Concannon-Gibney, T., Efthymiou, M., & Watkins, N. (2023, August 29). Interactive oral assessment case studies: An innovative, academically rigorous, authentic assessment approach. *Innovations in Education and Teaching International*, 1–18. doi:10.1080/14703297.2023.2251967

Warschauer, M., Tseng, W., Yim, S., Webster, T., Jacob, S., Du, Q, & Tate, T. (2023). *The affordances and contradictions of AI-generated text for second language writers.*

Webb, M. (2023, September 18). *AI Detection – Latest Recommendations. Jisc National Centre for AI in Tertiary Education.* National Center for Education. https://nationalcentreforai.jiscinvolve.org/wp/2023/09/18/ai-detection-latest-recommendations/

Weber-Wulff, D. (2014). *False Feathers: A Perspective on Academic Plagiarism.* Springer. doi:10.1007/978-3-642-39961-9

Weber-WulffD.Anohina-NaumecaA.BjelobabaS.FoltýnekT.Guerrera-DibJ.PopoolaO.ŠigutP.WaddingtonL. (2023). Testing detection tools for AI-Generated Text. https://arxiv.org/abs/2306.15666

Welborn, A. (2023, March 9). ChatGPT and Fake Citations. *Duke University Libraries Blogs.* https://blogs.library.duke.edu/blog/2023/03/09/chatgpt-and-fake-citations/

Westine, C., Oyarzun, B., Ahlgrim-Delzell, L., Casto, A., Okraski, C., Park, G., Person, J., & Steele, L. (2019). Familiarity, current use, and interest in Universal Design for Learning among online university instructors. *International Review of Research in Open and Distance Learning, 20*(5), 21–41. doi:10.19173/irrodl.v20i5.4258

Wheaton, A. (2020). Shift happens; moving from the ivory tower to the mushroom factory. *Higher Education Research & Development, 39*(1), 67–80. doi:10.1080/07294360.2019.1670145

White, A. (2020). Interactive approaches to learning about academic integrity: The role of fun and games. In T. Bretag (Ed.), *A Research Agenda for Academic Integrity* (pp. 86–99). Edward Elgar Publishing Ltd. doi:10.4337/9781789903775.00013

Whitley, B. E. Jr, & Keith-Spiegel, P. (2001). *Academic dishonesty: An educator's guide.* Psychology Press. doi:10.4324/9781410604279

Whitley, B. E. Jr, & Keith-Spiegel, P. (2001). Academic integrity as an institutional issue. *Ethics & Behavior, 11*(3), 325–342. doi:10.1207/S15327019EB1103_9

Wiggins, G. (1990). The Case for Authentic Assessment. *Practical Assessment, Research & Evaluation, 2*(2), 28–37.

Wiggins, G. (1993). *Assessing Student Performance.* Jossey-Bass.

Wiggins, G. (1999). *Assessing student performance: Exploring the purpose and limits of testing.* Jossey-Bass Publishers.

Wiggins, G., & McTighe, J. (2006). Examining the Teaching Life. *Educational Leadership, 63*(6), 26–29.

Wilhelm, I. (2023, June 12). Nobody Wins in an Academic-Integrity Arms Race: How artificial intelligence is changing the way colleges think about cheating. *The Chronicle of Higher Education.* Retrieved, January 05, 2024, from https://www.chronicle.com/article/nobody-wins-in-an-academic-integrity-arms-race

Williams, A., Miceli, M., & Gebru, T. (2022). The Exploited Labor Behind Artificial Intelligence. *Noema.* https://www.noemamag.com/the-exploited-labor-behind-artificial-intelligence/

Williams, R. (2023, July 07). AI-text detection tools are really easy to fool. *MIT Technology Review.* https://www.technologyreview.com/2023/07/07/1075982/ai-text-detection-tools-are-really-easy-to-fool/

Williams, R. M. (@FractalEcho@kolektiva. social). (2023, July 29). *I shared "the email" because it was interesting to me that this happened to me when it's actually something I write about academically …* [Mastodon post]. Mastodon. https://kolektiva.social/@FractalEcho/110800085168655662

Wolany, G. (2023, June 23). *In curiosity we trust: AI scouting for the ZHDK* [Online]. Beyond ChatGPT - what next for generative AI in higher education? https://eua.eu/events/277:beyond-chatgpt-what-next-for-generative-ai-in-higher-education.html

Wood, P. (2023, February 28). Oxford and Cambridge ban ChatGPT over plagiarism fears but other universities choose to embrace AI bot. *iNews*. https://inews.co.uk/news/oxford-cambridge-ban-chatgpt-plagiarism-universities-2178391

Wood, S. G., Moxley, J. H., Tighe, E. L., & Wagner, R. K. (2018). Does use of text-to-speech and related read-aloud tools improve reading comprehension for students with reading disabilities? A meta-analysis. *Journal of Learning Disabilities*, *51*(1), 73–84. doi:10.1177/0022219416688170 PMID:28112580

Wooldridge, M. (2018). The road to conscious machines: The story of AI. Penguin UK.

Wylie, A. (2018, February 22). Flesch-Kincaid Grade Level: How hard is it? Master the art of readable writing. *Medium*. https://medium.com/@annwylie/flesch-kincaid-grade-level-how-hard-is-it-ebb0bfcdfa87

XiaoP.ChenY.BaoW. (2023). *Waiting, banning, and embracing: An empirical analysis of adapting policies for Generative AI in higher education*. https://arxiv.org/abs/2305.18617

Xie, Y., Wu, S., & Chakravarty, S. (2023, October 2023). AI Meets AI: Artificial Intelligence and Academic Integrity - A Survey on Mitigating AI-Assisted Cheating in Computing Education. *ACM*, 79-83. doi:10.1145/3585059.3611449

Yang, M. (2023, January 6). New York City schools ban AI chatbot that writes essays and answers prompts. *The Guardian*. https://www.theguardian.com/us-news/2023/jan/06/new-york-city-schools-ban-ai-chatbot-chatgpt

Yang, M. (2023, January 7). New York City schools ban AI chatbot that writes essays and answers prompts. *The Guardian*. https://www.theguardian.com/us-news/2023/jan/06/new-york-city-schools-ban-ai-chatbot-chatgpt

Yeadon, W., Inyang, O. O., Mizouri, A., Peach, A., & Testrow, C. P. (2023). The death of the short-form physics essay in the coming AI revolution. *Physics Education*, *58*(3), 58. doi:10.1088/1361-6552/acc5cf

Youmans, R. J. (2011). Does the adoption of plagiarism-detection software in higher education reduce plagiarism? *Studies in Higher Education*, *36*(7), 749–761. doi:10.1080/03075079.2010.523457

Young, F. (2022, 28 February). Affordances of innovative learning environments. In *Scholarly Community Encyclopedia online*. https://encyclopedia.pub/entry/19677

Young, F., Cleveland, B., & Imms, W. (2019). The affordances of innovative learning environments for deep learning: Educators' and architects' perceptions. *Australian Educational Researcher*, *47*(4), 693–720. doi:10.1007/s13384-019-00354-y

Yu, H., & Guo, Y. (2023). Generative artificial intelligence empowers educational reform: Current status, issues, and prospects. *Frontiers in Education*, *8*, 1–10. doi:10.3389/feduc.2023.1183162

Zainuddin, Z., & Halili, S. H. (2016). Flipped Classroom Research and Trends from Different Fields of Study. *International Review of Research in Open and Distance Learning*, *17*(3). doi:10.19173/irrodl.v17i3.2274

Zajic, M. C., McIntyre, N., Swain-Lerro, L., Novotny, S., Oswald, T., & Mundy, P. (2018). Attention and written expression in school-age, high-functioning children with autism spectrum disorders. *Autism*, *22*(3), 245–258. doi:10.1177/1362361316675121 PMID:27940570

Zajko, M. (2022). Artificial intelligence, algorithms, and social inequality: Sociological contributions to contemporary debates. *Sociology Compass*, *16*(3), e12962. doi:10.1111/soc4.12962

Zauderer, D. G. (1992, October). Integrity: An essential executive quality. *Business forum*, *17*(4), 12.

Zawacki-Richter, O., Marín, V. I., Bond, M., & Gouverneur, F. (2019). Systematic review of research on AI applications in higher education–where are the educators? *International Journal of Educational Technology in Higher Education*, *16*(1), 1–27. doi:10.1186/s41239-019-0171-0

Zessoules, R., & Gardner, H. (1991). Authentic assessment: Beyond the buzzword and into the classroom. In V. Perrone (Ed.), *Expanding student assessment* (pp. 47–71). ASCD.

Zhai, X. (2022). *ChatGPT user experience: Implications for education.*

Zhai, X., Chu, X., Chai, C., Jong, M., Istenic, A., Spector, M., & C, N. (2021). *A Review of Artificial Intelligence (AI) in Education from 2010 to 2020.* New York City: Hoboken: Hindawi Coplexity.

ZhaiX. (2022) ChatGPT User Experience: Implications for Education. SSRN. https://ssrn.com/abstract=4312418 doi:10.2139/ssrn.4312418

Zhang, J. (2005). *Content analysis of web sites from 2000 to 2004: a thematic meta-analysis.* Texas A&M University.

Zhang, K., & Aslan, A. (2021). AI technologies for education: Recent research & future directions. *Computers and Education: Artificial Intelligence*, *2*, 100025. Advance online publication. doi:10.1016/j.caeai.2021.100025

Zhang, Y., Lin, H., Zhang, X., & Ye, Q. (2021). The next steps in academic integrity—Education, awareness, norms, duty and law. *Forensic Sciences Research*, *6*(4), 341–346. doi:10.1080/20961790.2021.1970887 PMID:35111353

Zhao, I., & Brookes, S. (2023). International students and researchers concerned tools to detect AI-generated text may be inaccurate. *ABC News*. https://www.abc.net.au/news/2023-06-02/international-students-say-ai-detectors-are-inaccurate/1023948944

Zhao, Y., Ni, L., & Li, D. (2021). Unpacking AI education for K–12: Comprehensive, equitable, and effective. *Educational Technology Research and Development*, *69*(3), 953–976.

About the Contributors

Saadia Mahmud is an Online Facilitator at the Australian Institute of Business. Her doctoral research at the University of South Australia applied complexity theory to the handling of rapid change by SMEs. After completing her MBA as the top student, she pursued a career in banking and finance with Citibank. In higher education, she has managed large research projects to improve the quality of teaching and learning funded by the Commonwealth Government of Australia. The vital role of honest communication, trust and a strong value system in organisations is a recurrent theme in her work from enhancing adaptive capability in complex systems to creating a culture of integrity. Her work has been published in peer reviewed journals and incorporated into industry relevant outcomes. Her research with colleagues is referred to on the Australian Tertiary Education Quality and Standards Agency (TEQSA) guidance on good practice in academic integrity.

***

Brent Anders has worked in higher education for over twenty years, concentrating on media and online instruction. Brent has worked as a professor and as an educational media consultant dealing with video production, live webcasting, student engagement, user experience, and instructional technology as well as course development and instructional design. Anders also served in the U.S. Army for 26 years, first as an airborne infantryman, then as a certified military instructor. Anders also does periodic speaking events as well as authoring books, research articles, and blog posts dealing with different aspects of instruction, online learning, and educational technology.

Janine Arantes is a researcher and academic with Victoria University. Her area of expertise lies in exploring the impact of digital technology in education, with a particular focus on critical algorithm studies, data metrics, education policy, and the evolving identities of teachers in digital classrooms. Janine obtained her PhD, titled 'Big Data, Black Boxes, and Bias: The Algorithmic Identity and Educational Practice,' from the University of Newcastle in 2021, and prior to joining Victoria University in 2019, she held positions in both TAFE and Secondary School settings across Victoria, Australia. Janine's contributions to the field have been recognized with three VU Fellowships (2019-2022) and a Cengage Fellowship in 2019. She has presented her research at national and international forums, concentrating on the implications of digital education, predictive analytics, big data, and algorithmic bias for educators.

Amy Emanuel is the Director of Online Learning and a Lecturer at Christian Heritage College, a private Higher Education Institution in Brisbane, Australia. In addition to these roles, she serves as the Chief Academic Integrity Officer. She received a Masters of Learning Sciences and Technology from the University of Sydney is passionate about understanding how people learn and how to incorporate technology into the learning process and equity in access to education. Recently, she has taken on additional roles Chairing the Student Success and Retention Committee and is heading up an assessment review project in response to opportunities and challenges of GenAI. Her research areas of interest include learning analytics and retention, contemporary technology and human behaviour, brain-based learning, brain-based teaching, character formation in online learning and generative artificial intelligence.

Whitney Gegg-Harrison studied Linguistics and Computer Science at The Ohio State University, earning their Bachelor's degree in 2005 before completing a Master's degree in Computational Linguistics in 2006. As a graduate student in Brain and Cognitive Sciences at the University of Rochester, Whitney studied psycholinguistics, earning a Ph.D in 2014. Since 2010, Whitney has taught first-year academic writing as well as upper-level writing in the Writing, Speaking, and Argument Program at the University of Rochester, where they are now an associate professor. Whitney received the Georgen Award for Excellence in Undergraduate Teaching in 2023.

Lynn Gribble is an Internationally, nationally and UNSW awarded Education Focused academic using her keen interest in transformative learning through engagement, belonging and personalisation of each student's learning experience. Over the past three years she has extensively considered how to develop authentic assessment and has worked on University wide feedback projects to enhance the student experience. In developing the Master's course, Responsible Business Professionalism, Lynn looked to bring her corporate experience to university learning focusing on ethics and sustainability as the future differentiator for her students. Today, that course has evolved further to focus on Ethical use of AI in the workplace. Known for her continual innovation, Lynn uses technology to connect with her students and personalise their experience. Her work on teaching innovation dissemination through "The 4Cs (Classroom, Corridor, Campus and Community) Strategy" has seen her practices adopted and adapted both locally and globally through her approaches to Scholarship of Teaching and Learning (SoTL). As a regularly invited guest to share her practice and insights, and as Co-lead of Digital, Online learning & Innovation CoP, Lynn's innovations are changing practice across the university and beyond particularly in the online and blended learning space.

Rob Howe is Head of Learning Technology at The University of Northampton. Accepted to CMALT and IADIS in 2007. Awarded University teaching fellowship in 2008. Achieved Senior Fellowship of the HEA in 2014. Has led four national projects (HEA BITE; HEA TIGER; JISC e4L and ELESIG - Midlands) in addition to local manager for the TLTP TALENT project and 5 internally funded projects. For details on research outputs please see - He is available to contact on twitter (@rjhowe) and also on LinkedIn ()

Maya Jaber, a seasoned social entrepreneur and visionary with two decades of business expertise, is dedicated to redefining the business landscape with a profound emphasis on humanity. Over the past ten years, she has been on a relentless quest to drive market transformation towards a sustainable future. With a multifaceted background that spans leadership roles within organizations and independent consultancy, Dr. Jaber has consistently fostered education and awareness. She champions holistic strategies that catalyze cultural shifts, optimize operations, expand organizational growth, and enhance the bottom line, all while weaving in crucial Environmental, Social, and Governance imperatives. Dr. Jaber's dynamic approach encompasses a blend of creativity, analytical prowess, research acumen, and tactical finesse. She uniquely navigates the intricate interplay between macro and micro perspectives, crafting solutions enriched by qualitative and quantitative data. Her central ethos revolves around placing humanity at the core of every endeavor. Her pioneering research has revolved around Sustainability Management challenges, culminating in the development of a comprehensive strategy framework that triggers a transformative mindset shift. This framework is instrumental in driving organizational behavior change, paving the way for a more sustainable future. Dr. Jaber firmly believes that every individual holds intrinsic value, and her commitment to equality, empathy, communication, and collaboration resonates deeply in every corporate community and culture she influences. Her work is a testament to the enduring power of human-centric business strategies that fuse value and purpose with lasting, positive change.

Sonja Johnston has more than 12 years of experience as an entrepreneur, consultant, and post-secondary instructor; this innovative researcher and practitioner is at the intersection of theory and praxis. Sonja is a PhD candidate at the Werklund School of Education at the University of Calgary with a specialization in Learning Sciences. Her dissertation explores reframing and redesign techniques of business capstone through an educational research lens and utilizing a design-based research methodology.

Blake Kanewischer is an award-winning faculty member at the Southern Alberta Institute of Technology, with over a decade of teaching experience. His background spans over 15 years in diverse professional roles, primarily in information systems and project management contexts. He is a PhD candidate at the Sobey School of Business, and an active researcher in the fields of adoption of artificial intelligence, equity, diversity, and inclusion, and management education.

Nadia Koren received her Bachelor of Science in Computer Science from the University of NSW and her Master of Applied Science in Information Technology from RMIT University. She has primarily worked as a lecturer but has also taken on various leadership roles in tertiary education. Currently, she serves as the Academic Integrity Lead for Technical and Further Education New South Wales (TAFE NSW), which has approximately half a million annual enrolments. She is ambitious in encouraging TAFE NSW teachers to embrace Generative AI in order to minimise academic integrity breaches and address root causes of breaches.

Edyta Kostanek is a Senior Teaching Fellow at UCL School of Management, University College London. Her research interests span gamification and playfulness in education, EdTech and AI, project management, and female entrepreneurship.

Brenda McDermott, PhD, is the Senior Manager of the Student Accessibility Services at the University of Calgary. Brenda McDermott uses an EDIA lens to reflect on teaching and learning practices in post-secondary education – striving to create a sense of belonging for all students and staff. In addition to over 10+ of post-secondary teaching experience, Brenda has supported instructors with academic integrity education, writing pedagogy, universal design for learning, and assessment design. She has a recent chapter on ableism and academic integrity practices published in the 2nd edition of the Handbook of Academic Integrity. She is currently part of the interdisciplinary team examining the ethics of artificial intelligence at the University of Calgary. As part of the project, she has presented to many groups on the intersection of artificial intelligence and diversity.

Lynsey Meakin is a Senior Lecturer of Education in the Institute of Education. Lynsey delivers initial teacher training to trainee teachers, on campus in person to full-time and school-based Beginning Teachers, and in a remote environment to Beginning Teachers around England and to international students around the world. Lynsey supports teaching and learning across multiple Programmes and modules, enhancing the knowledge and application of Professional Theory and Professional Practice of trainees. This is done with the aim of ensuring that teachers of tomorrow are reflective practitioners who are best prepared to be outstanding in education. Lynsey's current focus of research is in the challenges and opportunities offered by generative artificial intelligence and believes that AI will revolutionise education.

Anna Michalska is Associate Professor (Teaching Focussed) at the University of Warwick and Academic Integrity Lead for Warwick Business School, where she has a lead departmental responsibility for promoting ethical behaviour and academic integrity standards in professional practice. She specialises in academic integrity and student plagiarism. Her research focuses on differences in attitudes and practices of students towards academic misconduct, and reasons behind their dishonest academic behaviour.

Roopa Aruvanahalli Nagaraju is a Senior Lecturer at Oxford Brookes. Her teaching and research interests are in the areas of Innovation strategy and Management, High Technology SMEs, Technology Entrepreneurship, public policy to support entrepreneurship, Social Entrepreneurship and women entrepreneurship in emerging markets.

Claire Quarterman studied at McGill University, earning a Bachelors of Science in Mathematics with a minor concentration in French Language and Literature in 2021. In 2022, Claire began working as a data scientist for a financial technology company, and recently has been focusing on leveraging generative AI for business purposes. Since March 2023, Claire occasionally consults on the defenses of students falsely accused of AI cheating.

David Stone, PhD, is a lecturer and learning designer who specialises in the fields of digital communication and visual theology. He has professional experience in the education industry, primarily in curriculum development and design. His doctoral research explores the multimodality of illumination, specifically the use of light-centric semiotics and allegory as narrative teaching devices in screen media. His practice-led methodology is showcased in his published films which have received nominations and awards at international exhibitions.

Janis Wardrop is the Education Director at the Centre for Social Impact UNSW (CSI UNSW). Janis is an award-winning academic leader, educational change agent and commentator on management education, business ethics and governance. With 15+ years' experience in academia as both lecturer, program leader and manager, her expertise lies in adopting a holistic approach to curriculum design and delivery.

Index

A

B

C

D

E

F

G

H

I

www.ingramcontent.com/pod-product-compliance
Lightning Source LLC
LaVergne TN
LVHW080634011026
849160LV00014B/1216
* 9 7 9 8 3 6 9 3 0 2 4 1 5 *